The History of
Scottish Rugby

Sandy Thorburn

Johnston & Bacon
London

List of Plates

A Johnston & Bacon book published by
CASSELL LTD. 35 Red Lion Square, London WC1R 4SG
and at Sydney, Auckland, Toronto, Johannesburg
an affiliate of Macmillan Publishing Co. Inc., New York.

First published 1980
© Sandy Thorburn 1980
ISBN   0 7179 4275 9

Typeset by Inforum Ltd., Portsmouth
Printed in Great Britain by
Richard Clay (The Chaucer Press) Ltd., Bungay, Suffolk

Contents

Preface

In 1946 there came into my hands the first Minute Book of the Royal High School Former Pupils Cricket Club, an acquisition which set me off to record the history and statistics of that body. Inevitably the research widened to cover the rugby club, the two Scottish Cricket Unions and the Scottish Rugby Union.

Some of the rugby material found its way into the Club's Centenary History and into a manuscript dealing with the history of the SRU. There remained a mass of material of wider interest which I have drawn on here to sketch the growth of the rugby game in Scotland, to give brief descriptions of all matches played by Scottish teams and to provide some facts and figures about these matches and the players.

The bulk of the research was done in the National Library or in the file rooms of the *Evening News* and the former *Evening Dispatch* in Edinburgh and I must express my most sincere thanks to the Librarian and Editors of those establishments for the many privileges extended to me over the years.

It is simply not possible to thank individually the many club officials, former players and correspondents whose ready response to my queries added so much to the fabric of the book but I would mention two friends in Bob Ironside and Bruce Stenhouse whose rugby knowledge and advice so often augmented, guided and corrected my writings.

I am much indebted to Miss Heather Jones of Messrs Cassell, Bill McMurtrie of the *Glasgow Herald* and Bill Brady of *The Scotsman* for their help in procuring suitable photographs and to Messrs R.W. Forsyth, Edinburgh, who, from their splendid collection, at once provided copies of the Scottish XVs which played in the seasons when the Triple Crown was won. My thanks also go to my two typists, Mrs C.E. Braithwaite and Mrs D.W. Thorburn, who so speedily produced such competent copy from my scripts.

And lastly my thanks to my fellow Teri, Bill McLaren, not only for his delightful foreword but also for the word in the right ear which brought this book to life. Like so many other rugby lovers I was very happy to see that his 'Magisterial Broadcasting Expertise' had been regally and justly recognised.

Edinburgh: March 1980   AMCT

Foreword

It might pay the Scottish Tourist Board to make Sandy Thorburn's inner sanctum at his pleasantly secluded Edinburgh home an official tourist attraction! The sanctum I refer to is his own special room in which he stores all his Rugby Union and cricket records. I still remember my feeling of awe on the memorable occasion when I was first privileged to enter that Holy of Holies.

That sanctum, and the wealth of information it houses, bear rich testimony to Sandy Thorburn's feel for sporting history and his meticulous attention to detail in setting down on record facts, figures and anecdotes. When that experienced Welsh television producer, Dewi Griffiths, sought to trace the history of the Rugby Union game in Scotland for a series of programmes covering the world scene, Sandy Thorburn fascinated him and the interviewer, John Reason, with the depth of his knowledge and his gift for making the dry bones of history come alive with interest and vitality.

So it seems entirely appropriate that the task of recording the development of Rugby Union in Scotland should have been undertaken by Sandy Thorburn, whose greatest claim to fame, of course, is that he is a Hawick man! As another product of that blessed place, I also feel privileged to have been invited to write this foreword.

Scotland has been badly in need of a composite written record of her Rugby Union fortunes and of the distinctive contribution made by Scots to the game at large. Nowhere, for instance until now, has one come across complete coverage, under one cover, of every single match which Scotland have played. In thus providing details of teams, score, scorers and play, Sandy Thorburn has supplied the means of settling thousands of friendly disputes in office and factory for the next hundred years.

As one turns the pages, memories come flooding back. One of my boyhood idols was that remarkable personality, Jock Beattie. There is his name in the complete list of Scottish captains, which is just one of several very interesting appendices to this book. It was in his very last international, the Calcutta Cup match at Twickenham in 1936, that Jock was captain of Scotland. On that day I was at Twickenham for the very first time, a twelve-year-old schoolboy on one of the famous Cook's tours by rail along with my father and some of his factory friends. Another of my Hawick heroes, Rob Barrie, was carried off with a broken collar bone early in the game. My heart was broken too, for Scotland lost. Two years later I was lucky enough to be back at Twickenham for 'Wilson Shaw's match' and Scotland's last Triple Crown and Championship success. What a thrill to read about both these games in this book.

Life is constantly subject to change. It is important that Rugby Union, too, stays abreast of the times. Yet there is so much to be learned from the past, not least that all change is not necessarily for the good, that many of the old values and attitudes are still essential in the game today. It is good for us to be reminded, every now and again, of the rich heritage that has been handed on by the great pioneers and, indeed, of the huge part played by some of the famous former pupils' clubs which have fallen recently on hard times. Nor is there much in the modern game that is really new. Coaching, for instance, has brought about a minor revolution in preparation and play method over the past decade. Yet it is fascinating to read in the following pages that as long ago as 1859 the first seeds of coaching were being sown, as Merchistonians made the point that order and organisation had been brought to their game, 'each player now having a place assigned to him for which he is most suited. . . .' And in the same school magazine, a reference to the then Merchiston captain surely stresses to those who watch the modern game the similarities between then and now: 'His way of ridding himself of those who press upon him too closely in the maul by stamping on their toes, is admirable'!

By his care in research and his attention to detail, Sandy Thorburn has produced a most valuable addition to rugby literature whilst underlining the part Scots have played in the game's evolution. There are those who contend that had it been left to the Scottish Rugby Union, handling in rugby would never have been legalized! Yet one of the stories that will give infinite pleasure to the thousands of Scots who will read this book is of Harry Stevenson (Edinburgh Academicals), capped fifteen times as a back in 1888 to 1893, quietly informing a group of Englishmen that rugby had been played in Scotland long before William Webb Ellis first picked up the ball and ran with it at Rugby School in 1823. They were doing that, he said, at the High School of Edinburgh in 1810. Even at the outset, Scotland led the way!

Bill McLaren

Part 1: The Early Years

Prehistory

The football historian suffers from the same handicap as any other in that he can only begin his definite story at a period for which some written record of his subject exists. As far as Britain is concerned we have to wait until after the Norman Conquest to get a mention of football being played in London. Nevertheless it may be plausibly argued that some such pastime had existed throughout the island from the time of the Roman occupation.

The Roman soldiers were known to play an organised game, harpastum, before they came to Britain. Harpastum, played within a rectangular area marked with a centre line, involved two teams who tried to force a small hard ball over their opponents' end line. Running with the ball, passing or throwing the ball and forms of tackling were allowed — all features so closely resembling those found in ball games recorded throughout the whole of what was Roman-occupied Britain that it is tempting to claim harpastum as their common but distant progenitor.

The Romans, who reinvaded Britain in AD 43, were by about AD 78 in fairly firm control of the whole of England south of a line from Carlisle to the Tyne, an area they were to occupy and administer for some further 350 years. Their later advance into Scotland was governed by the need to flank the hostile Selgovae who occupied the middle and upper Tweed basin, so one route ran from Carlisle to the upper Clyde valley before striking east to the coast at Inveresk, and it seems likely that there was a link past Loudon Hill to the west coast near Irvine. The other route, Dere Street, ran from Corbridge over the Cheviots near Carter Bar, past Jedburgh and Ancrum to Newstead (Trimontium) on the Tweed near Melrose before going on to Inveresk. From there a northern continuation crossed the Forth near Stirling and the Tay near Perth to reach the large fort of Inchtuthil at Caputh near Dunkeld. Between Dere Street and the sea lay the territory of the friendly Votadini who occupied the lower Tweed valley and the coastal strip from the Tyne to the Lothians. Dere Street, whose line is still clearly visible, became the main route north and Newstead was established as the largest garrison fort and administrative centre north of the Cheviots. It and the inevitable native settlement which sprung up beside it, lasted, with one short break, until about AD 196 when the final withdrawal was made to the line of Hadrian's Wall. Even then contact with the Lowlands was not lost, for strong scouting parties were sent by a few routes over the Cheviots and apparently one of the recognised meeting points was at or near Jedburgh. These patrols continued until about AD 369 when pressure from the Picts and Scots forced the defence to concentrate along the Wall.

Dere Street passed through the middle of that Border region where the majority of Scottish Ba' games have been recorded and survive — for the game still takes place annually at Jedburgh and has been played at Hawick, Hobkirk, Lilliesleaf, Denholm, Ancrum, Selkirk, Galashiels, St Boswells, Melrose, Kelso, Duns, Yetholm and Morebattle. These games were played by the inhabitants who, divided into two bands according to some local criterion, tried to hail the ba' by carrying it beyond some target at the rear of their opponents' area. The ba', being quite small and hard, was carried or thrown. Kicking was almost impossible because of the mass of players involved and in any case would have achieved little other than a bruised foot.

Football or ball games have been recorded at many places outside the Borders, but it is surprising how many of those towns lie close to Roman camps on the two routes mentioned. The 400 years of Roman occupation in England and the shorter period in the Scottish Lowlands were both quite long enough for harpastum to have been observed and imitated by the natives who lived in the areas of Roman forts or camps. However, at the time of the Roman withdrawal from Teviotdale (and indeed for many centuries afterwards) the inhabitants, mainly herdsmen or farmers, lived in very small scattered communities situated above the forest level on the lower Cheviot foothills. Life was hard and little time existed for profitless exercises. Probably the only breaks would be the tribal gatherings at times and places nominated by the Newstead administrators operating the normal Roman occupation rules.

The Celtic tribes divided their year into four equal periods marked by festive holidays on the first day of the months of February, May, August and November and it is quite probable that the Romans accepted the February date as one suitable for a Spring meeting with the local tribes. These festivals were always occasions for relaxation and it is likely that in time a form of football appeared as part of the day's fun.

In later years the Church also adopted some of those holidays and, in particular, Candlemas was eventually celebrated on February 2. At Jedburgh two Ba' games were played; the first at Candlemas and the second on Fastern's E'en (which usually falls on Shrove Tuesday), the two dates being linked by the rhyme:

First comes Candlemas, then the new mune
And the first Tuesday after is Fastern's E'en.

There are so many other ball games played on those two dates that a link with harpastum does seem possible.

Another theory is proposed by Henri Garcia in his comprehensive *La Fabuleuse Histoire du Rugby*. Here he considers that the Brittany–Normandy game of La Soule had developed from harpastum but goes on to suggest that since none of the earlier European invaders of the island had any records of ball games, football in England was a descendant of La Soule introduced by the Normans after 1066. He supports his argument by pointing out that the earliest mention of a ball game in Britain is found in a work which appeared about 1175.

This not only ignores the lengthy Roman background in England but also the facts that when Magnus Maximus crossed from England into Gaul in his ill-fated campaign of AD 381–87 the numerous Britons in his legions finally settled in that north-western region of France to which they gave their name, and then later, in the first half of the sixth century, there was another large migration of Britons from England into the same area. Since Pierre Larousse in his nineteenth-century Dictionary has an entry 'Soule; sorte de jeu pratiqué surtout en Bretagne' one could suggest that La Soule was not only a derivative of harpastum but one with a solid British background before it returned to England with the Normans.

After the withdrawal of the Roman forces sometime about AD 410 the island suffered a succession of invasions from Europe which only ended with the Norman Conquest of 1066 and it is not surprising that the few chroniclers of those troubled times failed to mention anything so trivial as football.

During this period in Scotland the Picts and Scots had been merged to form a unified nation which by the time of Malcolm Canmore had also absorbed those Anglo-Saxons who had moved north from the Humber and Tyne regions into the former territory of the Votadini, and there is at least one writer who considers that the development of football in the Border and East Coast areas of Scotland owed much to this infiltration from the south.

From 1066 onwards the two countries, each governed by a

single authority, were able to develop relatively peacefully. Towns and industries were established and soon there was evidence that football began to play a part in the life of the people, especially for those living in populated areas. It is only fair to M. Garcia to admit that a Norman influence existed not only in London but also in Scone or Perth where Malcolm's second consort, the saintly Queen Margaret with her continental background, encouraged the introduction of many European customs and trades into Scotland. What effect this influence had on football is debatable. It could be that Fair days such as Candlemas and Shrove Tuesday were firmly established and also recognised as suitable days for the playing of organised games, but it seems more likely that the formation of larger fixed communities provided not only the necessary mass of players but also the craftsmen who could make a larger leather-cased ball filled with feathers, straw or an air-filled animal bladder.

Certainly it is from one such community, London, that the first written mention of football comes.

Early Records

About 1175 William Fitzstephen, a London-born monk of Canterbury, wrote in Latin a history of London in which he stated that the youths of the town had open spaces allotted to them near the town where they practised leaping, wrestling, casting of the stone and playing with the ball. He goes on to add that annually on Shrove Tuesday in the afternoon all the youth of the city go to a flat patch of ground just outside the city for the famous game of ball. The students of every faculty have their own ball and those who are engaged in the various trades of the city also have their own ball. The older men, the fathers and men of substance, come on horseback to watch the competitions of the younger men.

The extract makes it clear that the Shrove Tuesday game had existed for some time and that the city authorities did not object to it, almost certainly because it was played on a recognised Fair Day and, more important, it was not played through the narrow city streets for, as we shall see, the majority of the later references to the game spring from the displeasure of Town Councils or Church authorities at the damage to property or the desecration of the Sabbath by the players. In the latter case, certainly in Scotland, it seems that the churchyard immediately after the morning service was often used as the place and time for a Sunday afternoon's game.

4

In both countries right up to the Union of the Crowns the governments also frowned upon the game, considering that it interfered with the practising of archery and other warlike arts. In England from the time of Edward II to Henry VIII there appeared a succession of edicts banning play, a repetition which reveals how popular and strongly entrenched the game had become.

It is a similar edict which gives us the first Scottish reference. James I, immediately after his release from imprisonment in England, held a Council meeting in Scone in 1424 and issued the much quoted Act 'It is statut and the king forbiddis that na man play at the fute ball under the payne of xl.s.'.

This ban was no more successful than those in England, for the next three references are found in similar Acts issued in 1458, 1471 and 1491 by the next three James's, so we may safely assume that the game was as popular in Scotland as it was in England.

Another reference is found in the Lord High Treasurer's accounts for 1497, 'Item (the xxij day of Aprile) . . . giffen to Jame Dog to by fut ballis to the King . . . ij.s'. At first sight it would appear that James IV was ignoring his own edict but, noting the date of payment, one may more safely assume that the King was providing balls for use in the recognised Candlemas or Shrove Tuesday festivities. Similar recognition of these Fair days is seen in the St Andrews references of 1497 and 1537 and in the Glasgow ones of 1575 and 1609.

These early references spring from a need to be ready to take up arms, and it was only after the death of Henry VIII that the two countries were able to settle down to a fairly peaceful co-existence. Later references, listed elsewhere, came mainly from Kirk or Town Council sources.

The Kirk, deeply affected by the Calvinistic thunderings of John Knox who had returned to Scotland from Europe in 1559, became morally very stern, severe and unrelenting and their references were practically all condemnations of parishioners whose choice of time and place of play displeased them. It has nothing to do with football but it is amusing to note the famous rebuke wrenched out of Cromwell when he addressed the General Assembly in 1650. 'I beseech you, in the bowels of Christ, think it possible you may be mistaken.'

The Town Councils, who often permitted an annual Fair game, were more concerned with damage to property caused by unruly and boisterous play through the streets, a problem which had increased with the growth in town populations. Yet by 1800 there is evidence, on both sides of the Border, that the game, except for some annual Fair day games, was no longer a popular pastime. Almost certainly this was a result of the great industrial upsurge of that period — an upsurge which led to the working classes being faced with six long days of hard work per week so leaving them with little time or energy for play. Indeed the game might well have disappeared had it not been for many years an accepted recreation in schools and universities. In particular the schools during the next century, not only kept the game alive but developed it, codified it and eventually through their former pupils saw it established as a robust exercise acceptable to men of their social and professional status. This last point is worth noting for it was during the 1800s that the public schools and universities produced a new class of men who, well endowed and well educated, moved as a matter of course into the higher circles of their professions and, as will be seen, it was men of such background and authority who were to govern the game during its early years.

Returning to the schools we find that in general they played a very simple game which differed in several essentials from typical Fair day games. In the latter a small hard ball was usual; there was little or no kicking but running with or passing the ball was allowed. The schools tended to use a larger air-filled ball which could be kicked but only handled if caught directly from a kick, an action which permitted the catcher to halt play while he took a kick which could be charged. There was no running with or passing the ball. The game was governed by the senior pupils who over the years accumulated a traditional set of decisions which formed the rules of play. Inevitably there developed as many varieties of the basic game as there were schools — a diversity which became only too obvious at the universities when men from different schools tried to play football together, and it was their attempts to produce a mutually acceptable set of rules that led to an important step in the history of the game.

Here let us examine some of the conclusions reached in 1895 by a group of Old Rugbeians:

1 In 1820 the form of football in vogue at Rugby was something approximating more closely to Association than what is known as Rugby Football today.

2 That at some date between 1820 and 1833 the innovation was introduced of running with the ball.

3 That this was in all probability done in the latter half of 1823 by Mr W. Webb Ellis. . . .

6

To this we would add that the innovation was regarded as of doubtful legality for some time and only gradually became accepted as part of the game but obtained a customary status between 1830 and 1840 and was duly legalised first in the season 1841-42 and finally by the rules of 1846.

This reveals how slowly the school accepted the idea of running with the ball although this was nothing novel since it had been for years an accepted feature of many annual games. There is also evidence that a handling game existed in the High School of Edinburgh round about 1810.

Much more significant was the printing in 1846 of the Rugby rules of play, for this provided a definite code which their former pupils could follow and show to others. As a result these men, at University or in city circles, stuck firmly to the principles of their handling game in all the disputes that lay ahead. In Cambridge in 1838 an attempt had been made to form a club to play by the Rugby rules, only to meet with the opposition of men from other schools who did not approve of hacking, lengthy mauls and handling; and it was not until 1863 that representatives of several clubs at two meetings, one in Cambridge and a later one in London, produced an agreed set of rules which excluded handling. This was the beginning of the Football Association.

Blackheath, who had printed their own version of the Rugby rules in 1862, declined to join the Association especially as the handling game had been carried (usually by schoolmasters) to other new public schools such as Cheltenham and Marlborough and adult clubs were springing up.

The new Association proved remarkably active and it is surprising that another eight years were to pass before a similar Rugby Union was formed.

The Scottish Scene

In Scotland, as in England, play in the streets had almost vanished, but Fair Day annual games were still found in a few areas, notably the Borders at Candlemas and it appears that the Ettrick and Yarrow shepherds occupied that day with games which included a football match. One well-recorded game took place in 1815 outside Selkirk at Carterhaugh on the Duke of Buccleuch's estate at Bowhill. Here the two sets of shepherds combined to play against townsmen from the whole Border region, and one estimate reckons that about 750 played before a great crowd which included most of the local noblemen and gentry. The moving spirit seems to have been Sir Walter Scott with the support of the Duke of Buccleuch and the Earl of Home. The Hawick players, who included 'Wemyss, the best thrower of a stone or ball in the Borders', walked over early and on reaching Selkirk were treated to a dram each . . . a gesture which cost the Burgh of Selkirk about 2 gallons of whisky costing £1.11s.4d (£1.57). The proceedings were begun by Sir Walter's son who, suitably attired and mounted, carried the ancient Buccleuch standard (still to be seen in Bowhill) round the field whereafter the Duke started play by throwing the ball into the centre of the field. The ball was small, leather-skinned and packed with wool so the game was more handball than football.

This game is very well recorded in several papers contributed to the transactions of the Hawick Archaeological Society and here we only note an incident which confirms that handling and passing of the ball was permitted. During the first session a shepherd, Walter Laidlaw, lifted the ball and threw it wide of the mass of players to William Riddell, a noted runner who was ready and stripped. He would have hailed the ba' had he not been ridden down by a mounted spectator whose action proved so unacceptable that he found it prudent to gallop from the scene. Anyone who can keep a straight face may now claim that it was two Border half backs who invented the long attacking pass!

The four Scottish universities, established between 1400 and 1600, had permitted their students to indulge in outdoor exercise. The Glasgow students almost certainly used the Green but in Edinburgh the Town Council had by 1586 granted the use of a field near the Gallows and then in 1591 allocated an area on the Burgh Muir, known as the College pitch, where the students were taken on official play days for an afternoon of supervised exercise. (Perhaps it was the golfers who managed in 1659 to have the second-year students banned from playing football on the Muir.) It should be remembered that many Scots left their parish or grammar schools to enter university at the comparatively early age of fourteen or fifteen.

This would explain the need for the supervision of games and it seems more than likely that as far as football was concerned these youngsters would not bring any major variations with them so that the university game would remain a relatively simple one. Certainly the Scottish universities played no great part in developing the handling game in their areas.

8

Residential schools did not exist, for as early as 1496 an Act of James IV had required grammar schools to be opened in the larger towns. In Edinburgh, however, the High School, although claiming a much earlier beginning, could show evidence of its existence in 1378 and by 1696 that its pupils, in a six day week, were allowed a free afternoon for refreshment and play. As already noted it seems that some form of handling game was played by 1810.

During the second half of the eighteenth century Edinburgh not only increased its working population but produced a higher society of such calibre that the 'Athens of the North' became an acknowledged literary, medical and legal centre in Britain. One result was a movement of those upper classes away from the narrow confines of the Royal Mile to create the New Town north of the line of Princes Street. Then about 1822, when it became apparent that the High School was overcrowded, it was men of this standing who, in 1824, established the Edinburgh Academy in their own area, leaving the city to erect a new High School on the Calton Hill in 1829. This breakaway was not an isolated event for in and around the city there appeared many new schools, mainly residential, of which Loretto (1827), Merchiston Castle (1833) and later Fettes College (1870) were destined with the Academy to play vital rôles in the history of the game.

In other areas there appeared similar schools such as Dollar Institution (1819), Glasgow Academy (1845) and Trinity College, Glenalmond (1847), all known to have played a simple form of football from their earliest days; but it was in Edinburgh where the seeds of the handling game took root, grew and spread.

Here within a comparatively small region there lay several boarding schools whose pupils were encouraged to exercise themselves by playing cricket and football on their own fields. Their early form of football which allowed some handling of an air-filled ball, did not differ greatly from the pre-1823 Rugby game, and in time they readily accepted the idea of running with the ball introduced to them by pupils or masters coming from the English public schools or universities. Having no transport difficulties it was not long before inter-school matches were begun and continued as an acceptable form of rivalry between the young gentlemen. Soon former pupils were mingling with the scholars during their matches and, when their numbers were sufficient, breaking away to form the first adult clubs— not only in Edinburgh but also in Glasgow where the Glasgow Academical and West of Scotland clubs welcomed many valuable recruits returning to that city from

9

the Edinburgh boarding schools. Men from these and similar backgrounds, during the formative years, not only provided the bulk of the international players, but also, as members of the Union Committee, governed the game in Scotland.

The Game comes to Edinburgh

It was two brothers, the Crombies from Thornton Castle near Laurencekirk who brought the running game to the Academy. In 1852 they entered Durham Grammar School where the Rugby rules had already been adopted. In December 1853 Alex, then seventeen, left to study Law in Edinburgh whilst Francis, two years younger, came six months later to study in the Academy from 1854 to 1856. In his last year he became the first recorded Captain of Football, an office which suggests that with the opening of Raeburn Place in 1854 the game in the school had reached another stage of development. During this time Alex Crombie had continued to play, joining with some former pupils who mixed with the scholars in their games on the new field and events suggest that it was during this period that the Rugby rules were adopted by the players. Certainly in January 1858 we find the adults forming the first FP Football Club in Scotland and it seems significant that Alex Crombie was elected Captain, a position he retained for eight seasons, and also that the new club stated that it would play according to the rules at Rugby School.

The High School, who acquired a field at Holyrood in 1860, also had the Rugby rules brought to them by one Hamilton who came as a pupil from an English public school.

These pupils, however, cannot be given the entire credit for introducing the Rugby rules into the Edinburgh area for there also arrived three Scottish schoolmasters whose immediate impact at Merchiston and Loretto was definitely equally important and whose subsequent influence on the development of the game in the schools cannot be ignored.

Thomas Harvey, a native of Glasgow, was educated at Glasgow University and Balliol College, Oxford before becoming a master at Edinburgh Academy from 1847 to 1856. So he was there when Raeburn Place was opened and the Crombies arrived. During this latter period he was commended for the unusual habit of joining the pupils in their games. He went as Headmaster to Merchiston from 1856 to 1863 and eventually returned to the Academy as Rector from 1869 to 1888. A believer in the value of outdoor

10

exercises he encouraged his staff to take an active interest in the pupils' games.

John J. Rogerson was educated at Moffat Academy before graduating at Edinburgh University. After three years as a master at Loretto and a short spell at Cheltenham he came to Merchiston in 1858, taking over from Harvey as Headmaster from 1863 to 1898. He had a great regard for games, especially Rugby football and his spell as Headmaster 'was remembered as days of unbeaten rugby sides'.

Hely-Hutchinson Almond, also a native of Glasgow, was at the University before finishing in Balliol College, Oxford. After one year at Loretto he came to Merchiston from 1858 to 1862 and then returned to Loretto to reign as Headmaster from 1862 until his death in 1902.

So all three had come in contact with football in England and were together at Merchiston during the crucial period 1858–62. They believed in the virtues of supervised outdoor exercise and as friendly Headmasters were happy to encourage their pupils to engage in inter-school matches. Almond was probably the best known, even outside Scotland. He has been aptly described as 'the great apostle of muscular Christianity in Scotland' and indeed the Spartan regime he established at Loretto startled his contemporaries by its insistence on an educational system which trained not only the minds but also the bodies of his pupils. Loretto was no place for a Billy Bunter since the food, clothing, fresh air and outdoor sports were given as much importance and consideration as the lessons and moral guidance. As Headmaster he continued the practice of playing in some of the rugby and many of the cricket matches, and strangers to the Loretto pavilion are often puzzled to find his name appearing for so many seasons in the team lists displayed on the walls.

At Merchiston, a pupil named Adriaan Van der Byl who was born in Cape Colony in 1840, arrived in the school in 1855 and left in 1858. Since he had previously been at Marlborough College (1843) from 1853 to 1855 he may well have brought some hint of the rugby rules with him. But Dr David Murray, an acknowledged antiquary who was at Merchiston between 1855 and 1857 writes that in his time the football was 'the good old Scottish game as it had been played for centuries . . . there were no rules except that the ball must be kicked not carried but it might be caught, and if it was, the captor was entitled to a free and clear kick. . . . The rugby rules had not then been heard of in the

11

North. . . .' He also mentioned that Merchiston captained by Van der Byl played football on 13 February 1858 against the High School and on 11 December 1858 against the Edinburgh Academy. This latter fixture has continued to this date and must surely be the oldest in the history of the game. It is doubtful what rules were followed in the High School game, for the school magazine of January 1859 reports that 'Football at Merchiston this year is very different and superior to the game played last year (i.e. the winter of 1857-58). For this improvement we have to thank the rugby rules and those who introduced them. Last year there was no order in the game whatever; it was each for himself, each kicking recklessly ahead, very little running with the ball and 'off side' scarcely heard of. Now it is far different, each one has that place assigned to him for which he is most suited. . . .' It is difficult to ignore the conclusion that it was the newcomers, Almond and Rogerson, who were responsible for the organising particularly since masters, especially Almond, appeared as players in several of the Merchiston teams of that time.

The Senior Clubs appear

So by the end of 1858 we find that there were three schools in the Edinburgh area which had adapted their game to the Rugby rules and had begun to play matches with one another. The Academicals had progressed a stage further to form a senior club which at once managed to arrange two fixtures. Their first match against an Edinburgh University team was an extraordinary affair since it was played on four Saturdays starting on 26 December 1857 and finishing on 16 January 1858. There was no university club at this time and this team would be a group of students on vacation in the city. Nevertheless this encounter would appear to be the earliest recorded senior game in Scotland.

It was for the best of seven goals with 25 players on each side — conditions which show how vague the rules of play were in those early days. On the first day the students scored one goal; there followed two scoreless days but on the fourth Saturday, with the teams increased to 30, the Academicals between 2 pm and 3.30 pm had kicked the four goals required to win. Although outweighted, the winners 'owed much to three or four of their number who had learned the drop kick and played the game in England' — the first reference to that rugby curiosity, the drop kick. A look at the numbers involved makes it obvious that schoolboys as well as

12

former pupils (FPs) must have been involved.

A week later the Academicals played a military team, a match which cost them 7s 6d for beer plus £2 for a tent, flags and flag posts. The garrison officers and men had been familiar opponents on the cricket field for at least twenty years and as noted in Appendix 2 they had staged at least two inter-regimental games of football in earlier years.

The Academical Football Club's first AGM must have followed during the last week of January for this latter game is mentioned in the accounts. A copy of the rules of play approved at this meeting has been found in the Academy and appears in Appendix 5 since it would seem to be the earliest set printed by a Scottish club.

Apart from the report in the *Edinburgh Evening Courant* of the Academicals–University match of 1857–58, the local newspapers carry no references to football until about 1868, and it is fortunate that we can pick a few items from the Merchiston school magazine, Dr Murray's book on the school, and the Academicals' Minute Books or Secretary's letters.

From Dr Murray we learn that Merchiston had hoped to play their first match against the Academy in November 1857 but illness in the school forced a cancellation so that the match against the High School in February 1858 became the first inter-school game. It is interesting to note that the Merchiston captain, Van der Byl, returned to Cape Colony and played in the first recorded football match in South Africa. This took place in Cape Town in August 1862 and he was described as the best man on the field in a match labelled 'Civilians v. Military'.

The Merchiston Chronicle which appeared from November 1858 to February 1861 records the following items:

1 The first Academy game at Raeburn Place in December 1858. Some extracts of interest are to be found in Appendix 10.
2 A match, EAFC v. XX of Merchiston and Academy at Raeburn Place in January 1859. The schools' team was made up of ten Academy pupils, eight Merchiston pupils and two masters, one of whom was Almond.
3 A drawn match against 22 of High School in January 1859.
4 The return match against the Academy. The Academy team included two FPs whilst Merchiston kept strictly to residents at the school which meant that Almond and another master turned out.
5 Two matches against the Academy in the 1859-60 season.
6 In the 1860–61 season a Merchistonian team played two matches against the Academicals. In the first match the Merchistonians played six FPs, twelve pupils and two masters whilst the Academicals had sixteen FPs and four boys but in the second match both Clubs agreed to play seven adults.

So the winter of 1860–61 saw the appearance of a second FP club, but, compared with the Academicals, the Merchistonians were handicapped by the greater scattering of the pupils when they left school. Some returned to their homes and family businesses in the Glasgow area and played a part in establishing the West of Scotland (1865) and Glasgow Academical (1866) Clubs.

This was an indication of things to come, for the next ten years saw the game pass through another phase marked by the formation in various regions of more school and senior clubs which, making use of the relatively new railway links, began to play matches with one another.

Another school magazine, the *Merchistonian*, appeared in 1864 and its reports show that by 1868 later school opponents included Craigmount and Dreghorn College in Edinburgh, Blairlodge at Polmont, Madras College in St Andrews and Loretto in Musselburgh (Almond, now their Headmaster, appeared in the Loretto team).

But much more significant opponents noted were the two Glasgow senior clubs mentioned above for they had also arranged fixtures with the Merchistonians and Edinburgh Academicals so forming a link between the senior clubs of the two cities which proved to be a foundation on which arose the adult game in Scotland. It is possible that this inter-city connection may have owed something to the West of Scotland Cricket Club which was formed in 1862, for their early members included several Glasgow Academicals, Edinburgh Academicals and Merchistonians and two of their earliest opponents were Merchiston Castle and the Grange whose own players included many Edinburgh Academicals, Merchistonians and Lorettonians. So when the West's Football Club was added in 1865 it is more than likely that the cricket links would be continued during the winter.

The Green Book

It was not long before the spread and increase in the number of fixtures revealed that the rules followed by each club were anything but uniform and play in matches was often halted while the captains tried to settle some point of difference that had arisen. Those more deeply interested may care to turn to the appendices and compare the four sets of rules found in print during the decade, noting not only the variations but also the lack of information on points later to be regarded as essential.

There are brief descriptions of games in the Dreghorn College magazine, *The Echo*, which suggest that in 1865 that school was still playing an early form of the handling game while the *Merchistonian* in 1867 records: 'As the Blair Lodge knew nothing about 'rugby rules' we were forced to play theirs'.

By 1865 the Edinburgh Academical FC who controlled both the school and FP clubs, were considering an approach to the other Edinburgh clubs on the subject of the rules but nothing happened until November 1867 when their committee, taking up a suggestion from Almond at Loretto, authorised their Captain, H. Cheyne, and their Secretary, G.T. Chiene, 'to meet with delegates from Loretto, Merchiston and, if possible, the West of Scotland, to have the rules adjusted so as to prevent confusion and disputes in future matches'. Several meetings did take place in Edinburgh and one after a game at Partick with the final result that Chiene was able in February 1868 to send a proof of a set of rules to Almond who had undertaken to see them printed. Chiene finished his letter thus: 'After we have got the proof finally adjusted, clear proofs should, I think, be sent to St Andrews, Merchiston and the West of Scotland. I hope the two former will adopt them though I have considerable doubts about Merchiston doing so.' He added a postscript: 'I think we may put on the title page "The Laws of Football as played by the Principal Clubs of Scotland" '. So three years before the formation in London of the Rugby Union the Scottish Clubs had produced and printed their set of Laws, which became known as the Green Book. It is disappointing to find that so far no copy has turned up, for almost certainly it would be these Laws that were used in the first International match in March 1871.

A few of the variations that existed can be picked out of reports in the *Merchistonian*. Thus on their first visit to Raeburn Place in 1858 they noted that the goal posts there offered an easier target being wider and lower and that the pitch was narrower . . . a detail also to be commented on by the first English XX in 1871. During the game they had to yield a try to a player who touched down in the area we now designate 'touch in goal' for the Academy assured them that the touch rules only applied to the side touch lines. In the second match in 1859 they gave up a try because it was claimed that the scorer had taken the ball 'off his side' in a maul but they commented 'we had always thought that if a player went into a maul on his right side he was not off side if turned round in it, but this turned out to be a mistake'. It is interesting to find that it is this later view which is known to be accepted in the Green Book.

From the Minutes and Secretary's letter of the EAFC we learn in October 1860 that it was resolved that a ball going into touch should be brought back and put into play from the spot where it crossed the line, so doing away with the scramble after a rolling ball which had to be restarted from a spot opposite to where it was captured. It was not until 1874 that the Rugby Union incorporated this feature into their Laws.

During the preparation of the Green Book both the EAFC and the West were strongly in favour of adding a rule which read: 'In the event of no goal being obtained by either side the match will be decided by the number of tries obtained by either side and one try will be held to decide the match'. This was eventually withdrawn from the rules but apparently added as a note at the end making it a matter of agreement between clubs if so desired. This radical change in the method of scoring made its way into the Rugby Union Laws in 1875.

The publication of the Green Book not only marked the end of a decade of development but ushered in a period during which the game took a decisive forward step in the establishing of international matches.

Here one cannot ignore the part played by the newspapers which by 1868 had wakened up to the fact that football was no longer just a schoolboys' game but had become a recreation indulged in by men of some social standing, and so began to insert reports of inter-club matches. By the close of the 1869–70 season such reports show the existence of the following clubs:

SCHOOLS: Edinburgh Academy; Merchiston; Royal High; Loretto; Craigmount; Blairlodge; Madras College; Glasgow Academy.

FP CLUBS: Edinburgh Academicals; Merchistonians; Glasgow Academicals; Royal High School FP.

UNIVERSITIES: St Andrews; Edinburgh; Glasgow.

OPEN CLUBS: Roland's Rooms (Edinburgh); West of Scotland; Edinburgh Wanderers.

These clubs had arranged many mutual fixtures but other sources show that the following clubs, with limited fixture lists, were also in existence: Blairgowrie, Kilmarnock (1869), Ayr, Dollar, Alloa and Perth.

At this stage it should be noted that the public schools, notably Merchiston, Loretto and later Fettes, were perfectly capable of playing against the senior clubs. The schools had a fair number of eighteen- or nineteen-year-olds but they were usually much fitter and better drilled in their team work. As we shall see several later innovations in the style of play originated in those schools before being passed on to the senior clubs.

Roland's Fencing and Gymnastic Academy, off Queen Street in Edinburgh, was run by the Roland family, some of whom were educated at The Academy or at Merchiston. Walter M. Roland and Ernest T. Roland were good all-round sportsmen, the first playing in Scottish cricket XIs and the latter being capped twice in 1884 when playing for Edinburgh Wanderers.

The First International Game

When the FA, formed at a meeting in London in 1863, was formulating its rules of play, attention was paid to the views expressed at the Cambridge meeting held earlier in the same year, but no contact was made with several clubs who had been playing a form of football for at least five years in the Sheffield area. Eventually, with the object of widening and strengthening its area of control, the FA arranged a match in London against the Sheffield clubs, and this aroused so much attention that other similar district games were organised. Then in March 1870 the FA arranged a match at the Oval cricket ground under the title 'England v Scotland'. The Scottish XI was entirely comprised of players from the London area, some of whose claims to be Scottish were rather tenuous. Perhaps one had a Scottish father and another owned an estate over the Border but it was rumoured that one qualified because of his admiration for whisky and another because he went north every year to shoot grouse!

Nevertheless, the match was a success and so C.W. Alcock, the Secretary of the FA, arranged another under the same heading, to be played in London in November 1870, only this time he wrote to several Scottish newspapers inviting clubs to nominate players for the Scottish XI. This appeal produced a single player (who in fact had already gone to business in London), which is not surprising for there were only four clubs, all in the Glasgow area, playing under the FA rules: Queen's Park (1867), Thistle (1868), Hamilton (1869) and Airdrie (1870).

After the match there arose a newspaper correspondence in *The Scotsman* started off by a Glaswegian who suggested that the Scottish (Rugby) clubs should send ten down to join a like number

17

in London and challenge the FA. Alcock replied more or less accepting a challenge and added 'More than eleven we do not care to play as with greater numbers it is our opinion that the game becomes less scientific and more a trial of charging and brute force'. This provoked a letter from one H.M (whom R.S. Phillips in his *History of Scottish Rugby*, identifies as Almond, Headmaster of Loretto) who retorted: 'Mr Alcock is a very leading supporter of what is called the 'association game' which is to Rugby football or whatever its detractors may please to call it as moonlight unto sunlight and as water unto wine'.

However, it became obvious that the Scottish clubs had been discussing such matters amongst themselves for on 8 December 1870 there appeared in *Bell's Life in London* and *The Scotsman* the following historic letter signed by the captains of five senior Scottish clubs:

Sir,
    There is a pretty general feeling among Scotch football players that the football power of the old country was not properly represented in the late so-called International Football Match. Not that we think the play of the gentlemen who represented Scotland otherwise than very good — for that it was so is amply proved by the stout resistance they offered to their opponents and by the fact that they were beaten by only one goal — but that we consider the Association rules, in accordance with which the late game was played, not such as to bring together the best team Scotland could turn out. Almost all the leading clubs play by the Rugby code, and have no opportunity of practising the Association game even if willing to do so. We therefore feel that a match played in accordance with any rules other than those in general use in Scotland, as was the case in the last match, is not one that would meet with support generally from her players. For our satisfaction, therefore, and with a view of really testing what Scotland can do against an English team we, as representing the football interests of Scotland, hereby challenge any team selected from the whole of England, to play us a match, twenty-a-side, Rugby rules either in Edinburgh or Glasgow on any day during the present season that might be found suitable to the English players. Let this count as the return to the match played in London on 19th November, or, if preferred, let it be a separate match. If it be entered into we can promise England a hearty welcome and a first-rate match. Any communications addressed to any one of us will be attended to.
    We are, etc.,
      A.H. Robertson, West of Scotland FC
      F. Moncreiff, Edinburgh Academical FC
      B. Hall Blyth, Merchistonian FC
      J.W. Arthur, Glasgow Academical FC
      J.H. Oatts, St Salvator FC, St Andrews

As one might expect this challenge was ignored by Alcock and the FA but an acceptance on behalf of the rugby-playing clubs in the London area was received from B.H. Burns, Secretary of the oldest established club, Blackheath. So in Edinburgh a committee of six — H.H. Almond (Loretto), J.W. Arthur (Glas. Acads.), B.H. Blyth (Merchistonians), A. Buchanan (RHSFP), Dr J. Chiene and F.J. Moncreiff (Edin. Acads.) was formed to make the necessary arrangements and the match was fixed to be played on the Academical ground at Raeburn Place on Monday, 27 March. It was decided to stage one trial in Glasgow on 11 March and another in Edinburgh on 20 March before selecting the final team. In London a similar committee with B.H. Burns as Secretary undertook the English arrangements but no trials were run and their team was made up of twelve from the London region strengthened by four each nominated by the two main northern Clubs, Liverpool and Manchester. There had been some changes in mind about the number of players. The original challenge suggested twenty; by the end of February this had changed to fifteen but by 15 March Burns let it be known that he was able to bring twenty, which number was finally accepted.

The *Glasgow Herald* on 25 March reported that the Rugby School rules were to be used, with two minor alterations, both of which were customary round London:

1 The ball, on going into touch, is to be thrown into the ground again from the spot where it crossed the line, and not where it first pitched in touch.
2 For a try at goal, the ball is brought out in a straight line from where it was touched down. (This would eliminate the alternative choice of punting out after a touch down.)

It was also noted that round London it was a rule generally observed that the ball may be taken up whether rolling or bounding. The Scottish clubs only allowed it in the latter case — and this was the condition accepted.

Here some brief comments on a few of the players are of interest.

A.G. Colville, listed as a Merchistonian, had been playing with Blackheath since 1867 so is our first Anglo–Scot cap. The London committee had pressed him to play in the English XX but he preferred to play for Scotland.

B.H. Burns, already noted as the Blackheath Secretary, filled a last minute vacancy in the English XX, so creating another precedent for he was born in Scotland (probably Perth or St Andrews) and was educated in St Andrews and the Edinburgh Academy before going south to be a banker in London.

Two others could be regarded as our first Colonial caps for J.H.L. Macfarlane was born in Jamaica although educated at Craigmount and Edinburgh Institution while Alfred Clunies-Ross being one of the famous Cocos Island family was partly Scottish and partly Malaysian. He spent seven years at Madras College before studying at St Andrews and Edinburgh Universities.

J.H.L. Macfarlane like A. Buchanan, W. Cross and F.J. Moncreiff, had been placed amongst the forwards although all four were more than competent performers at half back for their clubs. Perhaps this was at the back of the writer's mind when he wrote the following letter which appeared in *The Scotsman* on the morning of the match:

Sir,
 Our Scottish team is a very heavy one and the play of the backs and half backs is very fine. Will you allow me a corner of your columns to remind *some* of the rest of the Twenty that their proper place is 'forward' and that habitually. Assuming the positions as they did last Wednesday (i.e. at the Edinburgh Trial) of quarter backs and three quarter backs is an annoyance to the best players and very bad play. The business of a forward is not to hang about promiscuously waiting for something to turn up but to FOLLOW UP.

There is a terribly familiar ring about that exhortation!

It is of interest to examine the choice of venue for the match. The Challenge Letter suggested either Edinburgh or Glasgow but basically this meant Raeburn Place or Hamilton Crescent in Partick. But at this time Hamilton Crescent lay some distance outside Glasgow and its transport system, a point known to G.T. Chiene when as Secretary of the EAFC he wrote to W.H. Dunlop of the West of Scotland FC saying: 'We intend to come through by the 11.30 train which will give us time to dress and drive out to your ground by 2.30. . . . If not too much trouble, might I ask you to look in at the Bedford and tell them to have some bedrooms ready. Would it be a good plan to have an omnibus out to the ground if such a thing can be got? If you think this is better than cabs, would you ask the Bedford also to order one for us.' Obviously then Raeburn Place was more convenient for it lay within a ten minutes' cab ride from the New Town area where the players would almost certainly lodge and change and of course the spectators could use the local service to Stockbridge. It was also a more sensible choice firstly for the Committee who had only J.W. Arthur from the Glasgow area and then for the players since thirteen of the Scottish XX were resident in the city. The London contingent would wish to use the East Coast route and the Lancashire group would travel via Carstairs to the Princes Street Station.

So the Edinburgh Academical Cricket Club Committee (who controlled Raeburn Place) was approached and after discussion 'resolved by a majority that the ground be granted', a statement that leaves one curious about the objections that had been raised. However, they were happier later on for their Treasurer's report noted 'the large sum of £13 was obtained from the Football Fund, being balance of gate money on the day of the First International Match after deducting expenses'.

The next home International in 1873 was taken to Hamilton Crescent but this venue did not find favour for only a further three matches were played there while Raeburn Place was used up to 1895. Whatever the reasons, this preference must have played a part when the Union Committee decided to place their own field in Edinburgh.

At Raeburn Place the playing area lay more or less in its present position but was bounded on the west and north by an open burn which then ran along the back of the Grange CC ground to join the Water of Leith. The pitch measured 120 yards by 55 yards, a narrowness which did not suit the visitors for they had speedy backs who favoured a semicircular path to the goal line. Since neither North Park Terrace nor Inverleith Pond existed, the open rising ground over the burn to the west and north was used by the spectators whilst the east touch line and the famous mound was reserved for Academicals and their guests. The spectators probably entered at the south-west corner (where the Wright Memorial Gates now stand) for there was a bridge over the burn at that spot. They paid their 1s. (5p) to J.H.A. Macdonald who sat behind a deal table with an earthenware bowl to hold the taking. We shall meet this official later in 1890 when as Lord Kingsburgh he played an even more important part in the history of rugby football.

Later the pitch was not only widened but moved 20 yards both to the north and east which placed the playing area that much further away from the main roadway at Raeburn Place and the open burn on the west side (which was not completely covered over until about 1891 and whose exit point into the Water of Leith is still clearly visible).

For 24 years this field was used for Scotland's home matches but eventually points of difference between the Union and the Academical club developed as the number of International and

ENGLAND   Raeburn Place   27 March 1871

SCOTLAND: 1 goal, 1 try   Win
ENGLAND: 1 try

Scotland: W.D. Brown (*Glas. Acads.*), T. Chalmers (*Glas. Acads.*), A. Clunies-Ross (*St Andrews Univ.*); T.R. Marshall (*Edin. Acads.*), J.W. Arthur (*Glas. Acads.*), W. Cross (*Glas. Acads.*); A. Buchanan (*RHSFP*), A.G. Colville (*Merchistonians*), D. Drew (*Glas. Acads.*), J.F. Finlay (*Edin. Acads.*), J. Forsyth (*Edin. Univ.*), R.W. Irvine (*Edin. Acads.*), W.J.C. Lyall (*Edin. Acads.*), J.L.H. Macfarlane (*Edin. Univ.*), J.A.W. Mein (*Edin. Acads.*), F.J. Moncreiff* (*Edin. Acads.*), R. Munro (*St Andrews Univ.*), G. Ritchie (*Merchistonians*), A.H. Robertson (*West of Scot.*), J.S. Thomson (*Glas. Acads.*)

England: A. Lyon (*Liverpool*), A.G. Guillemard (*West Kent*), R.R. Osborne (*Manchester*); W. McLaren (*Manchester*); F. Tobin (*Liverpool*), J.E. Bentley (*Gipsies*), J.F. Green (*West Kent*); R.H. Birkett (*Clapham Rovers*), B.H. Burns (*Blackheath*), J.H. Clayton (*Liverpool*), C.A. Crompton (*Blackheath*), A. Davenport (*Ravenscourt Park*), J.M. Dugdale (*Ravenscourt Park*), A.S. Gibson (*Manchester*), A.St.G. Hamersley (*Marl. Nomads*), J.H. Luscombe (*Gipsies*), C.W. Sherrard (*Blackheath*), F. Stokes* (*Blackheath*), D.P. Turner (*Richmond*), H.J.C. Turner (*Manchester*)

Umpires: H.H. Almond, A. Ward

No scoring at half time. A Buchanan scored and W. Cross converted; R.H. Birkett scored but F. Stokes failed; W. Cross scored but failed to convert.

Shortly after 3 pm Scotland kicked off from the Inverleith end with the slight north-easterly breeze behind them. Play was fairly even during the first half. Scotland carried the ball over the line once but the umpires decided on a hack off at five yards as both sides claimed the touch. Turner narrowly missed a drop at goal from a free kick and McLaren, not permitted to pick up a rolling ball, tried but failed to kick a field goal from some 15 yards in front of the posts.

Early in the second half a maul formed about a yard from the English line and Ritchie with the ball was pushed over with half-a-dozen on top of him. One of his opponents also claimed the touch and as the two could not agree the umpires decided on a hack off at five yards. To the end of his days Ritchie maintained that he had scored. However, no sooner had the maul formed when the Scottish forwards drove the entire mass over the line where Buchanan with Macfarlane beside him, grounded the ball. This was loudly disputed on the grounds that the ball had not been put down before the surge was made, but the umpires were unable to make out the exact nature of the objection and so granted the try which was converted from near the east touch line by Cross.

Now the English backs began to show their speed and had some splendid runs, but hard tackling and the narrowness of the pitch halted their efforts. Green was particularly good but was so heavily tackled by Chalmers that he had to leave the field. Then H.J.C. Turner, catching a drop out after a touch down, passed the ball to Birkett who ran in close to touch. Stokes missed the long difficult kick across the wind.

Towards the end the better training of the Scots began to tell, and near full time their pack forced the ball into touch near the English line. From there a long throw in went beyond the forwards to Arthur who, attempting to catch the ball, knocked it forward over the heads of the defenders and Cross, following up quickly, touched down for a try which was at once disputed by the Englishmen who objected to the knock forward catching them out of position. But at this time such knocks were not illegal and the umpires, deciding that it was not intentional, gave the score. Cross failed to convert against the wind and the game finished some two minutes later, Scotland thus winning by the only goal.

Since both Scottish scores were disputed on the field and adversely spoken of in later years, some comments on the points of law involved must be made here.

The first score followed a hack off at five yards. For this a Scottish forward, holding the ball, was surrounded by the forwards of both sides, each standing upright, head in the air, shoulder to shoulder and facing his opponents' goal line. The ball was then pushed down onto the ground and all tried by pushing, hacking and kicking to force the ball forward through the mass. H.H. Almond later wrote: 'The ball had certainly been scrummaged over the line by Scotland and touched down first by a Scotchman. The try was vociferously disputed by the English team but upon what ground I was then unable to discover. Had the good rule of the Green Book been kept, viz. that no one except the captain should speak in any dispute unless appealed to, I should have understood that the point raised was that the ball had never been fairly grounded in the scrummage but had got mixed up among Scottish feet or legs. This I only learned afterwards. Indeed when the game was played twenty-a-side, the ball, at the beginning of a scrummage, was quite invisible to anyone outside, nor do I know how I could have decided the point had I known what it was.'

A study of the contemporary drawing of such a scrummage reveals the accuracy of Almond's observation and I would add that having staged two old-style exhibition games I not only agree with Almond but am sure that in the scrummage only the holder of the ball could tell if it had been put down correctly. In view of Almond's initial remarks it may well have been the case that the Scots went into the maul so fast that they caught their opponents unprepared, for after all they did succeed in mauling the ball forward the five yards to the line for the score.

Almond's trenchant final comment on his decision has often been quoted: 'I must say, however, that when an umpire is in doubt, I think he is justified in deciding against the side which makes most noise. They are probably in the wrong.'

The second Scottish score raises no great problem. Undoubtedly by 1883 the try would have been disallowed as resulting from a knock on, but the original Rugby Union Laws which were approved in 1871 defined a knock on as 'deliberately hitting the ball with the hand' and so Arthur's unintentional deflection of the ball did not constitute a fault. It is recorded that in the 1879–80 season, H.T. Twynam, a Richmond cap, knocked the ball forward at the tail of a line out, followed up, caught the ball and scored against Oxford University. F.R. Adams, the Richmond captain and another cap, refused to admit that the knock on was deliberate and claimed the score. It is believed that the dead-lock that followed eventually caused the Union to amend the Law by omitting the word 'deliberately'.

Now while the Challenge Letter of 8 December 1870 certainly initiated a new stage in the history of the game, it may also have been the stimulus that prompted the English clubs to form their Rugby Union, for a letter over the names of the Blackheath and Richmond secretaries appeared on 26 December proposing a meeting of all rugby-playing clubs in order to produce an acceptable and uniform code of play. Such a meeting of 21 clubs took place in London on 26 January 1871, but the outcome was the formation of a Rugby Union with a constitution designed to produce and keep up to date the rules of the game and of the Union itself. The Committee of this Union duly produced a new set of Laws of play which were formally adopted at the first AGM in October 1871.

The Scottish clubs, who had worked by the Green Book since 1868, at once appreciated that this new code was more comprehensive and up-to-date, so accepted it by joining the new Union: West of Scotland, Glasgow Academicals and Edinburgh University in 1871 and Edinburgh Academicals, Royal High School FP and Edinburgh Wanderers in 1872. This immediate Scottish acceptance of the new Union as a Rule maker must be noted, and it could be recalled that a dispute over a try between Glasgow Academicals and West of Scotland in February 1870 had to be settled by referring the matter to the Editor of *Bell's Life in London*.

By November 1871 the Scottish clubs had received and accepted an invitation from the Rugby Union to repeat the International fixture in London and *The Scotsman* reported: 'It was now intended to make the event an annual affair to take place in Scotland and England alternately'. So the Scottish Committee met, arranged two trial games (rather ruined by the weather and the absence of nominated players) and eventually selected their XX. The Rugby Union asked each of their member clubs to nominate four players, reduced these to a pool of 40 and then ran two trials before picking their team, which at the Oval ground proved not only too heavy but too fit for their opponents.

Scotland once more included players from south of the Border: A.G. Colville (Black-heath), known as a very fast forward, adept at dribbling, was in again and there were three Army men in F.T. Maxwell, R.P. Maitland and H.W. Renny-Tailyour, the last two having made their names as fine back players while training at the R.M.A., Woolwich. This triggered off some discussion on the qualifications for inclusion in an International team: England favoured a residential basis but Scotland insisted on a birth qualification since they were losing so many players to business appointments down south, to the two Universities and to the Army. However, as we shall see this was a problem with so many facets that even today it is doubtful if a tidy answer has been found.

ENGLAND   Kennington Oval   5 February 1872

SCOTLAND: 1 drop goal   **Loss**

ENGLAND: 1 goal, 1 drop goal, 2 tries

Scotland: W.D. Brown (*Glas. Acads.*), T. Chalmers (*Glas. Acads.*), L.M. Balfour (*Edin. Acads.*); T.R. Marshall (*Edin. Acads.*), R.P. Maitland (*Royal Artillery*), J.W. Arthur (*Glas. Acads.*), W. Cross (*Glas. Acads.*), F.J. Moncreiff* (*Edin. Acads.*); J.W. Anderson (*West of Scot.*), E.M. Bannerman (*Edin. Acads.*), C.W. Cathcart (*Edin. Univ.*), A.G. Colville (*Merchistonians*), J.F. Finlay (*Edin. Acads.*), R.W. Irvine (*Edin. Acads.*), J.H. McClure (*West of Scot.*), J.L.H. Macfarlane (*Edin. Univ.*), W. Marshall (*Edin. Acads.*), F.T. Maxwell (*Royal Engineers*), J.A.W. Mein (*Edin. Acads.*), R.W. Renny-Tailyour (*Royal Engineers*)

England: F.W. Mills (*Marl. Nomads*), W.O. Moberley (*Ravenscourt Park*), A.G. Guil-lemard (*West Kent*); H. Freeman (*Marl. Nomads*), J.E. Bentley (*Gipsies*), S. Finney (*RIEC*), P. Wilkinson (*Law Club*); T. Batson (*Blackheath*), J.A. Body (*Gipsies*), J.A. Bush (*Clifton*), F.I. Currey (*Marl. Nomads*), F.B.G. D'Aguilar (*Royal Engineers*), A.St.G. Hamersley (*Marl. Nomads*), F.W. Isherwood (*Ravenscourt Park*), F. Luscombe (*Gipsies*), J.E.H. Mackinlay (*St George's*), W.W. Pinching (*Guy's*), C.W. Sherrard (*Royal Engineers*), F. Stokes* (*Blackheath*), D.P. Turner (*Richmond*)

Umpires: B. Hall Blyth, A. Rutter

C.W. Cathcart dropped a goal. A. St.C. Hamersley scored and F.W. Isherwood converted. (H.T). H. Freeman dropped a goal. F.B. D'Aguilar scored and Isherwood failed. S. Finney scored and Isherwood failed.

Played in favourable weather before some 4000 spectators. The pitch measured 120 × 70 yards, an increase in width which suited the English backs. This year the English had prepared by several trial games and were much fitter than their opponents.

Scotland began well with a drop goal inside ten minutes but thereafter the English pack took charge. The nearest Scotland came to scoring again was from a free kick taken by L.M. Balfour from a 'fair catch' by T. Chalmers. The West Kent Club lent their goal posts and the touch lines were marked out by white flags borrowed from Union clubs. One Scot had his flannels torn off and was surrounded by the players until 'he was handed a macintosh in which he encased himself and amid considerable amusement repaired to the pavilion to obtain another garment'.

ENGLAND   Hamilton Crescent, Glasgow   3 March 1873

SCOTLAND: Nil   **Draw**
ENGLAND: Nil

Scotland: J.L.P. Sanderson (*Edin. Acads.*), W.D. Brown (*Glas. Acads.*), T. Chalmers (*Glas. Acads.*); T.R. Marshall (*Edin. Acads.*), W. St.C. Grant (*Craigmount School*); G.B. McClure (*West of Scot.*), J.L.H. Macfarlane (*Edin. Univ.*); P. Anton (*St Andrews Univ.*), H.W. Allen (*Glas. Acads.*), E.M. Bannerman (*Edin. Acads.*), C.C. Bryce (*Glas. Acads.*), C.W. Cathcart (*Edin. Univ.*), J.P. Davidson (*RIEC*), R.W. Irvine (*Edin. Acads.*), J.A.W. Mein (*Edin. Acads.*), F.J. Moncreiff* (*Edin. Acads.*), A.G. Petrie (*RHSFP*), T.P. Whittington (*Merchistonians*), R.W. Wilson (*West of Scot.*), A. Wood (*RHSFP*)

England: F.W. Mills (*Marl. Nomads*), C.H.R. Vanderspar (*Richmond*), W.R.B. Fletcher (*Marl. Nomads*); H. Freeman (*Marl. Nomads*); C.W. Boyle (*Oxford Univ.*), S. Finney (*RIEC*), S. Morse (*Law Club*); J.A. Body (*Gipsies*), H.A. Bush (*Clifton*), E.C. Cheston (*Law Club*), A.St.G. Hamersley (*Marl. Nomads*), Hon. H.A. Lawrence (*Richmond*), F. Luscombe (*Gipsies*), J.E.H. Mackinlay (*St George's*), H. Marsh (*RIEC*), M.W. Marshall (*Blackheath*), C.H. Rickards (*Gipsies*), E.R. Still (*Oxford Univ.*), F. Stokes* (*Blackheath*), D.P. Turner (*Richmond*)

Umpires: B. Hall Blyth, A.G. Guillemard

A crowd of some 4000 saw the game played under the most disagreeable conditions for snow and frost had given way to heavy rain which fell throughout. There ensued a tremendous forward battle; the nearest to a score came from Freeman who, claiming a fair catch some 50 yards out, had a magnificent soaring drop kick which went so high that the umpires could only declare it 'a poster'.

Before the game the English players sent their boots to a local cobbler to have bars fixed to the soles. When the boots came back Boyle and Freeman found themselves one boot short and had to play with a dress boot on one foot.

A match card exists and shows Fletcher as a third back with Morse making a third half back.

The Formation of the Scottish Union

In May 1872 the Grange Cricket Club, having settled into their new ground just across the lane from the Academical field at Raeburn Place, opened it with a grand match 'Edinburgh v. Glasgow' and this was so successful that it may well have been the reason why the rugby men staged two inter-city matches, one in Glasgow in December 1872 and a return in Edinburgh in January 1873. Certainly the cricket and rugby fraternities of these days were closely linked, because they shared not only many players but also playing areas. Indeed it is interesting to check when Scotland first played an International rugby match on a non-cricket field.

The two inter-city matches and the trials for the 1873 International in Glasgow were arranged by the quondam Scottish Committee but obviously the aims and success of the new English Union had not gone unnoticed, and sometime during the autumn or early winter of 1872 the first steps to form a Scottish Union were taken at a small dinner session in the University Club in Edinburgh. Those present were Dr John Chiene, James Wallace, R. Craigie Bell and Harry Cheyne (Edinburgh Academicals), B. Hall-Blyth (Merchistonians) and Albert Harvey (Glasgow Academicals) — a group of players of considerable professional standing which was later to provide the first three Presidents, one Vice President and the first Secretary of the future Scottish Football Union. All, except Harvey, were graduates of Edinburgh University: Chiene finished as a very distinguished Professor of medicine; Wallace, an Advocate, became a Sheriff; Bell and Cheyne were Writers to the Signet; Hall-Blyth was a noted Civil Engineer, whilst Harvey, from a family of distillers, was a prominent merchant in Glasgow.

The eventual outcome of their discussion was a notice calling a meeting on Monday, 3 March 1873 to be held in the old Glasgow Academy in Elmbank Street at 4.30 pm (i.e. immediately after the end of the English match at Hamilton Crescent) to consider 'the propriety of forming a Football Union in Scotland on a similar basis to the Rugby Union in England'.

This meeting duly took place with Dr Chiene called to the Chair and it was agreed that such a Union should be created with the objects of (1) providing funds for a Cup (2) bringing into closer connection the clubs then playing (3) the formation of a committee by whom the Scotch International team might in future be chosen.

A provisional committee consisting of the Captain and one other member from each of the following clubs: Edinburgh, Glasgow and St Andrews Universities, Edinburgh and Glasgow Academicals, West of Scotland, Royal High School FP and Merchistonians, with James Wallace as Secretary, was nominated to draw up the Bye Laws of a Union to be submitted at a General Meeting to be held before the opening of the next season. There must have been little doubt about the outcome of this meeting for the International dinner card for that same evening not only carried a toast to the Rugby Union but also one for this embryonic Scottish Football Union.

Eventually then the First AGM of the Scottish Football Union was held in Keith & Co's Rooms, 65A George Street, Edinburgh at 4.30 pm on Thursday, 9 October 1873. Harry Cheyne, WS, was in the Chair and the meeting first approved and passed the Bye Laws of the new Union. It is interesting to note that the idea of providing a Cup had been discarded — a decision that was to be maintained for many years to come. It was, however, agreed that the new Union should co-operate with the Rugby Union but, as we shall see, this was a relationship that after some ten years became badly strained. It was also decided that the working committee should consist of a President, Vice President, Honorary Secretary and Treasurer with the Captains of all the member clubs.

The Bye Laws having been passed the meeting then admitted the Wanderers FC (Edinburgh) and Warriston FC as members, so whilst the eight original clubs may be termed founder members those two additional clubs now join them as original members of the Union.

Here we may look ahead and review briefly the changes in the composition of the committee that were to follow up to the war in 1914. The original set-up remained until 1876 by which time the number of member clubs had risen to 21, and it was then passed that the committee should consist of the three office bearers with two representatives from both the Eastern and Western Districts — a number that was increased to three each in 1880. By then the game had become firmly established in areas outside the two cities and recognition of this came in 1889 when the Northern and Southern Districts both added a single member to the committee. Not content with this the Borders (who, to put it bluntly, had their reservations about being controlled by the Old School Tie Brigade) succeeded in 1894 in raising the South representation to

29

two while reducing the West to the same number. The proposer stated: 'This was not dictated by any hostility to Glasgow but from a sense of justice to the South who boasted as many clubs as the West and who were not deficient in play'. Needless to say the Western contingent protested vigorously, even more so when in 1896 the London District were granted a single additional representative, and the question of numbers was raised and voted on without result until 1905 when a sub-committee produced a report on the matter. This report, amongst other points, suggested that the East and South representation should drop to two and one respectively. Again for two years these numbers were discussed without result until in 1908 when they accepted in spite of the continued opposition of the South who maintained that one man could not do justice to the needs of their scattered community. The next significant change came in 1910 when it was decided to appoint A.D. Flett, CA (Edinburgh Wanderers) as Treasurer — the first paid official of the Union. Finally, in March 1914, with no knowledge of the disruption that lay ahead, J. Aikman Smith, acting on medical advice, announced his intention to demit office at the next AGM. So a new Constitution was prepared which retained the seven District representatives, proposed the addition to the committee of five Special Representatives, who, without vote, would serve for a period of five years and allowed the engagement of a paid Secretary. At the AGM, changed to a new date in May, this Consititution was passed and A.D. Flett was appointed to the dual position of paid Secretary and Treasurer.

ENGLAND   **Kennington Oval**   **23 February 1874**

SCOTLAND: 1 try   **Loss**

ENGLAND: 1 drop goal

Scotland: W.D. Brown* (*Glas. Acads.*), T. Chalmers (*Glas. Acads.*); T.R. Marshall (*Edin. Acads.*), W.H. Kidston (*West of Scot.*), H.M. Hamilton (*West of Scot.*); W.St.C. Grant (*Craigmount School*), A.K. Stewart (*Edin. Univ.*); C.C. Bryce (*Glas. Acads.*), J.P. Davidson (*RIEC*), J.F. Finlay (*Edin. Acads.*), G. Heron (*Glas. Acads.*), R.W. Irvine (*Edin. Acads.*), J.A.W. Mein (*Edin. Acads.*), T. Neilson (*West of Scot.*), A.G. Petrie (*RHSFP*), J. Reid (*Edin. Wrs.*), J.K. Todd (*Glas. Acads.*), R.W. Wilson (*West of Scot.*), A. Wood (*RHSFP*), A.H. Young (*Edin. Acads.*)

England: J.W. Batten (*Camb. Univ.*), M.J. Brooks (*Oxford Univ.*); H. Freeman (*Marl. Nomads*); W.H. Milton (*Marl. Nomads*), S. Morse (*Marl. Nomads*), W.E. Collins (*Old Cheltonians*); T. Batson (*Blackheath*), H.A. Bryden (*Clapham Rovers*), E.C. Cheston

(*Richmond*), C.W. Cross (*Oxford Univ.*), F.L. Cunliffe (*RMA*), J.S.M. Genth (*Manchester*), A. St.G. Hamersley* (*Marl. Nomads*), E. Kewley (*Liverpool*), Hon. H.A. Lawrence (*Richmond*), M.W. Marshall (*Blackheath*), Hon. S. Parker (*Liverpool*), W.F.H. Stafford (*RE*), D.P. Turner (*Richmond*), R. Walker (*Manchester*)

J.F. Finlay scored but T. Chalmers failed. (H.T.). H. Freeman dropped a goal.

Another wet day for some 4000 spectators. Accidents to Macfarlane and Sanderson caused Scotland to alter their formation in the backs. One of the newcomers, A.K. Stewart, was noted as a pioneer of passing away from the mauls to the backs and during the day the 'chucking' between Stewart, Grant and Hamilton raised much comment. One report noted 'the Scotchmens' happy knack of "heeling" the ball out to their own quarterbacks several times stood them in good stead'.

Early on Stewart touched down between the posts, but the try was disallowed in the erroneous belief that he had played a dead ball. In the second half Morse nearly scored a field goal by kicking a rolling ball, but it was close to 'no side' when Freeman won the match with a tremendous drop kick estimated at 80 yards.

ENGLAND   Raeburn Place   8 March 1875

SCOTLAND: Nil   Draw

ENGLAND: Nil

Scotland: W.D. Brown* (*Glas. Acads.*), T. Chalmers (*Glas. Acads.*); N.J. Finlay (*Edin. Acads.*), M. Cross (*Merchistonians*), H.M. Hamilton (*West of Scot.*); J.R. Hay-Gordon (*Edin. Acads.*), J.K. Tod (*Glas. Acads.*); A. Arthur (*Glas. Acads.*), J.W. Dunlop (*West of Scot.*), A.B. Finlay (*Edin. Acads.*), J.F. Finlay (*Edin. Acads.*), G.R. Fleming (*Glas. Acads.*), G. Heron (*Glas. Acads.*), R.W. Irvine (*Edin. Acads.*), A. Marshall (*Edin. Acads.*), J.A.W. Mein (*Edin. Acads.*), A.G. Petrie (*RHSFP*), J. Reid (*Edin. Wrs.*), D. Robertson (*Edin. Acads.*), A. Wood (*RHSFP*)

England: L. Birkett (*Clapham Rovers*), S. Morse (*Marl. Nomads*), A.W. Pearson (*Guy's*); W.A.D. Evanson (*Richmond*); W.E. Collins (*Old Cheltonians*), A.T. Mitchell (*Oxford Univ.*); F.R. Adams (*Richmond*), R.H. Birkett (*Clapham Rovers*), J.A. Bush (*Clifton*), E.C. Cheston (*Richmond*), W.R.B. Fletcher (*Oxford Univ.*), J.S.M. Genth (*Manchester*), H.J. Graham (*Wimbledon Hornets*), E. Kewley (*Liverpool*), Hon. H.A. Lawrence* (*Richmond*), F. Luscombe (*Gipsies*), M.W. Marshall (*Blackheath*), Hon. S. Parker (*Liverpool*), J.E. Paul (*RIEC*), D.P. Turner (*Richmond*)

A record crowd of 7000 watched in excellent conditions. The field had been increased to 130 × 85 yards. England had to make three changes, for R. Walker called off, whilst C.W. Crosse and E.H. Nash were refused leave of absence by the Oxford University authorities. Ninian Finlay, who became one of the finest backs and drop kickers of his time, was still at school and joined his two brothers for this game. The Birketts were also brothers.

There were many near things, especially in the second half when the English backs continually dropped at goal. Finlay actually dropped a goal but it was disallowed 'because the ball had been called "down" by its possessor'. Once Cross fumbled a towering kick behind his line; Bush and Collins fell on him and claimed a touch down which, however, was not given. One account notes that R.H. Birkett came out of the maul and played in the backs.

31

A Change in the Scoring System

Up to this season a match was won by a majority of goals only, which meant that tries had no scoring value. So for example when RHSFP drew with Edinburgh University in 1872 the scores were one goal, seven tries to one goal one try. The University scored and converted their second try with the last kick of the match and if RHS had not converted their seventh try they would have been beaten. Results such as this caused the RU at their AGM in October 1875 to discuss a points scoring system which gave ten points to any goal, five points to a try and one point to a touch down or touch in goal. This scheme was rejected but at another meeting in November Rule Seven was altered to read: A match shall be decided by a majority of goals, but if the number of goals be equal, or no goal be kicked, by a majority of tries; if no goal be kicked or try obtained, the match shall be drawn.

The SFU Committee at a meeting in December, not only adopted this ruling but also decreed that it should operate as from the beginning of the new season.

SCOTLAND: Nil   **Loss**
ENGLAND: 1 goal, 1 try

Scotland: T. Chalmers (*Glas. Acads.*), J.S. Carrick (*West of Scot.*); M. Cross (*Glas. Acads.*), N.J. Finlay (*Edin. Acads.*); G.Q. Paterson (*Edin. Acads.*), A.K. Stewart (*Edin. Univ.*); A. Arthur (*Merchistonians*), W.H. Bolton (*West of Scot.*), N.T. Brewis (*Edin. Inst. FP*), C.W. Cathcart (*Edin. Univ.*), D. Drew (*Glas. Acads.*), G.R. Fleming (*Glas. Acads.*), J.H.S. Graham (*Edin. Acads.*), R.W. Irvine* (*Edin. Acads.*), J.E. Junor (*Glas. Acads.*), D. Lang (*Paisley*), A.G. Petrie (*RHSFP*), J. Reid (*Edin. Wrs.*), C. Villar (*Edin. Wrs.*), D.H. Watson (*Glas. Acads.*)

England: A.H. Heath (*Oxford Univ.*), A.W. Pearson (*Blackheath*); T.S. Tetley (*Bradford*), L. Stokes (*Blackheath*), R.H. Birkett (*Clapham Rovers*); W.E. Collins (*Old Cheltonians*), W.C. Hutchinson (*RIEC*); F.R. Adams (*Richmond*), J.A. Bush (*Clifton*), E.C. Cheston (*Richmond*), H.J. Graham (*Wimbledon Hornets*), W. Grey (*Manchester*), W.H. Hunt (*Preston Grasshoppers*), E. Kewley (*Liverpool*), F.H. Lee (*Oxford Univ.*), F. Luscombe* (*Gipsies*), M.W. Marshall (*Blackheath*), W.C.W. Rawlinson (*Blackheath*), G.R. Turner (*St George's*), R. Walker (*Manchester*)

Referee: A. Rutter   **Umpires:** H.M. Hamilton, C.D. Heatley

No scoring at half time. F.H. Lee scored and L. Stokes converted. W.E. Collins scored and L. Stokes failed.

About 4000 were present on a fine but cold and windy day. Early in the second half Scotland carried the ball inside the English 25 area and looked like scoring. However, Hutchinson seized a dropped pass and had a magnificent run to the Scottish 25 where he was tackled, but got a pass out to Lee who, noted for following up, was able to score between the posts. After this Watson was brought into the backs (his club position). This is the first team selection recorded in the SFU Minutes, and it had been decided to play six men behind the maul instead of the usual seven. R.H. Birkett had also started in the maul, but finished as a back. Scotland were outplayed at half where Stewart had dislocated a thumb and Paterson (8 st 12 lb) had not the physique to be effective in defence.

The Change to Fifteens

It is surprising to note that from 1846 when Rugby School first printed their Rules, no published set makes any mention of the number of players in a team until the Home Unions in their Rules of 1892 laid down: 'The game should be played by fifteen players on each side'.

Of course in the early days the public schools in their domestic games expected everyone to take part and in Scotland it was only after inter-scholastic matches began in 1858 that the playing of twenties became established. Right up to 1870 the schools were prepared to play twenties and the early Merchiston reports show their team structure to be: Goalkeepers four; Halfbacks four; Bulldogs twelve. One may recall the variations in numbers taking part in the Academical-University game of 1857–58 but the senior clubs, obviously short of players, soon settled down to play fifteens, generally placed as: Backs four; Half backs two; Quarter backs two; Forwards nine. The letter file of the Edinburgh Academical FC for 1867 reveals that their Secretary was in touch with the West of Scotland FC asking: 'I presume you commence play about two. Please let me know as to this and also how many men you are to play'. He also wrote to Dr Almond at Loretto: 'I understand you used to play fifteen a side; please let me know if you still do so'.

Yet as we have seen the 1870 challenge to the English clubs suggested a game with twenties — a number that was finally accepted and maintained for the first six Internationals. However, the Scottish Union after a Committee meeting in December 1875 wrote suggesting a change to fifteens but the Rugby Union decided that it was too late in the season to accept the proposal. The SFU repeated their suggestion after their AGM in October 1876 and this time the RU agreed with the result that the English–Irish match at the Oval in February 1877 was the first to be played with fifteens. A fortnight later the Irish–Scottish match at Belfast saw Scotland field fifteen for the first time.

Prominent Players 1871–1876

R.W. Irvine stands out as one of the great figures in the early history of the game for not only was he a powerful forward, skilled in the arts of dribbling, line out work and destructive tackling but was regarded by all as a good captain and organiser. A man of some strength he won the Hammer throw at Edinburgh University sports in 1872 and 1873, and after graduating in medicine in 1876 practised in Pitlochry where he was a prominent promoter of local athletics.

N.J. Finlay, one of the youngest caps in the history of the game, was still at the Academy when he joined his two brothers to play in the 1875 game — and he had already figured prominently in the two inter-city games of that season before his seventeenth birthday. As heavy as most of the forwards in that match, he had real pace and so was difficult to halt when on the run but he was particularly noted for the length and accuracy of his drop kicking. Even an English writer of that time considered him 'the longest drop in Britain, Leonard Stokes not excepted' and although Finlay was firmly tackled it was one of his characteristic efforts that drew the 1879 English game. A graduate of Edinburgh University, he practised as a WS in Edinburgh.

At 6 feet three inches and weighing some thirteen stones, A.G. Petrie was one of the giants in the early years of the game. A man of exceptional strength, he also made his mark in other strenuous sports such as weight lifting, hammer throwing and rowing. His non-election to the captaincy in 1881 raised a storm which rocked the young Union.

Many fine cricketers, by any standards, were to gain their caps; T. Chalmer and T.R. Marshall were the first. Chalmers, a splendid fielder, safe tackler and good drop kicker was our first great full back.

SCOTLAND: 4 goals, 2 drop goals, 2 tries   **Win**

IRELAND: Nil

Scotland: H.H. Johnston (*Edin. Collegians*); M. Cross (*Glas. Acads.*), R.C. Mackenzie (*Glas. Acads.*); J.R. Hay Gordon (*Edin. Acads.*), E.J. Pocock (*Edin. Wrs.*); J.H.S. Graham (*Edin. Acads.*), R.W. Irvine* (*Edin. Acads.*), J.E. Junor (*Glas. Acads.*), D. Lang (*Paisley*), H.M. Napier (*West of Scot.*), A.G. Petrie (*RHSFP*), J. Reid (*Edin. Wrs.*), S.H. Smith (*Glas. Acads.*), C. Villar (*Edin. Wrs.*), D.H. Watson (*Glas. Acads.*)

Ireland: H. Moore (*Windsor*), G.M. Shaw (*Windsor*); R.B. Walkington (*NIFC*), F.W. Kidd (*Lansdowne*); J. Heron (*NIFC*), T.G. Gordon (*NIFC*); W.H. Ash (*NIFC*), T. Brown (*Windsor*), H.L. Cox (*Dublin Univ.*), J. Currell (*NIFC*), W. Finlay (*NIFC*), H.C. Kelly (*NIFC*), J.A. Macdonald (*Windsor: Methodist Coll.*), H.W. Murray (*Dublin Univ.*), W.H. Wilson* (*Dublin Univ.*)

Referee: A. Buchanan   **Umpires:** A.R. Stewart, R. Bell

E.J. Pocock scored but Cross failed; R.C. Mackenzie dropped a goal: R.C. Mackenzie scored and Cross converted; (H.T.). R.C. Mackenzie dropped a goal; R.C. Mackenzie scored but Cross failed; R.W. Irvine scored and Cross converted; R.C. Mackenzie scored and Cross converted; J. Reid scored and Cross converted.

For this initial match against Ireland, Scotland for the first time played fifteen with a single fullback. There was a good attendance in spite of the unfavourable weather, rain falling throughout.

The Irish, averaging about a stone less, were outweighted and outplayed. Pocock (an Englishman educated at Clifton), a destructive runner against a weak defence, had a good match, but also note R.C. Mackenzie's tally of three tries and two drop goals.

The First Irish Matches

In 1877 Ireland had two Unions; the first, the Irish Football Union, being formed in Dublin in 1874 and the other, the Northern Football Union of Ireland, in Belfast in 1875. These two bodies, not without dissension, managed to co-operate and arrange matches against England, the third in December 1876 being the first ever to be played with XVs. The first against Scotland, also with XVs, was played in February 1877 but the offer of a return game in Glasgow in 1878 fell through because of further disagreements between the two Unions who, however, eventually settled their differences by producing a single Irish Rugby Football Union during 1879 and this allowed the resumption of the fixture in that same year.

ENGLAND	Raeburn Place	5 March 1877

SCOTLAND:	1 drop goal	**Win**
ENGLAND:	Nil	

Scotland: J.S. Carrick (*Glas. Acads.*); H.H. Johnston (*Edin. Collegians*); M. Cross (*Glas. Acads.*), R.C. Mackenzie (*Glas. Acads.*); J.R. Hay Gordon (*Edin. Acads.*), E.I. Pocock (*Edin. Wrs.*); J.H.S. Graham (*Edin. Acads.*), R.W. Irvine* (*Edin. Acads.*), J.E. Junor (*Glas. Acads.*), H.M. Napier (*West of Scot.*), A.G. Petrie (*RHSFP*), J. Reid (*Edin. Wrs.*), T.J. Torrie (*Edin. Acads.*), C. Villar (*Edin. Wrs.*), D.H. Watson (*Glas. Acads.*)

England: L. Birkett (*Clapham Rovers*), A.W. Pearson (*Blackheath*); A.N. Hornby (*Preston Grasshoppers*), L. Stokes (*Blackheath*); W.A.D. Evanson (*Richmond*), P.L.A. Price (*Richmond*); C.C. Bryden (*Clapham Rovers*), H.W.T. Garnett (*Bradford*), G. Harrison (*Hull*), W.H. Hunt (*Preston Grasshoppers*), E. Kewley* (*Liverpool*), A.F. Law (*Richmond*), M.W. Marshall (*Blackheath*), R. Todd (*Manchester*), C.J.C. Touzell (*Camb. Univ.*)

Referee: W. Cross **Umpire:** A. Buchanan

No scoring at half time; M. Cross dropped a goal.

Scotland reverted to six behind the scrum to counter the strong running English backs. They held their own against the wind in the first half. Later the English were put under some pressure and only good defence by their backs prevented a score until close on time, when M. Cross dropped a great goal from near half way. Hay Gordon had a good match but Pocock, a good attacking player, proved too weak in defence so was put into the forwards, his place being taken by Watson who played half for his club.

ENGLAND Kennington Oval **4 March 1878**

SCOTLAND: Nil **Draw**
ENGLAND: Nil

Scotland: W.E. Maclagan (*Edin. Acads.*); M. Cross (*Glas. Acads.*), N.J. Finlay (*Edin. Acads.*); J.A. Campbell (*Merchiston Castle*), J.A. Neilson (*Glas. Acads.*); L.J. Auldjo (*Abertay*), N.T. Brewis (*Edin. Inst. FP*), J.H.S. Graham (*Edin. Acads.*), D.R. Irvine (*Edin. Acads.*), R.W. Irvine* (*Edin. Acads.*), J.E. Junor (*Glas. Acads.*), G.W.L. MacLeod (*Edin. Acads.*), H.M. Napier (*West of Scot.*), A.G. Petrie (*RHSFP*), S.H. Smith (*Glas. Acads.*)

England: A.W. Pearson (*Blackheath*), H.E. Kayll (*Sunderland*); L. Stokes (*Blackheath*), A.N. Hornby (*Preston Grasshoppers*); P.L.A. Price (*RIEC*), W.A.D. Evanson (*Richmond*); F.R. Adams (*Richmond*), J.M. Biggs (*Univ. Coll. Hospital*), H. Fowler (*Oxford Univ.*), F.D. Fowler (*RIEC*), E.T. Gurdon (*Richmond*), E. Kewley* (*Liverpool*), M.W. Marshall (*Blackheath*), G.T. Thomson (*Halifax*), G.F. Vernon (*Blackheath*)

Referee: A.G. Guillemard **Umpires:** A.R. Stewart, C.D. Heatley

Some 4000 watched in favourable weather. Scotland had the better of the first half; Campbell missing a scoring chance and Cross coming near with a drop. The call of half time halted a maul in goal between Napier and Pearson. Stokes was prominent in the second half narrowly missing a drop and scoring a try. Adams did touch down but the Scots had halted because of an infringement and the English captain 'was courteous enough to give way'. A score by Neilson was disallowed as he had picked up a dead ball. This was the last match played at the Oval.

IRELAND Ormeau Belfast **17 February 1879**

SCOTLAND: 1 goal, 1 drop goal, 1 try **Win**
IRELAND: Nil

Scotland: W.E. Maclagan (*Edin. Acads.*), M. Cross (*Glas. Acads.*), N.J. Finlay (*Edin. Acads.*); W.H. Masters (*Edin. Inst. FP.*), J.A. Campbell (*Merchistonians*); R. Ainslie (*Edin. Inst. FP*), N.T. Brewis (*Edin. Inst. FP*), J.B. Brown (*Glas. Acads.*), J.H.S. Graham (*Edin. Acads.*), D.R. Irvine (*Edin. Acads.*), R.W. Irvine* (*Edin. Acads.*), H.M. Napier (*West of Scot.*), A.G. Petrie (*RHSFP*), E.R. Smith (*Edin. Acads.*), D. Somerville (*Edin. Inst. FP*)

Ireland: R.B. Walkington (*NIFC*), T. Harrison (*Cork*); R.N. Matier (*NIFC*), J.C. Bagot (*Dublin Univ.*); A.M. Whitestone (*Dublin Univ.*), W.J. Goulding (*Cork*); A.M. Archer (*Dublin Univ.*), W.E.A. Cummins (*QC Cork*), W. Finlay (*NIFC*), H.C. Kelly (*NIFC*), J.A. Macdonald (*Methodist Coll.*), W.C. Neville* (*Dublin Univ.*), H. Purdon (*NIFC*), G. Scriven (*Dublin Univ.*), J.W. Taylor (*NIFC*)

Referee: Dr Chiene **Umpires:** A.R. Stewart, Mr Ball

38

J.B. Brown scored and M. Cross kicked a disputed goal. D. Somerville scored and M. Cross converted. (H.T.). M. Cross dropped a goal.

As Cross was about to convert Brown's try the Irish charged out and kicked the ball away, claiming that the rule concerning the taking out of the ball had been broken. After a long dispute Cross was allowed to take the kick but it was agreed to refer the matter to the Rugby Union who later decreed that the Irish action was correct. Apparently Irvine had lifted the ball to bring it out for the place kick and Cross took it out of his hands to show him the position in which it was to be held. The Irish maintained that under Rule 55 they could charge the instant that Irvine was about to place the ball since the kicker had also handled it.

The Scottish pack was too strong and Masters had a great game, being 'busy from start to finish'.

ENGLAND   Raeburn Place   10 March 1879

SCOTLAND: 1 drop goal   **Draw**
ENGLAND: 1 goal

Scotland: W.E. Maclagan (*Edin. Acads.*); M. Cross (*Glas. Acads.*), N.J. Finlay (*Edin. Acads.*); J.A. Campbell (*Glas. Acads.*), J.A. Neilson (*Glas. Acads.*); R. Ainslie (*Edin. Inst. FP*), N.T. Brewis (*Edin. Inst. FP*), J.B. Brown (*Glas. Acads.*), E.N. Ewart (*Glas. Acads.*), J.H.S. Graham (*Edin. Acads.*), D.R. Irvine (*Edin. Acads.*), R.W. Irvine* (*Edin. Acads.*), J.E. Junor (*Glas. Acads.*), H.M. Napier (*West of Scot.*), A.G. Petrie (*RHSFP*)

England: H. Buth (*Huddersfield*), W.J. Penney (*United Hospitals*); L. Stokes (*Blackheath*); W.A.D. Evanson (*Richmond*). H.H. Taylor (*St George's*); F.R. Adams* (*Richmond*), A. Budd (*Blackheath*), G.W. Burton (*Blackheath*), F.D. Fowler (*Manchester*), G. Harrison (*Hull*), N.F. McLeod (*RIEC*), S. Neame (*Old Cheltonians*), H.C. Rowley (*Manchester*), H. Springmann (*Liverpool*), R. Walker (*Manchester*).

Referee: G.R. Fleming   **Umpires:** A. Buchanan, J. Maclaren

G.W. Burton scored and L. Stokes converted; (H.T.). N.J. Finlay dropped a goal.

This, the first contest for the beautiful Calcutta Cup, was watched in dull weather by a record crowd of 10,000. England, with the wind, started strongly. Their backs ran well and Stokes' drop kicking continually landed play near the Scottish line but powerful play by their pack returned play to the English half. Unfortunately on one occasion Cross miskicked and gave an easy run in for Burton. In the second half the Scottish pack again drove the ball down to the goal line only to be thwarted by a back stepping deliberately behind and touching down — a move that was loudly hissed by the crowd 'not because it lost a rare chance to Scotland but that it showed a want of pluck not normal with Britons'! However, later both Stokes and Maclagan were loudly cheered for running the ball from behind the posts into play. The Scottish pack continued their pressure and eventually a passing run by Graham, Petrie and Ewart got the ball to Finlay who, although tackled near the line, managed to drop a goal. Throughout the match Maclagan's tackling was ferocious and he undoubtedly halted several scoring runs by the English backs.

A Decade of Development 1870–1880

At the beginning of this period play was largely confined to the forwards who, whenever play was halted, put the ball down in the middle of a maul and tried to force it forward through the mass. With 26 forwards involved this was almost entirely a matter of blind shoving enlivened by some hearty hacking if the ball was seen or felt at the feet. Once XVs were established there gradually developed a habit of stooping in the mauls so that the ball could be watched and be better controlled.

The quarter backs (the English term of half back was adopted at the turn of the century), usually two in number, stood some five yards back from the scrum, one on either side, watching for the ball to emerge. The player had then to swoop on to the ball, pick it up and make a run, finishing with a kick if his way was blocked and he had not been tackled. So the quarter backs had to be fast, alert players who did the bulk of the running and scoring.

The backs were basically defenders, tackling the runners or fielding the kicks and replying with a return kick. If circumstances were favourable they would drop at goal: N.J. Finlay, H. Freeman and L. Stokes were all famous for their successful long range drops at goal. Practically every kick was taken as a drop and indeed spectators were given to barracking a punt! Remember that the earlier, less pointed shape of the ball favoured both drop kicking and close dribbling but tended to slow up swift directed passing. In fact an intentional long pass was sometimes achieved by throwing a ball that could be taken on the bounce.

The number and positioning of the back players also varied at this time but it appears that both countries up to 1876 played seven behind the maul. There is an SFU committee minute of 1876 which records their decision to play six behind in the approaching English match instead of seven as on previous occasions. However, during the actual game D.H. Watson was brought out of the forwards to play as a back — his usual club position. England frequently stationed one of their three full backs in a forward position as a three quarter back.

By 1880 the lowering of the heads in the mauls accompanied by linking with the arms had produced important variations in the manner of play. Thus instead of always trying to force the ball forward through the scrum, the players would steer it to the side (remember there was yet no set scrum formation) and then break away in a dribbling rush. The Blackheath pack were famed for this

40

wheeling manoeuvre while in Edinburgh the Merchiston forwards were constantly praised for their combined play which included fast breaking as a mass from the mauls.

The moving of the ball to the edge of the scrum produced another much debated trick. The *Lorettonian*, during 1880, commenting on the Fettes games notes: 'Just before the match began our Captain was informed by theirs that they played heeling out on their ground' (and later) 'I noticed a great deal of hoicking done by the Fettes forwards, that is, going to the side of the scrummage, thrusting in one leg and hoicking out the ball with it for the quarter back.' The Fettes captain concerned was A.R. Don Wauchope who, although one of the greatest individual scoring quarter backs of his age, was also deeply concerned to develop combined play amongst the college backs so naturally he had good reasons to get the ball back out of the scrums.

Such closer co-operation between the back players only became feasible after the schools began to use a formation of one full back, three halves and two quarters. This set-up has been credited to the Fettes team of 1878–79 who took R.A. Carruthers out of the forwards into the backs to strengthen the defence against two dangerous Academy halves (A.P. Reid and F.T. Wright), but in fact both Merchiston and Fettes had experimented with the added half back during the previous season while the Academy and Loretto followed their example by 1880. Curiously enough it was at Loretto where deliberate attacking passing really began and developed. In the early '70s passing was despised as it rather suggested a lack of moral fibre in the passer. *The Scotsman*, reporting on an Academy–Loretto game in 1869, comments 'The Loretto players made some determined runs but were invariably collared and almost suffered their heads to be wrenched off ere they would deliver up the ball'. It was Almond, their Headmaster, who began the transformation.

A.S. Blair, a Blue in the Oxford XV of 1884, while discussing the part played by H. Vassall in producing a running game at Oxford during the early '80s, wrote: 'I have always thought it scarcely accurate to call Vassall the inventor of the modern game. To my mind he was rather the great genius who thought out and worked out for his own team ideas which already existed. . . . He was in truth the master builder, but without the straw he could not have made the bricks. . . . If by the modern game is meant the present fast open game with its quick passing, kicking and breaking up, I am inclined to think that Dr Almond . . . was perhaps the real inventor. At any rate most Lorettonians who were at School in the latter '70s and early '80s have vivid recollections of Almond in his quintuple capacity of Headmaster, captain, forward, umpire and coach, rushing about the field crying out to his boys "Pass, pass, pass," and "Kick, kick, kick" and there can be no doubt whatever that much of the phenomenal success of the Oxford teams in the early '80s was due to the Old Lorettonians in those teams.' As a matter of fact the Oxford XV of 1880 contained five Blues from Loretto while the 1884 team had seven, but while credit must be given to those from Loretto who brought their background of combined play, it must also be admitted that they found themselves in the company of gifted players who, realising its virtues, were at once able to adopt this new style of play. In particular there was A. Rotherham who arrived to partner the Lorettonian, A.G.G. Asher, at quarter back for three seasons, during which time that pair played a tremendous part in establishing the Oxford teams as the exponents of a new and superior style of aggressive, running rugby. One result of this was that the new style was taken up earlier by the English clubs than by the Scottish.

IRELAND   **Hamilton Crescent**   **14 February 1880**

SCOTLAND: 1 goal, 2 drop goals, 2 tries   **Win**

IRELAND: Nil

Scotland: W.E. Maclagan (*Edin. Acads.*); M. Cross (*Glas. Acads.*), N.J. Finlay (*Edin. Acads.*); W.H. Masters (*Edin. Inst. FP*), W.S. Brown (*Edin. Inst. FP*); R. Ainslie (*Edin. Inst. FP*), N.T. Brewis (*Edin. Inst. FP*), J.B. Brown (*Glas. Acads.*), E.N. Ewart (*Glas. Acads.*), J.H.S. Graham (*Edin. Acads.*), R.W. Irvine* (*Edin. Acads.*), D. McCowan (*West of Scot.*), A.G. Petrie (*RHSFP*), C.R. Stewart (*West of Scot.*), J.G. Tait (*Edin. Acads.*)

Ireland: R.B. Walkington (*NIFC*); J.C. Bagot (*Dublin Univ.*), T. Harrison (*Cork*); M. Johnston (*Dublin Univ.*), W.T. Heron (*NIFC*); A.P. Cronyn (*Lansdowne*), J.L. Cuppaidge (*Dublin Univ.*), W. Finlay (*NIFC*), A.J. Forrest (*Wanderers*), R.W. Hughes (*NIFC*), H.C. Kelly* (*NIFC*), A. Millar (*Kingston*), G. Scriven (*Dublin Univ.*), J.W. Taylor (*NIFC*), W.A. Wallis (*Wanderers*)

Referee: A Buchanan **Umpires:** H.W. Little, Dr Neville

N.J. Finlay dropped two goals; W.H. Masters scored and M. Cross converted (H.T.). E.N. Ewart scored two tries which Cross failed to convert.

The favourable weather suited the Scottish backs, Masters and Brown being especially brilliant, but it was the forwards who were highly praised for their rare combined play, dribbling and passing. The first try came from 'some of the prettiest chucking probably ever seen in Scotland', for the ball was passed via Stewart, Petrie, Graham and Ainslie to Brewis, who left Masters a clear run in. Ewart's two scores also came from strong forward play. In the first half Finlay dropped what appeared to be a second goal. The Irish disputed this and the umpires and referee were appealed to. Both umpires said they did not see the point and the referee thought it was a clear goal and it appears to have been accepted. However, the score was disallowed pending an appeal to the SFU. This was the first International match to be played on a Saturday.

ENGLAND   **Whalley Range**   **28 February 1880**

SCOTLAND: 1 goal   **Loss**

ENGLAND: 2 goals, 3 tries

Scotland: W.E. Maclagan (*Edin. Acads.*); N.J. Finlay (*Edin. Acads.*), M. Cross (*Glas. Acads.*); W.H. Masters (*Edin. Inst. FP*), W.S. Brown (*Edin. Inst. FP*); R. Ainslie (*Edin. Inst. FP*), N.T. Brewis (*Edin. Inst. FP*), J.B. Brown (*Glas. Acads.*), D.Y. Cassels (*West of Scot.*), E.N. Ewart (*Glas. Acads.*), J.H.S. Graham (*Edin. Acads.*), R.W. Irvine* (*Edin. Acads.*), D. McCowan (*West of Scot.*), A.G. Petrie (*RHSFP*), C.R. Stewart (*West of Scot.*)

England: T.W. Fry (*Queen's House*); L. Stokes* (*Blackheath*), C.M. Sawyer (*Broughton*); R.T. Finch (*Camb. Univ.*), H.H. Taylor (*St George's*); G.W. Burton (*Blackheath*), C.H. Coates (*Camb. Univ.*), C. Gurdon (*Richmond*), E.T. Gurdon (*Richmond*), G. Harrison (*Hull*), S. Neame (*Old Cheltonians*), C. Phillips (*Oxford Univ.*), H.C. Rowley (*Manchester*), G.F. Vernon (*Blackheath*), R. Walker (*Manchester*)

Referee: A.G. Guillemard **Umpires:** A.R. Stewart, J. McLaren

H.H. Taylor scored twice but L. Stokes failed to convert. (H.T.). T.W. Fry scored and L. Stokes converted; W.S. Brown scored and M. Cross converted; E.T. Gurdon and G.W. Burton scored, L. Stokes converted the latter try.

This was the first English match to be played on a Saturday and the change to a venue in the north was a success. The conditions were reasonable and with the breeze in the first half the Scots had four near misses with drops but the somewhat slippery conditions affected the Scots backs more than the English whose superiority brought them five tries, one being the first to be run in by a full back.

This was 'Bulldog' Irvine's tenth successive, and last, match against England.

IRELAND Ormeau Belfast 19 February 1881

| **SCOTLAND:** | 1 try | **Loss** |
| **IRELAND:** | 1 drop goal | |

Scotland: T.A. Begbie (*Edin. Wrs.*); W.E. Maclagan (*Edin. Acads.*), N.J. Finlay (*Edin. Acads.*), R.C. Mackenzie (*Glas. Acads.*); J.A. Campbell (*Glas. Acads.*), P.W. Smeaton (*Edin. Acads.*); R.B. Allan (*Glas. Acads.*), J.B. Brown (*Glas. Acads.*), D.Y. Cassels (*West of Scot.*), J.H.S. Graham* (*Edin. Acads.*), J.E. Junor (*Glas. Acads.*), D. McCowan (*West of Scot.*), C. Reid (*Edin. Academy*), G.H. Robb (*Glas. Univ.*), A. Walker (*West of Scot.*)

Ireland: R.E. McLean (*Dublin Univ.*); J.C. Bagot (*Dublin Univ.*), W.W. Pike (*Kingstown*); M. Johnston (*Dublin Univ.*), H.F. Spunner (*Wanderers*); D.R. Browning (*Wanderers*), A.J. Forrest* (*Wanderers*), R.W. Hughes (*NIFC*), J. Johnston (*Belfast Albion*), J.A. Macdonald (*Methodist Coll.*), A.R. McMullan (*Cork*), H.B. Morell (*Dublin Univ.*), H. Purdon (*NIFC*), J.W. Taylor (*NIFC*), W.A. Wallis (*Wanderers*)

No scoring at half time; J.H.S. Graham scored but T.A. Begbie failed; J.C. Bagot dropped a goal.

This match, the first International win by Ireland, is best told by quoting Jacques McCarthy, an Irish reporter with a colourful turn of phrase.

They commenced fiercely but after Spunner and big Jock Graham had gotten black eyes, and a certain hot Scotsman had come second best out of an independent boxing match with Browning, milder methods were adopted. No tangible score was gained in the first half, but in the second McMullen making a miscatch at a long kick (. . . from Maclagan) placed the whole of the Scottish team onside, and Graham, who was leaning against the Irish goal post, rubbing his shin after a recent hack, leisurely limped over and touched the ball down. . . . some slight relief was forthcoming when Begbie missed the kick which was as easy as possible. . . . Only five minutes remained . . . Taylor got possession after a drop out and ran and worried his way amidst frantic exhortations up

44

to the Scottish 25 where he passed to Johnston who returned him the leather on the very verge of the Scottish line. Here it was heeled out to Johnston who amidst vociferous profanity missed his pick-up and Campbell shot the ball into touch ten yards down. Hughes, however, rapidly realised the situation and threw it out to Taylor before the Scotsmen could line up, and Taylor transferred to Johnston, who quicker than you could think or write tossed to Bagot who dropped the ball over the goal.

By 1880 club rivalries were well established and there was none fiercer than that between the Royal High School FPs and the Edinburgh Academicals which of course stemmed from the foundation of the Academy in 1824. Referring to some of their earlier matches a sports article in 1889 noted: 'It was never quite clear what the football was brought onto the field for, as after the first kick most of the players forgot it was there and they are said to have marched off the field one time and left the ball behind them'. (This must remind one of the spectator at the Hawick–Gala game who gave vent to the appeal 'Never mind the ba', get on wi' the game'.)

So when the XV to meet Ireland in 1881 was announced and it was seen that the captaincy held for the previous five years by R.W. Irvine had been passed to a relatively new cap in his clubmate, J.H.S. Graham, the indignation in certain areas that the senior cap in the High Scholar, A.G. Petrie, had been passed over, was tremendous. Phillips wrote that the lads met in crowds in their howffs and vented their displeasure on the Union. The outcome was a Special General Meeting which called for the resignation of the Union Committee, but after some considerable discussion the motion was withdrawn, the Committee having made some concessions which included a suggestion that the XV should be allowed to chose its own captain.

The affair then died down but there were two repercussions. Firstly the strong High School, Edinburgh Institution and Edinburgh University forward choices withdrew from the XV which lost to Ireland for the first time. Then at the next AGM of the Union there were wholesale changes in the Committee headed by the election of A.G. Petrie to the Presidency.

ENGLAND	Raeburn Place	19 March 1881

SCOTLAND:	1 goal, 1 try	**Draw**
ENGLAND:	1 drop goal, 1 try	

Scotland: T.A. Begbie (*Edin. Wrs.*); W.E. Maclagan (*Edin. Acads.*), N.J. Finlay (*Edin. Acads.*), R.C. Mackenzie (*Glas. Acads.*); A.R. Don Wauchope (*Camb. Univ.*), J.A. Campbell (*Glas. Acads.*); R. Ainslie (*Edin. Inst. FP*), T. Ainslie (*Edin. Inst. FP*), J.B. Brown (*Glas. Acads.*), J.W. Fraser (*Edin. Inst. FP*), J.H.S. Graham* (*Edin. Acads.*), D. McCowan (*West of Scot.*), R. Maitland (*Edin. Inst. FP*), W.A. Peterkin (*Edin. Univ.*), C. Reid (*Edin. Academy*)

England: A.N. Hornby (*Manchester*); R. Hunt (*Manchester*), L. Stokes* (*Blackheath*); F.T. Wright (*Edin. Academy*), H.C. Rowley (*Manchester*); A. Budd (*Blackheath*), G.W. Burton (*Blackheath*), C.H. Coates (*Leeds*), C.W.L. Fernandes (*Leeds*), H. Fowler (*Walthamstow*), C. Gurdon (*Richmond*), E.T. Gurdon (*Richmond*), W.W. Hewitt (*Queen's House*), C. Phillips (*Birkenhead Park*), H. Vassall (*Oxford Univ.*)

Referee: D.H. Watson **Umpires:** J. Reid, J. McLaren

R. Ainslie scored but T.A. Begbie failed; (H.T.). L. Stokes dropped a goal; H.C. Rowley scored but L. Stokes failed; J.B. Brown scored and T.A. Begbie converted.

This match was twice postponed and J.E. Junor missed a cap as he had left for India. H.H. Taylor reported to the wrong station, saw no team mates and so went home. F.T. Wright, still at the Edinburgh Academy, was pulled into the team to replace him, so the Edinburgh Academy had two pupils playing in this match.

A temporary stand had been erected and 12,000 watched a fast and open game in good conditions. Scotland with the wind had the better of the first half but England, playing with ten forwards, dominated the second half.

R. Ainslie, who played magnificently both in defence and attack, opened the scoring but Begbie, taking a difficult kick, hit the post. C. Reid got over the line but lost a maul in goal to three opponents. Right on half time Campbell touched down at the north-east corner but the score was disputed and eventually yielded because he had knocked the corner flag down.

Midway through the second half L. Stokes dropped a historic 80 yards goal from the touchline sixteen yards inside his own half and then Rowley scored an unconverted try. Right on time Finlay broke away and after a long run dropped at goal but missed. J.B. Brown followed up, got the ball and although tackled, managed to touch down for Begbie to save the match by converting. This score was also disputed as some of the opponents raised a question of off side but the claim was not accepted. This score rankled, for the President of the Rugby Union at their AGM was reported as saying 'They certainly did not win the Scotch match but that was no fault of theirs, for they sent a team that was fairly strong, but the Scotch team was strong also, their strength being in umpiring. Since that match, however, they had made such representation to the Scotch authorities that they hoped in future to have unbiassed referees who understood their duties.' Needless to say, this more than upset the Scottish committee and some acrimonious correspondence followed but it must be noted that a neutral referee officiated for the first time in the 1882 game.

IRELAND   Hamilton Crescent   18 February 1882

SCOTLAND: 2 tries   **Win**

IRELAND: Nil

Scotland: T. Anderson (*Merchiston Castle*); W.E. Maclagan (*Edin. Acads.*), F. Hunter (*Edin. Univ.*); W.S. Brown (*Edin. Inst. FP*), A.G.G. Asher (*Oxford Univ.*); R. Ainslie* (*Edin. Inst. FP*), T. Ainslie (*Edin. Inst. FP*), J.B. Brown (*Glas. Acads.*), D.Y. Cassels (*West of Scot.*), A.F.C. Gore (*London Scot.*), D. McCowan (*West of Scot.*), G.W.L. McLeod (*Edin. Wrs.*), R. Maitland (*Edin. Inst. FP*), C. Reid (*Edin. Acads.*), D. Somerville (*Edin. Inst. FP*)

Ireland: R.B. Walkington (*NIFC*); R.E. McLean (*Dublin Univ.*), J.R. Atkinson (*Dublin Univ.*), J.W.R. Morrow (*QC Belfast*); W.W. Fletcher (*Kingstown*), J. Pedlow (*Bessbrook*); J.B. Buchanan (*Dublin Univ.*), W. Finlay (*NIFC*), R.W. Hughes (*NIFC*), J. Johnston (*Albion*), J.A. Macdonald (*Methodist Coll.*), R. Nelson (*QC Belfast*), A.C. O'Sullivan (*Dublin Univ.*), G. Scriven (*Dublin Univ.*), J.W. Taylor* (*NIFC*)

Referee: A.G. Petrie **Umpires:** W. Cross, R.D. Bell

W.S. Brown scored. (H.T.). D. McCowan scored; T. Anderson failed with both kicks.

The Irish team was weakened by some eight withdrawals yet managed to make a very even game of it. Scotland were clearly superior at quarter back where Asher had a good attacking match and Brown scored a typical solo try following on a forward rush. Tom Anderson, then nearly nineteen years old, was still at Merchiston and in September was capped for a Scottish Cricket XI v. Australians.

ENGLAND   Whalley Range, Manchester   4 March 1882

SCOTLAND: 2 tries   Win
ENGLAND: Nil

Scotland: J.P. Veitch (*RHSFP*); W.E. Maclagan (*Edin. Acads.*), A. Philp (*Edin. Inst. FP*); W.S. Brown (*Edin. Inst. FP*), A.R. Don Wauchope (*Camb. Univ.*); R. Ainslie (*Edin. Inst. FP*), T. Ainslie (*Edin. Inst. FP*), J.B. Brown (*Glas. Acads.*), D.Y. Cassels* (*West of Scot.*), D. McCowan (*West of Scot.*), R. Maitland (*Edin. Inst. FP*), C. Reid (*Edin. Acads.*), A. Walker (*West of Scot.*), J.G. Walker (*West of Scot.*), W.A. Walls (*Glas. Acads.*)

England: A.N. Hornby* (*Manchester*); E. Beswick (*Swinton*), W.N. Bolton (*Blackheath*); H.H. Taylor (*Blackheath*), J.H. Payne (*Broughton*); C.H. Coates (*York Wrs.*), H.G. Fuller (*Camb. Univ.*), C. Gurdon (*Richmond*), E.T. Gurdon (*Richmond*), J.T. Hunt (*Manchester*), P.A. Newton (*Blackheath*), H.C. Rowley (*Manchester*), W.M. Tatham (*Oxford Univ.*), G.T. Thomson (*Halifax*), H. Vassall (*Oxford Univ.*)

Referee: Mr Robinson (*Ireland*)   **Umpires:** J.H.S. Graham, J. Maclaren

R. Ainslie scored a try in each half; J.G. Walker failed with both kicks.

This was the first match in which a neutral referee officiated and it was the first away win between the two countries. The game was badly interfered with, and nearly abandoned because of the spectators encroaching on the field. In the first half R. Ainslie took a pass from Wauchope and rushing against the crowd, managed to ground the ball over the goal line. The crowd were partly responsible for preventing J.H. Payne from scoring. The Scottish forwards were in tremendous form on a heavy greasy pitch and they fairly upset the strong English backs in the loose. R. Ainslie had a field day with two tries and also dealt severely with W.N. Bolton whenever he got on the move. A goal by Maclagan from a free kick was successfully disputed on the ground that he had not properly made his mark when claiming the free kick.

Seven-a-Side Tournaments

At the close of the 1882 season the Melrose Club, in an endeavour to supplement their funds, organised an athletic sports meeting which included a new event in a knockout football tournament. So that this novel competition could be completed during the afternoon the ties were limited to fifteen minutes play and the teams reduced to seven — the distribution being one full back, two quarters and four forwards. It was not long before one of the forwards was removed to become a centre standing behind the quarters and this arrangement has lasted except that the full back is now classed as a winger.

The new competition was a success and was quickly copied by Gala (1884), Hawick (1885) and later by Jedforest (1894) and Langholm (1908). Before 1914 several City clubs were invited and took part in those Border sevens and it was not long before the SFU began to worry about the payment of travelling expenses and the provision of handsome prizes to the finalists. Eventually, after consulting with the Border clubs, they assumed control of all sevens tournaments in 1905.

After the 1914–18 War Selkirk (1919) and Kelso (1920) started the autumn series and then in 1923 the Edinburgh Clubs got permission to run a tournament at Inverleith with the proceeds going to the Royal Infirmary and other city hospitals. Later the venue was moved to Murrayfield and, after the nationalisation of the hospitals, the proceeds were allocated to series of charities.

This later idea was taken up in England when in 1926 the Middlesex sevens tournament was begun and run to provide funds for charitable purposes. Attracting a large number of competing clubs this must now be the largest such tournament. Several preliminary rounds are held and it is only the last sixteen who play in the final ties at Twickenham.

Finally the SRU set another precedent when as part of their Centenary Season celebrations, they ran an International sevens tournament at Murrayfield in April 1973. Teams from Australia, England, France, Ireland, New Zealand, Scotland and Wales and a President's VII took part and to the dismay of all good Scots their seven failed to reach the final in which England beat Ireland.

WALES　　　　　Raeburn Place　　　　8 January 1883

SCOTLAND:　　3 goals　　　　　　　　**Win**

WALES:　　　1 goal

Scotland: D.W. Kidston (*Glas. Acads.*); W.E. Maclagan (*London Scot.*), D.J. McFarlan (*London Scot.*); A.R. Don Wauchope (*Camb. Univ.*), W.S. Brown (*Edin. Inst. FP*); T. Ainslie (*Edin. Inst. FP*), J.B. Brown (*Glas. Acads.*), D.Y. Cassels* (*West of Scot.*), J. Jamieson (*West of Scot.*), J.G. Mowat (*Glas. Acads.*), C. Reid (*Edin. Acads.*), D. Somerville (*Edin. Inst. FP*), A. Walker (*West of Scot.*), J.G. Walker (*West of Scot.*), W.A. Walls (*Glas. Acads.*)

Wales: C.P. Lewis* (*Llandovery*); C.H. Newman (*Newport*), W.B. Norton (*Cardiff*); W.F. Evans (*Rhymney*), G.F. Harding (*Newport*); A. Cattell (*Llanelli*), T.J.S. Clapp (*Newport*), R. Gould (*Newport*), A. Griffen (*Edin. Univ.*), J.A. Jones (*Cardiff*), T.B. Jones (*Newport*), J.H. Judson (*Llandovery*), H.S. Lyne (*Newport*), G.L. Morris (*Swansea*), F.T. Purdon (*Swansea*)

　Referee: G. Rowland Hill (*England*)　**Umpires:** W. Cross, Mr Mullock

D.J. McFarlan scored and Maclagan converted. (H.T.). A.R. Don Wauchope and D.J. McFarlan scored and Maclagan converted both; J.H. Judson scored and C.P. Lewis converted.

The first Welsh match was played on a hard pitch before some 4000 spectators. Some confusion exists over R.H. Bridie (who came to Swansea from Greenock). He was selected for Wales, is named in one report but really seems to have been replaced by W.B. Norton. This is the first match where Wales played with a single full back. J.G. Walker and A.R. Don Wauchope were playing for the Fettesian-Lorettonians on Saturday, 6 January. Wauchope had a good game, his famous dodging play producing two tries, but J.G. Walker had to go off with a twisted knee within fifteen minutes of the start. Near the end a fine run by T.J.S. Clapp saw the ball pass to Gould, Cattell and Judson who scored.

IRELAND　　　Ormeau, Belfast　　　17 February 1883

SCOTLAND:　　1 goal, 1 try　　　　　　**Win**

IRELAND:　　　Nil

Scotland: J.P. Veitch (*RHSFP*); W.E. Maclagan (*London Scot.*), M.F. Reid (*Loretto School*); P.W. Smeaton (*Edin. Acads.*), G.R. Aitchison (*Edin. Wrs.*); T. Ainslie (*Edin. Inst. FP*), J.B. Brown (*Glas. Acads.*), D.Y. Cassels* (*West of Scot.*), J. Jamieson (*West of Scot.*), D. McCowan (*West of Scot.*), W.A. Peterkin (*Edin. Univ.*), C. Reid (*Edin. Acads.*), D. Somerville (*Edin. Inst. FP*), A. Walker (*West of Scot.*), W.A. Walls (*Glas. Acads.*)

Ireland: J.W.R. Morrow (*QC Belfast*); W.W. Pike (*Kingstown*), R.E. McLean (*NIFC*);

S.R. Collier (*QC Belfast*), A.M. Whitestone (*Dublin Univ.*); S.A.M. Bruce (*NIFC*), F.S. Heuston (*Kingstown*), R.W. Hughes (*NIFC*), H. King (*Dublin Univ.*), J.A. Macdonald (*Methodist Coll.*), D.F. Moore (*Wanderers*), R. Nelson (*QC Belfast*), G. Scriven* (*Dublin Univ.*), J.W. Taylor (*NIFC*), W.A. Wallis (*Wanderers*)

No scoring at half time; C. Reid and D. Somerville scored; W.E. Maclagan converted the second.

A dreadful week of rain had turned the pitch into a sea of slush and water and both players and spectators were well nigh blinded with the liquid mud flung up from the scrimmages. By the finish no one tried to pick up the ball but aimed flying kicks at it. Initially there was little between the sides but Ireland were terribly handicapped by injuries — Morrow was concussed and carried off, Wallis and Macdonald had to go off and Whitestone and Scriven finished quite crippled. Maclagan's defence was much priased. M.F. Reid, who was still at Loretto, was a very late replacement for D.J. McFarlan.

ENGLAND   Raeburn Place   3 March 1883

SCOTLAND:	1 try	**Loss**
ENGLAND:	2 tries	

Scotland: D.W. Kidston (*Glas. Acads.*); W.E. Maclagan (*London Scot.*), M.F. Reid (*Loretto School*); P.W. Smeaton (*Edin. Acads.*), W.S. Brown (*Edin. Inst. FP*), T. Ainslie (*Edin. Inst. FP*), J.B. Brown (*Glas. Acads.*), D.Y. Cassels* (*West of Scot.*), J. Jamieson (*West of Scot.*), D. McCowan (*West of Scot.*), J.G. Mowat (*Glas. Acads.*), C. Reid (*Edin. Acads.*), D. Somerville (*Edin. Inst. FP*), A. Walker (*West of Scot.*), W.A. Walls (*Glas. Acads.*)

England: H.B. Tristram (*Oxford Univ.*); W.N. Bolton (*Blackheath*), A.M. Evanson (*Richmond*), C.G. Wade (*Oxford Univ.*); A. Rotherham (*Oxford Univ.*), J.H. Payne (*Broughton*); H.G. Fuller (*Camb. Univ.*), C. Gurdon (*Richmond*), E.T. Gurdon* (*Richmond*), R.S.F. Henderson (*Blackheath*), E.J. Moore (*Oxford Univ.*), R.M. Pattison (*Camb. Univ.*), W.M. Tatham (*Oxford Univ.*), G.T. Thomson (*Halifax*), C.S. Wooldridge (*Oxford Univ.*)

Referee: Mr Kelly (*Ireland*)   **Umpires:** J.H.S. Graham: J.S. McLaren

A Rotherham scored but J.H. Payne failed. (H.T.). C. Reid scored but W.E. Maclagan failed; W.N. Bolton scored but A.M. Evanson failed.

England, with seven Oxford men in the team played six backs against Scotland's five so that the game rather resolved itself into a trial between a fine fast dribbling pack and backs who put on 'an exhibition of passing the like of which has never previously been seen here'. Rotherham, who did so much to establish the new passing style of play at Oxford, saw to it that the forwards slipped the ball out of the side of the scrum and that his backs were given the ball to run with. Scotland, without Don Wauchope and McFarlan, were weak at back but Maclagan, although not fully fit, showed what a tremendous defender he could be and England only led by a try at half time. After the restart C. Reid, who was really outstanding as a forward, scored a try which was disputed but eventually granted but a great solo run by the powerful Bolton produced the winning try. This score or the kick at goal was surprisingly hissed by the spectators — an action which produced an apology from an angry Scottish President at the evening dinner. W.S. Brown and P.W. Smeaton both took the ball over the line but did not get the score — a decision that Smeaton never accepted!

WALES   Rodney Parade, Newport   12 January 1884

SCOTLAND: 1 drop goal, 1 try   **Win**
WALES: Nil

Scotland: J.P. Veitch (*RHSFP*); W.E. Maclagan* (*London Scot.*), D.J. McFarlan (*London Scot.*), G.C. Lindsay (*Fet.-Lor.*); A.R. Don Wauchope (*Fet.-Lor.*), A.G.G. Asher (*Oxford Univ.*); T. Ainslie (*Edin. Inst. FP*), J.B. Brown (*Glas. Acad.*), J. Jamieson (*West of Scot.*), R. Maitland (*Edin. Inst. FP*), W.A. Peterkin (*Edin. Univ.*), C. Reid (*Edin. Acads.*), D. Somerville (*Edin. Inst. FP*), J. Tod (*Watsonians*), W.A. Walls (*Glas. Acads.*)

Wales: C.P. Lewis (*Llandovery*); C.P. Allen (*Beaumaris*), C.G. Taylor (*Ruabon*), W.B. Norton (*Cardiff*); C.H. Newman* (*Newport*), W.H. Gwynn (*Swansea*); F.G. Andrews (*Swansea*), T.J.S. Clapp (*Newport*), R. Gould (*Newport*), T.B. Jones (*Newport*), H.S. Lyne (*Newport*), F.L. Margrave (*Llanelli*), G.L. Morris (*Swansea*), W.D. Phillips (*Cardiff*), H.J. Simpson (*Cardiff*)

Referee: J.S. McLaren (*England*) **Umpires:** J.A. Gardner, R. Mullock

No scoring at half time; A.G.G. Asher dropped a goal; T. Ainslie scored but McFarlan failed.

From a line out Reid passed to Asher who dropped a splendid goal from near half way. Don Wauchope, who played brilliantly throughout, had a typical run to near the line where he was tackled but got the ball away to Ainslie who scored at the corner. Both scores were disputed but not cancelled. The two Scottish quarter backs were in great form, and Maclagan's defence was very sound. Gwynn did well 'playing the passing game'. This match was originally meant to be played a week earlier.

IRELAND   Raeburn Place   16 February 1884

SCOTLAND: 2 goals, 2 tries   **Win**
IRELAND: 1 try

Scotland: J.P. Veitch (*RHSFP*); W.E. Maclagan* (*London Scot.*), E.T. Roland (*Edin. Wrs.*), D.F. McFarlan (*London Scot.*); A.R. Don Wauchope (*Fet.-Lor.*), A.G.G. Asher (*Oxford Univ.*); T. Ainslie (*Edin. Inst. FP*), C.W. Berry (*Fet.-Lor.*), J.B. Brown (*Glas. Acads.*), J. Jamieson (*West of Scot.*), D. McCowan (*West of Scot.*), W.A. Peterkin (*Edin. Univ.*), C. Reid (*Edin. Acads.*), J. Tod (*Watsonians*), W.A. Walls (*Glas. Acads.*)

Ireland: J.M. O'Sullivan (*Limerick*); R.E. McLean (*NIFC*), G.H. Wheeler (*QC Belfast*), L.M. McIntosh (*Dublin Univ.*); M. Johnson (*Dublin Univ.*), W.W. Higgins (*NIFC*); J.B. Buchanan (*Dublin Univ.*), A. Gordon (*Dublin Univ.*), T.H.M. Hobbs (*Dublin Univ.*), R.W. Hughes (*NIFC*), J. Johnston (*NIFC*), W. Kelly (*Wanderers*), J.A. Macdonald* (*Methodist Coll.*), J.F. Maguire (*Cork*), W.G. Rutherford (*Lansdowne*)

Referee: G. Rowland Hill (*England*) **Umpires:** J.H.S. Graham, H.C. Kelly

L. McIntosh scored but R.E. McLean failed; W.A. Peterkin scored but C.W. Berry failed; J. Tod scored but C.W. Berry failed. (H.T.). A.R. Don Wauchope and A.G.G. Asher scored for C.W. Berry to convert both.

A temporary stand was set up along the east touch line and 8,000 watched in clear but cold weather. Ireland were handicapped by having to make eight changes and while their forwards did quite well their backs could not cope with a brilliant pair of quarter backs in Asher and Don Wauchope. The latter was at his elusive best, the second Scottish score coming 'by one of these unequalled wriggling runs for which he is famous. He went from near the centre through the Irish forwards and backs but when just on the line was tackled but Tod being in close attendance got hold and scored.' His own score came from a run in course of which he crossed from one side of the field to the other. Peterkin's score came from a long solo run and it should be recalled that at that time he was the Scottish 440 yards title holder. The Irish score, within five minutes of the start, was made by a good break by a forward who gave McIntosh a scoring pass.

ENGLAND   Blackheath   1 March 1884

SCOTLAND: 1 try   Loss
ENGLAND: 1 goal

Scotland: J.P. Veitch (*RHSFP*); W.E. Maclagan* (*London Scot.*), E.T. Roland (*Edin. Wrs.*), D.J. McFarlan (*London Scot.*); A.R. Don Wauchope (*Fet.-Lor.*), A.G.G. Asher (*Fet.-Lor.*); T. Ainslie (*Edin. Inst. FP*), C.W. Berry (*Fet.-Lor.*) J.B. Brown (*Glas. Acads.*), J. Jamieson (*West of Scot.*), D. McCowan (*West of Scot.*), W.A. Peterkin (*Edin. Univ.*), C. Reid (*Edin. Acads.*), J. Tod (*Watsonians*), W.A. Walls (*Glas. Acads.*)

England: H.B. Tristram (*Oxford Univ.*); A.M. Evanson (*Richmond*), C.G. Wade (*Oxford Univ.*), W.N. Bolton (*Blackheath*); A. Rotherham (*Oxford Univ.*), H.T. Twynam (*Richmond*); C. Gurdon (*Richmond*), E.T. Gurdon* (*Richmond*), R.S.F. Henderson (*Blackheath*), R.S. Kindersley (*Exeter*), C.J.B. Marriott (*Blackheath*), E.L. Strong (*Oxford Univ.*), W.M. Tatham (*Oxford Univ.*), G.T. Thomson (*Halifax*), C.S. Wooldridge (*Blackheath*)

Referee: A Scriven (*Ireland*) **Umpires:** J.H.S. Graham, J. McLaren

J. Jamieson scored but C.W. Berry failed. (H.T.). R.S. Kindersley scored and W.N. Bolton converted.

This was the first International to be played on the Rectory field at Blackheath. The excellence of the dribbling rushes by the Scots was matched by the strength of the English backs, the powerful Bolton always being dangerous. Asher and Don Wauchope, however, had a good match. Jamieson's try was the result of one hard forward rush. After the interval Kindersley scored a try which was to leave its mark on the history of the game. The Scots objected to the score and after a lengthy discussion allowed the kick to be taken under protest, the point to be referred to the Rugby Union Committee.

The Formation of the International Board

Since Kindersley's disputed try was destined to start discussions which led to the formation of the International Rugby Football Board, the course of events may be set out now.

Two versions of the incident may be quoted, the first by G. Rowland Hill, the Secretary of the RU: 'In the course of play the ball was knocked back by a Scotsman (C.W. Berry), one of the English team secured it and a try was obtained. The Scots claimed that 'knocking back' was illegal; the English held that it was not an illegal act and even though it had been, the act was done by a Scotsman and as no Englishman claimed for it, the Scotsmen could not claim for or profit by their own infringement.'

The other account came from A.R. Don Wauchope who played in the game: 'In those days there were two umpires who carried sticks, not flags, and a referee without a whistle. The ball was thrown out of touch, an appeal was made, the umpire on the touch line (J.H.S. Graham) held up his stick, all the players with the exception of four Englishmen and two Scotsmen, stopped playing and England scored a try. The only question of fact decided by the referee was that a Scotsman knocked the ball back. This, according to the Scottish view of the reading of the rule, was illegal and the whole question turned on the interpretation. The point that no Englishman had appealed was never raised at the time and to judge by the fact that eleven of the English team ceased play, it would appear that their idea was that the game should stop.'

If we note that the Advantage Law was not introduced until 1896, some of the Scottish resentment over the try may be better understood and the basic cause of the trouble revealed as a lack of uniformity in the interpretation of the rules.

Following the match the SFU entered into a correspondence with the RU and while maintaining that the try was invalid, eventually offered to have the question adjudicated by some neutral body. The RU, while more or less agreeing that a difference in interpretation existed, would not accept arbitration, maintaining that the referee, having made a decision on a question of fact, must have his authority on the field upheld. These two views could not be reconciled and as a result the mutual fixture for 1885 was not arranged.

At their AGM in 1885 the Irish Union suggested that the four Unions should meet to discuss the possible formation of a body which would be useful for the settling of International disputes.

Such a meeting did take place in Dublin in February 1886 and one outcome was that Scotland agreed to cede the 1884 game to England on the understanding that the latter would join an International Board composed of equal numbers of representatives of each Union and whose duty would be to decide on such points of law that might arise in International matches. This Board was duly inaugurated in Manchester in early 1886 but the RU were not represented and later refused to accept the constitutional terms agreed on. At their own AGM in October 1886 they decided to alter their scoring system only to find the other Unions passing the decision to the new IB, which met in Liverpool in early 1887 and decreed that all International games should use the RU Rules of 1885.

By now it was clear that England was not prepared to yield her position as lawmaker for the game and in March 1887 the RU offered to allow representation from each Union to attend and vote at any committee meeting dealing with possible alterations in the rules. They received no replies but were faced by an IB ultimatum in December 1887 which decreed that the IB Rules must be used in all International games and that no English matches would be arranged unless the RU accepted this by joining the IB. This was not taken up and as a result England played no International games in 1888 and 1889.

The IB's views were splendidly summed up in a manifesto issued in September 1888 but there was no reaction from the RU until December 1889 when they took the decisive step of offering to submit the dispute to arbitration before two persons, one nominated by the IB and one by the RU. As a result Lord Kingsburgh, the Lord Justice Clerk (whom we last met taking the gate money at Raeburn Place in 1871), and Major Marindin, President of the Football Association, were nominated, met and by April 1890 produced their judgment which established the present International Rugby Football Board.

Basically the new constitution satisfied the three Unions by establishing that all Internationals should be played under one Code of Laws maintained and administered by the new board, while the RU were satisfied by having six members on the board as compared with two each from the other Unions.

WALES   Hamilton Crescent   10 January 1885

SCOTLAND: Nil   **Draw**

WALES: Nil

Scotland: P.R. Harrower (*London Scot.*); W.E. Maclagan* (*London Scot.*), A.E. Stephen (*West of Scot.*), G. Maitland (*Edin. Inst. FP*); A.R. Don Wauchope (*Fet.-Lor.*), A.G.G. Asher (*Fet.-Lor.*); T. Ainslie (*Edin. Inst. FP*), C.W. Berry (*Fet.-Lor.*), J. Jamieson (*West of Scot.*), R. Maitland (*Edin. Inst. FP*), J.G. Mitchell (*West of Scot.*), W.A. Peterkin (*Edin. Univ.*), C. Reid (*Edin. Acads.*), G.H. Robb (*Glas. Acads.*), J. Tod (*Watsonians*)

Wales: A.J. Gould (*Newport*); C.G. Taylor (*Ruabon*), F.E. Hancock (*Cardiff*), H.M. Jordan (*Newport*); C.H. Newman* (*Newport*), W.H. Gwyn (*Swansea*); E.P. Alexander (*Brecon*), T.J.S. Clapp (*Newport*), S. Goldsworthy (*Swansea*), R. Gould (*Newport*), A.F. Hill (*Cardiff*), T.B. Jones (*Newport*), D. Morgan (*Swansea*), L.C. Thomas (*Cardiff*), W.H. Thomas (*Llandovery*)

Referee: G. Rowland Hill (England)   **Umpires:** M. Cross, A. Duncan.

A soft ground and wet conditions hampered both teams. This and good tackling earned Wales their first drawn match, for the Scottish backs, particularly Don Wauchope, were full of running. Both sides also came near to scoring with drops at goal. W.H. Thomas, aged nineteen, was still at Llandovery College. A.R. Don Wauchope, A.G.G. Asher and C.W. Berry played for the Fet.-Lor. XV against Glasgow Academicals on Thursday, 8 February.

IRELAND   Ormeau, Belfast   21 February 1885

SCOTLAND   1 try   **Abandoned**

IRELAND: Nil

Scotland: J.P. Veitch (*RHSFP*); W.E. Maclagan* (*London Scot.*), H.L. Evans (*Edin. Univ.*), G.C. Lindsay (*Fet.-Lor.*); A.R. Don Wauchope (*Fet.-Lor.*), P.H. Don Wauchope (*Fet.-Lor.*); T. Ainslie (*Edin. Inst. FP*), C.W. Berry (*Fet.-Lor.*), J.B. Brown (*Glas. Acads.*), T.W. Irvine (*Edin. Acads.*), J. Jamieson (*West of Scot.*), J.G. Mitchell (*West of Scot.*), W.A. Peterkin (*Edin. Univ.*), C. Reid (*Edin. Acads.*), J. Tod (*Watsonians*)

Ireland: J.W.R. Morrow (*QC Belfast*); R.E. McLean (*NIFC*), J.P. Ross (*Lansdowne*), D.J. Ross (*Albion*); J.C. Crawford (*Dublin Univ.*), R.G. Warren (*Lansdowne*); T.C. Allen (*NIFC*), H.M. Brabazon (*Dublin Univ.*), R.M. Bradshaw (*Wanderers*), J. Johnson (*Albion*), T.R. Lyle (*Dublin Univ.*), H.J. Neil (*NIFC*), W.G. Rutherford* (*Tipperary*), T. Shanahan (*Lansdowne*), R.G. Thompson (*Cork*)

Referee: H.C. Kelly (*Ireland*)   **Umpires:** J.H.S. Graham, J.W. Taylor

J. Jamieson scored before the game was abandoned.

After a clear morning a fearful storm broke out and when a start was made the Irish team on a waterlogged pitch was forced to face into an appalling gale force wind of sleet. No sensible football was possible and when after twenty minutes Jamieson scored and the Irish full back had to leave the field, the game by mutual consent was abandoned. In the evening it was agreed that this would stand as a win for Scotland unless Ireland played a second match in Edinburgh. This of course they did, so that this game stands as an abandoned match and surprisingly has been ignored in previous records.

IRELAND   Raeburn Place   7 March 1885

SCOTLAND: 1 goal, 2 tries   **Win**

IRELAND: Nil

Scotland: J.P. Veitch (*RHSFP*); W.E. Maclagan* (*London Scot.*), G. Maitland (*Edin. Inst. FP*), H.L. Evans (*Edin. Univ.*); A.R. Don Wauchope (*Fet.-Lor.*), P.H. Don Wauchope (*Fet.-Lor.*); T. Ainslie (*Edin. Inst. FP*), J.B. Brown (*Glas. Acads.*), T.W. Irvine (*Edin. Acads.*), J. Jamieson (*West of Scot.*), J.G. Mitchell (*West of Scot.*), W.A. Peterkin (*Edin. Univ.*), C. Reid (*Edin. Acads.*), J.G. Tait (*Camb. Univ.*), J. Tod (*Watsonians*)

Ireland: J.W.R. Morrow (*Albion*); J.P. Ross (*Lansdowne*), D.J. Ross (*Albion*), E.H. Greene (*Dublin Univ.*); R.G. Warren (*Lansdowne*), D.V. Hunter (*Dublin Univ.*); R.M. Bradshaw (*Wanderers*), A.J. Forrest* (*Wanderers*), W. Hogg (*Dublin Univ.*), J. Johnstone (*Albion*), T.R. Lyle (*Dublin Univ.*), F.W. Moore (*Wanderers*), H.J. Neill (*NIFC*), T. Shanahan (*Lansdowne*), J.A. Thompson (*Queen's*)

Referee: H.C. Kelly   **Umpires:** M. Cross, W.A. Walls

C. Reid scored but J.P. Veitch failed. (H.T.). W.A. Peterkin and A.R. Don Wauchope scored; J.P. Veitch converted the latter try.

Both teams showed changes and in fact there is a doubt about the correct Irish XV, which, incidentally, played in white jerseys. A grandstand was erected along the east side of the pitch.
    The Scottish pack dominated play and the first score came from a fine handling run by Reid, Ainslie, Peterkin, Tod and Jamieson which was finished off by Reid. Peterkin, already noted as the Scottish sprint champion in 1883, scored the second try by outpacing the Irish backs during a run up the touch line. A.R. Don Wauchope was at his elusive best, the last try coming after one of his typical dodging runs.

WALES   Cardiff   9 January 1886

SCOTLAND: 2 goals, 1 try   **Win**
WALES: Nil

Scotland: F. McIndoe (*Glas. Acads.*); W.F. Holms (*London Scot.*), D.J. Macfarlan (*London Scot.*), R.H. Morrison (*Edin. Univ.*); A.R. Don Wauchope (*Fet.-Lor.*), P.H. Don Wauchope (*Fet.-Lor.*); J.B. Brown* (*Glas. Acads.*), A.T. Clay (*Edin. Acads.*), J. French (*Glas. Acads.*), T.W. Irvine (*Edin. Acads.*), W.M. Macleod (*Edin. Wrs.*), C.J.B. Milne (*West of Scot.*), C. Reid (*Edin. Acads.*), J. Tod (*Watsonians*), W.A. Walls (*Glas. Acads.*)

Wales: D.H. Bowen (*Llanelli*); F.E. Hancock* (*Cardiff*), W.M. Douglas (*Cardiff*), A.J. Gould (*Newport*), C.G. Taylor (*Ruabon*); W.H. Stadden (*Cardiff*), A.A. Matthews (*Lampeter*); E.P. Alexander (*Camb. Univ.*), W. Bowen (*Swansea*), T.J.S. Clapp (*Newport*), A.F. Hill (*Cardiff*), D.H. Lewis (*Cardiff*), D. Morgan (*Swansea*), W.H. Thomas (*Llandovery Coll.*), G.A. Young (*Cardiff*)

A.T. Clay scored and W.M. Macleod converted. (H.T.). J. Tod and A.R. Don Wauchope scored; W.M. Macleod converted the second.

For the first time Wales began with four threequarters but the nine Scottish forwards so dominated play that D.H. Bowen was sent into the pack and A.J. Gould went to full back.

IRELAND   Raeburn Place   20 February 1886

SCOTLAND: 3 goals, 1 drop goal, 2 tries   **Win**
IRELAND: Nil

Scotland: F. McIndoe (*Glas. Acads.*); A.E. Stephen (*West of Scot.*), D.J. Macfarlan (*London Scot.*), R.H. Morrison (*Edin. Univ.*); A.R. Don Wauchope (*Fet.-Lor.*), A.G.G. Asher (*Fet.-Lor.; Edin. Wrs.*); J.B. Brown* (*Glas. Acads.*), A.T. Clay (*Edin. Acads.*), T.W. Irvine (*Edin. Acads.*), D.A. Macleod (*Glas. Univ.*), W.M. Macleod (*Fet.-Lor.; Edin. Wrs.*), C.J.B. Milne (*West of Scot.*), C. Reid (*Edin. Acads.*), J. Tod (*Watsonians*), W.A. Walls (*Glas. Acads.*)

Ireland: J.W.R. Morrow (*Lisburn*); J.P. Ross* (*Lansdowne*), D.J. Ross (*Albion*), M.J. Carpendale (*Monkstown*); R.W. Herrick (*Dublin Univ.*), J.F. Ross (*NIFC*); J. Chambers (*Dublin Univ.*), J. McMordie (*QC Belfast*), F.H. Miller (*Wanderers*), F.W. Moore (*Wanderers*), V.C. Le Fanu (*Camb. Univ.*), H.J. Neil (*NIFC*), R. Nelson (*QC Belfast*), F.O. Stoker (*Wanderers*), J. Waites (*Bective Rangers*)

Referee: G. Rowland Hill (*England*) **Umpires:** J.S. Carrick, Mayne

A.R. Don Wauchope scored twice but W.M. Macleod failed with both; R.H. Morrison scored twice and D.J. Macfarlan converted both. (H.T.). A.G.G. Asher dropped a goal; D.J. Macfarlan scored and converted.

The Irish team was badly weakened by withdrawals of players unable to travel and found themselves up against backs who were full of running. Straightaway Don Wauchope had two typical dodging 'deer–like runs' which brought tries. Then Morrison, the Edinburgh University sprinter, ran in another two before half time. In the second half the Scottish backs were still active but selfishness cost them scores. Apart from Asher, their tackling came in for some criticism. A grandstand, double the size of last year's one, was erected along the east side of the field.

ENGLAND	**Raeburn Place**	**13 March 1886**

SCOTLAND:	Nil	**Draw**
ENGLAND:	Nil	

Scotland: J.P. Veitch (*RHSFP*); W.F. Holms (*RIEC*), G.R. Wilson (*RHSFP*), R.H. Morrison (*Edin. Univ.*); A.R. Don Wauchope (*Fet.-Lor.*), A.G.G. Asher (*Fet.-Lor; Edin. Wrs.*); J.B. Brown* (*Glas. Acads.*), A.T. Clay (*Edin. Acads.*), T.W. Irvine (*Edin. Acads.*), M.C. McEwan (*Edin. Acads.*), D.A. MacLeod (*Glas. Univ.*), C.J.B. Milne (*West of Scot.*), C. Reid (*Edin. Acads.*), J. Tod (*Watsonians*), W.A. Walls (*Glas. Acads.*)

England: C.H. Sample (*Durham*); A.E. Stoddart (*Blackheath*), R. Robertshaw (*Bradford*), E.B. Brutton (*Camb. Univ.*); A. Rotherham (*Richmond*), F. Bonsor (*Bradford*); W.G. Clibborn (*Richmond*), C. Gurdon (*Richmond*), E.T. Gurdon* (*Richmond*), R.E. Inglis (*Blackheath*), G.L. Jeffery (*Camb. Univ.*), C.J.B. Marriott (*Blackheath*), N. Spurling (*Blackheath*), A. Teggin (*Broughton Rangers*), E. Wilkinson (*Bradford*)

Referee: H. Cook (*Ireland*) **Umpires:** J.S. Carrick; G. Rowland Hill

In spite of the bitterly cold weather the resumption of the English fixture brought out a large crowd and the Railway Companies ran several special trains. A police force of 36 constables was reinforced for the first time by mounted police. This was a hard and fast game in which all the Scottish backs showed up well, but early on Bonsor hurt a knee which handicapped him throughout. As a result England was on the defensive for three-quarters of the game yet put in a tremendous finish. G.R. Wilson actually touched down but the score was disallowed as he was judged to have fumbled the ball in taking his pass. R.H. Morrison also crossed the line but was knocked into touch in goal before he could put the ball down. A.R. Don Wauchope and A.G.G. Asher were again very effective and Reid was very prominent and might have scored once but put out a pass which did not go to hand. R. Robertshaw played well at centre three quarter. A scene from this game is depicted in a painting by W.H. Overend and L.P. Smythe.

IRELAND	**Belfast**	**19 February 1887**

SCOTLAND:	1 goal, 1 mark goal, 2 tries	**Win**
IRELAND:	Nil	

Scotland: W.F. Holms (*London Scot.*); A.N. Woodrow (*Glas. Acads.*), W.E. Maclagan (*London Scot.*), D.J. Macfarlan (*London Scot.*); P.H. Don Wauchope (*Fet.-Lor.; Edin. Wrs.*), C.E. Orr (*West of Scot.*); C.W. Berry (*Edin. Wrs.*), A.T. Clay (*Edin. Acads.*), J. French (*Glas. Acads.*), T.W. Irvine (*Edin. Acads.*), H.T. Ker (*Glas. Acads.*), M.C. McEwan (*Edin. Acads.*), R.G. McMillan (*West of Scot.*), D.S. Morton (*West of Scot.*), C. Reid* (*Edin. Acads.*)

Ireland: J.M. O'Sullivan (*Cork*); R. Montgomery (*Camb. Univ.*), D.F. Rambant (*Dublin Univ.*), C.R. Tillie (*Dublin Univ.*); R.G. Warren* (*Lansdowne*), J.H. McLoughlin (*Derry*); J. Chambers (*Dublin Univ.*), J.S. Dick (*QC Cork*), J. Johnston (*Albion*), T.R. Lyle (*Dublin Univ.*), J. Macaulay (*Limerick*), C.M. Moore (*Dublin Univ.*), H.J. Neill (*NIFC*), R. Stevenson (*Lisburn*), E.J. Walsh (*Lansdowne*)

Referee: G. Rowland Hill (*England*) **Umpires:** J.S. Carrick, J. Pinion

C.W. Berry kicked a goal from a mark by D.J. Macfarlan; W.E. Maclagan scored: C.W. Berry converted. (H.T.). M.C. McEwan scored; C.W. Berry failed; D.S. Morton scored but the kick failed.

This game was played in fine weather on the NIFC ground at Ormeau. In the first half there was a lot of counter-kicking rather than running but Scotland held a clear advantage in the second half.

WALES Raeburn Place 26 February 1887

SCOTLAND: 4 goals, 8 tries Win
WALES: Nil

Scotland: A.W. Cameron (*Watsonians*); W.E. Maclagan (*London Scot.*), G.C. Lindsay (*London Scot.*), A.N. Woodrow (*Glas. Acads.*); P.H. Don Wauchope (*Edin. Wrs.*), C.E. Orr (*West of Scot.*); C.W. Berry (*Edin. Wrs.*), A.T. Clay (*Edin. Acads.*), J. French (*Glas. Acads.*), T.W. Irvine (*Edin. Acads.*), H.T. Ker (*Glas. Acads.*), M.C. McEwan (*Edin. Acads.*), R.G. Macmillan (*West of Scot.*), D.S. Morton (*West of Scot.*), C. Reid* (*Edin. Acads.*)

Wales: H. Hughes (*Cardiff*); D. Gwynn (*Swansea*), A.J. Gould (*Newport*), W.M. Douglas (*Cardiff*); G.E. Bowen (*Swansea*), O.J. Evans (*Cardiff*); A.F. Bland (*Cardiff*), W. Bowen (*Swansea*), T.J.S. Clapp (*Newport*), R. Gould* (*Newport*), T.W. Lockwood (*Newport*), D. Morgan (*Swansea*), E.S. Richards (*Swansea*), W.H. Thomas (*Camb. Univ.*), W.E.O. Williams (*Cardiff*)

Referee: F.I. Currey (*England*) **Umpires:** J.S. Carrick, A. Duncan

P.H. Don Wauchope scored; C.W. Berry failed: G.C. Lindsay scored; C.W. Berry converted: C.E. Orr scored; C.W. Berry converted: G.C. Lindsay scored; M.C. McEwan failed. (H.T.). C. Reid and G.C. Lindsay scored; C.W. Berry failed with both: R.G. Macmillan scored; A.N. Woodrow converted: M.C. McEwan scored; A.N. Woodrow failed: G.C. Lindsay scored but failed to convert: W.E. Maclagan scored; C.W. Berry failed: D.S. Morton scored; A.W. Cameron failed: G.C. Lindsay scored; A.N. Woodrow failed.

This match originally set for January was postponed because of frost and both sides were forced to make changes. In particular G.C. Lindsay came in for D.J. Macfarlan, and his brilliant fast dodging running brought him five tries — an individual record which still stands. Scotland from the beginning were completely on top. Their forwards with Reid outstanding proved much too powerful, not only with foot rushes but with handling runs. McEwan's score came when he and Clay won a maul in goal with a lone Welsh forward. The backs too were devastating form, their passing and combined play being a delight, and it seems that the Welsh tackling eventually cracked. It was reported, however, that they lost O.J. Evans through injury during the second half.

ENGLAND   Whalley Range   5 March 1887

SCOTLAND: 1 try   Draw
ENGLAND: 1 try

Scotland: W.F. Holms (*London Scot.*); W.E. Maclagan (*London Scot.*), G.C. Lindsay (*London Scot.*), A.N. Woodrow (*Glas. Acads.*); P.H. Don Wauchope (*Edin. Wrs.*), C.E. Orr (*West of Scot.*); C.W. Berry (*Edin. Wrs.*), A.T. Clay (*Edin. Acads.*), J. French (*Glas. Acads.*), T.W. Irvine (*Edin. Acads.*), H.T. Ker (*Glas. Acads.*), M.C. McEwan (*Edin. Acads.*), R.G. Macmillan (*London Scot.*), D.S. Morton (*West of Scot.*), C. Reid* (*Edin. Acads.*)

England: H.B. Tristram (*Richmond*); W.N. Bolton (*Blackheath*), R. Robertshaw (*Bradford*), R.E. Lockwood (*Dewsbury*), A. Rotherham* (*Richmond*), F. Bonsor (*Bradford*); C.R. Cleveland (*Oxford Univ.*), W.G. Clibborn (*Richmond*), J.H. Dewhurst (*Camb. Univ.*), J.L. Hickson (*Bradford*), G.L. Jeffery (*Blackheath*), R.L. Seddon (*Broughton Rangers*), H.H. Springmann (*Liverpool*), A. Teggin (*Broughton Rangers*), E. Wilkinson (*Bradford*)

Referee: J. Lyle (*Ireland*)   **Umpires:** J.S. Carrick, R. Stokes

F.L. Jeffery scored; W.N. Bolton failed. (H.T.). D.S. Morton scored; C.W. Berry failed.

The match was played in a fog so thick that at times it was difficult to see across the field. Scotland started confidently, Maclagan and Orr being seen in attacks as was Lockwood in defence but it was England who opened the scoring with a try by Jeffery whose play pleased the English critics. After half time England maintained their pressure but gradually Scotland got down to their 25 and Maclagan got over but was recalled before Morton scored the equaliser. Play appeared to be fairly even but five minutes from the end there came a tackle which is one of the game's legends. Maclagan slipped past Rotherham, knocked Lockwood over and although hemmed in on one side had only Tristram between himself and the goal line. He had no room to dodge so charged down on Tristram who sprang forward to meet him and the pair went down with a fearful crash — but no score for Scotland.

61

WALES   Newport   4 February 1888

SCOTLAND: Nil   **Loss**
WALES: 1 try

Scotland: H.F.T. Chambers (*Edin. Univ.*); W.E. Maclagan (*London Scot.*), H.J. Stevenson (*Edin. Acads.*), M.M. Duncan (*Camb. Univ.*); C.E. Orr (*West of Scot.*), C.J.P. Fraser (*Glas. Univ.*); C.W. Berry (*Fet.-Lor.*), A.T. Clay (*Edin. Acads.*), A. Duke (*RHSFP*), T.W. Irvine (*Edin. Acads.*), M.C. McEwan (*Edin. Acads.*), D.S. Morton (*West of Scot.*), C. Reid* (*Edin. Acads.*), L.E. Stevenson (*Edin. Univ.*), T.B. White (*Edin. Acads.*)

Wales: E.J. Roberts (*Llanelli*); T.J. Pryce-Jenkins (*London Welsh*), A.J. Gould (*Newport*), G.E. Bowen (*Swansea*); W.H. Stadden (*Cardiff*), O.J. Evans (*Cardiff*); A.F. Bland (*Cardiff*), T.J.S. Clapp* (*Newport*), A.F. Hill (*Cardiff*), W.H. Howells (*Swansea*), T.D. Kedzli (*Cardiff*), J. Meredith (*Swansea*), R.W. Powell (*Newport*), W.H. Thomas (*London Welsh*), T. Williams (*Swansea*)

Referee: J. Chambers (*Ireland*) **Umpires:** W.S. Brown, A. Duncan

T.J. Pryce-Jenkins scored; T.D. Kedzli failed. (H.T.).

This was Wales' first win over Scotland who, however, were rather critical about the winning try. R.J. Phillips wrote later 'Pryce-Jenkins scored from a run remarkable in that a goodly part of its course was in touch. Some of the Scottish defenders allowed him to go and although his tracks were quite discernible, he got his try. Scotland were not so fortunate. Five times the ball was touched down over the Welsh line and on each occasion it was disallowed.' H.J. Stevenson left an equally blunt comment on those points for it was he, Duncan and Chambers who did not bother to put in a tackle. So Scotland put in a lot of pressure with no result. On the Welsh side A.J. Gould for once played well against Scotland.

IRELAND   Raeburn Place   10 March 1888

SCOTLAND: 1 goal   **Win**
IRELAND: Nil

Scotland: H.F.T. Chambers (*Edin. Univ.*); W.E. Maclagan (*London Scot.*); H.J. Stevenson (*Edin. Acads.*), D.J. McFarlan (*London Scot.*); A.R. Don Wauchope* (*Fet.-Lor.*), C.E. Orr (*West of Scot.*); C.W. Berry (*Edin. Wrs.*), A. Duke (*RHSFP*), T.W. Irvine (*Edin. Acads.*), H.T. Ker (*Glas. Acads.*), M.C. McEwan (*Edin. Acads.*), A.G. Malcolm (*Glas. Univ.*), D.S. Morton (*West of Scot.*), C. Reid (*Edin. Acads.*), T.B. White (*Edin. Acads.*)

Ireland: J.W.R. Morrow (*Lisburn*); C.R. Tillie (*Dublin Univ.*), A. Walpole (*Dublin Univ.*), M.J. Carpendale (*Monkstown*); R.G. Warren (*Lansdowne*), J.H. McLaughlin (*Derry*); W. Ekin (*QC Belfast*), V.C. Le Fanu (*Lansdowne*), R.H. Mayne (*Albion*), J. Moffatt (*Albion*),

C.M. Moore (*Dublin Univ.*), W.A. Morton (*Dublin Univ.*), H.J. Neill* (*NIFC*), T. Shanahan (*Lansdowne*), E.W. Stoker (*Wanderers*)

Referee: J. McLaren (*England*) **Umpires:** W.S. Brown, E. McAllister

D.J. McFarlan scored and C.W. Berry converted. (H.T.).

This was a very even game where fast open play by both sides moved the ball from end to end and only good defence kept the score down to a single try. This was the result of wonderful passing between Don Wauchope, Stevenson and McFarlan who ran in for the score. Scotland lost Orr injured before half time but White who took over played very well. For Ireland, Le Fanu and Walpole frequently caught the eye. For the Scots, Don Wauchope did some fine saving by halting rushes by the Irish forwards; Stevenson again impressed as a centre half who could co-operate with his wingers but the biggest laugh of the afternoon came when Reid had a long run 'with the bulk of the Irish forwards hanging onto him'.

WALES   Raeburn Place   2 February 1889

SCOTLAND: 2 tries   **Win**

WALES: Nil

Scotland: H.F.T. Chambers (*Edin. Univ.*); W.F. Holms (*Edin. Wrs.*), H.J. Stevenson (*Edin. Acads.*), J. Marsh (*Edin. Inst. FP*); C.E. Orr (*West of Scot.*), C.F.P. Fraser (*Glas. Univ.*): W. Auld (*West of Scot.*), J.D. Boswell (*West of Scot.*), A. Duke (*RHSFP*), H.T. Ker (*Glas. Acads.*), M.C. McEwan (*Edin. Acads.*), W.A. Macdonald (*Glas. Univ.*), A. Methuen (*Camb. Univ.*), D.S. Morton* (*West of Scot.*), T.B. White (*Edin. Acads.*).

Wales: H. Hughes (*Cardiff*); R.M. Garrett (*Penarth*), J.E. Webb (*Newport*), E.H. Bishop (*Swansea*), H.M. Jordon (*Newport*); C.J. Thomas (*Newport*), R.Evans (*Cardiff*); W. Bowen (*Swansea*), D.W. Evans (*Cardiff*), J. Hannan (*Newport*), T. Harding (*Newport*), A.F. Hill* (*Cardiff*), S.H. Nicholls (*Cardiff*), R.L. Thomas (*London Welsh*), W.E.O. Williams (*Cardiff*).

Referee: A. McAllister (*Ireland*) **Umpires:** A.R. Don Wauchope, A. Duncan

C.E. Orr scored; J.D. Boswell failed. (H.T.). H.T. Ker scored; M.C. McEwan failed.

The Welsh selectors ran into difficulties when some Cardiff and Llanelli players declined to travel as they wished to play in that local derby and eventually had to send a much altered team, which, however, used the four three quarter system that had been reintroduced for their match against the Maoris. The game was played in poor conditions snow falling at intervals and two half hours were played. Nevertheless both sets of backs ran well and the Welsh forwards were praised for some fine dribbling. Yet again Stevenson distinguished himself by fine attacking play. J. Marsh was an Englishman who went south and was later capped for England against Ireland, a unique distinction.

63

SCOTLAND: 1 drop goal   **Win**
IRELAND: Nil

Scotland: H.F.T. Chambers (*Edin. Univ.*); W.F. Holms (*London Scot.*), H.J. Stevenson (*Edin. Acads.*), J. Marsh (*Edin. Inst. FP*); C.E. Orr (*West of Scot.*), D.G. Anderson (*London Scot.*); A.I. Aitken (*Edin. Inst. FP.*), J.D. Boswell (*West of Scot.*), A. Duke (*RHSFP*), T.W. Irvine (*Edin. Acads.*), M.C. McEwan (*Edin. Acads.*), J.G. McKendrick (*West of Scot.*), A. Methuen (*Camb. Univ.*), D.S. Morton* (*West of Scot.*), J.E. Orr (*West of Scot.*)

Ireland: L.J. Holmes (*Lisburn*); R.A. Yeates (*Dublin Univ.*), T.B. Pedlow (*Queen's*), D.C. Woods (*Bessbrook*); J. Stevenson (*Lisburn*), R.G. Warren* (*Lansdowne*); H.W. Andrews (*NIFC*), T.M. Donovan (*QC Cork*), G.E. Forrest (*Wanderers*), J.S. Jameson (*Lansdowne*), J. Moffatt (*Albion*), L.C. Nash (*QC Cork*), C.R.R. Stark (*Dublin Univ.*), R. Stevenson (*Lisburn*), F.O. Stoker (*Wanderers*)

Referee: W. Phillips (*Wales*)   **Umpires:** J.A. Smith, J. Chambers

H.J. Stevenson dropped a goal. (H.T.).

On a soft ground Scotland started with the wind and sun at their backs and almost at once Anderson sent out a pass to Stevenson who dropped a fine goal down wind. After the restart Holms went off with an injured knee and Boswell took his place. In spite of this the Scottish forwards continued to dominate play and kept Ireland out. Yet again Stevenson was the outstanding back.

Prominent players of the 1880s

A.R. Don Wauchope, already noted for his encouragement of combined play by the backs when captain of Fettes, developed into the finest, individual, attacking quarter back of the early days. Although fast, a relatively short stride helped him to side step and dodge at pace in the most astonishing manner — skills that produced scores after some remarkable winding runs. A graduate of Cambridge University, he spent some time at the Scottish Bar before becoming a stockbroker in London.

A.G.G. Asher was another outstanding quarter back and his Scottish partnership with Wauchope was one of the most successful in any country during this period. A triple Blue at Oxford, he captained the XV in 1884 and throughout his four years in the team played a significant part in establishing the running and passing style of game that made the Oxford teams so famous. His Oxford partner for the last three years was the English cap, Alan

Rotherham, who although never captain, gets much credit for the Oxford style of play from southern writers.

W.E. Maclagan was first capped as the second single full back for Scotland and then became a splendid aggressive back. His tackling was not only sound but destructively ferocious although always fair, and he played several memorable defensive games from both positions. A most determined runner, he was always a potential scorer if given the ball inside the opposition's 25. In 1880 he too moved to London as a stockbroker and as a player and office bearer played a prominent part in establishing the young London Scottish club. In 1891 he captained the first touring side sent to South Africa.

One of the youngest players to have been capped, Charles Reid, chosen while still at the Academy, is still regarded as having been one of the game's greatest forwards. Standing 6 feet 3 inches and weighing some fifteen and a half stones he was (especially in the 1880s) physically outstanding but, carrying no surplus weight, he was also a very speedy active forward who could handle and his tackling was feared. A medical graduate of Edinburgh University he practised in Selkirk and Swindon.

The Edinburgh Institution FP team during the early 1880s was very strong for behind a pack, seven of whom were eventually capped, they had a splendid pair of quarter backs in W. Sorley Brown and W.H. Masters — two small but extremely alert and lively men who were continually breaking away from the mauls as an interpassing and scoring partnership. In the pack the most prominent were the brothers Robert and Tom Ainslie, the former earning a reputation as a forward with a deadly tackle who was fast enough to get amongst and fell the opposing backs.

James Aikman Smith

1887–1890 — East Representative: 1890–1910 — Hon. Secretary & Treasurer: 1910–1914 — Hon. Secretary: 1915–1919 — Acting Secretary & Treasurer: 1914–1925 and 1927–1931 — Special Representative: 1925, 1926 and 1927 — Vice President & President.

The controversy over the captaincy which shook up the SFU in 1881 was merely one of several matters which had been causing concern. Another was the number of committee members who were voting themselves into the XV, e.g. in 1883 and 1884 there were five current caps among the six representatives and four during the next three seasons, but it is only fair to add that players such as A.R. Don Wauchope, C. Reid, T. Ainslie, J.B. Brown and J. Jamieson were practically automatic choices.

The RHSFP delegate to the AGMs, J. Aikman Smith, a Chartered Accountant by profession, had been most critical about the mode of presentation of information about the Union funds and finally had a motion carried that a proper printed summary must be produced by the Hon. Treasurer for the 1887 AGM.

The situation that developed after the 1884 dispute made it obvious that the committee should now contain men with the qualifications, ability and stature needed to formulate and establish the newly formed International Board. The sudden tragic death of the Hon. Secretary and Treasurer, J.A. Gardner, three weeks before the date of the 1887 AGM allowed his offices to be filled by A.S. Blair, WS, a splendid choice to handle the discussions over the IB that were now coming to a head.

The outspoken J. Aikman Smith was also elected as a new East representative and so began a period of unique service to the Union and the IB which only finished with his death in 1931. For 44 years his continued presence in a changing committee, his ability in office, his burning belief in the high quality and standing of rugby in Scotland, his bitter opposition to anything which smacked of professionalism allowed him to develop and exert a tremendous influence over the game, the players and clubs in Scotland.

He was not long in office before he had the real authority of the Union clearly established by a Special General Meeting in 1893 which endorsed a motion that the committee, so long as it worked within its Bye Laws, had the power to formulate and enforce resolutions without prior consultation with the clubs. Barely a year later this authority was challenged when, following a complaint by a referee, the Union suspended play for the remainder of the season on the Gala field at Mossilee, severely censured and later suspended *sine die* the Gala captain. The latter, aided by a fund subscribed to by some well known club members, opened a law suit against the Union (and the referee) on the grounds that it had no powers to suspend. This action was firmly met and when it was dismissed the Union not only continued its suspension on the captain but also denied the privilege of membership of any Union club to the subscribers to the fund — a most convincing demonstration of the new authority of the Union.

Himself a product of Geo. Watson's College and the Royal High School, Aikman Smith saw the game develop as an amateur sport until the schism of 1895 in England which saw the formation of professional rugby in the North of England. A year later a proposed testimonial of considerable value raised for the great Welsh player, A.J. Gould, brought the Welsh Union into conflict with the IB and the subsequent complications were not smoothed over until January 1898, but since the Welsh Union had withdrawn from the IB between February 1897 and February 1898, the Scottish Union cancelled their mutual fixtures for these years. It must be said that the Welsh Union found itself in a difficult position for while it remained clear that the player was being financially rewarded for his skill, his Union withdrew their own donation and pointed out that neither had they any control over the testimonial fund nor were they breaking any rules referring to professionalism laid down by the IB. The whole rather unsatisfactory affair was only really settled by the player who retired from the game.

Aikman Smith never halted in his fight against professionalism, for even on the evening of his last journey in 1931 two rather apprehensive young caps were summoned to his compartment and after asking if they had had any contact with rugby league scouts, he firmly warned them to steer clear of such infamous characters.

It was this stern background that was reflected in his committee's opposition to the daily payments made to the 1905 New Zealand tourists, the presentation of goods as prizes for the finalists in Border Sevens, and in 1923 the gift of a £21 watch to each member of a very successful Newport team which included Neil Macpherson, a current Scottish cap.

Even the numbering of the players in an International was frowned upon for he quite openly maintained that the game must be run for the players and not the spectators and so was also dead against any legislation which tended to make play faster thus demanding more in the way of training and preparation from amateur players. One wonders what he would have said about the squad training and tours of today!

Yet it was his careful handling and investing of the Union funds which permitted them to be the first to possess their own field with facilities for the spectators and Press and it is equally clear that he was the instigator of the move from the quite spacious Inverleith to the vast enclosure of Murrayfield which housed over 70,000 spectators for the opening match against England in 1925 but burst at the seams when over 104,000 watched the 1975 Welsh match with several thousand unable to get in — a world record for a rugby attendance.

Incidentally, the late Dr MacMyn and other caps have recalled with relish how he, normally a mild spoken man, had the habit of appearing, wearing his bowler hat, in the dressing room just before the XV went out and there delivering a blistering condemnation of the opposition and a fiercesome exhortation to go out and take them apart!

Needless to say he was one of the permanent Scottish representatives on the IB and here we may note that he was one of a half dozen who, while remaining loyal to the demands and interests of their own Unions, played significant rôles in nursing and developing the IB during its earlier years. These six, with dates and number of attendances, were: R.G. Warren (Ireland): 1887–1938 (68); H.S. Lyne (Wales): 1887–1938 (60); J.A. Smith (Scotland): 1888–1930 (59); E.T. Gurdon (England): 1890–1928 (51); W. Cail (England): 1890–1925 (45); Sir G. Rowland Hill (England): 1890–1928 (39).

WALES	**Cardiff**	**1 February 1890**

SCOTLAND:	1 goal, 2 tries	8	**Win**
WALES:	1 try	2	

Scotland: G. MacGregor (*Camb. Univ.*); W.E. Maclagan* (*London Scot.*), H.J. Stevenson (*Edin. Acads.*), G.R. Wilson (*RHSFP*); C.E. Orr (*West of Scot.*), D.G. Anderson (*London Scot.*); W. Auld (*West of Scot.*), J.D. Boswell (*West of Scot.*), A. Dalgleish (*Gala*), A. Duke (*RHSFP*), F.W.J. Goodhue (*London Scot.*), M.C. McEwan (*Edin. Acads.*), I. McIntyre (*Edin. Wrs.*), R.G. Macmillan (*West of Scot.*), J.E. Orr (*West of Scot.*)

Wales: W.J. Bancroft (*Swansea*); D.P.M. Lloyd (*Llanelli*), R.M. Garrett (*Penarth*), A.J. Gould (*Newport*), C.J. Thomas (*Newport*); E. James (*Swansea*), W.H. Stadden (*Cardiff*); A.F. Bland (*Cardiff*), W. Brown (*Swansea*), W.R. Evans (*Swansea*), J. Hannan (*Newport*), A.F. Hill* (*Cardiff*), J. Meredith (*Swansea*), S. Thomas (*Llanelli*), W.E.O. Williams (*Cardiff*)

Referee: A. McAllister (*Ireland*)   **Umpires:** A.R. Don Wauchope, A. Duncan

D.G. Anderson scored; M.C. McEwan failed (2–0): J.D. Boswell scored; M.C. McEwan failed (4–0): W.E. Maclagan scored; M.C. McEwan converted (8–0). (H.T.). A.J. Gould scored; W.J. Bancroft failed (8–2).

The ground was very wet and so not in great condition. Some good play in the first half by the Scottish pack let Anderson score early on and later a forward, believed to be Boswell, also went over. Near half time Maclagan scored after a typical hard dodging run. The four

68

Welsh backs had always been full of running and near full time Gould, who had shown up well, scored in the corner after a great crossfield run.

This match was played using the new International Board scoring rules: Try — 2; drop or mark goal — 3; goal from try — 4.

IRELAND   Raeburn Place   22 February 1890

SCOTLAND: 1 drop goal, 1 try   5   **Win**

IRELAND: Nil   0

Scotland: G. MacGregor (*Camb. Univ.*); W.E. Maclagan (*London Scot.*), H.J. Stevenson (*Edin. Acads.*), G.R. Wilson (*RHSFP*); C.E. Orr (*West of Scot.*), D.G. Anderson (*London Scot.*); J.D. Boswell (*West of Scot.*), A. Duke (*RHSFP*), F.W.J. Goodhue (*London Scot.*), H.T. Ker (*Glas. Acads.*), M.C. McEwan* (*Edin. Acads.*), I. MacIntyre (*Edin. Wrs.*), R.G. Macmillan (*West of Scot.*), D.S. Morton (*West of Scot.*), J.E. Orr (*West of Scot.*)

Ireland: H.P. Gifford (*Wanderers*); R. Dunlop (*Dublin Univ.*), R.W. Johnstone (*Dublin Univ.*), T. Edwards (*Lansdowne*); R.G. Warren* (*Lansdowne*), A.C. McDonnell (*Dublin Univ.*); W.J.N. Davis (*Bessbrook*), E.F. Doran (*Lansdowne*), E.G. Forest (*Wanderers*), J. Moffatt (*Albion*), J.H. O'Conor (*Bective Rangers*), H.A. Richey (*Dublin Univ.*), J. Roche (*Wanderers*), R. Stevenson (*Dungannon*), J. Waites (*Bective Rangers*)

Referee: H.L. Ashmore (*England*)   **Umpires:** A.R. Don Wauchope, J. Chambers

J.D. Boswell dropped a goal (3–0); J.E. Orr scored; M.C. McEwan failed (5–0). (H.T.).

Much of the play was confined to the midfield area but a dropped pass was fly-kicked on by Wilson to the Irish posts where Boswell got the ball from the loose and dropped a goal, a move he was much given to doing. Stevenson again was quite outstanding in attack and defence. He also got over the line only to lose the ball after a maul in goal — surely one of the last in International matches. J.E. Orr came out of the pack and stayed out and eventually taking a pass from his brother (which some thought suspiciously forward) used his pace to score far out. He was probably lucky to get a pass for C.E. Orr was considered a very selfish player! Ireland improved in the second half and although they could not score they were able to counter more clever play by Stevenson.

ENGLAND   Raeburn Place   1 March 1890

SCOTLAND: Nil   0   **Loss**

ENGLAND: 1 goal, 1 try   6

Scotland: G. MacGregor (*Camb. Univ.*); W.E. Maclagan* (*London Scot.*), H.J. Stevenson (*Edin. Acads.*), G.R. Wilson (*RHSFP*); C.E. Orr (*West of Scot.*), D.G. Anderson (*London Scot.*); J.D. Boswell (*West of Scot.*), A. Dalgleish (*Gala*), F.W.J. Goodhue (*London Scot.*),

69

H.T. Ker (*Glas. Acads.*), M.C. McEwan (*Edin. Acads.*), I. MacIntyre (*Edin. Wrs.*), R.G. Macmillan (*West of Scot.*), D.S. Morton (*West of Scot.*), J.E. Orr (*West of Scot.*)

England: W.G. Mitchell (*Richmond*); P.H. Morrison (*Camb. Univ.*), R.L. Aston (*Camb. Univ.*), J.W. Dyson (*Huddersfield*); F.H. Fox* (*Wellington*), M.T. Scott (*Northern*); H. Bedford (*Morley*), F. Evershed (*Burton*), J.L. Hickson (*Bradford*), E. Holmes (*Manningham*), D. Jowett (*Heckmondwike*), A. Robinson (*Blackheath*), J.H. Rogers (*Moseley*), J.T. Toothill (*Bradford*), S.M.J. Woods (*Camb. Univ.*)

Referee: J. Chamber (*Ireland*) **Umpires:** A.R. Don Wauchope, G. Rowland Hill

F. Evershed scored; W.G. Mitchell failed (0–2). (H.T.). J.W. Dyson scored; J. Jowett converted (0–6).

This match marked the resumption of fixtures with England following on the settlement of the dispute by arbitration. Conditions were reasonable although some snow fell during play. Maclagan against his wish (he had been suffering from sciatica) was induced to play and was sadly below form; his tackling, previously devastating, let him down especially when Evershed scored. Wilson, who had been on a medical course in Vienna, was not match fit and as a result Stevenson was the only effective back, although once again J.E. Orr was as often with the backs as in the pack. England, on the other hand, had two fast and effective wingers fed by Aston who was in tremendous form. Their pack with a hard core of burly Yorkshire men came in for much praise — none more so than Evershed. One English report noted the presence of the Cameron pipers who 'played what, to a certain proportion of the crowd, was doubtless stirring music'.

WALES　　　　　Raeburn Place　　　7 February 1891

SCOTLAND:　　1 goal, 2 drop goals, 6 tries　　15　**Win**

WALES:　　　　Nil　　　　　　　　　　　　　　0

Scotland: H.J. Stevenson (*Edin. Acads.*); W. Neilson (*Merchiston*), G. MacGregor (*Camb. Univ.*), P.R. Clauss (*Oxford Univ.*); C.E. Orr (*West of Scot.*), D.G. Anderson (*London Scot.*); J.D. Boswell (*West of Scot.*), A. Dalgleish (*Gala*), F.W.J. Goodhue (*London Scot.*), H.T.O. Leggatt (*Watsonians*), M.C. McEwan* (*Edin. Acads.*), I. McIntyre (*Edin. Wrs.*), R.G. Macmillan (*London Scot.*), G.T. Neilson (*West of Scot.*), J.E. Orr (*West of Scot.*)

Wales: W.J. Bancroft (*Swansea*); R.M. Garrett (*Penarth*), D. Gwynn (*Swansea*), G. Thomas (*Newport*), W. McCutcheon (*Swansea*); R.B. Sweet-Escott (*Cardiff*), H.M. Ingledew (*Cardiff*); P. Bennett (*Cardiff Harlequins*), W. Bowen (*Swansea*), D.J. Daniell (*Llanelli*), T.C. Graham (*Newport*), S.H. Nicholls (*Cardiff*), W. Rice Evans (*Swansea*), R.L. Thomas (*Llanelli*), W.H. Thomas* (*Llanelli*)

Referee: H.L. Ashmore (*England*) **Touch judges:** G. Mitchell, A. Duncan

C.E. Orr scored; M.C. McEwan failed (1–0): J.E. Orr scored; M.C. McEwan failed (2–0): F.W.J. Goodhue scored; J.D. Boswell failed (3–0): P.R. Clauss scored; M.C. McEwan failed (4–0). (H.T.). W. Neilson dropped a goal (7–0): H.T.O. Leggatt scored; M.C. McEwan converted (10–0): H.J. Stevenson dropped a goal (13–0): P.R. Clauss scored; M.C. McEwan failed (14–0): J.D. Boswell scored; M.C. McEwan failed (15–0).

Scotland completely dominated this game for Wales had no answer to a pack which scored four of the seven tries while giving their backs plenty of the ball. Scotland were still playing the three back formation and MacGregor, who specialised in feeding his wide set wingers with long accurate passes, struck up a good partnership with Clauss, a small man but fast and aggressive.

Stevenson who had been an automatic and outstanding choice as centre back for four seasons, refused to play this passive type of game, but being too good to omit, was placed at full back. Even here his ability to turn defence into attack was not lost and on several occasions he dashed up field and set the backs off in a passing run. Indeed he could well be classed as the first attacking full back. On the Welsh side, the day of the four back formation was still to come, and only Gwynn and McCutcheon were seen to advantage. Even the famous Bancroft had a bad day. One Welsh writer suggested his team's poor form was the aftermath of a visit earlier in the day to the dissecting rooms of the Royal Infirmary!

IRELAND   Belfast   21 February 1891

SCOTLAND: 3 goals, 1 drop goal, 2 tries   14   **Win**

IRELAND: Nil   0

Scotland: H.J. Stevenson (*Edin. Acads.*); P.R. Clauss (*Oxford Univ.*), G. MacGregor (*Camb. Univ.*), G.R. Wilson (*RHSFP*); C.E. Orr (*West of Scot.*), W. Wotherspoon (*Camb. Univ.*); J.D. Boswell (*West of Scot.*), A. Dalgleish (*Gala*), W.R. Gibson (*RHSFP*), F.W.J. Goodhue (*London Scot.*), H.T.O. Leggatt (*Watsonians*), M.C. McEwan* (*Edin. Acads.*), I. McIntyre (*Edin. Wrs.*), G.T. Neilson (*West of Scot.*), J.E. Orr (*West of Scot.*)

Ireland: D.B. Walkington* (*NIFC*); H.G. Wells (*Bective Rangers*), S. Lee (*NIFC*), R. Dunlop (*NIFC*); B.B. Tuke (*Bective Rangers*), E.D. Cameron (*Bective Rangers*); G. Collopy (*Bective Rangers*), W.J.N. Davis (*Bessbrook*), E.F. Fraser (*Bective Rangers*), J.N. Lytle (*NIFC*), J. Moffatt (*Albion*), L.C. Nash (*QC Cork*), J.H. O'Conor (*Bective Rangers*), J. Roche (*Wanderers*), R.D. Stokes (*QC Cork*)

Referee: G. Rowland Hill (*England*)   **Touch judges:** G. Mitchell, Kane

W. Wotherspoon scored; J.D. Boswell converted (3–0): P.R. Clauss scored; J.D. Boswell failed (4–0): M.C. McEwan dropped a goal (7–0). (H.T.). W. Wotherspoon scored twice; J.D. Boswell converted the first (11–0): G. MacGregor scored; J.D. Boswell converted (14–0).

Played in fine weather on the Ulster ground at Ballynafeigh. This was a good open game with plenty of action from the Irish forwards and some hard running from their backs but overall Scotland were in control. Wotherspoon and Clauss were outstanding in attack. For Ireland Lee played well and Wells had one run the length of the field and touched down for a score that was disallowed. D.B. Walkington was reported as regularly wearing a monocle when playing, taking it off when making a tackle! Note that touch judges have replaced the umpires on the field.

ENGLAND   **Richmond**   **7 March 1891**

| **SCOTLAND:** | 2 goals, 1 drop goal | 9 | **Win** |
| **ENGLAND:** | 1 goal | 3 | |

Scotland: H.J. Stevenson (*Edin. Acads.*); P.R. Clauss (*Oxford Univ.*), G. MacGregor (*Camb. Univ.*), W. Neilson (*Merchiston*); C.E. Orr (*West of Scot.*), D.G. Anderson (*London Scot.*); J.D. Boswell (*West of Scot.*), W.R. Gibson (*RHSFP*), F.W.J. Goodhue (*London Scot.*), H.T.O. Leggatt (*Watsonians*), M.C. McEwan* (*Edin. Acads.*), I. McIntyre (*Edin. Wrs.*), R.G. Macmillan (*London Scot.*), G.T. Neilson (*West of Scot.*), J.E. Orr (*West of Scot.*)

England: W.G. Mitchell (*Richmond*); P. Christopherson (*Blackheath*), F.H.R. Alderson* (*Hartlepool Rovers*), R.E. Lockwood (*Heckmondwike*); J. Berry (*Tyldesley*), W.R.M. Leake (*Harlequins*); E. Bonham-Carter (*Oxford Univ.*), R.T.D. Budworth (*Blackheath*), D. Jowett (*Heckmondwike*), T. Kent (*Salford*), E.H.G. North (*Oxford Univ.*), J. Richards (*Bradford*), J.H. Rogers (*Moseley*), R.P. Wilson (*Liverpool OB*), S.M.J. Woods (*Camb. Univ.*)

Referee: J. Chambers (*Ireland*)   **Touch judges:** D.G. Findlay, E.T. Gurdon

P.R. Clauss dropped a goal (3–0). (H.T.). J.E. Orr scored; G. MacGregor converted (6–0): W. Neilson scored; G. MacGregor converted (9–0): R.E. Lockwood scored; F.H.R. Alderson converted (9–3).

A severe storm and rain did not keep away a crowd of 20,000 who came hoping to see England win the Triple Crown but they had to go away bitterly disappointed. The critics blamed the forwards and halves who were completely outplayed by their opponents. Scotland began well, for within ten minutes C.E. Orr, getting the ball from a scrum, let MacGregor away, and when he passed to Clauss the winger dropped a very good left footed goal. After the restart MacGregor got the ball back from a line out and sent J.E. Orr off on a fast run round the English forwards and backs to score between the posts. Then D.G. Anderson, who had been playing very well, let MacGregor away and a good pass let W. Neilson (who was still at Merchiston) away for another try. The English defence had crumbled badly but Lockwood, who had tackled well, showed his paces and scored just on time. At full back H.J. Stevenson again showed himself to be a player of infinite resource and skill in defence and attack.

The Introduction of the Penalty Kick

Admiral Royd in his comprehensive *History of the Laws of Rugby Football* notes that in the early codes while some acts were classed as 'unlawful' no specific penalty was demanded and usually the offence was followed by a scrummage. Difficulties arose especially following cases of off-side play but the Rugby Union was reluctant to introduce further rules, preferring to trust to the sportsmanship of the players. It appears, however, that a judicious 'hack' was often used as an acceptable method of advising an opponent that he should get back 'on his side' or keep within the letter of the law!

However, by 1882 a penalty kick was introduced for offside but no goal could be dropped or placed from this. Then in 1888, during the dispute, the RU decided that a goal could now be scored from such an award but this ruling was not accepted by the new International Board until 1891 after the arbitration settlement.

This of course was a period when the game had spread to areas where most of the players were 'artisans' and 'lacked' the public school or 'Varsity' background. This viewpoint is clearly revealed in an article which appeared in the magazine of one Scottish school in May 1893:

> Legislation against intentionally handling the ball in a scrummage or wilfully putting the ball unfairly into a scrummage would have been regarded as an insult by the old fashioned football men. The fact that rugby football was hardly played by any except public school men goes a long way to explain such a state of matters. The gradual alteration in the rules and method of play corresponds with the gradual extension of the game to other classes of players. So in the old days penalties were unknown because unnecessary. If a player did make a mistake there was a scrummage and it was not until 1881 [sic] that any free kick penalty was introduced; and then the openly avowed reason for the change was that players, hailing principally from Yorkshire clubs, found it was an advantage under certain circumstances, to play offside. But the Yorkshire players for the most part were not public school men and those who have played against them in later years will, I think, be ready to admit that it is not among them that we must look for the Sir Nigel Lorings of Rugby Football.

It was against such a background that the South clubs in 1889 succeeded in getting one representative on to the Union committee but this did not satisfy them, for in 1891 their representatives, meeting at St Boswells, openly expressed their dissatisfaction with the SFU and even talked of forming a separate South of Scotland RU. Apparently the 1894 decision to double their representation seems to have produced an uneasy peace.

It is equally clear that the selection in 1890 of the first Border cap in the Gala forward, Adam Dalgleish, marked another break through. Dalgleish was an excellent choice for on more than one occasion it was he who was pulled out of the pack as a most successful replacement for an injured back player.

WALES **Swansea** **6 February 1892**

SCOTLAND:	1 goal, 1 try	7	**Win**
WALES:	1 try	2	

Scotland: H.J. Stevenson (*Edin. Acads.*); W. Neilson (*Camb. Univ.*), G.T. Campbell (*London Scot.*), P.R. Clauss (*Oxford Univ.*); C.E. Orr* (*West of Scot.*), D.G. Anderson (*London Scot.*); J.D. Boswell (*West of Scot.*), A. Dalgleish (*Gala*), W.R. Gibson (*RHSFP*), F.W.J. Goodhue (*London Scot.*), H.T.O. Leggatt (*Watsonians*), R.G. Macmillan (*London Scot.*), J.N. Millar (*West of Scot.*), G.T. Neilson (*West of Scot.*), J.E. Orr (*West of Scot.*)

Wales: W.J. Bancroft (*Swansea*); T.W. Pearson (*Cardiff*). A.J. Gould* (*Newport*), W.M. McCutcheon (*Swansea*), J.C. Rees (*Llanelli*); D. James (*Swansea*), E. James (*Swansea*); P. Bennett (*Cardiff Harlequins*), A.W. Boucher (*Newport*), J. Deacon (*Swansea*), T.C. Graham (*Newport*), J. Hannan (*Newport*), F. Mills (*Swansea*), C.B. Nicholl (*Llanelli*), W.H. Watts (*Newport*)

Referee: J.R. Hodgson (*England*)

J. Hannen scored; W.J. Bancroft failed (0–2); J.D. Boswell scored; P.R. Clauss failed (2–2); G.T. Campbell scored; J.D. Boswell converted (7–2). (H.T.).

An incessant downpour of rain had left the field so sodden that with a heavier pack the Scots were able to control the scrummages and smother the back play on which Wales depended so much. Yet throughout, the game was quite open and evenly contested and it was good forward play that gave Wales the opening score. Then the Scottish pack livened up and made the game safe. Wales played four backs and J.E. Orr came out of the pack 'to stop the chucking' but this was a frequent move for him. Indeed he must be one of the first winging forwards for he was often slated for doing more work out of the maul than in it. The referee did not please the crowd and he received some rough handling at the end of the match.

IRELAND **Raeburn Place** **20 February 1892**

SCOTLAND:	1 try	2	**Win**
IRELAND:	Nil	0	

Scotland: H.J. Stevenson (*Edin. Acads.*); G.T. Campbell (*London Scot.*), W. Neilson (*Camb. Univ.*), J.C. Woodburn (*Kelvinside Acads.*); C.E. Orr* (*West of Scot.*), W. Wotherspoon (*Camb. Univ.*); J.D. Boswell (*West of Scot.*), W.R. Gibson (*RHSFP*), F.W.J. Goodhue (*London Scot.*), N.F. Henderson (*London Scot.*), H.T.O. Leggatt (*Watsonians*), W.A. Macdonald (*Glas. Univ.*), R.G. Macmillan (*London Scot.*), J.N. Millar (*West of Scot.*), J.E. Orr (*West of Scot.*)

Ireland: T. Peel (*Bective Rangers*); R. Dunlop (*Dublin Univ.*), S. Lee (*NIFC*), W. Gardiner (*NIFC*); T. Thornhill (*Wanderers*), F.E. Davies (*Lansdowne*); A.D. Clinch (*Dublin Univ.*), G. Collopy (*Bective Rangers*). W.J.N. Davis (*Edin. Univ.*), E.F. Frazer

(*Bective Rangers*), T.J. Johnston (*QC Belfast*), V.C. Le Fanu* (*Lansdowne*), C.V. Rooke (*Dublin Univ.*), A.K. Wallis (*Wanderers*), E.J. Walsh (*Lansdowne*)

Referee: H.L. Ashmore (*England*) **Touch judges:** T. Ainslie, A. McAllister

J.N. Millar scored; J.D. Boswell failed (2–0). (H.T.).

There was a slight covering of snow which kept off until the last few minutes, for the game finished in a blinding storm. This was a fine open game with play swaying from end to end. Thornhill was much praised for some dangerous running but the Scottish backs were blamed for too much selfish play. Their defence, however, was very sound, Stevenson at full back being very safe and again he showed his ability to change defence into attack when, near the end, he made a fine solo run through nearly the whole of the opposition. Wotherspoon was very effective behind the scrum. Boswell produced one of his characteristic drop goals which, however, was turned down by the referee.

ENGLAND Raeburn Place 5 March 1892

| SCOTLAND: | Nil | 0 | **Loss** |
| ENGLAND: | 1 goal | 5 | |

Scotland: H.J. Stevenson (*Edin. Acads.*); P.R. Clauss (*Oxford Univ.*), W. Neilson (*Camb. Univ.*), G.T. Campbell (*London Scot.*); C.E. Orr* (*West of Scot.*), D.G. Anderson (*London Scot.*); J.D. Boswell (*West of Scot.*), W.R. Gibson (*RHSFP*), F.W.J. Goodhue (*London Scot.*), W.A. Macdonald (*Glas. Univ.*), M.C. McEwan (*Edin. Acads.*), R.G. Macmillan (*London Scot.*), J.N. Millar (*West of Scot.*), G.T. Neilson (*West of Scot.*), J.E. Orr (*West of Scot.*)

England: T. Coop (*Leigh*); J.W. Dyson (*Huddersfield*), F.H.R. Alderson* (*Hartlepool Rovers*), R.E. Lockwood (*Heckmondwike*); A. Briggs (*Bradford*), H. Varley (*Liversedge*); H. Bradshaw (*Bramley*), W.E. Bromet (*Todcaster*), E. Bullough (*Wigan*), F. Evershed (*Blackheath*), T. Kent (*Salford*), W. Nichol (*Brighouse Rovers*), J.T. Toothill (*Bradford*), S.M.J. Woods (*Wellington*), W. Yiend (*Hartlepool Rovers*)

Referee: Warren (*Ireland*) **Touch judges:** T. Ainslie, A. Budd.

W.E. Bromet scored; R.E. Lockwood converted (0–5). (H.T.).

After the rout of their pack last year England put eight Yorkshiremen into the team, and this stiffening certainly played its part for all three matches were won without a point being scored against them, but it also introduced an element of toughness into their play. One English report notes, 'Activity and skill were at a discount and very rough play was indulged in by both sides, the brandy bottle having frequently to be requisitioned for the knocked out ones'. The game then, although evenly contested, was mainly a forward battle but Briggs and Varley incensed the spectators by continually arriving too rapidly at the Scottish side of the scrums. As a result they fairly hammered Orr and Anderson and the Scottish backs suffered accordingly. Since the referee failed to penalise this and also disallowed two Scottish touchdowns, he too fell out of favour with the crowd, and some indignant letters appeared later in the local papers. Of the players, Lockwood was praised for his pace and skill, and Stevenson for his defence and willingness to attack from full back.

Before the start of the next season the Union Committee resolved that for the past 1891–92 season and for the future, the trophy caps should be presented by the Union.

Up to this time each player had purchased his own cap locally. Initially the style resembled a plain skullcap but about 1880 the front peak was added.

WALES	Raeburn Place	4 February 1893

SCOTLAND:	Nil	0	**Loss**
WALES:	1 penalty goal, 3 tries	9	

Scotland: A.W. Cameron (*Watsonians*); D.D. Robertson (*Camb. Univ.*), G. MacGregor (*London Scot.*), J.J. Gowans (*Camb. Univ.*); R.C. Greig (*Glas. Acads.*), W. Wotherspoon (*West of Scot.*); W.B. Cownie (*Watsonians*), A. Dalgleish (*Gala*), W.R. Gibson (*RHSFP*), T.L. Hendry (*Clydesdale*), H.T.O. Leggatt (*Watsonians*), R.G. Macmillan* (*London Scot.*), H.F. Menzies (*West of Scot.*), J.N. Millar (*West of Scot.*), G.T. Neilson (*West of Scot.*)

Wales: W.J. Bancroft (*Swansea*); W.M. McCutcheon (*Oldham*), A.J. Gould* (*Newport*), G.H. Gould (*Newport*), N.M. Biggs (*Cardiff*); F.C. Parfitt (*Newport*), H.P. Phillips (*Newport*); A.W. Boucher (*Newport*), H.T. Day (*Newport*), T.C. Graham (*Newport*), J. Hannan (*Newport*), A.F. Hill (*Cardiff*), F. Mills (*Swansea*), C.B. Nicholl (*Camb. Univ.*), W.H. Watts (*Newport*)

Referee: Humphrey (*England*) **Touch judges:** D.S. Morton, W. Wilkins

There was no scoring before half time. G.H. Gould scored (0–2); N.M. Biggs scored (0–4); W. J. Bancroft drop kicked a penalty goal (0–7); W.M. McCutcheon scored (0–9). W.J. Bancroft failed to convert the three tries.

For the first time Scotland was beaten by the 4 back formation and indeed the second half produced such an exhibition of continuous running and passing that the virtues of the system were apparent to all. Yet men of the stature of A.R. Don Wauchope, C. Reid and R.G. Macmillan maintained that it would fail against a team which played the traditional Scottish forward game with wheeling, close dribbling rushes, fast following up and hard tackling, and they predicted that since the ball was needed for the backs these characteristic Scottish skills would in time be lost.

Since this game played a decisive part in establishing the four back formation it is interesting, with hindsight, to note that the win was achieved against a relatively poor side. H.J. Stevenson had not been picked, G.T. Campbell, W. Neilson, J.D. Boswell and J.E. Orr had withdrawn and had these five been present things might have gone differently.

As for the actual play the reports praised the Welsh backs for their spectacular running, A.J. Gould being frequently mentioned. H.F. Menzies got over the line in a forward rush but the score was disallowed. W.J. Bancroft dropped a goal from a penalty awarded for an off-side decision.

76

IRELAND   **Belfast**   **20 February 1893**

SCOTLAND:	Nil	**0**	**Draw**
IRELAND:	Nil	**0**	

Scotland: H.J. Stevenson (*Edin. Acads.*); G.T. Campbell (*London Scot.*), G. MacGregor (*London Scot.*), W. Neilson (*Camb. Univ.*); J.W. Simpson (*RHSFP*), W.P. Donaldson (*Oxford Univ.*); J.M. Bishop (*Glas. Acads.*), J.D. Boswell* (*West of Scot.*), W.B. Cownie (*Watsonians*), D. Fisher (*West of Scot.*), J.R. Ford (*Gala*), W.R. Gibson (*RHSFP*), T.L. Hendry (*Clydesdale*), H.F. Menzies (*West of Scot.*), J.E. Orr (*West of Scot.*)

Ireland: S. Gardiner (*Albion*); W. Gardiner (*NIFC*), S. Lee* (*NIFC*), L.H. Gwynn (*Dublin Univ.*); W.S. Brown (*Dublin Univ.*), F.E. Davies (*Lansdowne*); E.G. Forrest (*Wanderers*), H. Forrest (*Wanderers*), T.J. Johnston (*Queen's Coll.*), J.S. Jameson (*Lansdowne*), H. Lindsay (*Armagh*), B.O'Brien (*Derry*), J.H. O'Conor (*Bective Rangers*), C.V. O'Rooke (*Dublin Univ.*), R. Stevenson (*Dungannon*)

Referee: G. Rowland Hill (*England*)   **Touch judges:** J. Stewart, J. Blood

This was played on the Ulster ground which was in poor condition and by half time more resembled a bog than a rugby ground so the game was largely a forward battle, the ball seldom moving out from the half backs. It was recorded that 'J.E. Orr came out of the pack to which he was seldom any more than a hanger on, to stop the rushes of the big Irish forwards.'

ENGLAND   **Leeds**   **4 March 1893**

SCOTLAND:	2 drop goals	**8**	**Win**
ENGLAND:	Nil	**0**	

Scotland: H.J. Stevenson (*Edin. Acads.*); G.T. Campbell (*London Scot.*), G. MacGregor (*London Scot.*), W. Neilson (*Camb. Univ.*); J.W. Simpson (*RHSFP*), W. Wotherspoon (*West of Scot.*); J.D. Boswell* (*West of Scot.*), W.B. Cownie (*Watsonians*), R.S. Davidson (*RHSFP*), W.R. Gibson (*RHSFP*), T.L. Hendry (*Clydesdale*), H.T.O. Leggatt (*Watsonians*), R.G. Macmillan (*London Scot.*), J.E. Orr (*West of Scot.*), T.M. Scott (*Melrose*)

England: W.G. Mitchell (*Richmond*); J.W. Dyson (*Huddersfield*), A.E. Stoddart* (*Blackheath*), F.P. Jones (*North Brighton*); H. Duckett (*Bradford*), C.M. Wells (*Camb. Univ.*); H. Bradshaw (*Bramley*), T. Broadley (*Bingley*), W.E. Bromet (*Richmond*), F. Evershed (*Burton*), L.J. Percival (*Rugby*), J.J. Robertson (*Camb. Univ.*), F. Soane (*Bath*), J.T. Toothill (*Bradford*), W. Yiend (*Hartlepool Rovers*)

Referee: W. Wilkins (*Wales*)   **Touch judges:** D.S. Morton, W. Gail

J.D. Boswell dropped a goal (4–0). (H.T.). G.T. Campbell dropped a goal (8–0).

This was played on the fairly new Headingley field which was rather bare and also soft after some rain. The strong Scottish pack was quite at home on this and dominated play but the loose slippy surface hampered both sets of backs. Scotland started well; a dash by MacGregor was followed by a pass from Simpson to Neilson whose drop kick hit a post before dropping over, but to their dismay the referee disallowed the score. However he did accept a drop by Boswell, that noted exponent of unexpected drop kicks. The Scottish backs, with Campbell outstanding, did some strong running before half time but were held by good tackling. Shortly after the break Campbell got the ball from a loose scrum and made a good run which finished when Dyson knocked him down with a tackle. In a flash, not having lost the ball, he was back on his feet to drop a fine goal. Dyson and Duckett were praised for their defence but the English backs had too little of the ball to be effective in attack. Wotherspoon was admirable in feeding MacGregor who in turn fed his wing halves effectively. MacGregor, of course, had been selected as centre half for this very purpose. A Test Match wicketkeeper, he was a magnificent handler of the ball, taking all manner of passes and could throw long accurate passes to his wide set wings. The man he had displaced, H.J. Stevenson, was here playing his last game. As a centre half with his club and Scotland he had not been content to be a feeder and tackler but showed an aggression, agility and resource which time and time again allowed him to halt an attack and immediately set up a counter attack. A determined and outspoken man he bluntly refused to change his style when the Union asked him to do so in 1891. He was far too good to drop so they put him at full back and discovered that they now had a full back with a solid defence and a distinct taste for attacking from that position. Undoubtedly he was one of the outstanding backs in the game at this time. Even in cricket his aggression was in evidence for he bowled underhand spin and took many astonishing off-the-bat catches by whipping up the pitch after the delivery. One of his victims commented that this was the first time he had batted against a silly mid on, a silly mid off and a silly bowler.

WALES　　　　　　　Newport　　　　　3 February 1894

SCOTLAND:　　Nil　　　　　　　　　　　　　0　　**Loss**

WALES:　　　1 drop goal, 1 try　　　　　7

Scotland: J. Rogerson (*Kelvinside Acads.*); G.T. Campbell (*London Scot.*), G. MacGregor (*London Scot.*), J.J. Gowans (*Camb. Univ.*), H.T.S. Gedge (*London Scot.*); W. Wotherspoon (*West of Scot.*), J.W. Simpson (*RHSFP*); W.B. Cownie (*Watsonians*), A. Dalgleish (*Gala*), W.R. Gibson (*RHSFP*), W.M.C. McEwan (*Edin. Acad.*); R.G. Macmillan* (*London Scot.*), H.F. Menzies (*West of Scot.*), G.T. Neilson (*West of Scot.*), H.B. Wright (*Watsonians*)

Wales: W.J. Bancroft (*Swansea*); W.L. Thomas (*Newport*), D. Fitzgerald (*Cardiff*), A.J. Gould* (*Newport*), T.W. Pearson (*Cardiff*); F.C. Parfitt (*Newport*), H.P. Phillips (*Newport*); D.J. Daniell (*Llanelli*), H.T. Day (*Newport*), T.C. Graham (*Newport*), J. Hannon (*Newport*), A.F. Hill (*Cardiff*), F. Mills (*Swansea*), C.B. Nicholl (*Camb. Univ.*), W.H. Watts (*Newport*)

Referee: J. Holmes (*England*)　　**Touch judges:** J.A. Smith, W.E. Rees

D. Fitzgerald scored but Bancroft failed (0–3). (H.T.). D. Fitzgerald dropped a goal (0–7).

J.D. Boswell (the elected captain), W. Neilson and H.T.O. Leggatt were replaced by H.B. Wright, J.J. Gowans and W.M.C. McEwan, the last being still at the Academy. He eventually went to Johannesburg and was capped for South Africa in 1903. Wales had to make four changes. For the first time Scotland played four halves and labelled them 'three quarters'. Their pack held its own but the backs were weaker than their opponents who frequently made ground by passing runs, one of which produced the first try.

IRELAND   Lansdowne Road   24 February 1894

SCOTLAND: Nil   0   **Loss**

IRELAND: 1 goal   5

Scotland: A.W. Cameron (*Watsonians*); G.T. Campbell (*London Scot.*), G. MacGregor (*London Scot.*), W. Wotherspoon (*West of Scot.*), H.T.S. Gedge (*Edin. Wrs.*); J.W. Simpson (*RHSFP*), W.P. Donaldson (*Oxford Univ.*); A.H. Anderson (*Glas. Acads.*), J.D. Boswell* (*West of Scot.*), W.B. Cownie (*Watsonians*), A. Dalgleish (*Gala*), W.R. Gibson (*RHSFP*), H.T.O. Leggatt (*Watsonians*), R.G. Macmillan (*London Scot.*), G.T. Neilson (*West of Scot.*)

Ireland: P.J. Grant (*Bective Rangers*); W. Gardiner (*NIFC*), S. Lee (*NIFC*), L.H. Gwynn (*Dublin Univ.*), H.G. Wells (*Bective Rangers*); W.S. Brown (*Dublin Univ.*), B.B. Tuke (*Bective Rangers*); A.T.W. Bond (*Derry*), T.J. Crean (*Wanderers*), E.G. Forrest* (*Wanderers*), H. Lindsay (*Dublin Univ.*), J.H. Lytle (*NIFC*), J.N. Lytle (*NIFC*), J.H. O'Conor (*Bective Rangers*), C.V. Rooke (*Dublin Univ.*)

     Referee: H.L. Ashmore (*England*)   **Touch judges:** J.A. Smith, Garrett

No scoring at half time. H.G. Wells scored; J. Lytle converted (0–5).

Once again an Irish game was played on a rain sodden ground and play was largely confined to the forwards who were fairly evenly matched. There were one or two near misses with drop kicks, but Ireland won with a late run by the backs which let Wells score. The spectators were not amused at an extra long interval during which the two captains were introduced to the Lord Lieutenant.

ENGLAND   Raeburn Place   17 March 1894

SCOTLAND: 2 tries   6   **Win**

ENGLAND: Nil   0

Scotland: G. MacGregor (*London Scot.*); G.T. Campbell (*London Scot.*), W. Neilson (*Camb. Univ.*), H.T.S. Gedge (*Edin. Wrs.*), J.J. Gowans (*Camb. Univ.*); W. Wotherspoon (*West of Scot.*), J.W. Simpson (*RHSFP*); J.D. Boswell* (*West of Scot.*), W.B. Cownie (*Watsonians*), W.R. Gibson (*RHSFP*), H.T.O. Leggatt (*Watsonians*), W.M.C. McEwan (*Edin. Academy*), R.G. Macmillan (*London Scot.*), H.F. Menzies (*West of Scot.*), W.G. Neilson (*Merchiston Castle*)

England: J.F. Byrne (*Moseley*); C.A. Hooper (*Middlesex Wrs.*), W.J. Jackson (*Halifax*), S. Morfitt (*W. Hartlepool*), F. Firth (*Halifax*); E.W. Taylor* (*Rockcliff*), C.M. Wells (*Harlequins*); A. Allport (*Blackheath*), H. Bradshaw (*Bramley*), T. Broadley (*Bingley*), A.E. Elliot (*St Thomas's*), H. Hall (*N. Durham*), F. Sloane (*Bath*), H. Speed (*Castleford*), W. Walton (*Castleford*)

Referee: W. Wilkins (*Wales*) **Touch judges:** W.E. Maclagan, W. Cail

No scoring at half time. J.D. Boswell scored twice; Wotherspoon and Boswell failed with the kicks (6–0).

Both teams retained the four three quarter formation. Scotland were very much on top throughout. Their forwards played well but the backs indulged in too many speculative drops at goal. Wotherspoon was hurt during the first half but resumed on the wing after the interval. Scotland played two schoolboys in McEwan and W.G. Neilson. The latter joined his brother, Willie, when he replaced another injured brother, George. The XV had played a practice match against Merchiston on 15 March and the committee, after strong representation from the captain and others, decided to nominate young Gordon as first reserve forward.

WALES   Raeburn Place   26 January 1895

SCOTLAND:	1 goal	5	**Win**
WALES:	1 drop goal	4	

Scotland: A.R. Smith (*Oxford Univ.*); J.J. Gowans (*London Scot.*), G.T. Campbell (*London Scot.*), W. Neilson (*London Scot.*), R. Welsh (*Watsonians*); J.W. Simpson (*RHSFP*), M. Elliot (*Hawick*); W.B. Cownie (*Watsonians*), J.H. Dods (*Edin. Acads.*), W.R. Gibson* (*RHSFP*), W.M.C. McEwan (*Edin. Acads.*), R.G. Macmillan (*London Scot.*), G.T. Neilson (*West of Scot.*), T. Scott (*Hawick*), H.O. Smith (*Watsonians*)

Wales: W.J. Bancroft (*Swansea*); E. Lloyd (*Llanelli*), A.J. Gould* (*Newport*), O. Badger (*Llanelli*), T.W. Pearson (*Cardiff*); F.C. Parfitt (*Newport*), S. Biggs (*Cardiff*); A.W. Boucher (*Newport*), E. George (*Pontypridd*), T.C. Graham (*Newport*), J. Hannan (*Newport*), F. Mills (*Cardiff*), C.B. Nicholl (*Llanelli*), H. Packer (*Newport*), T. Pook (*Newport*)

Referee: E.B. Holmes (*England*)

No scoring at half time. J.J. Gowans scored; H.O. Smith converted (5–0): W.J. Bancroft dropped a goal (5–4).

After the protective straw had been removed from the field, the north end was found to be too hard and at the request of the Welsh — who refused to play otherwise — the pitch was shortened by some eighteen yards to eliminate this area. Even so the ground remained unpleasantly hard, and one dangerous run by Gould later on finished when he swerved and slipped. There was a lot of fine play, nevertheless, with the Scottish pack showing up well in the loose. Behind them, Elliot in his first game, did well in attack and defence. In the second half Wales did a fair amount of attacking but Campbell's defence and kicking saved several situations. Ironically, it was a weak drop at goal by him which produced the first score for Bancroft, having fielded the kick, had his own kick charged down and Gowans went over for a try converted by H.O. Smith. Wales fought back but the defence, notably A.R. Smith, was sound. Then McEwan, on his own goal line, marked a dangerous kick ahead and kicked for touch, only to see Bancroft catch the ball, move deliberately infield and drop a fine goal from near half way. This finished the scoring although Gowans had one fine run to be collared on the line in front of the posts.

The Scottish XV had been chosen in two sessions for five places were left vacant until the committee had seen the South v. North game and it is interesting to note that W.R. Gibson, the captain, was one of the second batch.

IRELAND   Raeburn Place   2 March 1895

SCOTLAND:	2 tries	6	**Win**
IRELAND:	Nil	0	

Scotland: A.R. Smith (*Oxford Univ.*); J.J. Gowans (*London Scot.*), G.T. Campbell (*London Scot.*), W. Neilson (*London Scot.*), R. Welsh (*Watsonians*); J.W. Simpson (*RHSFP*), P.R. Clauss (*Birkenhead Park*); W.B. Cownie (*Watsonians*), J.H. Dods (*Edin. Acads.*), W.R. Gibson (*RHSFP*), T.L. Hendry (*Clydesdale*), R.G. Macmillan* (*London Scot.*), J.N. Millar (*West of Scot.*), G.T. Neilson (*West of Scot.*), T.M. Scott (*Hawick*)

Ireland: J. Fulton (*NIFC*); W. Gardiner (*NIFC*), J.T. Magee (*Bective Rangers*), A. Montgomery (*NIFC*), J. O'Conor (*Garryowen*); L.M. Magee (*Bective Rangers*), B.B. Tuke (*Bective Rangers*); A.D. Clinch (*Wanderers*), T. Crean (*Wanderers*), W.J.N. Davis (*Edin. Univ.*), M.S. Egan (*Garryowen*), H.C. McCoull (*Albion*), E.H. McIlwaine (*NIFC*), W. O'Sullivan (*QC Cork*), C.V. Rooke (*Monkstown*)

Referee: H.L. Ashmore (*England*)   **Touch judges:** M.C. McEwan, Macaulay

No scoring at half time. R. Welsh scored; T.M. Scott failed (3–0); G.T. Campbell scored; W.B. Cownie failed (6–0).

This match was postponed twice from January and both team selections were much influenced by influenza. Play was fairly even in the first half, both sides showing good defence but R. Welsh ran dangerously. Ireland started the second half confidently with a fine run by J.T. Magee but Scotland gradually got on top. Cownie had a run, passed to Simpson and the ball went via W. Neilson to Welsh who scored. Shortly afterwards Simpson and Clauss had a good passing run before giving the ball to W. Neilson who sent Campbell off on a grand dodging run through a mass of opponents to score. One reference book shows J.H. Lytle playing with J.T. Magee missing.

ENGLAND   Richmond   9 March 1895

SCOTLAND:	1 penalty goal, 1 try	6	**Win**
ENGLAND:	1 penalty goal	3	

Scotland: A.R. Smith (*Oxford Univ.*); R. Welsh (*Watsonians*), W. Neilson (*London Scot.*), J.J. Gowans (*London Scot.*), G.T. Campbell (*London Scot.*); J.W. Simpson (*RHSFP*), W.P. Donaldson (*West of Scot.*); W.B. Cownie (*Watsonians*), J.H. Dods (*Edin. Acads.*), W.R. Gibson (*RHSFP*), W.M.C. McEwan (*Edin. Acads.*), R.G. Macmillan* (*London Scot.*), J.N. Millar (*West of Scot.*), G.T. Neilson (*West of Scot.*), T.M. Scott (*Hawick*)

England: J.F. Byrne (*Moseley*); J.H.C. Fegan (*Blackheath*), W.B. Thomson (*Blackheath*), E.M. Baker (*Oxford Univ.*), T.H. Dobson (*Bradford*); R.H.B. Cattell (*Moseley*), E.W. Taylor (*Rockcliff*); W.E. Bromet (*Richmond*), G.M. Carey (*Oxford Univ.*), W.H. Finlinson (*Blackheath*), F. Mitchell (*Camb. Univ.*), F.O. Poole (*Oxford Univ.*), C. Thomas (*Barnstaple*), W.E. Tucker (*Camb. Univ.*), S.M.J. Woods* (*Bridgewater*)

Referee: W. Wilkins (*Wales*) Touch judges: D.G. Findlay, R.S. Whalley

J.F. Byrne kicked a penalty goal (0–3); G.T. Neilson kicked a penalty goal (3–3); G.T. Neilson scored but failed to convert (6–3). (H.T.).

The Scottish pack controlled the game throughout and tended to keep the ball tight so there was relatively little back play especially as Donaldson, as was his custom, did a lot of kicking to touch. Scotland started well and were startled to find themselves trailing when Byrne kicked England's first ever penalty goal from mid field. However, G.T. Neilson with an equally fine kick from the touchline equalised with Scotland's first penalty goal and it is interesting to note that it took 30 years before another penalty goal was kicked in a Calcutta Cup match. Before half time G.T. Neilson caught Byrne with the ball and securing it was able to run in for a try. A match programme exists for this game and the backs are set out in the formation shown above.

WALES   Cardiff   25 January 1896

SCOTLAND:	Nil	0	**Loss**
WALES:	2 tries	6	

Scotland: A.R. Smith (*Oxford Univ.*); G.T. Campbell (*London Scot.*), A.B. Timms (*Edin. Wrs.*), T. Scott (*Langholm*), R. Welsh (*Watsonians*); J.W. Simpson (*RHSFP*), D. Patterson (*Hawick*); A. Balfour (*Watsonians*), J.H. Couper (*West of Scot.*), J.H. Dods (*London Scot.*), W.M.C. McEwan (*Edin. Acads.*), M.C. Morrison (*RHSFP*), G.T. Neilson* (*West of Scot.*), T. Scott (*Hawick*), H.O. Smith (*Watsonians*)

Wales: W.J. Bancroft (*Swansea*); F.H. Dauncey (*Newport*), A.J. Gould* (*Newport*), E.G. Nicholls (*Cardiff*), C. Bowen (*Llanelli*); F.C. Parfitt (*Newport*), S. Biggs (*Cardiff*); W. Cope (*Blackheath*), W. Davies (*Cardiff*), D. Evans (*Penygraig*), J. Evans (*Llanelli*), F. Hutchinson (*Neath*), W. Morris (*Llanelli*), C.B. Nicholls (*Llanelli*), H. Packer (*Newport*)

Referee: G.H. Barnett (*England*) Touch judges: D.G. Findlay, W. Davies

No scoring at half time. C. Bowen and A.J. Gould scored but W.J. Bancroft failed in each case (0–6).

After a week of rain Cardiff Arms Park was a sea of mud and while this suited the Scottish pack in the loose they were beaten in the mauls. The handling of the Scottish backs continually broke down and they were completely outclassed by the Welsh backs who

82

passed, kicked and ran as if the conditions were perfect. Both Welsh scores came from fine passing runs by the backs. So the game became a series of Welsh attacks with intermittent raids by the Scottish forwards who in the last ten minutes strove hard to score, pinning their opponents on their goal line. It is worth recording that two of the game's greatest figures in M.C. Morrison and E.G. Nicholls gained their first caps.

IRELAND   Lansdowne Road   15 February 1896

| **SCOTLAND:** | Nil | 0 | **Draw** |
| **IRELAND:** | Nil | 0 | |

Scotland: A.R. Smith (*Oxford Univ.*); W. Neilson (*London Scot.*), G.T. Campbell (*London Scot.*), J.J. Gowans (*London Scot.*), C.J.N. Fleming (*Edin. Wrs.*); J.W. Simpson (*RHSFP*), W.P. Donaldson (*West of Scot.*); A. Balfour (*Watsonians*), J.H. Couper (*West of Scot.*), J.H. Dods (*London Scot.*), W.M.C. McEwan (*Edin. Acads.*), M.C. Morrison (*RHSFP*), G.T. Neilson* (*West of Scot.*), H.O. Smith (*Watsonians*), G.O. Turnbull (*West of Scot.*)

Ireland: G.H. McAllan (*Dungannon*); W. Gardiner (*NIFC*), S. Lee* (*NIFC*), T.H. Stevenson (*Edin. Univ.*), L.Q. Bulger (*Dublin Univ.*); L.M. Magee (*Bective Rangers*), G.G. Allen (*Derry*); W.G. Byron (*NIFC*), A.D. Clinch (*Wanderers*), T.J. Crean (*Wanderers*), H. Lindsay (*Armagh*), J.H. Lytle (*NIFC*), J.H. O'Conor (*Bective Rangers*), C.V. Rooke (*Monkstown*), J. Sealey (*Dublin Univ.*)

Referee: E. Holmes (*England*)   **Touch judges:** D.G. Findlay, R.G. Warren

A draw was a fair result for a fast exciting game, full of incident and remarkable for the number of penalties missed by the two recognised goalkickers, H.O. Smith and L.Q. Bulger. Both packs had their spells of domination and the Irish barrage of the last five minutes stretched the defence to its limit. Young McAllan, still at school, had one break through in the second half but passed instead of going on and Gardiner could not get the ball. Later Gowans, who had been handicapped by a damaged finger also had a fine touch line run which was halted just short of the line.

ENGLAND   Old Hampden Park   14 March 1896

| **SCOTLAND:** | 1 goal, 2 tries | 11 | **Win** |
| **ENGLAND:** | Nil | 0 | |

Scotland: G. MacGregor (*London Scot.*); H.T.S. Gedge (*London Scot.*), G.T. Campbell (*London Scot.*), C.J.N. Fleming (*Edin. Wrs.*), J.J. Gowans (*London Scot.*); M. Elliot (*Hawick*), W.P. Donaldson (*West of Scot.*); A. Balfour (*Watsonians*), J.H. Dods (*London Scot.*), W.M.C. McEwan (*Edin. Acads.*), M.C. Morrison (*RHSFP*), G.T. Neilson (*West of Scot.*), T.M. Scott (*Hawick*), H.O. Smith (*Watsonians*), G.O. Turnbull (*West of Scot.*)

England: R.W. Poole (*Hartlepool Rovers*); S. Morfitt (*Hull KR*), E.M. Baker (*Oxford Univ.*), J. Valentine (*Swinton*), E.F. Fookes (*Sowerby Bridge*); C.M. Wells (*Harlequins*), R.H. Cattell (*Blackheath*); J.H. Barron (*Bingley*), T. Broadley (*Bingley*), G.E. Hughes (*Barrow*), E. Knowles (*Millom*), .F Mitchell (*Camb. Univ.*), J. Rhodes (*Castleford*), H. Speed (*Castleford*), J.W. Ward (*Castleford*)

Referee: Douglas (Wales) **Touch judges:** D.G. Findlay, R. Walker

H.T.S. Gedge scored; H.O. Smith failed (3–0). (H.T.). J.J. Gowans scored; T.M. Scott failed (6–0); C.J.N. Fleming scored; T.M. Scott converted (11–0).

The Scottish pack dominated the play and although Donaldson kicked too much to touch, Elliot, who replaced J.W. Simpson, played very well and the aggressive Scottish backs had a good supply of the ball. Gedge was fast, Campbell was always a good attacking player and Fleming, weighing some fifteen stones, proved difficult to hold. After some Scottish pressure a good run by Speed and Cattell saw Baker just fail to score. Good touch kicking by Gowans and Gedge took play back and Gedge having made a good run, dropped at goal when he was actually clear. Elliot then broke from a line out and the ball passed from Donaldson and Fleming to Gedge whose pace and swerve let him score at the posts only to see Smith miss the kick. The second half began like the first: Scottish pressure was relieved by some good running by the English backs but they were inclined to run across the field and good tackling halted progress. Then Gedge intercepted a pass and after a strong run a passing movement between himself and Campbell let Fleming score.

IRELAND   Powderhall   20 February 1897

SCOTLAND: 1 goal, 1 penalty goal   8   **Win**

IRELAND: 1 try   3

Scotland: A.R. Smith (*Oxford Univ.*); G.T. Campbell (*London Scot.*), W. Neilson (*London Scot.*), C.J.N. Fleming (*Edin. Wrs.*), T. Scott (*Hawick*); M. Elliot (*Hawick*), R.C. Greig (*Glas. Acads.*); J.H. Dods (*Edin. Acads.*), A. Laidlaw (*Hawick*), W.M.C. McEwan (*Edin. Acads.*), R.G. Macmillan* (*London Scot.*), M.C. Morrison (*RHSFP*), T.M. Scott (*Hawick*), R.C. Stevenson (*London Scot.*), G.O. Turnbull (*London Scot.*)

Ireland: P.E. O'Brien-Butler (*Monkstown*); W. Gardiner (*NIFC*), L.Q. Bulger (*Dublin Univ.*), T.H. Stevenson (*Albion*), L.H. Gwynn (*Dublin Univ.*); L.M. Magee (*Bective Rangers*), G.G. Allen (*Derry*); W.G. Byron (*NIFC*), A.D. Clinch (*Wanderers*), E.F. Forrest* (*Wanderers*), J.H. Lytle (*NIFC*), J.E. McIlwaine (*NIFC*), C.V. Rooke (*Monkstown*), M. Ryan (*Rockwell*), J. Sealey (*Dublin Univ.*)

Referee: A. B. Holmes (*England*) **Touch judges:** D.G. Findlay, J.E. Dodds

L.Q. Bulger scored but failed (0–3). (H.T.). G.O. Turnbull scored; T.M. Scott converted (5–3); T.M. Scott kicked a penalty (8–3).

Ireland had the benefit of a strong westerly wind but could only score once during the first half and that mainly due to shaky play by Fleming who had a real off day. M. Elliot showed up well, continually halting the Irish forwards who indulged in their familiar rushing tactics. Scotland got well on top in the second half. Morrison took the ball over the line but was not given the score and T.M. Scott had a penalty goal kick turned down before Turnbull scored the decisive try.

ENGLAND Fallowfield 13 March 1897

SCOTLAND: 1 try   3   **Loss**

ENGLAND: 1 goal, 1 drop goal, 1 try   12

Scotland: A.R. Smith (*Oxford Univ.*); A.M. Bucher (*Edin. Acads.*), W. Neilson (*London Scot.*), T. Scott (*Hawick*), A.W. Robertson (*Edin. Acads.*); M. Elliot (*Hawick*), J.W. Simpson (*RHSFP*); A. Balfour (*Camb. Univ.*), J.H. Dods (*Edin. Acads.*), W.M.C. McEwan (*Edin. Acads.*), R.G. Macmillan* (*London Scot.*), M.C. Morrison (*RHSFP*), T.M. Scott (*Hawick*), R.C. Stevenson (*London Scot.*), G.O. Turnbull (*London Scot.*)

England: J.F. Byrne (*Moseley*); E.F. Fookes (*Sowerby Bridge*), W.L. Bunting (*Richmond*), O.G. Mackie (*Camb. Univ.*), G.C. Robinson (*Percy Park*); E.W. Taylor* (*Rockcliff*), C.M. Wells (*Harlequins*); Jas. Davidson (*Aspatria*), H.W. Dudgeon (*Richmond*), L.F. Giblin (*Camb. Univ.*), F. Jacob (*Camb. Univ.*), E. Knowles (*Millom*), R.F. Oakes (*Hartlepool Rovers*), J. Pinch (*Lancaster*), W.B. Stoddart (*Liverpool*)

Referee: J.T. Magee (*Ireland*)   Touch judges: D.G. Findlay, R.S. Whalley

No scoring at half time. E.F. Fookes and G.C. Robinson scored; J.F. Byrne converted the first (0–8); A.M. Bucher scored; T.M. Scott failed (3–8); J.F. Byrne dropped a goal (3–12).

Scotland came to Manchester as favourites but were outplayed in all departments. The English half backs dominated the game and Robinson on the wing had a great attacking afternoon. R.G. Macmillan often came out of the pack to strengthen the defence although A.R. Smith was very sound at full back. The Scottish score came when Bucher dribbled up to the full back, kicked the ball on and won the race for the touch down.

IRELAND Belfast 19 February 1898

SCOTLAND: 1 goal, 1 try   8   **Win**

IRELAND: Nil   0

Scotland: J.M. Reid (*Edin. Acads.*); A.R. Smith* (*Oxford Univ.*), E. Spencer (*Clydesdale*), R.T. Neilson (*West of Scot.*), T. Scott (*Hawick*); M. Elliot (*Hawick*), J.T. Mabon (*Jedforest*); J.M. Dykes (*Clydesdale*), G.C. Kerr (*Durham*), W.M.C. McEwan (*Edin. Acads.*), A. Mackinnon (*London Scot.*), M.C. Morrison (*RHSFP*), R. Scott (*Hawick*), T.M. Scott (*Hawick*), H.O. Smith (*Watsonians*)

Ireland: P.E. O'Brien-Butler (*Monkstown*); F.C. Purser (*Dublin Univ.*), F.F.S. Smithwick

(*Monkstown*), L.H. Gwynn (*Dublin Univ.*), L.Q. Bulger (*Lansdowne*); G.G. Allen* (*Derry*), L.M. Magee (*Edin. Wrs.*); W.G. Byron (*NIFC*), J.L. Davis (*Monkstown*), J.G. Franks (*Dublin Univ.*), H. Lindsay (*Wanderers*), J.H. Lytle (*NIFC*), J.E. McIlwaine (*NIFC*), J. Ryan (*Rockwell*), M. Ryan (*Rockwell*)

Referee: E.T. Gurdon (*England*)   **Touch judges:** R.D. Rainie, Rev. R. Huggard

No scoring at half time. T. Scott scored twice and T.M. Scott converted the first only (8–0).

Played on the Show Ground at Balmoral before 12,000 spectators. Smithwick was recorded as a seventeen year old replacement in the Irish backs. Scotland had the benefit of a strong wind in the first half but with eight new caps played a very disjointed game and Ireland were jubilant to be on equal terms at half time. They restarted strongly and only a good tackle by Reid prevented M. Ryan from scoring. Then McEwan was more or less crippled yet Scotland went on the offensive and Tom Scott's pace brought them two winning scores.

ENGLAND   Powderhall   12 March 1898

SCOTLAND:	1 try	3	**Draw**
ENGLAND:	1 try	3	

Scotland: J.M. Reid (*Edin. Acads.*); A.R. Smith* (*Oxford Univ.*), T.A. Nelson (*Oxford Univ.*), R.T. Neilson (*West of Scot.*), T. Scott (*Hawick*); M. Elliot (*Hawick*), J.T. Mabon (*Jedforest*); J.M. Dykes (*Clydesdale*), G.C. Kerr (*Durham*), W.M.C. McEwan (*Edin. Acads.*), A. MacKinnon (*London Scot.*), M.C. Morrison (*RHSFP*), T.M. Scott (*Hawick*), H.O. Smith (*Watsonians*), R.C. Stevenson (*Northumberland*)

England: J.F. Byrne* (*Moseley*); W.N. Pilkington (*Camb. Univ.*), W.L. Bunting (*Richmond*), P.M.R. Royds (*Blackheath*), P.W. Stout (*Gloucester*); G.T. Unwin (*Blackheath*), A. Rotherham (*Richmond*); W. Ashford (*Exeter*), Jas. Davidson (*Aspatria*), H.W. Dudgeon (*Richmond*), F. Jacob (*Richmond*), R.F. Oakes (*Hartlepool Rovers*), H.E. Ramsden (*Bingley*), J.F. Shaw (*RIEC*), F.M. Stout (*Gloucester*)

Referee: J. Dodds (*Ireland*)   **Touch judges:** R.D. Rainie, R.S. Whalley

No scoring at half time. P.M.R. Royds scored; J.P. Byrne failed (0–3); W.M.C. McEwan scored; T.M. Scott failed (3–3).

Powderhall was used again since the new ground at Inverleith was not ready. Scotland did quite well against the wind in the first half, Tom Scott nearly scoring thrice but their backs were not at their best. In the second half England opened the scoring when Reid's touch kick rebounded off Royds who ran on to score. Fortunately the Scottish pack was in fine fettle and continued pressure saw McEwan burst through for a try that T.M. Scott couldn't convert.

86

IRELAND   Inverleith   18 February 1899

SCOTLAND: 1 penalty goal **3** **Loss**
IRELAND: 3 tries **9**

Scotland: J.M. Reid (*Edin. Acads.*); G.T. Campbell (*London Scot.*), D.B. Monypenny (*London Scot.*), R.T. Neilson (*West of Scot.*), T. Scott (*Langholm*); W.P. Donaldson* (*West of Scot.*), J.T. Mabon (*Jedforest*); J.H. Couper (*West of Scot.*), L. Harvey (*Greenock Wrs.*), G.C. Kerr (*Durham*), W.M.C. McEwan (*Edin. Acads.*), A. Mackinnon (*London Scot.*), M.C. Morrison (*RHSFP*), H.O. Smith (*Watsonians*), R.C. Stevenson (*Northumberland*)

Ireland: P.E. O'Brien-Butler (*Monkstown*); G.P. Doran (*Lansdowne*), J.B. Allison (*Campbell Coll.*), C. Reid (*NIFC*), E.F. Campbell (*Monkstown*); L.M. Magee* (*Bective Rangers*), A. Barr (*Methodist Coll.*); W.G. Byron (*NIFC*), T.J. Little (*Bective Rangers*), J.H. Lytle (*NIFC*), T.M.W. McGown (*NIFC*), A.W.D. Meares (*Dublin Univ.*), J. Ryan (*Rockwell*), M. Ryan (*Rockwell*), J. Sealy (*Dublin Univ.*)

Referee: E.T. Gurdon (*England*)   **Touch judges:** J.D. Boswell

E.F. Campbell and C. Reid scored; J.H. Lytle failed with both (0–6). (H.T.). J. Sealy scored; L.M. Magee failed (0–9); W.P. Donaldson dropped a penalty goal (3–9).

The Welsh match having been postponed this became the opening match on the Union's new field at Inverleith. Ireland had to make six changes to Scotland's three. The match was won by the Irish pack behind which Magee was particularly brilliant for his elusive running set up two scores in the first half. Early in the second half a tremendous rush by the Irish forwards put Sealy over for another try and put Reid off the field with a dislocated shoulder. Later Monypenny in his own line kicked the ball clear of the Irish halves, reached it and kicked on again to reach the full back. He put the ball past the full back, over the line and was running on to touch down when he was tackled from behind and brought down. Donaldson dropped a goal from the resultant penalty kick.

WALES   Inverleith   4 March 1899

SCOTLAND: 1 mark goal, 2 drop goals, 3 tries **21** **Win**
WALES: 2 goals **10**

Scotland: H. Rottenburg (*London Scot.*); H.T.S. Gedge (*London Scot.*), D.B. Monypenny (*London Scot.*), G.A.W. Lamond (*Kelvinside Acads.*), T. Scott (*Langholm*); R.T. Neilson (*West of Scot.*), J.W. Simpson (*RHSFP*); J.M. Dykes (*London Scot.*), G.C. Kerr (*Edin. Wrs.*), W.M.C. McEwan (*Edin. Acads.*), A. Mackinnon (*London Scot.*), M.C. Morrison* (*RHSFP*), H.O. Smith (*Watsonians*), R.C. Stevenson (*London Scot.*), W.J. Thomson (*West of Scot.*)

Wales: W.J. Bancroft* (*Swansea*); W.M. Llewellyn (*Llwynypia*), R.T. Skirmshire (*New-*

port), E.G. Nicholls (*Cardiff*), H.V.P. Huzzey (*Cardiff*); G.L. Lloyd (*Newport*), S. Biggs (*Cardiff*); W.H. Alexander (*Llwynypia*), J. Blake (*Cardiff*), A. Brice (*Aberavon*), T. Dobson (*Cardiff*), R. Hellings (*Llwynypia*), J.J. Hodges (*Newport*), W. Parker (*Swansea*), F. Scrimes (*Swansea*)

Referee: M.G. Delaney (*Ireland*)   **Touch judges:** J.D. Boswell, T.D. Schofield

H.T.S. Gedge scored; G.A.W. Lamond failed (3–0); G.L. Lloyd scored; W.J. Bancroft converted (3–5); W.M. Llewellyn scored; W.J. Bancroft converted (3–10). (H.T.). D.B. Monypenny scored; W.J. Thomson failed (6–10); W.J. Thomson kicked a goal from a mark by J.W. Simpson (10–10); G.A.W. Lamond dropped a goal (14–10); H.O. Smith scored; W.J. Thomson failed (17–10); H.T.S. Gedge dropped a goal (21–10).

This was a much postponed match and Wales having thrashed England came as favourites. Scotland however started well when the backs sent Gedge away to score after a fine dodging run but the Welsh backs were equally fast and effective and good running produced two tries before half time. After the restart the home pack got well on top and right away Monypenny scored. Then Neilson had his nose fractured and some of the fluency amongst the backs vanished, the only try coming from a charged down kick. The last score was a surprise for Gedge was given the ball in the clear but decided to drop at goal instead of running.

ENGLAND   Blackheath   11 March 1899

SCOTLAND:	1 goal	5	**Win**
ENGLAND:	Nil	0	

Scotland: H. Rottenburg (*London Scot.*); H.T.S. Gedge (*London Scot.*), D.B. Monypenny (*London Scot.*), G.A.W. Lamond (*Kelvinside Acads.*), T. Scott (*Langholm*); J.I. Gillespie (*Edin. Acads.*), J.W. Simpson (*RHSFP*); J.M. Dykes (*London Scot.*), G.C. Kerr (*Edin. Wrs.*), W.M.C. McEwan (*Edin. Acads.*), A.Mackinnon (*London Scot.*), M.C. Morrison* (*RHSFP*), H.O. Smith (*Watsonians*), R.C. Stevenson (*London Scot.*), W.J. Thomson (*West of Scot.*)

England: H.T. Gamlin (*Wellington*); E.F. Fookes (*Sowerby Bridge*), W.L. Bunting (*Richmond*), J.C. Matters (*RNEC*), P.W. Stout (*Gloucester*); A. Rotherham* (*Richmond*), R.O. Schwarz (*Richmond*); Jas. Davidson (*Aspatria*), Jos. Davidson (*Aspatria*), A.O. Dowson (*Moseley*), H.W. Dudgeon (*Richmond*), R.F.A. Hobbs (*Blackheath*), R.F. Oakes (*Hartlepool Rovers*), J.P. Shooter (*Morley*), F.M. Stout (*Gloucester*)

Referee: J.T. Magee (*Ireland*)   **Touch judges:** J.D. Boswell

No scoring at halftime. J.I. Gillespie scored; W.J. Thomson converted (5–0).

Scotland had rather the better of the first half but both sides lost tries by repeatedly knocking on scoring passes. Tom Scott, however, was prominent with much dangerous running. Before half time J.W. Simpson twisted a knee and although remaining on the field as an extra full back was of no use. H.O. Smith took his place at quarter and played really well there. In spite of this the Scottish pack controlled the game but the English backs, especially Gamlin, defended very well and the only score came from a very long dribbling run by Gillespie who just managed to touch down short of the dead ball line. Gillespie who played well throughout, had replaced the injured Neilson so Scotland for the first time since 1890 were without one of the famous family.

Prominent Players of the 1890s

During this period Scottish rugby was particularly well served by their forwards; men such as M.C. and W.M.C. McEwan, W.R. Gibson, R.G. MacMillan, J.D. Boswell and H.T.O. Leggatt were feared for the ferocity of their dribbling rushes and their tackling. Adam Dalgleish of Gala was the first to be capped from a Border Club and probably the first not to have come from the established FP Clubs. J.D. Boswell also had an uncanny knack of dropping goals from the most unexpected positions. But the decade saw the advent of Mark C. Morrison, one of the greatest forwards in the history of the game. A big strong man by any standards, he was quite fast, could handle well and was a destructive tackler.

Amongst the backs H.J. Stevenson has already been noted as the most outstanding defensive yet attacking back or full back of his time. W. Neilson and G.T. Campbell were excellent centres while Tom Scott and H.T.S. Gedge were most elusive scoring wingers.

WALES	Swansea		27 January 1900
SCOTLAND:	1 try	3	**Loss**
WALES:	4 tries	12	

Scotland: H. Rottenburg (*London Scot.*); T. Scott (*Langholm*), A.B. Timms (*Edin. Univ.*), W.H. Morrison (*Edin. Acads.*), J.E. Crabbie (*Edin. Acads.*); J.I. Gillespie (*Edin. Acads.*), F.H. Fasson (*London Scot.*); D.R. Bedell-Sivright (*Camb. Univ.*), J.M. Dykes (*London Scot.*), F.W. Henderson (*London Scot.*), G.C. Kerr (*Durham*), W.M.C. McEwan (*Edin. Acads.*), M.C. Morrison* (*RHSFP*), T.M. Scott (*Hawick*), W.J. Thomson (*West of Scot.*)

Wales: W.J. Bancroft (*Swansea*); W.M. Llewellyn (*Llwynypia*), E.G. Nicholls (*Cardiff*), G. Davies (*Swansea*), W.J. Trew (*Swansea*); G.L. Lloyd (*Newport*), L.A. Phillips (*Newport*); J. Blake (*Cardiff*), J.G. Boots (*Newport*), A. Brice (*Aberavon*), G. Dobson (*Cardiff*), J.J. Hodges (*Newport*), F. Miller (*Mountain Ash*), R. Thomas (*Swansea*), W.H. Williams (*Pontyminster*)

Referee: A. Hartley (*England*)

W.M. Llewellyn scored (0–3); J.M. Dykes scored; T.M. Scott failed (3–3); W.G. Nicholls scored (3–6). (H.T.). W.M. Llewellyn and W.H. Williams scored (3–12); W.J. Bancroft failed with all four conversions.

The Welsh pack was clearly on top and with a plentiful supply of the ball a fine set of backs were continually making brilliant passing runs. Lloyd and Nicholls were especially good and the latter gave Llewellyn many opportunities to utilise his pace on the wing. Play was quite one-sided and the only redeeming feature for Scotland was the determined defence maintained by their backs, Tom Scott in particular. The Scottish try came from a rush in which McEwan and Dykes were prominent and the latter scored when Bancroft made a slip.

IRELAND   Dublin   24 February 1900

| **SCOTLAND:** | Nil | | 0 | **Draw** |
| **IRELAND:** | Nil | | 0 | |

Scotland: H. Rottenburg (*London Scot.*); T. Scott (*Langholm*), A.R. Smith (*London Scot.*), A.B. Timms (*Edin. Univ.*), W.H. Welsh (*Edin. Univ.*); R.T. Neilson (*West of Scot.*), J.T. Mabon (*Jedforest*); J.A. Campbell (*Camb. Univ.*), J.M. Dykes (*London Scot.*), J.R.C. Greenlees (*Camb. Univ.*), F.W. Henderson (*London Scot.*), G.C. Kerr (*Durham*), R. Scott (*Hawick*), T.M. Scott* (*Hawick*), W.P. Scott (*West of Scot.*)

Ireland: C.A. Boyd (*Dublin Univ.*); G.P. Doran (*Lansdowne*), B.R.W. Doran (*Lansdowne*), J.B. Allison (*QC Belfast*), I.G. Davidson (*NIFC*); L.M. Magee* (*Bective Rangers*), J.H. Ferris (*QC Belfast*); C.E. Allen (*Liverpool*), F. Gardiner (*NIFC*), S.T. Irwin (*QC Belfast*), T.J. Little (*Bective Rangers*), P.C. Nicholson (*Dublin Univ.*), J.Ryan (*Rockwell*), M. Ryan (*Rockwell*), J. Sealey (*Dublin Univ.*)

Referee: Dr Badger (*England*)   **Touch judges:** I McIntyre, S. Lee

The spell of frosty weather which caused a week's postponement of this match had also left the teams short of match practice so that in spite of the good conditions this was a scrambling game largely confined to the forwards. There were several stops for injuries as rather forcible tactics were indulged in by both teams. Both sides made some good runs but the defences were always sound. W.H. Welsh, however, had a fine debut, his pace being very much in evidence. T.M. Scott was the first from a Border Club to captain the XV.

ENGLAND   Inverleith   10 March 1900

| **SCOTLAND:** | Nil | | 0 | **Draw** |
| **ENGLAND:** | Nil | | 0 | |

Scotland: H. Rottenburg (*London Scot.*); T. Scott (*Langholm*), G.T. Campbell (*London Scot.*), A.R. Smith (*London Scot.*), W.H. Welsh (*Edin. Univ.*); R.T. Neilson (*West of Scot.*), J.I. Gillespie (*Edin. Acads.*); L.H.I. Bell (*Edin. Acads.*), G.C. Kerr (*Edin. Wrs.*), W.M.C. McEwan (*Edin. Acads.*), A. Mackinnon (*London Scot.*), M.C. Morrison* (*RHSFP*), R. Scott (*Hawick*), W.P. Scott (*West of Scot.*), H.O. Smith (*Watsonians*)

England: H.T. Gamlin (*Blackheath*); R. Forrest (*Blackheath*), W.L. Bunting (*Richmond*), G.W. Gordon-Smith (*Blackheath*), A.C. Robinson (*Percy Park*); J.C. Marquis (*Birkenhead*

Park), G.H. Marsden (*Morley*); H. Alexander (*Birkenhead Park*), J. Baxter (*Birkenhead Park*), R.W. Bell (*Northern*), J. Daniell* (*Camb. Univ.*), A.F.C.C. Luxmore (*Richmond*), S. Reynolds (*Richmond*), J.P. Shooter (*Morley*), A.F. Todd (*Blackheath*)

Referee: M. Delaney (*Ireland*) **Touch judges:** I. McIntyre, J.W.H. Thorpe

A draw was a fair result for a hard struggle largely confined to the forwards where England, good in the scrums, could not match the Scots in the loose. England had the better of the first half where two or three individual efforts nearly brought scores. Both Robinson and Bunting broke clear but in each case the player instead of going on, passed in field to another who was promptly floored, for the Scottish cover defence was fast and effective. The Scottish forwards, with H.O. Smith, McEwan and Morrison prominent, made some telling rushes only to find Gamlin in good form but just on half time he was badly shaken in tackling Morrison. The restart was held up because Shooter and A.R. Smith were receiving attention and the ball was mislaid! Scotland were clearly on top in the second half, their forwards putting great pressure on the defence. Welsh and Gillespie, who knocked down the corner flag, came near to scoring and later on Gillespie missed a kickable penalty.

WALES   Inverleith   9 February 1901

SCOTLAND:	3 goals, 1 try	18	**Win**
WALES:	1 goal, 1 try	8	

Scotland: A.W. Duncan (*Edin. Univ.*); W.H. Welsh (*Edin. Univ.*), A.B. Timms (*Edin. Univ.*), P. Turnbull (*Edin. Acads.*), A.N. Fell (*Edin. Univ.*); J.I. Gillespie (*Edin. Acads.*), F.H. Fasson (*Edin. Univ.*); D.R. Bedell-Sivright (*Camb. Univ.*), J.A. Bell (*Clydesdale*), J.M. Dykes (*Glas. HSFP*), A.B. Flett (*Edin. Univ.*), A. Frew (*Edin. Univ.*), M.C. Morrison* (*RHSFP*), J. Ross (*London Scot.*), R.S. Stronach (*Glas. Acads.*)

Wales: W.J. Bancroft* (*Swansea*); W.M. Llewellyn (*London Welsh*), E.G. Nicholls (*Cardiff*), G. Davies (*Swansea*), W.J. Trew (*Swansea*); G.L. Lloyd (*Newport*), L.A. Phillips (*Newport*); W.N. Alexander (*Llwynypia*), J. Blake (*Cardiff*), J.G. Boots (*Newport*), A. Brice (*Aberavon*), H. Davies (*Swansea*), R. Hellings (*Llwynypia*), J.J. Hodges (*Swansea*), F. Millar (*Mountain Ash*)

Referee: R.W. Jeffares (*Ireland*) **Touch judges:** R.G. Macmillan, D.H. Bowen

J.I. Gillespie scored and converted (5–0); A.B. Flett scored; J.I. Gillespie converted (10–0). (H.T.). J.I. Gillespie scored; A.B. Flett converted (15–0); P. Turnbull scored; A.B. Flett failed (18–0); G.L. Lloyd scored; W.J. Bancroft converted (18–5); J.G. Boots scored; W.J. Bancroft failed (18–8).

This match was postponed because of the death of Queen Victoria and as a mark of respect the spectators were predominently in black.

The Scottish team had eight new caps and contained seven of the outstanding Edinburgh University XV. J.T. Tulloch (Kelvinside Acads.) had been an original selection but after a special practice game he was considered unfit and replaced by Timms.

The heavy Welsh forwards (who were criticised for rough play) played well in the scrums but could not match the Scots in the loose and the Welsh backs were greatly troubled by the speedy and clever Scottish backs. On starting Fell nearly scored, Llewellyn just kicked the ball dead as he dived at it to score. Nicholls and Llewellyn got away with only Duncan to pass but the full back managed to put Llewellyn into touch and shortly after made a saving tackle on Trew. Then came the turning point in the match. From a maul the ball came out on Gillespie's side. He pounced on it, tricked two opponents with a dummy and with a sprint fell over the line with a Welshman hanging on to him. Then Turnbull with his characteristic ability to slip past defenders, wandered through the backs up to Bancroft and gave a scoring pass to Flett. The Scottish backs continued their brilliant running in the second half, Turnbull making several deceptive weaving runs and two more tries were added. A late rally in which Nicholls and Trew were outstanding brought two consolation tries to Wales.

IRELAND   Inverleith   23 February 1901

SCOTLAND: 3 tries   9   **Win**

IRELAND: 1 goal   5

Scotland: A.W. Duncan (*Edin. Univ.*); W.H. Welsh (*Edin. Univ.*), A.B. Timms (*Edin. Univ.*), P. Turnbull (*Edin. Acads.*), A.N. Fell (*Edin. Univ.*); J.I. Gillespie (*Edin. Acads.*), F.H. Fasson (*Edin. Univ.*); D.R. Bedell-Sivright (*Fet.-Lor.*), J.A. Bell (*Clydesdale*), F.P. Dods (*Edin. Acads.*), J.M. Dykes (*Glas. HSFP*), A.B. Flett (*Edin. Univ.*), A. Frew (*Edin. Univ.*), M.C. Morrison* (*RHSFP*), J. Ross (*London Scot.*)

Ireland: C.A. Boyd (*Wanderers*); A.E. Freear (*Lansdowne*), B.R.W. Doran (*Lansdowne*), J.B. Allison (*Edin. Univ.*), I.G. Davidson (*NIFC*); L.M. Magee* (*Bective Rangers*), A. Barr (*Methodist Coll.*); C.E. Allan (*Derry*), T.A. Harvey (*Dublin Univ.*), P. Healey (*Limerick*), H.A.S. Irvine (*Collegians*), T.J. Little (*Bective Rangers*), T.M.W. McGowan (*NIFC*), J. Ryan (*Rockwell*), M. Ryan (*Rockwell*)

   Referee: G. Harnett (*England*)

J.I. Gillespie scored; A.B. Flett failed (3–0); W.H. Welsh scored twice; A.B. Flett failed (9–0); B.R.W. Doran scored; H.A.S. Irvine converted (9–5). (H.T.).

Ireland pressed with good forward rushes checked by Timms. Almost at once Boyd was caught with the ball; the Scottish forwards worked the ball loose and a passing run by Fell and Dykes let Gillespie score. The Scottish backs continued to attack and well timed passing by Turnbull and Timms let Welsh away on a run where his great pace took him round the defenders for a score. From the kick off an almost similar move by the same three gave Welsh a second high speed try — three inside ten minutes. The Irish forwards again came away finely and good play by Magee and Allison put Doran in at the posts. The Scottish backs made several other fine runs but did not break through, Boyd putting in some fine tackles on Welsh.

   In the second half there was no scoring but plenty action. Bedell-Sivright broke away and Freear was hurt stopping him. Fell had a hard run halted by a splendid tackle by Magee who was so hurt that he had to go off. Duncan halted the Irish pack several times but eventually was caught with the ball and the game was halted until he recovered. Although badly dazed he managed to halt the two powerful Ryans who threatened trouble with a strong rush. One comment on Mike Ryan ran 'If not over refined is all the same a brilliant forward'. Welsh's great pace was much in evidence. Note with J.B. Allison playing for Ireland, all the Edinburgh University threes and full back were present.

ENGLAND   Blackheath   9 March 1901

SCOTLAND: 3 goals, 1 try   18   **Win**

ENGLAND: 1 try   3

Scotland: A.W. Duncan (*Edin. Univ.*); W.H. Welsh (*Edin. Univ.*), A.B. Timms (*Edin. Univ.*), P. Turnbull (*Edin. Acads.*), A.N. Fell (*Edin. Univ.*); J.I. Gillespie (*Edin. Acads.*), R.M. Neill (*Edin. Acads.*); D.R. Bedell-Sivright (*Fet.-Lor.*), J.A. Bell (*Clydesdale*), J.M. Dykes (*Glas. HSFP*), A.B. Flett (*Edin. Univ.*), A. Frew (*Edin. Univ.*), M.C. Morrison* (*RHSFP*), J. Ross (*London Scot.*), R.S. Stronach (*Glas. Acads.*)

England: H.T. Gamlin (*Wellington*); E.W. Elliot (*Sunderland*), N.S. Cox (*Sunderland*), W.L. Bunting* (*Richmond*), G.C. Robinson (*Percy Park*); B. Oughtred (*Hartlepool Rovers*), P.D. Kendall (*Birkenhead Park*); H. Alexander (*Birkenhead Park*), C.S. Edgar (*Birkenhead Park*), N.C. Fletcher (*OMT*), G.R. Gibson (*Northern*), C. Hall (*Gloucester*), B.C. Hartley (*Camb. Univ.*), A. O'Neill (*Torquay A*), H.T.F. Weston (*Northampton*)

Referee: R.W. Jeffares (*Ireland*)   **Touch judges:** R.G. Macmillan, F.H. Fox

J.I. Gillespie scored and converted (5–0); W.H. Welsh and A.B. Timms scored; J.I. Gillespie converted both (15–0). (H.T.). G.C. Robinson scored; H. Alexander failed (15–3); A.N. Fell scored; J.I. Gillespie failed (18–3).

Early on Frew went over but the referee gave Gamlin the benefit of the touch down. England pressed for fifteen minutes, Oughtred and Elliot having a fine run only halted by Fell who came across from the other wing to tackle Elliot. But from here onwards Scotland were clearly on top and scored thrice in ten minutes. Their pack was in good form with dribbling rushes whilst the backs combined beautifully at full pace. Fell and Turnbull combined to put Gillespie in (which meant that he had scored first in every match this season). Bell from the middle of a crowd of forwards flung the ball wide to Welsh whose pace carried him clear to score behind the posts and then Fell and Turnbull made another opening for Timms to score. The second half was less spectacular. Turnbull missed a chance when with Fell outside him, he kicked past Gamlin but lost the touch. Some slack defence let Robinson go through two tackles for the only English score and later from a scrum the ball passed right along the line to Fell who got over for the last score. Gamlin's defence was again splendid especially against a set of Scottish backs whose attacking ability and pace was so great.

WALES   Cardiff   1 February 1902

SCOTLAND: 1 goal   5   **Loss**

WALES: 1 goal, 3 tries   14

Scotland: A.W. Duncan (*Edin. Univ.*); W.H. Welsh (*Edin. Univ.*), A.B. Timms (*Edin. Univ.*), P. Turnbull (*Edin. Acads.*), A.N. Fell (*Edin. Univ.*); J.I. Gillespie (*Edin. Acads.*),

F.H. Fasson (*Edin. Univ.*); D.R. Bedell-Sivright (*Camb. Univ.*), J.V. Bedell-Sivright (*Camb. Univ.*), J.A. Bell (*Clydesdale*), A.B. Flett (*Edin. Univ.*), J.R.C. Greenlees (*Camb. Univ.*), W.E. Kyle (*Hawick*), M.C. Morrison* (*RHSFP*), J. Ross (*London Scot.*)

Wales: J. Strand Jones (*Oxford Univ.*); W.M. Llewellyn (*Llwynypia*), E.G. Nicholls* (*Cardiff*), R.T. Gabe (*Cardiff*), E.T. Morgan (*Guy's*); G.L. Lloyd (*Newport*), R.M. Owen (*Swansea*); J.G. Boots (*Newport*), A. Brice (*Aberavon*), A.F. Harding (*Cardiff*), J.J. Hodges (*Newport*), D. Jones (*Aberdare*), H. Jones (*Penygraig*), W.W. Joseph (*Swansea*), W.T. Osborne (*Mountain Ash*)

Referee: P. Gilliard (*England*)

W.M. Llewellyn scored twice but A. Brice failed (0–6); R.T. Gabe scored twice; J. Strand Jones converted the second only (0–14). (H.T.). W.H. Welsh scored; J.I. Gillespie converted (5–14).

Scotland were beaten at all quarters, especially forward so that their backs had few chances to attack. Fell was hurt in the first few minutes but returned with a bandage over a cut forehead. Straightway the Welsh backs with a good supply of the ball began fast passing attacks and Llewellyn after dropping one scoring pass, scored twice inside fifteen minutes. After a further 15 minutes Gabe had scored a further two tries, combining well with his winger, Morgan. Right on half time the Scottish backs had one chance to demonstrate their ability and Welsh getting the ball, showed his pace by passing Llewellyn.

Scotland resumed with the wind but although both sets of three-quarters indulged in good combined runs no scores developed. Gillespie made several dribbling runs from the scrums — a well known feature of his play as a half back. The Welsh backs were all good with Lloyd and the very fast Morgan outstanding.

IRELAND Belfast 22 February 1902

| **SCOTLAND:** | Nil | 0 | **Loss** |
| **IRELAND:** | 1 goal | 5 | |

Scotland: A.W. Duncan (*Edin. Univ.*); W.H. Welsh (*Edin. Univ.*), A.S. Drybrough (*Edin. Wrs.*), P. Turnbull (*Edin. Acads.*), J.E. Crabbie (*Oxford Univ.*); J.I. Gillespie (*Edin. Acads.*), R.M. Neill (*Edin. Acads.*); D.R. Bedell-Sivright (*Camb. Univ.*), J.A. Bell (*Clydesdale*), H.H. Bullmore (*Edin. Univ.*), A.B. Flett (*Edin. Univ.*), J.R.C. Greenlees (*Camb. Univ.*), W.E. Kyle (*Hawick*), M.C. Morrison* (*RHSFP*), W.P. Scott (*West of Scot.*)

Ireland: J. Fulton* (*NIFC*); I.G. Davidson (*NIFC*), J.B. Allison (*Edin. Univ.*), B.R.W. Doran (*Lansdowne*), G.P. Doran (*Lansdowne*); L.M. Magee (*Bective Rangers*), H.H. Corley (*Dublin Univ.*); J.J. Coffey (*Lansdowne*), F. Gardiner (*NIFC*), G.T. Hamlet (*Old Wesley*), T.A. Harvey (*Dublin Univ.*), P. Healy (*Limerick*), S.T. Irwin (*QC Belfast*), J.C. Pringle (*RIEC*), A. Tedford (*Malone*)

Referee: A. Hill (*England*)

No scoring at half time. G.P. Doran scored; H.H. Corley converted (0–5).

The Irish pack, helped by some poor defensive kicking against the wind, kept play in the Scottish half. Magee initiated many attacks which failed against a sound defence, Drybrough's tackling being very effective.

The Scottish forwards restarted well, Bell, Morrison and Bedell-Sivright dribbled the ball well into the Irish 25; then Kyle and Bell took it over the line and appeared to touch down before it went over the dead ball line. The referee, however, gave no score. Scotland continued to press and Welsh had two dangerous runs, the first halted by a good tackle and the second finished when Drybrough dropped a scoring pass right on the line. Ireland then improved and from a scrum on the Scottish 25 a passing run put G.B. Doran in for the only score of the game. Again the Scottish pack was mastered but the Irish backs, with the exception of Magee, were not brilliant and so the score was kept down.

ENGLAND   Inverleith   15 March 1902

SCOTLAND:	1 try	3	**Loss**
ENGLAND:	2 tries	6	

Scotland: A.W. Duncan (*Edin. Univ.*); A.N. Fell (*Edin. Univ.*), P. Turnbull (*Edin. Acads.*), A.B. Timms (*Edin. Univ.*), W.H. Welsh (*Edin. Univ.*); F.H. Fasson (*Edin. Univ.*), E.D. Simson (*Edin. Univ.*); D.R. Bedell-Sivright (*Camb. Univ.*), J.A. Bell (*Clydesdale*), J.M. Dykes (*Glas. HSFP*), J.R.C. Greenlees (*Camb. Univ.*), W.E. Kyle (*Hawick*), M.C. Morrison* (*RHSFP*), W.P. Scott (*West of Scot.*), H.O. Smith (*Watsonians*)

England: H.T. Gamlin (*Devonport Albion*); T. Simpson (*Rockcliff*), J.T. Taylor (*West Hartlepool*), J.E. Raphael (*Oxford Univ.*), R. Forrest (*Wellington*); B. Oughtred (*Hartlepool Rovers*), E.J. Walton (*Castleford*); J. Daniel* (*Richmond*), D.D. Dobson (*Newton Abbot*), G. Fraser (*Richmond*), P. Hardwick (*Percy Park*), R.C. Hartley (*Blackheath*), J.J. Robinson (*Headingley*), L.R. Tosswill (*Bart's*), S.G. Williams (*Devonport Albion*)

Referee: F.M. Hamilton (*Ireland*)   **Touch judges:** G.T. Neilson, M. Newsome

S.G. Williams scored but J.T. Taylor failed (0–3); J.T. Taylor scored but H.T. Gamlin failed (0–6). (H.T.). A.N. Fell scored but D.R. Bedell-Sivright failed (3–6).

A record crowd of 20,000 watched in brilliant sunshine. There was, however, a strong breeze and the famous 'Inverleith swirl' was in evidence. England played with the wind in the first half and the swirl and sun badly affected Duncan who was sadly off form. A misfield gave Williams a simple score and England were rather fortunate to turn round with two tries advantage. In the second half Scotland attacked for most of the time only to fail against some splendid tackling. Welsh was felled by one vigorous tackle and left the field with an injury which finished his rugby career.

One report notes that Walton was working the scrum, opposed to Fasson, and that Oughtred, receiving the ball, was playing a short punting game.

WALES   Inverleith   7 February 1903

SCOTLAND: 1 penalty goal, 1 try   6   **Win**
WALES: Nil   0

Scotland: W.T. Forrest (*Hawick*); A.N. Fell (*Edin. Univ.*), A.B. Timms (*Edin. Univ.*), H.J. Orr (*London Scot.*), J.E. Crabbie (*Oxford Univ.*); E.D. Simson (*Edin. Univ.*), J. Knox (*Kelvinside Acads.*); D.R. Bedell-Sivright (*Camb. Univ.*), A.G. Cairns (*Watsonians*), J.R.C. Greenless (*Kelvinside Acads.*), N. Kennedy (*West of Scot.*), W.E. Kyle (*Hawick*), M.C. Morrison* (*RHSFP*), W.P. Scott (*West of Scot.*), L. West (*Edin. Univ.*)

Wales: J. Strand-Jones (*Llanelli*); W.R. Arnold (*Llanelli*), R.T. Gabe (*Llanelli*), D. Rees (*Swansea*), W.J. Trew (*Swansea*); G.L. Lloyd* (*Newport*), R.M. Owen (*Swansea*); J.G. Boots (*Newport*), A. Brice (*Aberavon*), A.F. Harding (*Cardiff*), J.J. Hodges (*Newport*), D. Jones (*Treherbert*), W.W. Joseph (*Swansea*), W.T. Osborne (*Mountain Ash*), G. Travers (*Pill Harriers*)

Referee: A. Martelli (*Ireland*)   **Touch judges:** Revd. R.S. Davidson, J. James

A.B. Timms dropped a penalty goal (3–0). (H.T.). W.E. Kyle scored; W.T. Forrest failed (6–0).

Conditions were appalling for the game was played in a fierce gale of wind and blinding rain coming from the south-west. The water logged pitch was swept clear of pools by workmen just before the start.

Scotland began with the gale behind them but could only score a penalty goal, given for feet up in the scrum and and drop kicked by Timms from just inside halfway. The Welsh pack played to their backs who made one or two sallies only to be halted by stern tackling and the conditions which were really against all handling.

On restarting against the gale the Scottish forwards in a most determined manner gradually took control of the game. Wales did get into the Scottish 25 for a while but firm defence by the forwards and backs, especially Forrest, kept them out. Eventually good play by Orr and Crabbie took play well up field and the momentum was maintained by their forwards, a great surge being crowned by Kyle forcing his way over for a try. It was remarked that the Welsh backs were none too happy about checking the Scottish forwards in their foot rushes.

IRELAND   Inverleith   28 February 1903

SCOTLAND: 1 try   3   **Win**
IRELAND: Nil   0

Scotland: W.T. Forrest (*Hawick*); C. France (*Kelvinside Acads.*), A.S. Drybrough (*Edin. Wrs.*), J.H. Orr (*London Scot.*), J.E. Crabbie (*Oxford Univ.*); E.D. Simson (*Edin. Univ.*), J. Knox (*Kelvinside Acads.*); D.R. Bedell-Sivright (*Camb. Univ.*), A.G. Cairns (*Watson-*

ians), J.R.C. Greenlees (*Kelvinside Acads.*), N. Kennedy (*West of Scot.*), W.E. Kyle (*Hawick*), M.C. Morrison* (*RHSFP*), W.P. Scott (*West of Scot.*), L. West (*Edin. Univ.*)

Ireland: J. Fulton (*NIFC*); C.C. Fitzgerald (*Glas. Univ.*), G.A.D. Harvey (*Wanderers*), J.B. Allison (*Edin. Univ.*), H.J. Anderson (*Old Wesley*); L.M. Magee (*Bective Rangers*), H.H. Corley* (*Wanderers*); C.E. Allen (*Derry*), J.J. Coffey (*Lansdowne*), G.T. Hamlet (*Old Wesley*), P. Healy (*Limerick*), S.T. Irwin (*NIFC*), R.S. Smyth (*Dublin Univ.*), A. Tedford (*Malone*), Jos. Wallace (*Wanderers*)

Referee: F.R. Alderson (*England*)

No scoring at half time. J.E. Crabbie scored; W.T. Forrest failed (3–0).

The Irish contingent had a rough crossing and this may have left some effects for apart from Magee their backs were not in form and their pack faded in the second half. They began well enough but could not break a steady defence. Forrest was his usual frightening self — wonderful at times but every now and then making a terrifying mistake only to bring off an astonishing recovery. Corley broke away and when faced with Forrest passed to Magee but Forrest managed to collar Magee and the ball and clear with a run and kick. Magee, Allison and Harvey combined to give Anderson an open field but Simson came across and tackled him.

In the second half the Scottish pack got on top, Morrison and Bedell-Sivright showing up well, and from one rush and scrimmage Simson, Knox and Orr let Crabbie make a sprint for the corner and score.

France came in for Timms who got a bad kick on the mouth at a practice session held on the Tuesday.

ENGLAND Richmond 21 March 1903

SCOTLAND: 1 drop goal, 2 tries 10 **Win**

ENGLAND: 2 tries 6

Scotland: W.T. Forrest (*Hawick*); A.N. Fell (*Edin. Univ.*), H.J. Orr (*London Scot.*), A.B. Timms (*Edin. Univ.*), J.S. Macdonald (*Edin. Univ.*); E.D. Simson (*Edin. Univ.*), J. Knox (*Kelvinside Acads.*), A.G. Cairns (*Watsonians*), J.D. Dallas (*Watsonians*), J.R.C. Greenlees* (*Kelvinside Acads.*), N. Kennedy (*West of Scot.*), W.E. Kyle (*Hawick*), J. Ross (*London Scot.*), W.P. Scott (*West of Scot.*), L. West (*Edin. Univ.*)

England: H.T. Gamlin (*Devonport A*); R. Forrest (*Blackheath*), E.I.M. Barrett (*Lennox*), A.T. Brettargh (*Liverpool OB*), T. Simpson (*Rockcliff*); W.V. Butcher (*Streatham*), P.D. Kendall* (*Birkenhead Park*); V.H. Cartwright (*Oxford Univ.*), D.D. Dobson (*Newton Abbot*), N.C. Fletcher (*OMT*), P.F. Hardwick (*Percy Park*), B.A. Hill (*Blackheath*), R.Pierce (*Liverpool*), F.M. Stout (*Richmond*), S.G. Williams (*Devonport A*)

Referee: W.N. Douglas (*Wales*)

R. Forrest scored; N.C. Fletcher failed (0–3); A.B. Timms dropped a goal (4–3); J.D. Dallas scored but failed to convert (7–3). (H.T.). D.D. Dobson scored; V.H. Cartwright failed (7–6); E.D. Simson scored; J.S. Macdonald failed (10–6).

This was an undistinguished and rather scrambling game. The Scottish pack, although without two of its most powerful members in Morrison and Bedell-Sivright, gave a good account of itself. Early on a sudden English back attack produced a score but soon a fine forward rush followed by a scrimmage saw the ball flung out to Timms who immediately dropped an excellent goal. After another rush Simson started a passing run with the forwards which finished with Dallas scoring. Early in the second half Fell had a good run but could not pass Gamlin and then Brettargh broke clear and although tackled by Fell, got the ball out to Kendall who was stopped short of the line by Simson who actually overhauled him. The score was only delayed, for from a scrummage Dobson went over to reduce the lead to a single point. However, Scotland kept cool and when the forwards caught Gamlin with the ball, it broke to Simson who had a splendid dodging run for a solo try. Forrest again played well. Once with several opponents bearing down on him he failed to gather the ball, fell on it, jumped up with it, dodged the attackers and then put in his clearance. The Scottish threes had a colonial aspect for Timms and Orr were Australians, Fell was from New Zealand and Macdonald had a South African connection.

WALES   Swansea   6 February 1904

SCOTLAND:	1 try	3	**Loss**
WALES:	3 goals, 1 penalty goal, 1 try	21	

Scotland: W.T. Forrest (*Hawick*); H.J. Orr (*London Scot.*), G.E. Crabbie (*Edin. Acads.*), L.M. MacLeod (*Camb. Univ.*), J.S. Macdonald (*Edin. Univ.*); E.D. Simson (*Edin. Univ.*), A.A. Bisset (*RIEC*); D.R. Bedell-Sivright (*West of Scot.*), L.H.I. Bell (*Edin. Acads.*), A.G. Cairns (*Watsonians*), W.E. Kyle (*Hawick*), M.C. Morrison* (*RHSFP*), E.J. Ross (*London Scot.*), W.P. Scott (*West of Scot.*), G.O. Turnbull (*Edin. Wrs.*)

Wales: H.B. Winfield (*Cardiff*); W.M. Llewellyn* (*Newport*), C.C. Pritchard (*Newport*), R.T. Gabe (*Cardiff*), E.T. Morgan (*London Welsh*); R. Jones (*Swansea*), R.M. Owen (*Swansea*); A. Brice (*Aberavon*), D.H. Davies (*Neath*), A.F. Harding (*Cardiff*), J.J. Hodges (*Newport*), W.W. Joseph (*Swansea*), W. Neill (*Cardiff*), E. Thomas (*Newport*), H.V. Watkins (*Llanelli*)

    Referee: Nicholls (*England*)   **Touch judges:** R.C. Greig, H. Bowen

H.B. Winfield kicked a penalty goal (0–3); R.T. Gabe and R. Jones scored; H.B. Winfield converted both (0–13). (H.T.). E.T. Morgan scored; H.B. Winfield failed (0–16); H.J. Orr scored; J.S. Macdonald failed (3–16); A. Brice scored; H.B. Winfield converted (3–21).

Wales always had this game well in hand, their light forwards giving their backs plenty of the ball. Gabe and Morgan were a most effective wing and the score would have been greater but for some splendid tackling of the two by Forrest. Gabe on one occasion tried to jump over a tackle and the game was held up while he recovered after being caught by the ankles and bounced on his head. Winfield opened the scoring with a touch line penalty for 'feet up' and the Welsh backs added two good tries before half time. Scotland restarted well. Simson made an opening for Crabbie who sent Macdonald over the line only to be brought back for a foot in touch a yard out. The Gabe-Morgan wing broke away again and although Forrest got in his tackle he could not stop the scoring pass. Scotland's only score followed a good forward rush from which Simson started a passing movement for Bisset to put Orr clear away and score. Wales replied with a similar effort when Brice after a scrimmage picked up a loose ball and scored. Scotland rallied fiercely in the last ten minutes but could not break through. It was reported that the referee rebuked Bedell-Sivright for roughing up one or two of his opponents.

IRELAND　　　　Lansdowne Road　　　28 February 1904

SCOTLAND:	2 goals, 3 tries		19	**Win**
IRELAND:	1 try		3	

Scotland: W.T. Forrest (*Hawick*); H.J. Orr (*London Scot.*), A.B. Timms (*Cardiff*), L.M. MacLeod (*Camb. Univ.*), J.S. Macdonald (*Edin. Univ.*); E.D. Simson (*Edin. Univ.*), J.I. Gillespie (*Edin. Acads.*); D.R. Bedell-Sivright (*West of Scot.*), L.H.I. Bell (*Edin. Acads.*), A.G. Cairns (*Watsonians*), W.E. Kyle (*Hawick*), W.M. Milne (*Glas. Acads.*), M.C. Morrison* (*RHSFP*), W.P. Scott (*West of Scot.*), J.B. Waters (*Camb. Univ.*)

Ireland: J. Fulton (*NIFC*); J.E. Moffatt (*Old Wesley*), J.C. Parker (*Dublin Univ.*), H.H. Corley* (*Wanderers*), C.G. Robb (*QC Belfast*); T.T.H. Robinson (*Dublin Univ.*), E.D. Caddell (*Dublin Univ.*); C.E. Allen (*Derry*), F. Gardiner (*NIFC*), G.T. Hamlet (*Old Wesley*), P. Healy (*Limerick*), M. Ryan (*Rockwell*), A. Tedford (*Malone*), Jas. Wallace (*Wanderers*), Jos. Wallace (*Wanderers*)

　Referee: Williams (*England*)

D.R. Bedell-Sivright scored; J.S. Macdonald failed (0–3). (H.T.). A.B. Timms and D.R. Bedell-Sivright scored; J.S. Macdonald converted both (13–0); J.E. Moffatt scored; J.C. Parke failed (13–3); J.S. Macdonald and E.D. Simson scored; J.S. Macdonald failed with both (19–3).

The Irish pack made its usual rousing start and Gardiner appeared to have touched down but the referee gave a drop out. Timms' kick landed play in the Irish 25 and after some scrimmaging the ball was rushed over the line for Bedell-Sivright and Kyle to throw themselves on it for a score. However, the Irish pack were rather on top and made several fierce rushes only halted by some fearless defence by MacLeod, Timms and Forrest. Parke broke away but on meeting Forrest flung out a wretched pass and a scoring chance was lost. Soon after the restart Simson threw out from the scrum to Gillespie who set Macdonald off on a weaving run. A pass to Timms let him break through to score. The Scottish pack livened up after this and put in several foot rushes. In one, Bedell-Sivright kicked the ball too hard but Fulton missed it and Bedell-Sivright with Orr beside him flung himself on the ball for a try. The Irish backs struck back with a nice run which put Moffatt in at the corner and Robb got over only to be brought back for a forward pass. From a scrum in the Irish 25 Gillespie put the ball along the threes from one touch line to the other. Timms made a lot of ground and then Macdonald got in at the corner but ran round behind the posts only to miss the easy kick. Near the close Simson twice dummied opponents and scored a fine solo try. He had been always very deceptive when carrying the ball. Forrest's defence and kicking was again first rate while Morrison and Bedell-Sivright were prominent in the forwards.

100

ENGLAND   Inverleith   19 March 1904

| SCOTLAND: | 2 tries | 6 | **Win** |
| ENGLAND: | 1 try | 3 | |

Scotland: W.T. Forrest (*Hawick*); J.E. Crabbie (*Edin. Acads.*), L.M. MacLeod (*Camb. Univ.*), A.B. Timms (*Cardiff*), J.S. Macdonald (*Edin. Univ.*); J.I. Gillespie (*Edin. Acads.*), E.D. Simson (*Edin. Univ.*); D.R. Bedell-Sivright (*West of Scot.*), A.G. Cairns (*Watsonians*), H.M. Fletcher (*Edin. Univ.*), W.E. Kyle (*Hawick*), W.M. Milne (*Glas. Acads.*), M.C. Morrison* (*RHSFP*), W.P. Scott (*West of Scot.*), J.B. Waters (*Camb. Univ.*)

England: H.T. Gamlin (*Blackheath*); T. Simpson (*Rockcliff*), A.T. Brettargh (*Liverpool OB*), E.W. Dillon (*Harlequins*), E.J. Vivyan (*Devonport Albion*); P.S. Hancock (*Richmond*), W.V. Butcher (*Bristol*); V.H. Cartwright (*Oxford Univ.*), J. Daniel* (*Richmond*), P.F. Hardwick (*Percy Park*), G.H. Keeton (*Richmond*), J.G. Milton (*Bedford GS*), N.J.N.H. Moore (*Bristol*), C.J. Newbold (*Blackheath*), F.M. Stout (*Richmond*)

Referee: S. Lee (*Ireland*)   **Touch judges:** R.C. Greig, M. Newsome

J.E. Crabbie scored but J.S. Macdonald failed (3–0). (H.T.). E.J. Vivyan scored but J.S. Macdonald failed (3–0). (H.T.). E.J. Vivyan scored but failed to convert (3–3); J.S. Macdonald scored but failed to convert (6–3).

The first half was fairly evenly contested and both sides missed scores by mishandling. Hancock had a clear run in when Forrest slipped but passed inside and the chance was lost. The Scottish score came from a fine passing by Gillespie, MacLeod and Crabbie. In the second half Scotland had rather the better of the play but Vivyan, intercepting a pass, put Brettargh away and was up to take the scoring pass. Intensive pressure on the English line produced a try when Simson lofted a kick that was misfielded and Macdonald got the touch. Both Daniell and Timms were off the field for a while with injuries. One report makes it evident that the old half back style of play was employed.

WALES   Inverleith   4 February 1905

| SCOTLAND: | 1 try | 3 | **Loss** |
| WALES: | 2 tries | 6 | |

Scotland: W.T. Forrest (*Hawick*); J.S. Macdonald (*Edin. Univ.*), J.L. Forbes (*Watsonians*), L.M. MacLeod (*Camb. Univ.*), J.E. Crabbie (*Oxford Univ.*); P. Munro (*Oxford Univ.*), E.D. Simson (*Edin. Univ.*); A.G. Cairns (*Watsonians*), H.N. Fletcher (*Edin. Univ.*), W.E. Kyle (*Hawick*), A.W. Little (*Hawick*), W.M. Milne (*Glas. Acads.*), A. Ross (*RHSFP*), W.P. Scott* (*West of Scot.*), R.S. Stronach (*Glas. Acads.*)

Wales: G. Davies (*Swansea*); W.M. Llewellyn* (*Newport*), D. Rees (*Swansea*), R.T. Gabe (*Cardiff*), E.T. Morgan (*London Welsh*); W.J. Trew (*Swansea*), R.M. Owen (*Swansea*);

A.F. Harding (*London Welsh*), J.J. Hodges (*Newport*), D. Jones (*Treherbert*), W.W. Joseph (*Swansea*), W. Neill (*Cardiff*), C.M. Pritchard (*Newport*), G. Travers (*Pill Harriers*), H.V. Watkins (*Llanelli*)

Referee: H. Kennedy (*Ireland*)

A.W. Little scored but J.S. Macdonald failed (3–0); W.M. Llewellyn scored but G. Davies failed (3–3). (H.T.). W.M. Llewellyn scored but G. Davies failed (3–6).

Some 12,000 spectators watched in clear but uncomfortable conditions for a strong stormy wind blew from the north-west. In the first half the Scottish backs, with the wind, did most of the attacking but could only score once. The Welsh backs were equally active, and right on half time a good run by Rees put Llewellyn in at the corner. In the second half the Welsh had most of the play but good defence, particularly by Forrest, prevented any scoring until near the close of play when a fine run by Llewellyn saw him score again. E.D. Simson at half played brilliantly throughout.

IRELAND   Inverleith   25 February 1905

SCOTLAND: 1 goal   5   **Loss**

IRELAND: 1 goal, 2 tries   11

Scotland: W.T. Forrest (*Hawick*); W.T. Ritchie (*Camb. Univ.*), L.M. MacLeod (*Camb. Univ.*), A.B. Timms (*Cardiff*), R.H. McCowat (*Glas. Acads.*); E.D. Simson (*Edin. Univ.*), P. Munro (*Oxford Univ.*); A.G. Cairns (*Watsonians*), M.R. Dickson (*Edin. Univ.*), W.E. Kyle (*Hawick*), W.M. Milne (*Glas. Acads.*), A. Ross (*RHSFP*), W.P. Scott* (*West of Scot.*), R.S. Stronach (*Glas. Acads.*), L. West (*Carlisle*)

Ireland: M.F. Landers (*Cork Const.*); J.E. Moffatt (*Old Wesley*), B. Maclear (*Cork County*), G.A.D. Harvey (*Wanderers*), H. Thrift (*Dublin Univ.*); T.T.H. Robinson (*Dublin Univ.*), E.D. Caddell (*Dublin Univ.*); C.E. Allen* (*Derry*), J.J. Coffey (*Lansdowne*), G.T. Hamlet (*Old Wesley*), H.J. Knox (*Dublin Univ.*), H.J. Millar (*Markstown*), A. Tedford (*Malone*), Jos. Wallace (*Wanderers*); H.G. Wilson (*Glas. Univ.*)

Referee: P. Coles (*England*)

A Tedford scored; B. Maclear converted (0–5). (H.T.). J. Wallace and J.E. Moffatt scored; B. Maclear failed with both (0–11); A.B. Timms scored; W.T. Forrest converted (5–11).

This might have been a fairly even game had Maclear not been playing, for the big centre was always dangerous. Not only did he create openings but he was extremely difficult to bring down on the move. It was the Irish forwards, however, who took the ball the length of the field for Tedford to score before half time and for Jos. Wallace to score after the restart. Maclear made the opening which let Moffatt score later. In the closing minutes Munro broke away and crosskicked to Timms who scored. The Scottish forwards and halves played quite well but the threes were not up to standard. Forrest, however, was in his best form.

102

ENGLAND   Richmond   18 March 1905

SCOTLAND: 1 goal, 1 try   8   **Win**

ENGLAND Nil   0

Scotland: D.G. Schulze (*London Scot.*); W.T. Ritchie (*Camb. Univ.*), G.A.W. Lamond (*Bristol*), A.B. Timms* (*Cardiff*), T. Elliot (*Gala*); E.D. Simson (*Edin. Univ.*), P. Munro (*Oxford Univ.*); A.G. Cairns (*Watsonians*), W.E. Kyle (*Hawick*), J.C. MacCallum (*Watsonians*), H.G. Monteith (*Camb. Univ.*), A. Ross (*RHSFP*), W.P. Scott (*West of Scot.*), R.S. Stronach (*Glas. Acads.*), L. West (*Carlisle*)

England: J.T. Taylor (*Castleford*); S.F. Cooper (*Blackheath*), J.E. Raphael (*OMT*), A.T. Brettargh (*Liverpool OB*), T. Simpson (*Rockcliff*); A.D. Stoop (*Oxford Univ.*), W.V. Butcher (*Streatham*); V.H. Cartwright (*Nottingham*), T.A. Gibson (*Northern*), C.E.L. Hammond (*Harlequins*), J.L. Mathias (*Bristol*), J.G. Milton (*Camborne*), C.J. Newbold (*Blackheath*), S.H. Osborne (*St Bees*), F.M. Stout (*Richmond*)

Referee: H.D. Bowen (*Wales*).

No scoring at half time. E.D. Simson and R.S. Stronach scored; W.P. Scott converted the second only (8–0).

England had had a very poor season before this but here they started and finished well. It was only for a while in the second half that the Scottish pack got on top and made the vital scores possible. Play was fairly even during the first half with some individual efforts being made, Simpson being dangerous on the wing. After the restart the Scottish forwards improved greatly and gave their two very active halves chances to open up the game. From one scrum Simson kicked high into the English 25 and followed up so quickly that he caught the ball and was over at the corner before the English defence realised the danger. Later Munro passed to Lamond who gave the ball to Ritchie. He dodged two opponents and then the ball went from Cairns and West before arriving at Stronach who suddenly spurted for the line and just got there as he was tackled. England rallied towards the end without success. This was Stoop's first cap and he played at left half.

NEW ZEALAND   Inverleith   18 November 1905

SCOTLAND: 1 drop goal, 1 try   7   **Loss**

NEW ZEALAND: 4 tries   12

Scotland: J.G. Scoular (*Camb. Univ.*); J.T. Simson (*Watsonians*), K.G. MacLeod (*Camb. Univ.*), L.M. MacLeod (*Camb. Univ.*), T. Sloan (*Glas. Acads.*); L.L. Greig (*Un. Services*); E.D. Simson (*Edin. Univ.*), P. Munro (*London Scot.*); D.R. Bedell-Sivright* (*Edin. Univ.*), W.E. Kyle (*Hawick*), J.C. MacCallum (*Watsonians*), J.M. Mackenzie (*Edin. Univ.*), W.L. Russell (*Glas. Univ.*), W.P. Scott (*West of Scot.*), L. West (*Carlisle*)

New Zealand: G.A. Gillett (*Canterbury*); G.W. Smith (*Auckland*), R.G. Deans (*Canter-*

bury), W.J. Wallace (*Wellington*); J.W. Stead (*Southland*), J. Hunter (*Taranaki*); F. Roberts (*Wellington*); S. Casey (*Otago*), W. Cunningham (*Auckland*), D. Gallaher* (*Auckland*), F.T. Glasgow (*Taranaki*), A. McDonald (*Otago*), J.J. O'Sullivan (*Taranaki*), C.E. Seeling (*Auckland*), G.A. Tyler (*Auckland*)

Referee: W. Kennedy (*Ireland*)

E.D. Simson dropped a goal (4–0); F.T. Glasgow scored but W.J. Wallace failed (4–3); G.W. Smith scored but W.J. Wallace failed (4–6); J.C. MacCallum scored but K.G. MacLeod failed (7–6). (H.T.). G.W. Smith scored but G.A. Gillett failed (7–9); W. Cunningham scored but W.J. Wallace failed (7–12).

Much to the annoyance of the Union, Dr Fell called off rather than play against his countrymen. He was replaced by L.L. Greig who was required to play as a third half back outside Simson and Munro — a move designed to counter the formation of seven forwards, one roving forward and seven backs. With hindsight this did not work, for the three half backs were quite unaccustomed to playing this formation and as a result the Scottish back play and defence were disorganised. The New Zealand forwards, packing two-three-two, were very strong and gave their backs much of the ball from the tight and line out, but the ground and ball were slippery after a morning of frost and their handling which was really very poor, lost them several scores. The Scottish pack, however, was formidable in the loose, their dribbling rushes, fierce following up and heavy tackling thoroughly upsetting their opponents. It was from such rushes that both Scottish scores came.

Early in the second half L.M. MacLeod went off with an ankle injury and could only resume with a bad limp, a handicap which played a part during the last five minutes when strong running saw New Zealand score two tries.

E.D. Simson had a good game but K.G. MacLeod, still under eighteen, had a great debut for his great pace and power of kicking were outstanding. On one occasion when the ball was kicked past the full back, he ran back, picked up the ball in the field and 'then cantered off behind the posts and got in a fine kick'.

The First Touring Teams

The first rugby touring team was one taken to Australia and New Zealand during the home summer of 1888 by Messrs Shaw and Shrewsbury, two professional cricketers who had just returned from a successful cricket tour of Australia. Three Scots were included in the party: W. Burnet, R. Burnet and A.J. Laing, all from Hawick, and on their return were promptly interviewed by the SFU about the terms, management and conduct of the tour. However, they were able to give satisfactory assurances about any alleged professionalism and the matter was dropped. Incidentally, Laing at a dinner given by the Hawkes Bay FC sang 'an untranslatable Scotch dialect song'. I wonder if it was 'Teribus' or more likely 'Pauky Paiterson's Auld Grey Yaud'?

There followed a tour of Britain by the 'Maori' team during the 1888–89 season but only one match was played in Scotland when Hawick, playing on their new ground at Mansfield Park, was beaten by 3–5.

With the IB dispute behind them, the Home Unions began to co-operate in staging a succession of rugby tours to the Colonies — South Africa in 1891, 1896, 1903, and Australia/New Zealand in 1899 and 1904. The inevitable return visit was first sought by New Zealand in 1902 but this did not materialise until the 1905–6 season while the first South African visit took place during the following season.

The first New Zealand tour did not pass without controversy. Firstly the visitors adopted a novel formation of seven forwards packing two-three-two and always tried to pack down not on the opposition middle man but on one of the flank forwards so leaving the other 'prop' with no one to push against. This not only gave them the loose head but provided an extremely rapid heel. This was made good use of by having three half backs. One put the ball into the scrum but generally remained at his mid-way position to become what most considered to be a quite illegal offside obstruction. The second half played in the scrum half position with the third 'standing off'. The result was an extremely rapid and unobstructed supply of the ball to their very efficient backs.

Well before the tour was even begun the SFU had made it clear that they would not accede to the New Zealand request for a guaranteed sum from each match but offered instead the nett gates, after deduction of expenses, from their two matches. Later comments by J. Aikman Smith, as Treasurer, revealed that his committee, while genuinely anxious to do everything possible to assist the visitors, was faced with a fairly hefty Debenture Debt and Bond on the new ground, so was not prepared to ask its Trustees to undertake a further guarantee. However, as a result of the agreement reached the tourists received nearly £1700, a sum something like four times the amount a guarantee would have given them and as a result the SFU was later frequently made the butt of sarcastic humour over the outcome. It is only fair to make two points here: first, a committee which contained men of the professional background and quality such as W. Neilson, J.D. Dallas, J.C. Findlay (a barrister, Sheriff and solicitor), Robin Welsh (gentleman farmer), A.B. Flett, J.W. Simpson (doctors) and steered by J. Aikman Smith (Chartered Accountant), lacked neither legal, financial nor business sense. These men knew what they were doing and, secondly, showed this by offering precisely the same terms to the South Africans for their visit in the following season.

Nevertheless the SFU remained perturbed about the amateur status of the New Zealand players, making it known that they did not feel justified in handing over money without knowing what was to be done with it and once the South African tour was over asked for copies of the accounts of both tours. Those for the South African tour soon arrived and were accepted but the New Zealand set came much later and at once the SFU queried an entry therein of 3s (15p) per day for players' expenses. When they learned that this had been authorised by the RU they were so disturbed that they wrote cancelling the next Calcutta Cup match. The whole question was at once laid before the IB who ruled: (1) that Scotland were not entitled to cancel the fixture without reference to the Board; (2) that the question of those daily payments to players should not be pressed; (3) that in future no such allowances be made to any player. These findings the SFU accepted, feeling that it would be in the best interests of the game that they should do so. Yet it had been noted that the Scottish motion on the payments had failed by a vote of six–six so it was no surprise to find the SFU making a request to the IB for equal representation of the four countries for all purposes. This was debated and eventually in 1910 a compromise was achieved by England reducing its representation to four thus permitting the other countries to have a majority vote if desired.

WALES   Cardiff   3 February 1906

SCOTLAND;   1 penalty goal   3   **Loss**

WALES: 3 tries   9

Scotland: J.G. Scoular (*Camb. Univ.*); W.C. Church (*Glas. Acads.*), T. Sloan (*Glas. Acads.*), K.G. MacLeod (*Camb. Univ.*), A.B.H.L. Purves (*London Scot.*); E.D. Simson (*Edin. Univ.*), P. Munro (*Oxford Univ.*); D.R. Bedell-Sivright (*Edin. Univ.*), A.G. Cairns (*Watsonians*), W.E. Kyle (*Hawick*), J.C. MacCallum (*Watsonians*), H.G. Monteith (*Camb. Univ.*), W.L. Russell (*Glas. Acads.*), W.P. Scott (*West of Scot.*), L. West* (*Hartlepool Rovers*)

Wales: H.B. Winfield (*Cardiff*); E.T. Morgan (*London Welsh*), C.C. Pritchard (*Pontypool*), E.G. Nicholls* (*Cardiff*), H.T. Maddocks (*London Welsh*); W.J. Trew (*Swansea*), R.A. Gibbs (*Cardiff*); R.M. Owen (*Swansea*), A.F. Harding (*London Welsh*), J.J. Hodges (*Newport*), D. Jones (*Treherbert*), W.W. Joseph (*Swansea*), C.M. Pritchard (*Newport*), G. Travers (*Pill Harriers*), J.F. Williams (*London Welsh*)

Referee: J.W. Allen (*Ireland*)   **Touch judges:** J.T. Tulloch, J. Garrett

J.J. Hodges scored; H.B. Winfield failed (0–3); C.C. Pritchard scored; R.A. Gibbs failed (0–6) (H.T.). H.T. Maddocks scored; H.B. Winfield failed (0–9); K.G. MacLeod dropped a penalty goal (3–9).

Wales played seven forwards with Travers acting as a recognised hooker but the system was not a success against a good Scottish pack which was again good in the loose with Kyle and Bedell-Sivright outstanding. The latter actually touched down early in the match but as the ball had rebounded off the Chief Constable who was walking about in the in-goal area, the referee gave no score but dead ball. However, the Scottish threes, with the brilliant exception of MacLeod, were not effective although Simson at half was always dangerous. Nor were the Welsh backs much better — all three scores coming from individual efforts rather than team work. A cross kick by Owen was picked up by Morgan who put Hodges over; Nicholls dropped at goal but the ball flew very wide and Pritchard was able to get to it first; while Maddocks only got in because of some poor tackling in the backs. MacLeod who had narrowly missed a drop goal from halfway, converted a penalty kick by a drop.

IRELAND   Lansdowne Park   24 February 1906

SCOTLAND: 2 goals, 1 mark goal   13   **Win**

IRELAND: 2 tries   6

Scotland: J.G. Scoular (*Camb. Univ.*); K.G. MacLeod (*Camb. Univ.*), J.L. Forbes (*Watsonians*), M.W. Walter (*London Scot.*), A.B.H.L. Purves (*London Scot.*); E.D. Simson (*Edin. Univ.*), P. Munro (*Oxford Univ.*); D.R. Bedell-Sivright (*Edin. Univ.*), A.G. Cairns (*Watsonians*), W.E. Kyle (*Hawick*), J.C. MacCallum (*Watsonians*), H.G. Monteith (*Lon-

don Scot.), W.L. Russell (*Glas. Acads.*), W.P. Scott (*West of Scot.*), L. West* (*London Scot.*)

Ireland: G.J. Henebrey (*Garryowen*); C.G. Robb (*QC Belfast*), J.C. Parke (*Dublin Univ.*), F. Casement (*Dublin Univ.*), H.J. Anderson (*Old Wesley*); B. Maclear (*Cork County*), E.D. Caddell (*Dublin Univ.*), W.B. Purdon (*QC Belfast*); C.E. Allen* (*Derry*), J.J. Coffey (*Lansdowne*), F. Gardiner (*NIFC*), H.J. Know (*Lansdowne*), A. Tedford (*Malone*), M. White (*QC Cork*), H.G. Wilson (*Malone*)

Referee: V.H. Cartwright (*England*)

D.R. Bedell-Sivright scored; J.C. MacCallum converted (5–0); P. Munro scored; J.C. MacCallum converted (10–0).(H.T.). K.G. MacLeod dropped a goal from a mark (13–0); J.C. Parke scored but failed to convert (13–3); C.G. Robb scored; B. Maclear failed (13–6).

Ireland also tried the seven forward formation but the extra back formation was not a success and was merely a handicap to their best back, Maclear, who apparently at one time went into the pack to help the hard pressed forwards. The Scottish pack was well on top yet the Irish forwards broke quickly and by fine tackling kept the score down. Simson and Munro again played well, each working the scrum in their own side of the field. These two started the game with some persistent attacks which failed against a good defence. Then Russell broke away on a good dribbling run and when the ball went to Bedell-Sivright he crashed over for a try. Ten minutes later Simson from a scrum started a passing run where the ball went from Munro to Forbes to MacLeod and back to Munro for a fine score. Good Irish tackling kept the Scots out during the second half and their only score came when MacLeod marked the ball at midfield and dropped a goal. Then with four minutes to go an Irish passing run saw Parke score and from the kick off the Irish forwards rushed the ball back for Robb to touch down but the final whistle went after the unsuccessful kick. It is of interest to note that M.W. Walter had been invited but declined to play for England v. Ireland on 10 February.

ENGLAND	**Inverleith**	**17 March 1906**

SCOTLAND:	1 try	3	**Loss**
ENGLAND:	3 tries	9	

Scotland: J.G. Scoular (*Camb. Univ.*); K.G. MacLeod (*Camb. Univ.*), J.L. Forbes (*Watsonians*), M.W. Walter (*London Scot.*), A.B.H.L. Purves (*London Scot.*); E.D. Simson (*Edin. Univ.*), P. Munro (*Oxford Univ.*); D.R. Bedell-Sivright (*Edin. Univ.*), A.G. Cairns (*Watsonians*), W.E. Kyle (*Hawick*), J.C. MacCallum (*Watsonians*), H.G. Monteith (*London Scot.*), W.L. Russell (*Glas. Acads.*), W.P. Scott (*West of Scot.*), L. West* (*London Scot.*)

England: E.J. Jackett (*Falmouth*); J.E. Raphael (*OMT*), H.E. Shewring (*Bristol*), J.G.G. Birkett (*Harlequins*), T. Simpson (*Rockcliff*); J. Peters (*Plymouth*), A.D. Stoop (*Harlequins*); V.H. Cartwright* (*Nottingham*), R. Dibble (*Bridgewater A*), J. Green (*Skipton*), C.E.L. Hammond (*Harlequins*), T.S. Kelly (*Exeter*), A.L. Kewney (*Rockcliff*), W.A. Mills (*Devonport A*), C.H. Shaw (*Moseley*)

Referee: J.W. Allen (*Ireland*)

J.E. Raphael scored; V.H. Cartwright failed (0–3); A.B.H.L. Purves scored; J.C. MacCallum failed (3–3). (H.T.). T. Simpson and W.A. Mills scored; V.H. Cartwright failed to convert both (3–9).

England, having lost to Wales and Ireland, were not expected to win but did so deservedly. Their pack were much livelier and for once Simson and Munro were well held, Peters and Stoop being definitely the better pair. The English backs were sound while the Scottish defence was poor, but both MacLeod and Bedell-Sivright were injured fairly early on. In the first half Raphael picked up a dropped pass and dashed 40 yards to score. After some Scottish forward pressure Munro went off on his own from a scrum and made an easy opening for Purves to score. Early in the second half a limping MacLeod could not get to a ball; Simpson picked up, cut diagonally across the field, brushed aside two weak tackles and scored. The Scottish pack put in some pressure but the defence, where Raphael showed up well, was too sound and later a good passing run put Mills in for a third try.

SOUTH AFRICA   Hampden Park   17 November 1906

SCOTLAND:	2 tries	6	Win
SOUTH AFRICA:	Nil	0	

Scotland: J.G. Scoular (*Camb. Univ.*); K.G. MacLeod (*Camb. Univ.*), T. Sloan (*Glas. Acads.*), M.W. Walter (*London Scot.*), A.B.H.L. Purves (*London Scot.*); P. Munro (*Oxford Univ.*), L.L. Greig* (*Un. Services*); D.R. Bedell-Sivright (*Edin. Univ.*), G.M. Frew (*Glas. HSFP*), I.C. Geddes (*London Scot.*), J.C. MacCallum (*Watsonians*), H.G. Monteith (*London Hospitals*), W.P. Scott (*West of Scot.*), L.M. Spiers (*Watsonians*), W.H. Thomson (*West of Scot.*)

South Africa: A.F. Marsburg (*GW*); A.C. Stegmann (*WP*), H.A. de Villiers (*WP*), J.D. Krige (*WP*), J.A. Loubser (*WP*); H.W. Carolin* (*WP*), F.J. Dobbin (*GW*); D.J. Brink (*WP*), D. Brookes (*B*), A.F. Burkett (*WP*), W.A. Burger (*B*), H.J. Daneel (*WP*), D. Mare (*T*), W.S. Morkel (*T*), J.W.E. Raaf (*GW*)

Referee: H.H. Chorley (*Ireland*)

There was no scoring at half time. K.G. MacLeod and A.B.H.L. Purves scored but J.C. MacCallum failed to convert either (6–0).

Since this was a third home match for the season it was played at Hampden Park in Glasgow where a record crowd of 32,000 watched a game made memorable by a historic try by K.G. MacLeod. After two days of heavy rain the ground was sodden and heavy, conditions which made running and accurate passing very difficult but which suited a splendid Scottish pack whose fiercesome play in the loose really controlled the game. Behind them P. Munro and K.G. MacLeod were quite outstanding.

In spite of constant pressure there was no scoring at half time although Scotland had the ball twice over the line and MacLeod narrowly missed with a couple of long range drop kicks. Shortly after the resumption Munro broke away to his left from a scrum at the centre and when faced by the cover defence he hoisted a high kick clear across the field to the right wing where MacLeod, running full out, caught the wet ball cleanly and outpaced the defence along the touch line to score at the corner.

A little later, Marsburg who had worked wonders keeping the rampant Scottish pack at bay, had to retire with a head injury got by stopping a rush headed by Bedell-Sivright. Morkel took his place but with five minutes to go could not check another forward rush headed by MacCallum and Purves was able to follow up and score. It is fair to note that South Africa had to struggle against injuries for Brink was off for fifteen minutes with a twisted ankle while Mare finished with two broken fingers.

(Many years later I asked Sir Tennant Sloan about Munro's crosskick and he replied 'Oh, I saw it all right and ran for it but couldn't get near it. It was only MacLeod's tremendous pace that allowed him to get under the ball and then he caught it safely at full pace'.)

WALES   Inverleith   2 February 1907

SCOTLAND:	2 tries	6	**Win**
WALES:	1 penalty goal	3	

Scotland: T. Sloan (*Glas. Acads.*); K.G. MacLeod (*Camb. Univ.*), D.G. MacGregor (*Pontypridd*), W.M. Walter (*London Scot.*), A.B.H.L. Purves (*London Scot.*); E.D. Simson (*London Scot.*), L.L. Greig* (*Un. Services*); D.R. Bedell-Sivright (*Edin. Univ.*), G.M. Frew (*Glas. HSFP*), I.C. Geddes (*London Scot.*), J.C. MacCallum (*Watsonians*), H.G. Monteith (*London Scot.*), G.A. Sanderson (*RHSFP*), W.P. Scott (*West of Scot.*), L.M. Spiers (*Watsonians*)

Wales: H.B. Winfield (*Cardiff*); H.T. Maddocks (*London Welsh*), J. Evans (*Pontypool*), R.T. Gabe (*Cardiff*), J.L. Williams (*Cardiff*); R.M. Owen (*Swansea*), W. Trew* (*Swansea*); R.A. Gibbs (*Cardiff*), J. Brown (*Cardiff*), W. Dowell (*Newport*), T. Evans (*Llanelli*), C.M. Pritchard (*Newport*), G. Travers (*Pill Harriers*), J. Watts (*Llanelli*), J. Webb (*Abertillary*)

Referee: J. Lefevre (*Ireland*)

W.B. Winfield kicked a penalty (0–3). (H.T.). A.B.H.L. Purves scored but K.G. MacLeod failed (3–3); H.G. Monteith scored but J.C. MacCallum failed (6–3).

Wales, after a good win over England, again adopted the seven forward formation, but this failed against a good defence and a vigorous Scottish pack whose only fault was a tendency to get offside during their dribbling rushes, a fault which cancelled out one touch down. Yet play was fairly even in the first half, the only score being a penalty for offside kicked by Winfield. Early in the second half the Scottish pack took the ball right down to the line and from a line out swift passing right across the field gave Purves the chance to hand off Maddocks and run in at the corner. Shortly afterwards, Winfield courageously halted another tremendous dribbling rush, but was so injured that he had to leave the field. Near the end Purves had a good run finishing with a cross kick which was picked up by MacGregor and passed to Monteith who scored. Wales put in a great finish; Gibbs touched down after a good run but was brought back for a foot in touch and the Scottish pack cleared the ball from the line out. MacGregor had a fine debut; born in Pontypridd he had a Scottish father and was educated at Watson's College, Edinburgh. He was captain of Pontypridd but played so well for the Watsonians on their Xmas tour at Newport that the Welsh selectors picked him as a reserve for this game only to find him amongst the opposition.

IRELAND   Inverleith   **23 February 1907**

SCOTLAND:	3 goals	15	**Win**
IRELAND:	1 penalty goal	3	

Scotland: D.G. Schulze (*London Scot.*); A.B.H.L. Purves (*London Scot.*), M.W. Walter (*London Scot.*), D.G. MacGregor (*Pontypridd*), K.G. McLeod (*Camb. Univ.*); E.D. Simson (*London Scot.*), P. Munro* (*London Scot.*); D.R. Bedell-Sivright (*Edin. Univ.*), G.M. Frew (*Glas. HSFP*), I.C. Geddes (*London Scot.*), J.C. MacCallum (*Watsonians*), H.G. Monteith (*London Scot.*), G.A. Sanderson (*RHSFP*), W.P. Scott (*West of Scot.*), L.M. Spiers (*Watsonians*)

Ireland: C. Thompson (*Collegians*); H. Thrift (*Dublin Univ.*), J.C. Parke (*Dublin Univ.*), T.J. Greeves (*NIFC*), B. MacLear (*Cork Const.*); E.D. Cadell (*Wanderers*), T.T.H. Robinson (*Wanderers*); C.E. Allen* (*Derry*), W. St.J. Cogan (*QC Cork*), F. Gardiner (*NIFC*), G.T. Hamlet (*Old Wesley*), H.S. Sugars (*Dublin Univ.*), J.A. Sweeny (*Blackrock Coll.*), A. Tedford (*Malone*), H.G. Wilson (*Malone*)

  Referee: A.O. Jones (*England*)

J.C. Parke kicked a penalty (0–3). (H.T.). G.A. Sanderson scored and K.G. MacLeod converted (5–3); A.B.H.L. Purves and G.M. Frew scored for I.C. Geddes to convert both (15–3).

Conditions were good but the usual Inverleith breeze was in evidence. Play in the first half was quite even, both sets of backs making some good runs. MacLear had two fine runs halted by firm tackles and this was the occasion when he handed-off Bedell-Sivright so fiercely that the latter, who was probably the hardest forward ever to play for Scotland, was knocked out and spent quite a while recovering on the straw on the touch line! After the restart the strength of the Scottish pack and the pace of their backs began to tell and Scotland finished good winners.

ENGLAND   Blackheath   **16 March 1907**

SCOTLAND:	1 goal, 1 try	8	**Win**
ENGLAND:	1 try	3	

Scotland: D.G. Schulze (*London Scot.*); A.B.H.L. Purves (*London Scot.*), T. Sloan (*Glas. Acads.*), D.G. MacGregor (*Pontypridd*), K.G. McLeod (*Camb. Univ.*); P. Munro* (*London Scot.*), E.D. Simson (*London Scot.*); D.R. Bedell-Sivright (*Edin. Univ.*), G.M. Frew (*Glas. HSFP*), I.C. Geddes (*London Scot.*), J.C. MacCallum (*Watsonians*), G.A. Sanderson (*RHSFP*), J.M.B. Scott (*Edin. Acads.*), W.P. Scott (*West of Scot.*), L.M. Spiers (*Watsonians*)

England: E.J. Jackett (*Falmouth*); W.C. Wilson (*Richmond*), J.G.G. Birkett (*Harlequins*),

H.E. Shewring (*Bristol*), A.W. Newton (*Blackheath*); S.P. Start (*Un. Services*), J. Peters (*Plymouth*); J. Green (*Skipton*), T.S. Kelly (*Exeter*), W.A. Mills (*Devonport Albion*), E. Roberts* (*RN*), G.D. Roberts (*Oxford Univ.*), C.H. Shaw (*Moseley*), L.A.N. Slocock (*Liverpool*), S.G. Williams (*Devonport Albion*)

Referee: T.D. Schofield (*Wales*)

No scoring at half time. E.D. Simson and A.B.H.L. Purves scored and I.C. Geddes converted the second (8–0); J. Peters scored but G.D. Roberts failed (8–3).

England started well especially as their pack seemed to be more than holding their own and Scotland were not using the wind sensibly. MacLeod, however, had about six lengthy drops at goal which narrowly missed, one from halfway which rebounded from an upright. In the second half both sets of backs had some exciting thrusts stopped by good tackling but suddenly Simson broke away from midfield to score a magnificent solo try after a long dodging run. It was noted that Bedell-Sivright kept up with him and acted as some form of shield! The Scottish pack finished strongly and from one rush the ball was put over the line for Purves to touch down.

WALES	Swansea	1 February 1908

SCOTLAND:	1 goal	5	**Loss**
WALES:	2 tries	6	

Scotland: D.G. Schulze (*Dartmouth RN Coll.*); H.G. Martin (*Oxford Univ.*), T. Sloan (*London Scot.*), M.W. Walter (*London Scot.*), A.B.H.L. Purves (*London Scot.*); L.L. Greig* (*Un. Services*), G. Cunningham (*Oxford Univ.*); D.R. Bedell-Sivright (*Edin. Univ.*), J.A. Brown (*Glas. Acads.*), G.M. Frew (*Glas. HSFP*), I.C. Geddes (*London Scot.*), G.C. Gowlland (*London Scot.*), J.C. MacCallum (*Watsonians*), J.M.B. Scott (*Edin. Acads.*), L.M. Spiers (*Watsonians*)

Wales: H.B. Winfield (*Cardiff*); J.L. Williams (*Cardiff*), R.T. Gabe (*Cardiff*), W.J. Trew (*Swansea*), R.A. Gibbs (*Cardiff*); P.F. Bush (*Cardiff*), T.H. Vile (*Newport*); J. Brown (*Cardiff*), W.H. Dowell (*Pontypool*), A.F. Harding (*London Welsh*), G. Hayward (*Swansea*), W. Neill (*Cardiff*), G. Travers* (*Pill Harriers*), J. Watts (*Llanelli*), J. Webb (*Abertillery*)

Referee: W. Williams (*England*)

W.J. Trew scored but H.B. Winfield failed (0–3); A.B.H.L. Purves scored and I.C. Geddes converted (5–3). (H.T.). J.L. Williams scored but H.B. Winfield failed (5–6).

This was a hard slogging game that Scotland were most unlucky to lose. In the first half Purves with a clear run in slipped and was caught, while Walter also clear of the defence was tripped and did not even gain a penalty for the offence. Then in the dying moments Geddes

112

had a winning try disallowed. J.M.B. Scott later recorded that he was up with Geddes who dived and touched down a foot over the line, but, as was claimed by Deans of New Zealand in 1905, he was pulled back into the field and when the referee arrived and saw the ball short of the line he gave a scrum. It was noted that Purves had scored in six consecutive matches.

IRELAND   Lansdowne Road   29 February 1908

SCOTLAND:	1 goal, 1 penalty goal, 1 try 11	**Loss**
IRELAND:	2 goals, 2 tries 16	

Scotland: D.G. Schulze (*London Scot.*); H. Martin (*Oxford Univ.*), K.G. MacLeod (*Camb. Univ.*), M.W. Walter (*London Scot.*), A.B.H.L. Purves (*London Scot.*); L.L. Greig* (*Un. Services*), G. Cunningham (*Oxford Univ.*); D.R. Bedell-Sivright (*Edin. Univ.*), J.A. Brown (*Glas. Acads.*), G.M. Frew (*Glas. HSFP*), J.C. MacCallum (*Watsonians*), G.A. Sanderson (*RHSFP*), J.M.B. Scott (*Edin. Acads.*), L.M. Spiers (*Watsonians*), J.S. Wilson (*London Scot.*)

Ireland: W.P. Hinton (*Old Wesley*); H. Thrift* (*Dublin Univ.*), J.C. Parke (*Monkstown*), G.G.P. Beckett (*Dublin Univ.*), C. Thompson (*Collegians*); E.D. Caddell (*Wanderers*), F.N.B. Smartt (*Dublin Univ.*); F. Gardiner (*NIFC*), G.T. Hamlet (*Old Wesley*), T.G. Harper (*Dublin Univ.*), H.J. Knox (*Lansdowne*), T. Smyth (*Malone*), B. Solomans (*Dublin Univ.*), A. Tedford (*Malone*), H.G. Wilson (*Malone*)

Referee: W. Williams (*England*)

H. Thrift scored and J.C. Parke converted (0–5); K.G. MacLeod scored but failed to convert (3–5); C. Thompson scored but J.C. Parke failed (3–8); G. Beckett scored and W.P. Hinton converted (3–13). (H.T.). H. Martin scored and K.G. MacLeod converted (8–13); K.G. MacLeod dropped a penalty goal (11–13); H. Thrift scored but J.C. Parke failed (11–16).

Scotland were badly handicapped by injury for M.W. Walter retired with a broken collar bone after five minutes' play and K.G. MacLeod also had to come off towards the end. Lansdowne Road had just been acquired by the Irish Rugby Union.

ENGLAND   Inverleith   21 March 1908

SCOTLAND:	1 goal, 2 drop goals, 1 try 16	**Win**
ENGLAND:	2 goals 10	

Scotland: D.G. Schulze (*London Scot.*); H. Martin (*Oxford Univ.*), K.G. MacLeod (*Camb. Univ.*), C.M. Gilray (*London Scot.*), A.B.H.L. Purves (*London Scot.*); J. Robertson (*Clydesdale*), A.L. Wade (*London Scot.*); G.M. Frew (*Glas. HSFP*), I.C. Geddes* (*London Scot.*), W.E. Kyle (*Hawick*), J.C. MacCallum (*Watsonians*), H.G. Monteith (*London Scot.*), L. Robertson (*London Scot.*), J.M.B. Scott (*Edin. Acads.*), L.M. Spiers (*Watsonians*)

England: G.H.D. Lyon (*Un. Services*); D. Lambert (*Harlequins*), J.G.G. Birkett (*Harlequins*), W.N. Lapage (*Un. Services*), A. Hudson (*Gloucester*); J. Davey (*Redruth*), R.H. Williamson (*Oxford Univ.*); F. Boylen (*Hartlepool Rovers*), R. Dibble (*Bridgwater Albion*), R. Gilbert (*Devonport Albion*), T.S. Kelly (*Exeter*), W.L. Oldham (*Coventry*), L.A.N. Slocock* (*Liverpool*), F.B. Watson (*Un. Services*), T. Woods (*Bridgwater Albion*)

Referee: H.H. Corley (*Ireland*) **Touch judges:** Dr A.B. Flett, W. Williams

J.G.G. Birkett scored and D. Lambert converted (0–5); K.G. Macleod scored but I.C. Geddes failed (3–5); L.A.N. Slocock scored and D. Lambert converted (3–10); A.B.H.L. Purves dropped a goal (7–10). (H.T.). K.G. MacLeod scored and I.C. Geddes converted (12–10); D.G. Schulze dropped a goal (16–10).

A record crowd of 20,000 watched a fast game in excellent conditions. Inside 3 minutes Birkett scored after a brilliant run from near halfway. However, MacLeod, playing in his last International at the age of twenty, was in devastating form. He frequently sent Martin away and being as fast as his winger was up with him twice to accept scoring passes. Many regard these two to be the fastest pair ever to play for Scotland. One report talks of Robertson as 'the stand off-man'.

WALES Inverleith 6 February 1909

SCOTLAND:	1 penalty goal	3	**Loss**
WALES:	1 goal	5	

Scotland: D.G. Schulze (*London Scot.*); H. Martin (*Edin. Acads.*), A.W. Angus (*Watsonians*), C.M. Gilray (*London Scot.*), J.T. Simson (*Watsonians*); G. Cunningham (*London Scot.*), J.M. Tennent (*West of Scot.*); G.M. Frew (*Glas. HSFP*), G.C. Gowlland (*London Scot.*), W.E. Kyle (*Hawick*), J.C. MacCallum (*Watsonians*), J.M. Mackenzie (*Edin. Univ.*), A. Ross (*RHSFP*), J.M.B. Scott* (*Edin. Acads.*), J.S. Wilson (*London Scot.*)

Wales: J. Bancroft (*Swansea*); A.M. Baker (*Newport*), J.P. Jones (*Newport*), W.J. Trew* (*Swansea*), J.L. Williams (*Cardiff*); R. Jones (*Swansea*), R.M. Owen (*Swansea*); T.H. Evans (*Llanelli*), I. Morgan (*Swansea*), E. Thomas (*Newport*), E.J.R. Thomas (*Mountain Ash*), G. Travers (*Pill Harriers*), P.D. Waller (*Newport*), J. Watts (*Llanelli*), J. Webb (*Abertillery*)

Referee: J.W. Jeffares (*Ireland*)

No scoring at half time, G. Cunningham kicked a penalty (3–0); W.J. Trew scored; J. Bancroft converted (3–5).

This was a poor ragged game; both sets of backs played below standard and the packs were dull, indulging in few rushes, yet the Welsh forwards' tactics continually displeased the referee who awarded many penalties to Scotland. Gilray was badly knocked about early on and only resumed, badly shaken, after half time. Scott was also hurt and the pack, with MacCallum at centre, were two short for a while. Bancroft, who was apt to fall on the ball in defence, took a considerable mauling from the Scottish pack. A poor first half was marked by bad handling and finishing by both sides and after some uneventful to and fro play after

114

restarting Cunningham converted a penalty to put Scotland in the lead. Then with ten minutes to go some Welsh pressure saw Trew score a try converted by Bancroft. There followed a desperate finish by Scotland. Simson was hurled into touch in goal. Then Tennent dribbled away only to be halted by Bancroft getting down on the ball again but, as he was too dazed to get off it, a penalty was awarded to Scotland. Cunningham narrowly missed the kick and the final whistle went at once.

IRELAND   Inverleith   27 February 1909

SCOTLAND:	3 tries	**9**	**Win**
IRELAND:	1 penalty goal	**3**	

Scotland: D.G. Schulze (*London Scot.*); R.H. Lindsay-Watson (*Hawick*), T. Sloan (*London Scot.*), J. Pearson (*Watsonians*), J.T. Simson (*Watsonians*); J.R. McGregor (*Edin. Univ.*), J.M. Tennent (*West of Scot.*); G.M. Frew (*Glas. HSFP*), W.E. Kyle (*Hawick*), W.G. Lely (*London Scot.*), J.C. MacCallum (*Watsonians*), J.M. Mackenzie (*Edin. Univ.*), A. Ross (*RHSFP*), J.M.B. Scott* (*Edin.Acads.*), C.D. Stuart (*West of Scot.*)

Ireland: W.P. Hinton (*Old Wesley*); H. Thrift (*Dublin Univ.*), J.C. Parke (*Monkstown*), C. Thompson (*Collegians*), R.M. Magrath (*Cork Const.*); G. Pinion (*Collegians*), F. Gardiner* (*NIFC*); J.C. Blackham (*QC Cork*), M.G. Garry (*Bective Rangers*), T. Halpin (*Garryowen*), G.T. Hamlet (*Old Wesley*), O.J.S. Piper (*Cork Const.*), T. Smyth (*Malone*), B. Solomons (*Dublin Univ.*), H.G. Wilson (*Malone*)

    Referee: V.H. Cartwright (*England*)

R.H. Lindsay-Watson scored; J.C. MacCallum failed (3–0).(H.T.). J.C. Parke kicked a penalty (3–3); J.R. McGregor and W.E. Kyle scored; J.C. MacCallum failed with both (9–3).

The Irish pack was on top for most of the first half but their backs made no use of their possession. So Tennent and McGregor had a rough time to begin with and an early arrangement which saw Tennent working the scrum with McGregor standing back was abandoned. As the Scottish pack improved McGregor was able to get the ball out to the threes while Tennent fairly roamed about the field in attack and defence. Gardiner, normally a forward, was not a success in his new rôle as a half back. Early play, then, favoured the Irish and most of the game was in the Scottish half. However, near half time, their threes had two good runs from the second of which Pearson made a nice opening for Lindsay-Watson who had to sprint with the greatest determination to get over for a try. In the second half the Scottish pack came on to a game but Simson, lying offside, fielded a kick by Schulze and Parke kicked a fine penalty to level the scores. However, fairly continuous pressure saw McGregor break away from a scrum inside the Irish 25 to score and later Kyle touched down (with MacCallum doing the same to make sure) for the last try. There is evidence that Pearson and Sloan changed places at centre.

SCOTLAND:	3 goals, 1 try	18	**Win**
ENGLAND:	1 goal, 1 try	8	

Scotland: D.G. Schulze (*London Scot.*); H. Martin (*Oxford Univ.*), J. Pearson (*Watsonians*), C.M. Gilray (*Oxford Univ.*), J.T. Simson (*Watsonians*); J.M. Tennent (*West of Scot.*), G. Cunningham* (*Oxford Univ.*); G.M. Frew (*Glas. HSFP*), G.C. Gowlland (*London Scot.*), J.R. Kerr (*Greenock Wrs.*), W.E. Kyle (*Hawick*), J.C. MacCallum (*Watsonians*), J.M. Mackenzie (*Edin. Univ.*), A.R. Moodie (*St Andrews Univ.*), J.M.B. Scott (*Edin. Acads*)

England: E.J. Jackett (*Falmouth*); A.C. Palmer (*London Hospitals*), C.C.G. Wright (*Camb. Univ.*), R.W. Poulton (*Oxford Univ.*), E.R. Mobbs (*Northampton*); F. Hutchison (*Headingley*), H.J.H. Sibree (*Harlequins*); R. Dibble* (*Bridgewater A*), F.G. Handford (*Manchester*), H.C. Harrison (*RN*), E.D. Ibbotson (*Headingley*), W.A. Johns (*Gloucester*), A.L. Kewney (*Rockcliff*), H.J.S. Morton (*Camb. Univ.*), F.B. Watson (*RN*)

Referee: E.G. Nicholls (*Wales*)   **Touch judges:** Dr A.B. Flett, T.C. Pring

J.T. Simson scored; G. Cunningham failed (3–0); E.R. Mobbs and F.B. Watson scored; A.C. Palmer converted the second (3–8). (H.T.). C.M. Gilray and J.M. Tennent (2) scored; G. Cunningham converted all three (18–8).

This was the last Calcutta Cup match to be played at Richmond and among the 20,000 spectators was HRH, The Prince of Wales. They saw a fine forward battle but the continued agression of the Scottish halves had much to do with the result. Early on a move by Tennent and Cunningham set Gilray off on a fine run. He passed to Simson who sprinted along the touch line, broke through a tackle at the corner and scored behind the posts only to see the easy kick missed. The English forwards then exerted some considerable pressure and before half time the home team had taken the lead by scoring twice.

After half time the Scottish pack began to get on top and saw Gilray dummy and dodge in for a good try. Then Tennent scored twice. The first came from a very fast solo dash and the second when, after following a forward rush, he picked up and although heavily tackled by Jackett, held on and fell over for a try. At this stage Pearson was hurt but carried on limping and Scotland had to face up to a terrific onslaught. Wright hit the posts with a drop while Mobbs and Harrison both narrowly failed to get over.

FRANCE   Inverleith   22 January 1910

SCOTLAND: 3 goals, 4 tries   27   **Win**
FRANCE: Nil   0

Scotland: F.G. Buchanan (*Kelvinside Acads.*); I.P.M. Robertson (*Watsonians*), A.W.
Angus (*Watsonians*), J. Pearson (*Watsonians*), J.T. Simson (*Watsonians*); G. Cunningham*
(*Oxford Univ.*), J.M. Tennent (*West of Scot.*); G.M. Frew (*Glas. HSFP*), G.C. Gowlland
(*London Scot.*), J.C. MacCallum (*Watsonians*), A.R. Moodie (*St Andrews Univ.*), J.M.B.
Scott (*Edin. Acads.*), L.M. Spiers (*Watsonians*), R.C. Stevenson (*St Andrews Univ.*), C.D.
Stuart (*West of Scot.*)

France: J. Combe (*SF*); E. Lesieur (*SF*), J. Dedet (*SF*), M. Burgun (*RCF*), C. Vareilles
(*SF*); C. Martin (*Lyon*), A. Theuriet (*SCUF*); M. Boudreau (*SCUF*), J. Cadenat
(*SCUF*), M. Communeau (*SF*), P. Guillemin (*RCF*), M. Hourdebaigt (*SBUC*), R.
Lafitte (*SCUF*), H. Masse (*SBUC*), P. Mauriat (*Lyon*)

Referee: G.A. Harris (*Ireland*)   **Touch judges:** C.J.N. Fleming, C.F. Rutherford

I.P.M. Robertson, A.W. Angus and J.M. Tennent scored; J.C. MacCallum converted the
second only (11–0). (H.T.). J.M. Tennent, I.P.M. Robertson, G.C. Gowlland and J.M.
Tennent scored; J.C. MacCallum converted the last two only (27–0).

For this first match against France a full Scottish XV was selected but no caps were
awarded, this being a distinction retained for appearances against the home countries. The
final selection included the complete Watsonian three-quarter line and indeed so strong
was the club side at that time that their two half backs could have been added without
weakening the team.

The visitors could not match up to this strong opposition: the forwards did not play as a
pack and their threes did not combine but were keen and fast as individuals. They were all
inclined to get offside and tackle opponents who did not have the ball; one claimed a mark
from a kick made behind him but the referee allowed them considerable latitude to keep the
game flowing. The Scottish players at first were inclined to halt but eventually got the idea
and kept on playing till the whistle went. Scotland played in white jerseys so that France
could wear their light blue strip.

The First Contacts with France

The first Scottish contact with French rugby came in April 1896 when a strong Edinburgh XV, which included one Irish and four Scottish caps, travelled to play a Paris XV in that city. In 1898 a French XV made a return visit playing one game at Myreside, Edinburgh and a second at Hamilton Crescent, Glasgow. These trips were organised by J. Welsh (RHSFP) and J.B. Hatt (London Scottish) and both were later suspended by the Union who demanded and then disproved of the accounts relating to the second visit.

Rugby in France at this time was one of several sports controlled by a composite body formed in 1887 — the *Union des Sociétés Françaises des Sports Athlétiques*. This body succeeded in arranging France's first International matches against New Zealand (1906), England (1906), Wales (1908) and Ireland (1909) but although it had first approached the SFU in 1907 it was not until 1910 that the first fixture against Scotland was played in Edinburgh. Scotland in this match played in white, a courtesy which the host nation in this fixture continued until the 1979–80 season.

The USFSA continued to control the game until 1920 when its function was taken over a completely separate body — the *Fédération Française de Rugby*.

WALES   Cardiff   5 February 1910

| **SCOTLAND:** | Nil | 0 | **Loss** |
| **WALES:** | 1 goal, 3 tries | 14 | |

Scotland: D.G. Schulze (*London Scot.*); W.R. Sutherland (*Hawick*), A.W. Angus (*Watsonians*), J. Pearson (*Watsonians*), J.T. Simson (*Watsonians*); J.M. Tennent (*West of Scot.*), E.Milroy (*Watsonians*); G.M. Frew* (*Glas. HSFP*), G.C. Gowlland (*London Scot.*), W.E. Kyle (*Hawick*), J.C. MacCallum (*Watsonians*), J.M. Mackenzie (*Edin. Univ.*), J.M.B. Scott (*Edin. Acads.*), L.M. Spiers (*Watsonians*), C.D. Stuart (*West of Scot.*)

Wales: J. Bancroft (*Swansea*); R.A. Gibbs (*Cardiff*), W.J. Spiller (*Cardiff*), W.J. Trew* (*Swansea*), A.M. Baker (*Newport*); P.F. Bush (*Cardiff*), W.L. Morgan (*Cardiff*); T.H. Evans (*Llanelli*), B. Gronow (*Bridgend*), H. Jarman (*Newport*), E. Jenkins (*Newport*), J. Morgan (*Swansea*), J. Pugsley (*Cardiff*), D.J. Thomas (*Swansea*), J. Webb (*Abertillery*)

Referee: G.H.B. Kennedy (*Ireland*)   **Touch judges:** C.J.N. Fleming, J. Jarrett

J. Pugsley and W.J. Spiller scored; J. Bancroft converted the second (0–8). (H.T.). A.M. Baker and J. Morgan scored; J. Bancroft failed with both (0–14).

Steady and heavy rain had made the pitch so wet that after ten minutes play it was an utter quagmire. There was little handling by any of the backs but the Welsh forwards with fine footwork were quite irresistible and laid the foundation for all the scores. Tennent had to leave the field before half time with an injured elbow. He came back but almost at once after the interval he was badly hurt again and had to retire for good, MacCallum coming out of the pack to replace him. Tennent's injuries were caused by studs and this undoubtedly led to legislation on such matters before the next season. In a team forced on the defensive Schulze was quite outstanding. For the first time special trains were run to Cardiff from Edinburgh and Glasgow.

IRELAND   Belfast   26 February 1910

| **SCOTLAND:** | 1 goal, 3 tries | 14 | **Win** |
| **IRELAND:** | Nil | 0 | |

Scotland: D.G. Schulze (*Northampton*); D.G. Macpherson (*London Hospital*), M.W. Walter (*London Scot.*), J. Pearson (*Watsonians*), J.D. Dobson (*Glas. Acads.*); G. Cunningham* (*Oxford Univ.*), A.B. Lindsay (*London Hospitals*); C.H. Abercrombie (*Un. Services*), G.M. Frew (*Glas. HSFP*), G.C. Gowlland (*London Scot.*), J.C. MacCallum (*Watsonians*), J.M. Mackenzie (*Edin. Univ.*), J.M.B. Scott (*Edin. Acads.*), R.C. Stevenson (*St Andrews Univ.*), C.D. Stuart (*West of Scot.*)

Ireland: W.P. Hinton (*Old Wesley*); J.P. Quinn (*Dublin Univ.*), C. Thompson (*Collegians*), A.R. Foster (*QU Belfast*), A.S. Taylor (*Queen's*); R.A. Lloyd (*Dublin Univ.*), H.M. Read

(Dublin Univ.); J.C. Blackham *(Wanderers)*, T. Halpin *(Garryowen)*, G.T. Hamlet* *(Old Wesley)*, G. McIldowie *(Malone)*, H. Moore *(QU Belfast)*, O.J.S. Piper *(Cork Const.)*, T. Smyth *(Newport)*, B. Solomans *(Wanderers)*

Referee: V.H. Cartwright *(England)*

J.D. Dobson scored but C.H. Abercrombie failed (3–0). (H.T.). M.W. Walter scored twice but G. Cunningham failed with both (9–0); C.D. Stuart scored and J.C. MacCallum converted (14–0).

This match was played on the Royal Ulster Agricultural Society's ground in Belfast before 12,000 spectators. Scotland were the better team but the score rather flattered them. The packs were well matched although Scotland finished stronger. The Irish pack tried many foot rushes only to be completely frustrated by some splendid defensive play by Cunningham who was well backed up by Lindsay. The Scottish backs did not combine well in the first half but improved greatly later.

ENGLAND   Inverleith   19 March 1910

SCOTLAND:	1 goal	5	**Loss**
ENGLAND:	1 goal, 3 tries	14	

Scotland: D.G. Schulze *(London Scot.)*; W.R. Sutherland *(Hawick)*, J. Pearson *(Watsonians)*, A.W. Angus *(Watsonians)*, D.G. Macpherson *(London Hospitals)*; G. Cunningham* *(Oxford Univ.)*, J.M. Tennent *(West of Scot.)*; C.H. Abercrombie *(Un. Services)*, G.C. Gowlland *(London Scot.)*, J.C. MacCallum *(Watsonians)*, J.M. Mackenzie *(Edin. Univ.)*, J.M.B. Scott *(Edin. Acads.)*, L.M. Spiers *(Watsonians)*, R.C. Stevenson *(St Andrews Univ.)*, C.D. Stuart *(West of Scot.)*

England: W.R. Johnston *(Bristol)*; P.W. Lawrie *(Leicester)*, F.M. Stoop *(Harlequins)*, J.G.G. Birkett* *(Harlequins)*, F.E. Chapman *(Hartlepool Rovers)*; A.D. Stoop *(Harlequins)*, A.L.H. Gotley *(Oxford Univ.)*; L.E. Barrington-Ward *(Edin. Univ.)*, H. Berry *(Gloucester)*, R. Dibble *(Bridgewater A)*, R.H.M. Hands *(Oxford Univ.)*, L. Haigh *(Manchester)*, G.R. Hind *(Guy's)*, C.H. Pillman *(Blackheath)*, J.A.S. Ritson *(Newcastle N.)*

Referee: G.B. Kennedy *(Ireland)*   **Touch judge:** C.J.N. Fleming

D.G. Macpherson scored; J.C. MacCallum converted (5–0); J.G.G. Birkett scored; F.E. Chapman converted (5–5). (H.T.). J.G.G. Birkett, H. Berry and J.A.S. Ritson scored; F.E. Chapman failed with each (5–14).

A record crowd of 25,000 saw England take complete charge after half time and practically run Scotland off their feet. The Scottish pack began well but hard running by the English backs nearly brought scores. Then a solo effort by Sutherland took play right into the English half and after some sustained pressure, Macpherson scored at the posts. However, a fine run started by A.D. Stoop left Birkett with a clear run in to equalise before half time. In the second half the English pack took command and their backs, enjoying an almost continuous supply of the ball ran in three good tries. A late move by Angus and Pearson set Sutherland away on a magnificent run from the centre to be tackled just short of the line.

England became champions for the first time since 1892 and owed a great deal to the attacking skills of Adrian Stoop not to mention the highly developed wing forward play of Pillman. For Scotland 'Wattie' Sutherland showed that he had real pace allied with football skills.

FRANCE	Colombes	2 January 1911

SCOTLAND:	1 goal, 1 drop goal, 2 tries	15	Loss
FRANCE:	2 goals, 2 tries	16	

Scotland: H.B. Tod (*Gala*); W.R. Sutherland (*Hawick*), T.E.B. Young (*Durham*), F.G. Buchanan (*Oxford Univ.*), J. Pearson (*Watsonians*); P. Munro* (*London Scot.*), F. Osler (*Edin. Univ.*); C.H. Abercrombie (*Un. Services*), R. Fraser (*Camb. Univ.*), J.C. MacCallum (*Watsonians*), A.R. Moodie (*St Andrews Univ.*), J.M.B. Scott (*Edin. Acads.*), A.M. Stevenson (*Glas. Univ.*), R.C. Stevenson (*St Andrews Univ.*), F.H. Turner (*Oxford Univ.*)

France: J. Coombe (*SF*); P. Failliot (*RCF*), M. Burgun (*RCF*), A. Francquenelle (*Vaugirard*), G. Lane (*RCF*); A. Laterrade (*Tarbes*), M. Peyroutou (*Perigueux*); J. Bavozet (*Lyon*), M. Communeau* (*Beauvais*), P. Decamps (*RCF*), F. Forgues (*Bayonne*), P. Guillemin (*RCF*), M. Legrain (*SF*), P. Mauriat (*Lyon*), P. Mounicq (*Toulouse*)

Referee: M.A.S. Jones (*England*)

J.C. MacCallum scored; H.B. Tod failed (3–0); A. Laterrade scored; P. Decamps converted (3–5); P. Failliot and M. Peyroutou scored; M. Communeau failed to convert (3–11); P. Munro scored; F.H. Turner converted (8–11). (H.T.). J. Pearson dropped a goal (12–11); P. Failliot scored; P. Decamps converted (12–16); C.H. Abercrombie scored; H.B. Tod failed (15–16).

This, France's first win in international rugby, undoubtedly gave the game a boost in that country and a warning to the other nations. One of the established Scottish players had some sour comments to make in his scrap book: (1) The Scottish Union, still not awarding caps against France, regarded this match as a trial for the home country games still to come and so picked several newcomers as trialists. (2) Pearson, a small light man and normally a centre, was placed on the wing and found himself marking Failliot, who at fourteen stones and six feet tall was probably the fastest amateur sprinter in France. As a result Failliot more or less ran through, rather than round, Pearson. (3) The referee, until the last half hour, held Scotland to the rules while allowing the opposition a fair amount of latitude with offsides, forward passes and knocks-on and only tightened up later when he saw what was happening. (4) In the last minute one of the trialists knocked on a pass which merely needed holding and laying over the line for the winning score.

France had their troubles before the start. M. Garcia in his *Histoire* relates that Vareilles, a centre, had hopped out of his carriage at Melun station to grab a sandwich only to see the train move away at once leaving him stranded on the platform and he only arrived at the field after the game was in progress. Near the time of kick off the reserve, Francquenelle, was also missing so the committee went out looking for a player and indeed approached two — 'Mais, en ces jours de fête, ils ont tous deux fait un trop bon déjeuner et ils se récusent'. Eventually they got someone who had begun to change when Francquenelle (who had missed *his* train at Saint Lazare station) arrived breathless, stripped and got onto the field some minutes after the start!

121

WALES　　　　　　Inverleith　　　　4 February 1911

SCOTLAND:	1 drop goal, 2 tries	10	**Loss**
WALES:	2 goals, 1 drop goal, 6 tries	32	

Scotland: D.G. Schulze (*London Scot.*); D.M. Grant (*Elstow School*), A.W. Angus (*Watsonians*), F.G. Buchanan (*Kelvinside Acads.*); J.M. Macdonald (*Edin. Wrs.*); P. Munro* (*London Scot.*), F. Osler (*Edin. Univ.*); C.H. Abercrombie (*London Scot.*), R. Fraser (*Camb. Univ.*), J.M. Mackenzie (*Edin. Univ.*), L. Robertson (*London Scot.*), A.R. Ross (*Edin. Univ.*), J.M.B. Scott (*Edin. Acads.*), R.C. Stevenson (*St Andrews Univ.*), F.H. Turner (*London Scot.*)

Wales: F.W. Birt (*Newport*); R.A. Gibbs (*Cardiff*), W.J. Spiller (*Cardiff*), L.M. Dyke (*Cardiff*), J.L. Williams (*Cardiff*); W.J. Trew* (*Swansea*), R.M. Owen (*Swansea*); J. Birch (*Neath*), A.P. Coldrich (*Newport*), T.H. Evans (*Llanelli*), J. Pugsley (*Cardiff*), D.J. Thomas (*Swansea*), R. Thomas (*Pontypool*), G. Travers (*Newport*), J. Webb (*Abertillery*)

Referee: J.G. Davidson (*Ireland*)

W.J. Spiller dropped a goal (0–4); J.L. Williams scored; F.W. Birt failed to convert (0–7); P. Munro dropped a goal (4–7). (H.T.). R. Thomas and R.A. Gibbs scored; R.A. Gibbs failed with both kicks (4–13); W.J. Spiller scored; F.W. Birt failed to convert (4–16); W.J. Spiller, J.L. Williams and R.A. Gibbs scored; L.M. Dyke failed with the first but converted the other two (4–29); J.M.B. Scott and F.H. Turner scored; D.M. Grant failed to convert either (10–29); R.A. Gibbs scored; L.M. Dyke failed (10–32).

This was Scotland's heaviest defeat to date. They more or less held their own up to half time but then the Welsh pack took control and played to their threes who combined beautifully for their scores. Shortly after half time Macdonald had to go off with a leg injury and Abercrombie (an extraordinary choice) was put out on the wing. This weakness was exploited at once and Wales ran in four tries before he (much to his relief) was replaced by Scott. Almost at once Angus had a good run and passed to Scott who by sheer strength and determination forced his way over for a try. Scotland kept up some pressure and Turner plunged in from a line out but in the last mintue Gibbs ran in for the last score. There is evidence that D.M. Grant was still at Elstow School although some reports name his club as East Midlands or London Scottish.

IRELAND　　　　　　Inverleith　　　　25 February 1911

SCOTLAND:	1 drop goal, 2 tries	10	**Loss**
IRELAND:	2 goals, 2 tries	16	

Scotland: A. Greig (*Glas. HSFP*); J.T. Simson (*Watsonians*), A.W. Angus (*Watsonians*), C. Ogilvy (*Hawick*), D.M. Grant (*Elstow School*); P. Munro* (*London Scot.*), A.B. Lindsay (*London Hospitals*); R. Fraser (*Camb. Univ.*), G.M. Frew (*Glas. HSFP*), J.C. MacCallum

(Watsonians), J.M. Mackenzie *(Edin. Univ.)*, J.M.B. Scott *(Edin. Acads.)*, R.C. Stevenson *(St Andrews Univ.)*, C.D. Stuart *(West of Scot.)*, F.H. Turner *(Oxford Univ.)*

Ireland: W.P. Hinton *(Old Wesley)*; C.T. O'Callaghan *(OMT)*, A.R. Foster *(QU Belfast)*, A.R.V. Jackson *(Wanderers)*, J.P. Quinn *(Dublin Univ.)*; R.A. Lloyd *(Dublin Univ.)*, H.M. Read *(Dublin Univ.)*; C. Adams *(Old Wesley)*, S.B.B. Campbell *(Derry)*, M.G. Garry *(Bective Rangers)*, T. Halpin *(Garryowen)*, G.T. Hamlet* *(Old Wesley)*, M.R. Heffernan *(Cork Const.)*, P.J. Smyth *(Collegians)*, T. Smyth *(Malone)*

Referee: V.H. Cartwright *(England)*

C.T. O'Callaghan and A.R. Foster scored; W.P. Hinton converted the first only (0–8); J.T. Simson scored; D.M. Grant failed (3–8). (H.T.). C. Adams scored; R.A. Lloyd converted (3–13); P. Munro dropped a goal (7–13); A.W. Angus scored; D.M. Grant failed (10–13); J.P. Quinn scored; the kick failed (10–16).

Ireland attacked from the beginning and scored twice inside ten minutes, their backs with Lloyd outstanding, running well. There followed some aggression by the Scottish threes and eventually Simson, getting the ball ten yards out, got over by a most determined run although tackled by two defenders. On the restart the Irish pack forced a score by Adams but increasing Scottish pressure saw Munro drop a goal and Angus score. At this stage Campbell came out of the pack to strengthen the defence but had a hand in a fast break by the backs which let Quinn score the last try. Ireland throughout were quicker onto the ball and sounder in defence while Scotland's handling too often let them down, Lindsay was recorded as a 'scrum-half'. This was Pat Munro's last match and his leave of absence having expired he left the same evening for London to return to duty in the Sudan as a District Commissioner.

Years later a former member of the Sudan Political Service, an Edinburgh Academical, related that Munro, when transferred from the Shilluk Province, gave his Scottish Cap to the tribal chief who was so delighted with it that thereafter he always wore it on state occasions instead of the traditional fez.

ENGLAND	Twickenham		18 March 1911

SCOTLAND:	1 goal, 1 try	**8**	**Loss**
ENGLAND:	2 goals, 1 try	**13**	

Scotland: C. Ogilvy *(Hawick)*; W.R. Sutherland *(Hawick)*, G. Cunningham *(London Scot.)*, R.F. Simson *(London Scot.)*, S.S.L. Steyn *(London Scot.)*; E. Milroy *(Watsonians)*, J.Y.M. Henderson *(Watsonians)*; D.M. Bain *(Oxford Univ.)*, J. Dobson *(Glas. Acads.)*, R. Fraser *(Camb. Univ.)*, G.M. Frew *(Glas. HSFP)*, W.R. Hutchison *(Glas. HSFP)*, J.C. MacCallum* *(Watsonians)*, C.D. Stuart *(West of Scot.)*, F.H. Turner *(Oxford Univ.)*

England: S.H. Williams *(Newport)*; P.W. Lawrie *(Leicester)*, R.W. Poulton *(Oxford Univ.)*, J.G.G. Birkett *(Harlequins)*, A.D. Roberts *(Newcastle N.)*; A.D. Stoop *(Harlequins)*, A.L.H. Gotley* *(Blackheath)*, L.G. Brown *(Oxford Univ.)*, R. Dibble *(Bridgewater A)*, L. Haigh *(Manchester)*, A.L. Kewney *(Rockcliff)*, J.A. King *(Headingley)*, R.O. Lagden *(Oxford Univ.)*, C.H. Pillman *(Blackheath)*, N.A. Wodehouse *(RN)*

Referee: T.D. Schofield *(Wales)*

W.R. Sutherland scored; F.H. Turner failed (3–0); N.A. Wodehouse scored; R.O. Lagden converted (3–5); P.W. Lawrie scored; R.O. Lagden failed (3–8). (H.T.). J.G.G. Birkett scored; R.O. Lagden converted (3–13); R.F. Simson scored; J.C. MacCallum converted (8–13).

The English threes threatened danger early on but were well held. Then Cunningham broke through and when tackled, the ball got to Milroy who passed to Sutherland. The winger beat three men by pace to open the scoring. England struck back at once and a passing run saw Wodehouse up with the backs to score. Sutherland again ran away from the backs but Williams got him on the touch line. Again good passing by the English threes put Lawrie over. Before half time Cunningham broke clear hotly pursued by Birkett and Stoop but looking round for someone to pass to, was tackled. It was reported that modesty dictated the move for he had lost his shorts in the initial burst! In the second half Henderson injured his arm and went to full back. Cunningham moved to half while Ogilvy came into the threes. Another fine run by Stoop and Birkett saw the latter run round the injured Henderson to score. England continued to press but Simson picked up a bad pass, ran clear to Williams, kicked over his head and after nearly colliding with a goal post, managed to get the touch down. Scotland continued to press but the defence had no trouble in holding out.

FRANCE   Inverleith   20 January 1912

SCOTLAND:	5 goals, 1 penalty goal, 1 try	31	**Win**
FRANCE:	1 try	3	

Scotland: W.M. Dickson (*Blackheath*); W.R. Sutherland (*Hawick*), A.W. Angus (*Watsonians*), J. Pearson (*Watsonians*), J.G. Will (*Camb. Univ.*); A.W. Gunn (*RHSFP*), J. Hume. (*RHSFP*); D.M. Bain (*Oxford Univ.*), J. Dobson (*Glas. Acads.*), C.C.P. Hill (*St Andrews Univ.*), D.D. Howie (*Kirkcaldy*), J.C. MacCallum* (*Watsonians*), W.D.C.L. Purves (*Camb. Univ.*), R.D. Robertson (*London Scot.*), F.H. Turner (*Oxford Univ.*)

France: F. Dutour (*Toulouse*); P. Failliot (*RCF*), D. Ihingone (*BEC*), J. Dufau (*Biarritz*), M. Burgun (*RCF*); J. Dedet (*SF*), L. Larribau (*Perigueux*); M. Boyou (*SBUC*), M. Communeau (*Beauvais*), J. Conil De Beyssac (*SBUC*), J. Domercq (*Bayonne*), P. Mauriat (*Lyon*), R. Monnier (*SBUC*), R. Paoli (*SF*), P. Vallot (*SCUF*)

Referee: J.J. Coffey (*Ireland*)   **Touch judges:** J.D. Dallas, C.F. Rutherford

J. Pearson dropped a penalty goal (3–0); A.W. Gunn scored; F.H. Turner converted (8–0); M. Communeau scored; M. Boyou failed (8–3); J. Pearson scored; F.H. Turner converted (13–3).(H.T.). J.G. Will scored; F.H. Turner converted (18–3); F.H. Turner scored but failed to convert (21–3); W.R. Sutherland scored twice and F.H. Turner converted both (31–3).

France played better than the score suggests, but poor handling not only lost them tries but gave Scotland chances from which they scored. Dutour at full back had a good game, his tackling of Will saving at least three scores. One report places Dedet at centre with Burgun at stand off. For Scotland, who played in white jerseys, Gunn played well while Will proved to be one of the fastest wingers ever picked for Scotland. Gunn was definitely selected to play as stand-off to Hume.

WALES   Swansea   3 February 1912

SCOTLAND: 2 tries   6   **Loss**

WALES: 2 goals, 2 drop goals, 1 try   21

Scotland: W.M. Dickson (*Blackheath*); W.R. Sutherland (*Hawick*), A.W. Angus (*Watsonians*), J. Pearson (*Watsonians*), J.G. Will (*Camb. Univ.*); A.W. Gunn (*RHSFP*), E. Milroy (*Watsonians*); D.M. Bain (*Oxford Univ.*), J. Dobson (*Glas. Acads.*), D.D. Howie (*Kirkcaldy*), J.C. MacCallum* (*Watsonians*), W.D.C.L. Purves (*London Scot.*), L. Robertson (*London Scot.*), J.M.B. Scott (*Edin. Acads.*), F.H. Turner (*Liverpool*)

Wales: J. Bancroft (*Swansea*); G.L. Hirst (*Newport*), W. Davies (*Aberavon*), F.W. Birt (*Newport,*) R.C.S. Plummer (*Newport*); W.J. Trew (*Swansea*), R.M. Owen* (*Swansea*); A.P. Coldrick (*Newport*), H.J. Davies (*Neath*), I. Morgan (*Swansea*), G. Stephens (*Neath*), R. Thomas (*Pontypool*), L. Tramp (*Newport*), H. Uzzell (*Newport*), J. Webb (*Abertillery*)

Referee: F.C. Potter-Irwin (*England*)   **Touch judge:** J.S. Jones

G.L. Hirst scored; J. Bancroft failed (0–3); W.J. Trew dropped a goal (0–7); J.G. Will scored; F.H. Turner failed (3–7). (H.T.). E. Milroy scored; F.H. Turner failed (6–7); I. Morgan scored; J. Bancroft converted (6–12); F.W. Birt dropped a goal (6–16); R.C.S. Plummer scored; J. Bancroft converted (6–21).

The game was threatened by a heavy fall of snow during the morning but the staff were able to clear the field in time. Scotland made a good fight of it but the excellence of a lively and heavier Welsh pack coupled with the greater individual cleverness of the Swansea halves won the match for Wales. For Scotland Angus was conspicuous in defence and attack.

IRELAND   Lansdowne Park   24 February 1912

SCOTLAND: 1 goal, 1 try   8   **Loss**

IRELAND: 1 drop goal, 1 penalty goal, 1 try   10

Scotland: C. Ogilvy (*Hawick*); S.S.L. Steyn (*Oxford Univ.*), A.W. Angus (*Watsonians*), C.M. Gilray (*London Scot.*), J.G. Will (*Camb. Univ.*); A.W. Gunn (*RHSFP*), E. Milroy (*Watsonians*); J. Dobson (*Glas. Acads.*), C.C.P. Hill (*St Andrews Univ.*), D.D. Howie (*Kirkcaldy*), J.C. MacCallum* (*Watsonians*), W.D.C.L. Purves (*London Scot.*), L. Robertson (*London Scot.*), J.M.B. Scott (*Edin. Acads.*), F.H. Turner (*Liverpool*)

Ireland: R.A. Wright (*Monkstown*); J.P. Quinn (*Dublin Univ.*), A.R. Foster (*Derry*), M. Abraham (*Bective Rangers*), C.V. McIvor (*Dublin Univ.*); R.A. Lloyd* (*Dublin Univ.*), H.M. Read (*Dublin Univ.*); C. Adams (*Old Wesley*), G.S. Brown (*Monkstown*), S.B.B. Campbell (*Derry*), T. Halpin (*Garryowen*), R. Hemphill (*Dublin Univ.*), G.V. Killeen (*Garryowen*), H. Moore (*QU Belfast*), R.D. Patterson (*Wanderers*)

R.A. Lloyd kicked a penalty and dropped a goal (0–7); J.G. Will scored; F.H. Turner failed (3–7). (H.T.). F.H. Turner scored; J.C. MacCallum converted (8–7); A.R. Foster scored; R.A. Lloyd failed (8–10).

Although this was a fast and exciting game play did not really reach a high standard. The Scottish forwards were quite effective but the backs had a bad day, their handling being poor. Early on Lloyd kicked a penalty for 'feet up' and then dropped a good goal. Before half time Gilray put up a kick ahead and a good bounce let Will, following up very fast, score. In the second half Will had two good runs, finishing the second off with a cross kick which Turner held and took over. Then Lloyd, who had played well throughout, seized on a bad pass by Milroy, put in a high kick which Angus could not hold and Foster got the ball and went on to score.

ENGLAND   Inverleith   16 March 1912

SCOTLAND:	1 goal, 1 try	8	**Win**
ENGLAND:	1 try	3	

Scotland: W.M. Dickson (*Blackheath*); W.R. Sutherland (*Hawick*), W. Burnet (*Hawick*), A.W. Angus (*Watsonians*), J.G. Will (*Camb. Univ.*); J.L. Boyd (*Un. Services*), E. Milroy (*Watsonians*); D.M. Bain (*Oxford Univ.*), J. Dobson (*Glas. Acads.*), D.D. Howie (*Kirkcaldy*), J.C. MacCallum* (*Watsonians*), L. Robertson (*London Scot.*), J.M.B. Scott (*Edin. Acads.*), F.H. Turner (*Liverpool*), C.M. Usher (*London Scot.*)

England: W.R. Johnston (*Bristol*); A.D. Roberts (*Northern*), R.W. Poulton (*Harlequins*), J.G.G. Birkett (*Harlequins*), H. Brougham (*Harlequins*); A.D. Stoop (*Harlequins*), J.A. Pym (*Blackheath*); R. Dibble* (*Newport*), J.H. Eddison (*Headingley*), D. Holland (*Devon Albion*), A.L. Kewney (*Rockcliff*), J.A. King (*Headingley*), A.H. MacIlwaine (*Un. Services*), R.C. Stafford (*Bedford*), N.A. Wodehouse (*Un. Services*)

Referee: F. Gardiner (*Ireland*) **Touch judges:** W.A. Walls, J. Baxter

There was no scoring at half time. W.R. Sutherland scored; J. MacCallum failed (3–0); D. Holland scored; A.H. MacIlwaine failed (3–3); C.M. Usher scored; J.C. MacCallum converted (8–3).

Scotland deserved to win this match but England were badly handicapped by losing King with two broken ribs early in the first half. While this was an accident there is no doubt that the Scottish forwards were in magnificent form in the loose and their tackling fairly upset the opposition including the much lauded Harlequin backs. Johnston, at full back, took a hammering either in tackling Will in full cry or in halting forward rushes. Angus had another good game and Sutherland was always very penetrative.

SOUTH AFRICA   **Inverleith**   **23 November 1912**

SCOTLAND:	Nil	0	**Loss**
SOUTH AFRICA:	2 goals, 2 tries	16	

Scotland: W.M. Dickson (*Oxford Univ.*); W.R. Sutherland (*Hawick*), A.W. Gunn (*RHSFP*), A.W. Angus (*Watsonians*), J. Pearson (*Watsonians*); J.L. Boyd (*Un. Services*), E. Milroy (*Watsonians*); D.M. Bain (*Oxford Univ.*), P.C.B. Blair (*Camb. Univ.*), J. Dobson (*Glas. Acads.*), D.D. Howie (*Kirkcaldy*), W.D.C.L. Purves (*London Scot.*), L. Robertson (*London Scot.*), J.M.B. Scott (*Edin. Acads.*), F.H. Turner* (*Liverpool*)

South Africa: P.G. Morkel (*WP*); J.A. Stegmann (*T*), R.R. Luyt (*WP*), J.W.H. Morkel (*WP*), E. McHardy (*Orange FS*); F.P. Luyt (*WP*), F.J. Dobbin* (*GW*); J.A.J. Francis (*T*), A.S. Knight (*T*), S.H. Ledger (*GW*), J.D. Luyt (*EP*), D.F.T. Morkel (*T*), W.H. Morkel (*WP*), G. Thompson (*WP*), T.F. Van Vuuren (*EP*)

  Referee: F.C. Potter-Irwin (*England*)   **Touch judges:** J.D. Dallas, M. Honnet

E.E. McHardy scored; P.G. Morkel failed (0–3). (H.T.). J.A. Stegmann scored twice; P.G. Morkel converted the first only (0–11); W.H. Morkel scored; D.T.F. Morkel converted (0–16).

Scotland had an equal share territorially of the game but there was never any real doubt about the outcome for South Africa were both heavier and faster. Sutherland alone had the necessary pace to cope with his opponents and indeed it needed good tackling to prevent him from scoring. In the second half the visitors backs fairly opened out and two of the scores resulted from passing movements which crossed the width of the field at least twice.

FRANCE   **Parc des Princes**   **1 January 1913**

SCOTLAND:	3 goals, 2 tries	21	**Win**
FRANCE:	1 try	3	

Scotland: W.M. Dickson (*Oxford Univ.*); W.R. Sutherland (*Hawick*), R.E. Gordon (*Un. Services*), A.W. Angus (*Watsonians*), W.A. Stewart (*London Hospitals*); A.W. Gunn (*RHSFP*), E. Milroy (*Watsonians*); C.H. Abercrombie (*Un. Services*), D.M. Bain (*Oxford Univ.*), P.C.B. Blair (*Camb. Univ.*), D.D. Howie (*Kirkcaldy*), G.A. Ledingham (*Aberdeen GSFP*), J.B. McDougall (*Greenock Wrs.*), F.H. Turner* (*Liverpool*), C.M. Usher (*London Scot.*)

France: F. Dutour (*Toulouse*); L. Larribau (*Perigueux*), G. Lane* (*RCF*), J. Sentilles (*Tarbes*), P. Jaureguy (*Toulouse*); M. Burgun (*RCF*), A. Hedembaigt (*Bayonne*); F. Forgues (*Bayonne*), M. Legrain (*SF*), M. Leuvielle (*Bordeaux*), P. Mauriat (*Lyon*), P. Mounicq (*Toulouse*), M. Pascarel (*TOEC*), J. Sebadio (*Tarbes*), P. Thil (*Nantes*)

J. Sebadio scored an unconverted try (0–3); W.A. Stewart scored twice; F.H. Turner converted the first (8–3). (H.T.). R.E. Gordon (2) and W.A. Stewart scored; F.H. Turner converted two (21–3).

Colombes Stadium was rendered unplayable by heavy rain and flooding and Cyril Rutherford, the French secretary, worked a minor miracle by making within 24 hours all the necessary arrangements to shift the game to the Parc des Princes.

The teams were much more evenly matched than the score suggests. There was little to choose between the forwards but the Scottish backs were clearly better, especially in combined work. France opened the scoring early on when an unexpected short throw to the front of a line out let Sebadio hurl himself in for a try but eventually some fine play by Gordon and the tremendous pace of Stewart produced five tries for Scotland.

On this occasion the refereeing was from the start firm, even strict, and as a result France was frequently penalised. As the game proceeded the spectators became more and more enraged at Mr Baxter and there were some ugly scenes after the final whistle when the police and many of the players found it necessary to protect and escort the referee from the field. W.M. Dickson, who was quite deaf, completely misinterpreted the crowd scenes at the close and while making his way to the dressing room remarked to Charles Usher how sporting the spectators were in applauding the Scots so enthusiastically.

However, there were repercussions. The Rugby Union let it be known that they would not supply any referees for future matches in France but did relent to let an Englishman referee the France–South Africa match in Bordeaux later in the season.

The SFU took a much sterner stand for they refused to renew the 1914 fixture even though it would have been at Inverleith. They made it quite clear that they had no fault to find with the French committee and team but were equally emphatic that they could not accept a situation where the referee's decisions, authority and safety were threatened by the spectators. World War I intervened before further action could be discussed and it may be noted that four of the French XV and nine of the Scots did not survive to see the fixture resumed in 1920.

WALES   Inverleith   1 February 1913

SCOTLAND:	Nil	0	**Loss**
WALES:	1 goal, 1 try	8	

Scotland: W.M. Dickson (*Oxford Univ.*); W.A. Stewart (*London Hospitals*), R.E. Gordon (*Un. Services*), A.W. Angus (*Watsonians*), W.R. Sutherland (*Hawick*); J.H. Bruce Lockhart (*London Scot.*), E. Milroy (*Watsonians*); C.H. Abercrombie (*Un. Services*), D.M. Bain (*Oxford Univ.*), P.C.B. Blair (*Camb. Univ.*), D.D. Howie (*Kirkcaldy*), L. Robertson (*London Scot.*), J.M.B. Scott (*Edin. Acads.*), F.H. Turner* (*Liverpool*), C.M. Usher (*London Scot.*)

Wales: R.F. Williams (*Cardiff*); H. Lewis (*Swansea*), W.J. Trew* (*Swansea*), T. Jones (*Pontypool*), G.L. Hirst (*Newport*); J.M.C. Lewis (*Cardiff*), R. Lloyd (*Pontypool*); F. Andrews (*Pontypool*), A. Davies (*Swansea*), W. Jenkins (*Cardiff*), P. Jones (*Newport*), F. Perrett (*Neath*), R. Richards (*Aberavon*), G. Stephens (*Neath*), H. Uzzell (*Newport*)

Referee: S.H. Crawford (*Ireland*)   **Touch judges:** J.D. Dallas, W.M. Douglas

J.M.C. Lewis scored but failed to convert (0–3). (H.T.). T. Jones scored; J.M.C. Lewis converted (0–8).

This was rather a dreary game consisting mainly of a series of scrums. The Welsh pack was clearly on top but their backs did not play well. Lewis, the stand off, however, was in excellent form and had the opening score in what was a very even first half. Wales' domination up front saw the second half played mainly in the Scottish half but a good defence prevented any score until late on Lewis dropped at goal, the ball went wide, and a wicked bounce beat two defenders to let Jones get there first to score.

IRELAND	Inverleith	22 February 1913

SCOTLAND:	4 goals, 3 tries	29	**Win**
IRELAND:	2 goals, 1 drop goal	14	

Scotland: W.M. Dickson (*Oxford Univ.*); W.R. Sutherland (*Hawick*), R.E. Gordon (*Un. Services*), J. Pearson (*Watsonians*), W.A. Stewart (*London Hospitals*); T.C. Bowie (*Watsonians*), E. Milroy (*Watsonians*); D.M. Bain (*Oxford Univ.*), P.C.B. Blair (*Camb. Univ.*), G.H.H.P. Maxwell (*Edin. Acads.*), W.D.C.L. Purves (*London Scot.*), L. Robertson (*London Scot.*), J.M.B. Scott (*Edin. Acads.*), F.H. Turner* (*Liverpool*), C.M. Usher (*London Scot.*).

Ireland: J.W. McConnell (*Lansdowne*); C.V. McIvor (*Dublin Univ.*), G.W. Holmes (*Dublin Univ.*), J.B. Minch (*Bective Rangers*), F. Bennett (*Collegians*); H.M. Read (*Dublin Univ.*), R.A. Lloyd* (*Liverpool*); S.B.B. Campbell (*Edin. Univ.*), J.E. Finlay (*QC Belfast*); E.W. Jeffares (*Wanderers*), A.V. Killeen (*Garyowen*), R.D. Patterson (*Wanderers*), F.G. Schute (*Dublin Univ.*), P. Stokes (*Blackrock*), W. Tyrell (*QU Belfast*).

Referee: J. Baxter (*England*)　**Touch judges:** J.D. Dallas, R. Stevenson

W.A. Stewart scored; F.H. Turner converted (5–0); F.G. Schute scored; R.A. Lloyd converted (5–5); W.A. Stewart (2) and C.M. Usher scored; F.H. Turner converted the first two (18–5). (H.T.). T.C. Bowie and W.A. Stewart scored; F.H. Turner converted one (26–5); P. Stokes scored; C.A. Lloyd converted (26–10); R.A. Lloyd dropped a goal (26–14); W.D.C.L. Purves scored; F.H. Turner failed (29–14).

This was the antithesis of the Welsh match, being full of open play and incidents. In spite of losing Dickson with a shoulder injury during the first half, the Scottish pack with Scott in the backs, more than held their own and good play by the threes produced some fine tries. The Watsonian half backs played well as a pair while Stewart, with four tries, proved much too fast for his opponents, yet for his second score he had to hand off and beat several defenders in a 70 yards run. Later on Campbell came out of the pack as an extra defender. A late Irish rally brought a score by Stokes and an excellent 40 yards drop goal by Lloyd.

129

ENGLAND   Twickenham   **15 March 1913**

SCOTLAND: Nil   0   **Loss**
ENGLAND: 1 try   3

Scotland: W.M. Wallace (*Camb. Univ.*); J.B. Sweet (*Glas. HSFP*), J. Pearson (*Watson-ians*), E.G. Loudoun-Shand (*Oxford Univ.*), W.R. Sutherland (*Hawick*); T.C. Bowie (*Watsonians*), E.Milroy (*Watsonians*); D.M. Bain (*Oxford Univ.*), P.C.B. Blair (*Camb. Univ.*), G.H.H.P. Maxwell (*Edin. Acads.*), W.D.C.L. Purves (*London Scot.*), L. Robert-son (*London Scot.*), J.M.B. Scott (*Edin. Acads.*), F.H. Turner* (*Oxford Univ.*), C.M. Usher (*London Scot.*)

England: W.R. Johnston (*Bristol*); V.H.M. Coates (*Bath*), R.W. Poulton (*Harlequins*), F.N. Tarr (*Leicester*), C.N. Lowe (*Camb. Univ.*); W.J.A. Davies (*RN*), F.E. Oakeley (*RN*); L.G. Brown (*Blackheath*), J.E. Greenwood (*Camb. Univ.*), J.A. King (*Headingley*), C.H. Pillman (*Blackheath*), J.A.S. Ritson (*Newcastle N*), S. Smart (*Gloucester*), G. Ward (*Leicester*), N.A. Wodehouse* (*RN*)

   Referee: T.D. Schofield (*Wales*)

L.G. Brown scored but J.E. Greenwood failed (0–3). (H.T.).

This was a game made memorable by the play of Sutherland. Always dangerous in attack he achieved wonders in defence after Loudoun-Shand was crippled and changed to the wing. For the rest of the game Sutherland, playing at centre, blotted out single-handed the potentially great wing pair of Poulton and Coates, and England could only manage a scrambled try scored in the first half. Scott also defended well and had one great run which might have produced a score had Loudoun-Shand been able to keep up with him.

WALES   Cardiff   **7 February 1914**

SCOTLAND: 1 goal   5   **Loss**
WALES: 2 goals, 2 drop goals,   24
               1 penalty goal, 1 try

(*RMA*), W.R. Sutherland (*Hawick*), J.G. Will (*Camb. Univ.*); A.T. Sloan (*Edin. Acads.*), A.S. Hamilton (*Headingley*); D.M. Bain* (*Oxford Univ.*), D.G. Donald (*Oxford Univ.*), A.D. Laing (*RHSFP*), G.H.H.P. Maxwell (*Edin. Acads.*), A.R. Ross (*Edin. Univ.*), A.M. Stewart (*Edin. Acads.*), A.W. Symington (*Camb. Univ.*), A. Wemyss (*Gala*)

Wales: J. Bancroft (*Swansea*); I.T. Davies (*Llanelli*), W.H. Evans (*Llwynypia*), J. Wetter (*Newport*), G.L. Hirst (*Newport*); J.M.C. Lewis (*Cardiff*), R. Lloyd (*Pontypool*); J.A. Davies* (*Llanelli*), J.B. Jones (*Abertillery*), P. Jones (*Pontypool*), T.C. Lloyd (*Neath*), E. Morgan (*Swansea*), H. Uzzell (*Newport*), D. Watts (*Maesteg*), T. Williams (*Swansea*)

Referee: V. Drennon (*Ireland*) **Touch judges:** Dr J.R.C. Greenlees, A. Llewellyn

W.A. Stewart scored; A.D. Laing converted (5–0); G.L. Hirst dropped a goal (5–4); J. Bancroft kicked a penalty (5–7). (H.T.). I.T. Davies and J. Wetter scored; J. Bancroft converted the second (5–15); J.M.C. Lewis dropped a goal (5–19); G.L. Birst scored; J. Bancroft converted (5–24).

This was a very rough game, one paper commented that there were no drawing-room tactics indulged in. D.M. Bain had six stitches put in a head wound and later commented that the dirtier team won. 'Podger' Laing was one of the first to be felled — a challenge that he gladly accepted and returned in full measure. Scotland did relatively well up to half time but Sutherland was lamed and although he stayed on the field on the wing, was practically useless. Wales in the second half exploited this weak wing effectively.

IRELAND   Lansdowne Park   28 February 1914

SCOTLAND:	Nil	**0**	**Loss**
IRELAND:	2 tries	**6**	

Scotland: W.M. Wallace (*Camb. Univ.*); J.B. Sweet (*Glas. HSFP*), R.M. Scobie (*RMA*), J.R. Warren (*Glas. Acads.*), J.G. Will (*Camb. Univ.*); T.C. Bowie (*Watsonians*), E. Milroy* (*Watsonians*); D.M. Bain (*Oxford Univ.*), D.G. Donald (*Oxford Univ.*), A.D. Laing (*RHSFP*), J.B. McDougall (*Greenock Wrs.*), G.H.H.P. Maxwell (*Edin. Acads.*), A.R. Ross (*Edin. Univ.*), F.H. Turner (*Liverpool*), A. Wemyss (*Gala*)

Ireland: F.P. Montgomery (*Queen's*); J.P. Quinn* (*Dublin Univ.*), A.R.V. Jackson (*Wanderers*), J.B. Minch (*Bective Rangers*), A.R. Foster (*NIFC*); H.W. Jack (*UC Cork*); H.W. Jack (*UC Cork*), V. McNamara (*UC Cork*), C. Adams (*Old Wesley*), W.P. Collopy (*Bective Rangers*), J.C.A. Dowse (*Monkstown*), G.V. Killeen (*Garryowen*), P. O'Connell (*Bective Rangers*), J.S. Parr (*Wanderers*), J. Taylor (*Collegians*), W. Tyrell (*QU Belfast*)

Referee: J. Baxter (*England*)

No scoring at half time. J.P. Quinn and V. McNamara scored; H.W. Jack failed to convert (0–6).

In drizzling rain Scotland began well but Ireland developed their characteristic forward rushes which improved as the game went on; the Scottish backs were largely committed to defence. After half time the rain became very heavy and the game developed mainly into a fierce forward battle. Ireland got the ball over the line twice for tries but in spite of great efforts by Will and Sweet Scotland could not score. It was noted that Laing played well and that Turner was useful in 'hooking'.

SCOTLAND:　　1 goal, 1 drop goal, 2 tries　　15　　**Loss**

ENGLAND:　　2 goals, 2 tries　　　　　　　16

Scotland: W.M. Wallace (*Camb. Univ.*); J.L. Huggan (*London Scot.*), R.M. Scobie (*Un. Services*), A.W. Angus (*Watsonians*), J.G. Will (*Camb. Univ.*); T.C. Bowie (*Watsonians*), E. Milroy* (*Watsonians*); A.D. Laing (*RHSFP*), G.H.H.P. Maxwell (*Edin. Acads.*), I.M. Pender (*London Scot.*), A.R. Ross (*Edin. Univ.*), A.W. Symington (*Camb. Univ.*), F.H. Turner (*Liverpool*), C.M. Usher (*London Scot.*), E.T. Young (*Glas. Acads.*)

England: W.R. Johnston (*Bristol*); C.N. Lowe (*Camb. Univ.*), J.H.D. Watson (*Blackheath*), R.W. Poulton (*Liverpool*), A.J. Dingle (*Hartlepool Rovers*); W.J.A. Davies (*RN*), F.E. Oakeley (*RN*); L.G. Brown (*Blackheath*); J. Brunton (*North Durham*), J.E. Greenwood (*Camb. Univ.*), H.C. Harrison (*Un. Services*), A.F. Maynard (*Camb. Univ.*), C.H. Pillman (*Blackheath*), S. Smart (*Gloucester*), G. Ward (*Leicester*)

Referee: T.D. Schofield (*Wales*)

J.G. Will scored; F.H. Turner failed (3–0); C.N. Lowe scored; J.E. Greenwood failed (3–3). (H.T.). J.L. Huggan scored; F.H. Turner failed (6–3); C.N. Lowe scored twice; H.C. Harrison converted both (6–13); R.W. Poulton scored; H.C. Harrison failed (6–16); T.C. Bowie dropped a goal (10–16); J.G. Will scored; F.H. Turner converted (15–16).

This was a great and exciting game. Scotland who completed the season without a win came within a goal kick of beating England who finished as undefeated champions. The match was marked throughout by some splendid attacking rugby by both sides. Milroy got over but was brought back for a forward pass and then Wallace had to touch down in defence but at once Maxwell made ground. Ross and Turner carried the movement on and the ball went to Will who outpaced Lowe to score far out. Turner's long kick just failed. Just before the interval Watson put Lowe over to score with Will hanging on to him.

Early in the second half a great forward rush involving most of the Scottish pack finished by Huggan scoring — again too far out for Turner to convert. Almost at once a brilliant English run involving their whole back division gave Lowe room to sprint round Wallace and score between the posts. This was the prelude to further fine moves by the English threes and they seemed to have made the game safe by scoring two more sparkling tries. Harrison, having converted two, unaccountably missed the third which was relatively easy. Yet Scotland did not give in for getting well up field Bowie dropped a good goal and immediately after, he set Will away at midfield. The winger held off a challenge by Lowe and scored in a position where Turner's conversion brought the scores to 15–16. England then put in a strong attack in which Pillman had to retire with a bad leg injury and Scotland finished with some good running, Will again being prominent, but could not get the vital score.

With the coming of World War I this splendid Calcutta Cup match marked the close of an epoch. Before the close of 1914 three of the players were gone, and by 1918 five of the English and six of the Scottish XV had been killed in action.

Prominent Players 1900–1914

The typical Scottish style of hard forward play was maintained by players like J.M. Dykes, W.P. Scott, W.E. Kyle, J.M. Mackenzie, J.R.C. Greenlees, C.D. Stuart and A.D. Laing while later J.C. MacCallum, J.M.B. Scott and C.M. Usher excelled in the more open game that developed with the four threequarter formation. Others as good like F.H. Turner and D.M. Bain had just come to the fore when World War I claimed them as victims.

D.R. Bedell-Sivright, however, cannot be passed over lightly for without doubt he was the hardest forward ever to play for Scotland. Strong in the line out, a magnificent dribbler and a murderous tackler, he had many critics of his uncompromising desire and ability to be first onto the ball. After watching him play for Cambridge University against the Racing Club de France a local newspaper commented: *'Il travaille avec vigueur, plaquant, chargeant, bousculant, carambolant sans lassitude'* while a famous Welsh cap contented himself with 'He is very rough'. He captained Cambridge and graduated BA before captaining the British tour in South Africa in 1904. After his return he captained Edinburgh University and was Scottish Amateur Heavy Weight Boxing Champion before he qualified as a doctor. As a surgeon in the Royal Navy he died of blood poisoning during the Dardanelles campaign.

As early half backs J.I. Gillespie, E.D. Simson and P. Munro were justly noted for their ability to make openings from the scrum base while later J. Hume and A.W. Gunn appear to have been the first pair selected to play as scrum half and stand off. E. Milroy, another war casualty, was a later scrum half of the highest calibre.

At centre Phipps Turnbull had the skill to glide deceptively fast through the defence whilst the Australian student, A.B. Timms, was equally successful in a more direct manner. Later J. Pearson and A.W. Angus were fine centres coming from the outstanding Watsonian Club XV.

There was a succession of wingers of genuine pace in W.H. Welsh, H. Martin, W.R. Sutherland, W.A. Stewart and J.G. Will, but the young K.G. MacLeod was in a class by himself as an attacking wing or centre for he had the pace of a sprinter allied to a wickedly good swerve and was constantly dropping goals of enormous range. His try in the South African game of 1906 is one of the game's historic scores. After the sudden death of his older brother, L.M. MacLeod, in 1907 he, a year later at the age of twenty, gave up the game at the request of his father and turned to playing aggressive and successful cricket for Lancashire.

At full back Scotland were well served by H. Rottenburg, A.W. Duncan, D.G. Schulze and W.M. Dickson but W.T. Forrest deserves mention for while his defence and kicking were consistently of the highest order he now and then committed an appalling blunder which was immediately retrieved by some extraordinary piece of virtuosity.

FRANCE	**Parc des Princes**	**1 January 1920**

SCOTLAND:	1 goal	5	**Win**
FRANCE:	Nil	0	

Scotland: G.L. Pattullo (*Panmure*); A.T. Sloan (*Edin. Acads.*), E.C. Fahmy (*Abertillery*), A.W. Angus* (*Watsonians*), G.B. Crole (*Oxford Univ.*); A.S. Hamilton (*Headingley*), J. Hume (*RHSFP*); D.D. Duncan (*Oxford Univ.*), R.A. Gallie (*Glas. Acads.*), F. Kennedy (*Stewart's FP*), A.D. Laing (*RHSFP*), W.A.K. Murray (*London Scot.*), G. Thom (*Kirkcaldy*), C.M. Usher (*London Scot.*), A. Wemyss (*Edin. Wrs.*)

France: A. Chilo (*RCF*); A. Jaureguy (*RCF*), R. Lasserre (*Bayonne*), R. Crabos (*RCF*), P. Serre (*Perpignan*); E. Billac (*Bayonne*), P. Struxiano* (*Toulouse*); J. Sebedio (*Beziers*), P. Pons (*Toulouse*), M.F. Lubin-Lebrere (*Toulouse*), A. Cassayet (*Tarbais*), L. Puech (*Toulouse*), R. Thierry (*RCF*), R. Marchand (*Poitiers*), J. Laurent (*Bayonne*)

Referee: F.C. Potter-Irwin (*England*)   **Touch judges:** J.R.C. Greenlees, C.F. Rutherford

There was no scoring in the first half. G.B. Crole scored and F. Kennedy converted (5–0).

The game was played in heavy rain on a muddy and slippery ground. The Scottish forwards were much praised especially for their excellent dribbling. The Scottish try came from a fast dribble by Usher and Thom which was carried on by Crole.

WALES	**Inverleith**	**7 February 1920**

SCOTLAND:	2 penalty goals, 1 try	9	**Win**
WALES:	1 goal	5	

Scotland: G.L. Patullo (*Panmure*); E.B. Mackay (*Glas. Acads.*), A.W. Angus (*Watson-*

ians), E.C. Fahmy (*Abertillery*), G.B. Crole (*Oxford Univ.*); A.T. Sloan (*Edin. Acads.*), J.A.R. Selby (*Watsonians*); D.D. Duncan (*Oxford Univ.*), R.A. Gallie (*Glas. Acads.*), F. Kennedy (*Stewart's FP*), A.D. Laing (*RHSFP*), N. Macpherson (*Newport*), G.H.H.P. Maxwell (*RAF*), G. Thom (*Kirkcaldy*), C.M. Usher* (*London Scot.*)

Wales: J. Rees (*Swansea*); W.J. Powell (*Cardiff*), J. Shea (*Newport*), A. Jenkins (*Llanelli*), B. Williams (*Llanelli*); B. Beynon (*Swansea*), J. Wetter (*Newport*); C.W. Jones (*Bridgend*), J. Jones (*Aberavon*), S. Morris (*Crosskeys*), G. Oliver (*Pontypool*), T. Parker (*Swansea*), J. Whitfield (*Newport*), J. Williams (*Blaina*), H. Uzzell* (*Newport*)

Referee: J.F. Crawford (*Ireland*)   **Touch judges:** T. Scott, H. Parker

A. Jenkins scored and converted (0–5). (H.T.). F. Kennedy kicked a penalty (3–5); A.T. Sloan scored but Kennedy failed (6–5); F. Kennedy kicked a penalty (9–5).

Wales, having decisively beaten England, came to Inverleith in perfect conditions fully expecting to win. The packs were fairly evenly matched but the Welsh backs were clearly faster. J. Shea was blamed since he continually dropped at goal or tried to go through on his own. A.T. Sloan's try came from a brilliant diagonal solo run from mid field to the corner. F. Kennedy's two penalties were long range efforts; the first was taken from near touch ten yards inside the Welsh half. It was a hard game and both teams had two men hurt or off.

IRELAND   Inverleith   28 February 1920

SCOTLAND: 2 goals, 1 penalty goal, 2 tries   19   **Win**
IRELAND: Nil   0

Scotland: G.L. Pattullo (*Panmure*); A. Browning (*Glas. HSFP*), A.W. Angus (*Watsonians*), A.T. Sloan (*Edin. Acads.*), G.B. Crole (*Oxford Univ.*); E.C. Fahmy (*Abertillery*), J.A.R. Selby (*Watsonians*); D.D. Duncan (*Oxford Univ.*), R.A. Gallie (*Glas. Acads.*), F. Kennedy (*Stewart's FP*), A.D. Laing (*RHSFP*), N. Macpherson (*Newport*), W.A.K. Murray (*London Scot.*), G. Thom (*Kirkcaldy*), C.M. Usher* (*London Scot.*)

Ireland: W.E. Crawford (*Lansdowne*); C.H. Bryant (*Cardiff*), T. Wallace (*Cardiff*), P.J. Roddy (*Bective Rangers*), B.A.T. McFarland (*Londonderry*); W. Duggan (*UC Cork*), J.B. O'Neill (*QU Belfast*); H.H. Coulter (*QU Belfast*), A.W. Courtney (*UC Dublin*), R.Y. Crichton (*Dublin Univ.*), W.D. Doherty* (*Guy's*), J.E. Finlay (*Cardiff*), A.H. Price (*Dublin Univ.*), W.J. Roche (*UC Cork*), P. Stokes (*Garryowen*)

Referee: J. Baxter (*England*)   **Touch judges:** T. Scott, A. Tedford

G.B. Crole scored and F. Kennedy converted (5–0); F. Kennedy kicked a penalty (8–0); G.B. Crole scored and Kennedy converted (13–0). (H.T.). A.W. Angus scored (16–0); A. Browning scored but F. Kennedy failed with both (19–0).

The Irish forwards lacked fire while the Scottish pack improved as the match went on. The Irish backs defended well especially as they had to contend with many unexpected moves by their opponents. E.C. Fahmy, moved from centre, had a good match; one dummy and a run followed by a cross kick gave Angus his score. G.B. Crole had a brilliant match. His ability to short punt over an opponent and use his great pace to regain the ball gave him two tries and caused endless trouble to the defence.

ENGLAND Twickenham **20 March 1920**

SCOTLAND: 1 drop goal 4 **Loss**
ENGLAND: 2 goals, 1 try 13

Scotland: G.L. Pattullo (*Panmure*); A.T. Sloan (*Edin. Acads.*), A.W. Angus (*Watsonians*), J.H. Bruce Lockhart (*London Scot.*), G.B. Crole (*Oxford Univ.*); E.C. Fahmy (*Abertillery*), C.S. Nimmo (*Watsonians*); D.D. Duncan (*Oxford Univ.*), R.A. Gallie (*Glas. Acads.*), F. Kennedy (*Stewart's FP*), N. Macpherson (*Newport*), G.H.H.P. Maxwell (*RAF*), G. Thom (*Kirkcaldy*), C.M. Usher* (*London Scot.*), A. Wemyss (*Edin. Wrs.*)

England: B.S. Cumberlege (*Blackheath*); C.N. Lowe (*Blackheath*), E. Myers (*Bradford*), E.D.G. Hammett (*Newport*), S.W. Harris (*Blackheath*); W.J.A. Davies (*Un. Services*), C.A. Kershaw (*Un. Services*); A.F. Blakiston (*Northampton*), G.S. Conway (*Camb. Univ.*), J.E. Greenwood* (*Camb. Univ.*), F.W. Mellish (*Blackheath*), S. Smart (*Gloucester*), A.T. Voyce (*Gloucester*), W.W. Wakefield (*Harlequins*), T. Woods (*RN*)

Referee: T.D. Schofield (*Wales*)

C.N. Lowe scored and J.E. Greenwood converted (0–5); S.W. Harris scored and Greenwood converted (0–10); J.H. Bruce Lockhart dropped a goal (4–10). (H.T.). C.A. Kershaw scored but Greenwood failed (4–13).

A record crowd of 40,000 saw the teams presented to HM King George V. The Scottish pack showed some aggression in the tight but had no answer to the fine open play by their opponents in the loose. The English backs were obviously better and very ready and quick to capitalise on an error. The new partnership of Fahmy and Nimmo was not a success and it is interesting to note that Nimmo had been selected to replace Selby, his club-fellow half back.

FRANCE Inverleith **22 January 1921**

SCOTLAND: Nil 0 **Loss**
FRANCE: 1 try 3

Scotland: H.H. Forsayth (*Oxford Univ.*); I.J. Kilgour (*RMA*), A.E. Thomson (*Un. Services*), A.L. Gracie (*Harlequins*), J.H. Carmichael (*Watsonians*); A.T. Sloan (*Edin. Acads.*), J. Hume* (*RHSFP*); J.M. Bannerman (*Glas. HSFP*), R.S. Cumming (*Aber. Univ.*), R.A. Gallie (*Glas. Acads.*), A.D. Laing (*RHSFP*), J.B. McDougall (*Wakefield*), N. Macpherson (*Newport*), G.H.H.P. Maxwell (*London Scot.*), W.A.K. Murray (*Kelvinside Acads.*)

France: J. Clement (*RCF*); R. Got (*Perpignan*), R. Crabos* (*RCF*); F. Borde (*RCF*), J. Lobies (*RCF*); E. Billac (*Bayonne*), R. Piteu (*Pau*); M. Biraben (*Dax*), J. Boubee (*Tarbes*), J. Coscoll (*Beziers*), R. Lasserre (*Bayonne*), G. Lubin-Lebrere (*Toulouse*), P. Pons (*Toulouse*), E. Soulie (*CASG*), F. Vaquer (*Perpignan*)

E. Billac scored but Crabos failed (0–3). (H.T.).

This was France's first win in Scotland and was well deserved for their entire XV was faster and more alert. The forwards were fairly evenly matched but the Scottish backs had a bad day. J. Hume was most consistent but got no support. One fumbled pass was smartly seized on by Borde and passed to Billac for the only score. Towards the end the French defence held out against fierce forward pressure.

WALES　　　　　　　Swansea　　　　　5 February 1921

SCOTLAND:　　1 goal, 1 penalty goal, 2 tries　　14　　**Win**

WALES:　　　　2 drop goals　　　　　　　　　　8

Scotland: H.H. Forsayth (*Oxford Univ.*); A.T. Sloan (*Edin. Acads.*), A.L. Gracie (*Harlequins*), A.E. Thomson (*Un. Services*), J.H. Carmichael (*Watsonians*); R.L.H. Donald (*Glas. HSFP*), J. Hume* (*RHSFP*); J.M. Bannerman (*Glas. HSFP*), J.C.R. Buchanan (*Stewart's FP*), R.S. Cumming (*Aber. Univ.*), G. Douglas (*Jedforest*), R.A. Gallie (*Glas. Acads.*), G.H.H.P. Maxwell (*RAF*), J.N. Shaw (*Edin. Acads.*), C.M. Usher (*Edin. Wrs.*)

Wales: J. Rees (*Swansea*); M.G. Thomas (*Bart's*), A. Jenkins (*Llanelli*), P.E.R. Baker-Jones (*Army*), F. Evans (*Llanelli*); W. Bowen (*Swansea*), T.H. Vile* (*Newport*); L. Attewell (*Newport*), W. Hodder (*Pontypool*), J. Jones (*Aberavon*), E. Morgan (*Llanelli*), T. Parker (*Swansea*), T. Roberts (*Risca*), J. Williams (*Blaina*), S. Winmill (*Cross Keys*)

Referee: J. Baxter (*England*)

A.E. Thomson scored but Maxwell failed (3–0); J.C.R. Buchanan scored and Maxwell converted (8–0); G.H.H.P. Maxwell kicked a penalty goal (11–0). (H.T.). A. Jenkins dropped two goals (11–8); A.T. Sloan scored but Maxwell failed (14–8).

This was the first win in Wales since 1892 and the match was remarkable for the unprecedented crowd scenes, for play was held up on several occasions to move spectators from the touch line and goal areas. At one time the referee conferred with the captains about abandoning the game and although Scotland really deserved their win there is no doubt that a crucial break after Jenkins' second drop goal with the score at 11–8 halted the Welsh revival. Wales elected to play against the wind and found themselves 11–0 down at half time. In the second half Jenkins and Vile dropped at goal continually, Jenkins getting two including one from the touchline. Near the end Sloan clinched things with a run down the wing but he only got his try by touching down amongst the spectators who were sitting packed in the Welsh goal area.

This was not the end of a hectic day for the Scottish XV who had to grab their clothes, rush into their bus, and catch their train where they washed and changed.

IRELAND   Lansdowne Road   26 February 1921

SCOTLAND: 1 goal, 1 try   8   **Loss**

IRELAND: 3 tries   9

Scotland: H.H. Forsayth (*Oxford Univ.*); J.W.S. McCrow (*Edin. Acads.*), A.L. Gracie (*Harlequins*), A.T. Sloan (*Edin. Acads.*), J.H. Carmichael (*Watsonians*); R.L.H. Donald (*Glas. HSFP*), J. Hume* (*RHSFP*); J.M. Bannerman (*Glas. HSFP*), J.C.R. Buchanan (*Stewart's FP*), R.A. Gallie (*Glas. Acads.*), J.B. McDougall (*Wakefield*), G.H.H.P. Maxwell (*London Scot.*), G.M. Murray (*Glas. Acads.*), J.N. Shaw (*Edin. Acads.*), J.L. Stewart (*Edin. Acads.*)

Ireland: W.E. Crawford (*Lansdowne*); H.S.T. Cormac (*Clontarf*), G.V. Stephenson (*QU Belfast*), A.R. Foster (*Derry*), D.J. Cussen (*Dublin Univ.*); W. Cunningham (*Lansdowne*), T. Mayne (*NIFC*); J.J. Bermingham (*Blackrock*), W.P. Collopy (*Bective Rangers*), A.W. Courtney (*UC Dublin*), W.D. Doherty* (*Camb. Univ.*), C.F.G.T. Hallaran (*RN*), T.A. McClelland (*QU Belfast*), N.M. Purcell (*Lansdowne*), P. Stokes (*Blackrock*)

  Referee: J. Baxter (*England*)

J. Hume scored and Maxwell converted (5–0); D.J. Cussen scored but Crawford failed (5–3); A.T. Sloan scored but Maxwell failed (8–3). (H.T.). G.V. Stephenson scored but Crawford failed (8–6); W. Cunningham scored but Hallaran failed (8–9).

Scotland were beaten forward although the Irish pack was described as robust rather than brilliant. However the Irish backs were poor finishers and faced by some good tackling. Sloan was crippled early on and Scotland were rather fortunate to lead at half time.

ENGLAND   Inverleith   19 March 1921

SCOTLAND: Nil   0   **Loss**

ENGLAND: 3 goals, 1 try.   18

Scotland: H.H. Forsayth (*Oxford Univ.*); A.T. Sloan (*Edin. Acads.*), A.E. Thomson (*Un. Services*), C.J.G. Mackenzie (*Un. Services*), A.L. Gracie (*Harlequins*); R.H.L. Donald (*Glas. HSFP*), J. Hume* (*RHSFP*); J.M. Bannerman (*Glas. HSFP*), J.C.R. Buchanan (*Stewart's FP*), R.A. Gallie (*Glas. Acads.*), F. Kennedy (*Stewart's FP*), J.B. McDougall (*Wakefield*), N. Macpherson (*Newport*), G.H.H.P. Maxwell (*London Scot.*), C.M. Usher (*Edin. Wrs.*)

England: B.S. Cumberlege (*Blackheath*); C.N. Lowe (*Blackheath*), E.D.G. Hammett (*Newport*), A.M. Smallwood (*Leicester*), Q.E.M.A. King (*Army*); W.J.A. Davies* (*Un. Services*); C.A. Kershaw (*Un. Services*); A.F. Blakiston (*Northampton*), L.G. Brown (*Blackheath*), R. Cove-Smith (*Camb. Univ.*), R. Edwards (*Newport*), E.R. Gardner (*RN*), A.T. Voyce (*Gloucester*), W.W. Wakefield (*Harlequins: RAF*), T. Woods (*Devonport Services*)

E.R. Gardner scored but B.S. Cumberlege failed (0–3); T. Woods scored and Hammett converted (0–8). (H.T.). L.G. Brown and Q.E.M.A. King scored for Hammett to convert both (0–18).

The placing of Gracie on the wing was a mistake especially as his centre had a terrible day of mishandling. There was fairly even play for half an hour but the ability of the entire English XV to develop play from Scottish mistakes won the match. The open play and handling of their pack was quite outstanding. Brown's try is often recalled: Davies dropped at goal and the ball rebounded off a post to Brown who instinctively caught it and scored. It was said that he was so far offside that he admitted feeling embarrassed at getting the decision.

FRANCE	Colombes	2 January 1922

SCOTLAND:	1 try	3	**Draw**
FRANCE:	1 try	3	

Scotland: W.C. Johnston (*Glas. HSFP*); A. Browning (*Glas. HSFP*), G.P.S. Macpherson (*Oxford Univ.*), A.L. Gracie (*Harlequins*), E.H. Liddell (*Edin. Univ.*); J.C. Dykes (*Glas. Acads.*), J. Hume (*RHSFP*); A. Wemyss (*Edin. Wrs.*), D.M. Bertram (*Watsonians*), A.K. Stevenson (*Glas. Acads.*), D.S. Davies (*Hawick*), J.M. Bannerman (*Glas. HSFP*), J.R. Lawrie (*Melrose*), C.M. Usher* (*Edin. Wrs.*), G.H.H.P. Maxwell (*London Scot.*)

France: J. Clement (*Valence*); A. Jaureguy (*Toulouse*), F. Borde (*Toulouse*), R. Crabos* (*St Severs*), R. Got (*Perpignan*); J. Pascot (*Perpignan*), R. Piteu (*Pau*); R. Lasserre (*Cognac*), J. Sebedio (*Carcassone*), F. Cahuc (*St Girons*), P. Moureu (*Beziers*), A. Cassayet (*St Gaudens*), M. Biraben (*Dax*), P. Pons (*Toulouse*), G. Lubin-Lebrere (*Toulouse*)

Referee: H.C. Harrison (*England*)   **Touch judges:** J.M. Dykes, C.F. Rutherford

A. Jaureguy scored but Crabos failed: (0–3); A. Browning scored but Maxwell failed (3–3). (H.T.).

The ground was soft after some heavy rain but the dismal conditions did not keep away a record crowd of 37,000. The game was fairly even up to half-time; then rain fell continually so that handling became very difficult. The Scottish pack dominated the second half but no score came from many near things, the French defence being desperate but successful.

WALES	Inverleith	4 February 1922

SCOTLAND:	1 penalty goal, 2 tries.	9	**Draw**
WALES:	1 goal, 1 drop goal	9	

139

Scotland: H.H. Forsayth (*Oxford Univ.*); A. Browning (*Glas. HSFP*), R.C. Warren (*Glas. Acads.*), A.L. Gracie (*Harlequins*), E.H. Liddell (*Edin. Univ.*); G.P.S. Macpherson (*Oxford Univ.*), W.E. Bryce (*Selkirk*); A. Wemyss (*Edin. Wrs.*), D.M. Bertram (*Watsonians*), W.G. Dobson (*Heriot's FP*), D.S. Davies (*Hawick*), J.M. Bannerman (*Glas. HSFP*), J.R. Lawrie (*Melrose*), C.M. Usher* (*Edin. Wrs.*), J.C.R. Buchanan (*Stewart's FP*)

Wales: F. Samuel (*Mountain Ash*); F. Palmer (*Swansea*), I. Evans (*Swansea*), B.E. Evans (*Llanelli*), C. Richards (*Pontypool*); W. Bowen (*Swansea*), W.J. Delahay (*Bridgend*); T. Parker* (*Swansea*), J. Whitfield (*Newport*), S. Morris (*Cross Keys*), D.D. Hiddlestone (*Neath*), T. Roberts (*Risca*), J.G. Stephens (*Llanelli*), W. Cummings (*Treorchy*), T. Jones (*Newport*)

Referee: R.A. Lloyd (*England*) **Touch judges:** J.M. Dykes, W.W. James

There was no scoring at half time. W. Bowen scored and Samuel converted (0–6); A. Browning scored but Bertram failed (3–5); A. Browning kicked a penalty and scored a try which he did not convert (9–6); I. Evans dropped a goal (9–9).

The Scottish forwards played well but their backs did not make good use of a plentiful supply of the ball. Bryce had a fine game making several good breaks one of which gave Browning his first try. The winger also had a good game, scoring all the points. The opening score came when Forsayth, catching a high kick under the posts, had his kick charged down by Bowen who ran on to drop on the rebound. Evans' equaliser came in the last minute and a very disappointed crowd left in stunned silence.

IRELAND Inverleith 25 February 1922

SCOTLAND:	2 tries	6	**Win**
IRELAND:	1 try	3	

Scotland: H.H. Forsayth (*Oxford Univ.*); A. Browning (*Glas. HSFP*), R.C. Warren (*Glas. Acads.*), A.L. Gracie (*Harlequins*), E.H. Liddell (*Edin. Univ.*); G.P.S. Macpherson (*Oxford Univ.*), W.E. Bryce (*Selkirk*); A. Wemyss (*Edin. Wrs.*), D.M. Bertram (*Watsonians*), W.G. Dobson (*Heriot's FP*), D.S. Davies (*Hawick*), J.M. Bannerman (*Glas. HSFP*), J.R. Lawrie (*Melrose*), C.M. Usher* (*Edin. Wrs.*), J.C.R. Buchanan (*Stewart's FP*)

Ireland: W.E. Crawford (*Lansdowne*); H.W.V. Stephenson (*Un. Services*), G.V. Stephenson (*QU Belfast*), D.B. Sullivan (*UC Dublin*), T.G. Wallis (*Wanderers*); J.R. Wheeler (*QU Belfast*), J.B. Clarke (*Bective Rangers*); W.P. Collopy* (*Bective Rangers*), M.J. Bradley (*Dolphin*), I. Popham (*Cork Const.*), F.G.T. Hallaran (*Un. Services*), S. McVicker (*QU Belfast*), R.H. Owens (*Dublin Univ.*), J.K.S. Thompson (*Dublin Univ.*), J.D. Egan (*Bective Rangers*)

Referee: T.D. Schofield (*Wales*) **Touch judges:** J.M. Dykes, R.M. Mcgrath

J.A. Clarke scored but Wallis failed (0–3).(H.T.). W.E. Bryce and E.H. Liddell scored but Browning failed to convert (6–3).

A strong wind made handling difficult and play often surged from end to end. The Scottish pack, held in the first half, finished strongly to give Bryce, who had another good game, and the backs the chances they needed for the Irish defence was fast and effective. G.P.S. Macpherson did not please the critics as a stand-off half.

ENGLAND   Twickenham   18 March 1922

SCOTLAND: 1 goal   5   **Loss**

ENGLAND: 1 goal, 2 tries   11

Scotland: H.H. Forsayth (*Oxford Univ.*); J.M. Tolmie (*Glas. HSFP*), A.L. Gracie (*Harlequins*), G.P.S. Macpherson (*Oxford Univ.*), E.B. Mackay (*Glas. Acads.*); J.C. Dykes (*Glas. Acads.*), W.E. Bryce (*Selkirk*); J.C.R. Buchanan (*Stewart's FP*), D.M. Bertram (*Watsonians*), W.G. Dobson (*Heriot's FP*), D.S. Davies (*Hawick*), J.M. Bannerman (*Glas. HSFP*), J.R. Lawrie (*Melrose*), C.M. Usher* (*London Scot.*), G.H.H.P. Maxwell (*Edin. Acads.*)

England: J.A. Middleton (*Richmond*); I.J. Pitman (*Oxford Univ.*), A.M. Smallwood (*Leicester*), E. Myers (*Headingley*), C.N. Lowe (*Camb. Univ.*); W.J.A. Davies* (*RN*), C.A. Kershaw (*RN*); W.W. Wakefield (*Harlequins*), G.S. Conway (*Camb. Univ.*), A.T. Voyce (*Gloucester*), R. Cove-Smith (*Camb. Univ.*), J.E. Maxwell-Hyslop (*Oxford Univ.*), R.F.H. Duncan (*Guy's*), H.L. Price (*Oxford Univ.*), P.B.R.W. Williams-Powlett (*RN*)

   Referee: R.A. Lloyd (*Ireland*)

J.C. Dykes scored and Bertram converted (5–0). (H.T.). C.N. Lowe scored twice and then W.J.A. Davies once; G.S. Conway converted the second only (5–11).

Another large crowd in fine weather saw the teams presented to HM King George V. Scotland had a good first half but England came away in the end. Again the English pack were splendid in the loose but it was a brilliant display by Davies which, in the second half, brought about their win. G.P.S. Macpherson often showed his skill as an attacker but the wingers were not fast enough to match their opponents.

FRANCE   Inverleith   20 January 1923

SCOTLAND: 2 goals, 2 tries   16   **Win**

FRANCE: 1 mark goal   3

Scotland: D. Drysdale (*Heriot's FP*); A.C. Wallace (*Oxford Univ.*), E. McLaren (*RHSFP*), A.L. Gracie* (*Harlequins*), E.H. Liddell (*Edin. Univ.*); S.B. McQueen (*Waterloo*), W.E. Bryce (*Selkirk*); D.S. Kerr (*Heriot's FP*), D.M. Bertram (*Watsonians*), A.K. Stevenson (*Glas. Acads.*), L.M. Stuart (*Glas. HSFP*), J.M. Bannerman (*Glas. HSFP*), J.R. Lawrie (*Melrose*), D.S. Davies (*Hawick*), J.C.R. Buchanan (*Stewart's FP*)

France: J. Clement (*Valence*); M. Lalande (*RCF*), R. Crabos* (*St Sever*), F. Bordes

141

(*Toulouse*), A. Jaureguy (*Toulouse*); J. Pascot (*Toulon*), C. Dupont (*Lourdes*); A. Bernon (*Lourdes*), J. Bayard (*Toulouse*), L. Beguet (*RCF*), P. Moureu (*Beziers*), A. Casseyet (*St Gaudens*), J. Larrieu (*Tarbes*), J. Sebedio (*Carcassone*), A. Guichemerre (*Dax*)

Referee: T.H. Vile (*Wales*)   **Touch judges:** H.S. Dixon, C.F. Rutherford

E. McLaren scored and Drysdale converted (5–0). (H.T.). W.E. Bryce and E. McLaren scored and Drysdale converted the first (13–0); L. Beguet dropped a goal from a mark (13–3); E.H. Liddell scored but Drysdale failed (16–3).

The Scots were not really too impressive; rather that the French proved ineffective. Scotland opened strongly but continually wasted scoring situations and it took a solo dash by McLaren to score. However, against the wind in the second half their forwards kept up the pressure and the backs combined better for their three scores. France were handicapped by injuries to Pascot and Bordes.

WALES   Cardiff   3 February 1923

SCOTLAND: 1 goal, 2 tries   11   **Win**
WALES: 1 goal, 1 penalty goal   8

Scotland: D. Drysdale (*Heriot's FP*); A. Browning (*Glas. HSFP*), E. McLaren (*RHSFP*), A.L. Gracie* (*Harlequins*), E.H. Liddell (*Edin. Univ.*); S.B. McQueen (*Waterloo*), W.E. Bryce (*Selkirk*); D.S. Kerr (*Heriot's FP*), D.M. Bertram (*Watsonians*), A.K. Stevenson (*Glas. Acads.*), L.M. Stuart (*Glas. HSFP*), J.M. Bannerman (*Glas. HSFP*), J.R. Lawrie (*Melrose*), D.S. Davies (*Hawick*), J.C.R. Buchanan (*Stewart's FP*)

Wales: B.O. Male (*Cardiff*); W.R. Harding (*Camb. Univ.*), A. Jenkins (*Llanelli*), R.A. Cornish (*Cardiff*), T. Johnson (*Cardiff*); J.M.C. Lewis* (*Camb. Univ.*), W.J. Delahay (*Cardiff*); A. Baker (*Neath*), S. Morris (*Cross Keys*), D.G. Davies (*Cardiff*), T. Parker (*Swansea*), G. Michael (*Swansea*), G. Thomas (*Llanelli*), L. Jenkins (*Aberavon*), T. Roberts (*Newport*)

Referee: J.W. Baxter (*England*)

A. Jenkins kicked a penalty (0–3). (H.T.). E.H. Liddell scored but Browning failed (3–3); J.M.C. Lewis scored and Jenkins converted (3–8); L.M. Stuart scored but Browning failed (6–8); A.L. Gracie scored and D. Drysdale converted (11–8).

Although the police closed the gates before the start, a record crowd got in and lined the playing area. They were to witness a hard game which finished with one of the most famous tries in the history of the game. Wales failed to take their chances in the first half and only led by a penalty goal. Straightway Eric Liddell showed his pace by scoring a fine try only for Wales to increase their lead to 3–8 with a converted try. Then with fifteen minutes to go the Scottish pack put in a tremendous finish. Firstly L.M. Stuart scored after a fine forward rush. Then came two scoring attacks by the backs but Liddell and Gracie were both tackled short of the line. With three minutes to go the ball was heeled from a scrum on the 25; Bryce passed to McQueen who went to the left and seeing that McLaren was covered, threw a long pass over his head to Gracie. Now in his own words: 'Running slightly diagonally to the left to go between Arthur Cornish and 'Codger' Johnson I saw in a flash that the latter was in

142

two minds — whether to go for me or run between me and Liddell and prevent me passing to the latter . . . as I went on the way opened up for me and the tactics to be adopted were as plain as a pikestaff. Whether I dummied or not I do not remember but I was just able to swerve round my opposite number and in doing so saw I had Male on the wrong foot and all I had to do was to carry on over the line. But here I nearly spoilt everything. The dead ball line at Cardiff was desperately close to the goal line and in trying to touch down near the posts I recklessly ran along the dead ball line, only inches off it, till the close proximity of Cornish and Jenkins made me decide to drop on the ball.' It is recorded that he was so close to the dead ball line that a small boy, sitting there, was struck by Gracie's boot and lost some teeth. One can only add that the disappointed Welsh supporters swarmed onto the field and carried Gracie off the field shoulder high.

IRELAND   Lansdowne Road   24 February 1923

SCOTLAND:	2 goals, 1 try	13	**Win**
IRELAND:	1 try	3	

Scotland: D. Drysdale (*Heriot's FP*); A. Browning (*Glas. HSFP*), E. McLaren (*London Scot.*), A.L. Gracie* (*Harlequins*), E.H. Liddell (*Edin. Univ.*); S.B. McQueen (*Waterloo*), W.E. Bryce (*Selkirk*); N. Macpherson (*Newport*), D.M. Bertram (*Watsonians*), J.C.R. Buchanan (*Stewart's FP*), L.M. Stuart (*Glas. HSFP*), J.M. Bannerman (*Glas. HSFP*), J.R. Lawrie (*Melrose*), D.S. Davies (*Hawick*), R.S. Simpson (*Glas. Acads.*).

Ireland: W.E. Crawford (*Lansdowne*); D.J. Cussen (*Dublin Univ.*), G.V. Stephenson (*Queen's*), J.B. Gardiner (*NIFC*), R.O. McClenahan (*Instonians*); W.H. Hall (*Instonians*), W. Cunningham (*Lansdowne*); M. Bradley (*Dolphin*), R. Collopy (*Bective Rangers*), W.P. Collopy (*Bective Rangers*), D.M. Cunningham (*NIFC*), P.E.F. Dunn (*Bective Rangers*), R.D. Gray (*Old Wesley*), T.A. McClelland (*Queen's*), J.K.S. Thompson* (*Dublin Univ.*)

   Referee: T.H. Vile (*Wales*)

D.J. Cusson scored (0–3); E.H. Liddell scored and Browning converted (5–3); A. Browning scored but failed to convert (8–3). (H.T.). S.B. McQueen scored and Browning converted (13–3).

In drizzling rain Ireland played a spoiling game and gave Gracie and McLaren little scope. Nevertheless the two wingers were successes, Liddell showing that he was not only very fast but determined. It was considered that McQueen, given a good supply of the ball from the scrums, did not vary his play enough. Drysdale was praised for his defence.

ENGLAND   Inverleith   17 March 1923

SCOTLAND:	2 tries	6	**Loss**
ENGLAND:	1 goal, 1 try	8	

Scotland: D. Drysdale (*Heriot's FP*); A. Browning (*Glas. HSFP*), E. McLaren (*London Scot.*), A.L. Gracie* (*Harlequins*), E.H. Liddell (*Edin. Univ.*); S.B. McQueen (*Waterloo*), W.E. Bryce (*Selkirk*); N. Macpherson (*Newport*), D.M. Bertram (*Watsonians*), A.K. Stevenson (*Glas. Acads.*), L.M. Stuart (*Glas. HSFP*), J.M. Bannerman (*Glas. HSFP*), J.R. Lawrie (*Melrose*), D.S. Davies (*Hawick*), J.C.R. Buchanan (*Stewart's FP*)

England: T.E. Holliday (*Aspatria*); C.N. Lowe (*Blackheath*), E. Myers (*Bradford*), H.M. Locke (*Birkenhead Park*), A.M. Smallwood (*Leicester*); W.J.A. Davies* (*Un. Services*), C.A. Kershaw (*Un. Services*); A.F. Blakiston (*Northampton*), G.S. Conway (*Rugby*), R. Cove-Smith (*OMT*), E.R. Gardner (*Devonport Services*), W.G.E. Luddington (*Devonport Services*), F.W. Sanders (*Plymouth Albion*), A.T. Voyce (*Gloucester*), W.W. Wakefield (*Camb. Univ.*)

Referee: T.H. Vile (*Wales*) **Touch judges:** H.S. Dixon, J. Baxter

A.M. Smallwood scored but W.G.E. Luddington failed (0–3); E. McLaren scored but A. Browning failed (3–3). (H.T.). A.L. Gracie scored but D. Drysdale failed (6–3); A.T. Voyce scored and W.G.E. Luddington converted (6–8).

The match was played in brilliant weather before a crowd of 30,000 which included the Duke of York. The teams were quite evenly matched but England were expert at seizing chances, their pack being very ready to run with the ball. Smallwood had a good solo try after beating the defenders and this was later matched when Gracie taking the ball on at his feet, kicked it past the full back and only his speed enabled him to fall on the ball just before it went over the dead ball line. The winning score came from an interception by Locke which was carried on by the forwards for Voyce to score.

FRANCE Stade Pershing 1 January 1924

SCOTLAND:	1 drop goal, 1 penalty goal, 1 try 10	**Loss**
FRANCE:	4 tries	12	

Scotland: D. Drysdale (*Heriot's FP*); A.C. Wallace (*Oxford Univ.*), A.L. Gracie (*Harlequins*), E. McLaren (*London Scot.*), C.E.W.C. Mackintosh (*London Scot.*); H. Waddell (*Glas. Acads.*), W.E. Bryce (*Selkirk*); D.S. Kerr (*Heriot's FP*), A. Ross (*Kilmarnock*), R.A. Howie (*Kirkcaldy*), L.M. Stuart (*Glas. HSFP*), J.M. Bannerman (*Glas. HSFP*), J.C.R. Buchanan* (*Stewart's FP*), D.S. Davies (*Hawick*), K.G.P. Hendrie (*Heriot's FP*)

France: E. Besset (*Grenoble*); A. Jaureguy (*SF*), A. Behoteguy (*Bayonne*), R. Crabos* (*St Sever*), L. Cluchague (*Biarritz*); H. Galau (*Toulouse*), C. Dupont (*Rouen*); L. Lepatey (*Mazamet*), A. Gonnet (*RCF*), L. Beguet (*RCF*), P. Moureu (*Beziers*), A. Cassayet (*St Gaudeas*), R. Lasserre (*Grenoble*), E. Piquaral (*RCF*), J. Etcheberry (*Cognac*)

Referee: E. Roberts (*Wales*) **Touch judges:** C.F. Rutherford

A. Jaureguy scored (0–3); A. Piquaral scored but Crabos failed (0–6); A.C. Wallace scored but Davies failed (3–6). (H.T.). D.S. Davies kicked a penalty (6–6); H. Waddell dropped a goal (10–6); H. Galau and P. Maureu scored unconverted tries (10–12).

The Colombes pitch was flooded by the Seine but C.F. Rutherford worked a major miracle

144

in transferring the match to the Stade Pershing in 36 hours. It was expected that the heavy conditions would suit the Scottish pack but in fact the French forwards thoroughly outplayed their opponents. The winning try in a scramble following a line out came in the last five minutes.

WALES	**Inverleith**	**2 February 1924**

SCOTLAND:	4 goals, 1 penalty goal, 4 tries	35	**Win**
WALES:	2 goals	10	

Scotland: D. Drysdale (*Heriot's FP*); I.S. Smith (*Oxford Univ.*), G.P.S. Macpherson (*Oxford Univ.*), G.G. Aitken (*Oxford Univ.*); A.C. Wallace (*Oxford Univ.*); H. Waddell (*Glas. Acads.*), W.E. Bryce (*Selkirk*); A. Ross (*Kilmarnock*), D.M. Bertram (*Watsonians*), R.A. Howie (*Kirkcaldy*), J.C.R. Buchanan* (*Stewart's FP; Exeter*), J.M. Bannerman (*Glas. HSFP*), J.R. Lawrie (*Leicester*), K.G.P. Hendrie (*Heriot's FP*), A.C. Gillies (*Watsonians*)

Wales: B.O. Male (*Cardiff*); H. Davies (*Newport*), M.A. Rosser (*Penarth*), J.E. Evans (*Llanelli*), T. Johnson (*Cardiff*); V.M. Griffiths (*Newport*), E. Watkins (*Neath*); J. Whitfield* (*Newport*), S. Morris (*Cross Keys*), J.I. Morris (*Swansea*), I. Jones (*Llanelli*), T. Jones (*Newport*), C. Pugh (*Maestig*), W.J. Ould (*Cardiff*), D.G. Francis (*Llanelli*)

Referee: J.B. McGowan (*Ireland*)   **Touch judges:** R.T. Neilson, I.D. Thomas

I.S. Smith scored and Drysdale converted (5–0); Drysdale kicked a penalty (8–0); W.E. Bryce scored and Drysdale converted (13–0); D.M. Bertram scored but Drysdale failed (16–0); I.S. Smith scored but Drysdale failed (19–0); A.C. Wallace scored but Drysdale failed (22–0). (H.T.). H. Waddell scored but Gillies failed (25–0); G.P.S. Macpherson scored and Drysdale converted (30–0); I.S. Smith scored and Drysdale converted (35–0); V. Griffiths and I. Jones scored for Male to convert both (35–10).

A.L. Gracie could not play so Scotland fielded the entire Oxford University backs and this combination proved too fast and clever for the Welshmen. I.S. Smith had a splendid day, showing up the opposition by his pace and power. The Scottish pack laid the foundation of the win, being on top in the scrum and loose play. The Welsh tries came during the last six minutes of the game when Scotland, leading 35–0, were easing up.

IRELAND	**Inverleith**	**23 February 1924**

SCOTLAND:	2 goals, 1 try	13	**Win**
IRELAND:	1 goal, 1 try	8	

Scotland: D. Drysdale (*Heriot's FP*); I.S. Smith (*Oxford Univ.*), G.G. Aitken (*Oxford Univ.*), J.C. Dykes (*Glas. Acads.*), R.K. Millar (*London Scot.*); H. Waddell (*Glas. Acads.*),

145

W.E. Bryce (*Selkirk*); R.G. Henderson (*Newcastle N*), D.M. Bertram (*Watsonians*), R.A. Howie (*Kirkcaldy*), J.C.R. Buchanan* (*Stewart's FP*), J.M. Bannerman (*Glas. HSFP*), J.R. Lawrie (*Leicester*), A.C. Gillies (*Watsonians*), K.G.P. Hendrie (*Heriot's FP*)

Ireland: W.J. Stewart (*QU Belfast*); H.W.V. Stephenson (*Un. Services*), G.V. Stephenson (*QU Belfast*), J.B. Gardiner (*NIFC*), A.C. Douglas (*Instonians*); W.H. Hall (*Instonians*), J.A.B. Clarke (*Bective Rangers*); J.D. Clinch (*Dublin Univ.*), W.P. Collopy* (*Bective Rangers*), R. Collopy (*Bective Rangers*), R.Y. Crichton (*Dublin Univ.*), C.F.G.T. Hallaran (*Un. Services*), T.A. McClelland (*QU Belfast*), J. McVicker (*Collegians*), I.M.B. Stuart (*Dublin Univ.*)

Referee: T.H. Vile (*Wales*) **Touch judges:** R.T. Neilson, H. Thrift

H. Waddell scored and D. Drysdale converted (5–0); D.M. Bertram scored and D. Drysdale converted (10–0); G.V. Stephenson scored and converted (10–5). (H.T.). G.V. Stephenson scored but failed to convert (10–8); H. Waddell scored but D. Drysdale failed (13–8).

This was essentially a robust forward game played mainly in the Scottish half. The Irish backs set out to play a spoiling game which nearly succeeded since two of the Scottish scores came from defensive blunders. For a while in the second half Ireland attacked, the two Stephensons combining well but the Scottish forwards were on top during the last vital quarter. J.D. Clinch was praised as were W.E. Bryce and H. Waddell. The Scottish team changes were puzzling, for R.K. Millar, usually a right wing, was placed on the left while J.C. Dykes and H. Waddell reversed their club positions.

ENGLAND Twickenham 15 March 1924

SCOTLAND: Nil 0 **Loss**

ENGLAND: 3 goals, 1 drop goal 19

Scotland: D. Drysdale (*Heriot's FP*); I.S. Smith (*Oxford Univ.*), G.P.S. Macpherson (*Oxford Univ.*), G.G. Aitken (*Oxford Univ.*), A.C. Wallace (*Oxford Univ.*); H. Waddell (*Glas. Acads.*), W.E. Bryce (*Selkirk*); D.S. Davies (*Hawick*), D.M. Bertram (*Watsonians*), R.A. Howie (*Kirkcaldy*), R.G. Henderson (*Newcastle N*), J.M. Bannerman (*Glas. HSFP*), J.R. Lawrie (*Leicester*), A.C. Gillies (*Watsonians*), J.C.R. Buchanan* (*Stewart's FP*)

England: B.S. Chantrill (*Bristol*); H.C. Catcheside (*Percy Park*), L.J. Corbett (*Bristol*), H.M. Locke (*Birkenhead Park*), H.P. Jacobs (*Oxford Univ.*); E. Myers (*Bradford*), A.T. Young (*Camb. Univ.*); A.F. Blakiston (*Liverpool*), C.S. Conway (*Rugby*), R. Cove-Smith (*OMT*), R. Edwards (*Newport*), W.G.E. Luddington (*Devonport Services*), A. Robson (*Newcastle N*), A.T. Voyce (*Gloucester*), W.W. Wakefield* (*Leicester*)

Referee: T.H. Vile (*Wales*)

W.W. Wakefield scored and C.S. Conway converted (0–5). (H.T.). E. Myers dropped a goal and scored for C.S. Conway to convert (0–14); H.C. Catcheside scored and C.S. Conway converted (0–19).

146

England started very strongly but Scotland eventually rallied and would have scored but for good final tackling. Near half time a fine combined run by the English backs finished with a cross kick which bounced awkwardly to give Wakefield possession and a try between the posts. From the restart Scotland attacked and again came near to scoring. Then came a burst of scoring from Myers who dropped a good goal and scored a fine solo dodging try. The last score came by another solo effort by Catcheside who picked up a fumbled pass in his own half and after rounding Drysdale and handing Wallace off twice, scored a great try. England were the more resourceful but Scotland had chances enough to have scored several times and some praise must go to Chantrill who three times reached Smith in full flight and put in try-saving tackles.

Murrayfield

We have already noted that the Union, in 1913, seeking space for junior clubs, had considered asking for a lease of the Polo Ground at Murrayfield. The Edinburgh Polo Club had occupied the area since 1888 and during the early 1900s had leased their field and pavilion to various pioneer hockey clubs, notably the Edinburgh (later Edinburgh Northern) Hockey Club, and this may have been a reason why the approach was not followed up.

After World War I a similar request to the Union in 1920 was met by their renting the Corstorphine ground (just vacated by the Royal High School PP and FP Clubs who had moved to Jock's Lodge) but a year later this lease was terminated when the town acquired the ground.

The Union, however, had its own ground worries for it had already become clear that Inverleith could not, without considerable expense, be expanded to handle the larger crowds now attending the International games. So in 1922 it announced the purchase of the Polo ground at Murrayfield and later issued debentures to finance this purchase and the cost of the stand, embankments and other buildings.

There was some discussion with the town over the placing of a new road running past the ground but the work went on well and everything was ready by the end of the 1924–25 season. The French match of 1925 was the last to be played at Inverleith and since it and the Welsh and Irish games were all won it was an interested and expectant crowd that came to watch the Calcutta Cup match chosen to open the field.

Now by 1914 the greatest attendances at Inverleith had reached some 25,000 and this had risen to 30,000 at the English game of 1923 but the Union were really caught out when over 70,000 came to see this opening game. Looking ahead we may note that this figure was reached at several later English and Welsh matches, but a real crisis came at the 1975 Welsh game when over 104,000 got into the ground with several thousands locked out. As a result further matches were made 'all ticket' with a stated maximum attendance.

In 1936 the addition of the two end extensions to the stand more than doubled the seating capacity to over 15,000 and about the same time a committee box was added with access to improved committee rooms inside.

Two ex-Presidents in Sir David Gowan and J. Aikman Smith

presented the Clock Tower (1929) and the original score board (1930) while Sheriff Watt K.C. presented a flag staff and flag (1931), but the most startling improvement followed the gift by Dr C.A. Hepburn in 1959 of the undersoil heating system which has ensured that the pitch has remained playable in spite of frost or snow.

FRANCE	**Inverleith**	**24 January 1925**

SCOTLAND:	2 goals, 5 tries	25	**Win**
FRANCE:	1 drop goal	4	

Scotland: D. Drysdale (*Heriot's FP*); I.S. Smith (*Oxford Univ.*), G.P.S. Macpherson* (*Oxford Univ.*), G.G. Aitken (*Oxford Univ.*), A.C. Wallace (*Oxford Univ.*); J.C. Dykes (*Glas. Acads.*), J.B. Nelson (*Glas. Acads.*); J.C.R. Buchanan (*Exeter*), J. Gilchrist (*Glas. Acads.*), W.H. Stevenson (*Glas. Acads.*), D.J. MacMyn (*Camb. Univ.*), J.M. Bannerman (*Glas. HSFP*), J.W. Scott (*Stewart's FP*), A.C. Gillies (*Carlisle*), J.R. Paterson (*Birkenhead Park*)

France: J. Ducousso (*Tarbes*); F. Raymond (*Toulouse*), J. Ballari (*Toulouse*), M. Baillette (*Perpignan*), J. Halet (*Strasbourg*); Y. du Manoir (*RCF*), C. Dupont (*Havre*); A. Montade (*Perpignan*), C. Marcet (*Albi*), A. Maury (*Toulouse*), A. Cassayet (*Narbonne*), A. Laurent (*Biarritz*), A. Biousa (*Toulouse*), J. Boubee* (*Agen*), E. Ribere (*Perpignan*)

Referee: Dr E. De Courcy Wheeler (*Ireland*)   **Touch judges:** Sir Robert C. Mackenzie, C.F. Rutherford

A.G. Gillies scored and converted (5–0); Y. du Manoir dropped a goal (5–4). (H.T.). A.C. Wallace scored but Gillies failed (8–4); I.S. Smith scored and Drysdale converted (13–4); A.C. Wallace scored but Drysdale failed (16–4); I.S. Smith scored thrice; Dykes failed with the first and Gillies with the other two (25–4).

20,000 turned out to watch the last International to be played at Inverleith, a game marked by a partial eclipse of the sun which reached its maximum during the second half without interrupting play. In spite of the score the critics were unhappy with the display of the Scottish pack which did not dominate play. I.S. Smith, with four tries, and J.B. Nelson both had good games while G.P.S. Macpherson had a hand in practically every score. Y. du Manoir's goal was a really fine one from well out. The French team was numbered and frequently packed down 3–4 with Bioussa acting as a rover and even putting the ball into the scrum. The story goes that at the dinner a Frenchman asked I.S. Smith what his time was over 100 yards, and not quite catching the question, he replied 'four' — an answer which fairly astounded the enquirer.

WALES   **Swansea**   **7 February 1925**

SCOTLAND: 1 goal, 1 drop goal, 5 tries   24   **Win**

WALES: 1 goal, 1 penalty goal, 2 tries   14

Scotland: D. Drysdale (*Heriot's FP*); I.S. Smith (*Oxford Univ.*), G.P.S. Macpherson* (*Oxford Univ.*), G.G. Aitken (*Oxford Univ.*), A.C. Wallace (*Oxford Univ.*); J.C. Dykes (*Glas. Acads.*), J.B. Nelson (*Glas. Acads.*); D.S. Davies (*Hawick*), J.C.H. Ireland (*Glas. HSFP*), R.A. Howie (*Kirkcaldy*), D.J. MacMyn (*Camb. Univ.*), J.M. Bannerman (*Glas. HSFP*), J.W. Scott (*Stewart's FP*), A.C. Gillies (*Carlisle*), J.R. Paterson (*Birkenhead Park*)

Wales: T. Johnson (*Cardiff*); C. Thomas (*Bridgend*), E. Williams (*Aberavon*), R.A. Cornish (*Cardiff*), W.P. James (*Aberavon*); W.J. Hopkins (*Aberavon*), W.J. Delahay (*Cardiff*); C. Pugh (*Maesteg*), S. Morris* (*Cross Keys*), B. Phillips (*Aberavon*), S. Herrara (*Cross Keys*), W.I. Jones (*Llanelli*), D. Parker (*Swansea*), I. Richards (*Cardiff*), S. Lawrence (*Bridgend*)

Referee: J. Baxter (*England*)   **Touch judges:** Sir Robert C. Mackenzie, R.P. Thomas

I.S. Smith scored thrice and Drysdale converted the first only (11–0); D. Drysdale dropped a goal (15–0); A.C. Wallace scored but Gillies failed (18–0). (H.T.). A.C. Wallace scored but Gillies failed (21–0); W.J. Hopkins scored and Parker converted (21–5); I.S. Smith scored but Gillies failed (24–5); I. Jones and R.A. Cornish scored but Parker failed each time (24–11); D. Parker kicked a penalty (24–14).

In the first half the speed and skill of the Scottish backs were quite devastating and once again I.S. Smith scored four tries. However during the last fifteen minutes the Welsh pack lifted its game to put in a storming finish. On occasions in the first half Pugh came out of the pack to help in defence. The Welsh team was numbered.

IRELAND   **Lansdowne Road**   **28 February 1925**

SCOTLAND: 2 goals, 1 drop goal   14   **Win**

IRELAND: 1 goal, 1 penalty goal   8

Scotland: D. Drysdale* (*Heriot's FP*); I.S. Smith (*Oxford Univ.*), J.C. Dykes (*Glas. Acads.*), G.G. Aitken (*Oxford Univ.*), A.C. Wallace (*Oxford Univ.*); H. Waddell (*Glas. Acads.*), J.B. Nelson (*Glas. Acads.*); D.S. Davies (*Hawick*), J.C.H. Ireland (*Glas. HSFP*), R.A. Howie (*Kirkcaldy*), D.J. MacMyn (*Camb. Univ.*), J.M. Bannerman (*Glas. HSFP*), J.W. Scott (*Stewart's FP*), J.C.R. Buchanan (*Exeter*), J.R. Paterson (*Birkenhead Park*)

Ireland: W.E. Crawford* (*Lansdowne*); H.W.V. Stephenson (*Un. Services*), G.V. Stephenson (*QU Belfast*), J.B. Gardiner (*NIFC*), T.R. Hewitt (*QU Belfast*); F.S. Hewitt (*Instonians*), M. Sugden (*Dublin Univ.*); G.R. Beamish (*Leicester; RAF*), W.F. Browne (*Un. Services*), J.D. Clinch (*Dublin Univ.*), W.R.F. Collis (*Wanderers*), R. Collopy (*Bective Rangers*), R.Y. Crichton (*Dublin Univ.*), J. McVicker (*Collegians*), M.J. Bradley (*Dolphin*)

150

Referee: A.E. Freethy (*Wales*)

A.C. Wallace scored and Drysdale converted (5–0). (H.T.). W.E. Crawford kicked a penalty (5–3); D.J. MacMyn scored and Dykes converted (10–3); H.W.V. Stephenson scored and Crawford converted (10–8); H. Waddell dropped a goal.

As against Wales the speed and handling of the Scottish backs was splendid. The absence of Macpherson had much to do with the comparative quietness of I.S. Smith but the return of Waddell outside to Nelson compensated for this. The second Scottish score was the result of great handling which started in midfield. The ball went from Nelson, Waddell, Dykes, Aitken to Wallace who after a 30-yard run passed the ball back to Dykes and thence via Scott to MacMyn who scored under the posts. The Irish try came from a dodge by H.W.V. Stephenson. Inside the Scottish half he flung the ball in from touch, caught the throw himself and sprinted to score in the corner before a surprised defence could tackle him. As a result of this the touch law was later altered. Ireland was handicapped by an injury to T. Hewitt and W.F. Browne came out of the pack to help the defence.

ENGLAND Murrayfield 21 March 1925

SCOTLAND: 2 goals, 1 drop goal 14 **Win**
ENGLAND: 1 goal, 1 penalty goal, 1 try 11

Scotland: D. Drysdale (*Heriot's FP*); I.S. Smith (*Oxford Univ.*), G.P.S. Macpherson* (*Oxford Univ.*), G.G. Aitken (*Oxford Univ.*), A.C. Wallace (*Oxford Univ.*); H. Waddell (*Glas. Acads.*), J.B. Nelson (*Glas. Acads.*); D.S. Davies (*Hawick*), J.C.H. Ireland (*Glas. HSFP*), R.A. Howie (*Kirkcaldy*), D.J. MacMyn (*London Scot.*), J.M. Bannerman (*Glas. HSFP*), J.W. Scott (*Stewart's FP*), A.C. Gillies (*Carlisle*), J.R. Paterson (*Birkenhead Park*)

England: T.E. Holliday (*Aspatria*); R.H. Hamilton-Wickes (*Harlequins*), L.J. Corbett (*Bristol*), H.M. Locke (*Birkenhead Park*), A.M. Smallwood (*Leicester*); E. Myers (*Bradford*), E.J. Massey (*Leicester*); D.C. Cumming (*Camb. Univ.*), R.R.F. MacLennan (*OMT*), W.G.E. Luddington (*RN*), J.S. Tucker (*Bristol*), A.F. Blakiston (*Liverpool*), A.T. Voyce (*Gloucester*), R. Cove-Smith (*OMT*), W.W. Wakefield* (*Harlequins*)

Referee: A.E. Freethy (*Wales*) **Touch judges:** R. Welsh, G.C. Robinson.

W.G.E. Luddington kicked a penalty goal (0–3); J.B. Nelson scored and Drysdale converted (5–3); R.H. Hamilton-Wickes scored and Luddington converted (5–8). (H.T.). W.W. Wakefield scored but Luddington failed (5–11); A.C. Wallace scored and Gillies converted (10–11); H. Waddell dropped a goal (14–11).

Beautiful weather for the opening of the new ground at Murrayfield brought out a record crowd of at least 70,000 who watched one of the most exciting matches ever played. The lead changed hands thrice and England's great fight to save the game during the last minutes only failed because of some tremendous tackling by the Scots and the utter exhaustion of the attackers.

W.G.E. Luddington had opened the scoring with an early penalty shortly before G.P.S. Macpherson, with a typical dummy and side step, broke through and the ball passed via H. Waddell to J.B. Nelson, who, fending off a tackler with a killing hand-off, scored under the posts. D. Drysdale's conversion put Scotland into the lead but just before half-time

England went ahead when R.H. Hamilton scored after a fine interpassing run with A.T. Voyce.

Shortly after the restart Corbett had a good run, finishing with a cross-kick which H. Waddell, on his line, could not hold and W.W. Wakefield seized the ball to score. W.G.E. Luddington, when about to take the conversion, was startled to find D.J. MacMyn rush out and kick the ball away from the mark — a move accepted by the referee. (Younger readers may be reminded that, at this period, the ball, just before a conversion attempt, was held clear of the ground by a placer. When he put the ball down in the mark for the kick, the defenders were allowed to charge.)

There followed an excellent try in the right-hand corner by A.C. Wallace and a magnificent conversion from the touch-line by A.C. Gillies brought the score to 10–11. At this point I must challenge several statements made about this try in the Calcutta Cup match programme of 1979. Therein it is stated that 'Wakefield and Voyce tackled Ian Smith into touch near the line . . . that Smith never got anywhere near the line . . . the touch judge was usually the local president, or something, and he was hardly ever within twenty yards . . . a photograph . . . shows Smith, clearly in touch, still on his feet, with Voyce and Wakefield tackling him and the line nowhere near'.

There is, of course, no doubt that the scorer was Johnny Wallace. He had been given an overlap inside the 25 and sprinted for the corner where he dived under Holliday's tackle to touch down just over the line. The photograph on page xi shows that the corner flag was still upright and the next nearest Englishman still some two yards away. The nearest Scot, G.P.S. Macpherson, was following up in support about five yards away, ready for a possible inside pass and I know that he had no doubts about the try. The touch judge concerned was Robin Welsh, the then Vice President of the SRU, a man whose integrity is beyond question. He was, in 1925, a very active and high grade tennis player and may be seen running five yards back, ideally placed to give a decision on a touch line matter. Later in the evening, when questioned about the score by the late Dr A.C. Gillies, he was quite adamant that the try was good, a point that he made when the referee checked with him at the time.

Scotland now attacked for the next twenty minutes and several times came near to scoring. A.C. Wallace was halted by a forward pass; J.W. Scott beat the full back only to be felled by A.M. Smallwood cutting across in defence; G.G. Aitken dribbled through only to have the ball rebound wide off a goal post and H. Waddell narrowly missed with a drop goal. Then J.B. Nelson gave H. Waddell a clear pass which let him drop a goal from the 25.

With five minutes left England made desperate efforts to score. A.M. Smallwood broke away but was floored by D. Drysdale; E. Myers was halted on the line by sheer numbers and finally L.J. Corbett broke through only to stumble and fall through sheer exhaustion about a yard short of the line. In the maul that followed the spectators were much incensed at the very unnecessary kick which badly stunned D. Drysdale. There remained a final thrill for Holliday, with practically the last kick of the match, narrowly missed with a very long range drop kick.

It was noted that when the final whistle went, this final desperate burst by England had so exhausted some of their players that they literally staggered off the field.

FRANCE	Colombes	2 January 1926

SCOTLAND:	1 goal, 1 penalty goal, 4 tries	20	**Win**
FRANCE;	1 penalty goal, 1 try		

Scotland: D. Drysdale (*Oxford Univ.*); I.S. Smith (*Edin. Univ.*), R.M. Kinnear (*Heriot's FP*), J.C. Dykes (*Glas. Acads.*), A.C. Wallace (*Oxford Univ.*); H. Waddell (*Glas. Acads.*),

J.B. Nelson (*Glas. Acads.*); D.S. Davies (*Hawick*), J.C.H. Ireland (*Glas. HSFP*), W.V. Berkley (*Oxford Univ.*), D.J. MacMyn (*London Scot.*), J.M. Bannerman (*Glas. HSFP*), J.W. Scott (*Stewart's FP*), A.C. Gillies (*Watsonians*), J.R. Paterson (*Birkenhead Park*)

France: L. Destarac (*Tarbes*); M. Besson (*CASG*), C. Magnanou (*Bayonne*), M. Chapuy (*SF*), A. Jaureguy (*SF*); Y. du Manoir (*RCF*), R. Llary (*Carcassone*); J. Etcheberry (*Vienne*), A. Gonnet (*RCF*), A. Maury (*Toulouse*), A. Puig (*Perpignan*), A. Cassayet* (*Narbonne*), E. Ribere (*Perpignan*), E. Piquiral (*RCF*), A. Bioussa (*Toulouse*)

Referee: W.M. Llewellyn (*Wales*) **Touch judge:** R. Welsh

A.C. Gillies kicked a penalty (3–0); A.C. Wallace scored twice but Gillies failed to convert (9–0). (H.T.). D.J. MacMyn scored but Gillies failed (12–0); A.C. Wallace scored but Gillies failed (15–0); A. Gonnet kicked a penalty (15–3); E. Piquiral scored but Gonnet failed (15–6); J.M. Bannerman scored and Drysdale converted (20–6).

The ground was heavy after rain and this suited the Scottish pack who really controlled the game. This was Wallace's last game. He had just graduated in Law and left for Australia after the match. Ribere and Bioussa were both hurt and off for some time in the second half. Bioussa again acted as scrum half to a three-four scrum. A French report tells that the ball often fell into the water-logged ditch around the pitch and that the groundsman had to recover it with a butterfly net — 'Il faut bien rire un peu'.

WALES   Murrayfield   6 February 1926

SCOTLAND:	1 goal, 1 penalty goal	8	**Win**
WALES:	1 goal	5	

Scotland: D. Drysdale* (*Oxford Univ.*); I.S. Smith (*Edin. Univ.*), R.M. Kinnear (*Heriot's FP*), J.C. Dykes (*Glas. Acads.*), W.M. Simmers (*Glas. Acads.*); H. Waddell (*Glas. Acads.*), J.B. Nelson (*Glas. Acads.*); D.S. Davies (*Hawick*), J.C.H. Ireland (*Glas. HSFP*), G.M. Murray (*Glas. Acads.*), D.J. MacMyn (*London Scot.*), J.M. Bannerman (*Glas. HSFP*), J.W. Scott (*Stewart's FP*), A.C. Gillies (*Watsonians*), J.R. Paterson (*Birkenhead Park*)

Wales: W.A. Everson (*Newport*); G.E. Andrews (*Newport*), A.R. Stock (*Newport*), R.A. Cornish* (*Cardiff*), W.C. Powell (*London Welsh*); R. Jones (*Northampton*), W.J. Delahay (*Cardiff*); D.M. Jenkins (*Treorchy*), J.H. John (*Swansea*), T. Hopkins (*Swansea*), S. Hinam (*Cardiff*), R.C. Herrera (*Crosskeys*), D.L Jones (*Newport*), S. Lawrence (*Bridgend*), E. Watkins (*Blaina*)

Referee: D. Hallewell (*England*) **Touch judges:** R. Welsh, E. Thomas

R.C. Herrera scored and Everson converted (0–5). (H.T.). A.C. Gillies kicked a penalty (3–5); H. Waddell scored and Drysdale converted (8–5).

The Welsh captain Rowe Harding called off late and W.C. Powell, a scrum half, took his place on the wing. He was given some credit in that I.S. Smith did not score but the Scottish backs had a thin afternoon being denied much of the ball by a very strong Welsh pack. Fortunately the Welsh backs made little of their chances. Their single score came from a good break by Delahay who was well backed up by his pack. The Scottish scores came within ten minutes of the restart. Gillies kicked a 30-yard penalty and then Waddell with a dummy and cut back went clean through the defence for a fine solo try. Thereafter some solid tackling kept the Welsh at bay.

IRELAND   Murrayfield   27 February 1926

SCOTLAND:	Nil	0	**Loss**
IRELAND:	1 try	3	

Scotland: D. Drysdale* (*Oxford Univ.*); I.S. Smith (*Edin. Univ.*), J.C. Dykes (*Glas. Acads.*), R.M. Kinnear (*Heriot's FP*), W.M. Simmers (*Glas. Acads.*); H. Waddell (*Glas. Acads.*), J.B. Nelson (*Glas. Acads.*); D.S. Davies (*Hawick*), J.C.H. Ireland (*Glas. HSFP*), D.S. Kerr (*Heriot's FP*), D.J. MacMyn (*London Scot.*), J.M. Bannerman (*Glas. HSFP*), J. Graham (*Kelso*), J.W. Scott (*Stewart's FP*), J.R. Paterson (*Birkenhead Park*)

Ireland: W.E. Crawford* (*Lansdowne*); D.J. Cussen (*Dublin Univ.*), G.V. Stephenson (*NIFC*), T.R. Hewitt (*QU Belfast*), J.H. Gage (*QU Belfast*); E.O. Davy (*Univ. Coll*), M. Sugden (*Dublin Univ.*); M.J. Bradley (*Dolphin*), W.F. Browne (*Army*), A.M. Buchanan (*Dublin Univ.*), S.J. Cagney (*London Irish*), J.D. Clinch (*Wanderers*), J.L. Farrell (*Bective Rangers*), C.J. Hanrahan (*Dolphin*), J. McVicker (*Collegians*)

Referee: B.S. Cumberlege (*England*)   **Touch judges:** R. Welsh, F. Strain

No scoring at half-time. J.H. Gage scored but Stephenson failed (0–3).

Heavy rain during the morning left the ground sodden and it cut up heavily during the game. It was a hard and evenly balanced match. Simmers touched down twice only to have the scores cancelled for previous infringements. Ten minutes before full time Waddell had to be carried off concussed so Paterson came out of the pack onto the wing. Then in injury time the Irish backs started a movement which finished with Gage getting in at the corner and the whistle went after the conversion kick. Both full backs tackled and kicked well under difficult conditions.

ENGLAND   Twickenham   20 March 1926

SCOTLAND:	2 goals, 1 drop goal, 1 try	17	**Win**
ENGLAND:	3 tries	9	

Scotland: D. Drysdale* (*Oxford Univ.*); I.S. Smith (*Edin. Univ.*), J.C. Dykes (*Glas. Acads.*), W.M. Simmers (*Glas. Acads.*), G.M. Boyd (*Glas. HSFP*); H. Waddell (*Glas. Acads.*), J.B. Nelson (*Glas. Acads.*); D.S. Davies (*Hawick*), J.C.H. Ireland (*Glas. HSFP*), D.S. Kerr (*Heriot's FP*), D.J. MacMyn (*London Scot.*), J.M. Bannerman (*Glas. HSFP*), J.W. Scott (*Stewart's FP*), J. Graham (*Kelso*), J.R. Paterson (*Birkenhead Park*)

England: T.E. Holliday (*Aspatria*); H.L.V. Day (*Leicester*), T.E.S. Francis (*Blackheath*), A.R. Aslett (*Army*), R.H. Hamilton-Wickes (*Harlequins*); H.J. Kittermaster (*Harlequins*), J.T. Young (*Army*); R. Webb (*Northampton*), H.G. Periton (*Waterloo*), R.J. Hanvey (*Aspatria*), C.K.T. Faithful (*Army*), E. Stanbury (*Plymouth Albion*), J.S. Tucker (*Bristol*), T.T. Voyce (*Gloucester*), W.W. Wakefield* (*Harlequins*)

Referee: W.H. Acton (*Ireland*)

J.C. Dykes dropped a goal (4–0); H. Waddell scored and converted (9–0); I.S. Smith scored and H. Waddell converted (14–0); A.T. Voyce scored but H.L.V. Day failed (14–3). (H.T.). J.S. Tucker scored but H.L.V. Day failed (14–6); I.S. Smith scored but D. Drysdale failed (17–6); E. Stanbury scored but T.E.S. Francis failed (17–9).

H.L.V. Day replaced Sir T.G. Devitt at the last minute and the wingers changed over. In dull and cold weather 50,000 people saw the teams presented to HM King George V. The English full back had a bad day for the Scottish tries were scored from errors forced on him by awkward kicks. I.S. Smith was prominent, his pace making two of the scores. The Scottish forwards, although outweighed played well as a pack, making several fine dribbling rushes and giving their backs the chances they needed. The English team was numbered but the Scots were not, in spite of a request for the change from the Rugby Union. Comments on this at the dinner nettled the SRU Officials. There is a story that the King had been encouraged to ask J. Aikman Smith about numbering and received the dour reply that 'This was a rugby match and not a cattle sale'. This was the first time England had been defeated by a Home Country at Twickenham since it was opened in 1910.

FRANCE **Murrayfield** **22 January 1927**

SCOTLAND:	4 goals, 1 penalty goal	23	**Win**
FRANCE:	2 tries	6	

Scotland: D. *Drysdale* (*Heriot's FP*); I.S. Smith (*Edin. Univ.*), G.P.S. Macpherson* (*Edin. Acads.*), J.C. Dykes (*Glas. Acads.*), W.M. Simmers (*Glas. Acads.*); H. Waddell (*Glas. Acads.*), J.B. Nelson (*Glas. Acads.*); D.S. Davies (*Hawick*), J.C.H. Ireland (*Glas. HSFP*), J.W. Allan (*Melrose*), J.M. Bannerman (*Glas. HSFP*), J.W. Scott (*Stewart's FP*), J. Graham (*Kelso*), A.C. Gillies (*Watsonians*), J.R. Paterson (*Birkenhead Park*)

France: M. Piquemal (*Tarbes*); R. Revillon (*CASG*), R. Graciet (*SBUC*), V. Graule (*Perpignan*), R. Houdet (*SF*); Y du Manoir* (*RCF*), E. Bader (*Primveres*); G.A. Gonnet (*RCF*), R. Hutin (*CASG*), J. Etcheberry (*Vienne*), R. Bousquet (*Albi*), A. Cassayet (*Narbonne*), A. Prevost (*Albi*), E. Ribere (*Quillan*), E. Piquiral (*Lyon*)

Referee: B.S. Cumberlege (*England*) **Touch judges:** J.M. Mackenzie, C.F. Rutherford

H. Waddell scored and A.C. Gillies converted (5–0); I.S. Smith scored and A.C. Gillies converted (10–0); H. Waddell scored and D. Drysdale converted (15–0); R. Hutin scored but G. Gonnet failed (15–3); I.S. Smith scored and A.C. Gillies converted (20–3). (H.T.). A.C. Gillies kicked a penalty (23–3); E. Piquiral scored but G. Gonnet failed (23–6).

The Scottish pack faded noticeably in the second half but the skill and pace of the backs in

155

the first half produced a winning total. I.S. Smith again used his pace to good effect whil
G.P.S. Macpherson produced many clever touches. The French XV was numbered.

WALES   Cardiff   5 February 192

SCOTLAND: 1 goal   5   Wi
WALES: Nil   0

Scotland: D. Drysdale (*Heriot's FP*); E.G. Taylor (*Oxford Univ.*), G.P.S. Macpherson
(*Edin. Acads.*), J.C. Dykes (*Glas. Acads.*), W.M. Simmers (*Glas. Acads.*); H. Wadde
(*Glas. Acads.*), J.B. Nelson (*Glas. Acads.*); D.S. Davies (*Hawick*), J.C.H. Ireland (*Gla*
HSFP), D.S. Kerr (*Heriot's FP*), J.W. Scott (*Stewart's FP*), J.M. Bannerman (*Glas*
HSFP), J. Graham (*Kelso*), A.C. Gillies (*Watsonians*), J.R. Paterson (*Birkenhead Park*

Wales: B.O. Male* (*Cardiff*); J.D. Bartlett (*Llandovery Coll.*), B.R. Turnbull (*Cardiff*), .
Roberts (*Cardiff*), W.R. Harding (*Camb. Univ.*); G. Richards (*Cardiff*), W.J. Delaha
(*Cardiff*); I. Jones (*Llanelli*), J.H. John (*Swansea*), T. Arthur (*Neath*), E.M. Jenkir
(*Aberavon*), T. Lewis (*Cardiff*), H. Phillips (*Newport*), W. Thomas (*Llanelli*), W. William
(*Crumlin*)

Referee: W.H. Jackson (*England*)   **Touch judges:** J. McGill, M. Moses

D.S. Kerr scored and A.C. Gillies converted (5–0). (H.T.).

40,000 spectators, including the Prince of Wales, watched a match played on a sodden pitc
which turned to a sea of mud and water. Wales looked more dangerous to begin with an
missed one chance to score. However the Scottish backs broke through repeatedly only
be kept out by some desperate last minute tackling. Shortly before the interval a high kic
was misfielded and in a fine forward rush Davies pushed a foot pass to Kerr who scoope
the ball up to score near the corner and Gillies converted the very difficult kick. In th
second half the Scottish forwards began to dictate the play with some fine rushes but Wale
were handicapped by an injury to T. Arthur.
  Windsor Lewis was the original choice at stand off and when he called off the Wels
selectors stood down W.C. Powell from scrum half so that the Cardiff pair could play. Th
Welsh team was numbered from one to sixteen, there being no number thirteen!

IRELAND   Lansdowne Road   26 February 192

SCOTLAND: Nil   0   Los
IRELAND: 2 tries   6

Scotland: D. Drysdale (*Heriot's FP*); I.S. Smith (*Edin. Univ.*), G.P.S. Macpherson
(*Edin. Acads.*), J.C. Dykes (*Glas. Acads.*), W.M. Simmers (*Glas. Acads.*); H. Wadde

156

Glas. Acads.), J.B. Nelson (*Glas. Acads.*); D.S. Davies (*Hawick*), J.C.H. Ireland (*Glas. SFP*), D.S. Kerr (*Heriot's FP*), J.W. Scott (*Stewart's FP*), J.M. Bannerman (*Glas. HSFP*), J. Graham (*Kelso*), A.C. Gillies (*Watsonians*), J.R. Paterson (*Birkenhead Park*)

Ireland: W.E. Crawford* (*Lansdowne*); J.B. Ganly (*Monkstown*), F.S. Hewitt (*Instonians*), G.V. Stephenson (*NIFC*), J.H. Gage (*QU Belfast*); E. Davy (*Lansdowne*), M. Sugden (*Wanderers*); A.M. Buchanan (*Dublin Univ.*), W.F. Browne (*Army*), T.O. Pike (*Lansdowne*), H. McVicker (*Richmond*), J.L. Farrell (*Bective Rangers*), J. McVicker (*Collegians*), C.T. Payne (*NIFC*), C.F. Hanrahan (*Dolphin*)

Referee: B.S. Cumberlege (*England*)

T.O. Pike and J.B. Ganly scored but G.V. Stephenson failed to convert (0–6). (H.T.).

The conditions were worse than those in the Welsh match for a continual fierce gale of wind and rain swept down the field. Once again the field became a morass and the players were so caked with mud as to be indistinguishable. A crowd of 40,000, some huddled in the newly erected but unroofed stand, were literally soaked to the skin while reporters had a miserable time trying to write on pulped notebooks. The Irish team was numbered.

Ireland, starting with the gale, got over twice for unconverted tries in the first half. Conditions got worse after the interval but Scotland although getting a fair share of the ball just couldn't score. Before the end G.V. Stephenson had collapsed and was taken off and at no side some had to be assisted into the dressing rooms. W.F. Browne took half an hour to come to while the referee was also in a poor state, his left hand being lifeless.

ENGLAND	Murrayfield	19 March 1927

SCOTLAND:	1 goal, 1 drop goal, 4 tries	21	**Win**
ENGLAND:	2 goals, 1 penalty goal	13	

Scotland: D. Drysdale* (*Heriot's FP*); I.S. Smith (*Edin. Univ.*), G.P.S. Macpherson (*Edin. Acads.*), J.C. Dykes (*Glas. Acads.*), W.M. Simmers (*Glas. Acads.*); H. Waddell (*Glas. Acads.*), J.B. Nelson (*Glas. Acads.*); J.W. Scott (*Stewart's FP*), J.C.H. Ireland (*Glas. HSFP*), D.S. Kerr (*Heriot's FP*), D.J. MacMyn (*London Scot.*), J.M. Bannerman (*Glas. HSFP*), J. Graham (*Kelso*), A.C. Gillies (*Watsonians*), J.R. Paterson (*Birkenhead Park*)

England: K.A. Sellar (*RN*); J.C. Gibbs (*Harlequins*), L.J. Corbett* (*Bristol*), H.M. Locke (*Birkenhead Park*), H.C. Catcheside (*Percy Park*); H.C.C. Laird (*Harlequins*), A.T. Young (*Army & Blackheath*); K.J. Stark (*Old Alleynians*), J.S. Tucker (*Bristol*), E. Stanbury (*Plymouth Albion*), R. Cove-Smith (*OMT*), W.E. Pratten (*Blackheath*), H.G. Periton (*Waterloo*), W.W. Wakefield (*Harlequins*), J. Hamley (*Plymouth Albion*).

Referee: N.M. Purcell (*Ireland*) **Touch judges:** J.C. Sturrock, G.C. Robinson

G.P.S. Macpherson scored but A.C. Gillies failed (3–0); J.C. Gibbs scored and E. Stanbury converted (3–5); I.S. Smith scored twice but A.C. Gillies failed to convert (9–5); K.J. Stark kicked a penalty (9–8). (H.T.). H. Waddell dropped a goal (13–8); J.C. Dykes scored and A.C. Gillies converted (18–8); H.C.C. Laird scored and K.J. Stark converted (18–13); J.W. Scott scored but D. Drysdale failed (21–13).

157

Some 70,000 watched a fast game in good conditions which suited the Scottish backs wh
were in great attacking form. Macpherson was at his elusive best, Smith was fast, Wadde
and Nelson made a fine half back pair, whilst Dykes' solo try was the best of the match
Waddell's drop goal was queried by Wakefield who claimed to have touched it but th
referee gave the score. For most of the second half England had to play with Hanley on th
wing as Catcheside retired with a leg injury. The English team were numbered.

NEW SOUTH WALES   Murrayfield   17 December 192

SCOTLAND:	2 goals	10	**Wi**
NEW SOUTH WALES:	1 goal, 1 try	8	

Scotland: D. Drysdale* (*London Scot.*); E.G. Taylor (*Oxford Univ.*), R.F. Kelly (*Wats
nians*), J.C. Dykes (*Glas. Acads.*), W.M. Simmers (*Glas. Acads.*); H.D. Greenlees (*Leice
ter*), P.S. Douty (*London Scot.*); J.W. Scott (*Stewart's FP*), W.N. Roughead (*Londo
Scot.*), W.G. Ferguson (*RHSFP*), D.J. MacMyn (*London Scot.*), J.M. Bannerman (*Gla
HSFP*), J. Graham (*Kelso*), W.B. Welsh (*Hawick*), J.R. Paterson (*Birkenhead Park*.)

N.S.W.: A.W. Ross (*University*); E.E. Ford (*Glebe Balmain*), W.B.J. Sheehan (*Univer
sity*), S.C. King (*Western Suburbs*), A.C. Wallace* (*Glebe Balmain*); T. Lawton (*Wester
Suburbs*), S.J. Malcolm (*Newcastle*); H.F. Woods (*YMCA*), J.G. Blackwood (*Easter
Suburbs*), B. Judd (*Randwick*), A.N. Finlay (*Sydney Univ.*), G.P. Storey (*Western Suburbs
J.W. Breckonridge (*Glebe Balmain*), J.A. Ford (*Glebe Balmain*), A.J. Tancred (*Gleb
Balmain*)

Referee: W.J. Llewellyn (*Wales*) **Touch judges:** M.M. Duncan, K. Tarleton.

E.E. Ford scored and T. Lawton converted (0–5); J. Graham scored and D. Drysda
converted (5–5). (H.T.). W.B. Welsh scored and D. Drysdale converted (10–5); J.A. For
scored but T. Lawton failed (10–8).

In a fairly even game the Scottish pack, although outweighted, held its own until the last te
minutes but their backs were better, Simmers in particular playing very well. He wa
responsible for both scores. In each case he broke away up the wing and crosskicked fr
Graham and Welsh to run on to the ball and score under the posts. Drysdale also was h
usual cool and competent self. The New South Wales team was numbered and played i
light blue jerseys.

FRANCE   Colombes   2 January 192

SCOTLAND:	5 tries	15	**Wi**
FRANCE:	2 tries	6	

Scotland: D. Drysdale* (*Heriot's FP*); G.P.S. Macpherson (*Edin. Acads.*), R.F. Kell

Watsonians), J.C. Dykes (*Glas. HSFP*), W.M. Simmers (*Glas. Acads.*); H.D. Greenlees
Leicester), P.S. Douty (*London Scot.*); W.B. Welsh (*Hawick*), W.N. Roughead (*London
Scot.*), W.G. Ferguson (*RHSFP*), D.J. MacMyn (*London Scot.*), J.M. Bannerman (*Glas.
HSFP*), J. Graham (*Kelso*), J.W. Scott (*Stewart's FP*), J.R. Paterson (*Birkenhead Park*)

France: M. Magnol (*Toulouse*); A. Jaureguy* (*SF*), G. Gerald (*RCF*), J. Coulon (*Greno-
ble*), C. Dulaurens (*Toulouse*); H. Haget (*CASG*), G. Daudignon (*SF*); A. Loury (*RCF*),
F. Camicas (*Tarbes*), J. Morere (*Marseilles*), J. Galia (*Quillan*), A. Camel (*Toulouse*), A.
Cazenave (*Paloise*), G. Branca (*SF*), E. Ribere (*Quillan*)

Referee: R. McGrath (*Ireland*) **Touch judges:** R.T. Neilson, M. Muntz

W.M. Simmers scored; D. Drysdale failed (3–0); H. Haget scored but failed to convert
3–3); J.R. Paterson and J.C. Dykes scored unconverted tries (9–3). (H.T.). P.S. Douty
and J.W. Scott scored unconverted tries (15–3); A. Camel scored an unconverted try
(15–6).

Scotland showed the better team work for the backs played well together and the forwards
were good as a pack in the loose. Bad passing by the French backs lost them several chances
and certainly one score for Drysdale picked up a loose pass, ran and kicked ahead. Magnol
fielded but was caught by the forwards who worked the ball free for Scott to plunge over.
The referee did not please the crowd who found him too ready with the whistle and they
became especially vocal after he granted Douty a try which they believed had been pushed
by a hand over the line. The papers noted that he only blew for 'no side' when he was
opposite the tunnel down which he vanished at a fair pace.

WALES Murrayfield 4 February 1928

SCOTLAND:	Nil	0	**Loss**
WALES:	2 goals, 1 try	13	

Scotland: D. Drysdale (*London Scot.*); J. Goodfellow (*Langholm*), G.P.S. Macpherson
Edin. Acads.), R.F. Kelly (*Watsonians*), W.M. Simmers (*Glas. Acads.*); H.D. Greenlees
Leicester), P.S. Douty (*London Scot.*); J.H. Ferguson (*Gala*), W.N. Roughead (*London
Scot.*), W.G. Ferguson (*RHSFP*), J.W. Scott (*Stewart's FP*), J.M. Bannerman* (*Glas.
HSFP*), J. Graham (*Kelso*), W.B. Welsh (*Hawick*), J.R. Paterson (*Birkenhead Park*)

Wales: B.O. Male* (*Cardiff*); J.D. Bartlett (*London Welsh*), J. Roberts (*Cardiff*), A.
Jenkins (*Llanelli*), W.C. Powell (*London Welsh*); A. John (*Llanelli*), D. John (*Llanelli*);
F.A. Bowdler (*Cross Keys*), C. Pritchard (*Pontypool*), H. Phillips (*Newport*), E. Jenkins
Aberavon), A. Skym (*Llanelli*), Y. Jones (*Llanelli*), T. Hollingdale (*Neath*), I. Jones
Llanelli)

Referee: R.W. Harland (*Ireland*) **Touch judges:** A.A. Lawie, J. Jarrett

A. Jenkins, D. John and J. Roberts scored; B.O. Male converted the first two but failed
with the third (0–13). (H.T.).

Wales started with a strong wind and rain at their backs and after fifteen minutes had scored
two tries, adding a third later. In the second half, with the ground cutting up they were

content to hold on to their lead and did some good defensive kicking. The Scots, however were a disjointed team. The forwards put in some good dribbling rushes but otherwise were poor and their ragged scrummaging gave the backs few chances. This was Wales' first win in Scotland since 1913.

IRELAND   Murrayfield   25 February 1928

SCOTLAND: 1 goal   5   Loss

IRELAND: 2 goals, 1 try   13

Scotland: D. Drysdale* (*London Scot.*); J. Goodfellow (*Langholm*), J.W.G. Hume (*Oxford Univ.*), J.C. Dykes (*Glas. Acads.*), W.M. Simmers (*Glas. Acads.*); H. Lind (*Dunfermline*), J.B. Nelson (*Glas. Acads.*); J.W. Allan (*Melrose*), W.N. Roughead (*London Scot.*), D.S. Kerr (*Heriot's FP*), W.G. Ferguson (*RHSFP*), J.M. Bannerman (*Glas. HSFP*), J. Graham (*Kelso*), W.B. Welsh (*Hawick*), J.R. Paterson (*Birkenhead Park*)

Ireland: W.J. Stewart (*NIFC*); R.M. Byers (*NIFC*), G.V. Stephenson* (*NIFC*), J.B. Ganly (*Monkstown*), A.C. Douglas (*Instonians*); E.O. Davy (*Lansdowne*), M. Sugden (*Wanderers*); T.O. Pike (*Lansdowne*), S.J. Cagney (*London Irish*), W.F. Browne (*US*), C.T. Payne (*NIFC*), C.J. Hanrahan (*Dolphin*), J.L. Farrell (*Bective Rangers*), J.D. Clinch (*Wanderers*), G.R. Beamish (*RAF*)

Referee: B.S. Cumberlege (*England*)   Touch judges: A.W. Angus, Judge Sealey

J.B. Ganly scored an unconverted try (0–3); D.S. Kerr scored: D. Drysdale converted (5–3). (H.T.). E.O. Davy and G.V. Stephenson scored; G.V. Stephenson converted both (5–13).

Some early Scottish attacks failed against fine tackling but the superior resolution and incisiveness of the Irish backs, supported by a robust set of forwards, had the match well won by the close. Scotland certainly did not deserve to be ahead at the interval.

ENGLAND   Twickenham   17 March 1928

SCOTLAND: Nil   0   Loss

ENGLAND: 2 tries   6

Scotland: D. Drysdale* (*London Scot.*); J. Goodfellow (*Langholm*), G.P.S. Macpherson (*Edin. Acads.*), W.M. Simmers (*Glas. Acads.*), R.F. Kelly (*Watsonians*); A.H. Brown (*Heriot's FP*), J.B. Nelson (*Glas. Acads.*); L.M. Stuart (*Glas. HSFP*), W.N. Roughead (*London Scot.*), D.S. Kerr (*Heriot's FP*), W.G. Ferguson (*RHSFP*), J.M. Bannerman (*Glas. HSFP*), J. Graham (*Kelso*), J.W. Scott (*Stewart's FP*), J.R. Paterson (*Birkenhead Park*)

160

England: T.W. Brown (*Bristol*); W.J. Taylor (*Blackheath*), C.D. Aarvold (*Camb. Univ.*), J.V. Richardson (*Birkenhead Park*), G.V. Palmer (*Richmond*); H.C.C. Laird (*Harlequins*), A.T. Young (*Blackheath*); R.H.W. Sparkes (*Plymouth Albion*), J.S. Tucker (*Bristol*), J. Hanley (*Plymouth Albion*), K.J. Stark (*Old Alleynians*), F.D. Prentice (*Leicester*), E. Stanbury (*Plymouth Albion*), H.G. Periton (*Waterloo*), R. Cove-Smith* (*OMT*)

Referee: T.H. Vile (*Wales*)

H.C.C. Laird scored; J.V. Richardson failed (0–3). (H.T.). J. Hanley scored; F.D. Prentice failed (0–6).

England won all five of their matches this season yet this was one that Scotland with a little luck, could have drawn for their backs, with Macpherson in form, came near to scoring on several occasions. A.H. Brown missed a score when after a good break, his kick ahead bounced out of his reach. Defence was the strongest part of the English back play although A.T. Young proved most elusive. The English pack was the better for they handled well, followed up fast and were physically stronger.

FRANCE Murrayfield 19 January 1929

| **SCOTLAND:** | 1 penalty goal, 1 try | 6 | **Win** |
| **FRANCE:** | 1 try | 3 | |

Scotland: D. Drysdale* (*London Scot.*); I.S. Smith (*Edin. Univ.*), G.G. Aitken (*London Scot.*), J.C. Dykes (*Glas. Acads.*), W.M. Simmers (*Glas. Acads.*); A.H. Brown (*Heriot's FP*), *J.B. Nelson* (*Glas. Acads.*); J.W. Allan (*Melrose*), H.S. Mackintosh (*West of Scot.*), R.T. Smith (*Kelso*), J.A. Beattie (*Hawick*), J.M. Bannerman (*Glas. HSFP*), K.M. Wright (*London Scot.*), W.V. Berkley (*London Scot.*), J.R. Paterson (*Birkenhead Park*)

France: M. Magnol (*Toulouse*); A. Jaureguy* (*SF*), A. Behoteguy (*Cognac*), G. Gerald (*RCF*), R. Houdet (*SF*); C. Magnanou (*Bayonne*), C. Lacazedieu (*Dax*); J. Hauc (*Toulon*), F. Camicas (*Tarbes*), J. Sayrou (*Perpignan*), A. Camel (*Toulouse*), R. Majerus (*SF*), A. Bioussa (*Toulouse*), G. Branca (*SF*), J. Auge (*Dax*)

Referee: B.S. Cumberlege (*England*) **Touch judges:** T.H.H. Warren, C.F. Rutherford

A.H. Brown kicked a penalty (3–0); J.R. Paterson scored and D. Drysdale failed (6–0); A. Behoteguy scored and M. Magnol failed (6–3). (H.T.).

This was anything but a decisive win, for France were full of running especially during the last fifteen minutes when their pack came on to a game and Scotland were lucky to survive several near things. The veteran Jaureguy was in fine form throughout and made the opening for Behoteguy's try. Magnol at full back delighted the crowd with a sound but often acrobatic display. A.H. Brown's penalty was a good 30-yarder. The French were numbered but no numbers appeared in the programme.

161

WALES   Swansea   2 February 1929

SCOTLAND: 1 drop goal, 1 penalty goal   7   **Loss**

WALES: 1 goal, 3 tries   14

Scotland: T.G. Aitchison (*Gala*); I.S. Smith (*Edin. Univ.*), J.C. Dykes (*Glas. Acads.*), W.M. Simmers (*Glas. Acads.*), T.G. Brown (*Heriot's FP*); A.H. Brown (*Heriot's FP*), J.B. Nelson (*Glas. Acads.*); J.W. Allan (*Melrose*), H.S. Mackintosh (*Glas. Univ.*), R.T. Smith (*Kelso*), J.A. Beattie (*Hawick*), J.M. Bannerman* (*Glas. HSFP*), K.M. Wright (*London Scot.*), W.V. Berkley (*London Scot.*), J.R. Paterson (*Birkenhead Park*)

Wales: J. Bassett (*Penarth*); J.C. Morley (*Newport*), H.M. Bowcott (*Camb. Univ.*), W.G. Morgan* (*Camb. Univ.*), J. Roberts (*Camb. Univ.*); F.L. Williams (*Cardiff*), W.C. Powell (*London Welsh*); A.E. Broughton (*Treorchy*), I. Jones (*Llanelli*), H. Peacock (*Newport*), H. Jones (*Neath*), T. Arthur (*Neath*), F.A. Bowdler (*Cross Keys*), C. Pritchard (*Pontypool*), A. Barrel (*Cardiff*)

     Referee: D. Helliwell (*England*)   **Touch judge:** E. Thomas

J. Roberts scored but I. Jones failed (0–3); A.H. Brown kicked a penalty (3–3). (H.T.). A.H. Brown dropped a goal (7–3); H. Peacock scored and I. Jones converted (7–8); J. Roberts scored but I. Jones failed (7–11); W.G. Morgan scored but W.C. Powell failed (7–14).

The Scots, although putting up a hard fight with a fine rally in the last quarter, were not good enough. Their pack was outplayed so that the Welsh backs with an ample supply of the ball were constantly on the attack and in spite of a wet ball and treacherous ground handled and ran very well. Scotland, without crossing the line, were fortunate to lead just after the restart but from the kick off the Welsh forwards took the ball right up to the line for a score and Wales continued this domination until the late revival. Right on time Simmers broke through and set Smith off on a sprint which only finished when he was hurled into touch taking the corner flag with him.

IRELAND   Lansdowne Road   23 February 1929

SCOTLAND: 2 goals, 2 tries   16   **Win**

IRELAND: 1 drop goal, 1 try   7

Scotland: T.G. Aitchison (*Gala*); I.S. Smith (*Edin. Univ.*), G.P.S. Macpherson (*Edin. Acads.*), J.C. Dykes (*Glas. Acads.*), W.M. Simmers (*Glas. Acads.*); H.D. Greenlees (*Leicester*), J.B. Nelson (*Glas. Acads.*); R.T. Smith (*Kelso*), H.S. Mackintosh (*Glas. Univ.*), J.W. Allan (*Melrose*), W.V. Berkley (*London Scot.*), J.M. Bannerman* (*Oxford Univ.*), J.R. Paterson (*Birkenhead Park*), K.M. Wright (*London Scot.*), W.B. Welsh (*Hawick*)

Ireland: W.J. Stewart (*Bolton*); R.M. Byers (*NIFC*), P.F. Murray (*Wanderers*), J.B. Ganly

(*Monkstown*), J.E. Arigho (*Lansdowne*); E. Davy* (*Lansdowne*), M. Sugden (*Wanderers*); G.R. Beamish (*RAF*), H.C. Browne (*Un. Services*), S.J. Cagney (*London Irish*), J.D. Clinch (*Wanderers*), M.J. Dunne (*Lansdowne*), J.L. Farrell (*Bective Rangers*), C.J. Hanrahan (*Dolphin*), J.S. Synge (*Lansdowne*)

Referee: B.S. Cumberlege (*England*)   **Touch judges:** J. Anderson, H.J. Millar

G.P.S. Macpherson scored and J.C. Dykes converted (5–0); E. Davy dropped a goal (5–4); J.E. Arigho scored but P.F. Murray failed (5–7). (H.T.). J.M. Bannerman scored and J.W. Allan converted (10–7); I.S. Smith and W.M. Simmers scored but J.W. Allan failed with both (16–7).

Ireland had already beaten France and England and a fine day brought out a record crowd of 40,000 for their first home match. Unfortunately the spectators encroached on the field of play and play had to be halted several times to clear the goal area. Arigho could not run behind the posts when he got over and the referee was forced to refuse a score to Byers who was tackled over the line by Aitchison and flung amongst the crowd.

The Scots started well when Dykes intercepted a pass and gave Macpherson a clear run in but the Irish pack dominated play during the first half. Their backs, apart from the move that gave Arigho his score, were only capable of solo efforts. After half time the Scottish pack took over and fine team work brought three scores. Macpherson had a good game latterly. Dykes was hurt and changed places with Aitchison.

ENGLAND   Murrayfield   16 March 1929

SCOTLAND: 4 tries   12   **Win**
ENGLAND: 2 tries   6

Scotland: T.G. Aitchison (*Gala*); I.S. Smith (*Edin. Univ.*), G.P.S. Macpherson (*Edin. Acads.*), W.M. Simmers (*Glas. Acads.*), C.H.C. Brown (*Dunfermline*); H.D. Greenlees (*Leicester*), J.B. Nelson (*Glas. Acads.*); R.T. Smith (*Kelso*), H.S. Mackintosh (*Glas. Univ.*), J.W. Allan (*Melrose*), J.W. Scott (*Bradford*), J.M. Bannerman* (*Oxford Univ.*), J.R. Paterson (*Birkenhead Park*), K.M. Wright (*London Scot.*), W.B. Welsh (*Hawick*)

England: T.W. Brown (*Bristol*); R.W. Smeddle (*Camb. Univ.*), A.R. Aslett (*Richmond*), G.M. Sladen (*RN*); A.L. Novis (*Army*); S.C.C. Meikle (*Waterloo*), E.E. Richards (*Plymouth Albion*); E. Stanbury (*Plymouth Albion*), R.H.W. Sparks (*Plymouth Albion*), R. Webb (*Northampton*), T.W. Harris (*Northampton*), H. Rew (*Army*), H. Wilkinson (*Halifax*), D. Turquand-Young (*Richmond*), H.G. Periton* (*Waterloo*)

Referee: Dr J.R. Wheeler (*Ireland*)   **Touch judges:** J. Magill, G.C. Robinson

A.L. Novis scored but T.W. Harris failed (0–3). (H.T.). J.B. Nelson scored but J.W. Allan failed (3–3); S.C.C. Meikle scored but A.L. Novis failed (3–6); C.H. Brown and I.S. Smith (2) scored but J.W. Allan failed to convert (12–6).

The conditions were good but cold and dull. After a fairly even first half there was a burst of scoring which left the scores level. Then I.S. Smith, running with great determination scored twice. On each occasion he was firmly tackled by Brown but his impetus carried them both over the line. Neither side was numbered. This was Bannerman's last game.

163

FRANCE   Colombes   1 January 1930

SCOTLAND:	1 try	3	Loss
FRANCE:	1 drop goal, 1 try	7	

Scotland: R.W. Langrish (*London Scot.*); I.S. Smith (*London Scot.*), G.P.S. Macpherson* (*Edin. Acads.*), J.W.G. Hume (*Edin. Wrs.*), W.M. Simmers (*Glas. Acads.*); W.D. Emslie (*RHSFP*), J.B. Nelson (*Glas. Acads.*); J.W. Allan (*Melrose*), H.S. Mackintosh (*Glas. Univ.*), R.T. Smith (*Kelso*), J.W. Scott (*Waterloo*), J. Stewart (*Glas. HSFP*), W.B. Welsh (*Hawick*), R. Rowand (*Glas. HSFP*), F.H. Waters (*Camb. Univ.*)

France: M. Piquemal (*Tarbes*); R.R. Samatan (*Agen*), M. Baillette (*Quillan*), G. Gerald (*RCF*), R.R. Houdet (*SF*); C. Magnanou (*Bayonne*), L. Serin (*Beziers*); A. Ambert (*Toulouse*), C. Bigot (*Quillan*), J. Choy (*Narbonne*), R. Majerus (*SF*), A. Camel (*TOEC*), E. Ribere* (*Quillan*), J. Galia (*Quillan*), A. Bioussa (*Toulouse*)

Referee: D. Helliwell (*England*) **Touch judges:** Dr G.W. Simpson

A. Bioussa scored an unconverted try (0–3); W.M. Simmers scored an unconverted try (3–3). (H.T.). C. Magnanou dropped a goal (3–7).

France thoroughly deserved their win for Scotland although physically the stronger were beaten for speed and virility. Magnanou was always dangerous, making the opening for Bioussa's try in the first five minutes and then winning the match in the dying minutes with a splendid 30-yards drop. The French pack, although poor in the set scrums, handled brilliantly in the loose and for once proved to be as fierce and tough as their opponents. The Scottish backs could not penetrate a speedy defence although Macpherson cut through beautifully several times only to find his passes go astray. Both packs were depleted in the second half, Allan having to go off before half time while a collision laid two Frenchmen out for a spell.

WALES   Murrayfield   1 February 1930

SCOTLAND:	1 goal, 1 drop goal, 1 try	12	Win
WALES:	1 goal, 1 drop goal	9	

Scotland: R.C. Warren (*Glas. Acads.*); I.S. Smith (*London Scot.*), G.P.S. Macpherson* (*Edin. Acads.*), T.M. Hart (*Glas. Univ.*), W.M. Simmers (*Glas. Acads.*); H. Waddell (*Glas. Acads.*), J.B. Nelson (*Glas. Acads.*); R.T. Smith (*Kelso*), H.S. Mackintosh (*Glas. Acads.*), R. Foster (*Hawick*), J.A. Beattie (*Hawick*), F.H. Waters (*London Scot.*), W.C.C. Agnew (*Stewart's FP*), R. Rowand (*Glas. HSFP*), W.B. Welsh (*Hawick*)

Wales: J. Bassett (*Penarth*); G. Davies (*Cheltenham*), B.R. Turnbull (*Cardiff*), G. Jones (*Cardiff*), R. Boon (*Carmarthen College*); F. Williams (*Cardiff*), W.C. Powell (*London Welsh*); T. Arthur (*Neath*), H.C. Day (*Newport*), A. Skym (*Cardiff*), E. Jenkins (*Aberavon*), A. Lemon (*Neath*), H. Peacock (*Newport*), D. Thomas (*Swansea*), I. Jones* (*Llanelli*)

W.M. Simmers scored and F.H. Waters converted (5–0); G. Jones scored and I. Jones converted (5–5); G. Jones dropped a goal (5–9); W.M. Simmers scored but F.H. Waters failed (8–9). (H.T.). H. Waddell dropped a goal (12–9).

A drizzle cleared before the start and about 60,000 were present. Scotland had much defending to do in the first half and were indebted to some good backing up by Simmers to be only one point behind at half time. The second half was more equally contested although at one time when Hart was hurt Rowand came out of the pack to act as an extra defender. However the game had a sensational finish when in the last minutes Waddell dropped a goal following a scrum in front of the posts. This was a game that Wales could have won but their backs could not turn a plentiful supply of the ball into scores.

IRELAND	Murrayfield	22 February 1930

SCOTLAND:	1 goal, 2 tries	11	**Loss**
IRELAND:	1 goal, 3 tries	14	

Scotland: R.C. Warren (*Glas. Acads.*); I.S. Smith (*London Scot.*), G.P.S. Macpherson* (*Edin. Acads.*), W.M. Simmers (*Glas. Acads.*), D.St.C. Ford (*Un. Services*); T.M. Hart (*Glas. Univ.*), J.B. Nelson (*Glas. Acads.*); H.S. Mackintosh (*Glas. Univ.*), W.N. Roughmead (*London Scot.*), R.T. Smith (*Kelso*), W.C.C. Agnew (*Stewart's FP*), L.M. Stuart (*Glas. HSFP*), W.B. Welsh (*Hawick*), J. Graham (*Kelso*), F.H. Waters (*London Scot.*)

Ireland: F.W. Williamson (*Dolphin*); J.E. Arigho (*Lansdowne*), M.F. Crowe (*Lansdowne*), E.O. Davy (*Lansdowne*), G.V. Stephenson* (*London Hospitals*); P.F. Murray (*Wanderers*), M. Sugden (*Wanderers*); H.O. O'Neill (*QU Belfast*), T.C. Casey (*Young Munsters*), C.J. Hanrahan (*Dolphin*), C.T. Payne (*NIFC*), M.J. Dunne (*Lansdowne*), J.L. Farrell (*Bective Rangers*), J.D. Clinch (*Dublin Univ.*), G.R. Beamish (*RAF*)

D. St.C. Ford scored but F.H. Waters failed (3–0); E.O. Davy scored but P.F. Murray failed (3–3); E.O. Davy scored and P.F. Murray converted (3–8); E.O. Davy scored but G.V. Stephenson failed (3–11). (H.T.). G.P.S. Macpherson scored and F.H. Waters converted (8–11); M.P. Crowe scored but P.F. Murray failed (8–14); F.H. Waters scored but failed to convert (11–14).

Again the Scottish pack failed to match their opponents, who held their own in the scrums but set a fierce pace in the loose. Scotland were actually on top during the first half hour for Nelson sent Ford away for a good try inside five minutes while two further scores were lost by knocks on. Then Ireland came to life and some good handling put Davy in for three tries in ten minutes' play before half time. Soon after the restart a good run and crosskick by Smith was taken in for a try by Macpherson but this was countered by Crowe scoring after a forward rush. Then the Scottish pack rallied in the last ten minutes but could only manage a single try before time.

ENGLAND   Twickenham   15 March 1930

SCOTLAND:	Nil	0	**Draw**
ENGLAND:	Nil	0	

Scotland: R.C. Warren (*Glas. Acads.*); W.M. Simmers (*Glas. Acads.*), G.P.S. Macpherson* (*Edin. Acads.*), J.E. Hutton (*Harlequins*), D.St.C. Ford (*Un. Services*); H.D. Greenlees (*Leicester*), J.B. Nelson (*Glas. Acads.*); H.S. Mackintosh (*West of Scot.*), W.N. Roughead (*London Scot.*), J.W. Allan (*Melrose*), W.B. Welsh (*Hawick*), L.M. Stuart (*Glas. HSFP*), A.H. Polson (*Gala*), J. Graham (*Kelso*), F.H. Waters (*London Scot.*)

England: J.C. Hubbard (*Harlequins*); C.C. Tanner (*Richmond*), M. Robson (*Oxford Univ.*), F.W.S. Malir (*Otley*), J.C.R. Reeve (*Harlequins*); R.S. Spong (*Old Millhillians*), W.H. Sobey (*Old Millhillians*); H. Rew (*Army*), J.S. Tucker* (*Bristol*), A.H. Bateson (*Otley*), J.W. Forrest (*Un. Services*), B.H. Black (*Oxford Univ.*), H.G. Periton (*Waterloo*), P.D. Howard (*Oxford Univ.*), P.W.P. Brook (*Camb. Univ.*)

Referee: R.W. Jeffares (*Ireland*)

The pointless draw was a fairly accurate reflection of a fiercely contested struggle in which defence triumphed over attack. For England Sobey was a very alert scrum half and had one splendid solo run which narrowly failed to bring a score. For Scotland Macpherson had one typical sidestepping run and his final crosskick found Waters clear but given off-side — a very close decision.

FRANCE   Murrayfield   24 January 1931

SCOTLAND:	2 penalty goals	6	**Win**
FRANCE:	1 drop goal	4	

Scotland: R.W. Langrish (*London Scot.*); I.S. Smith (*London Scot.*), J.E. Hutton (*Harlequins*), A.W. Wilson (*Dunfermline*), W.M. Simmers (*Glas. Acads.*); H. Lind (*Dunfermline*), J.B. Nelson (*Glas. Acads.*); J.W. Allan (*Melrose*), W.N. Roughead* (*London Scot.*), H.S. Mackintosh (*West of Scot.*), J.A. Beattie (*Hawick*), D.A. McLaren (*Durham Co.*), J.S. Wilson (*St Andrews Univ.*), A.W. Walker (*Camb. Univ.*), W.B. Welsh (*Hawick*)

France: M. Savy (*Montferrand*); L. Augras (*Agen*), G. Gerald (RCF), M. Baillette (*Toulon*), S.Samatan (*Agen*); M. Servolle (*Toulon*), M. Rousie (*Villeneuve*); R. Scohy (*BEC*), J. Dahan (*SBUC*), A. Duclos (*Lourdes*), A. Clady (*Lezignan*), J. Galia (*Villeneuve*), C. Bigot (*Lezignan*), E. Camo (*Villeneuve*), E. Ribere* (*Quillan*)

Referee: R.W. Jeffares (*Ireland*)   **Touch judges:** Dr G.W. Simpson, C.F. Rutherford

J.W. Allan kicked two penalty goals (6–0). (H.T.). L. Servolle dropped a goal (6–4).

The Scottish pack were well on top but the backs could not break through the splendid tackling and covering defence of the speedy French backs. Allan's penalties were both fine long range kicks. Conditions were good and about 50,000 were present. The French team were numbered; Scotland were not and played in white jerseys.

WALES	Cardiff	7 February 1931

SCOTLAND:	1 goal, 1 try	8	Loss
WALES:	2 goals, 1 try	13	

Scotland: R.W. Langrish (*London Scot.*); I.S. Smith (*London Scot.*), G.P.S. Macpherson (*Edin. Acads.*), W.M. Simmers (*Glas. Acads.*), G. Wood (*Gala*); H. Lind (*Dunfermline*), J.B. Nelson (*Glas. Acads.*); J.W. Allan (*Melrose*), W.M. Roughead* (*London Scot.*), H.S. Mackintosh (*West of Scot.*), A.W. Walker (*Camb. Univ.*), J.A. Beattie (*Hawick*), W.B. Welsh (*Hawick*), J.S. Wilson (*St Andrews Univ.*), D. Crichton-Miller (*Gloucester*)

Wales: J. Bassett* (*Penarth*); J.C. Morley (*Newport*), E.C. Davey (*Swansea*), T.E. Jones-Davies (*London Welsh*), R.W. Boon (*Cardiff*); H.M. Bowcott (*Cardiff*), W.C. Powell (*London Welsh*); A. Skym (*Cardiff*), H.C. Day (*Newport*), T. Day (*Swansea*), T. Arthur (*Neath*), E. Jenkins (*Aberavon*), N. Fender (*Cardiff*), A. Lemon (*Neath*), W.G. Thomas (*Swansea*)

Referee: J.E. Bott (*England*)

J.C. Morley scored but J. Bassett failed (0–3); D. Crichton-Miller scored but J.W. Allan failed (3–3). (H.T.). D. Crichton-Miller scored and J.W. Allan converted (8–3); W. Thomas scored and J. Bassett converted (8–8); R.W. Boon scored and J. Bassett converted (8–13).

50,000 spectators were present in fine weather. A minute's silence was observed to mark the passing of J. Aikman Smith who had died on the journey south. It was not a great game, both sides having chances of scoring which were not taken. Boon's try in the last minutes came from a pass that his opponents thought was forward and he was allowed to follow up his kick ahead and touch down unchallenged. Walker was lame for all the first half but Watcyn Thomas played for most of the match with a fractured collar bone and still managed to score. The Welsh team were lettered.

IRELAND	Lansdowne Road	28 February 1931

SCOTLAND:	1 goal	5	Loss
IRELAND:	1 goal, 1 try	8	

Scotland: R.W. Langrish (*London Scot.*); I.S. Smith (*London Scot.*), W.M. Simmers (*Glas. Acads.*), A.W. Wilson (*Dunfermline*), G. Wood (*Gala*); H. Lind (*Dunfermline*), J.B. Nelson (*Glas. Acads.*); J.W. Allan (*Melrose*), W.N. Roughead* (*London Scot.*), H.S.

Mackintosh (*West of Scot.*), A.W. Walker (*Camb. Univ.*), J.A. Beattie (*Hawick*), W.B. Welsh (*Hawick*), J.S. Wilson (*St Andrews Univ.*), D. Crichton-Miller (*Gloucester*)

Ireland: J.C. Entrican (*QU Belfast*); E.J. Lightfoot (*Lansdowne*), E.O. Davy (*Lansdowne*), M.P. Crowe (*Lansdowne*), J.E. Arigho (*Lansdowne*); P.F. Murray (*Wanderers*), M. Sugden* (*Wanderers*); H.C.C. Withers (*Army*), J.A.E. Siggins (*Collegians*), J. Russell (*UC Cork*), N.F. Murphy (*Cork Const.*), V.J. Pike (*Lansdowne*), J.L. Farrell (*Bective Rangers*), J.D. Clinch (*Wanderers*), G.R. Beamish (*RAF*)

Referee: B.S. Cumberlege (*England*) **Touch judges:** T.H.H. Warren, J.J. Coffey

M. Sugden scored: P.F. Murray failed (0–3); H.S. Mackintosh scored and J.W. Allan converted (5–3). (H.T.). V.J. Pike scored and P.F. Murray converted (5–8).

The conditions played a vital part, for Sugden won the toss and a strong icy wind with several snow showers pinned Scotland down to a persistent and gruelling defence. That it took Ireland half an hour to open the scoring was a tribute to the Scots' tenacity. The first try followed a typical Sugden dart and dummy from a scrum near the line. Pike's try came from a forward rush. The Scottish score followed from a break by Lind who flung a long pass inwards which Mackintosh, amongst a crowd of green jerseys, grabbed and fought his way over. With the wind Scotland had hopes but it seemed that they were too exhausted to beat the defence. I.S. Smith had one good run with a kick ahead, only to see the ball beat Walker down-wind to the dead ball line.

ENGLAND   Murrayfield   21 March 1931

SCOTLAND: 5 goals, 1 try   28   **Win**

ENGLAND: 2 goals, 1 penalty goal, 2 tries   19

Scotland: A.W. Wilson (*Dunfermline*); I.S. Smith (*London Scot.*), G.P.S. Macpherson* (*Edin. Acads.*), D.St.C. Ford (*RN*), W.M. Simmers (*Glas. Acads.*); H. Lind (*Dunfermline*), W.R. Logan (*Edin. Univ.*); J.W. Allan (*Melrose*), W.N. Roughead (*London Scot.*), H.S. Mackintosh (*West of Scot.*), A.W. Walker (*Camb. Univ.*), J.A. Beattie (*Hawick*), W.B. Welsh (*Hawick*), J.S. Wilson (*St Andrews Univ.*), D. Crichton-Miller (*Gloucester*)

England: E.C.P. Whiteley (*Old Alleynians*); J.S.R. Reeve (*Harlequins*), J.A. Tallent (*Camb. Univ.*), C.D. Aarvold* (*Headingley*); A.C. Harrison (*Hartlepool Rovers*); T.C. Knowles (*Birkenhead Park*), E.B. Pope (*Blackheath*); R.H.W. Sparkes (*Civil Service*), G.G. Gregory (*Taunton*), H. Rew (*Army*), J.W. Forrest (*RN*), B.H. Black (*Blackheath*), P.E. Dunkley (*Harlequin*), P.D. Howard (*Oxford Univ.*), P.C. Hordern (*Blackheath*)

Referee: Dr J.R. Wheeler (*Ireland*) **Touch judges:** R.B. Waddell, H.A. Haigh-Smith

D.St.C. Ford scored and J.W. Allan converted (5–0); H.S. Mackintosh scored and J.W. Allan converted (10–0); J.A. Tallent scored twice and B.H. Black converted (10–10); W.R. Logan scored and J.W. Allan converted (15–10); J.S.R. Reeve scored but B.H. Black failed (15–13); H.S. Mackintosh scored and J.W. Allan converted (20–13). (H.T.). I.S. Smith scored twice and J.W. Allan converted one (28–13); B.H. Black kicked a penalty (28–16); J.S.R. Reeve scored but B.H. Black failed (28–13).

75,000 watched this most spectacular match which produced some scoring records. The general opinion was that good attacking play faced by some rather moderate tackling was responsible for the flood of scoring. Certainly it was a day where Macpherson did a lot of shadow tackling but engineered many moves which bewildered the opposition and certainly led to two of the scores. Logan had an excellent debut, scoring one try and making another for Smith. There was some splendid goal kicking by Allan and Black. The English players were numbered.

SOUTH AFRICA   Murrayfield   16 January 1932

SCOTLAND:	1 try	3	Loss
SOUTH AFRICA:	2 tries	6	

Scotland: T.H.B. Lawther (*Old Millhillians*); I.S. Smith (*London Scot.*), G.P.S. Macpherson (*Edin. Acads.*), W.M. Simmers* (*Glas. Acads.*), J.E. Forrest (*Glas. Acads.*); H. Lind (*Dunfermline*), W.R. Logan (*Edin. Univ.*); J.W. Allan (*Melrose*), H.S. Mackintosh (*West of Scot.*), R.A. Foster (*Hawick*), M.S. Stewart (*Stewart's FP*), J.A. Beattie (*Hawick*), J. Graham (*Kelso*), F.H. Waters (*London Scot.*), W.B. Welsh (*Hawick*)

South Africa: G.H. Brand (*Hamiltons*); M. Zimmerman (*UCT*), B.G. Gray (*Villagers*), J.H. Van der Westhuizen (*Gardens*), F.D. Venter (*Pretoria*); B.L. Osler* (*Villagers*), D.H. Craven (*Un. Services*); P.J. Mostert (*Somerset*), H.G. Kipling (*Beaconsfield*), M.M. Louw (*Gardens*), G.M .Daneel (*PUC*), W.F. Bergh (*George*), P.J. Nel (*Greytown*), L.C.T. Strachan (*Police*), A.J. McDonald (*Un. Services*)

Referee: B.S. Cumberlege (*England*) **Touch judges:** Dr G.W. Simpson, Pienaar

H. Lind scored but J.W. Allan failed (3–0). (H.T.). B.L. Osler and D.H. Craven scored but B.L. Osler and G.H. Brand failed (3–6).

65,000 attended in a day of very poor conditions. A gale of wind and icy rain blew down the length of the field hampering handling and kicking and testing the endurance of the players. This made it almost entirely a forward game and the South African pack with an obvious weight and height advantage played a major part in the win. Early in the first half Lind broke through and with Welsh running beside him, dummied the full back and ran on to score. Scotland held this lead until shortly after the restart. The South Africans were numbered.

WALES   Murrayfield   6 February 1932

SCOTLAND:	Nil	0	Loss
WALES:	1 penalty goal, 1 try	6	

Scotland: T.H.B. Lawther (*Old Millhillians*); I.S. Smith (*London Scot.*), D.St.C. Ford

169

(*US*), W.M. Simmers* (*Glas. Acads.*), G. Wood (*Gala*); H. Lind (*Dunfermline*), W.R. Logan (*Edin. Univ.*); J.W. Allan (*Melrose*), W.N. Roughead (*London Scot.*), H.S. Mackintosh (*West of Scot.*), M.S. Stewart (*Stewart's FP*), J.A. Beattie (*Hawick*), J. Graham (*Kelso*), F.H. Waters (*London Scot.*), W.B. Welsh (*Hawick*)

Wales: J. Bassett* (*Penarth*); J.C. Morley (*Newport*), E.C. Davey (*Swansea*), F.L. Williams (*Cardiff*), R.W. Boon (*Cardiff*); A.R. Ralph (*Newport*), W.C. Powell (*London Welsh*); A. Skym (*Cardiff*), F.A. Bowdler (*Crosskeys*), T. Day (*Swansea*), W. Davies (*Swansea*), D. Thomas (*Swansea*), W.G. Thomas (*Swansea*), A. Lemon (*Neath*), E.M. Jenkins (*Aberavon*)

Referee: T. Bell (*Ireland*) **Touch judges:** F.J.C. Moffat, Captain J.N. Jones

R.W. Boon scored but J. Bassett failed (0–3). (H.T.). J. Bassett kicked a penalty.

About 60,000 watched in reasonable conditions. Although it was a fairly even first half Wales finished well on top. There was a bruising game up front but the Welsh backs were too fast for their opponents and only good tackling kept the score to a penalty in the second half. The Welsh team were identified by letters.

IRELAND   Murrayfield   27 February 1932

SCOTLAND:	1 goal, 1 try	8	Loss
IRELAND:	4 goals	20	

Scotland: A.H.M. Hutton (*Dunfermline*); I.S. Smith (*London Scot.*), G. Wood (*Gala*), D.St.C. Ford (*Un. Services*), W.M. Simmers* (*Glas. Acads.*); W.D. Emslie (*RHSFP*), W.R. Logan (*Edin. Univ.*); J.W. Allan (*Melrose*), H.S. Mackintosh (*West of Scot.*), R.A. Foster (*Hawick*), M.S. Stewart (*Stewart's FP*), J.A. Beattie (*Hawick*), A.W. Walker (*Birkenhead Park*), F.H. Waters (*London Scot.*), W.B. Welsh (*Hawick*)

Ireland: E.C. Ridgeway (*Wanderers*); S.L. Waide (*NIFC*), E.W.F. de V. Hunt (*Army*), M.P. Crowe (*Lansdowne*), E.J. Lightfoot (*Lansdowne*); E. Davy (*Lansdowne*), P.F. Murray (*Wanderers*); G.R. Beamish* (*RAF*), M.J. Dunne (*Lansdowne*), J.L. Farrell (*Bective Rangers*), N. Murphy (*Cork Const.*), V.J. Pike (*Lansdowne*), W.M. Ross (*QU Belfast*), J.A.E. Siggins (*Collegians*), C.J. Hanrahan (*Dolphin*)

Referee: B.S. Cumberlege (*England*) **Touch judges:** M.A. Allan, W.A. Clarke

E.J. Lightfoot scored and P.F. Murray converted (0–5). (H.T.). G. Wood scored but F.H. Waters failed (3–5); E.W.F. de V. Hunt, E.J. Lightfoot and S.L. Waide scored for P.F. Murray to convert all three (3–20); W.M. Simmers scored and J.W. Allan converted (8–20).

Ridgeway was a very late replacement for D.P. Morris but had a good match. The Scots were disorganised when after twenty minutes Emslie had to leave the field with an ankle injury. Simmers moved to half, not the best choice, and Welsh went out to the wing where he played very well. In one dash down the wing he kicked over Ridgeway's head only to be badly impeded and so missed a touch down.

170

SCOTLAND:	1 try	3	**Loss**
ENGLAND:	2 goals, 2 tries	16	

Scotland: A.S. Dykes (*Glas. Acads.*); I.S. Smith (*London Scot.*), G.P.S. Macpherson* (*Edin. Acads.*), G. Wood (*Gala*), W.M. Simmers (*Glas. Acads.*); H. Lind (*Dumfermline*), J.P. McArthur (*Waterloo*); R.A. Foster (*Hawick*), H.S. Mackintosh (*West of Scot.*), R. Rowand (*Glas. HSFP*), F.A. Wright (*Edin. Acads.*), J.A. Beattie (*Hawick*), W.B. Welsh (*Hawick*), G.F. Ritchie (*Dundee HSFP*), J.S. Wilson (*St Andrews Univ.*)

England: T.W. Brown (*Bristol*); C.C. Tanner (*Richmond*), D.W. Burland (*Bristol*), R.A. Gerrard (*Bath*), C.D. Aarvold (*Blackheath*); W. Elliot (*Un. Services*), B.C. Gadney (*Leicester*); A. Vaughan-Jones (*Un. Services*), R.J. Longland (*Northampton*), B.H. Black (*Blackheath*), J.M. Hodgson (*Northern*), G.G. Gregory (*Bristol*), R.G.S. Hobbs (*Richmond*), C.F.H. Wells (*Devonport Services*), N.L. Evans (*Un. Services*)

Referee: Dr J.R. Wheeler (*Ireland*)

I.S. Smith scored but A.S. Dykes failed (3–0); C.C. Tanner and C.D. Aarvold scored but D.W. Burland failed to convert (3–6). (H.T.). C.D. Aarvold and B.H. Black scored for D.W. Burland to convert both (3–16).

65,000 spectators, including the Duke of York, watched in brilliant weather. Although the Scottish backs showed some good touches in attack they were outpaced and the slightly built Wood had an unhappy second half trying to tackle the burly Burland, whose straight running set up two scores.

WALES   Swansea   **4 February 1933**

SCOTLAND:	1 goal, 1 penalty goal, 1 try	11	**Win**
WALES:	1 try	3	

Scotland: D.I. Brown (*Camb. Univ.*); I.S. Smith* (*London Scot.*), H.D.B. Lorraine (*Oxford Univ.*), H. Lind (*Dunfermline*), K.C. Fyfe (*Camb. Univ.*); K.L.T. Jackson (*Oxford Univ.*), W.R. Logan (*Edin. Wrs.*); J.A. Waters (*Selkirk*), J.M. Ritchie (*Watsonians*), J.R. Thom (*Watsonians*), J. A. Beattie (*Hawick*), M.S. Stewart (*Stewart's FP*), W.B. Welsh (*Hawick*), R. Rowand (*Glas. HSFP*), J.M. Henderson (*Edin. Acads.*)

Wales: G. Baylis (*Pontypool*); A. Hickman (*Neath*), E.C. Davey (*Swansea*), W. Wooller (*Rydal School*), A.H. Jones (*Cardiff*); R.R. Morris (*Swansea*), B. Evans (*Swansea*); A. Skym (*Cardiff*), B. Evans (*Llanelli*), E. Jones (*Llanelli*), R.B. Jones (*Camb. Univ.*), D. Thomas (*Swansea*), W.G. Thomas* (*Swansea*), T. Arthur (*Neath*), I. Isaacs (*Cardiff*)

Referee: J.G. Bott (*Ireland*)   **Touch judges:** M.A. Allan, J.S. Jones

I.S. Smith scored but K.C. Fyfe failed (3–0); K.C. Fyfe kicked a penalty (6–0). (H.T.). K.L.T. Jackson scored and K.C. Fyfe converted (11–0); T. Arthur scored but W. Wooller failed (11–3).

Wales were forced to make some late changes. M.J. Turnbull called off and it was decided that H.M. Bowcott should stand down to allow the Swansea halves to play together. R.W. Boon and V.G.J. Jenkins were also replaced at the last moment. Scotland had eight new caps including Brown at full back who misfielded the opening kick and thereafter never put a foot wrong.

Scotland who held a distinct territorial advantage in the first half, scored twice. Smith scored with a typical run to the corner flag and then Fyfe kicked a good penalty from near the centre. Wales started the second half without D. Thomas who had broken a collar bone and fell further behind when another long run by Smith finished with Jackson scoring. A late revival by the depleted Welsh pack gave Arthur a score after a good forward rush. Lind who defended well was subdued in attack, for Davey tackled viciously and never gave him room to move. Once again the Scots were numbered but this time the decision was not revoked.

After the match the SRU selection committee, headed by Dan Drysdale, retired to their hotel room to pick the XV for the next game in Dublin. Although delighted with the result, the committee found points to discuss and after a while deemed it sensible to ring for some further refreshments. When a head was poked round the door Dan said, 'Ah, the same again'. 'Oh, good!', said the face and vanished but nothing arrived and it took another approach before the drinks appeared. Suitably fortified the committee resumed its deliberations and eventually decided to play an unchanged team — which was just as well for one morning paper carried the news that 'the same' team had indeed been chosen!

ENGLAND   Murrayfield   18 March 1933

SCOTLAND:	1 try	3	Win
ENGLAND:	Nil	0	

Scotland: D.I. Brown (*Camb. Univ.*); I.S. Smith* (*London Scot.*), H.D.B. Lorraine (*Oxford Univ.*), H. Lind (*Dunfermline*), K.C. Fyfe (*Camb. Univ.*); K.L.T. Jackson (*Oxford Univ.*), W.R. Logan (*Edin. Wrs.*); J.A. Waters (*Selkirk*), J.R. Thom (*Watsonians*), J.M. Ritchie (*Watsonians*), W.B. Welsh (*Hawick*), J.M. Henderson (*Edin. Acads.*), M.S. Stewart (*Stewart's FP*), R. Rowand (*Glas. HSFP*), J.A. Beattie (*Hawick*)

England: T.W. Brown (*Bristol*); L.A. Booth (*Headingley*), D.W. Burland (*Bristol*), R.A. Gerrard (*Bath*), A.L. Novis* (*Army*); W. Elliot (*RN*), B.C. Gadney (*Leicester*); D.A. Kendrew (*Army*), G.G. Gregory (*Bristol*), R.J. Longland (*Northampton*), C.F.H. Webb (*RN*), A.S. Roncoroni (*Richmond*), W.H. Weston (*Northampton*), C.L. Troop (*Army*), E.H. Sadler (*Army*)

Referee: Dr J.R. Wheeler (*Ireland*)   **Touch judges:** F.J.C. Moffat, H.A. Haigh Smith

K.C. Fyfe scored but did not convert (3–0). (H.T.).

It was fortunate for England that they exercised a definite superiority forward, for during the game both their centres went lame and some desperate tackling was needed to keep the score down to a single try.

172

IRELAND   Lansdowne Road   1 April 1933

SCOTLAND:	2 drop goals	**8**	**Win**
IRELAND:	2 tries	**6**	

Scotland: D.I. Brown (*Camb. Univ.*); I.S. Smith* (*London Scot.*), H.D.B. Lorraine (*Oxford Univ.*), H. Lind (*Dunfermline*), P.M.S. Gedge (*Edin. Wrs.*); K.L.T. Jackson (*Oxford Univ.*), W.R. Logan (*Edin. Wrs.*); J.A. Waters (*Selkirk*), J.R. Thom (*Watsonians*), J.M. Ritchie (*Watsonians*), J.A. Beattie (*Hawick*), M.S. Stewart (*Stewart's FP*), W.B. Welsh (*Hawick*), R. Rowand (*Glas. HSFP*), J.M. Henderson (*Edin. Acads.*)

Ireland: R.H. Pratt (*Dublin Univ.*); J.J. O'Connor (*UC Cork*), P.B. Coote (*Leicester*), M.P. Crowe (*Lansdowne*), E.J. Lightfoot (*Lansdowne*); E.O. Davy* (*Lansdowne*), P.F. Murray (*Wanderers*); G.R. Beamish (*Leicester*), M.J. Dunne (*Lansdowne*), H. O'Neill (*UC Cork*), J. Russell (*UC Cork*), J.A.E. Siggins (*Collegians*), C.E. St.J. Beamish (*Harlequins*), V.J. Pike (*Lansdowne*), W.M. Ross (*QU Belfast*)

Referee: B.S. Cumberlege (*England*)   **Touch judges:** D. Drysdale

M.P. Crowe scored but failed to convert (0–3); K.L.T. Jackson dropped a goal (4–3). (H.T.). P.F. Murray scored but J.A.E. Siggins failed (4–6); H. Lind dropped a goal (8–6).

This game had been postponed from 25 February when an appalling blizzard not only left the ground under inches of slushy snow but also forced the Scottish team to lie off Dublin Bay for sixteen hours and they were in no condition to play when they got ashore on the Saturday morning.

For this game Scotland were forced to make the only change during the season when Gedge replaced Fyfe who had been injured in a car accident on the previous day. This was a really bruising match for the ground was very hard and both sides tackled fiercely. Lind suffered a nasty face scrape, Smith was lame for most of the match, Lorraine was tackled so heavily by Coote that he was dazed for the rest of the day, while Gedge broke a bone in his hand attempting a hand off. Scotland, however, led at half time but fell behind immediately after the start. Davy put in a long kick to the corner which, unnoticed by the touch judge and referee, went into touch off the corner post. From the resultant line out and scrum Murray slipped over for a try to put Ireland in the lead. The Scottish pack then set to and controlled play so well that Logan and Jackson, the only fit backs, were able to take play gradually into the Irish 25. With some ten minutes left, Logan from a scrum threw a long pass to Lind who just had time to drop a good goal. So in I.S. Smith's last season he had the satisfaction of captaining Scotland to the Triple Crown.

WALES   Murrayfield   3 February 1934

SCOTLAND:	1 penalty goal, 1 try	**6**	**Loss**
WALES:	2 goals, 1 try	**13**	

Scotland: K.W. Marshall (*Edin. Acads.*); R.W. Shaw (*Glas. HSFP*), R.C.S. Dick (*Camb.*

173

Univ.), H. Lind* (*Dunfermline*), J. Park (*RHSFP*); K.L.T. Jackson (*Oxford Univ.*), W.R. Logan (*Edin. Wrs.*); W.A. Burnet (*West of Scot.*), L.B. Lambie (*Glas. HSFP*), J.M. Ritchie (*Watsonians*), J.D. Lowe (*Heriot's FP*), M.S. Stewart (*Stewart's FP*), D.A. Thom (*London Scot.*), J.A. Waters (*Selkirk*), R. Rowand (*Glas. HSFP*)

Wales: V.G.J. Jenkins (*Bridgend*); B.T.V. Cowey (*Newport*), E.C. Davey* (*Swansea*), J.I. Rees (*Edin. Wrs.*), G.R.R. Jones (*London Welsh*); C.W. Jones (*Camb. Univ.*), B. Jones (*Llanelli*); Y. Evans (*London Welsh*), T. Day (*Swansea*), D.R. Prosser (*Neath*), G. Hughes (*Penarth*), W. Ward (*Cross Keys*), J. Lang (*Llanelli*), G. Prosser (*Neath*), A. Fear (*Newport*)

Referee: H.L.V. Day (*England*)   **Touch judges:** F.J.C. Moffat, A. Wyndham Jones

J.I. Rees scored and V.G.J. Jenkins converted (0–5). (H.T.). B.T.V. Cowey scored and V.G.J. Jenkins converted (0–10); J.M. Ritchie kicked a penalty (3–10); W.R. Logan scored but K.L.T. Jackson failed (6–10); B.T.V. Cowey scored but V.C.J. Jenkins failed (6–13).

Scotland had to find late replacements for D.I. Brown, K.C. Fyfe and J.A. Beattie and so had eight new caps with three in the backs so understandably were better in defence than in combined play. C.W. Jones played well at half and provided the capable Welsh backs with many opportunities for attack. A. Fear was conspicuous at wing forward, continually harassing Logan but was over inclined to be offside. Wales seemed comfortably placed with twenty minutes to go when Scotland started to fight back. Dick made a great break and kicked over Jenkins' head. Shaw whipped after the ball to get the touch but it bounced sideways off a post to Cowey who kicked it dead. The rally was sustained for Ritchie kicked a penalty and Logan, following good forward play scored to bring the score to 6–10. But the defence held firm and in the dying minutes Cowey, although knocking down the corner flag, scored in the corner to make the match safe.

IRELAND   Murrayfield   24 February 1934

SCOTLAND: 2 goals, 1 penalty goal, 1 try   16   **Win**

IRELAND: 3 tries   9

Scotland: K.W. Marshall (*Edin. Acads.*), R.W. Shaw (*Glas. HSFP*), R.C.S. Dick (*Camb. Univ.*), H. Lind (*Dunfermline*), J.A. Crawford (*Army*); J.L. Cotter (*Hillhead HSFP*), W.R. Logan (*Edin. Wrs.*); J.W. Allan (*Melrose*), G.S. Cottington (*Kelso*), J.M. Ritchie (*Watsonians*), J.A. Beattie (*Hawick*), M.S. Stewart* (*Stewart's FP*), L.B. Lambie (*Glas. HSFP*), J.A. Waters (*Selkirk*), J.G. Watherston (*Edin. Wrs.*)

Ireland: R.H. Pratt (*Dublin Univ.*); D. Lane (*UC Cork*), N.H. Lambert (*Lansdowne*), J.V. Reardon (*Cork Const.*), J.J. O'Connor (*UC Cork*); J.L. Reid (*London Irish*), G.J. Morgan (*Clontarf*); V.J. Pike (*Army*), W.M. Ross (*QU Belfast*), C.R. Graves (*Wanderers*), S. Walker (*Instonians*), J.A.E. Siggins* (*Collegians*), C.E.St.J. Beamish (*RAF*), M.J. Dunne (*Lansdowne*), J. Russell (*UC Cork*)

Referee: B.S. Cumberlege (*England*)   **Touch judges:** Dr G.W. Simpson, R.D. Gray

J. Russell scored but J.A.E. Siggins failed (0–3); R.C.S. Dick scored and R.W. Shaw converted (5–3); J.W. Allan kicked a penalty (8–3); J.A. Crawford scored but J.W. Allan

174

failed (11–3). (H.T.). R.C.S. Dick scored and R.W. Shaw converted (16–3); J.J. O'Connor and J. Russell scored unconverted tries (16–9).

This was Scotland's first win over Ireland at Murrayfield. The Irish forwards started in their usual bustling style, taking every scrum and it was no surprise when O'Connor gave Russell a chance to force his way over for the opening score. Then Scotland began to win some ball and it became obvious that the Scottish backs were in dangerous form. Cotter made a good break but his final pass to Shaw arrived with a tackler. Then he gave an awkward pass to Lind, who stooped and whipped the ball backwards through his legs to Dick. The defence was baffled and Dick shot off and swerved past the full back to score. After an Allan penalty further good passing set Crawford off along the touch line and a most determined run saw him go in at the corner with two defenders on his back. Shaw also got over but lost the try because of a defective touch down. In the second half Dick had another fine score but then the Irish pack rallied furiously, O'Connor and Russell scored after vigorous rushes. Beamish was only halted by a fierce tackle by Waters, then time ran out.

ENGLAND   Twickenham   17 March 1934

SCOTLAND: 1 try   3   **Loss**
ENGLAND: 2 tries   6

Scotland: K.W. Marshall (*Edin. Acads.*); R.W. Shaw (*Glas. HSFP*), R.C.S. Dick (*Camb. Univ.*), H. Lind (*Dunfermline*), K.C. Fyfe (*Camb. Univ.*); J.L. Cotter (*Hillhead HSFP*), W.R. Logan (*Edin. Wrs.*); J.W. Allan (*Melrose*), G.S. Cottington (*Kelso*), J.M. Ritchie (*Watsonians*), J.A. Beattie (*Hawick*), M.S. Stewart* (*Stewart's FP*), L.B. Lambie (*Glas. HSFP*), J.A. Waters (*Selkirk*), J.G. Watherston (*Edin. Wrs.*)

England: H.G. Owen-Smith (*St Mary's*); G.W.C. Meikle (*Waterloo*), R.A. Gerrard (*Bath*), P. Cranmer (*Oxford Univ.*), L.A. Booth (*Headingley*); C.F. Slow (*Leicester*), B.C. Gadney* (*Leicester*); H. Rew (*Blackheath*), G.G. Gregory (*Bristol*), R.J. Longland (*Northampton*), J.W. Forrest (*RN*), J. Dicks (*Northampton*), W.H. Weston (*Northampton*), D.A. Kendrew (*Army*), H.A. Fry (*Liverpool*)

Referee: F.W. Haslett (*Ireland*)   **Touch judges:** D. Drysdale, H.A. Haigh Smith

R.W. Shaw scored but K.C. Fyfe failed (3–0); G.W.C. Meikle scored but failed to convert (3–3). (H.T.). L.A. Booth scored but D.A. Kendrew failed (3–6).

This was an exciting game played at a tremendous pace. Scotland held the upper hand in the first half but only once got past some fine tackling. Dick had a slashing break through which Lind continued, to send Shaw in at the corner. The first English score came from a penalty kick taken by Forrest near mid-field. The ball hit a Scottish forward on the back and shot sideways to Fry who started a good passing run which gave Meikle a clear run along the touch-line to score. Near the close Lind made three good breaks through the centre but fell to good tackles. On the last break the ball bounced nicely for Booth who was left with a long clear run up to Marshall whose desperate tackle he broke through with a fast swerve.

WALES   Cardiff   2 February 1935

SCOTLAND: 2 tries   6   **Loss**
WALES: 1 drop goal, 2 tries   10

Scotland: K.W. Marshall (*Edin. Acads.*); W.G.S. Johnston (*Camb. Univ.*), R.C.S. Dick (*Guy's*), R.W. Shaw (*Glas. HSFP*), K.C. Fyfe* (*Camb. Univ.*); C.F. Grieve (*Oxford Univ.*), W.R. Logan (*Edin. Wrs.*); R.O. Murray (*Camb. Univ.*), G.S. Cottington (*Kelso*), R.M. Grieve (*Kelso*), J.A. Beattie (*Hawick*), W.A. Burnet (*West of Scot.*), D.A. Thom (*London Scot.*), J.A. Waters (*Selkirk*), L.B. Lambie (*Glas. HSFP*)

Wales: V.G.J. Jenkins (*Bridgend*); A. Bassett (*Aberavon*), W. Wooller (*Camb. Univ.*), E.C. Davey* (*Swansea*), J.I. Rees (*Edin. Wrs.*); C.W. Jones (*Camb. Univ.*), W.C. Powell (*Northampton*); T. Day (*Swansea*), S.C. Murphy (*Cross Keys*), T.J. Rees (*Newport*), D. Thomas (*Swansea*), T. Williams (*Cross Keys*), A.M. Rees (*Camb. Univ.*), J. Lang (*Llanelli*), A. Fear (*Newport*)

Referees: F.W. Haslett (*Ireland*)   **Touch judges:** D. Drysdale, J.L. Thorn

C.W. Jones scored but V.G.J. Jenkins failed (0–3); W. Wooller scored but V.G.J. Jenkins failed (0–6); D.A. Thom scored but R.W. Shaw failed (3–6). (H.T.). R.W. Shaw scored but K.C. Fyfe failed (6–6); V.G.J. Jenkins dropped a goal (6–10).

This was a match of three phases. At first C.W. Jones was in tremendous form, scoring one fine solo try and sending Wooller in for a second. Then the Scottish pack, with Beattie setting a fine lead, aroused itself; quick dribbling, short passing and keen following up kept the Welsh backs on the defensive but only one score was achieved. However, Jones stopping one such rush had an arm badly wrenched and had to go off, Rees coming to stand off with Fear on the wing. In the second half Wales had the wind which they used most judiciously but late on Shaw moved up to stand off and at once began to run through the Welsh defence. He brought the scores equal only to see Jenkins run back, pick up a kick ahead, turn and drop a magnificent 40 yards goal to win the match.

IRELAND   Lansdowne Road   23 February 1935

SCOTLAND: 1 goal   5   **Loss**
IRELAND: 4 tries   12

Scotland: K.W. Marshall (*Edin. Acads.*); W.G.S. Johnston (*Camb. Univ.*), R.C.S. Dick (*Guy's*), H. Lind (*London Scot.*), K.C. Fyfe (*Camb. Univ.*); R.W. Shaw* (*Glas. HSFP*), W.R. Logan (*Edin. Wrs.*); A.S.B. McNeil (*Watsonians*), G.S. Cottington (*Kelso*), R.M. Grieve (*Kelso*), J.A. Beattie (*Hawick*), W.A. Burnet (*West of Scot.*), D.A. Thom (*London Scot.*), J.A. Waters (*Selkirk*), L.B. Lambie (*Glas. HSFP*)

Ireland: D.P. Morris (*Bective Rangers*); J.J. O'Connor (*UC Cork*), E.C. Ridgeway (*Wanderers*), A.H. Bailey (*UC Dublin*), D. Lane (*UC Cork*); V.A. Hewitt (*Instonians*), G.J.

Morgan (*Clontarf*); S.J. Deering (*Bective Rangers*), J. Russell (*UC Cork*), P.J. Lawlor (*Bective Rangers*), C.R.A. Graves (*Wanderers*), S. Walker (*Instonians*), J.A.E. Siggins* (*Collegians*), C.E.St.J. Beamish (*RAF*), H.J.M. Sayers (*Army*)

Referee: J. Hughes (*England*) **Touch judges:** J.B. Nelson, Dr J. Wallace

J.J. O'Connor scored but E.J. Ridgeway failed (0–3); R.W. Shaw scored and K.C. Fyfe converted (5–3).(H.T.). P.J. Lawlor scored but J.A.E. Siggins failed (5–6); A.H. Bailey scored but E.J. Ridgeway failed (5–9); E.C. Ridgeway scored but H.J.M. Sayers failed (5–12).

In a day of misty rain the much heavier Irish pack ruled the game throughout and eventually an overworked Scottish defence broke down. The Irish backs were not outstanding and a goal kicker was badly needed. The first Irish score came from a bad pass by Morgan which trundled along the ground to O'Connor, who fly kicked it ahead and just beat the defence to the touch. The Scottish score also came from a loose ball. Dick broke through to be tackled inside the Irish half. Lind stabbed the ball forward and Shaw was on to it in a flash, kicking it over the line and getting there first. Then in the second half the continual Irish pressure eventually won the match comfortably. The two Borderers, Waters and Beattie, were the best in the beaten pack.

ENGLAND   Murrayfield   16 March 1935

SCOTLAND: 2 goals   10   **Win**

ENGLAND: 1 drop goal, 1 try   7

Scotland: K.W. Marshall (*Edin. Acads.*); J.E. Forrest (*Glas. Acads.*), R.C.S. Dick (*Guy's*), W.C.W. Murdoch (*Hillhead HSFP*), K.C. Fyfe (*Camb. Univ.*); R.W. Shaw* (*Glas. HSFP*), W.R. Logan (*Edin. Wrs.*); R.O. Murray (*Camb. Univ.*), P.W. Tait (*RHSFP*), R.M. Grieve (*Kelso*), J.A. Beattie (*Hawick*), W.A. Burnet (*West of Scot.*), D.A. Thom (*London Scot.*), J.A. Waters (*Selkirk*), L.B. Lambie (*Glas. HSFP*)

England: H. Boughton (*Gloucester*); L.A. Booth (*Headingley*), P. Cranmer (*Richmond*), J. Heaton (*Liverpool Univ.*), R. Leyland (*Waterloo*); J.R. Auty (*Headingley*), B.C. Gadney* (*Leicester*); J. Dicks (*Northampton*), E.S. Nicholson (*Oxford Univ.*), R.J. Longland (*Northampton*), A.J. Clark (*Coventry*), C.F.H. Webb (*RN*), W.H. Weston (*Northampton*), A.T. Payne (*Bristol*), A.G. Cridlan (*Blackheath*)

Referee: R.W. Jeffares (*Ireland*) **Touch judges:** F.J.C. Moffat, H.A. Haigh-Smith

P. Cranmer dropped a goal (0–4); K.C. Fyfe scored and converted (5–4); L.B. Lambie scored and K.C. Fyfe converted (10–4). (H.T.). L.A. Booth scored (10–7).

The English pack with a height and weight advantage had a double share of the ball from the scrum and line out, but were outshone in the loose, a factor which played a part in the only Scottish win of the season. In good conditions there was some fine running by both sets of backs although there was perhaps too much shadow tackling. After Cranmer had dropped a goal Murdoch intercepted a pass and set Shaw away on a move which finished when Fyfe kicked ahead and scored. Then Shaw ran down the touch line and beat two only

177

to be held up over the line, but the ball fell loose for Lambie to touch down. The only score in the second half by Booth came after a run by Cranmer but Leyland had one spectacular run beating man after man only to find his pass to Booth adjudged forward. Right on time Beattie finished a handling run by going over but again the final pass was ruled forward. Logan and Shaw were praised as a partnership.

NEW ZEALAND	Murrayfield	23 November 1935

SCOTLAND:	1 goal, 1 try	8	Loss
NEW ZEALAND:	3 goals, 1 try	18	

Scotland: J.M. Kerr (*Heriot's FP*); J.E. Forrest (*Glas. Acads.*), R.C.S. Dick (*Guy's*), W.C.W. Murdoch (*Hillhead HSFP*), K.C. Fyfe (*Camb. Univ.*); R.W. Shaw* (*Glas. HSFP*), W.R. Logan (*Edin. Wrs.*); R.M. Grieve (*Kelso*), G.L. Gray (*Gala*), G.D. Shaw (*Sale*), J.A. Beattie (*Hawick*), W.A. Burnet (*West of Scot.*), L.B. Lambie (*Glas. HSFP*), J.A. Waters (*Selkirk*), D.A. Thom (*London Scot.*)

New Zealand: G. Gilbert (*West Coast*); G.F. Hart (*Canterbury*), C.J. Oliver (*Canterbury*), M. Mitchell (*Southland*); T.H.C. Coughey (*Auckland*); J.L. Griffiths (*Wellington*), B.S. Sadler (*Wellington*); J. Hore (*Otago*), W.E. Hadley (*Auckland*), A. Lambourn (*Wellington*), R.M. McKenzie (*Manawatu*), R.R. King (*West Coast*), S.T. Reid (*Hawke's Bay*), J.E. Manchester* (*Canterbury*), A. Mahoney (*Bush Districts*)

Referee: C.H. Gadney (*England*)   **Touch judges:** F.J.C. Moffat, H. Brown

K.C. Fyfe scored but failed to convert (3–0); T.H.C. Caughey and W.E. Hadley scored and G. Gilbert converted both (3–10); T.H.C. Caughey scored but G. Gilbert failed (3–13). (H.T.). R.C.S. Dick scored and W.C.W. Murdoch converted (8–13); T.H.C. Caughey scored and G. Gilbert converted (8–18).

This was a fine fast game with plenty action from both sets of backs and forwards but New Zealand deserved their win being just that shade faster and more decisive. A good break by Shaw and Dick was finished off by Fyfe beating the defence to the corner, but then Murdoch was injured and eventually came back looking anything but fit. During his absence Caughey scored his first try. After half time Shaw made another good break to send Dick in at the posts and Scotland were back in the game. Indeed Murdoch gave Fyfe a scoring pass which was not taken and in the last minutes Sadler made a good break on the blind side which allowed Caughey to clinch the match.

WALES	Murrayfield	1 February 1936

SCOTLAND:	1 try	3	Loss
WALES:	2 goals, 1 try	13	

Scotland: K.W. Marshall (*Edin. Acads.*); W.C.W. Murdoch (*Hillhead HSFP*), R.C.S.

Dick* (*Guy's*), H.M. Murray (*Glas. Univ.*), K.C. Fyfe (*Camb. Univ.*); R.W. Shaw (*Glas. HSFP*), W.R. Logan (*Edin. Wrs.*); R.M. Grieve (*Kelso*), W.A.H. Druitt (*London Scot.*), J.A. Waters (*Selkirk*), J.A. Beattie (*Hawick*), W.A. Burnet (*West of Scot.*), M.McG. Cooper (*Oxford Univ.*), P.L. Duff (*Glas. Acads.*), G.D. Shaw (*Sale*)

Wales: V.G.J. Jenkins (*London Welsh*); J.I. Rees (*Edin. Wrs.*), C. Davey* (*Swansea*), W. Wooller (*Camb. Univ.*), B.E.W. McCall (*Welsh Regt.*); C.W. Jones (*Camb. Univ.*), H. Tanner (*Swansea*); T.J. Rees (*Newport*), B. Evans (*Llanelli*), T. Williams (*Cross Keys*), H. Thomas (*Neath*), G. Williams (*Aberavon*), A.M. Ross (*London Welsh*), J. Lang (*Llanelli*), E. Long (*Swansea*)

Referee: C.H. Gadney (*England*) **Touch judges:** J.B. Nelson, D. Jones

W. Wooller scored but V.J.G. Jenkins failed (0–3); C. Davey scored and V.C.J. Jenkins converted (0–8). (H.T.). H.M. Murray scored but K.C. Fyfe failed (388); C.W. Jones scored and V.G.J. Jenkins converted (3–13).

Wales began strongly and eventually a half break by Jones let Wooller race in for the opening score. Near half time a tackle on Murdoch produced a loose ball that was snatched up and Davey scored. Scotland restarted well and picked up a score when Jenkins, in possession, threw out a pass which Murray pounced upon to score at the corner. Shaw and Dick followed with some fine runs which threatened danger but Wales finished strongly and Jones, who had struck up a good partnership with Tanner, rounded off the game with a lovely solo dodging run.

IRELAND Murrayfield 22 February 1936

SCOTLAND: 1 drop goal **4** **Loss**

IRELAND: 1 drop goal, 2 tries **10**

Scotland: J.M. Kerr (*Heriot's FP*); W.C.W. Murdoch (*Hillhead HSFP*), R.C.S. Dick* (*Guy's*), H.M. Murray (*Glas. Univ.*), R.J.E. Whitworth (*London Scot.*); R.W. Shaw (*Glas. HSFP*), W.R. Logan (*Edin. Wrs.*); R.M. Grieve (*Kelso*), W.A.H. Druitt (*London Scot.*), J.A. Waters (*Selkirk*), J.A. Beattie (*Hawick*), W.A. Burnet (*West of Scot.*), M.McG. Cooper (*Oxford Univ.*), P.L. Duff (*Glas. Acads.*), V.G. Weston (*Kelvinside Acads.*)

Ireland: G.L. Malcolmson (*NIFC*); J.J. O'Conner (*UC Cork*), A.H. Bailey (*UC Dublin*), L.B. McMahon (*Blackrock Coll.*), C.V. Boyle (*Dublin Univ.*); V.A. Hewitt (*Instonians*), G.J. Morgan (*Clontarf*); R. Alexander (*NIFC*), S. Walker (*Instonians*), C.E.St.J. Beamish (*RAF*), H.J.M. Sayers (*Army*), S.J. Deering (*Bective Rangers*), J.A.E. Siggins* (*Collegians*), C.R.A. Graves (*Wanderers*), J. Russell (*UC Cork*)

Referee: J.W. Faull (*Wales*) **Touch judges:** R.M. Meldrum, S.T. Irwin

S. Walker scored but J.A.E. Siggins failed (0–3); L.B. McMahon scored but A.H. Bailey failed (0–6); V.A. Hewitt dropped a goal (0–10). (H.T.). W.C.W. Murdoch dropped a goal (4–10).

Play was fairly even during the first half but Ireland seized on two loose passes to score. McMahon picked both up and set the Irish forwards away on a good handling run for the first try but ran in on his own for the second. Just on half time Hewitt dropped a goal.

179

Murdoch moved to centre in the second half and although Scotland showed improved form the Irish defence was too sound and all that could be managed was a fine drop goal by Murdoch.

ENGLAND	**Twickenham**	**21 March 1936**

SCOTLAND:	1 goal, 1 penalty goal	8	**Loss**
ENGLAND:	3 tries	9	

Scotland: J.M. Kerr (Heriot's FP); R.W. Shaw (*Glas. HSFP*), H. Lind (*London Scot.*), R.C.S. Dick (*Guy's*), K.C. Fyfe (*Sale*); C.F. Grieve (*Oxford Univ.*), W.R. Logan (*Edin. Wrs.*); R.M. Grieve (*Kelso*), G.S. Cottington (*Headingley*), W.A.H. Druitt (*London Scot.*), J.A. Beattie* (*Hawick*), W.A. Burnet (*West of Scot.*), R.W. Barrie (*Hawick*), J.A. Waters (*Selkirk*), V.G. Weston (*Kelvinside Acads.*)

England: H.G. Owen-Smith (*St. Mary's*); H.S. Sever (*Sale*), P. Cranmer (*Richmond*), R.A. Gerrard (*Bath*), A. Obolensky (*Oxford Univ.*); P.L. Candler (*St. Bart's*), B.C. Gadney* (*Leicester*); R.J. Longland (*Northampton*), H.B. Toft (*Waterloo*), J. Dicks (*Northampton*), C.F.H. Webb (*RN*), P.E. Dunkley (*Harlequins*), R. Bolton (*Harlequins*), P.W.P. Brook (*Harlequins*), W.H. Weston (*Northampton*)

Referee: T.H. Phillips (*Wales*)   **Touch judges:** M.A. Allan, H.A. Haigh-Smith

R. Bolton scored but P. Cranmer failed (0–3); K.C. Fyfe kicked a penalty (3–3); P.L. Candler scored but P. Cranmer failed (3–6); H.S. Sever failed (3–9); R.W. Shaw scored and K.C. Fyfe converted (8–9). (H.T.).

In a day of sunshine there was some attractive but not outstanding play. After a fairly even first half, the second spell developed into an English siege, but their backs were well held by a good defence. Fyfe marked the dangerous Obolensky out of the game and Cranmer did some hard running spoiled by poor finishing. It was fortunate that England lacked a kicker for many scoring kicks were missed whereas Fyfe kicked one good 40 yard penalty and a conversion from the touch line. The English pack held an advantage throughout and Logan was handicapped by sluggish heeling and little ball. During the last few minutes one has a memory of England camped on the Scottish line; Gadney kicking to touch at the corner, Scotland taking scrums instead of line-outs, but losing the strike, for the whole process to be repeated for Gadney refused to open the game up.

WALES	**Swansea**	**6 February 1937**

SCOTLAND:	2 goals, 1 try	13	**Win**
WALES:	2 tries	6	

Scotland: J.M. Kerr (*Heriot's FP*); W.G.S. Johnston (*Richmond*), R.C.S. Dick (*Guy's*),

180

D.J. Macrae (*St Andrews Univ.*), R.W. Shaw (*Glas. HSFP*); W.A. Ross (*Hillhead HSFP*), W.R. Logan* (*Edin. Wrs.*); M.M. Henderson (*Dunfermline*), G.L. Gray (*Gala*), W.M. Inglis (*Camb. Univ.*), G.B. Horsburgh (*London Scot.*), C.L. Melville (*Army*), W.B. Young (*Camb. Univ.*), J.A. Waters (*Selkirk*), G.D. Shaw (*Gala*)

Wales: T.D. James (*Aberavon*); W.H. Clement (*Llanelli*), W. Wooller (*Cardiff*), J.I. Rees* (*Edin. Wrs.*), W.H. Hopkin (*Chepstow*); R.R. Morris (*Bristol*), H. Tanner (*Swansea*); T.J. Rees (*Newport*), W.H. Travers (*Newport*), T. Williams (*Cross Keys*), H. Thomas (*Neath*), H. Rees (*Cardiff*), E. Long (*Swansea*), E. Watkins (*Cardiff*), A.M. Rees (*London Welsh*)

Referee: C.H. Gadney (*England*) **Touch judges:** R.M. Meldrum, W.R. Thomas

W. Wooller scored but T.D. James failed (0–3); R.C.S. Dick scored but G.D. Shaw failed (3–3). (H.T.). R.C.S. Dick scored and G.D. Shaw converted (8–3); R.W. Shaw scored and G.D. Shaw converted (13–3); W. Wooller scored but T.D. James failed (13–6).

Scotland after a shaky start settled down and finished in firm control. The Welsh pack had the better of the set scrums, taking a count of 31–16, for Scotland, with five new caps in the pack, had selected four number eights, but by the end of the first half the back row, fast and tackling fiercely, had upset the fluency of the Welsh backs. Wooller, expected to be a match winner, did score both tries but was very firmly contained by Dick. Wales, with the sun and wind began strongly and Wooller, running on to a dropped pass, kicked ahead, got the bounce and ran in for the opening score. Gradually the Scottish loose play began to tell and Macrae with a hard swerving run made an opening for Dick to equalise before half time. Wales restarted strongly but some fine handling by the Scots brought a score. Beginning with Macrae, R.W. Shaw, Inglis and Waters handled before Dick scored again. Then Kerr, fielding an attacking kick ahead, burst up the left wing, drew Hopkins before passing to R.W. Shaw whose pace got him in at the corner. In the last minutes Wooller got into his stride and ran round Johnston to score far out. Logan was praised for his work behind a sluggish tight scrum and it is interesting to note that he and the rival captain were both playing for the same club.

IRELAND Lansdowne Road 27 February 1937

SCOTLAND:	1 drop goal	**4**	**Loss**
IRELAND:	1 goal, 2 tries	11	

Scotland: J.M. Kerr (*Heriot's FP*); W.G.S. Johnston (*Richmond*), D.J. Macrae (*St Andrews Univ.*), I. Shaw (*Glas. HSFP*), R.W. Shaw (*Glas. HSFP*); R.B. Bruce Lockhart (*Camb. Univ.*), W.R. Logan* (*Edin. Wrs.*); M.M. Henderson (*Dunfermline*), G.L. Gray (*Gala*), W.M. Inglis (*Camb. Univ.*), G.B. Horsburgh (*London Scot.*), C.L. Melville (*Army*), W.B. Young (*Camb. Univ.*), J.A. Waters (*Selkirk*), G.D. Shaw (*Gala*)

Ireland: G.L. Malcolmson (*RAF*); C.V. Boyle (*Dublin Univ.*), A.H. Bailey (*UC Dublin*), L.B. McMahon (*Blackrock*), F.G. Moran (*Clontarf*); G.E. Cromey (*QU Belfast*), G.J. Morgan* (*Clontarf*); C.R.A. Graves (*Wanderers*), T.S. Corken (*Collegians*), S. Walker (*Instonians*), S.J. Deering (*Bective Rangers*), J. Russell (*UC Cork*), P.J. Lawlor (*Bective Rangers*), J.A.E. Siggins (*Collegians*), R. Alexander (*NIFC*)

Referee: C.H. Gadney (*England*) **Touch judges:** R.K. Cuthbertson, E.C. Powell

R. Alexander scored but A.H. Bailey failed (0–3). (H.T.). L.B. McMahon and F.G. Moran scored and A.H. Bailey converted the second (0–11); I. Shaw dropped a goal (4–11).

Scotland were perhaps unlucky but Ireland deserved their win for the good first half display against a very strong bitter wind with many flurries of snow. There were some fierce exchanges and many stoppages. R.W. Shaw was concussed early during the first half and had to be taken off mid way through the second half; Waters left the field at half time to return later with three ribs strapped and Russell was also off for a while with a face injury. The Irish scores were snap efforts. Two came from loose passes while the third came after Moran had kicked ahead and the wind carried the ball half the length of the field. R.W. Shaw had to give the Irish sprint champion a yard but passed him with the ball short of the line. He plunged on the ball but only succeeded in knocking it on with the wind. He tried again but stumbled and Moran went past to touch down just short of the dead ball line. The depleted Scottish pack finished strongly but nothing came of it.

ENGLAND   Murrayfield   20 March 1937

SCOTLAND: 1 penalty goal   3   **Loss**
ENGLAND: 2 tries   6

Scotland: K.W. Marshall (*Edin. Acads.*); W.G.S. Johnston (*Richmond*), R.W. Shaw (*Glas. HSFP*), D.J. Macrae (*St Andrews Univ.*), R.H. Dryden (*Watsonians*); W.A. Ross (*Hillhead HSFP*), W.R. Logan* (*Edin. Wrs.*); M.M. Henderson (*Dunfermline*), G.L. Gray (*Gala*), W.M. Inglis (*Camb. Univ.*), G.B. Horsburgh (*London Scot.*), C.L. Melville (*Black Watch*), W.B. Young (*Camb. Univ.*), J.A. Waters (*Selkirk*), G.D. Shaw (*Sale*)

England: H.G. Owen-Smith* (*St Mary's*); E.J. Unwin (*Army*), P.L. Candler (*Bart's*), P. Cranmer (*Richmond*), H.S. Sever (*Sale*); F.J. Reynolds (*Army*), B.C. Gadney (*Leicester*); R.J. Longland (*Northampton*), H.B. Toft (*Waterloo*), H.F. Wheatley (*Coventry*), A.A. Wheatley (*Coventry*), T.F. Huskisson (*OMT*), J.G. Cook (*Bedford*), R. Bolton (*Harlequins*), W.H. Weston (*Northampton*)

Referee: S. Donaldson (*Ireland*)   **Touch judges:** F.J.C. Moffat, H.A. Haigh Smith

E.J. Unwin scored but P. Cranmer failed (0–3). (H.T.). H.S. Sever scored but J.G. Cook failed (0–6); G.D. Shaw kicked a penalty (3–6).

The English forwards were in fine form and their backs should have done better with a good supply of the ball. Some credit must go to the Scottish defence; Shaw and Macrae were too fast for the English centres, Marshall was sound and made at least three try-saving tackles while Logan had a fine game both in defence and attack. Given more ball the Scottish backs would probably have won the match. As it was G.D. Shaw, who had kicked one penalty, just failed to save the game with a last minute kick.

SCOTLAND: 1 goal, 1 penalty   8   **Win**

WALES: 2 tries   6

Scotland: G. Roberts (*Watsonians*); A.H. Drummond (*Kelvinside Acads.*), R.C.S. Dick (*Guy's*), D.J. Macrae (*St Andrews Univ.*), J.G.S. Forrest (*Camb. Univ.*); R.W. Shaw* (*Glas. HSFP*), T.F. Dorward (*Gala*); J.B. Borthwick (*Stewart's FP*), J.D. Hastie (*Melrose*), W.M. Inglis (*RE*), G.B. Horsburgh (*London Scot.*), A. Roy (*Waterloo*), W.B. Young (*Camb. Univ.*), P.L. Duff (*Glas. Acads.*), W.H. Crawford (*Un. Services*)

Wales: V.G.J. Jenkins (*London Welsh*); W.H. Clement (*Llanelli*), J.I. Rees (*Edin. Wrs.*), W. Wooller (*Cardiff*), A. Bassett (*Cardiff*); C.W. Jones* (*Cardiff*), H. Tanner (*Swansea*); M.E. Morgan (*Swansea*), W.H. Travers (*Newport*), H. Rees (*Cardiff*), F.L. Morgan (*Llanelli*), E. Watkins (*Cardiff*), A. McCarley (*Neath*), W. Vickery (*Aberavon*), A.M. Rees (*London Welsh*)

Referee: C.H. Gadney (*England*)   **Touch judges:** R.K. Cuthbertson, J.N. Jones

A McCarley scored twice but V.G.J. Jenkins failed both times (0–6). (H.T.). W.H. Crawford scored and converted (5–6); W.H. Crawford kicked a penalty (8–6).

This match will be remembered for the dramatic penalty goal kicked in the last minutes to give Scotland a win. During the first half Scotland had an equal share of the ball and hardly deserved to be behind at the interval for Shaw was in good form, clearly undisturbed by Jones, and had one saving touch down which showed that he was the fastest man in the game over 30 yards. Macrae and Dick were thrustful and the latter held Wooller from start to finish. Yet it was a run and good crosskick by Jones that put McCarley in for the first score and the same player seized on an inaccurate pass by Dorward to get his second try. Wales, however, ran into trouble when a rib injury to Morgan forced him to retire just before the interval. In the second half, Scotland with the numerical advantage pressed continuously. Drummond hit the bar with a penalty. He then picked up a pass and went over only to find that the whistle had gone for a Welsh forward pass. Dorward narrowly missed with a drop before Macrae and Forrest had a good run and found Crawford up to take a scoring pass. At this stage Wooller was limping, so McCarley came out of the pack leaving six forwards to contest the scrums. This they did very well although things became rather tousy, Dorward in particular coming in for some hammering. With less than five minutes to go Drummond tried another long range penalty which dropped short but the pressure was sustained. Man after man charged at the line and Dorward seemed to have grounded the ball but the Welsh pack fell on him. There followed a maul on the line in which a Welsh forward was judged to have interfered with the ball and a penalty was awarded. There followed a nerve-racking halt to allow the weary, the maimed and the concussed to get up and get on side whereupon Crawford kicked the goal to win the match.

IRELAND   Murrayfield   26 February 1938

SCOTLAND: 2 goals, 1 drop goal,   23   **Win**
              1 penalty goal, 2 tries

IRELAND: 1 goal, 3 tries   14

Scotland: G. Roberts (*Watsonians*); A.H. Drummond (*Kelvinside Acads.*), R.C.S. Dick (*Guy's*), D.J. Macrae (*St Andrews Univ.*), J.G.S. Forrest (*Camb. Univ.*); R.W. Shaw* (*Glas. HSFP*), T.F. Dorward (*Gala*); J.B. Borthwick (*Stewart's FP*), J.D. Hastie (*Melrose*), W.M. Inglis (*RE*), G.B. Horsburgh (*London Scot.*), A. Roy (*Waterloo*), W.B. Young (*Camb. Univ.*), P.L. Duff (*Glas. Acads.*), W.H. Crawford (*Un. Services*)

Ireland: R.G. Craig (*QU Belfast*); F.G. Moran (*Clontarf*), A.H. Bailey (*UC Dublin*), L.B. McMahon (*Blackrock*), J.J. O'Connor (*Blackrock*); G.E. Cromey (*QU Belfast*), G.J. Morgan* (*Old Belvedere*); E. Ryan (*Dolphin*), C.R.A. Graves (*Wanderers*), H. Kennedy (*Bradford*), D.B. O'Loughlin (*UC Cork*), D. Tierney (*UC Cork*), R. Alexander (*NIFC*), S. Walker (*Instonians*), J.W.S. Irwin (*NIFC*)

Referee: C.H. Gadney (*England*)   **Touch judges:** R.M. Meldrum, R.W. Jeffares

J.G.S. Forrest scored twice and W.H. Crawford converted the second (8–0); G.E. Cromey scored but A.H. Bailey failed (8–3); T.F. Dorward dropped a goal (12–3); A.H. Drummond kicked a penalty (15–3). (H.T.). D. O'Loughlin scored but H. Kennedy failed (15–6); F. Moran scored but A.H. Bailey failed (15–9); D.J. Macrae scored and W.H. Crawford converted (20–9); A.H. Drummond scored but failed (23–9); G.J. Morgan scored and S. Walker converted (23–14).

Scotland were full of brilliant running for Shaw, Macrae and Dick were quite explosive in attack. For Ireland Morgan had many dangerous dodging runs round the blind side but, with the exception of the sprinter Moran, the backs lacked pace and also seemed over anxious to curb Shaw. The Irish forwards opened with a burst that nearly brought a score but inside fifteen minutes Shaw intercepted a pass, was through at top speed and gave Forrest a clear run in. Shaw continued to worry the defence and found a chance to let Macrae away and give Forrest his second try. After the interval Ireland came back into the game when O'Loughlin charged down a kick and scored and a break by Morgan put Moran in but then a scissors move between Dick and Macrae saw the latter score. There followed a good dribbling run by Duff and Forrest which let Shaw snap up the ball and send Drummond in. With three minutes to go Morgan scored after a fine break.

ENGLAND Twickenham 19 March 1938

SCOTLAND: 2 penalty goals, 5 tries 21 **Win**

ENGLAND: 1 drop goal, 3 penalty goals, 1 try 16

Scotland: G. Roberts (*Watsonians*); W.N. Renwick (*London Scot.*), R.C.S. Dick (*Guy's*), D.J. Macrae (*St Andrews Univ.*), J.G.S. Forrest (*Camb. Univ.*); R.W. Shaw* (*Glas. HSFP*), T.F. Dorward (*Gala*); W.F. Blackadder (*West of Scot.*), J.D. Hastie (*Melrose*), W.M. Inglis (*Army*), G.B. Horsburgh (*London Scot.*), A. Roy (*Waterloo*), W.B. Young (*Camb. Univ.*), P.L. Duff (*Glas. Acads.*), W.H. Crawford (*Un. Services*)

England: G.W. Parker (*Blackheath*); H.S. Sever (*Sale*), P. Cranmer (*Moseley*), P.L. Candler (*St. Bart's*), E.J. Unwin (*Army*); F.J. Reynolds (*Army*), J.L. Giles (*Coventry*); H.F. Wheatley (*Coventry*), H.B. Toft* (*Waterloo*), R.J. Longland (*Northampton*), A.A. Wheatley (*Coventry*), R.M. Marshall (*Oxford Univ.*), A.A. Brown (*Exeter*), D.L.K. Milman (*Bedford*), W.H. Weston (*Northampton*)

Referee: I. David (*Wales*) **Touch judges:** J.C.H. Ireland, H.A. Haigh-Smith

W.N. Renwick scored but W.H. Crawford failed (3–0); G.W. Parker kicked two penalties (3–6); W.N. Renwick scored but W.H. Crawford failed (6–6); R.C.S. Dick scored but W.H. Crawford failed (9–6); E.J. Unwin scored but G.W. Parker failed (9–9); R.W. Shaw scored but W.H. Crawford failed (12–9). (H.T.). F.J. Reynolds dropped a goal (12–13); W.H. Crawford kicked two penalties (18–13); G.W. Parker kicked a penalty (18–16); R.W. Shaw scored but W.H. Crawford failed (21–16).

The King and Queen and 70,000 spectators saw what was probably the most spectacular and exciting Calcutta Cup match ever played and one made memorable by a superb personal performance by R.W. Shaw, who scored two magnificent solo tries, created a third and with the ball in his hands was a source of extreme anxiety to the English defence. Starved of the ball (the scrum count was four–one in England's favour), the Scottish forwards were splendid in the loose and get some credit for the other two tries. As for excitement a glance at the scores show that Scotland took the lead four times, England drew level three times, fluctuations which left the spectators absolutely shattered.

England made a good start and it took a touch down and good tackling to keep them out. Then a bad pass missed Reynolds and Shaw like a flash touched it ahead, picked it up and kicked ahead. Renwick ran on to the ball, also kicked ahead, got the bounce and fairly hurled himself in for a good try. Inside ten minutes Parker had kicked England into the lead only to have the Scottish forwards come back and a crashing run by Crawford let Renwick run in again. Then the Scottish forwards on their own 25 lost a scrum but the back row broke so effectively that they got the ball back and shot up field. Duff, Young and Crawford all made ground before the ball was suddenly passed in field to Dick who sprinted away for a great try. Almost at once a good run by Candler put Irwin in to equalise again. Just before half time, from some loose play at half field the ball was put out to Shaw who dummied Reynolds and cut out to the left touch line, leaving the defenders standing by his acceleration. Faced by Parker he produced a text-book right foot/left foot fast jink which left the full back sprawling in touch and ran in for a wonderful solo try.

On restarting England pressed in spite of another fine dash by Shaw which narrowly failed and from the 25 Reynolds dropped a nice goal to put England into the lead for the last time, for soon Crawford kicked two fairly lengthy penalties for offside. Parker brought the score to 18–16 with another penalty and Sever must have scored had he not collided with the goal post. With some three minutes left the ball, from a scrum near midfield on the right, came out to Shaw who shot diagonally to the left behind the English threes. With his acceleration he was clear and he finished with a five feet dive to score far out. The kick failed but that was the virtual end.

Wilson Shaw, who was carried off the field by his team and cheered by all, has two other memories of the afternoon. First the bus driver bringing the Scots to the ground got confused threading his way through the enormous crowd and delivered the players at the wrong gate. Once inside they had to walk a long way round to the dressing room through another dense crowd, who recognising them, offered a range of comments ranging from their chance of winning to the parsimony of the SRU who apparently made their team walk to the match!

Later, having showered and dressed, he made his way to the tea room which the players shared with a section of the general public. There he was glad to sink into a vacant chair beside an elderly gentleman and to start the conversation remarked: 'Pretty hard going out there to-day' and got the reply 'Yes, you must be glad you were not a player'.

WALES   Cardiff   4 February 1939

SCOTLAND: 1 penalty goal   3   **Loss**

WALES: 1 goal, 1 penalty goal, 1 try   11

Scotland: G. Roberts (*Watsonians*); J.B. Craig (*Heriot's FP*), D.J. Macrae (*St Andrews Univ.*), J.R.S. Innes (*Aberdeen Univ.*), W.N. Renwick (*Edin. Wrs.*); R.W. Shaw* (*Glas. HSFP*), W.R.C. Brydon (*Heriot's FP*); G.H. Gallie (*Edin. Acads.*), R.W.F. Sampson (*London Scot.*), W. Purdie (*Jedforest*), G.B. Horsburgh (*London Scot.*), A. Roy (*Waterloo*), W.B. Young (*King's Coll. Hosp.*), P.L. Duff (*Glas. Acads.*), W.H. Crawford (*Un. Services*)

Wales: C.H. Davies (*Swansea*); S. Williams (*Aberavon*), W. Wooller* (*Cardiff*), M.J. Davies (*Oxford Univ.*), E.L. Jones (*Llanelli*); W.T.H. Davies (*Swansea*), H. Tanner (*Swansea*); W.E.N. Davies (*Cardiff*), W.H. Travers (*Newport*), L. Davies (*Swansea*), E. Watkins (*Cardiff*), R.E. Price (*Weston-super-Mare*), E. Evans (*Llanelli*), L. Manfield (*Otley*), E. Long (*Swansea*)

Referee: A.S. Bean (*England*)   **Touch judges:** M.A. Allan, D. Jones

M.J. Davies scored but W. Wooller failed (0–3); W. Wooller kicked a penalty (0–6). (H.T.). W.H. Crawford kicked a penalty (3–6); W.H. Travers scored and W. Wooller converted (3–11).

Both sides had six new caps of whom the most controversial choice was that of Brydon for although he was a fine Sevens player he could not command a place in his Club's 1st XV. In the event Scotland were well beaten by a Welsh side which was workmanlike rather than good. The Scottish pack was weak and steady packing gave Wales a two–one strike count. G.B. Horsburgh played well but the back row were slated for contributing little in the loose and less to the scrums. At the start, Shaw, who had been quite unwell during the journey south, had a typical cut through but his kick ahead was safely touched down. Then before the interval a nice diagonal kick by W.T.H. Davies put M.J. Davies over and Wooller kicked a penalty. In the second half Tanner went off for a while with an arm injury and Crawford kicked a penalty. Shortly before the close Travers broke away from a line out and ran unattended between the right wing pair to score a simple try.

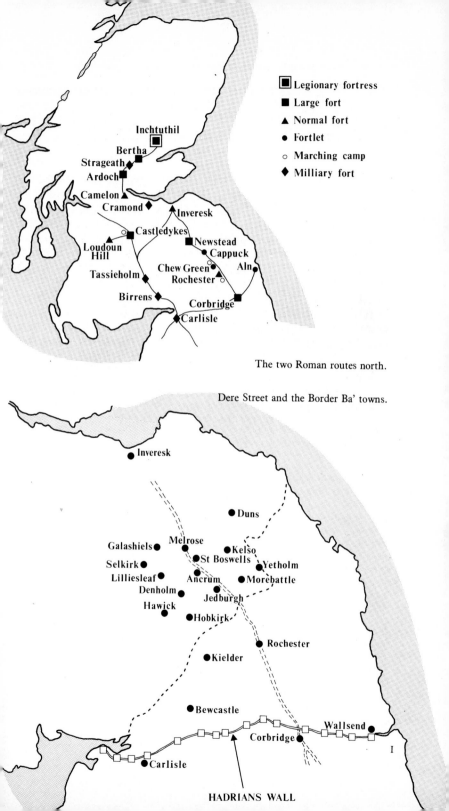

The two Roman routes north.

Dere Street and the Border Ba' towns.

Legend (top map):

■ (boxed) Legionary fortress
■ Large fort
▲ Normal fort
● Fortlet
○ Marching camp
◆ Milliary fort

Top map labels:

Inchtuthil
Bertha
Strageath
Ardoch
Camelon
Cramond
Inveresk
Castledykes
Loudoun Hill
Newstead
Cappuck
Chew Green
Rochester
Aln
Tassieholm
Birrens
Corbridge
Carlisle

Bottom map labels:

Inveresk
Duns
Galashiels
Melrose
Kelso
Selkirk
St Boswells
Yetholm
Lilliesleaf
Ancrum
Morebattle
Denholm
Jedburgh
Hawick
Hobkirk
Rochester
Kielder
Bewcastle
Wallsend
Corbridge
Carlisle
HADRIANS WALL

ITEM It is statute and the King forbiddis, that na mã play at the fute ball vnder the pane of.xl.s.to be rasit to the Lord of the land, als oft as he be taintit, or to the Schiref of the land or his ministers gif the Lordis will not punis sic trespassouris.

ITEM It is decretit and ordanit, that the wapinschawingis be haldin be the Lordis and Barronis spirituall and temporall,foure tymis in the zeir. And that the futball and golf be vtterly cryit downe, and not to be vsit. And that the bow markis be maid, at ilk paroche kirk a pair of buttis. And schuting be vsit ilk Sonday. And that ilk man schute. vj. schottis at the leist, vnder the pane to be rasit vpone thamme, that cummis not at the leist. ij. d. to be gewin to thamme that cummis to the bow markis to drink. And this to be vsit fra Pasche till Alhallowmes efter. And be the nixt midsomer to be reddy with al thair graith without failzie.And that thair be a bowar and a flegear in ilk heid towne of the Schire. And at the towne furneis hĩm of stuf and graith, efter as neidis him thairto, that thay may serue the cuntrie with. And as tuiching the futball and the golf to be punist be the Barronis vnlaw, and gif he takis not the vnlaw, that it be takin be the Kingis Officiaris. And gif the parochin be mekill,that thair be thre or foure or fyue bow markis in sic placis, as ganis thairfoir. And that all man,that is within fyftie and past. xij. zeiris sall vse schuting.

Acts of Parliament of Scotland. James I, 1424 (top); James II, 1457 (bottom). These are extracts from what are known as the Black Acts, the reference being to the density of the printing.

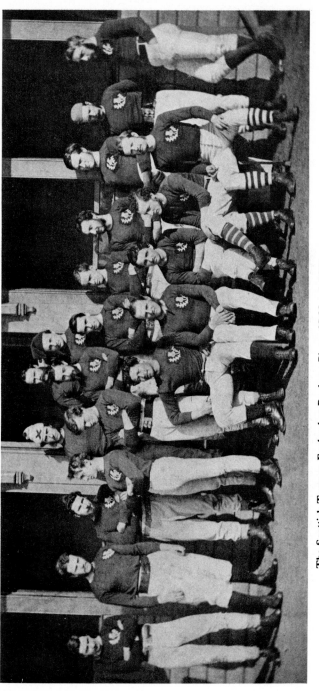

The Scottish Team v. England at Raeburn Place, 27 March 1871.
Left to right: top row: R. Munro (*St Andrews Univ.*), J.S. Thomson (*Glas. Acads.*), T. Chalmers (*Glas. Acads.*); *middle row:* A. Buchanan (*RHSFP*), A.G. Colville (*Merchistonians*), J. Forsyth (*Edin. Univ.*), J.A.W. Mein (*Edin. Acads.*), R.W. Irvine (*Edin. Acads.*), J.W. Arthur (*Glas. Acads.*), W.D. Brown (*Glas. Acads.*), D. Drew (*Glas. Acads.*), W. Cross (*Glas. Acads.*), J.F. Finlay (*Edin. Acads.*), F.J. Moncreiff* (*Edin. Acads.*), G. Ritchie (*Merchistonians*); *bottom row:* A. Clunies-Ross (*St Andrews Univ.*), W.J.C. Lyall (*Edin. Acads.*), T.R. Marshall (*Edin. Acads.*), J.L.H. McFarlane (*Edin. Acads.*), A.H. Robertson (*West of Scot.*).

SCOTTISH FOOTBALL UNION.

GRAND INTERNATIONAL MATCH,
SCOTLAND v. ENGLAND,

TO BE PLAYED AT THE

ACADEMICAL CRICKET GROUND, RAEBURN PLACE,
On MONDAY, 5th MARCH 1877.
Play to commence at 3 p.m.

STEWARDS—
THE COMMITTEE OF THE SCOTTISH FOOTBALL UNION, AND
THE OFFICERS AND COMMITTEE OF THE RUGBY FOOTBALL UNION.

◆

SCOTLAND. | ## ENGLAND.

FORWARDS.

SCOTLAND			ENGLAND		
R. W. Irvine, Captain,	.	Edinburgh Academicals.	E. Kewley, Captain,	.	Liverpool.
J. H. S. Graham,	.	Edinburgh Academicals.	M. W. Marshall,	.	Blackheath.
T. J. Torrie,	.	Edinburgh Academicals.	W. H. Hunt,	.	Preston.
J. Reid,	.	Wanderers.	G. Harrison,	.	Hull.
C. Villar,	.	Wanderers.	C. J. C. Touzell,	.	Cambridge University.
J. E. Junor,	.	Glasgow Academicals.	H. W. T. Garnett,	.	Bradford.
D. H. Watson,	.	Glasgow Academicals.	C. C. Bryden,	.	Clapham Rovers.
A. G. Petrie,	.	Royal High School F. P.	R. Todd,	.	Manchester.
H. M. Napier,	.	West of Scotland.	A. F. Law,	.	Richmond.

QUARTER-BACKS.

SCOTLAND			ENGLAND		
J. R. Hay Gordon,	.	Edinburgh Academicals.	P. L. Price,	.	Cooper's Hill.
E. I. Pocock,	.	Wanderers.	W. A. D. Evanson,	.	Richmond.

HALF-BACKS.

SCOTLAND			ENGLAND		
M. Cross,	.	Glasgow Academicals.	A. N. Hornby,	.	Preston.
R. C. Mackenzie,	.	Glasgow Academicals.	L. Stokes,	.	Blackheath.

BACKS.

SCOTLAND			ENGLAND		
J. S. Carrick,	.	Glasgow Academicals.	A. W. Pearson,	.	Blackheath.
H. H. Johnston,	.	Collegiate F. P.	L. Birkett,	.	Clapham Rovers.

THE SCOTTISH UNIFORM.—White knickerbockers and dark blue stockings, dark blue jerseys, with the Scottish Thistle as a badge; blue velvet caps, with silver badge and lace.

THE ENGLISH UNIFORM.—White knickerbockers and dark brown stockings, white jerseys, with the English Rose as a badge; rose velvet caps, with silver badge and lace.

Stewards and Representatives of the Press alone are allowed within the Ropes.
Spectators are particularly requested not to encroach upon the Field of Play.

A. R. STEWART, *Hon. Sec.*

Original Scottish cap and badge. This cap and badge belonged to J.W. Arthur and is reproduced here by courtesy of the family. Initially players purchased and dated their own caps; the plain skullcap type persisted to about 1880 when a front peak was added. The Union took control and issued the first official caps for the 1891–92 season.

Scotland v. Ireland at Powderhall, Edinburgh, 1897. This was the first of two matches played at Powderhall. The photograph was a gift from G.O. Turnbull who played and scored.

Scotland v. Wales at Inverleith, 1907. Note the splendid press box erected in 1901.

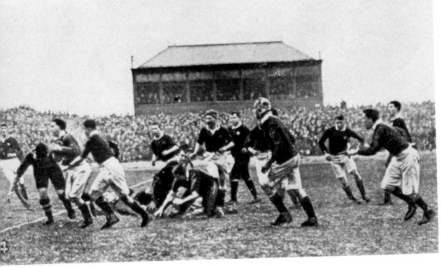

The Scottish Team v. England at Richmond, 7 March 1891.
Left to right: top row: G.T. Neilson (*West of Scot.*), J.D. Boswell (*West of Scot.*), J.E. Orr (*West of Scot.*), H.T.O. Leggatt (*Watsonians*), W.R. Gibson (*RHS*), R.G. MacMillan (*London Scot.*); *middle row*: F.W.J. Goodhue (*London Scot.*), H.J. Stevenson (*Edin. Acads.*), M.C. McEwan* (*Edin. Acads.*), C.E. Orr (*West of Scot.*), I. McIntyre (*Edin. Wrs.*); *bottom row*: G. MacGregor (*Camb. Univ.*), D.G. Anderson (*London Scot.*), P.R. Clauss (*Oxford Univ.* and *Fet.-Lor.*), W. Neilson (*Merchiston Castle*).

The Scottish Team v. Ireland at Raeburn Place, 26 January 1895.
Left to right: top row: T.M. Scott (*Hawick*), J.H. Dods (*Edin. Acads.*), J.N. Millar (*West of Scot.*) J.J. Gowans (*London Scot.*), T.L. Hendry (*Clydesdale*), A.R. Smith (*Oxford Univ.*), W.R. Gibson (*RHSFP*), G.T. Neilson (*West of Scot.*); *middle row*: G.T. Campbell (*London Scot.*), W. Neilson (*London Scot.*), R.G. Macmillan* (*London Scot.*), W.B. Cownie (*Watsonians*), R. Welsh (*Watsonians*); *bottom row*: J.W. Simpson (*RHSFP*), P.R. Clauss (*Birkenhead Park*).

VII

The Scottish team v. Wales at Inverleith, 9 February 1901.
Left to right: top row: D.R. Bedell-Sivright (*Fet.-Lor.*), J. Ross (*London Scot.*). J.A. Bell (*Clydesdale*), A.B. Flett (*Edin. Univ.*), R.S. Stronach (*Glas. Acads.*), A.W. Duncan (*Edin. Univ.*), A.B. Timms (*Edin. Univ.*), A.N. Fell (*Edin. Univ.*); *middle row*: J.M. Dykes (*Glas. High School*), J.I. Gillespie (*Edin. Acads.*), M.C. Morrison* (*RHSFP*), P. Turnbull (*Edin. Acads.*), A. Frew (*Edin. Univ.*); *bottom row*: W.H. Welsh (*Edin. Univ.*), F.H. Fasson (*Edin. Univ.*).

The Scottish team v. Wales at Inverleith, 7 February 1903.
Left to right: top row: A.G. Cairns (*Watsonians*), N. Kennedy (*West of Scot.*), W.P. Scott (*West of Scot.*), J.R.C. Greenlees (*Kel. Acads*), L. West (*Edin. Univ.*), W.E. Kyle (*Hawick*), A. Martelli (*Ireland*) (referee); *middle row*: J. Knox (*Kel. Acads.*), H.J. Orr (*London Scot.*), D.R. Bedell-Sivright (*Camb. Univ.*), M.C. Morrison* (*RHSFP*), W.T. Forrest (*Hawick*), A.N. Fell (*Edin. Univ.*), A.B. Timms (*Edin. Univ.*); *bottom row*: E.D. Simson (*Edin. Univ.*), J.E. Crabbie (*Edin. Acads.*).

VIII

The Scottish team v. Ireland at Inverleith, 23 February 1907.
left to right: top row: J.C. MacCallum (*Watsonians*), A.B.H.L. Purves (*London Scot.*), G.A. Anderson (RHSFP), I.C. Geddes (*London Scot.*), D.G. Schulze (*London Scot.*), G.M. rew (*Glas. HSFP*); *middle row:* H.G. Monteith (*London Scot.*), E.D. Simson (*London ot.*), P. Munro* (*London Scot.*), K.G. MacLeod (*Camb. Univ.*), D.R. Bedell-Sivright din. Univ.), L.M. Spiers (*Watsonians*); *bottom row:* M.W. Walter (*London Scot.*), D.G. acGregor (*Pontypridd*).

The Scottish team v. France at Inverleith, 24 January 1925.
left to right: top row: G.G. Aitken (*Oxford Univ.*), J.C. Dykes (*Glas. Acads.*), J. Gilchrist las. Acads.), J.W. Scott (*Stewart's FP*), W.H. Stevenson (*Glas. Acads.*), D.J. MacMyn amb. Univ.), I.S. Smith (*Oxford Univ.*); *middle row:* A.C. Wallace (*Oxford Univ.*), J.M. annerman (*Glas. HSFP*), J.C.R. Buchanan (*Exeter*), G.P.S. Macpherson* (*Oxford niv.*), D. Drysdale (*Heriot's FP*), A.C. Gillies (*Carlisle*); *bottom row:* J.B. Nelson (*Glas. ads.*), J.R. Paterson (*Birkenhead Park*).

IX

The Scottish team v. England at Murrayfield, 18 March 1933.
Left to right: top row: Dr J.R. Wheeler (*Ireland*) (referee), K.L.T. Jackson (*Oxford Univ.*), J.R. Thom (*Watsonians*), J.M. Ritchie (*Watsonians*), J.M. Henderson (*Edin. Acads.*), H.D.B. Lorraine (*Oxford Univ.*), D.I. Brown (*Camb. Univ.*); *middle row*: W.R. Logan (*Edin. Wrs.*), R Rowand (*Glas. HSFP*), W.B. Welsh (*Hawick*), I.S. Smith* (*London Scot.*), J.A. Beattie (*Hawick*), M.S. Stewart (*Stewart's FP*), J.A. Waters (*Selkirk*); *bottom row*: H. Lind (*Dunfermline*), K.C. Fyfe (*Camb. Univ.*).

The Scottish team v. Ireland at Murrayfield, 26 February 1938.
Left to right: top row: C.H. Gadney (*England*) (referee), D.J. Macrae (*St Andrews Univ.*), A.H. Drummond (*Kel. Acads.*), W.H. Crawford, (*Un. Services*), A. Roy (*Waterloo*), J.G.S. Forrest (*Camb. Univ.*), J.B. Borthwick (*Stewart's FP*); *middle row*: G.B. Horsburgh (*London Scot.*), J.D. Hastie (*Melrose*), R.C.S. Dick (*Guy's*), R.W. Shaw* (*Glas. HSFP*), P.L. Duff (*Glas. Acads.*), W.M. Inglis (*RE*), W.B. Young (*Camb. Univ.*); *bottom row*: G. Roberts (*Watsonians*), T.F. Dorward (*Gala*).

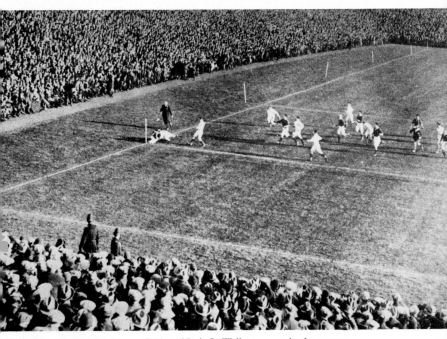

Scotland v. England at Murrayfield, 1925. A.C. Wallace scores in the corner.

England v. Scotland at Twickenham, 1938. R.W. Shaw's first score, having beaten the full back on the touch line.

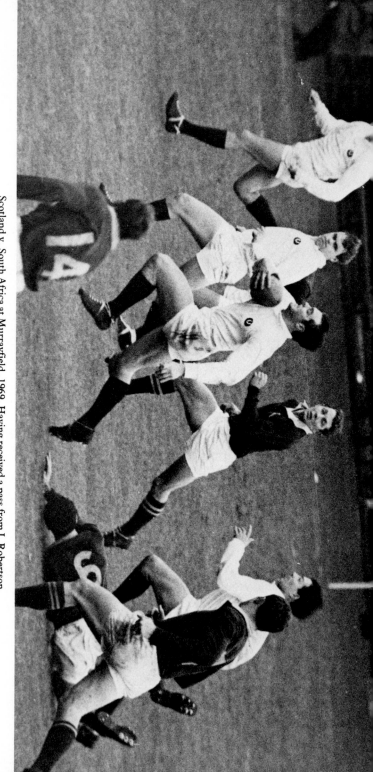

Scotland v. South Africa at Murrayfield, 1969. Having received a pass from I. Robertson, J.N.M. Frame makes a break. His pass to I.S.G. Smith let the full back sprint in for the only try of the match. A.G. Biggar is the winger running outside Smith.

Scotland v England at Murrayfield, 1971. J.N.M. Frame scores the fastest try in international rugby.

New Zealand v. Scotland at Auckland, 1975. The water polo match.

Scotland v. England, 1962. The two captains, A.R. Smith (*left*) and R.E.G. Jeeps (*right*), show the Calcutta Cup, without its lid, to Sir Tennent Sloan at the evening dinner. A.R. Smith (1955–1962) 33 caps; Sir Tennent Sloan (1905–1909) 7 caps; R.E.G. Jeeps (1957–1962) 24 caps.

A.R. Irvine (1973–1980) 37 caps.

A.B. Carmichael (*front*) (1967–1978) 50 caps; G.L. Brown (1969–1976) 30 caps.

P.C. Brown (1964–1973) 27 caps.

A.F. McHarg (1968–1979) 44 caps.

J.P. Fisher (1963–1980) 25 caps. D.M.D. Rollo (1957–1962) 40 caps.

Two Scottish Captains:
Ian McGeechan (*left*) (1969–1979) 32 caps
and Ian McLauchlan (1973–1979) 43 caps. Lord Bannerman (1921–1929) 37 caps.

IRELAND   Lansdowne Road   25 February 1939

SCOTLAND: 1 try   3   **Loss**
IRELAND: 1 penalty goal, 1 mark goal,   12
                  2 tries

Scotland: W.M. Penman (*RAF*); J.R.S. Innes (*Aberdeen Univ.*), D. J. Macrae (*St Andrews Univ.*), R.W. Shaw* (*Glas. HSFP*), K.C. Fyfe (*London Scot.*); R.B. Bruce Lockhart (*Camb. Univ.*), T.F. Dorward (*Gala*); I.C. Henderson (*Edin. Acads.*), I.N. Graham (*Edin. Acads.*), W. Purdie (*Jedforest*), G.B. Horsburgh (*London Scot.*), A. Roy (*Waterloo*), G.D. Shaw (*Sale*), D.K.A. Mackenzie (*Edin. Wrs.*), W.B. Young (*King's Coll. Hosp.*)

Ireland: C.J. Murphy (*Lansdowne*); W.J. Lyttle (*Bedford*), J.D. Torrens (*Bohemians*), H.R. McKibbin (*Instonians*), F.G. Morran (*Clontarf*); G.E. Cromey (*QU Belfast*), G.J. Morgan* (*Old Belvedere*); T.A. Headon (*UC Dublin*), C. Teehan (*UC Cork*), H.J.M. Sayers (*Army*), J.G. Ryan (*UC Dublin*), D.B. O'Loughlin (*Garryowen*), R.B. Mayne (*Malone*), J.W.S. Irwin (*NIFC*), R. Alexander (*RUC*)

Referee: C.H. Gadney (*England*)   **Touch judges:** R.M. Meldrum, E.O. Davy

F.G. Moran scored but H.R. McKibbin failed (0–3); H.R. McKibbin kicked a penalty (0–6); H.J. Sayers kicked a mark goal (0–9). (H.T.). J.R.S. Innes scored but D.J. Macrae failed (3–9); J.D. Torrens scored but H.R. McKibbin failed (3–12).

Scotland had to face sudden pelting showers of rain and sleet but by half time the wind had dropped and the field was churned to mud. This suited the Irish tactics for their forwards throughout played well being fiery in the loose. Early on Shaw and Macrae both cut through but the defence held and then the Irish pack really opened out and after some intense pressure Moran followed up a rush to score far out. Before half time Sayers had an unusual score when he marked a poor clearance and kicked a goal. Scotland had some bad luck on restarting for Macrae narrowly missed a penalty from half way. From the scramble Bruce Lockhart dropped at goal only to see a late swirl of wind carry the ball to hit the post high up and fall clear. With fifteen minutes to go Roy sent a ball back which went along the line to Shaw who cut through and passed to Macrae who sent Innes in for a try. However, the Irish forwards continued to press and Torrens was put over for the closing score.

ENGLAND   **Murrayfield**   **18 March 1939**

SCOTLAND:	2 tries	6	**Loss**
ENGLAND:	3 penalty goals	9	

Scotland: G. Roberts (*Watsonians*); J.R.S. Innes (*Aberdeen Univ.*), D.J. Macrae (*St Andrews Univ.*), R.W. Shaw* (*Glas. HSFP*), W.C.W. Murdoch (*Hillhead HSFP*); R.B. Bruce Lockhart (*London Scot.*), T.F. Dorward (*Gala*); I.C. Henderson (*Edin. Acads.*), I.N. Graham (*Edin. Acads.*), W. Purdie (*Jedforest*), G.B. Horsburgh (*London Scot.*), A. Roy (*Waterloo*), W.B. Young (*King's Coll. Hosp.*), D.K.A. Mackenzie (*Edin. Wrs.*), W.H. Crawford (*Un. Services*)

England: E.J. Parsons (*RAF*); R.H. Guest (*Liverpool Univ.*), J. Heaton (*Waterloo*), G.E. Hancock (*Birkenhead Park*), R.S.L. Carr (*Manchester*); T.A. Kemp (*St Mary's*), J. Ellis (*Wakefield*); D.E. Teden (*Richmond*), H.B. Toft* (*Waterloo*), R.E. Prescott (*Harlequins*), H.F. Wheatley (*Coventry*), T.F. Huskisson (*OMT*), J.K. Watkins (*RN*), R.M. Marshall (*Harlequins*), J.T.W. Berry (*Leicester*)

Referee: I. David (*Wales*) **Touch judges:** F.J.C. Moffat, H.A. Haigh Smith

W.C.W. Murdoch and R.W. Shaw scored but W.H. Crawford and W.C.W. Murdoch failed to convert (6–0); J. Heaton kicked two penalties (6–6). (H.T.). J. Heaton kicked a penalty (6–9).

Although it was disappointing to lose because of three penalties the result was fair, for a disciplined English pack dominated the game and a spark of enterprise in their backs would have seen Scotland routed. Yet Scotland began well; a dribble by Crawford and a run by Henderson and Shaw finished in touch only inches short. Then Innes had a run and cross-kicked. The bounce beat Heaton and Murdoch followed up to take the ball over. There followed a fine try from Shaw who had a typical accelerated burst past the defence. He was well covered about twenty yards out so changed pace, sold a dummy which halted the covering backs, and then another acceleration carried him to the line. England, with a lot of the ball (the scrum count was 48–12 in their favour), could not break through, but equalised before half time with two fine 40 yard penalties by Heaton. Immediately after half time he kicked a third which proved to be the winning score. Later in the game Shaw moved to stand off and there was one promising run by Bruce Lockhart which failed when he delayed his pass to Innes. So a year after the Triple Crown brought the Wooden Spoon.

Between the Wars

Scottish Rugby took some five years to recover from the long break and sad losses of the World War I before producing teams and players of the highest class — teams that won the mythical Triple Crown in 1925, 1933 and 1938, a distinction that sadly has evaded them since! This renaissance sprung from the strength of some half dozen or so Club sides, notably Heriot's FP, Watsonians and the Academicals in Edinburgh, the High School FP and Academicals in Glasgow and the most consistent Border team, Hawick. Club matches between those sides were thrillers watched by large crowds.

Men like D.S. Davies, D.S. Kerr, J.W. Scott, J.C.R. Buchanan and J.A. Waters maintained the vigorous pre-war standards of forward play whilst John Bannerman and Jock Beattie, outstanding in the line out and the loose, were recognised as two of the finest forwards in the game. R.A. Gallie, D.M. Bertram and J.C.H. Ireland were as effective in the open as they were at the now established art of hooking in the set scrum. J. Graham, J.R. Paterson and W.B. Welsh were back row forwards, not only sound in defence but fast enough and capable of joining the backs in attack. Then there were three in F. Kennedy, A.C. Gillies and J.W. Allan whose ability to kick goals from all ranges and angles literally won matches.

At scrum half J. Hume, also a pre-war player, was a quietly efficient player while W.E. Bryce, later also a hockey cap, was a speedy, attacking half. Two partnerships must be mentioned. J.B. Nelson was an aggressive half with a punishing hand-off and combined well with his clubmate, H. Waddell, who not only could make openings but still managed to maintain contact with his threes. His late match-winning drop goals against England in 1925 and Wales in 1930 were classics and his tally of five drop goals has tended to obscure the fact that he also ran in seven tries. Later W.R. Logan formed a fine partnership with R.W. Shaw. Ross Logan was apt to produce a rather flourishing dummy which amused the critics but annoyed his opponents who seldom failed to buy it. While often praised for his strong defensive play, he was also capable of the genuine destructive break round the scrum. Wilson Shaw was one of the game's outstanding players. Fast enough to be selected as a winger, his great asset was an ability to hit top speed inside two paces. In the memorable 1938 game at Twickenham it was this acceleration which let him set up the

189

opening score and shoot through for the final try. His ability to side step off either foot was never better seen than when, in the same match, he scored his first try by first halting the full back and then flashing between him and the touch line with a lightning left foot/right foot jink.

During the first decade we may note three outstanding partnerships in the threes. Firstly, there was E.H. Liddell, a resolute and intelligent winger with the pace of an Olympic sprinter. In fact he gave up rugby to concentrate on running. He was partnered by A.L. Gracie, an unorthodox centre who was said to do all the wrong things so fast that he became unpredictably brilliant. He added to the confusion by running with his head back and waving the ball about in front of him as though playing a concertina. His match winning try against Wales in 1923 is another classic score. Gracie, born in Ceylon, and Liddell, born in China, both attended the famous school for Sons of Missionaries at Eltham, as did that other excellent stand off, E.C. Fahmy who was also born in China.

Next two pairs who played as a complete line for Oxford University and Scotland — A.C. Wallace with G.G. Aitken and I.S. Smith with G.P.S. Macpherson. The first pair were fast, aggressive and fine handlers who combined well in attack. Both were Colonials, Wallace being born in Australia and Aitken in New Zealand. Smith was also born in Australia but Macpherson was a true clansman from Newtonmore. The pair formed a formidable and famous partnership. Smith was fast, somewhat leggy and ran with a high knee action which made tackling difficult and he had a habit of aiming at and scoring in the corner. His tally of 24 tries is quite outstanding as is his feat of scoring four tries in each of two successive games against France and Wales in 1925.

Macpherson must rank as one of the greatest attacking centres in the game. He was genuinely fast but employed a multitude of feints, side steps, swerves, dummies, changes of pace and tactical kicks to split the defence before setting Smith off on a run. He is credited with saying that he had no great objection to the opponents scoring twenty points so long as his side scored 21 and also that he considered that a man on the ground was out of the game. Certainly many who believed in an uncompromising tackle used to be infuriated by his habit of shadow tackling an opponent who, however, suddenly discovered that he was about to run into touch with no one to pass to. But tackle he could when the occasion demanded it.

H. Lind was a fine, perhaps individualistic, attacking half or centre with fine defensive qualities. His match-winning drop against Ireland in 1933 will not be forgotten. That afternoon he and the other Scottish backs took a terrible hammering, both in defence and when attacking, on a very hard pitch. Others such as A.T. Sloan, J.C. Dykes, W.M. Simmers, R.C.S. Dick, D.J. Macrae, W.C.W. Murdoch and K.C. Fyfe cannot be passed over for each was an outstanding back who played a significant part in one or more of the memorable wins of the period.

Dan Drysdale takes a place as one of the great full backs. A tidy unflurried player he seldom needed to chase after a kick for his positional play was really excellent. His fielding of the ball was consistently clean, his touch kicking was effortlessly lengthy and when required his goal kicking was accurate. Some critics maintained that he was lucky to play behind backs who could defend but like Macpherson, he could tackle solidly when necessary. When he retired in 1929 the next ten years saw twelve players fill the position, the longest serving being the very competent K.W. Marshall.

The War Years 1939–1946

By the close of the 1938–39 season the SRU had decided to resume relations with France, offering to play in Paris in January, 1940 but the outbreak of hostilities in September 1939 brought everything to a halt. It was at once decided to cancel all Union fixtures but the clubs were encouraged to continue and arrange what fixtures they could. Some clubs amalgamated (e.g. the Academicals and Wanderers in Edinburgh and Kelvinside Academicals with the West of Scotland in Glasgow) and many blank Saturdays were filled by games with sides drawn from Navy, Army and Air Force units stationed in their areas. No subscriptions were required from the clubs, the Debenture scheme was suspended and the Bye Laws were altered to allow the existing committee to continue to administer the Union affairs without calling General Meetings so long as the crisis required. The grounds and buildings at Murrayfield were taken over as a Supply Depot by the RASC so when the Services Sports authorities began to arrange Services International matches it was Inverleith that was used in 1942 and 1943, but a return was made to Murrayfield in 1944 when the ground was derequisitioned.

After the defeats of Germany and Japan during 1945 the committee selected Scottish XVs to play during 1946 in a series of

Victory Internationals against the other home countries and a strong New Zealand Army team, but these games were regarded as 'unofficial' and no caps were awarded to players.

In March 1946 the committee decided that the state of emergency had finished so restored the original Bye Laws and held the first post war AGM in May 1946.

SERVICES RUGBY   Inverleith   21 March 1942

SCOTLAND: 2 goals, 2 drop goals, 1 try   21   **Win**

ENGLAND: 1 penalty goal, 1 try   6

Scotland: Captain W.C.W. Murdoch (*Hillhead HSFP*); Lt J.R.S. Innes (*Aberdeen GSFP*), Captain W.H. Munro (*Glas. HSFP*), Ft Lt E.C. Hunter (*Watsonians*), Cadet E.C.K. Douglas (*Edin. Univ.*); Lt T. Gray (*Heriot's FP*), Cadet M.R. Dewar (*Watsonians*); Cpl J. Maltman (*Hawick*), Lt R.M. Grieve (*Kelso*), Lt N.W. Ramsay (*Army*), Lt S.G.A. Harper (*Watsonians*), Major C.L. Melville* (*London Scot.*), Lt A.W.B. Buchanan (*London Scot.*), Captain P.L. Duff (*Glas. Acads.*), Captain G.D. Shaw (*Sale*)

England: Major G.W. Parker (*Blackheath*); Lt E.J.H. Williams (*Camb. Univ.*), Sgt S. Brogden (*Army*), P.Off H. Kenyon (*Coventry*), Lt G.A. Hollis (*Oxford Univ.*); Captain J. Ellis (*Wakefield*), Gr Captain G.A. Walker (*Blackheath*); Captain R.E. Prescott* (*Harlequins*), Sq Ldr C.G. Gilthorpe (*Coventry*), Cpl R.J. Lougland (*Northampton*), Captain T.F. Huskisson (*OMT*), Lt Com R.J.L. Hammond (*RN*), Paymaster Lt J.K. Watkins (*RN*), Lt C.L. Newton-Thompson (*Camb. Univ.*), Cpl W.T. Reynolds (*Bristol*)

Referee: A.M. Buchanan (*Ireland*)   **Touch judges:** Lt Col D.J. MacMyn, Captain H.A. Haigh-Smith

G.D. Shaw scored (3–0); M.R. Dewar scored and W.C.W. Murdoch converted (8–0). (H.T.). G.W. Parker kicked a penalty (8–3); W.C.W. Murdoch dropped a goal (12–3): J. Ellis scored (12–6); T. Gray scored and W.C.W. Murdoch converted (17–6); W.C.W. Murdoch dropped a goal (21–6).

This was a good win rather inflated by Murdoch's two drop goals. The Scottish pack was held in the scrum but did well in the loose whilst the backs were much more enterprising than their opponents; Munro in particular showed up well.

SERVICES RUGBY   Wembley   11 April 1942

SCOTLAND: 1 goal, 1 try   8   **Win**

ENGLAND: 1 goal   5

Scotland: Captain W.C.W. Murdoch (*Hillhead HSFP*); Captain J.B. Craig (*Heriot's FP*), Cadet D.A. Roberts (*Edin. Acads.*), FtLt E.C. Hunter (*Watsonians*), Cadet E.C.K. Douglas (*Edin. Univ.*); Lt T. Gray (*Heriot's FP*), Cadet M.R. Dewar (*Watsonians*); Cpl J. Maltman (*Hawick*), Lt R.M. Grieve (*Kelso*), Lt N.W. Ramsay (*Army*), Captain J.B. McNeil (*Glas HSFP*), Major C.L. Melville* (*London Scot.*), Lt A.W.B. Buchanan (*London Scot.*), Captain P.L. Duff (*Glas. Acads.*), Captain G.D. Shaw (*Sale*)

England: PO R. Rankin (*Australia*); Lt G.A. Hollis (*Oxford Univ.*), Sub Lt A.C. Simmonds (*RNEC*), Lt P.R.H. Hastings (*Oxford Univ.*), Lt A.L. Evans (*Rosslyn Park*); Captain J. Ellis (*Wakefield*), PO H. Kenyon (*Coventry*); Captain R.E. Prescott* (*Harlequins*), Sq Ldr C.G. Gilthorpe (*Coventry*), Cpl R.J. Longland (*Northampton*), Captain T.F. Huskisson (*OMT*), Cpl J. Mycock (*Harlequins*), Sgt E. Hodgson (*Broughton Rangers*), PO W. Fallowfield (*Northampton*), Cpl W.T. Reynolds (*Bristol*)

Referee: Sq Ldr C.H. Gadney (*England*) **Touch judges:** Captain T.C. Wilson, Captain H.A. Haigh-Smith

J. Ellis scored and R. Rankin converted (0–5); G.D. Shaw scored and W.C.W. Murdoch converted (5–5). (H.T.). M.R. Dewar scored (8–5).

England rather lost this game by their own shortcomings for they certainly ruled the scrums. The Scottish pack held an advantage in the line out and loose and a nippy pair of halves played well to a set of fast backs.

SERVICES RUGBY   Inverleith   27 February 1943

| **SCOTLAND:** | 2 tries | 6 | **Loss** |
| **ENGLAND:** | 4 goals, 3 tries | 29 | |

Scotland: Captain W.C.W. Murdoch (*Hillhead HSFP*); Captain J.R.S. Innes (*Aberdeen GSFP*), Captain W.H. Munro (*Glas. HSFP*), Cadet E.C.K. Douglas (*Edin. Univ.*), Lt T.G.H. Jackson (*Cheltenham*); Lt T. Gray (*Heriot's FP*), Lt J.M. Blair (*Oxford Univ.*); W Cr W.F. Blackadder (*West of Scot.*), Captain I.N. Graham (*Edin. Acads.*), Captain N.W. Ramsay (*Army*), Sgt D. Maltman (*Hawick*), Cpl R. Cowe (*Melrose*), Lt C. McLay (*Edin. Acads.*), Major C.L. Melville* (*London Scot.*), Captain G.D. Shaw (*Sale*)

England: L Cpl E. Ward (*Bradford N.*); Sgt Inst R.L. Francis (*Dewsbury*), Captain M.M. Walford (*Oxford Univ.*), Sgt J. Lawrenson (*Wigan*), Major E.J. Unwin (*Rosslyn Park*); Major F.J.C. Reynolds (*Old Cranleigh*), Captain J. Ellis (*Wakefield*); Cpl R.J. Longland (*Northampton*), F Lt B.J. McMaster (*Bedford*), Captain R.E. Prescott* (*Harlequins*), Cpl J. Mycock (*Harlequins*), Surg Lt R.S. Hall (*Bart's*), Cpl E.H. Sadler (*Castleford*), Captain C.L. Newton-Thompson (*Camb. Univ.*), Cpl G. Hudson (*Gloucester*)

Referee: A.M. Buchanan (*Ireland*) **Touch judges:** Lt Col D.J. MacMyn, Captain H.A. Haigh-Smith

W.H. Munro scored twice; C.L. Newton-Thompson and M.M. Walford scored and E. Ward converted one (6–8). (H.T.). J. Lawrenson, (3) R.L. Francis and E.H. Sadler scored and E. Ward converted all three (6–29).

The first half was evenly contested but thereafter the five Rugby League players in the English threes took full advantage of their pack's superiority.

SERVICES RUGBY   Leicester   10 April 1943

SCOTLAND: 2 goals, 3 tries   19   **Loss**

ENGLAND: 1 goal, 1 drop goal, 5 tries   24

Scotland: Captain W.B. Biggart (*Army*); Captain J.R.S. Innes (*Army*), Major C.R. Bruce (*Glas. Acads.*), Cadet E.C.K. Douglas (*Army*), FO E. Grant (*RNZAF*); Lt T. Gray (*Army*), Lt J.M. Blair (*Army*); Sgt J. Maltman (*Army*), Captain I.N. Graham (*Army*), Lt M.D. Kennedy (*Army*), Major C.L. Melville* (*Army*), Captain J. McNeill (*Army*), Captain P.L. Duff (*Army*), Lt J.A. Waters (*Selkirk*), Captain G.D. Shaw (*Army*)

England: Lt R.T. Campbell (*Army*); Sgt Instr R.L. Francis (*Army*), Pte J. Stott (*St Helen's*), AC J. Lawrenson (*RAF*), Lt G. Hollis (*RN*); Captain P.R. Hastings (*Army*), Ft Lt J. Parsons (*RAF*); Sgt G.T. Dancer (RAF), Cpl R.J. Longland (*RAF*), Captain R.E. Prescott* (*Army*), Captain G.P.C. Vallence (*Army*), Surg-Lt R.L. Hall (*Bart's*), Cpl E.H. Sadler (*Castleford*), Captain D.L.K. Milman (*Army*), Cpl G. Hudson (*Gloucester*)

Referee: I. David (*Wales*) **Touch judges:** LtCol D.J. MacMyn, Captain H.A. Haigh-Smith

G. Hollis scored (0–3); J. Lawrenson scored and J. Stott converted (0–8); J.R.S. Innes scored and G.D. Shaw converted (5–8); C.R. Bruce scored but G.D. Shaw failed (8–8); P.R. Hastings, J.J. Parsons and J. Stott scored and J. Stott converted one (8–17); J. Stott dropped a goal (8–21); J.R.S. Innes, G.D. Shaw and M.D. Kennedy scored; G.D. Shaw converted one (19–21); R.L. Francis scored (19–24).

Both sides were handicapped by injuries but there was some good open play for even with Sadler out on the wing to replace Lawrenson, the English pack played well to their threes who ran well for their scores. Then Scotland staged a fine recovery to come within two points before Francis scored a good last try to clinch the win.

SERVICES RUGBY   Murrayfield   26 February 1944

SCOTLAND: 2 goals, 1 penalty goal   13   **Loss**

ENGLAND: 2 goals, 1 drop goal, 3 tries   23

Scotland: Captain W.C.W. Murdoch (*Hillhead HSFP*); Cadet A.E. Murray (*Oxford Univ.*), Major C.R. Bruce (*Glas. Acads.*), Captain W.H. Munro (*Glas. HSFP*), Captain J.R.S. Innes (*Aberdeen GSFP*); Lt T. Gray (*Heriot's FP*), Lt J.M. Blair (*Oxford Univ.*); Lt H.H. Campbell (*Camb. Univ.*), LCpl J.D.H. Hastie (*Melrose*), Cpl R. Cowe (*Melrose*), Major C.L. Melville (*London Scot.*), Captain F.H. Coutts (*Melrose*), Captain G.D. Shaw

(Sale), Captain J.A. Waters* *(Selkirk)*, CSM J.E. McClure *(Ayr)*

England: LCpl E. Ward *(Bradford N)*; Sgt Instr R.L. Francis *(Dewsbury)*, Cfn J. Stott *(St Helens)*, LAC J. Lawrenson *(Wigan)*, Lt G. Hollis *(Sale)*; Lt P.R. Hastings *(Army)*, SqLr J. Parsons *(Leicester)*; Captain R.E. Prescott* *(Harlequins)*, Cpl R.J. Longland *(Northampton)*, FSgt I. Dustin *(RNZAF)*, Cpl J. Mycock *(Harlequins)*, Schoolmaster J.B. Doherty *(Manchester)*, Cpl G. Hudson *(Gloucester)*, Sgt G.T. Dancer *(Bedford)*, F Lt R.G.H. Weighill *(Waterloo)*

Referee: A.M. Buchanan *(Ireland)*   **Touch judges:** Major A. Wemyss, Captain H.A. Haigh-Smith

T. Gray kicked a penalty (3–0); J. Parsons scored (3–3); G. Hudson scored and J. Lawrenson converted (3–8); J. Stott dropped a goal (3–12); G. Hudson scored (3–15); G. Hudson scored and J. Lawrenson converted (3–20). (H.T.). G. Hudson scored (3–23); T. Gray scored and W.C.W. Murdoch converted (8–23); J.M. Blair scored and W.C.W. Murdoch converted (13–23).

England had a slight advantage in the scrums but G. Hudson showed up well with four tries. The Rugby League players in the backs were outstanding. In the second half C.R. Bruce came to stand off and this set off a spirited rally and a strong finish put a better face on the result.

SERVICES RUGBY   Leicester   18 March 1944

SCOTLAND: 1 goal, 1 drop goal, 1 penalty   15   **Loss**
goal, 1 try

ENGLAND: 3 goals, 1 penalty goal, 3 tries   27

Scotland: Captain W.C.W. Murdoch *(Hillhead HSFP)*; Captain H.G. Uren *(Glas. Acads.)*, F Lt E. Grant *(RNZAF)*, Captain W.H. Munro *(Glas. HSFP)*, Captain J.R.S. Innes *(Aberdeen GSFP)*; Major C.R. Bruce *(Glas. Acads.)*, FO E. Anderson *(Camb. Univ.)*; Lt H.H. Campbell *(Camb. Univ.)*, C.S.M. J.R. McClure *(Ayr)*, Cpl R. Cowe *(Melrose)*, Major C.L. Melville *(London Scot.)*, Captain F.H. Coutts *(Melrose)*, Pte J.B. Lees *(Gala)*, Captain J.A. Waters* *(Selkirk)*, Captain G.D. Shaw *(Sale)*

England: L Cpl E. Ward *(Bradford N.)*; S Instr R.L. Francis *(Dewsbury)*, Cfn J. Stott *(St Helen's)*, Cadet LE. Oakley *(Bedford)*, Lt G. Hollis *(Sale)*; Lt P.R. Hastings *(Welsh Guards)*, Sq Lr J. Parsons *(Leicester)*; Sgt G.T. Dancer *(Bedford)*, Cpl R.J. Longland *(Northampton)*, Captain R.E. Prescott* *(Harlequins)*, Cpl J. Mycock *(Harlequins)*, Schoolmaster J.B. Doherty *(Sale)*, Cpl G. Hudson *(Gloucester)*, F Lt R.G.H. Weighill *(Waterloo)*, Captain F.W. Gilbert *(Coventry)*

Referee: W Cr C.H. Gadney *(England)*   **Touch judges:** Major A. Wemyss, Captain H.A. Haigh-Smith

Ward kicked a penalty (0–3); G. Hudson scored (0–6); J.R.S. Innes scored (3–6); G. Hollis scored and J. Stott converted (3–11).(H.T.). R. Cowe kicked a penalty (6–11); L.E. Oakley scored and J. Stott converted (6–16); W.C.W. Murdoch dropped a goal (10–16); P.R. Hastings, R.L. Francis (2) scored and J. Stott converted one (10–27); F.H. Coutts scored and R. Cowe converted (15–27).

The English pack get the credit for the success, constantly winning the ball yet good tackling by the Scottish threes and wing forwards really restrained the scoring. Indeed behind a winning pack the Scottish backs would have been dangerous.

SERVICES RUGBY Leicester 24 February 1945

SCOTLAND: 3 goals, 1 try 18 **Win**

ENGLAND: 1 goal, 1 penalty goal, 1 try 11

Scotland: Sq Lr K.I. Geddes* (*Wasps*); F Lt E. Grant (*RNZAF*), Surg Lt W.D. MacLennan (*Watsonians*), Captain J.R. Henderson (*Glas. Acads.*), Sq Lr J.B. Nicholls (*NSW*); FO D.D. McKenzie (*Merchistonians*), Cadet A.W. Black (*Edin. Univ.*); SSM J.R. McClure (*Ayr*), Cpl J.D.H. Hastie (*Melrose*), Cadet T.P.L. McGlashan (*RHSFP*), Sub Lt C. Wilhelm (*SA Services*), Pte R.M. McKenzie (*NZ*), PO J.H. Orr (*Heriot's FP*), FO A.L. Barcroft (*Heriot's FP*), Captain J.A.D. Thom (*Hawick*)

England: L Cpl E. Ward (*Bradford N.*); Lt G. Hollis* (*Sale*), AB E. Ruston (*RN*), Sgt M.P. Goddard (*RNZAF*), LAC R.J. Forbes (*RAF*); Lt Comr R.E. Bibby (*RN*), Sq Lr J. Parsons (*Leicester*); Cpl R.J. Longland (*Northampton*), Sq Lr C.G. Gilthorpe (*RAF*), Captain F.P. Dunkley (*Army*), Cpl J. Mycock (*Harlequins*), Schoolmaster J.B. Docherty (*Sale*), Sgt E. Bedford (*RAF*), OS J.D. Robins (*RN*), F Lt R.G.H. Weighill (*Waterloo*)

Referee: I. Jones (*Wales*) **Touch judges:** Major A. Wemyss, Captain L.M. Davies

R.M. McKenzie scored and K.I. Geddes converted (5–0); E. Ward kicked a penalty (5–3); E. Grant scored and K.I. Geddes converted (10–3).(H.T.). W.D. MacLennan scored but K.I. Geddes failed (13–3); E. Ward scored (13–6); J.H. Orr scored and K.I. Geddes converted (18–6); M.P. Goddard scored and C.G. Gilthorpe converted (18–11).

There were enforced changes which included playing J.B. Nicholls, a forward, on the wing. A young Scottish pack did well overall and their backs were better with Geddes a good full back. For England, Goddard, the New Zealander, made some capital runs at centre.

SERVICES RUGBY Murrayfield 17 March 1945

SCOTLAND: 1 goal 5 **Loss**

ENGLAND: 2 goals, 2 tries 16

Scotland: Sq Lr K.I. Geddes* (*Wasps*); Cadet D.W.C. Smith (*Aberdeen Univ.*), Surg Lt W.D. MacLennan (*Watsonians*), Captain J.R. Henderson (*Glas. Acads.*), Fl Lt. E. Grant (*RNZAF*); FO D.D. McKenzie (*Merchistonians*), Cadet A.W. Black (*Edin. Univ.*); CSM

J.R. McClure (*Ayr*), Cpl J.D.H. Hastie (*Melrose*), Cadet T.P.L. McGlashan (*RHSFP*), Lt E.A. Melling (*Sedbergh*), Pte R.M. McKenzie (*NZ*), PO J.H. Orr (*Heriot's FP*), Sq Lr J.B. Nicholls (*NSW*), FO A.L. Barcroft (*Heriot's FP*)

England: Lt M.T.A. Ackermann (*SAAF*); Lt G. Hollis (*RN*), L Cpl E. Ward (*Bradford N.*), Sgt M.P. Goddard (*RNZAF*), LAC R.J. Forbes (*RAF*); AB E. Ruston (*RN*), AC P.W. Sykes (*RAF*); Cpl R.J. Longland (*RAF*), WCom C.G. Gilthorpe (*RAF*), Cpl P. Plumpton (*RAF*), Cpl J. Mycock (*RAF*), Schoolmaster J.B. Doherty (*RN*), Cpl A.G. Hudson (*RAF*), FLt R.G.H. Weighill (*RAF*), Sgt E. Bedford (*RAF*)

    Referee: A.M. Buchanan (*Ireland*)   **Touch judges:** Major A. Wemyss, Captain A.L. Warr

G. Hollis scored twice and E. Ward converted one (0–8); W.D. MacLennan scored and K.I. Geddes converted (5–8). (H.T.). G. Hollis scored (5–11); A.G. Hudson scored and C.G. Gilthorpe converted (5–16).

The English pack was markedly on top and gave their backs plenty to do, Ward and Hollis being an outstanding pair. K.I. Geddes again shone in defence.

NEW ZEALAND ARMY   Murrayfield   19 January 1946

SCOTLAND: 1 goal, 2 tries   11   **Win**

N.Z. ARMY: 1 penalty goal, 1 try   6

Scotland: K.I. Geddes* (*London Scot.*); J. Anderson (*London Scot.*), W.H. Munro (*Glas. HSFP*), C.R. Bruce (*Glas. Acads.*), D.W.C. Smith (*Aberdeen Univ.*); I.J.M. Lumsden (*Watsonians*), A.W. Black (*Edin. Univ.*); I.C. Henderson (*Edin. Acads.-Wrs.*), G.G. Lyall (*Gala*), R. Aitken (*London Scot.*), A.G.M. Watt (*Edin. Acads.-Wrs.*), J. Kirk (*Edin. Acads.-Wrs.*), W.I.D. Elliot (*Edin. Acads.-Wrs.*), D.W. Deas (*Heriot's FP*), J.H. Orr (*Edin. City Police*)

New Zealand Army: H.E. Cooke (*Hawkes Bay*); J.R. Sherratt (*Wellington*), J.B. Smith (*N. Auckland*), W.G. Argus (*Canterbury*); F.R. Allen (*Canterbury*), J.C. Kearney (*Otago*); C.K. Saxton* (*Southland*); N.J. McPhail (*Canterbury*), F.N. Haigh (*Wellington*), J.G. Simpson (*Auckland*), K.D. Arnold (*N. Auckland*), S.W. Woolley (*Marlborough*), S.L. Young (*N. Auckland*), A.W. Blake (*Hawkes Bay*), J. Finlay (*Manawata*)

    Referee: G.D. Gadney (*England*)   **Touch judges:** F.J.C. Moffat, N.H. Thornton

S.W. Woolley scored but H.E. Cooke failed (0–3). (H.T.). J. Anderson scored but K.I. Geddes failed (3–3); W.H. Munro scored and D.W.C. Smith converted (8–3); H.E. Cooke kicked a penalty (8–6); J. Anderson scored but D.W.C. Smith failed (11–6).

This was the first of six International matches played during the season. These were regarded as 'unofficial' and no caps were awarded. This was a hard exciting game for the Scottish forwards stood up splendidly against a physically stronger pack and their backs more than held their own. The visitors scored first but Scotland might have been level at the interval for their forwards gave the defence a hard time. Half an hour after the interval Bruce had a lovely break through and passed to Anderson who sprinted in at the corner.

Then Cooke kicked a penalty and the Kiwis, with their first defeat looming up, stepped up their attack only to find the Scottish pack continually turning defence into offence by fine footwork. Then in the dying minutes Bruce made a break, was knocked down but seemed to drop at goal. The ball went wide to drop over the line at the corner and Anderson's pace let him get there to touch down for a try.

WALES	Swansea	2 February 1946

SCOTLAND:	2 goals, 1 penalty goal, 4 tries	25	**Win**
WALES:	2 tries		

Scotland: K.I. Geddes* (*London Scot.*); D.W.C. Smith (*Aberdeen Univ.*), C.R. Bruce (*Glas. Acads.*), W.H. Munro (*Glas. HSFP*), C.W. Drummond (*Melrose*); I.J.M. Lumsden (*Watsonians*), A.W. Black (*Edin. Univ.*); I.C. Henderson (*Edin. Acads.-Wrs.*), G.G. Lyall (*Gala*), R. Aitken (*London Scot.*), A.G.M. Watt (*Edin. Acads.-Wrs.*), J. Kirk (*Edin. Acads.-Wrs.*), W.I.D. Elliot (*Edin. Acads.-Wrs.*), D.W. Deas (*Heriot's FP*), J.H. Orr (*Heriot's FP*)

England: R.F. Trott (*Penarth*); L. Williams (*Llanelli*), J. Matthews* (*Cardiff*), B.L. Williams (*Cardiff*), W.E. Williams (*Newport*); G. Davies (*Pontypridd CS*), W. Davies (*Cardiff Univ.*); L. Manfield (*Cardiff*), J.R.G. Stephens (*Neath*), D.H. Steer (*Taunton*), G. Hughes (*Neath*), R. Hughes (*Aberavon*), F.E. Morris (*Pill Harriers*), M. James (*Cardiff*), G. Bevan (*Llanelli*)

Referee: H.L.V. Day (*England*) **Touch judges:** F.J.C. Moffat, I. Jones

W.I.D. Elliot scored but K.I. Geddes failed (3–0); C.R. Bruce scored and K.I. Geddes converted (8–0); C.W. Drummond scored but K.I. Geddes failed (11–0); J.H. Orr scored and K.I. Geddes converted (16–0). (H.T.). G. Davies scored (16–3); W.I.D. Elliot scored but K.I. Geddes failed (19–3); G. Bevan scored (19–6); A.W. Black scored but K.I. Geddes failed (22–6); K.I. Geddes kicked a penalty (25–6).

Scotland were clearly on top in spite of a strong rally by Wales after the interval when Glyn Davies scored after a magnificent solo swerving run of some 50 yards. The Scottish pack were always in command with Elliot outstanding in backing up and defence; he put in a fearsome score-saving tackle on L. Williams.

IRELAND	Murrayfield	23 February 1946

SCOTLAND:	1 goal, 1 drop goal	9	**Win**
IRELAND:	Nil	0	

Scotland: K.I. Geddes* (*London Scot.*); D.W.C. Smith (*Aberdeen Univ.*), C.R. Bruce (*Glas. Acads.*), W.H. Munro (*Glas. HSFP*), C.W. Drummond (*Melrose*); I.J.M. Lumsden (*Watsonians*), A.W. Black (*Edin. Univ.*); I.C. Henderson (*Edin. Acads.-Wrs.*), G.G. Lyall (*Gala*), R. Aitken (*London Scot.*), J.R. McClure (*Ayr*), J. Kirk (*Edin. Acads.-Wrs.*), W.I.D. Elliott (*Edin. Acads.-Wrs.*), D.W. Deas (*Heriot's FP*), J.H. Orr (*Heriot's FP*)

Ireland: C.J. Murphy (*Lansdowne*); B.T. Quinn (*Old Belvedere*), K. Quinn (*Old Belvedere*), T. Coveney (*St Mary's*), F.G. Moran (*Clontarf*); E.A. Carry (*Old Wesley*), E. Strathdee (*QU Belfast*); D. Hingerty (*Lansdowne*), H.G. Dudgeon (*Collegians*), D. McCourt (*Instonians*), E. Keeffe (*Sunday's Well*), C.P. Callan (*Lansdowne*), M.R. Neely (*RN*), C. Mullen (*Old Belvedere*), J.C. Corcoran (*UC Cork*)

Referee: I. Jones (*Wales*) **Touch judges:** R.M. Meldrum, R.W. Jeffares

W.H. Munro scored but K.I. Geddes converted (5–0). (H.T.). I.J.M. Lumsden dropped a goal (9–0).

After a strong Irish challenge had been halted, Elliot broke away from his own 25, kicked ahead, regained possession to set the backs moving and Munro cut in for a good try. Ireland, aided by a good pack, continued to press but rather orthodox play was held by a sound defence, the Irish wingers both being put into touch at the corner flags. In the second half Geddes hit the crossbar with a 50 yard penalty before a swift heel by the Scottish pack gave Lumsden a chance to drop a goal.

ENGLAND   Twickenham   16 March 1946

SCOTLAND: 1 goal, 1 try   8   Loss
ENGLAND: 1 goal, 1 drop goal, 1 penalty goal 12

Scotland: K.I. Geddes* (*London Scot.*); J.R.S. Innes (*Aberdeen GSFP*), C.R. Bruce (*Glas. Acads.*), W.H. Munro (*Glas. HSFP*), C.W. Drummond (*Melrose*); I.J.M. Lumsden (*Watsonians*), K.S.H. Wilson (*London Scot.*); I.C. Henderson (*Edin. Acads.-Wrs.*), G.G. Lyall (*Gala*), R. Aitken (*London Scot.*), A.G.M. Watt (*Edin. Acads.-Wrs.*), J. Kirk (*Edin. Acads.-Wrs.*), W.I.D. Elliot (*Edin. Acads.-Wrs.*), D.W. Deas (*Heriot's FP*), J.H. Orr (*Heriot's FP*)

England: H.J.M. Uren (*Waterloo*); H.F. Greasley (*Coventry*), E.K. Scott (*St Mary's*), J. Heaton* (*Waterloo*), R.S.L. Carr (*Manchester*); N.M. Hall (*St Mary's*), W.K.T. Moore (*Devonport Services*); J.W. Thornton (*Gloucester*), E. Bole (*Camb. Univ.*), D.B. Vaughan (*RNE Coll.*), H.R. Peel (*Headingley*), J. Mycock (*Sale*), G.A. Kelly (*Bedford*), F.C.H. Hill (*Bristol*), T.W. Price (*Gloucester*)

Referee: I. David (*Wales*) **Touch judges:** R.K. Cuthbertson, J.A. Haigh-Smith

J.R.S. Innes scored but K.I. Geddes failed (3–0); C.R. Bruce scored and K.I. Geddes converted (8–0).(H.T.). J. Heaton kicked a penalty (8–3); R.S.L. Carr scored and J. Heaton converted (8–8); E.K. Scott dropped a goal (8–12).

The English pack held the whip hand in the loose while their back row harassed Wilson unmercifully on his own heel so that the Scottish back play suffered in consequence. Yet it was a seemingly beaten English team which produced a winning challenge in the last twenty minutes.

199

WALES   Murrayfield   30 March 1946

SCOTLAND: 2 goals, 1 penalty goal   13   **Win**

WALES: 1 goal, 2 tries   11

Scotland: K.I. Geddes (*London Scot.*); J.R.S. Innes (*Aberdeen GSFP*), C.R. Bruce (*Glas. Acads.*), W.H. Munro (*Glas. HSFP*), C.W. Drummond (*Melrose*); I.J.M. Lumsden (*Watsonians*), A.W. Black (*Edin. Univ.*); I.C. Henderson (*Edin. Acads.-Wrs.*), G.G. Lyall (*Gala*), R. Aitken (*London Scot.*), A.G.M. Watt (*Edin. Acads.-Wrs.*), F.H. Coutts (*Melrose*), W.I.D. Elliot (*Edin. Acads.-Wrs.*), D.W. Deas* (*Heriot's FP*), J.H. Orr (*Heriot's FP*)

Wales: T. Griffiths (*Newport*); L. Williams (*Devonport Services*), B.L. Williams (*Cardiff*), J. Matthews (*Cardiff*), W.E. Williams (*Newport*); W.B. Cleaver (*Cardiff*), H. Tanner* (*Swansea*); J.H. Bale (*Newport*), W.J. Evans (*Pontypool*), C. Davies (*Cardiff*), D.J. Davies (*Swansea*), G. Parsons (*Abertillery*), L. Mansfield (*Cardiff*), R.T. Evans (*Newport*), H. Jones (*Cardiff*)

Referee: J.B.G. Whittaker (*England*)   **Touch judges:** W.A. Mackinnon, I. Jones

H. Jones scored and W.B. Cleaver converted (0–5); C.W. Drummond scored and K.I. Geddes converted (5–5).(H.T.). W.E. Williams scored but H. Tanner failed (5–8); K.I. Geddes kicked a penalty (8–8); L. Williams scored but H. Tanner failed (8–11); C.R. Bruce scored and K.I. Geddes converted (13–11).

After being three times in arrears Scotland overhauled a depleted Welsh team and held off a desperate final challenge. T. Griffiths suffered a broken rib after fifteen minutes and Mansfield went to full back until a bruising forward rush knocked him off the ball before Drummond scored, after which Cleaver took over.

ENGLAND   Murrayfield   13 April 1946

SCOTLAND: 3 goals, 1 penalty goal, 3 tries   27   **Win**

ENGLAND: Nil

Scotland: K.I. Geddes (*London Scot.*); W.D. MacLennan (*Watsonians*), C.R. Bruce (*Glas. Acads.*), W.H. Munro (*Glas. HSFP*), T.G.H. Jackson (*Cheltenham*); I.J.M. Lumsden (*Watsonians*), A.W. Black (*Edin. Univ.*); I.C. Henderson (*Edin. Acads.-Wrs.*), G.G. Lyall (*Gala*), R. Aitken (*London Scot.*), A.G.M. Watt (*Edin. Acads.-Wrs.*), F.H. Coutts (*Melrose*), W.I.D. Elliot (*Edin. Acads.-Wrs.*), D.W. Deas* (*Heriot's FP*), J.H. Orr (*Heriot's FP*)

England: H.J.M. Uren (*Waterloo*); R.S.L. Carr (*Manchester*), E.K. Scott (*St Mary's*), J. Heaton* (*Waterloo*), R.H. Guest (*Waterloo*); N.M. Hall (*St Mary's*), W.K.T. Moore (*Devonport Services*); J.W. Thornton (*Gloucester*), D.B. Vaughan (*RNE Coll.*), E. Bole (*Camb. Univ.*), H.R. Peel (*Headingley*), J. Mycock (*Sale*), G.A. Kelly (*Bedford*), F.C.H. Hill (*Bristol*), T.W. Price (*Gloucester*)

A.G.M. Watt scored but K.I. Geddes failed (3–0); K.I. Geddes kicked a penalty (6–0); C.R. Bruce scored but K.I. Geddes failed (9–0).(H.T.). I.J.M. Lumsden, A.G.M. Watt, W.H. Munro and W.D. MacLennan scored and K.I. Geddes converted the first three (27–0).

Inside 25 minutes Scotland had scored twice and appeared to have the game well in hand when Uren damaged a knee and had to retire, whereafter the game became quite one sided. The two new Scottish wingers played well; Jackson's pace, physique and determination were noticeable. Geddes again showed up as an attacking full back.

FRANCE   Colombes   1 January 1947

SCOTLAND: 1 penalty goal   3   **Loss**
FRANCE: 1 goal, 1 try   8

Scotland: K.I. Geddes* (*London Scot.*); T.G.H. Jackson (*Army*), C.R. Bruce (*Glas. Acads.*), C.W. Drummond (*Melrose*), W.D. MacLennan (*Un. Services*); I.J.M. Lumsden (*Bath*), A.W. Black (*Edin. Univ.*); A.G.M. Watt (*Edin. Acads.-Wrs.*), I.C. Henderson (*Edin. Acads.-Wrs.*), T.P.L. McGlashan (*RHSFP*), J.M. Hunter (*London Scot.*), G.L. Cawkwell (*Oxford Univ.*), W.I.D. Elliot (*Edin. Acads.-Wrs.*), D.W. Deas (*Heriot's FP*), J.H. Orr (*Edin. City Police*)

France: A. Alvarez (*Tyrosse*); E. Pebeyre (*Briviste*), L. Junquas* (*Bayonne*), M. Sorrondo (*Montalban*), J. Lassegue (*Toulouse*); M. Terreau (*Bressane*), Y. Bergougnan (*Toulouse*); E. Buzy (*Lourdes*), M. Jol (*Biarritz*), A. Moga (*Beglais*), R. Soro (*Romanaise*), J. Prat (*Lourdes*), G. Basquet (*Agen*), J. Mathew (*Castres*)

Referee: C.H. Gadney (*England*): **Touch judges:** D.S. Kerr, L. Carie

K.I. Geddes kicked a penalty (3–0); J. Lassegue scored (3–3); M. Terreau scored and J. Prat converted (3–8).(H.T.).

Scotland started well taking an early lead with a penalty goal but France recovered fairly quickly and persistent attacks put them ahead at the interval. They kept up the pressure in the second half but the Scottish defence held out, Geddes at full back doing much to keep the score down. There was some exciting running in the last quarter, Drummond in particular coming close to a score with a fine solo run which only failed against a crowded defence. France's tackling and speed on and off the ball were deciding factors in their win.

WALES   Murrayfield   1 February 1947

SCOTLAND: 1 goal, 1 penalty goal   8   **Loss**
WALES: 2 goals, 1 penalty goal, 3 tries   22

Scotland: K.I. Geddes* (*London Scot.*); T.G.H. Jackson (*Army*), C.W. Drummond (*Melrose*), C.R. Bruce (*Glas. Acads.*), D.D. Mackenzie (*Edin. Univ.*); I.J.M. Lumsden (*Bath*), A.W. Black (*Edin. Univ.*); I.C. Henderson (*Edin. Acads.-Wrs.*), R.W. Sampson (*London Scot.*), R. Aitken (*RN*), F.H. Coutts (*Melrose*), D.W. Deas (*Heriot's FP*), W.I.D. Elliot (*Edin. Acads.-Wrs.*), A.G.M. Watt (*Edin. Acads.-Wrs.*), J.H. Orr (*Edin. City Police*)

Wales: C.H. Davies (*Llanelli*); L. Williams (*Llanelli*), B.L. Williams (*Cardiff*), W.B. Cleaver (*Cardiff*), K. Jones (*Newport*); G. Davies (*Pontypridd*), H. Tanner* (*Cardiff*); C. Davies (*Cardiff*), W. Gore (*Newbridge*), W.J. Evans (*Pontypool*), W.E. Tamplin (*Cardiff*), S. Williams (*Llanelli*), O. Williams (*Llanelli*), R. Stephens (*Neath*), G. Evans (*Cardiff*)

Referee: M.J. Dowling (*Ireland*)   **Touch judges:** D.S. Kerr, R.A. Cornish

B.L. Williams scored but W.E. Tamplin failed (0–3); W.E. Tamplin kicked a penalty (0–6); K.I. Geddes kicked a penalty (3–6); W.I.D. Elliot scored and K.I. Geddes converted (8–6). (H.T.). W.B. Cleaver and K. Jones scored and W.E. Tamplin converted both (8–16); K. Jones and L. Williams scored but W.E. Tamplin failed (8–22).

In arctic conditions Scotland held their own up to half time and then faded badly especially during the last quarter. The Welsh pack were strong in the open and their back row were very hard on Black and Lumsden. Early on B.L. Williams intercepted a pass and a quick swerve put him past the defence for the first score. After two penalties Cleaver fumbled an unexpected pass from the line out and Elliot came up fast to go over for a converted try. The Welsh pack began the second half ominously well and Wales took the lead when B.L. Williams ran straight through to send Cleaver in although well tackled short of the line. Then Scotland faded and a late spate of scoring left Wales clear winners.

IRELAND   Murrayfield   22 February 1947

SCOTLAND: Nil   0   **Loss**

IRELAND: 1 try   3

Scotland: K.I. Geddes (*London Scot.*); W.D. Maclennan (*Un. Services*), C.W. Drummond (*Melrose*), C.R. Bruce (*Glas. Acads.*), D.D. Mackenzie (*Edin. Univ.*); W.H. Munro* (*Glas. HSFP*), E. Anderson (*Stewart's FP*); T.P.L. McGlashan (*RHSFP*), A.T. Fisher (*Waterloo*), H.H. Campbell (*London Scot.*), F.H. Coutts (*Melrose*), A.G.M. Watt (*Edin. Acads.-Wrs.*), D.D. Valentine (*Hawick*), J.B. Lees (*Gala*), D.I. McLean (*RHSFP*)

Ireland: J.A.D. Higgins (*Ulster CS*); B. O'Hanlan (*Dolphin*), J.D.E. Monteith* (*QU Belfast*), J. Harper (*Instonians*), B. Mullan (*Clontarf*); J.W. Kyle (*QU Belfast*), E. Strathdee (*QU Belfast*); M.R. Neely (*Collegians*), K.D. Mullen (*Old Belvedere*), J.C. Daly (*London Irish*), C.P. Callan (*Lansdowne*), E. Keefe (*Sunday's Well*), J.W. McKay (*QU Belfast*), R.D. Agar (*Malone*), D. Hingerty (*UC Dublin*)

Referee: C.H. Gadney (*England*)   **Touch judges:** D.S. Kerr, T.A. Brindley

No scoring at half time. B. Mullan scored but J.A.D. Higgins failed (0–3).

The Irish forwards were on top in the scrums and line outs but were held in the loose yet put in some ruthless spoiling. Their backs, although the halves combined well, had no real

202

penetration and were easily held by an excellent defence. Then with fifteen minutes to go Strathdee went round the blind side of a scrum, ran up to Geddes and gave B. Mullan a clear run for a try.

ENGLAND   Twickenham   15 March 1947

SCOTLAND: 1 goal   5   **Loss**

ENGLAND: 4 goals, 1 drop goal   24

Scotland: K.I. Geddes (*London Scot.*); T.G.H. Jackson (*London Scot.*), C.W. Drummond (*Melrose*), W.H. Munro (*Glas. HSFP*), D.D. Mackenzie (*Edin. Univ.*); C.R. Bruce* (*Glas. Acads.*), E. Anderson (*Stewart's FP*); T.P.L. McGlashan (*RHSFP*), A.T. Fisher (*Waterloo*), H.H. Campbell (*London Scot.*), F.H. Coutts (*Army*), I.C. Henderson (*Edin. Acads.-Wrs.*), D.D. Valentine (*Hawick*), D.I. McLean (*RHSFP*), W.I.D. Elliot (*Edin. Acads.-Wrs.*)

England: A. Gray (*Otley*); C.B. Holmes (*Manchester*), N.O. Bennett (*St Mary's*), J. Heaton* (*Waterloo*), R.H. Guest (*Waterloo*); N.M. Hall (*St Mary's*), J.O. Newton-Thompson (*Oxford Univ.*); H.W. Walker (*Coventry*), A.P. Henderson (*Camb. Univ.*), G.A. Kelly (*Bedford*), J.T. George (*Falmouth*), J. Mycock (*Sale*), M.R. Steele-Bodger (*Camb. Univ.*), R.H.G. Weighill (*RAF*), D.F. White (*Army*).

Referee: I. David (*Wales*)   **Touch judges:** M.A. Allan, H.A. Haigh Smith

N.M. Hall dropped a goal (0–4); C.B. Holmes and R.H. Guest scored and J. Heaton converted both (0–14).(H.T.). A.P. Henderson and N.O. Bennett scored and J. Heaton converted both (0–24); T.G.H. Jackson scored and K.I. Geddes converted (5–24).

This was a match which was bedevilled by the appalling wintry conditions that had persisted from mid-January. In Scotland clubs had not had a game since that time and the team members who travelled to London on Thursday afternoon had to endure a twenty hours journey. D.I. McLean who travelled later did not join his team mates until six a.m. on the Saturday morning, having spent all day and night on Friday in a train which had neither a restaurant nor sleeping carriage. M.R. Steele-Bodger (who was a student in the RD Vet. College in Edinburgh) had an equally appalling trip. His train had to be dug out of the snow twice before reaching Carlisle and he too only arrived in London in the early hours of Saturday morning.

The match was played on a hard pitch in bitterly cold weather which deteriorated to a blizzard of snow in the second half. While England were clearly the better team Scotland were badly handicapped by a succession of injuries. Within five minutes Elliot had to hirple off with a leg injury and he later returned limping to play at full back only to see Jackson limp off. Drummond then retired with a broken collar bone but after the restart Jackson returned so giving Scotland fourteen players, two of whom were sadly handicapped. But early in the second half Kelly went off with injured ribs and Holmes had a spell on the touch-line nursing severe cramp so for a while both teams had fourteen on the field.

England's first try came from an interception by Holmes who, with Geddes up with his threes, had a 70 yards sprint for a try. Their second try came from a kick ahead by Hall which bounced kindly for Guest who had followed up fast. Then Henderson dribbled in for a try before Holmes and Bennett moved onto a bad pass, kicked the ball ahead and the latter got the touch down. Scotland had a consolation score when a fine run by Munro put Jackson over.

AUSTRALIA Murrayfield 22 November 1947

SCOTLAND:	1 drop goal, 1 penalty goal	7	**Loss**
AUSTRALIA:	2 goals, 2 tries	16	

Scotland: I.J.M. Lumsden (*Bath*); T.G.H. Jackson (*London Scot.*), J.R.S. Innes* (*Aberdeen GSFP*), T. Wright (*Hawick*), C. McDonald (*Jedforest*); D.P. Hepburn (*Woodford*), W.D. Allardice (*Aberdeen GSFP*); R.M. Bruce (*Gordonians*), G.G. Lyall (*Gala*), I.C. Henderson (*Edin. Acads.*), L. Currie (*Dunfermline*), J.C. Dawson (*Glas. Acads.*), W.I.D. Elliot (*Edin. Acads.*), A.G.M. Watt (*Army*), J.B. Lees (*Gala*)

Australia: B.C.J. Piper (*NSW*); A.E.J. Tonkin (*NSW*), T. Allan* (*NSW*), M.L. Howell (*NSW*), J.W.T. McBride (*NSW*); N.A. Emery (*NSW*), C.T. Burke (*NSW*); C.J. Windon (*NSW*), A.J. Buchan (*NSW*), D.H. Keller (*NSW*), G.M. Cooke (*Queensland*), D.F. Kraefft (*NSW*), E.H. Davis (*Victoria*), K.H. Kearney (*NSW*), E. Tweedale (*NSW*)

Referee: N.H. Lambert (*Ireland*) **Touch judges:** D.S. Kerr, T.K. Bourke

C. McDonald kicked a penalty (3–0); K.H. Kearney scored but B.J.C. Piper failed (3–3)(H.T.). D.P. Hepburn dropped a goal (7–3); A.E.J. Tonkin, M.L. Howell and G.M. Cooke scored and B.J.C. Piper converted the first two (7–16).

The game was fairly evenly balanced until the last twenty minutes when Wright had to go off with a dislocated shoulder. Up till then the Scottish halves had been combining well while the opposing pair had been troubled by the wet and greasy ball, but now their pack got on top especially at the line out. A nice break by Allan put Tonkin over and the conversion saw Australia leading for the first time. Then Keller broke away from a line out to send Howell in and later a powerful forward rush let Cooke away along the touch line to score. Scotland did not give in and had one spirited counter-attack before the close.

FRANCE Murrayfield 24 January 1948

SCOTLAND:	2 penalty goals, 1 try	9	**Win**
FRANCE:	1 goal, 1 penalty goal	8	

Scotland: W.C.W. Murdoch (*Hillhead HSFP*); T.G.H. Jackson (*London Scot.*), J.R.S. Innes* (*Aberdeen GSFP*), C.W. Drummond (*Melrose*), D.D. Mackenzie (*Edin. Univ.*); D.P. Hepburn (*Woodford*), W.D. Allardice (*Aberdeen GSFP*); R.M. Bruce (*Gordonians*), G.G. Lyall (*Gala*), W.P. Black (*Glas. HSFP*), L.R. Currie (*Dunfermline*), J.C. Dawson (*Glas. Acads.*), W.I.D. Elliot (*Edin. Acads.*), A.G.M. Watt (*Army*), J.B. Lees (*Gala*)

France: A. Alvarez (*Tyrosse*); M. Pomathios (*Agen*), L. Junques (*Bayonne*), P. Dizabo (*Tyrosse*), R. Lacaussade (*Beglais*); L. Bordenave (*Toulon*), Y. Bergougnan (*Toulouse*); E. Buzy (*Lourdes*), L. Martin (*Paloise*), L. Aristouy (*Paloise*), R. Soro (*Romans*), A. Moga (*Beglais*), J. Prat (*Lourdes*), G. Basquet* (*Agen*), J. Matheu (*Castres*)

Referee: A.S. Bean (*England*)

R. Lacaussade scored and A. Alvarez converted (0–5); W.C.W. Murdoch kicked a penalty (3–5); J. Prat dropped a penalty goal (3–8).(H.T.). T.G.H. Jackson scored but W.C.W. Murdoch failed (6–8); W.C.W. Murdoch kicked a penalty (9–8).

Scotland showed a welcome stamina and spirit after France had taken a lead at half time and after they had edged in front with some fifteen minutes to go a determined defence saw them through. The game began with an unorthodox tackle on Drummond which laid him out but after a short spell off he returned fit enough. Early on Bergougnan, who was always ready to drop at goal, sent one such kick wide of the posts to pitch over the line. Several defenders did everything but head the ball before Lacaussade nipped in to touch down. There was almost a repeat shortly after but this time Hepburn kicked dead. A break by Mackenzie was halted but, to the obvious disagreement of the French touch judge, a penalty was given and converted by Murdoch. Near half time J. Prat dropped a penalty goal 40 yards out on the touch line to put France in the lead at the interval. Scotland resumed strongly and when Alvarez failed to collect a kick ahead Innes gathered and passed to Jackson who ran some 30 yards closely chased to score. Murdoch failed here but converted a penalty for a blatant offside at a scrum and this one point lead was held for the win, although J. Prat just missed with one huge drop kick penalty.

Murdoch, last capped in 1939, came in as a deputy reserve to make a fine come-back and also proved to be a welcome goal kicker.

The French style of play was obviously much changed since 1931 — both backs and forwards producing some adventurous handling but the pack, although heavy, were too inclined to barge at the line out and get offside in the open.

WALES   Cardiff   7 February 1948

SCOTLAND: Nil   0   Loss
WALES: 1 goal, 1 penalty goal, 2 tries   14

Scotland: W.C.W. Murdoch (*Hillhead HSFP*); T.G.H. Jackson (*London Scot.*), J.R.S. Innes* (*Aberdeen GSFP*), A. Cameron (*Glas. HSFP*), D.D. Mackenzie (*Edin. Univ.*); D.P. Hepburn (*Woodford*), W.D. Allardice (*Aberdeen GSFP*); R.M. Bruce (*Gordonians*), G.G. Lyall (*Gala*), L.R. Currie (*Dunfermline*), J.C. Dawson (*Glas. Acads.*), W.P. Black (*Glas. HSFP*), W.I.D. Elliot (*Edin. Acads.*), A.G.M. Watt (*Edin. Acads.*), J.B. Lees (*Gala*)

Wales: R.F. Trott (*Cardiff*); K.J. Jones (*Newport*), B.L. Williams (*Cardiff*), W.B. Cleaver (*Cardiff*), J. Matthews (*Cardiff*); G. Davies (*Pontypridd*), H. Tanner* (*Cardiff*); C. Davies (*Cardiff*), M. James (*Cardiff*), L. Anthony (*Neath*), S. Williams (*Llanelli*), W.E. Tamplin (*Cardiff*), O. Williams (*Llanelli*), L. Manfield (*Cardiff*), G. Evans (*Cardiff*)

Referee: T.N. Pearce (*England*)   **Touch judges:** H. Waddell, A. Cornish

No scoring at half time. B.L. Williams scored and W.E. Tamplin converted (0–5); J. Matthews scored but W.E. Tamplin failed (0–8); W.E. Tamplin kicked a penalty (0–11); K.J. Jones scored but W.E. Tamplin failed (0–14).

Wales were clearly the better team. Their halves were in fine form and gave an active set of backs good possession. This stemmed from a vigorous Welsh pack which controlled the scrums and line outs. As a result Allardice had to do much brave defending round the mauls and his backs saw little of the ball.

Scotland started with the wind and did well enough in the loose to keep play mainly in the Welsh half but could not break through before the interval. Murdoch, too, was unsuccessful with a run of five penalty kicks. After the interval Wales with the wind and a dominating pack were clearly on top and continuous fine play by their backs gave them a clear win.

IRELAND   Lansdowne Road   28 February 1948

| **SCOTLAND:** | Nil | **0** | **Loss** |
| **IRELAND:** | 2 tries | **6** | |

Scotland: W.C.W. Murdoch (*Hillhead HSFP*); T.G.H. Jackson (*London Scot.*), C.W. Drummond (*Melrose*), J.R.S. Innes* (*Aberdeen GSFP*), D.D. Mackenzie (*Edin. Univ.*); D.P. Hepburn (*Woodford*), W.D. Allardice (*Aberdeen GSFP*); I.C. Henderson (*Edin. Acads.*), G.G. Lyall (*Gala*), S. Coltman (*Hawick*), L.R. Currie (*Dunfermline*), H.H. Campbell (*London Scot.*), W.I.D. Elliot (*Edin. Acads.*), W.P. Black (*Glas. HSFP*), R.M. Bruce (*Gordonians*)

Ireland: J.A.D. Higgins (*Civil Service*); B. Mullan (*Clontarf*), M. O'Flanagan (*Lansdowne*), W.D. McKee (*NIFC*), B. O'Hanlon (*Dolphin*); J.W. Kyle (*Queen's*), H.de Lacy (*Harlequins*); A.A. McConnell (*Collegians*), K.D. Mullen* (*Old Belvedere*), J.C. Daly (*London Irish*), C.P. Callan (*Lansdowne*), J.E. Nelson (*Malone*), J.S. McCarthy (*Dolphin*), D.J. O'Brien (*London Irish*), J.W. McKay (*QU Belfast*)

Referee: C.H. Gadney (*England*) **Touch judges:** H. Waddell, I.F. Mahoney

No scoring at half time. B. Mullan scored but failed to convert (0–3); J.W. Kyle scored but B. Mullan failed (0–6).

The Irish pack laid the foundation of the win especially after half time when Scotland was continually on the defensive and it was only good tackling by their backs that kept the score down. Kyle, well supplied with the ball in the second half, kept his backs on the move. McKee made the opening for Mullan's try and following a fierce forward rush De Lacy got the ball out to Kyle who cut through to score. One other such forward rush carried the ball and Allardice some 25 yards!

ENGLAND   Murrayfield   20 March 1948

| **SCOTLAND:** | 2 tries | **6** | **Win** |
| **ENGLAND:** | 1 penalty goal | **3** | |

Scotland: W.C.W. Murdoch (*Hillhead HSFP*); T.G.H. Jackson (*London Scot.*), J.R.S. Innes* (*Aberdeen GSFP*), L. Bruce Lockhart (*London Scot.*), C.W. Drummond (*Melrose*); D.P. Hepburn (*Woodford*), A.W. Black (*Edin. Univ.*); I.C. Henderson (*Edin. Acads.*),

G.G. Lyall (*Gala*), H.H. Campbell (*London Scot.*), W.P. Black (*Glas. HSFP*), R. Finlay (*Watsonians*), W.I.D. Elliot (*Edin. Acads.*), J.B. Lees (*Gala*), W.B. Young (*London Scot.*)

England: R. Uren (*Waterloo*); R.H. Guest (*Waterloo*), N.O. Bennett (*Un. Services*), E.K. Scott* (*Redruth*), M.F. Turner (*Blackheath*); I. Preece (*Coventry*), R.J.P. Madge (*Exeter*); H. Walker (*Coventry*), A.P. Henderson (*Edin. Wrs.*), T. Price (*Gloucester*), S.V. Perry (*Camb. Univ.*), H.F. Luya (*Headingley*), M.R. Steele-Bodger (*Edin. Univ.*), R.H.G. Weighill (*RAF*), D.B. Vaughan (*Devonport Services*)

Referee: N.H. Lambert (*Ireland*)   Touch judges: H. Waddell, H.C. Catcheside

R. Uren kicked a penalty (0–3).(H.T.). C.W. Drummond scored but L.B. Lockhart failed (3–3); W.B. Young scored but W.C.W. Murdoch failed (6–3).

Play never reached a great standard but England were handicapped by losing Madge after ten minutes play. Steele-Bodger took his place and was quite outstanding even after being badly dazed by a heavy tackle in the second half. Against the wind England actually held the lead at half time although Hepburn did get over with the ball but being smother tackled the referee refused the score. Early in the second half Jackson raced up to a line out and was able to start a movement finished off by Innes giving Drummond a clear run for a good score at the corner. Later the English pack began to tire and after some slack play at a line out Young was able to grab a loose ball and charge over. After the game it was found that Scott, injured during the second half, had in fact played on with a fractured jaw.

FRANCE   Colombes   15 January 1949

SCOTLAND:	1 goal, 1 try	8	**Win**
FRANCE:	Nil	0	

Scotland: I.J.M. Lumsden (*Bath*); T.G.H. Jackson (*Army*), L.G. Gloag (*Camb. Univ.*), D.P. Hepburn (*Woodford*), D.W.C. Smith (*Army*); C.R. Bruce (*Glas. Acads.*), W.D. Allardice (*Aberdeen GSFP*); J.C. Dawson (*Glas. Acads.*), J.C. Abercrombie (*Edin. Univ.*), S. Coltman (*Hawick*), L.R. Currie (*Dunfermline*), G.A. Wilson (*Oxford Univ.*), D.H. Keller* (*London Scot.*), P.W. Kininmonth (*Oxford Univ.*), W.I.D. Elliot (*Edin. Acads.*)

France: N. Baudry (*Montferrand*); M. Pomathios (*Lyon*), M. Terreau (*Bressane*), P. Dizabo (*Tyrosse*), M. Siman (*Montferrand*); L. Bordenave (*Toulon*), Y. Bergougnan (*Toulouse*); E. Buzy (*Lourdes*), M. Jol (*Biarritz*), L. Caron (*Lyon*), R. Soro (*Romans*), A. Moga (*Beglais*), J. Prat (*Lourdes*), G. Basquet* (*Agen*), J. Matheu (*Castres*)

Referee: T.N. Pearce (*England*)   Touch judges: H. Waddell, M. Gos

W.I.D. Elliot scored (3–0).(H.T.). P.W. Kininmonth scored and W.D. Allardice converted (8–0).

D.H. Keller had played for Australia at Murrayfield during the previous season and his selection as player and captain raised a considerable amount of controversy. France attacked for most of the game for their pack fairly shoved their opponents about, the massive Soro, Moga and Basquet being particularly tough and aggressive. Even after France lost Bergougnan with a broken collar bone after half an hour, their pack continued

207

to dominate the scrums but although J. Pratt was an admirable substitute at scrum half the French threes were too prosaic — too often passing without purpose. Scotland were quite effective in the loose and following some good defensive play by Lumsden and Hepburn a fine breakaway by the backs and forwards let Elliot open the scoring after ten minutes' play. In the second half Allardice, who had been defending well, broke away in his own half. Jackson got the ball and kicked inside for Kininmonth to collect and score. France continued to attack but could not break through although they got the ball over the line once. The referee, to the wrath of their supporters, gave the defenders the benefit of the touch down.

WALES	Murrayfield	5 February 1949

SCOTLAND:	2 tries	6	**Win**
WALES:	1 goal	5	

Scotland: I.J.M. Lumsden (*Bath*); T.G.H. Jackson (*London Scot.*), L.G. Gloag (*Camb. Univ.*), D.P. Hepburn (*Woodford*), D.W.C. Smith (*London Scot.*); C.R. Bruce (*Glas. Acads.*), W.D. Allardice (*Aberdeen GSFP*); J.C. Dawson (*Glas. Acads.*), J.G. Abercrombie (*Edin. Univ.*), S. Coltman (*Hawick*), L.R. Currie (*Dunfermline*), G.A. Wilson (*Oxford Univ.*), D.H. Keller* (*London Scot.*), P.W. Kininmonth (*Oxford Univ.*), W.I.D. Elliot (*Edin. Acads.*)

Wales: R.F. Trott (*Cardiff*); K.J. Jones (*Newport*), J. Matthews (*Cardiff*), B.L .Williams (*Cardiff*), T. Cook (*Cardiff*); G. Davies (*Camb. Univ.*), H. Tanner* (*Cardiff*); E. Colman (*Newport*), W.H. Travers (*Newport*), D. Jones (*Swansea*), J.A. Gwilliam (*Camb. Univ.*), A. Meredith (*Devonport Services*), G. Evans (*Cardiff*), J.R.G. Stephens (*Neath*), W.R. Cole (*Newbridge*).

Referee: N.H. Lambert (*Ireland*)   **Touch judges:** D.A. Thom, J.W. Faull

L.G. Gloag scored but W.D. Allardice failed (3–0).(H.T.). D.W.C. Smith scored but L.R. Currie failed (6–0); B.I.. Williams scored and R.F. Trott converted (6–5).

Again the Scottish pack were beaten in the line out and scrums but their fiendishly aggressive back row, with Elliot quite outstanding, fairly demolished the Welsh attacks. Davies took a tremendous hammering and with the Scottish threes also tackling well, a formidable Welsh attack never really got on the move. The Scottish pack, however, were quite effective with their work in the loose yet it was at a line out where Allardice nipped through a gap and good interplay between Hepburn and Elliot finished with Gloag scoring. In the second half Wales continued their fruitless attacking but Smith twice intercepted passes and had one 50 yards dash before the Olympic sprinter, Jones, could catch him. After some loose play Dawson picked up and sent Smith off from midfield. This time he got over before Jones could tackle. With five minutes to go Tanner threw a long pass to B. Williams who jinked his way through a crowded defence to score a great try. The conversion reduced Scotland's lead to a point but a confident defence saw them through. This game was threatened by a thick fog which, however, lifted shortly before the kick off.

208

IRELAND　　　　Murrayfield　　　26 February 1949

SCOTLAND:	1 penalty goal	3	Loss
IRELAND:	2 goals, 1 penalty goal	13	

Scotland: I.J.M. Lumsden (*Bath*); T.G.H. Jackson (*London Scot.*), L.G. Gloag (*Camb. Univ.*), D.P. Hepburn (*Woodford*), D.W.C. Smith (*London Scot.*); C.R. Bruce (*Glas. Acads.*), W.D. Allardice (*Aberdeen GSFP*); J.C. Dawson (*Glas. Acads.*), J.G. Abercrombie (*Edin. Univ.*), S. Coltman (*Hawick*), L.R. Currie (*Dunfermline*), A.M. Thomson (*St Andrews Univ.*), D.H. Keller* (*London Scot.*), P.W. Kininmonth (*Oxford Univ.*), W.I.D. Elliot (*Edin. Acads.*)

Ireland: G.W. Norton (*Bective Rangers*); B. O'Hanlan (*Dolphin*), N.J. Henderson (*QU Belfast*), W.D. McKee (*NIFC*), M.F. Lane (*UC Cork*); J.W. Kyle (*Queen's*), E. Strathdee (*Queen's*); T. Clifford (*Young Munster*), K. Mullen* (*Old Belvedere*), L. Griffin (*Wanderers*), J.E. Nelson (*Malone*), R.D. Agar (*Malone*), J.W. McKay (*Queen's*), D.J. O'Brien (*London Irish*), J.S. McCarthy (*Dolphin*)

Referee: A.S. Bean (*England*)　　**Touch judges:** D.A. Thom, O.F. Murray

J.S. McCarthy scored and G.W. Norton converted (0–5).(H.T.). G.W. Norton kicked a penalty (0–8); J.S. McCarthy scored and G.W. Norton converted (0–13); W.D. Allardice kicked a penalty (3–13).

The Scottish pack failed to harass the Irish halves. Not only did the Irish pack rather dominate affairs but Kyle made use of good possession by kicking to touch until a winning lead had been established. In contrast the Scottish halves were always under pressure and their backs got little chance to shine. Elliot had one good run in the first half. On reaching the full back he kicked ahead just before he was heavily tackled and laid out but no obstruction was given.

ENGLAND　　　　Twickenham　　　19 March 1949

SCOTLAND:	1 penalty goal	3	Loss
ENGLAND:	3 goals, 3 tries	19	

Scotland: I.J.M. Lumsden (*Bath*); T.G.H. Jackson (*London Scot.*), L.G. Gloag (*Camb. Univ.*), D.P. Hepburn (*Woodford*), W.D.C. Smith (*Army*); C.R. Bruce (*Glas. Acads.*), W.D. Allardice (*Aberdeen GSFP*); S.T.H. Wright (*Stewart's FP*), J.A.R. Macphail (*Edin. Acads.*), S. Coltman (*Hawick*), L.R. Currie (*Dunfermline*), G.A. Wilson (*Oxford Univ.*), D.H. Keller* (*London Scot.*), P.W. Kininmonth (*Oxford Univ.*), W.I.D. Elliot (*Edin. Acads.*)

England: W.B. Holmes (*Camb. Univ.*); R.D. Kennedy (*Camborne*), C.B. Van Ryneveld (*Oxford Univ.*), L.B. Cannell (*Oxford Univ.*), R.H. Guest (*Waterloo*); I. Preece* (*Coven-*

try), W.K.T. Moore (*Leicester*); B.H. Travers (*Harlequins*), D.B. Vaughan (*Headingley*), V.G. Roberts (*Penryn*), G.R.D. Hosking (*Devonport Services*), J.R.C. Matthews (*Harlequins*), J.M. Kendall-Carpenter (*Oxford Univ.*), J.H. Steeds (*Middlesex Hospital*), T.W. Price (*Cheltenham*)

Referee: N.H. Lambert (*Ireland*)   **Touch judges:** D.A. Thom, H.A. Haigh-Smith

R.D. Kennedy scored but W.B. Holmes failed (0–3).(H.T.). C.B. Van Ryneveld scored and B.H. Travers converted (10–8); G.A. Wilson kicked a penalty (3–8); G.B. Van Rynefeld, G.R.D. Hosking and R.H. Guest scored, B.H. Travers converted the second only (3–19).

The teams were introduced to the Duke of Edinburgh. During the first half the Scottish pack did quite well in the open but their backs could not break through a firm and speedy defence. Later on the English forwards were on top and their backs attacked well. After 25 minutes Jackson, who started with a suspect knee, became very lame and as far as possible took the non-open wing position. Early on Kennedy went past Jackson and got over only to be brought back for a foot in touch. Then Roberts broke away at mid field and Van Ryneveld put Kennedy in. Early in the second half Lumsden fielded a cross kick by Preece but was brought down by two attackers. Van Ryneveld scooped up the ball and scored. After a Wilson penalty England pressed continually and good handling play by both forwards and backs produced two more good tries.

FRANCE   Murrayfield   14 January 1950

SCOTLAND: 1 goal, 1 try   8   **Win**

FRANCE: 1 goal   5

Scotland: G. Burrell (*Gala*); D.W.C. Smith (*Army*), R. Macdonald (*Edin. Univ.*), D.A. Sloan (*Edin. Acads.*), C.W. Drummond (*Melrose*); L. Bruce Lockhart (*London Scot.*), A.F. Dorward (*Camb. Univ.*); J.C. Dawson (*Glas. Acads.*), J.G. Abercrombie (*Edin. Univ.*), G.M. Budge (*Edin. Wrs.*), D.E. Muir (*Heriot's FP*), R. Gemmill (*Glas. HSFP*), W.I.D. Elliot* (*Edin. Acads.*), P.W. Kininmonth (*Richmond*), D.H. Keller (*Sheffield*)

France: R. Arcalis (*Brive*): M. Pomathios (*Lyon OU*), J. Merquey (*Toulon*), P. Dizabo (*RCF*), M. Siman (*Castres O*); P. Lauga (*Vichy*), G. Dufau (*RCF*); P. Lavergne (*Limoges*), L. Martin (*Paloise*), P. Aristouy (*Paloise*), R. Ferrien (*Tarbais*), F. Bonnus (*Toulon*), J. Prat (*Lourdes*), G. Basquet* (*Agen*), R. Bienes (*Cognac*)

Referee: T. Jones (*Wales*)   **Touch judges:** J.R.S. Innes, R. Lerou

R. Macdonald and G.M. Budge scored and L.B. Lockhart converted the second only (8–0).(H.T.). J. Merquey scored and J. Prat converted (8–5).

Scotland were more emphatic winners than the score suggests although J. Prat in the last minutes nearly saved the match with a drop kick penalty from 50 yards out which narrowly missed. The Scottish pack were on top but the French pack were distinctly fast about the field yet as a team they seemed to have abandoned a running game for a more defensive and destructive style. Budge had a good game and was surprisingly mobile for a prop of his size. After half an hour's play Scotland scored twice; first Budge and Bruce Lockhart combined to put Macdonald over and almost at once Drummond and Dawson put Budge in.

The French pack livened up in the second half and were helped a little when Burrell, Keller and Aristouy were all dazed in the one collision. Burrell went off for a while and Kininmonth deputised at full back. Towards the end Siman broke away, his crosskick beat Smith, and Merquey ran in for a converted try. About this time Arcalis was badly dazed when he halted Elliot who would have scored to make the score more appropriate and Scotland got a fright when J. Prat, 50 yards out, narrowly missed that drop kick from a penalty award.

WALES   Swansea   4 February 1950

SCOTLAND: Nil   0 **Loss**

WALES: 1 drop goal, 1 penalty goal, 2 tries   12

Scotland: G. Burrell (*Gala*); D.W.C. Smith (*Army*), R. Macdonald (*Edin. Univ.*), D.A. Sloan (*Edin. Acads.*), C.W. Drummond (*Melrose*); L. Bruce Lockhart (*London Scot.*), A.W. Black (*Edin. Univ.*); J.C. Dawson (*Glas. Acads.*), J.G. Abercrombie (*Edin. Univ.*), G.M. Budge (*Edin. Wrs.*), D.E. Muir (*Heriot's FP*), R. Gemmill (*Glas. HSFP*), W.I.D. Elliot* (*Edin. Acads.*), P.W. Kininmonth (*Richmond*), D.H. Keller (*Sheffield*)

Wales: B.J. Jones (*Devonport Services*); K.J. Jones (*Newport*), J. Matthews (*Cardiff*), M.C. Thomas (*Newport*), W. Major (*Maesteg*); W.B. Cleaver (*Cardiff*), W.R. Willis (*Cardiff*); C. Davies (*Cardiff*), D.M. Davies (*Somerset Police*), J.D. Robins (*Birkenhead Park*), R. John (*Neath*), J.D. Hayward (*Newbridge*), W.R. Cole (*Pontypool*), J.A. Gwilliam* (*Edin. Wrs.*), R.T. Evans (*Newport*)

    Referee: M.J. Dowling (*Ireland*)   **Touch judges:** J.R.S. Innes, V. Griffiths

M.C. Thomas scored but B.L. Jones failed (0–3).(H.T.). B.L. Jones kicked a penalty (0–6); K.J. Jones scored but B.L. Jones failed (0–9); W.B. Cleaver dropped a goal (0–12).

Scotland did some early attacking which was held by a solid defence. Then rather against the run of play Matthews (who was always dangerous) had a strong run which finished with Thomas scoring. In the second half Wales were clearly on top but both packs concentrated on spoiling tactics which produced a tiresome stream of penalties for offside and obstruction. Jones had kicked a goal from one before Matthews placed a kick ahead into the corner which Jones got to first for a score, and Cleaver finished the scoring with a drop goal.

IRELAND   Lansdowne Road   25 February 1950

SCOTLAND: Nil   0 **Loss**

IRELAND: 3 goals, 2 penalty goals   21

Scotland: G. Burrell (*Gala*); D.W.C. Smith (*Army*), R. Macdonald (*Edin. Univ.*), C.W.

Drummond (*Melrose*), D.M. Scott (*Langholm*); A. Cameron (*Glas. HSFP*), A.W. Black (*Edin. Univ.*); J.C. Dawson (*Glas. Acads.*), J.G. Abercrombie (*Edin. Univ.*), G.M. Budge (*Edin. Wrs.*), D.E. Muir (*Heriot's FP*), R. Gemmill (*Glas. HSFP*), W.I.D. Elliot* (*Edin. Acads.*), P.W. Kininmonth (*Richmond*), D.H. Keller (*Sheffield*)

Ireland: G.W. Norton (*Bective Rangers*); L. Crowe (*Old Belvedere*), J. Blayney (*Wanderers*), R.J.H. Uprichard (*RAF*), M.F. Lane (*UC Cork*); J.W. Kyle (*Queen's*), R. Carroll (*Lansdowne*); T. Clifford (*Young Munster*), K.D. Mullen* (*Old Belvedere*), D. McKibbin (*Instonians*), J.E. Nelson (*Malone*), J. Maloney (*UC Dublin*), A.B. Curtis (*Oxford Univ.*), D.J. O'Brien (*London Irish*), J.W. McKay (*Queen's*)

Referee: T. Pearce (*England*)   **Touch judges:** R.W. Shaw, B.V. Fox

G.W. Morton kicked two penalties (0–6).(H.T.). J. Blayney, A.B. Curtis and L. Crowe scored and G.W. Norton converted all three (0–21).

This was Scotland's biggest defeat in Dublin. Nothing went right whereas Ireland picked up everything that was going and Norton was right on target with his kicking. Scotland started brightly enough and produced one spectacular run by Drummond, Cameron, Macdonald and Smith which finished close to the line but they gradually faded. In the second half the Irish forwards were clearly on top. Even with the wind Scotland could not get moving whereas Ireland ran in three good tries.

ENGLAND   Murrayfield: 18 March 1950

SCOTLAND: 2 goals, 1 try   13   **Win**

ENGLAND: 1 goal, 1 penalty goal, 1 try   11

Scotland: T. Gray (*Northampton*); C.W. Drummond (*Melrose*), R. Macdonald (*Edin. Univ.*), D.A. Sloan (*Edin. Acads.*), D.M. Scott (*Langholm*); A. Cameron (*Glas. HSFP*), A.W. Black (*Edin. Univ.*); J.C. Dawson (*Glas. Acads.*), J.G. Abercrombie (*Edin. Univ.*), G.M. Budge (*Edin. Wrs.*), D.E. Muir (*Heriot's FP*), R. Gemmill (*Glas. HSFP*), W.I.D. Elliot (*Edin. Acads.*), P.W. Kininmonth* (*Richmond*), H. Scott (*St Andrews Univ.*)

England: M.B. Hofmeyr (*Oxford Univ.*); J.P. Hyde (*Army*), B. Boobyer (*Oxford Univ.*), L.B. Cannell (*Oxford Univ.*), J.V. Smith (*Camb. Univ.*); I. Preece* (*Coventry*), W.K.T. Moore (*Leicester*); J. L. Baume (*Army*), J.H. Steeds (*Saracens*), W.A. Holmes (*Nuneaton*) J.R.C. Matthews (*Harlequins*), S.J. Adkins (*Coventry*), H.D. Small (*Oxford Univ.*), J.M. Kendall-Carpenter (*Oxford Univ.*), V.G. Roberts (*Penryn*)

Referee: M.J. Dowling (*Ireland*)   **Touch judges:** J.R.S. Innes, G. Warden

D.A. Sloan scored but T. Gray failed (3–0); J.V. Smith scored but M.B. Hofmeyr failed (3–3); J.G. Abercrombie scored and T. Gray converted (8–3).(H.T.). M.B. Hofmeyr kicked a penalty (8–6); J.V. Smith scored and M.B. Hofmeyr converted (8–10); D.A. Sloan scored and T. Gray converted (13–11).

The Scottish forwards took some credit for the win; beaten in the scrums, they were good in the loose and finished very strongly. Continual rain made handling difficult but Hofmeyr fielded and kicked immaculately. After fifteen minutes an English passing movement broke down near their line; Scott and Sloan dribbled the ball in for the latter to be credited with the score. Within three minutes a rush by the English forwards put the defence in a tangle and when the ball rolled over the line, Smith, a fast and alert winger, got there first to score. Two minutes later Black broke away and getting the ball again after Cameron was held, passed to Abercrombie who scored near the posts. Straight after the break Hofmeyr kicked a fine long range penalty and within ten minutes England took the lead. Pearce placed a fine kick to the corner flag and Smith's pace allowed him to score. Hofmeyr converted with a fine kick. Scotland fought on until right on time some fine foot work by the Scottish forwards let Cameron get the ball and he put in a towering kick which Sloan ran on to and in spite of a mass of defenders got the ball and scored. In pelting rain Gray converted from half way to the touch-line and the whistle went almost immediately after.

FRANCE   Colombes   13 January 1951

SCOTLAND:	2 penalty goals, 2 tries	12	**Loss**
FRANCE:	1 goal, 2 penalty goals, 1 try	14	

Scotland: T. Gray (*Northampton*); A.D. Cameron (*Hillhead HSFP*), I.D.F. Coutts (*Old Alleynians*), F.O. Turnbull (*Kelso*), D.M. Rose (*Jedforest*); A. Cameron (*Glas. HSFP*), I.A. Ross (*Hillhead HSFP*); J.C. Dawson (*Glas. Acads.*), N.G.R. Mair (*Edin. Univ.*), R.L. Wilson (*Gala*), H.M. Inglis (*Edin. Acads.*), R. Gemmill (*Glas. HSFP*), W.I.D. Elliot (*Edin. Acads.*), P.W. Kininmonth* (*Richmond*), J.J. Hegarty (*Hawick*)

France: A.J. Alvarez (*Tyrosse*); A. Porthault (*RCF*), M. Terreau (*Bressane*), G. Brun (*Vienne*), M. Pomathios (*Lyon*); J. Carabignac (*Agen*), G. Dufau (*RCF*); R. Bernard (*Bergerac*), P. Pascalin (*Mont-de-Marsan*), R. Bienes (*Cognac*), L. Mias (*Mazamet*), H. Foures (*Toulouse*), J. Prat (*Lourdes*), G. Basquet* (*Agen*), J. Matheu (*Castres*)

Referee: T.N. Pearce (*England*)   **Touch judges:** R.W. Shaw, R. Le Roux

J. Prat kicked a penalty (0–3); T. Gray kicked a penalty (3–3); L. Mias scored but A.J. Alvarez failed (3–6); T. Gray kicked a penalty (6–6).(H.T.). D.M. Rose scored twice but T. Gray failed (12–6); A. Porthault scored and J. Prat converted (12–11); J. Prat kicked a penalty (12–14).

Scotland played nine new caps which included a whole new three quarter line while France had five new men. Scotland started well, the backs handling and running whenever possible but could only score by Gray's penalty kicks, two of which counted while a third struck the inside of an upright yet managed to rebound into play. The early French try followed a good touch-line run by Brun and his crosskick fell amongst the mass of the French pack for Mias to score. Prat's kick narrowly missed but the score board registered the full points for the remainder of the game and perhaps it was fortunate that Prat's final kick actually did win the match! After the interval Scotland forged ahead with two tries by Rose stemming from openings made by Coutts and Elliot but with 15 minutes left the French pack rose to the occasion. A fine rush put the ball past the defence over the line and Pomathios, who had been a constant threat, was able to race in to touch down. The try was magnificently converted by Prat but it needed an equally good penalty kick by him in the last minutes to win the match.

213

SCOTLAND: 2 goals, 1 drop goal,   19   **Win**
              1 penalty goal, 1 try

WALES: Nil   0

Scotland: I.H.M. Thomson (*Heriot's FP*); R. Gordon (*Edin. Wrs.*), D.A. Sloan (*Edin. Acads.*), D.M. Scott (*Langholm*), D. M. Rose (*Jedforest*); A. Cameron (*Glas. HSFP*), I.A. Ross (*Hillhead HSFP*); J.C. Dawson (*Glas. Acads.*), N.G.R. Mair (*Edin. Univ.*), R.L. Wilson (*Gala*), R. Gemmill (*Glas. HSFP*), H.M. Inglis (*Edin. Acads.*), W.I.D. Elliot (*Edin. Acads.*), P.W. Kininmonth* (*Richmond*), R.C. Taylor (*Kelvinside-West*)

Wales: G. Williams (*Llanelli*); M.C. Thomas (*Devonport Services*), B.L. Jones (*Devonport Services*), J. Matthews (*Cardiff*), K.J. Jones (*Newport*); G. Davies (*Camb. Univ.*), W.R. Willis (*Cardiff*); C. Davies (*Cardiff*), D.M. Davies (*Somerset Police*), J.D. Robins (*Birkenhead Park*), E.R. John (*Neath*), D.J. Hayward (*Newbridge*), A. Forward (*Pontypool*), J.A.Gwilliam* (*Edin. Wrs.*), R.T. Evans (*Newport*)

Referee: M.J. Dowling (*Ireland*)   **Touch judges:** D.A. Thom, I. Jones

I.H.M. Thomson kicked a penalty (3–0). (H.T.). P.W. Kininmonth dropped a goal (6–0); R. Gordon scored twice and H.M. Inglis converted the first (14–0); J.C. Dawson scored and I.H.M. Thomson converted (19–0).

In front of a record crowd of some 80,000 (which included about 20,000 Welsh supporters) a young Scottish XV achieved one of the most unexpected results of the season when they demolished a formidable Welsh team which included eleven Lions from the last tour. Wales made a very confident start but found the Scottish pack continually bringing the play back into the Welsh 25 area. The Welsh forwards were well held while their backs were harassed into making mistakes. Scotland actually led at the interval by a Thomson penalty and the twenty-year-old new cap had only come into the side that morning when Gray called off with a cold. On restarting Scotland, full of confidence, stepped up the pace and persistence of their attack and determined efforts by Gordon, Elliot and Rose nearly brought scores. After twenty minutes of this pressure Williams was forced to make a hurried clearance from his own line and his kick was caught cleanly by Kininmonth standing on the touch line at the Welsh 25 flag, whereupon he steadied himself, glanced at the distant posts and then dropped what must rank as one of the historic goals in the history of the game. Badly shaken, Wales moved Lewis Jones up to half and the Welsh pack staged a furious onslaught but achieved no break through. Scotland, however, raised their game in pace and vigour and began an attack which demoralised their opponents. A break away by Scott let Gordon race in for a try and he scored again following up a dribbling run by Elliot and Taylor. The rout was completed when a rush by the Scottish forwards was finished by Dawson scoring.

This excellent win was the more remarkable in that it was to be the last until the Welsh match in 1955 for Scotland was now about to enter on an appalling run of seventeen consecutive losses.

IRELAND　　　　　Murrayfield　　　24 February 1951

SCOTLAND:　　1 goal　　　　　　　　　5　　**Loss**

IRELAND:　　　1 drop goal, 1 try　　　6

Scotland: I.H.M. Thomson (*Heriot's FP*); K.J. Dalgleish (*Edin. Wrs.*), D.A. Sloan (*Edin. Acads.*), D.M. Scott (*Langholm*), D.M. Rose (*Jedforest*); A. Cameron (*Glas. HSFP*), I.A. Ross (*Hillhead HSFP*); J.C. Dawson (*Glas. Acads.*), N.G.R. Mair (*Edin. Univ.*), R.L. Wilson (*Gala*), H.M. Inglis (*Edin. Acads.*), R. Gemmill (*Glas. HSFP*), W.I.D. Elliot (*Edin. Acads.*), P.W. Kininmonth* (*Richmond*), R.C. Taylor (*Kelvinside-West*)

Ireland: A.W. Norton (*Bective Rangers*); M.F. Lane (*UC Cork*), R.C. Chambers (*Instonians*), N.J. Henderson (*QU Belfast*), W.H.J. Millar (*QU Belfast*); J.W. Kyle (*QU Belfast*), J. O'Meara (*UC Cork*); J.H. Smith (*QU Belfast*), K.D. Mullen* (*Old Belvedere*), D. McKibbin (*Instonians*), P.J. Lawlor (*Clontarf*), J.R. Brady (*CIYMS*), J.S. McCarthy (*Dolphin*), D.J. O'Brien (*London Irish*), J.W. McKay (*QU Belfast*)

　　Referee: T.N. Pearce (*England*)　　**Touch judges:** J.R.S. Innes, R.R. Butler

D.A. Sloan scored and I.H.M. Thomson converted (5–0); N.J. Henderson dropped a goal (5–3).(H.T.). D.J. O'Brien scored but D. McKibbin failed (5–6).

Ireland lost Norton after fifteen minutes yet controlled play for the rest of the afternoon. The Scottish pack never gave their halves a decent supply of the ball and they were harried continually by O'Brien and McCarthy. On the other hand Kyle was well served and used the possession to great advantage. For a while Scotland attacked. Thomson missed one penalty and hit the post with another; Cameron had a drop goal disallowed for a previous knock on; from a line out, Scott broke away and Cameron and Sloan backed up for the latter to score. Before half time an Irish quick heel let Henderson drop a goal from the 25. The second half, however, was almost entirely dominated by the short handed Irish pack who maintained a tremendous pace. Lane was nearly in three times before Kyle, who was in fine form, made a diagonal run to send O'Brien over for the winning score. Scotland reacted strongly but all they could achieve were several abortive drops at goal.

ENGLAND　　　　Twickenham　　　17 March 1951

SCOTLAND:　　1 try　　　　　　　　　3　　**Loss**

ENGLAND:　　　1 goal　　　　　　　　5

Scotland: T. Gray (*Northampton*); K.J. Dalgleish (*Edin. Wrs.*), D.A. Sloan (*Edin. Acads.*), D.M. Scott (*Langholm*), D.M. Rose (*Jedforest*); A. Cameron (*Glas. HSFP*), I.A. Ross (*Hillhead HSFP*); J.C. Dawson (*Glas. Acads.*), N.G.R. Mair (*Edin. Univ.*), R.L. Wilson (*Gala*), W.P. Black (*Glas. HSFP*), H.M. Inglis (*Edin. Acads.*), W.I.D. Elliot (*Edin. Acads.*), P.W. Kininmonth* (*Richmond*), R.C. Taylor (*Kelvinside-West*)

England: W.G. Hook (*Gloucester*); C.G. Woodruff (*Harlequins*), A.C. Towell (*Bedford*), J.M. Williams (*Penzance-Newlyn*), V.R. Tindall (*Liverpool Univ.*); E.M.P. Hardy (*Army*), D.W. Shuttleworth (*Army*); R.V. Stirling (*RAF*), E. Evans (*Sale*), W.A. Holmes (*Nuneaton*), D.T. Wilkins (*Navy*), B.A. Neale (*Army*), V.G. Roberts (*Penryn*), J.M. Kendall-Carpenter* (*Oxford Univ.*), D.F. White (*Northampton*)

Referee: M.J. Dowling (*Ireland*)

D.F. White scored and W.G. Hook converted (0–5).(H.T.). A. Cameron scored but H.M. Inglis failed (3–5).

This was a desperately hard and fast game on heavy going which got worse when heavy rain fell during the second half. The English forwards began well especially in the loose but some good running by their backs was checked by firm tackling. Cameron, who was always difficult to stop, had a good break but Scott could not hold a difficult, if not forward, pass. England had one run which finished with Hook missing a drop at goal. Cameron broke again with Elliot and Kininmonth in support but Towell got in a saving kick to touch from his own line. Then from a slack Scottish heel White pounced on the ball, sold a dummy and scored. Hook's conversion was to win the match. In heavy rain England started the second half by attacking but the Scottish pack were constantly dangerous with dribbling rushes. England had one counter-attack when Roberts was narrowly beaten to the touch by Gray. With five minutes left some more aggression by the Scottish pack let Cameron score near the corner, too far out for Inglis to overcome the distance and conditions.

SOUTH AFRICA   Murrayfield   24 November 1951

SCOTLAND: Nil   0   **Loss**
SOUTH AFRICA: 7 goals, 1 drop goal, 2 tries   44

Scotland: G. Burrell (*Gala*); J.G.M. Hart (*London Scot.*), D.M. Scott (*London Scot.*), F.O. Turnbull (*Kelso*), D.M. Rose (*Jedforest*); A. Cameron* (*Glas. HSFP*), A.F. Dorward (*Gala*); J.C. Dawson (*Glas. Acads.*), J.A.R. Macphail (*Edin. Acads.*), R.L. Wilson (*Gala*), H.M. Inglis (*Edin. Acads.*), J. Johnston (*Melrose*), W.I.D. Elliot (*Edin. Acads.*), P.W. Kininmonth (*Richmond*), R.C. Taylor (*Kelvinside Acads.*)

South Africa: J. Buchler (*T*); F. Marais (*Boland*), R. Van Schoor (*Rhodesia*), M.T. Lategan (*WP*), P. Johnstone (*WP*); J.D. Brewis (*NT*), P.W. Du Toit (*NT*); A. Geffin (*T*), W. Delport (*EP*), C. Kock (*Boland*), C.J. Van Wyk (*T*), J. Du Rand (*Rhodesia*), E. Dinkelman (*NT*), S.P. Fry (*WP*), H. Muller* (*T*)

Referee: M.J. Dowling (*Ireland*)   **Touch judges:** R.W. Shaw, S.S. Viviers

J. Du. Rand, R. Van Schoor and C. Koch scored and A. Geffin converted the last two (0–13); J.D. Brewis dropped a goal (0–16); C. Koch scored but A. Geffin failed (0–19).(H.T.). W. Delport, C.J. Van Wyk, H. Muller, M.T. Lategan and E. Dinkelman scored and A. Geffin converted the lot (0–44).

This became known as the Murrayfield Massacre — a defeat so devastating that in retrospect it seemed to inflict a wound on Scottish rugby that took four seasons to heal. In fine conditions Scotland for some fifteen minutes held their opponents and even had one dangerous break headed by Elliot. Then suddenly their weaknesses were piteously exposed and the game exploded into a magnificent exhibition of combined handling and attacking play by the South African backs and forwards, backed up by some accurate goal kicking by A. Geffin who converted seven of the nine tries scored. The South African play was described as seven-a-side rugby played by fifteen men and there is a much-quoted comment made by a dazed Scottish supporter who was asked later what the score was and answered '44–0 and we were bloody lucky to get nothing'.

FRANCE   Murrayfield   12 January 1952

SCOTLAND: 1 goal, 2 penalty goals   11   **Loss**

FRANCE: 2 goals, 1 penalty goal   13

Scotland: I.H.M. Thomson (*Heriot's FP*); R. Gordon (*Edin. Wrs.*), I.F. Cordial (*Edin. Wrs.*), J.L. Allan (*Melrose*), D.M. Scott (*London Scot.*); J.N.G. Davidson (*Edin. Univ.*), A.K. Fulton (*Edin. Univ.*); J.C. Dawson (*Glas. Acads.*), N.M. Munnoch (*Watsonians*), J. Fox (*Gala*), M. Walker (*Oxford Univ.*), J. Johnston (*Melrose*), W.I.D. Elliot (*Edin. Acads.*), P.W. Kininmonth* (*Richmond*), J.T. Greenwood (*Dunfermline*)

France: R. Labarthete (*Pau*); G. Brun (*Vienne*), M. Prat (*Lourdes*), R. Martine (*Lourdes*), F. Cazenave (*Mont-de-Marsan*); R. Furcade (*Perpignan*), P. Lasaosa (*Dax*); R. Brejassou (*Tarbes*), P. Labadie (*A Bayonnais*), R. Bienes (*Cognac*), B. Chevallier (*Montferrand*), F. Varenne (*RCF*), J. Prat (*Lourdes*), G. Basquet* (*Agen*), J.R. Bourdeu (*Lourdes*)

   Referee: I. David (*Wales*)   **Touch judges;** J.R.S. Innes: A. Verger

I.H.M. Thomson kicked a penalty (3–0); J. Prat kicked a penalty (3–3); J. Prat scored and converted (3–8).(H.T.). I.H.M. Thomson kicked a penalty (6–8); G. Basquet scored and J. Prat converted (6–13); I.F. Cordial scored and I.H.M. Thomson converted (11–13).

Each side played eight new caps and France won at Murrayfield for the first time. An early penalty by Thomson was matched by a 45 yard kick by J. Prat who, before the interval, supported a break by his brother to score a try which he also converted. After the interval Gordon had one good 40 yards run down the touch line which was halted by J. Prat but the game really came to life in the last ten minutes. Lasaosa went off down the blind side. Again J. Prat was in support and passed to Basquet who knocked two defenders aside before scoring. Scotland came back at once and after a line out a passing run by the Scottish halves was finished by Cordial scoring. Thomson's conversion left Scotland two points behind but time ran out on them. For France J. Prat was outstanding as a breakaway forward and goal kicker while for Scotland Elliot again showed up in attack and cover defence.

WALES   Cardiff   2 February 1952

SCOTLAND: Nil   0   **Loss**

WALES: 1 goal, 2 penalty goals   11

217

Scotland: I.H.M. Thomson (*Heriot's FP*); R. Gordon (*Edin. Wrs.*), I.F. Cordial (*Edin. Wrs.*), J.L. Allan (*Melrose*), D.M. Scott (*London Scot.*); J.N.G. Davidson (*Edin. Univ.*), A.F. Dorward (*Gala*); J.C. Dawson (*Glas. Acads.*), N.M. Munnoch (*Watsonians*), J. Fox (*Gala*), J. Johnston (*Melrose*), D.E. Muir (*Heriot's FP*), W.I.D. Elliot (*Edin. Acads.*), H.M. Inglis (*Edin. Acads.*), P.W. Kininmonth* (*Richmond*)

Wales: G. Williams (*Llanelli*); K.J. Jones (*Newport*), M.C. Thomas (*Newport*), B.L. Williams (*Cardiff*), A.G. Thomas (*Cardiff*); C.I. Morgan (*Cardiff*), W.R. Willis (*Cardiff*); W.O. Williams (*Swansea*), D.M. Davies (*Somerset Police*), D.J. Hayward (*Newbridge*), E.R. John (*Neath*), J.R.G. Stephens (*Neath*), L. Blyth (*Swansea*), J.A. Gwilliam* (*Edin. Wrs.*), A. Forward (*Pontypool*)

Referee: M.J. Dowling (*Ireland*) Touch judges: D.A. Thom, D. Jones

M.C. Thomas kicked a penalty (0–3); K.J. Jones scored and M.C. Thomas converted (0–8).(H.T.). M.C. Thomas kicked a penalty (0–11).

Although defeated this was actually a most creditable display by Scotland. The Welsh centres seemed handicapped by a soft slippery surface and their scrummaging was not good. It was really M.C. Thomas' place kicking which won the match. The only try stemmed from a strong diagonal run by A.G. Thomas; K.J. Jones moved inside and took a long pass to break clear at full pace. In the second half Scott, Davidson and Kininmonth came close to scoring but the latter was overtaken by Jones short of the line.

IRELAND   Lansdowne Road   23 February 1952

SCOTLAND: 1 goal, 1 penalty goal   8   **Loss**

IRELAND: 1 penalty goal, 3 tries   12

Scotland: I.H.M. Thomson (*Heriot's FP*); R. Gordon (*Edin. Wrs.*), I.F. Cordial (*Edin. Wrs.*), J.L. Allan (*Melrose*), D.M. Scott (*London Scot.*); J.N.G. Davidson (*Edin. Univ.*), A.F. Dorward (*Gala*); J.C. Dawson (*Glas. Acads.*), N.M. Munnoch (*Watsonians*), J. Fox (*Gala*), J. Johnston (*Melrose*), D.E. Muir (*Heriot's FP*), W.I.D. Elliot (*Edin. Acads.*), H.M. Inglis (*Edin. Acads.*), P.W. Kininmonth* (*Richmond*)

Ireland: J.G.M.W. Murphy (*Dublin Univ.*); W.H.J. Millar (*QU Belfast*), N.J. Henderson (*QU Belfast*), J.R. Notley (*Wanderers*), M.J. Lane (*UC Cork*); J.W. Kyle (*QU Belfast*), J.A. O'Meara (*UC Cork*); T. Clifford (*Young Munster*), K.D. Mullen (*Old Belvedere*), J.H. Smith (*Collegians*), P.J. Lawlor (*Clontarf*), A. O'Leary (*Cork Const.*), M. Dargan (*Old Belvedere*), D.J. O'Brien* (*Cardiff*), J.S. McCarthy (*Dolphin*)

Referee: J. Davies (*Wales*) Touch judges: D.A. Thom, R. Mitchell

I.H.M. Thomson kicked a penalty (3–0); N.J. Henderson kicked a penalty (3–3); M.F. Lane and J.W. Kyle scored but N.J. Henderson failed to convert (3–9); J.N.G. Davidson scored and I.H.M. Thomson converted (8–9).(H.T.). N.J. Henderson scored but failed to convert (8–12).

Scotland had an excellent start when right away Thomson kicked a penalty but this was matched almost at once by Henderson. After ten minutes O'Meara went off round the blind side; O'Brien backed up and sent an unmarked Lane in for a try. With Ireland doing well in the scrums, Henderson broke away but was brought down and from the resultant maul Kyle went clear through for a fine solo try. At this stage Lane had to go off with a broken wrist. Just short of half time a good run by Inglis, Kininmonth, Dawson and Fox put Kininmonth clear to give Davidson a try at the posts.

Soon after the interval O'Meara broke away again and sent the ball over the line. A hurried clearance by a defender fell into Millar's hands and a pass to Henderson saw him score at the corner and also get the conversion. The rest of the game was an even struggle with no scoring.

ENGLAND	Murrayfield	15 March 1952

SCOTLAND:	1 try		3	Loss
ENGLAND:	2 goals, 1 drop goal, 2 tries		19	

Scotland: N.W. Cameron (*Glas. Univ.*); R. Gordon (*Edin. Wrs.*), I.F. Cordial (*Edin. Wrs.*), I.D.F. Coutts (*Old Alleynians*), T.G. Weatherstone (*Stewart's FP*); J.N.G. Davidson (*Edin. Univ.*), A.F. Dorward* (*Gala*); J.C. Dawson (*Glas. Acads.*), J. Fox (*Gala*), J.M. Inglis (*Selkirk*), J. Johnston (*Melrose*), D.E. Muir (*Heriot's FP*), W.I.D. Elliot (*Edin. Acads.*), J.P. Friebe (*Glas. HSFP*), D.S. Gilbert-Smith (*London Scot.*)

England: P.J. Collins (*Camborne*); C.E. Winn (*Rosslyn Park*), B. Boobyer (*Rosslyn Park*), A.E. Agar (*Harlequins*), J.E. Woodward (*Wasps*); N.M. Hall* (*Richmond*), P.W. Sykes (*Wasps*); W.A. Holmes (*Nuneaton*), E. Evans (*Sale*), R.V. Stirling (*RAF*), J.R.C. Matthews (*Harlequins*), D.T. Wilkins (*RN*), D.F. White (*Northampton*), J.M. Kendall-Carpenter (*Penzance-Newlyn*), A.O. Lewis (*Bath*)

Referee: M.J. Dowling (*Ireland*) **Touch judges:** D.A. Thom, J.B.G. Whittaker

C.E. Winn scored and N.M. Hall converted (0–5).(H.T.). E. Evans, J.E. Woodward and J.M. Kendall-Carpenter scored and N.M. Hall converted the last (0–16); J. Johnston scored but N.W. Cameron failed (3–16); A.E. Agar dropped a goal (3–19).

The Scottish forwards worked hard but not as a pack, whilst the handling of the backs was most uncertain. From one breakdown early on Agar got the ball and broke through the confused defence. A cross kick went to Winn who ran through two tackles to score. Scotland lost further chances by bad handling although Weatherstone was nearly over once. England also had some good runs but there was no further scoring before half time. On restarting the Scottish passing continued to be poor but England improved as a striking force. Twice Boobyer, using the dummy, ran well and Winn nearly scored from the second. From a line out and maul Evans dived over. Further good running brought scores by Woodward and White and then in the closing minute Johnston scored after a forward rush but Agar finished the match with a drop goal.

FRANCE   Colombes   **10 January 1953**

SCOTLAND: 1 goal   5   **Loss**
FRANCE: 1 goal, 1 drop goal, 1 penalty goal 11

Scotland: N.W. Cameron (*Glas. Univ.*); K.J. Dalgleish (*Camb. Univ.*), D.A. Sloan (*London Scot.*), D.M. Scott (*Watsonians*), D.M. Rose (*Jedforest*); J.N.G. Davidson (*Edin. Univ.*), A.F. Dorward* (*Gala*); B.E. Thomson (*Oxford Univ.*), J.H.F. King (*Selkirk*), R.L. Wilson (*Gala*), J.H. Henderson (*Oxford Univ.*), J.J. Hegarty (*Hawick*), A.R. Valentine (*RNAS*), D.C. Macdonald (*Edin. Univ.*), K.H.D. McMillan (*Sale*)

France: J. Rouan (*Narbonne*); M. Pomathios (*Bressane*), J. Dauger (*Bayonne*), M. Prat (*Lourdes*), A. Porthault (*RCF*); J. Carabignac (*Agen*), G. Dufau (*RCF*); A. Sanac (*Perpignan*), P. Labadie (*Bayonne*), P. Bertrand (*Bressane*), P. Tignol (*Toulouse*), L. Mias (*Mazamet*), J. Prat* (*Lourdes*), R. Bienes (*Cognac*), J.R. Bourdeu (*Lourdes*)

Referee: O.B. Glasgow (*Ireland*)

P. Bertrand kicked a penalty (0–3); J. Carabignac dropped a goal (0–6); D.M. Rose scored and N.W. Cameron converted (5–6). (H.T.). J.R. Bourdeu scored and P. Bertrand converted (5–11).

The pitch was treacherous after frost, snow and sleet. The recast Scottish pack did remarkably well against a heavier and much more experienced set but the Scottish backs were disappointing both in attack and defence. The French were very fast onto the man and the ball but their back play was rather stereotyped.

After an early penalty goal Carabignac got the ball from a loose maul and from a long range dropped a rather speculative goal. Before half time a forward rush let Dorward pass to Rose who beat two defenders for a good score. Cameron's conversion kept the game very open. France resumed strongly and missed two chances of scoring before Hegarty, Sloan and MacDonald took play up to the French 25. Then some fine running by France brought play back and a quick heel started another burst of short sharp passing which produced a splendid try by Bourdeu. Scotland fought back; Valentine broke clear, Henderson carried on and passed to Rose who got to the corner flag but could not manage to ground the ball.

WALES   Murrayfield   **7 February 1953**

SCOTLAND: Nil   0   **Loss**
WALES: 1 penalty goal, 3 tries   12

Scotland: N.W. Cameron (*Glas. Univ.*); R. Gordon (*Edin. Wrs.*), K.J. Dalgleish (*Camb. Univ.*), J.L. Allan (*Melrose*), D.M. Rose (*Jedforest*); J.N.G. Davidson (*Edin. Univ.*), A.F. Dorward* (*Gala*); B.E. Thomson (*Oxford Univ.*), J.H.F. King (*Selkirk*), R.L. Wilson (*Gala*), J.H. Henderson (*Oxford Univ.*), J.J. Hegarty (*Hawick*), A.R. Valentine (*RNAS*), D.C. Macdonald (*Edin. Univ.*), K.H.D. McMillan (*Sale*).

Wales: T.J. Davies (*Devonport Services*); G.M. Griffiths (*Cardiff*), B.L. Williams* (*Cardiff*), A.G. Thomas (*Cardiff*), K.J. Jones (*Newport*); C.I. Morgan (*Cardiff*), W.R. Willis (*Cardiff*); W.O.G. Williams (*Devonport Services*), G. Beckingham (*Cardiff*), C.C. Meredith (*Neath*), J.R.G. Stephens (*Neath*), E.R. John (*Neath*), S. Judd (*Cardiff*), R.J. Robins (*Royal Signals*), R.C.C. Thomas (*Coventry*).

Referee: P.F. Cooper (*England*) **Touch judges:** J. Graham, D.G. Williams

T.J. Davies kicked a penalty (0–3); K.J. Jones scored but T.J. Davies failed (0–6).(H.T.). B.L. Williams scored twice but T.J. Davies failed (0–12).

Wales were too heavy forward and too alert in the backs yet in what was mainly a forward battle the Scottish pack held its own in the scrums and loose play. Both sets of backs struggled against good defensive play by the forwards.

After a Davies penalty a punt ahead by Morgan fell awkwardly for Cameron. Jones kicked the ball up to the line and had the pace to beat the defence. In the second half Willis hurt his shoulder; went off, came back but again had to retire. Both Welsh tries stemmed from poor Scottish passing. From one loose pass Williams started a passing movement and kept up to get a scoring pass from Jones. Later he snapped up another blind pass and ran some 30 yards to score.

IRELAND   Murrayfield   28 February 1953

SCOTLAND:	1 goal, 1 penalty goal	8	**Loss**
IRELAND:	4 goals, 2 tries	26	

Scotland: I.H.M. Thomson (*Army*); T.G. Weatherstone (*Stewart's FP*), A. Cameron* (*Glas. HSFP*), D. Cameron (*Glas. HSFP*), D.W.C. Smith (*London Scot.*); L. Bruce Lockhart (*London Scot.*), K.M. Spence (*London Scot.*); B.E. Thomson (*Oxford Univ.*), G.C. Hoyer-Millar (*Oxford Univ.*), J.H. Wilson (*Watsonians*), J.H. Henderson (*Oxford Univ.*), J.J. Hegarty (*Hawick*), A.R. Valentine (*RNAS*), E.H. Henriksen (*RHSFP*), K.H.D. McMillan (*Sale*)

Ireland: R.J. Gregg (*QU Belfast*); S.J. Byrne (*Lansdowne*), N.J. Henderson (*QU Belfast*), K. Quinn (*Old Belvedere*), M. Mortell (*Bective Rangers*); J.W. Kyle* (*NIFC*), J.A. O'Meara (*UC Cork*); F.E. Anderson (*QU Belfast*), R. Roe (*Dublin Univ.*), W.A. O'Neill (*UC Dublin*), J.R. Brady (*CIYMS*), T.E. Reid (*Garryowen*), W.E. Bell (*Collegians*), J.R. Kavanagh (*UC Dublin*), J.S. McCarthy (*Dolphin*)

Referee: I. David (*Wales*) **Touch judges:** Dr J.R.S. Innes, C.G. Morton

J.S. McCarthy and S.J. Byrne scored and R.J. Gregg converted both (0–10).(H.T.). S. Byrne scored and R.J. Gregg converted (0–15); I.H.M. Thomson kicked a penalty (3–15); R. Kavanagh scored but R.J. Gregg failed (3–18); J.H. Henderson scored and I.H.M. Thomson converted (8–18); M. Mortell and S. Byrne scored and R.J. Gregg converted the second (8–28).

The Irish forwards were good in the line out and loose play with McCarthy much in evidence and although Kyle was well held his backs were much too fast for their opponents. Bad tackling helped Ireland to score twice before half time although O'Meara's pass to put

McCarthy in was suspiciously forward.

Ireland restarted strongly and a dropped pass was picked up by Quinn who sent Byrne in for his second score. Thomson then kicked a penalty before Weatherstone had a fine 40 yards run but when he was tackled Kyle got the ball and started off a fine passing run which let Kavanagh score. A fierce revival by the Scottish pack let Lockhart try a drop which was charged down but regaining the ball he started some swift passing that let Henderson score. This effort died away and Kyle began a good passing movement which involved half a dozen players before Byrne went over for his third try.

ENGLAND	**Twickenham**	**21 March 1953**

SCOTLAND:	1 goal, 1 try	8	**Loss**
ENGLAND:	4 goals, 2 tries	26	

Scotland: I.H.M. Thomson (*Army*); T.G. Weatherstone (*Stewart's FP*), A. Cameron* (*Glas. HSFP*), D. Cameron (*Glas. HSFP*), J.S. Swan (*Army*); L. Bruce Lockhart (*London Scot.*), A.F. Dorward (*Gala*); J.C. Dawson (*Glas. Acads.*), J.H.F. King (*Selkirk*), R.L. Wilson (*Gala*), J.H. Henderson (*Oxford Univ.*), J.J. Hegarty (*Hawick*), W. Kerr (*London Scot.*), W.L.K. Cowie (*Edin. Wrs.*), K.H.D. McMillan (*Sale*)

England: N.M. Hall* (*Richmond*); R.C. Bazley (*Waterloo*), W.P.C. Davies (*Harlequins*), J. Butterfield (*Northampton*), J.E. Woodward (*Wasps*); M. Regan (*Liverpool*), D.W. Shuttleworth (*Army*); R.V. Stirling (*RAF*), E. Evans (*Sale*), W.A. Holmes (*Nuneaton*), D.T. Wilkins (*RN*), S.J. Adkins (*Coventry*), A.O. Lewis (*Bath*), J.M.K. Kendall-Carpenter (*Bath*), D.F. White (*Northampton*)

Referee: M.J. Dowling (*Ireland*)   **Touch judges:** J. Graham, Col. G. Warden

R.C. Bazley scored and N.M. Hall converted (0–5); T.G. Weatherstone scored but A. Cameron failed (3–5); R.C. Bazley and S.J. Adkins scored but N.M. Hall failed (3–11).(H.T.). R.V. Stirling and J. Butterfield scored and N.M. Hall converted both (3–21); J.H. Henderson scored and I.H.M. Thomson converted (8–21); J.E. Woodward scored and N.M. Hall converted (8–26).

Again the Scottish centres were guilty of bad marking and tackling. For fifteen minutes Scotland pressed missing two penalties but there was no real attacking power and all that resulted were three wild drops at goal. Then White made a fine break carried on by Regan who was tackled short of the line but the movement was continued and a cross-kick to Bazley saw him beat two defenders to score. After some further English pressure Weatherstone broke away twice down the touch line. On the second run he crosskicked for Dorward to get possession and the ball went via Cameron back to Weatherstone who scored at the corner. However continued forward pressure by England was rewarded by some good passing runs which produced two tries before half time.

On restarting the pressure was maintained and a somewhat demoralised Scottish defence gave away two tries inside ten minutes. A. Cameron then came up to stand-off and one break was carried on by Lockhart supported by Dawson and Henderson who finished by scoring. Before the close Woodward scored a fine try, running from near midfield and handing off a series of defenders.

FRANCE   Murrayfield   9 January 1954

SCOTLAND: Nil   0   **Loss**
FRANCE: 1 try   3

Scotland: J.C. Marshall (*London Scot.*); J.S. Swan (*London Scot.*), A.D. Cameron (*Hillhead HSFP*), D. Cameron (*Glas. HSFP*), T.G. Weatherstone (*Stewart's FP*); J.N.G. Davidson* (*Edin. Univ.*), A.K. Fulton (*Dollar Acads.*); T.P.L. McGlashan (*RHSFP*), R.K.G. MacEwen (*Camb. Univ.*), H.F. McLeod (*Hawick*), E.A.J. Fergusson (*Oxford Univ.*), E.J.S. Michie (*Aberdeen Univ.*), A. Robson (*Hawick*), P.W. Kininmonth (*Richmond*), J.H. Henderson (*Richmond*)

France: M. Vannier (*RCF*); L. Roge (*Beziers*), R. Martine (*Lourdes*), J. Bouquet (*Bourgoin*), M. Pomathios (*Bourg-en-Bresse*); A. Labazuy (*Lourdes*), G. Dufau (*RCF*); R. Bienes (*Cognac*), P. Labadie (*Bayonne*), R. Brejassou (*Tarbes*), B. Chevallier (*Montferrand*), L. Mias (*Mazamet*), H. Domec (*Lourdes*), R. Baulon (*Vienne*), J. Prat* (*Lourdes*)

Referee: I. David (*Wales*)   **Touch judges:** R.W. Shaw, R. Paries

No scoring at half time. R. Brejassou scored (0–3).

Scotland were a shade unlucky to lose but although a new pack showed promise the backs were weak. The halves suffered badly from much destructive tackling by the French forwards so there was much kicking to touch and little combined play. Scotland began briskly, playing some good open rugby and Weatherstone nearly scored. Then France came on to their game with speedy backing up and close passing and but for a forward pass and a knock-on would have scored twice. Weatherstone had another fine run from midfield and his pace and determination took him past Pomathios only to stumble and lose the ball short of the line. Shortly after the interval Labazuy got the ball from some loose play, broke away and passed to Pomathios who sent Brejasson off on a clear run in for the only score of the game.

NEW ZEALAND   Murrayfield   13 February 1954

SCOTLAND: Nil   0   **Loss**
NEW ZEALAND: 1 penalty goal   3

Scotland: J.C. Marshall (*London Scot.*), J.S. Swan (*London Scot.*), M.K. Elgie (*London Scot.*), D. Cameron (*Glas. HSFP*), T.G. Weatherstone (*Stewart's FP*); G.T. Ross (*Watsonians*), L.P. MacLachlan (*Oxford Univ.*); T.P.L. McGlashan (*RHSFP*), R.K.G. MacEwen (*Camb. Univ.*), H.F. McLeod (*Hawick*), E.A.J. Fergusson (*Oxford Univ.*), E.J.S. Michie (*Aberdeen Univ.*), W.I.D. Elliot* (*Edin. Acads.*), P.W. Kininmonth (*Richmond*), J.H. Henderson (*Richmond*)

New Zealand: R.W.H. Scott (*Auckland*); R.A. Jarden (*Wellington*), C.J. Loader (*Welling-

223

ton), M.J. Dixon (*Canterbury*), D.D. Wilson (*Canterbury*); L.S. Haig (*Otago*), K. Davi‐
(*Auckland*); P. Eastgate (*Canterbury*), R.C. Hemi (*Waikato*), K.L. Skinner (*Otago*), W.H‐
Clark (*Wellington*), R.A. White (*Poverty Bay*), G.N. Dalzell (*Canterbury*), P.F.H. Jone‐
(*North Auckland*), R.C. Stuart* (*Canterbury*)

Referee: I. David (*Wales*)   **Touch judges:** Dr J.R.S. Innes, J.T. Fitzgerald

No scoring at half time. R.W.H. Scott kicked a penalty (0–3).

This was another game that Scotland did not deserve to lose. Their pack, badly outweigh‐
ted, was never out-scrummaged in any phase of the play. Elliot made a quite outstanding
return to the team. With their pack held in the tight and often outplayed in the open, th‐
New Zealand backs' limitations were exposed. The Scottish tackling was very sound an‐
killed any attempt at running the ball. The Scottish backs, however, were equally well hel‐
but did appear smarter at snapping up chances. Before the interval Ross put out a long pass
to Weatherstone and a reverse pass to Elgie let Swan away to be held short of the line. Afte‐
the restart Ross had one cross kick which Weatherstone kicked on over the line only to b‐
narrowly beaten to the touch down. Then Scott took a penalty some 30 yards out and eigh‐
yards in from the touch and the kick fairly scraped over the bar for the only score of th‐
game. The Scottish pack still hammered away and one rush did get the ball over the line bu‐
again Weatherstone just could not get there first.

IRELAND   Belfast   27 February 195‐

SCOTLAND: Nil   0   Los‐
IRELAND: 2 tries   6

Scotland: J.C. Marshall (*London Scot.*); J.S. Swan (*London Scot.*), M.K. Elgie (*Londor
Scot.*), D. Cameron (*Glas HSFP*), T.G. Weatherstone (*Stewart's FP*); G.T. Ross (*Watson-
ians*), L.P. MacLachlan (*London Scot.*); T.P.L. McGlashan (*RHSFP*), R.K.G
MacEwen (*Camb. Univ.*), H.F. McLeod (*Hawick*), E.A.J. Fergusson (*Oxford Univ.*)
E.J.S. Michie (*Aberdeen Univ.*), W.I.D. Elliot* (*Edin. Acads.*), P.W. Kininmonth (*Rich-
mond*), J.H. Henderson (*Richmond*)

Ireland: R.J. Gregg (*QU Belfast*); M. Mortell (*Bective Rangers*), N.J. Henderson (*NIFC*)
R.P. Godfrey (*UC Dublin*), J.T. Gaston (*Dublin Univ.*); S. Kelly (*Lansdowne*), J.A
O'Meara (*Dolphin*); F.E. Anderson (*QU Belfast*), R. Roe (*Dublin Univ.*), B.G.M. Wood
(*Garryowen*), R.H. Thompson (*Instonians*), P.J. Lawler (*Clontarf*), G.F. Reidy (*Lans-
downe*), J.R. Kavanagh (*Wanderers*), J.S. McCarthy* (*Dolphin*)

Referee: V. Parfitt (*Wales*)

M. Mortell scored, (0–3).(H.T.). M. Mortell scored (0–6).

This was a poor game between two disappointing sides. The only noticeable incidents were
the two Irish tries for both sides kicked too much and there was a spate of penalties. In the
first half Kavanagh, on his own line, threw a long pass to Gaston who ran some 100 yards
before kicking ahead. Three Scots failed to gather the ball and Godfrey picked up, passed tc
Henderson who sent Mortell in for the try. In the second half Kelly, going off on the blind
side, ran 40 yards up to Marshall and a timely pass saw Mortell score again. Scotland los‐

MacEwen in the second half with a damaged knee. This game was played at Ravenshill in Belfast.

ENGLAND **Murrayfield** **20 March 1954**

SCOTLAND: 1 try 3 **Loss**

ENGLAND: 2 goals, 1 try 13

Scotland: J.C. Marshall (*London Scot.*); J.S. Swan (*London Scot.*), M.K. Elgie (*London Scot.*), D. Cameron (*Glas. HSFP*), T.G. Weatherstone (*Stewart's FP*); G.T. Ross (*Watson-ians*), L.P. MacLachlan (*Oxford Univ.*); T.P.L. McGlashan (*RHSFP*), J.H.F. King (*Selkirk*), H.F. McLeod (*Hawick*), E.A.J. Fergusson (*Oxford Univ.*), E.J.S. Michie (*Aberdeen Univ.*), W.I.D. Elliot* (*Edin. Acads.*), P.W. Kininmonth (*Richmond*), J.H. Henderson (*Richmond*)

England: N. Gibbs (*Harlequins*); J.E. Woodward (*Wasps*), J. Butterfield (*Northampton*), J.P. Quinn (*New Brighton*), C.E. Winn (*Rosslyn Park*); M. Regan (*Liverpool*), G. Rimmer (*Waterloo*); R.N. Stirling* (*RAF*), E. Robinson (*Coventry*), D.L. Sanders (*Ipswich YMCA*), P.D. Young (*Dublin Wanderers*), J.F. Bance (*Bedford*), D.S. Wilson (*Metropolitan Police*), V.H. Leadbetter (*Edin. Wrs.*), A.R. Higgins (*Army*)

Referee: O.B. Glasgow (*Ireland*) **Touch judges:** Dr J.R.S. Innes, W.N. Gillmore

P.D. Young scored and N. Gibbs converted (0–5).(H.T.). D.S. Wilson scored and N. Gibbs converted (0–10); M.K. Elgie scored but J.C. Marshall failed (3–10); D.S. Wilson scored but N. Gibbs failed (3–13).

The English backs were clearly superior whilst their pack slowly improved as the game progressed; D.S. Wilson in particular showed speed and initiative to score twice. For fifteen minutes the Scots held their own and better goal kicking could have given them the lead, for the English passing was shaky and one interception by Cameron nearly produced a score. Then Marshall was stranded by an awkward bounce during a forward rush and Robinson threw a pass to Young who ran twenty yards to score. Cameron had one break through to put Weatherstone away down the touch only to be well tackled by Young short of the corner flag. On the restart Elliot broke away from the loose and his final kick ahead found touch at the corner but nothing came of it. A counter attack saw Butterfield cover 40 yards to cross the line only to be bundled into touch in goal. Then a fast run by Quinn and Regan found Wilson up to score his first try. Cameron caught Quinn in possession and Elgie successfully chased a long boot ahead to score. In the last minutes a slow heel and pass back let Wilson dash in, intercept and be over the line before the defence could come alive.

WALES **Swansea** **10 April 1954**

SCOTLAND: 1 try 3 **Loss**

WALES: 1 penalty goal, 4 tries 15

Scotland: J.C. Marshall (*London Scot.*); J.S. Swan (*London Scot.*), M.K. Elgie (*London Scot.*), A.D. Cameron (*Hillhead HSFP*), T.G. Weatherstone (*Stewart's FP*); G.T. Ross (*Watsonians*), L.P. MacLachan (*Oxford Univ.*); T.P.L. McGlashan (*RHSFP*), R.K.G. MacEwen (*Camb. Univ.*), H.F. McLeod (*Hawick*), E.A.J. Fergusson (*Oxford Univ.*), J.W.Y. Kemp (*Glas. HSFP*), W.I.D. Elliot* (*Edin. Acads.*), P.W. Kininmonth (*Richmond*), J.H. Henderson (*Richmond*)

Wales: V. Evans (*Neath*); K.J. Jones* (*Newport*), G.M. Griffiths (*Cardiff*), B.L. Williams (*Cardiff*), R. Williams (*Llanelli*); C.I. Morgan (*Cardiff*), W.R. Willis (*Cardiff*); C.C. Meredith (*Neath*), B.V. Meredith (*St. Lukes*), W.O.G. Williams (*Swansea*), R.H. Williams (*Llanelli*), R.J. Robins (*Pontypridd*), R.C.C. Thomas (*Swansea*), S. Judd (*Cardiff*), L. Davies (*Llanelli*)

Referee: P.F. Cooper (*England*) **Touch judges:** R.W. Shaw, I. Jones

R.H. Williams and B.V. Meredith scored but V. Evans failed to convert (0–6).(H.T.). R. Williams scored but V. Evans failed (0–9); V. Evans kicked a penalty (0–12); C.I. Morgan scored but S. Judd failed (0–15); J.H. Henderson scored but M.K. Elgie failed (3–15).

This match had been postponed from January because of frost and was the last to be played on the historic St Helen's ground. Although four tries were scored the Welsh attack was not too convincing. They attacked continually during the first half but took 35 minutes to open the scoring and then it was a forward who went over from a short line out at the corner. Just before half time another forward, B.V. Meredith, took a pass from Robins to score. The Scottish pack, not so good at the line out, were doing well enough otherwise. In the second half Elliot had one burst, catching Evans who fumbled his kick ahead into the sun, but Morgan managed to clear. For once a good passing run put Ray Williams in at the corner and after an Evans penalty, Morgan kicked hard along the ground past Marshall and just beat Weatherstone to the touch down. With ten minutes to go Kininmonth and Fergusson got the ball across the line but missed the touch. Then Ross nearly put Henderson over. Evans managed to get a kick in but Marshall fielded and gave an inside pass to Elgie who sent Henderson in for the final score.

FRANCE   Colombes   8 January 1955

SCOTLAND:	Nil	0	**Loss**
FRANCE:	1 penalty goal, 4 tries	15	

Scotland: A. Cameron (*Glas. HSFP*); J.S. Swan (*London Scot.*), M.K. Elgie (*London Scot.*), M.L. Grant (*Harlequins*), T.G. Weatherstone (*Stewart's FP*); J.T. Docherty (*Glas. HSFP*), A.F. Dorward (*Gala*); H.F. McLeod (*Hawick*), W.K.L. Relph (*Stewart's FP*), I.R. Hastie (*Kelso*), J.J. Hegarty (*Hawick*), J.W.Y. Kemp (*Glas. HSFP*), H. Duffy (*Jedforest*), J.T. Greenwood* (*Dunfermline*), A. Robson (*Hawick*)

France: M. Vannier (*RCF*); J. Lepatey (*Mazamet*), L. Roge (*Beziers*), M. Prat (*Lourdes*), A. Boniface (*Montois*); R. Martine (*Lourdes*), G. Dufau (*RCF*); A. Domenech (*Vichy*), J. Labadie (*Bayonne*), R. Brejassou (*Tarbes*), B. Chevallier (*Montferrand*), J. Barthe (*Lourdes*), J. Prat* (*Lourdes*), M. Celaya (*Biarritz*), H. Domec (*Lourdes*)

Referee: H.B. Elliot (*England*)

A. Boniface scored (0–3); M. Vannier kicked a penalty (0–6); J. Prat scored (0–9).(H.T.). A. Domenech and G. Dufau scored (0–15).

The French team was in tremendous form, continually indulging in brilliant and bewildering movements in which the speed and handling even of their heavier forwards was noticeable. Scotland never really looked like scoring and on the odd occasions when they got into an attacking position they were met by a most merciless defence. Only Kemp, especially at the line out, with McLeod and Robson came in for any commendation. The French pack was so much in control that Daufau could vary his tactics as he pleased and J. Prat, hardly needing to push, had a happy afternoon joining in all the handling moves.

WALES   Murrayfield   5 February 1955

SCOTLAND:	1 goal, 1 drop goal, 1 penalty goal, 1 try	**14** **Win**
WALES:	1 goal, 1 try	**8**

Scotland: A. Cameron* (*Glas. HSFP*); A.R. Smith (*Camb. Univ.*), M.K. Elgie (*London Scot.*), R.G. Charters (*Hawick*), J.S. Swan (*London Scot.*); J.T. Docherty (*Glas. HSFP*), J.A. Nichol (*RHSFP*); H.F. McLeod (*Hawick*), W.K.L. Relph (*Stewart's FP*), T. Elliot (*Gala*), E.J.S. Michie (*Aberdeen Univ.*), J.W. Y. Kemp (*Glas. HSFP*), W.S. Glen (*Edin. Wrs.*), J.T. Greenwood (*Dunfermline*), A. Robson (*Hawick*)

Wales: A.B. Edwards (*London Welsh*); K.J. Jones (*Newport*), G.T. Wells (*Cardiff*), A.G. Thomas (*Llanelli*), T.J. Brewer (*London Welsh*); C.I. Morgan (*Bective Rangers*), W.R. Willis* (*Cardiff*); W.O. Williams (*Swansea*), B.V. Meredith (*Newport*), C.C. Meredith (*Neath*), R.J. Robins (*Pontypridd*), R.H. Williams (*Llanelli*), S. Judd (*Cardiff*), J.R.G. Stephens (*Neath*), R.C.C. Thomas (*Swansea*)

   Referee: M.J. Dowling (*Ireland*)   **Touch judges:** C.W. Drummond, I. Jones

T.J. Brewer scored (0–3).(H.T.). A.R. Smith scored but M.K. Elgie failed (3–3); J.T. Docherty dropped a goal (6–3); M.K. Elgie kicked a penalty (9–3); T.J. Brewer scored and J.R.G. Stephens converted (9–8); J.A. Nichol scored and M.K. Elgie converted (14–8).

At last Scotland broke the disheartening run of defeats with another unexpected win over Wales at Murrayfield. Wales began ominously well, for inside five minutes a well placed diagonal kick by Morgan laid the line wide open for Brewer to score. The success of this manoeuvre seemed to influence Morgan since he repeated it rather too often without success although passing movements just failed to put Brewer and K.J. Jones over before half time. On restarting the Scottish pack began a vigorous recovery showing a welcome mood of aggression especially in the loose. Suddenly Robson threw a pass to A.R. Smith hemmed in on the right touch line. The winger ran some 30 yards, shaking off a couple of tackles, punted the ball over Edward's head, tapped the ball on by foot and then picked it up to go in at the corner for one of the finest solo tries ever seen at Murrayfield. This fairly lifted the Scots and inside fifteen minutes they increased their lead by Docherty's drop and Elgie's penalty. Wales struck back when Morgan set his backs away and Stephen's conversion of a try by Brewer put them back in the game. However, the Scottish pack battled on and from a scrum near the Welsh line Willis was forced to throw back a bad pass which missed Morgan. Like a flash Nichol went past him to score the clinching try.

IRELAND   **Murrayfield**   **26 February 1955**

| **SCOTLAND:** | 1 drop goal, 2 penalty goals, 1 try | 12 | **Win** |
| **IRELAND:** | 1 penalty goal | 3 | |

Scotland: R.W.T. Chisholm (*Melrose*); A.R. Smith (*Camb. Univ.*), M.K. Elgie (*London Scot.*), R.G. Charters (*Hawick*), J.S. Swan (*Coventry*); A. Cameron* (*Glas. HSFP*), J.A. Nichol (*RHSFP*); H.F. McLeod (*Hawick*), W.K.L. Relph (*Stewart's FP*), T. Elliot (*Gala*), E.J.S. Michie (*Aberdeen Univ.*), J.W.Y. Kemp (*Glas. HSFP*), I.A.A. MacGregor (*Hillhead HSFP*), J.T. Greenwood (*Dunfermline*), A. Robson (*Hawick*)

Ireland: W.R. Tector (*Wanderers*); A.C. Pedlow (*QU Belfast*), A.J.F. O'Reilly (*Old Belvedere*), N.J. Henderson (*NIFC*), R.E. Roche (*UC Galway*); S. Kelly (*Lansdowne*), S.J. McDermott (*London Irish*); P.J. O'Donoghue (*Bective Rangers*), R. Roe (*Lansdowne*), F.E. Anderson (*NIFC*), T.E. Reid (*London Irish*), M.N. Madden (*Sunday's Well*), D.A. McSweeney (*Blackrock*), R.H. Thompson* (*London Irish*), M.J. Cunningham (*UC Cork*)

Referee: L.M. Boundy (*England*)   **Touch judges:** G.G. Crerar, A. Archer

S. Kelly kicked a penalty (0–3); M.K. Elgie kicked a penalty (3–3); J.S. Swan scored but M.K. Elgie failed (6–3).(H.T.). A. Cameron dropped a goal (9–3); M.K. Elgie kicked a penalty (12–3).

Scotland thoroughly deserved to win and indeed the margin would have been greater had Elgie not been off form with his place kicking. Docherty having called off, Cameron moved up to half and, more or less ignoring his threes, concentrated on some tactical kicking which sadly troubled the Irish defence. He was helped in this by the power of the pack, McLeod in the scrums, Kemp in the line out and Robson in the loose all being particularly effective. The backs not seen in attack nevertheless defended well — one report noted that young O'Reilly had the makings of a good player! Near the interval, with the score level, Swan intercepted a pass and sprinted about 40 yards diagonally away from everyone for his try. During the second half, Scotland remained clearly on top and after Cameron had fielded a drop out and replied with a drop goal, Elgie added a penalty to finish the scoring.

ENGLAND   **Twickenham**   **19 March 1955**

| **SCOTLAND:** | 1 penalty goal, 1 try | 6 | **Loss** |
| **ENGLAND:** | 1 penalty goal, 2 tries | 9 | |

Scotland: R.W.T. Chisholm (*Melrose*); A.R. Smith (*Camb. Univ.*), M.K. Elgie (*London Scot.*), R.G. Charters (*Hawick*), J.S. Swan (*Coventry*); A. Cameron* (*Glas. HSFP*), J.A. Nichol (*RHSFP*); H.F. McLeod (*Hawick*), W.K.L. Relph (*Stewart's FP*), T. Elliot (*Gala*), E.J.S. Michie (*Aberdeen Univ.*), J.W.Y. Kemp (*Glas. HSFP*), I.A.A. MacGregor (*Hillhead HSFP*), J.T. Greenwood (*Dunfermline*), A. Robson (*Hawick*)

England: N.S.D. Estcourt (*Blackheath*); F.D. Sykes (*Northampton*), J. Butterfield (*North-*

228

ampton), W.P.C. Davies (*Harlequins*), R.C. Bazley (*Waterloo*); D.G.S. Baker (*OMT*), J.E. Williams (*Old Millhillians*); G.W.D. Hastings (*Gloucester*), N.A. Labuschagne (*Guy's*), D. St.G. Hazell (*Leicester*), P.D. Young* (*Wanderers*), P.G. Yarranton (*Wasps*), D.S. Wilson (*Metropolitan Police*), I.D.S. Beer (*Harlequins*), R. Higgins (*Liverpool*)

Referee: D.C. Joynson (*Wales*)   **Touch judges:** C.W. Drummond, E.V. Barnes

D.S. Hazell kicked a penalty (0–3); F.D. Sykes scored but D.S. Hazell failed (0–6); A. Cameron dropped a penalty (3–6); I.D.S. Beer scored but D.S. Hazell failed (3–9).(H.T.). A. Cameron scored but M.K. Elgie failed (6–9).

Once again Scotland came to Twickenham and failed to lift the Triple Crown. A heavy English pack started well and their backs ran in two tries before the interval. Yet Scotland had some bad luck for an awkward bounce robbed Swan of a try and Elgie had several narrow misses with penalties. Cameron's penalty came from a majestic drop kick taken some 45 yards out. The Scottish pack greatly improved after the break but the only score started with Chisholm, who took a kick ahead and shot through a startled mass of attackers to pass to Cameron. He set Elgie off on a dummying run right up to the right hand corner and from some loose play Cameron got the ball again. This time he lifted a high kick to the posts and from the ensuing loose play Nichol broke on the blind side and passed to Cameron whose momentum sent him through a mass of defenders.

FRANCE   Murrayfield   14 January 1956

SCOTLAND: 2 penalty goals, 2 tries   12   **Win**
FRANCE: Nil

Scotland: R.W.T. Chisholm (*Melrose*); A.R. Smith (*Camb. Univ.*), A. Cameron* (*Glas. HSFP*), K.R. Macdonald (*Stewart's FP*), J.S. Swan (*Coventry*); M.L. Grant (*Harlequins*), N.M. Campbell (*London Scot.*); H.F. McLeod (*Hawick*), R.K.G. MacEwen (*London Scot.*), T. Elliot (*Gala*), E.J.S. Michie (*Aberdeen GSFP*), J.W.Y. Kemp (*Glas. HSFP*), I.A.A. MacGregor (*Llanelli*), J.T. Greenwood (*Dunfermline*), A. Robson (*Hawick*)

France: M. Vannier (*RCF*); J. Dupuy (*Tarbes*), A. Boniface (*Mont-de-Marsan*), G. Stener (*Paris Univ.*), S. Torreilles (*Perpignan*); J. Bouquet (*Vienne*), G. Dufau* (*RCF*); A. Domenech (*Brive*), R. Vigier (*Montferrand*), R. Bienes (*Cognac*), B. Chevallier (*Montferrand*), G. Roncaries (*Perpignan*), J. Carrere (*Vichy*), M. Celaya (*Biarritz*), R. Baulon (*Bayonne*)

Referee: M.J. Dowling (*Ireland*)   **Touch judges:** R.F. Kelly, S. Saulnier

A.R. Smith kicked a penalty (3–0); A. Cameron kicked a penalty (6–0).(H.T.). J.W.Y. Kemp scored twice but A. Cameron failed to convert (12–0).

On a wet murky day some traditional Scottish forward play was most effective, many fierce well controlled rushes greatly upsetting the French defence, yet Scotland could only manage two penalties before half time. In the second half, however, Kemp scored twice, once after a tremendous heave by the pack on the French line and later when Campbell broke to give him a scoring pass. During this half a great run by the French pack only finished when Bienes was heaved into touch at the corner flag.

WALES   Cardiff   4 February 1956

SCOTLAND:	1 penalty goal	3	**Loss**
WALES:	3 tries	9	

Scotland: R.W.T. Chisholm (*Melrose*); A.R. Smith (*Camb. Univ.*), A. Cameron* (*Glas. HSFP*), K.R. Macdonald (*Stewart's FP*), J.S. Swan (*Coventry*); M.L. Grant (*Harlequins*), N.M. Campbell (*London Scot.*); H.F. McLeod (*Hawick*), R.K.G. MacEwen (*London Scot.*), T. Elliot (*Gala*), E.J.S. Michie (*Aberdeen GSFP*), J.W.Y. Kemp (*Glas. HSFP*), I.A.A. MacGregor (*Llanelli*), J.T. Greenwood (*Dunfermline*), A. Robson (*Hawick*)

Wales: G.D. Owen (*Newport*); K.J. Jones (*Newport*), H.P. Morgan (*Newport*), M.C. Thomas (*Newport*), C.L. Davies (*Cardiff*); C.I. Morgan* (*Cardiff*), D.O. Brace (*Newport*); W.O.G. Williams (*Swansea*), B.V. Meredith (*Newport*), R. Prosser (*Pontypool*), R.H. Williams (*Llanelli*), J.R.G. Stephens (*Neath*), R.C.C. Thomas (*Swansea*), L.H. Jenkins (*Newport*), B. Sparks (*Neath*)

    Referee: L.M. Boundy (*England*)   **Touch judges:** C.W. Drummond, J. Jones

H.P. Morgan scored but G.D. Owen failed (0–3); A. Cameron kicked a penalty (3–3); C.L. Davies scored but G.D. Owen failed (3–6).(H.T.). C.I. Morgan scored but G.D. Owen failed (3–9).

The ground was only made playable by the use of dozens of braziers kept burning throughout the night and it looked a sorry mess when play began on a surface made treacherous by a misty rain. These conditions greatly troubled the Scottish halves and centres but in contrast Morgan fairly sparkled at half and continually set his backs attacking. The Scottish pack and the neglected wingers could be absolved for the defeat.

IRELAND   Lansdowne Road   25 February 1956

SCOTLAND:	2 goals	10	**Loss**
IRELAND:	1 goal, 3 tries	14	

Scotland: R.W.T. Chisholm (*Melrose*); A.R. Smith (*Camb. Univ.*), T. McClung (*Edin. Acads.*), K.R. Macdonald (*Stewart's FP*), J.S. Swan (*Coventry*); A. Cameron* (*Glas. HSFP*), A.F. Dorward (*Gala*); H.F. McLeod (*Hawick*), R.K.G. MacEwen (*London Scot.*), T. Elliot (*Gala*), E.J.S. Michie (*Aberdeen GSFP*), J.W.Y. Kemp (*Glas. HSFP*), I.A.A. McGregor (*Llanelli*), J.T. Greenwood (*Dunfermline*), A. Robson (*Hawick*)

Ireland: P.J. Berkery (*Lansdowne*); A.C. Pedlow (*QU Belfast*), A.J.F. O'Reilly (*Old Belvedere*), N.J. Henderson* (*NIFC*), W.J. Hewitt (*Instonians*); J.W. Kyle (*NIFC*), J.A. O'Meara (*Dolphin*); W.B. Fagan (*Moseley*), R. Roe (*London Irish*), B.G.M. Wood (*Garryowen*), B.M. Guerin (*Galwegians*), L.M. Lynch (*Lansdowne*), C.T.J. Lydon (*Galwegians*), J.R. Kavanagh (*Wanderers*), M.J. Cunningham (*Cork Const.*)

N.J. Henderson and A.J. O'Reilly scored but A.C. Pedlow failed (0–6); E.J.S. Michie scored and T. McClung converted (5–6).(H.T.). J.A. O'Meara scored and A.C. Pedlow converted (5–10); A.R. Smith scored and T. McClung converted (10–11); J.W. Kyle scored but A.C. Pedlow failed (10–14).

Almost at once Hewitt was over but called back for a forward pass and then Cameron, concussed in a tackle, went off and a reshuffle brought McClung to half, Swan to centre with MacGregor on the wing. Kyle was able to make use of some greater freedom and Henderson had one fine solo try while making another for O'Reilly. Before the interval Smith had a good run and his kick ahead was kicked on by Kemp for Michie to get the touch. After half time Macdonald made an opening for a Smith score but the Irish halves each engineered a good solo try. The short handed Scottish pack did not fade but the cover defence was weakened.

ENGLAND   Murrayfield   17 March 1956

| **SCOTLAND:** | 1 penalty goal, 1 try | 6 | **Loss** |
| **ENGLAND:** | 1 goal, 2 penalty goals | 11 | |

Scotland: R.W.T. Chisholm (*Melrose*); A.R. Smith (*Camb. Univ.*), J.T. Docherty (*Glas. HSFP*), G.D. Stevenson (*Hawick*), J.S. Swan (*Coventry*); T. McClung (*Edin. Acads.*), A.F. Dorward (*Gala*); H.F. McLeod (*Hawick*), R.K.G. MacEwen (*London Scot.*), T. Elliot (*Gala*), E.J.S. Michie (*Aberdeen GSFP*), J.W.Y. Kemp (*Glas. HSFP*), I.A.A. MacGregor (*Llanelli*), J.T. Greenwood* (*Dunfermline*), A. Robson (*Hawick*)

England: D.F. Allison (*Coventry*); J.E. Woodward (*Wasps*), J. Butterfield (*Northampton*), L.B. Cannell (*St Mary's*), P.H. Thompson (*Headingley*); M. Regan (*Liverpool*), J.E. Williams (*Old Millhillians*); D.L. Sanders (*Harlequins*), E. Evans* (*Sale*), C.R. Jacobs (*Northampton*), R.W.D. Marques (*Camb. Univ.*), J.D. Currie (*Oxford Univ.*), P.G.D. Robbins (*Oxford Univ.*), A. Ashcroft (*Waterloo*), V.G. Roberts (*Harlequins*)

J.D. Currie kicked a penalty (0–3); J.E. Williams scored and J.D. Currie converted (0–8); A.R. Smith kicked a penalty (3–8); J.D. Currie kicked a penalty (3–11); G.D. Stevenson scored but T. McClung failed (6–11).(H.T.).

In perfect conditions England deserved their success but were not too convincing for if Scotland had carried a goal kicker they could have won — at least five penalties were missed in a disappointing and scoreless second half. Again the Scottish pack did well in the first half and were noticeably dangerous as the game went on. However although the backs defended well they were not much seen in attack.

FRANCE   Colombes   **12 January 1957**

SCOTLAND: 1 drop goal, 1 penalty goal   6   **Win**
FRANCE: Nil   0

Scotland: K.J.F. Scotland (*Royal Signals*); A.R. Smith (*Camb. Univ.*), E. McKeating (*Heriot's FP*), G.D. Stevenson (*Hawick*), J.S. Swan (*Coventry*); M.L. Grant (*Harlequins*), A.F. Dorward (*Gala*); H.F. McLeod (*Hawick*), R.K.G. MacEwan (*London Scot.*), T. Elliot (*Gala*), E.J.S. Michie (*London Scot.*), J.W.Y. Kemp (*Glas. HSFP*), I.A.A. MacGregor (*Llanelli*), J.T. Greenwood* (*Perthshire Acads.*), A. Robson (*Hawick*)

France: M. Vannier (*RCF*); J. Dupuy (*Tarbes*), L. Roge (*Beziers*), M. Prat (*Lourdes*), A. Boniface (*Montois*); J. Bouquet (*Vienne*), G. Dufau (*RCF*); A. Domenech (*Brive*), R. Vigier (*Montferrand*), H. Lazies (*Toulouse*), B. Chevallier (*Montferrand*), A. Sanac (*Perpignan*), R. Baulon (*Bayonne*), M. Celaya* (*Biarritz*), J. Barthe (*Lourdes*)

Referee: L.M. Boundy (*England*)   **Touch judges:** W.C.W. Murdoch, R.B. Marie

No scoring at half time. K.J.F. Scotland dropped a goal and kicked a penalty (6–0).

France made a belligerent start but even after losing MacEwen after two minutes play the depleted Scottish pack held their own without him and was clearly on top after he returned some fifteen minutes later. About this time heavy rain began and continued to the end of the game. Barthe and Baulon, when not conducting a private feud with MacGregor, gave the Scottish halves a hard time and Grant, under the conditions, closed up the game. The backs defended solidly as did the new full back, Scotland. In the second half he dropped a calculated goal from 30 yards out and completed the scoring with an equally lengthy penalty.

WALES   **Murrayfield**   **2 February 1957**

SCOTLAND: 1 drop goal, 1 penalty goal, 1 try   9   **Win**
WALES: 1 penalty goal, 1 try   6

Scotland: K.J.F. Scotland (*Royal Signals*); A.R. Smith (*Camb. Univ.*), E. McKeating (*Heriot's FP*), K.R. Macdonald (*Stewart's FP*), J.S. Swan (*Coventry*); T. McClung (*Edin. Acads.*), A.F. Dorward (*Gala*); H.F. McLeod (*Hawick*), R.K.G. MacEwen (*London Scot.*), T. Elliot (*Gala*), E.J.S. Michie (*London Scot.*), J.W.Y. Kemp (*Glas. HSFP*), I.A.A. MacGregor (*Hillhead HSFP*), J.T. Greenwood* (*Perthshire Acads.*), A. Robson (*Hawick*)

Wales: T.J. Davies (*Llanelli*); K.J. Jones (*Newport*), G.M. Griffiths (*Cardiff*), M.C. Thomas* (*Newport*), G. Howells (*Llanelli*); C.I. Morgan (*Cardiff*), L.H. Williams (*Cardiff*); C.C. Meredith (*Neath*), B.V. Meredith (*London Welsh*), R. Prosser (*Pontypool*), R.H.

Williams (*Llanelli*), J.R.G. Stephens (*Neath*), R.H. Davies (*Oxford Univ.*), R.J. Robins (*Pontypridd*), B. Sparks (*Neath*)

Referee: R.C. Williams (*Ireland*)   **Touch judges:** R.F. Kelly; I. Jones

T.J. Davies kicked a penalty (0–3); K.J.F. Scotland kicked a penalty (3–3); R.H. Davies scored but T.J. Davies failed (3–6); A.R. Smith scored but K.J.F. Scotland failed (6–6).(H.T.). A.F. Dorward dropped a goal (9–6).

In fine conditions a capacity crowd watched a most exciting game. There was a most ferocious forward battle, well controlled by the referee, and the issue was in doubt until the close. Scoring started with splendid long range penalty kicks by each full back before R.H. Davies scored in a forward rush. Near half time Michie and Macgregor had a good clearance dribble to mid field where McClung placed a lovely kick into the left corner. From the maul he got the ball again and put an equally fine kick into the other corner for Smith to race up and score. Play was even after the interval and although Morgan always looked dangerous he could not break past good defence by the Scottish back row and backs. After twenty minutes T.J. Davies was forced to halt a rush by a mark but his kick was caught by Dorward who, standing 40 yards out and 10 yards from the touch, dropped a prodigous goal for a lead that was not lost.

IRELAND   Murrayfield   23 February 1957

SCOTLAND:	1 penalty goal	3	**Loss**
IRELAND:	1 goal	5	

Scotland: K.J.F. Scotland (*Royal Signals*); A.R. Smith* (*Camb. Univ.*), T. McClung (*Edin. Acads.*), K.R. Macdonald (*Stewart's FP*), J.L.F. Allan (*Camb. Univ.*); J.M. Maxwell (*Langholm*), A.F. Dorward (*Gala*); H.F. McLeod (*Hawick*), R.K.G. MacEwen (*London Scot.*), T. Elliot (*Gala*), E.J.S. Michie (*London Scot.*), J.W.Y. Kemp (*Glas. HSFP*), I.A.A. MacGregor (*Hillhead HSFP*), G.K. Smith (*Kelso*), A. Robson (*Hawick*)

Ireland: P.J. Berkery (*Lansdowne*); A.C. Pedlow (*QU Belfast*), N.J. Henderson* (*NIFC*), A.J.F. O'Reilly (*Old Belvedere*), R.E. Roche (*Galwegians*); J.W. Kyle (*NIFC*), A.A. Mulligan (*Camb. Univ.*); B.G.M. Wood (*Garryowen*), R. Roe (*London Irish*), J.I. Brennan (*CIYMS*), T.E. Reid (*London Irish*), J.R. Brady (*CIYMS*), J.R. Kavanagh (*Wanderers*), P.J.A. O'Sullivan (*Galwegians*), H.S. O'Connor (*Dublin Univ.*)

Referee: L.M. Boundy (*England*)   **Touch judges:** R. Tod, M.E. Holland

P.J.A. O'Sullivan scored and P.J. Berkery converted (0–5).(H.T.). K.J.F. Scotland kicked a penalty (3–5).

A heavy snowstorm which continued throughout the afternoon affected the pitch and ruined any hopes of a handling game for the players skidded and mishandled a slipping ball. The Irish pack adapted well to the conditions and dictated much of the play and it was from a diagonal kick by Kyle that the forwards rushed the ball over for a try by O'Sullivan. The pack maintained their control during the second half and all Scotland could manage was a good penalty by Scotland. Maxwell took a heavy tackle early on and later changed places with McClung.

ENGLAND Twickenham **16 March 1957**

| **SCOTLAND:** | 1 penalty goal | 3 | **Loss** |
| **ENGLAND:** | 2 goals, 1 penalty goal, 1 try | 16 | |

Scotland: K.J.F. Scotland (*Royal Signals*); A.R. Smith (*Camb. Univ.*), T. McClung (*Edin. Acads.*), K.R. Macdonald (*Stewart's FP*), J.L.F. Allan (*Camb. Univ.*); G.H. Waddell (*London Scot.*), A.F. Dorward (*Gala*); H.F. McLeod (*Hawick*), R.K.G. MacEwen (*London Scot.*), T. Elliot (*Gala*), E.J.S. Michie (*London Scot.*), J.W.Y. Kemp (*Glas. HSFP*), G.K. Smith (*Kelso*), J.T. Greenwood* (*Perthshire Acads.*), A. Robson (*Hawick*)

England: R. Challis (*Bristol*); P.B. Jackson (*Coventry*), J. Butterfield (*Northampton*), W.P.C. Davies (*Harlequins*), P.H. Thompson (*Headingley*); R.M. Bartlett (*Harlequins*), R.E.G. Jeeps (*Northampton*); C.R. Jacobs (*Northampton*), E. Evans* (*Sale*), G.W.D. Hastings (*Gloucester*), R.W.D. Marques (*Camb. Univ.*), J.D. Currie (*Oxford Univ.*), P.G.D. Robbins (*Oxford Univ.*), A. Ashcroft (*Waterloo*), R. Higgins (*Liverpool*)

Referee: R. Mitchell (*Ireland*) **Touch judges:** C.W. Drummond, S.C. Dwyer

J. Butterfield scored but R. Challis failed (0–3).(H.T.). R. Challis kicked a penalty (0–6); K.J.F. Scotland kicked a penalty (3–6); P.H. Thompson and R. Higgins scored and R. Challis converted both (3–16).

The Queen and Prince Philip joined with a crowd of 70,000 who saw England finish the season undefeated. Scotland were quite outclassed by the best team of the year. Their backs had pace and skill while their pack was always clearly on top. Even so a grim defence kept the lead to 3–6 until the last fifteen minutes when the English backs began to throw the ball about freely and soon put the issue beyond doubt. Scotland got so little of the ball that there was really no danger and their only score came from a penalty by K.J.F. Scotland who therefore had scored in every game during the year.

FRANCE Murrayfield **11 January 1958**

| **SCOTLAND:** | 1 goal, 1 penalty goal, 1 try | 11 | **Win** |
| **FRANCE:** | 2 penalty goals, 1 try | 9 | |

Scotland: R.W.T. Chisholm (*Melrose*); A.R. Smith* (*Camb. Univ.*), G.D. Stevenson (*Hawick*), J.T. Docherty (*Glas. HSFP*), J.S. Swan (*Leicester*); G.H. Waddell (*Devonport Services*), J.A.T. Rodd (*Un. Services*); H.F. McLeod (*Hawick*), N.S. Bruce (*Blackheath*), I.R. Hastie (*Kelso*), M.W. Swan (*Oxford Univ.*), J.W.Y. Kemp (*Glas. HSFP*), G.K. Smith (*Kelso*), J.T. Greenwood (*Perthshire Acads.*), M.A. Robertson (*Gala*)

France: M. Vannier (*RCF*); G. Mauduy (*Perigueux*), A. Boniface (*Mont-de-Marsan*), J. Bouguet (*Vienne*), J. Dupuy (*Tarbes*); C. Vignes (*RCF*), P. Danos (*Beziers*); A. Domenech

(*Brive*), R. Vigier (*Montferrand*), A. Quaglio (*Mazamet*), L. Mias (*Mazamet*), M. Celaya*
(*Biarritz*), M. Crauste (*RCF*), J. Barthe (*Lourdes*), J. Carrere (*Toulon*)

Referee: L.M. Boundy (*England*)   **Touch judges:** A.M. Nicol, M. Lavrent

R.W.T. Chisholm kicked a penalty (3–0); M. Vannier kicked a penalty (3–3); G.D.
Stevenson scored and R.W.T. Chisholm converted (8–3); J. Dupuy scored but M. Vannier
failed (8–6).(H.T.). M. Vannier kicked a penalty (8–9); I.R. Hastie scored but R.W.T.
Chisholm failed (11–9).

This was a hard punishing game where Scotland played orthodox rugby and by good
defence countered the ornate French attacks. Certainly France had two speedy centres and
a tricky stand off but all were inclined to be too individualistic. The Scottish pack
controlled the set scrums and line out but Waddell used the touch line so much that the
threes were more seen in defence than attack, yet, after a penalty by each full back, it was he
who made the opening for Stevenson's score. Before the interval Dupuy's pace allowed him
to score from a kick ahead which bounced unkindly for the defence. After the interval a
Vannier penalty put France ahead but the Scottish pack stepped up their game: G.K.
Smith and Stevenson came near to scoring before Hastie from a short line out caught an
astute throw in by Smith and bullocked his way over for the winning score.

WALES   Cardiff   1 February 1958

SCOTLAND:	1 penalty goal	3	**Loss**
WALES:	1 goal, 1 try	8	

Scotland: R.W.T. Chisholm (*Melrose*); A.R. Smith* (*Camb. Univ.*), G.D. Stevenson
(*Hawick*), J.T. Docherty (*Glas. HSFP*), T.G. Weatherstone (*Stewart's FP*); G.H. Wad-
dell (*Devonport Services*), J.A.T. Rodd (*Un. Services*); H.F. McLeod (*Hawick*), R.K.G.
MacEwen (*Lansdowne*), T. Elliot (*Gala*), M.W. Swan (*Oxford Univ.*), J.W.Y. Kemp
(*Glas. HSFP*), G.K. Smith (*Kelso*), J.T. Greenwood (*Perthshire Acads.*), A. Robson
(*Hawick*)

Wales: T.J. Davies (*Llanelli*); J.R. Collins (*Aberavon*), M.C. Thomas (*Newport*), C.A.H.
Davies (*Llanelli*), G.T. Wells (*Cardiff*); C.I. Morgan (*Cardiff*), L.H. Williams (*Cardiff*); R.
Prosser (*Pontypool*), B.V. Meredith (*Newport*), D. Devereux (*Neath*), R.H. Williams
(*Llanelli*), W.R. Evans (*Cardiff*), R.C.C. Thomas* (*Swansea*), J. Faull (*Swansea*), H.J.
Morgan (*Abertillery*)

Referee: N. McNeill-Parkes (*England*)   **Touch judges:** G. Burrell, D. Pritchard

G.T. Wells scored and T.J. Davies converted (0–5).(H.T.). A.R. Smith kicked a penalty
(3–5); J.R. Collins scored but T.J. Davies failed (3–8).

The strength of the Welsh pack was eventually a deciding factor and the Scottish halves,
much harassed by the back row, were not seen in attack. As a result their centres had little
useful ball whilst the wingers had to fend for themselves but at least their defence was
sound. Play was mainly in the Welsh half before the interval and Scotland missed two hard
but kickable penalties before Wells ran onto a kick ahead by C. Davies and beat Smith for
the touch. In the second half Wales came more into the game and after a Smith penalty

235

L.H. Williams and Collins had an interpassing run (which many thought had started with a forward pass) which finished with the latter scoring a vital try.

AUSTRALIA   Murrayfield   15 February 1958

| SCOTLAND: | 2 penalty goals, 2 tries | 12 | **Win** |
| AUSTRALIA: | 1 goal, 1 try | 8 | |

Scotland: R.W.T. Chisholm (*Melrose*); A.R. Smith* (*Gosforth*), G.D. Stevenson (*Hawick*), J.T. Docherty (*Glas. HSFP*), T.G. Weatherstone (*Stewart's FP*); G.H. Waddell (*Devonport Services*), J.A.T. Rodd (*Un. Services*); H.F. McLeod (*Hawick*), N.S. Bruce (*Blackheath*), T. Elliot (*Gala*), M.W. Swan (*Oxford Univ.*), J.W.Y. Kemp (*Glas. HSFP*), G.K. Smith (*Kelso*), J.T. Greenwood (*Perthshire Acads.*), A. Robson (*Hawick*)

Australia: T.G.P. Curley (*NSW*); K.J. Donald (*Queensland*), J.K. Lenehan (*NSW*), S.W. White (*NSW*), R. Phelps (*NSW*); A.J. Summons (*NSW*), D.M. Connor (*Queensland*); G.N. Vaughan (*Victoria*), J.V. Brown (*NSW*), R.A.L. Davidson* (*NSW*), A.R. Miller (*NSW*), D.M. Emanuel (*NSW*), E.M. Purkiss (*NSW*), N.M. Hughes (*NSW*), J.E. Thornett (*NSW*)

Referee: R.C. Williams (*Ireland*)   **Touch judges:** R.P. Burrell, R.M. Harvey

K.J. Donald scored and J.K. Lenehan converted (0–5); T.G. Weatherstone scored but A.R. Smith failed (3–5); J.E. Thornett scored (3–8); A.R. Smith kicked a penalty (6–8).(H.T.). A.R. Smith kicked a penalty (9–8); G.D. Stevenson scored but A.R. Smith failed (12–8).

Australia were perhaps unlucky to lose for a point behind with ten minutes left they lost White injured and concussed checking a fine forward rush. Up till then they had shown themselves to be the better running and attacking team with a pack that had an edge in the scrums and line out. From this point the Scottish pack took command, Waddell became more prominent and a run in which Chisholm took part saw Stevenson score — although some thought the move included a forward pass.

Australia took an early lead when Curley came into the threes and after a 30 yards run, kicked the ball over Chisholm's head. Donald, credited with 9.8 seconds for 100 yards, caught the ball and was not overtaken. However, ten minutes later a fast Scottish heel let Waddell make a break for Docherty to crosskick, Weatherstone gathered the ball and scored at the corner. Within minutes Summons made a break and Thornett was in support to score. Two penalties by Smith, the second after the interval being from near half field put Scotland in the lead then Australia lost White and the initiative.

IRELAND   Lansdowne Road   1 March 1958

| SCOTLAND: | 2 tries | 6 | **Loss** |
| IRELAND: | 2 penalty goals, 2 tries | 12 | |

Scotland: R.W.T. Chisholm (*Melrose*); A.R. Smith* (*Gosforth*), G.D. Stevenson (*Hawick*), J.T. Docherty (*Glas. HSFP*), T.G. Weatherstone (*Stewart's FP*); G.H. Waddell (*Devonport Services*), J.A.T. Rodd (*Un. Services*); H.F. McLeod (*Hawick*), N.S. Bruce (*Blackheath*), T. Elliot (*Gala*), M.W. Swan (*Oxford Univ.*), J.W.Y. Kemp (*Glas. HSFP*), D.C. Macdonald (*Edin. Univ.*), J.T. Greenwood (*Perthshire Acads.*), A. Robson (*Hawick*)

Ireland: P.J. Berkery (*London Irish*); A.C. Pedlow (*CIYMS*), D. Hewitt (*QU Belfast*), N.J. Henderson* (*NIFC*), A.J.F. O'Reilly (*Old Belvedere*); J.W. Kyle (*NIFC*), A.A. Mulligan (*Wanderers*); P.J. O'Donoghue (*Bective Rangers*), A.R. Dawson (*Wanderers*), B.G.M. Wood (*Garryowen*), J.B. Stevenson (*Instonians*), W.A. Mulcahy (*UC Dublin*), J.A. Donaldson (*Collegians*), J.R. Kavanagh (*Wanderers*), N.A.A. Murphy (*Cork Const.*)

Referee: W.N. Gillmore (*England*)   **Touch judges:** J.I. Morrison, S.V. Crawford

A.R. Smith scored but failed to convert (3–0); T.G. Weatherstone scored but A.R. Smith failed (6–0).(H.T.). N.J. Henderson kicked a penalty (6–3); A.C. Pedlow scored but P.J. Berkery failed (6–6); P.J. Berkery kicked a penalty (6–9); A.C. Pedlow scored but P.J. Berkery failed (6–12).

Rather against the run of play Scotland scored first when Stevenson picked up a missed pass and set Smith off on a spectacular 65 yards run for the first try. A few minutes later Rodd broke from a scrum and put Weatherstone in at the corner. Just on half time Chisholm was hurt checking a forward rush and was taken off. Smith went to full back with Robson on the wing but Ireland held the advantage during the second half and finished clear winners.

ENGLAND   Murrayfield   15 March 1958

| **SCOTLAND:** | 1 penalty goal | **3** | **Draw** |
| **ENGLAND:** | 1 penalty goal | **3** | |

Scotland: K.J.F. Scotland (*Heriot's FP*); C. Elliot (*Langholm*), G.D. Stevenson (*Hawick*), J.T. Docherty (*Glas. HSFP*), T.G. Weatherstone (*Stewart's FP*); G.H. Waddell (*Devonport Services*), J.A.T. Rodd (*Un. Services*); H.F. McLeod (*Hawick*), N.S. Bruce (*Blackheath*), I.R. Hastie (*Kelso*), M.W. Swan (*London Scot.*), J.W.Y. Kemp (*Glas. HSFP*), D.C. Macdonald (*Edin. Univ.*), J.T. Greenwood* (*Perthshire Acads.*), A. Robson (*Hawick*)

England: D.F. Allison (*Coventry*); P.B. Jackson (*Coventry*), J. Butterfield (*Northampton*), M.S. Phillips (*Oxford Univ.*), P.H. Thompson (*Headingley*); R.M. Bartlett (*Harlequins*), R.E.G. Jeeps (*Northampton*); C.R. Jacobs (*Northampton*), E. Evans* (*Sale*), G.W.D. Hastings (*Gloucester*), R.W.D. Marques (*Camb. Univ.*), J.D. Currie (*Oxford Univ.*), A.J. Herbert (*Wasps*), A. Ashcroft (*Waterloo*), P.G.D. Robbins (*Oxford Univ.*)

Referee: R.C. Williams (*Ireland*)   **Touch judges:** J.A. Cessford, D.A. Brown

No scoring at half time. C. Elliot kicked a penalty (3–0); G.W.D. Hastings kicked a penalty (3–3).

Scotland showed such improved form that they really deserved to win for they set a fierce pace from the start and never eased up. The much vaunted English threes never really got moving and only near half time did they show their class when Jackson ran the ball from his own line across field for five others to handle in a movement brought to a halt by a good tackle by K.J.F. Scotland. Their defence, however, was sound and the giants Marques and Currie were prominent at the line outs. Scotland attacked frequently; Waddell came close with a drop kick whilst Bruce and Weatherstone were both nearly over. Just before the close Jeeps was laid out when he tackled Elliot and so saved a certain score. The winger was a late replacement for A.R. Smith and raised a tremendous cheer when, after others had failed, he kicked a penalty shortly after the interval to give Scotland a rather short lived lead.

FRANCE Colombes 10 January 1959

SCOTLAND:	Nil	0	**Loss**
FRANCE:	2 drop goals, 1 try	9	

Scotland: K.J.F. Scotland (*Camb. Univ.*); A.R. Smith (*Gosforth*), T. McClung (*Edin. Acads.*), I.H.P. Laughland (*London Scot.*), C. Elliot (*Langholm*); G.H. Waddell (*Camb. Univ.*), S. Coughtrie (*Edin. Acads.*); H.F. McLeod (*Hawick*), N.S. Bruce (*Blackheath*), I.R. Hastie (*Kelso*), M.W. Swan (*London Scot.*), J.W.Y. Kemp (*Glas. HSFP*), G.K. Smith (*Kelso*), J.T. Greenwood* (*Perthshire Acads.*), A. Robson (*Hawick*)

France: P. Lacaze (*Lourdes*); J. Dupuy (*Tarbes*), A. Marquesuzaa (*RCF*), J. Bouquet (*Vienne*), H. Rancoule (*Lourdes*); A. Labazuy (*Lourdes*), P. Danos (*Beziers*); A. Qualio (*Mazamet*), R. Vigier (*Monteferrand*), A. Roques (*Cahors*), L. Mias (*Mazamet*), B. Mommejat (*Cahors*), F. Moncla (*RCF*), J. Barthe (*Lourdes*), M. Celaya (*Biarritz*)

Referee: G. Walters (*Wales*) **Touch judges:** J.A. Cessford, R.B. Marie

P. Lacaze dropped a goal (0–3); F. Moncla scored (0–6).(H.T.). P. Lacaze dropped a goal (0–9).

The score barely reflected France's superiority '*grâce à sa ligne d'avants et l'étonnant Pierre Danos*' and indeed the home pack were outstanding in a game that was fast from beginning to end. Coughtrie did well behind a beaten pack but the backs spent a busy afternoon in defence and never at any time looked like winning. The only try came from a movement started by Danos from a loose scrum and Moncla was involved twice before he crashed in for his try. Danos was also involved in getting the ball away to Lacaze when he dropped his second goal.
    Later at the official dinner Dr D.J. MacMyn, then President of the SRU, greatly pleased and moved his hosts of the FFR when he presented them with the jersey of the late Y. du Manoir, which he had kept since the game in 1926.

WALES Murrayfield 7 February 1959

SCOTLAND:	1 penalty goal, 1 try	6	**Win**
WALES:	1 goal	5	

Scotland: K.J.F. Scotland (*Camb. Univ.*); A.R. Smith (*Gosforth*), T. McClung (*Edin. Acads.*), G.D. Stevenson (*Hawick*), T.G. Weatherstone (*Stewart's FP*); G.H. Waddell (*Camb. Univ.*), S. Coughtrie (*Edin. Acads.*); H.F. McLeod (*Hawick*), N.S. Bruce (*Blackheath*), I.R. Hastie (*Kelso*), M.W. Swan (*London Scot.*), J.W.Y. Kemp (*Glas. HSFP*), G.K. Smith (*Kelso*), J.T. Greenwood* (*Perthshire Acads.*), A. Robson (*Hawick*)

Wales: T.E. Davies (*Llanelli*); J.R. Collins (*Aberavon*), H.J. Davies (*Camb. Univ.*), M.J. Price (*Pontypool*), D.I. Bebb (*Carmarthen TC*); C. Ashton (*Aberavon*), L.H. Williams (*Cardiff*); R. Prosser (*Pontypool*), B.V. Meredith (*Newport*), D.R̄. Main (*London Welsh*), R.H. Williams (*Llanelli*), I. Ford (*Newport*), R.C.C. Thomas* (*Swansea*), J. Faull (*Swansea*), J. Leleu (*London Welsh*)

Referee: R.C. Williams (*Ireland*)   **Touch judges:** R.P. Burrell, G. Thomas

M.J. Price scored and T.E. Davies converted (0–5); K.J.F. Scotland kicked a penalty (3–5); N.S. Bruce scored but K.J.F. Scotland failed (6–5).(H.T.).

The Scottish pack held their own in the scrums and line outs but were clearly on top in the loose, being very fast in following up. Waddell benefitted from Coughtrie's good and lengthy service and had one fine 60 yard run that narrowly failed to bring a score. Nevertheless Wales were first to score within five minutes when Price burst away from a line out and ran some 40 yards to score. 30 minutes later K.J.F. Scotland kicked a penalty. Then, just on the interval, the Welsh pack in a rush nearly scored, only to see the Scottish pack headed by G.K. Smith, take the ball 80 yards downfield in a dribbling rush, which finished with Waddell picking up and passing to Bruce who went for the corner to score. In the second half Scotland missed two penalties and only the sternest defence denied them at least two scores. Yet they nearly lost the match in the closing minutes when a long drop by Ashton dropped just short of the bar.

IRELAND   Murrayfield   28 February 1959

SCOTLAND:	1 penalty goal	3	**Loss**
IRELAND:	1 goal, 1 penalty goal	8	

Scotland: K.J.F. Scotland (*Camb. Univ.*); A.R. Smith (*Ebbw Vale*), T. McClung (*Edin. Univ.*), G.D. Stevenson (*Hawick*), T.G. Weatherstone (*Stewart's FP*); G.H. Waddell (*Camb. Univ.*), S. Coughtrie (*Edin. Acads.*); H.F. McLeod (*Hawick*), N.S. Bruce (*Blackheath*), I.R. Hastie (*Kelso*), M.W. Swan (*London Scot.*), J.W.Y. Kemp (*Glas. HSFP*), G.K. Smith (*Kelso*), J.T. Greenwood* (*Perthshire Acads.*), A. Robson (*Hawick*)

Ireland: N.J. Henderson (*NIFC*); N.H. Brophy (*UC Dublin*), D. Hewitt (*QU Belfast*), J.F. Dooley (*Galwegians*), A.F. O'Reilly (*Old Belvedere*); M.A.F. English (*Bohemians*), A.A. Mulligan (*London Irish*); B.G.M. Wood (*Garryowen*), A.R. Dawson* (*Wanderers*), S. Millar (*Ballymena*), W.A. Mulcahy (*UC Dublin*), M.G. Culliton (*Wanderers*), N.A.A. Murphy (*Cork Const.*), P.J.A. O'Sullivan (*Galwegians*), J.R. Kavanagh (*Wanderers*)

Referee: L.M. Boundy (*England*)   **Touch judges:** J.I. Morrison, P.J. Lavery

D. Hewitt kicked a penalty (0–3); J.F. Dooley scored and D. Hewitt converted (0–8).(H.T.). K.J.F. Scotland kicked a penalty (3–8).

239

After ten minutes Greenwood came off with a dislocated shoulder and before he came back to play as a complete passenger Hewitt had kicked a fine 40 yard penalty from a difficult angle. Just before the interval O'Reilly cut in from the wing to join a handling movement and smart handling saw Hewitt go through a gap and send Dooley in. Scotland never managed to produce the dash that they showed against Wales but their halves and backs were harried and spent most of the time in defence. In fact K.J.F. Scotland was probably their most penetrating runner at full back.

ENGLAND   Twickenham   21 March 1959

SCOTLAND:	1 penalty goal	3	**Draw**
ENGLAND:	1 penalty goal	3	

Scotland: K.J.F. Scotland (*Camb. Univ.*); A.R. Smith (*Ebbw Vale*), J.A.P. Shackleton (*London Scot.*), G.D. Stevenson (*Hawick*), T.G. Weatherstone (*Stewart's FP*); G.H. Waddell* (*Camb. Univ.*), S. Coughtrie (*Edin. Acads.*); D.M.D. Rollo (*Howe of Fife*), N.S. Bruce (*Blackheath*), H.F. McLeod (*Hawick*), F.H. ten Bos (*Oxford Univ.*), J.W.Y. Kemp (*Glas. HSFP*), G.K. Smith (*Kelso*), J.A. Davidson (*London Scot.*), A. Robson (*Hawick*)

England: J.G.G. Hetherington (*Northampton*); P.B. Jackson (*Coventry*), M.S. Phillips (*Oxford Univ.*), J. Butterfield* (*Northampton*), P.H. Thompson (*Waterloo*); A.B.W. Risman (*Manchester Univ.*), S.R. Smith (*Camb. Univ.*); St. L.H. Webb (*Bedford*), H.O. Godwin (*Coventry*), G.J. Bendon (*Wasps*), R.W.D. Marques (*Harlequins*), J.D. Currie (*Harlequins*), A.J. Herbert (*Wasps*), A. Ashcroft (*Waterloo*), J.W. Clements (*Old Cranleighans*)

Referee: G. Walters (*Wales*)   **Touch judges:** H.B. Laidlaw, J.V. Pollard

K.J.F. Scotland kicked a penalty (3–0); A.B.W. Risman kicked a penalty (3–3).(H.T.).

A heavy English pack were better in the scrums while Scotland showed up well in the open, Robson being particularly noticeable. The newcomer Rollo, in spite of a knock on the face, was a solid but active prop. Both stand-offs lay deep yet never really escaped the attention of the back row forwards. Waddell depended mainly on lofty punts but Hetherington was quite untroubled by this form of attack. In the first half a dangerous run by Phillips was halted by a fine tackle by Scotland who again showed his flair for attacking from the back position. The Scottish pack made a very vigorous start to the second half and nearly forced a score against a very good defence. The four very talented wingers were hardly brought into the play.

FRANCE   Murrayfield   9 January 1960

SCOTLAND:	1 goal, 1 penalty goal, 1 try	11	**Loss**
FRANCE:	2 goals, 1 try	13	

Scotland: K.J.F. Scotland (*Camb. Univ.*); A.R. Smith* (*Ebbw Vale*), J.J. McPartlin (*Harlequins*), I.H.P. Laughland (*London Scot.*), C. Elliot (*Langholm*); G. Sharp (*Stewart's FP*), J.A.T. Rodd (*Un. Services*); H.F. McLeod (*Hawick*), N.S. Bruce (*London Scot.*), D.M.D. Rollo (*Howe of Fife*), F.H. ten Bos (*Oxford Univ.*), J.W.Y. Kemp (*Glas. HSFP*), G.K. Smith (*Kelso*), K.R.F. Bearne (*Camb. Univ.*), A. Robson (*Hawick*)

France: M. Vannier (*RCF*); L. Roge (*Beziers*), J. Bouquet (*Vienne*), A. Marquesuzaa (*Lourdes*), S. Mericq (*Agen*); R. Martine (*Lourdes*), P. Danos (*Beziers*); A. Domenech (*Brive*), J. de Gregorio (*Grenoble*), A. Roques (*Cahors*), B. Mommejat (*Cahors*), M. Celaya (*Bordeaux*), F. Moncla* (*Pau*), M. Crauste (*Lourdes*), S. Meyer (*Perigueux*)

Referee: G. Walters (*Wales*) Touch judges: G. Burrell, M. Laurent

S. Meyer scored and M. Vannier converted (0–5).(H.T.). S. Mericq and F. Moncla scored and M. Vannier converted the second (0–13); A.R. Smith scored and C. Elliot converted (5–13); C. Elliot kicked a penalty (8–13); A.R. Smith scored but C. Elliot failed (11–13).

This was an exciting match which Scotland might have won had they changed their tactics early on. After some ten minutes Roge fractured his hand tackling Smith but remained on the field as an extra back and Meyer came out of the pack onto the wing. This arrangement worked because the depleted French pack held their own everywhere except in the set scrums and their ferocious tackling and speed onto the man and ball stifled all the Scottish attacks. Near half time Bouquet intercepted a pass at half field and when Smith ran him down a pass to Meyer produced a score at the posts. France restarted in tremendous fashion scoring two tries inside three minutes for a 13 points lead. Then Scotland began to play on the injured Roge. He was forced to fly kick at a high bouncing ball and a miss let Smith pick up and score for Elliot to convert this and almost at once kick a penalty for off-side. After a scrum Sharp kicked ahead and when two defenders collided Smith again picked up to streak round Vannier and score too far out for Elliot to convert — and then time ran out for Scotland.

WALES   Cardiff   6 February 1960

SCOTLAND: Nil   0   Loss
WALES: 1 goal, 1 penalty goal   8

Scotland: K.J.F. Scotland (*Camb. Univ.*); A.R. Smith* (*Ebbw Vale*), J.J. McPartlin (*Harlequins*), I.H.P. Laughland (*London Scot.*), G.D. Stevenson (*Hawick*); T. McClung (*Edin. Acads.*), J.A.T. Rodd (*Un. Services*); H.F. McLeod (*Hawick*), N.S. Bruce (*London Scot.*), D.M.D. Rollo (*Howe of Fife*), F.H. ten Bos (*Oxford Univ.*), J.W.Y. Kemp (*Glas. HSFP*), G.K. Smith (*Kelso*), K.R.F. Bearne (*Camb. Univ.*), C.E.B. Stewart (*Kelso*)

Wales: N. Morgan (*Newport*); F.C. Coles (*Pontypool*), M.J. Price (*RAF*), G.W. Lewis (*Richmond*), D.I. Bebb (*Carmarthen TC*); C. Ashton (*Aberavon*), D.O. Brace (*Llanelli*); R. Prosser (*Pontypool*), B.V. Meredith* (*Newport*), L.J. Cunningham (*Aberavon*), G.W. Payne (*Army*), D.J.E. Harris (*Cardiff*), B. Cresswell (*Newport*), G.D. Davidge (*Newport*), G. Whitson (*Newport*)

Referee: K. Kelleher (*Ireland*) Touch judges: J. Imrie, A. Williams

No scoring at half time. D.I. Bebb scored and N. Morgan converted (0–5); N. Morgan kicked a penalty (0–8).

There was a disappointing display by both sets of backs. Behind beaten forwards and receiving a poor service McClung had to rely mainly on placing diagonal kicks, especially as A.R. Smith was clearly the best back on the field. One long run by the latter would have given G.K. Smith a score had the final pass not been so wide. Brace did relatively well behind a strong pack but it was lucky for Scotland that his backs were so off form with their handling. The only try came early in the second half when a kick ahead by Brace was fumbled and Bebb nipped in to score.

IRELAND   Lansdowne Road   27 February 1960

SCOTLAND:	1 drop goal, 1 try	6	**Win**
IRELAND:	1 goal	5	

Scotland: K.J.F. Scotland (*Camb. Univ.*); A.R. Smith (*Ebbw Vale*), G.D. Stevenson (*Hawick*), I.H.P. Laughland (*London Scot.*), R.H. Thomson (*London Scot.*); G.H. Waddell* (*Camb. Univ.*), R.B. Shillinglaw (*KOSB*); D.M.D. Rollo (*Howe of Fife*), N.S. Bruce (*London Scot.*), H.F. McLeod (*Hawick*), T.O. Grant (*Hawick*), J.W.Y. Kemp (*Glas. HSFP*), G.K. Smith (*Kelso*), J.A. Davidson (*Edin. Wrs.*), D.B. Edwards (*Heriot's FP*)

Ireland: T.J. Kiernan (*UC Cork*); A.C. Pedlow (*CIYMS*), D. Hewitt (*QU Belfast*), J.C. Walsh (*UC Cork*), W.W. Bornemann (*Wanderers*); M.A.F. English (*Bohemians*), A.A. Mulligan* (*London Irish*); B.G.M. Wood (*Lansdowne*), B. McCallan (*Ballymena*), S. Millar (*Ballymena*), W.A. Mulcahy (*UC Dublin*), M.G. Culliton (*Wanderers*), N.A.A. Murphy (*Cork Const.*), T. McGrath (*Garryowen*), J.R. Kavanagh (*Wanderers*)

Referee: D.G. Walters (*Wales*)   **Touch judges:** D. McIntyre, A.B. Robertson

B.G.M. Wood scored and D. Hewitt converted (0–5); R.H. Thomson scored but K.J.F. Scotland failed (3–5); K.J.F. Scotland dropped a goal (6–5).(H.T.).

This was Scotland's first win in Dublin since 1933 and while Ireland had chances that they did not take, there were welcome signs of improvement in an altered Scottish team. Shillinglaw at scrum half had an excellent debut and Waddell, benefitting from a good long service, was much more able to dictate play, especially towards the close when Ireland fought hard to save the game. Then his ability to place lengthy but accurate kicks to touch was invaluable. During this period the threes, not great in attack, were immense in defence especially as both centres had earlier been injured. After an early Irish score K.J.F. Scotland, who fielded beautifully all afternoon, came up to join a movement and put Thomson over for his try. He failed with the conversion but shortly afterwards he dropped a goal after a set scrum in front of the posts — having come up deliberately to take the pass from the scrum.

ENGLAND   **Murrayfield**   **19 March 1960**

SCOTLAND: 3 penalty goals, 1 try   12   **Loss**
ENGLAND   2 goals, 1 drop goal,   21
               1 penalty goal

Scotland: K.J.F. Scotland (*Camb. Univ.*); A.R. Smith (*Ebbw Vale*), G.D. Stevenson (*Hawick*), I.H.P. Laughland (*London Scot.*), R.H. Thomson (*London Scot.*); G.H. Waddell* (*Camb. Univ.*), R.B. Shillinglaw (*KOSB*); D.M.D. Rollo (*Howe of Fife*), N.S. Bruce (*London Scot.*), H.F. McLeod (*Hawick*), T.O. Grant (*Hawick*), J.W.Y. Kemp (*Glas. HSFP*), G.K. Smith (*Kelso*), J.A. Davidson (*Edin. Wrs.*), D.B. Edwards (*Heriot's FP*)

England: D. Rutherford (*Percy Park*); J.R.C. Young (*Harlequins*), M.S. Phillips (*Oxford Univ.*), M.P. Weston (*Richmond*), J. Roberts (*Old Millhillians*); R.A.W. Sharp (*Oxford Univ.*), R.E.G. Jeeps* (*Northampton*); C.R. Jacobs (*Northampton*), S.A.M. Hodgson (*Durham City*), T.P. Wright (*Blackheath*), R.W.D. Marques (*Harlequins*), J.D. Currie (*Harlequins*), P.G.D. Robbins (*Moseley*), W.G.D. Morgan (*Medicals*), R.E. Syrett (*Wasps*)

Referee: R.C. Williams (*Ireland*)   **Touch judges:** J.A.S. Taylor, W. Howarth

R.A.W. Sharp dropped a goal (0–3); R.E. Syrett and J. Roberts scored and D. Rutherford converted both (0–13); D. Rutherford kicked a penalty (0–16); K.J.F. Scotland kicked two penalties (6–16).(H.T.). K.J.F. Scotland kicked a penalty (9–16); J.R.C. Young scored and D. Rutherford converted (9–21); A.R. Smith scored but K.J.F. Scotland failed (12–21).

This was a spectacular game, full of exciting action. England were particularly well served by Sharp at half and Phillips at centre. For Scotland Shillinglaw did well under constant pressure from Jeeps and the English back row but there was no penetration further back and the wingers saw little of the ball. Inside five minutes Sharp dropped a 35 yard goal and then England rattled on two tries converted by Rutherford who followed with a penalty for a 16 points lead. Before half time K.J.F. Scotland had reduced the deficit by kicking two long range penalties and ten minutes after the interval added another from 40 yards. Scotland had one chance of scoring spoiled by a dropped pass before Phillips made a fine opening to send Young in. Late on K.J.F. Scotland showed the threes what could be done when he came upfield and made an opening for A.R. Smith to show his pace and score.

SOUTH AFRICA   **Port Elizabeth**   **30 April 1960**

SCOTLAND: 2 goals   10   **Loss**
SOUTH AFRICA: 3 goals, 1 try   18

Scotland: R.W.T. Chisholm (*Melrose*); A.R. Smith (*Ebbw Vale*), P.J. Burnet (*London Scot.*), G.D. Stevenson (*Hawick*), R.H. Thomson (*London Scot.*); G.H. Waddell* (*Camb. Univ.*), R.B. Shillinglaw (*Gala*); H.F. McLeod (*Hawick*), N.S. Bruce (*London Scot.*),

D.M.D. Rollo (*Howe of Fife*), F.H. ten Bos (*Oxford Univ.*), J.W.Y. Kemp (*Glas. HSFP*), D.B. Edwards (*Heriot's FP*), T.O. Grant (*Hawick*), W. Hart (*Melrose*)

South Africa: M.C. Gerber (*EP*); J.P. Engelbrecht (*WP*), I.A. Kirkpatrick (*GW*), J.L. Gainford (*WP*), R.J. Twigge (*NT*); D.A. Stewart (*WP*), F.W. Gerike (*T*); D.N. Holton (*EP*), A.J. Van der Merwe (*Boland*), M.J. Bekker (*NT*), J.T. Claassen (*WT*), P.B. Allen (*EP*), D.C. Van Jaarsveldt* (*Rhodesia*), D.J. Hopwood (*WP*), G.H. Van Zyl (*WP*)

Referee: Dr E.A. Strasheim

N.S. Bruce scored and A.R. Smith converted (5–0); G.H. Van Zyl scored and M.C. Gerber converted (5–5).(H.T.). G.H. Van Zyl scored but M.C. Gerber failed (5–8); F.W. Gerike scored and M.C. Gerber converted (5–13); D.C. Van Jaarsveldt scored and M.C. Gerber converted (5–18); A.R. Smith scored and converted (10–18).

This, the first experimental short tour by any country, was a distinct success and clearly set a pattern for others in the future. Since it was the start of the South African season they were hoping that their physical advantages in the pack would compensate for a lack of match fitness. As it turned out the lighter Scottish forwards held their own in the scrums, were faster in the loose and did well at the line outs but their back row failed to subdue Gerike who engineered three vital tries by breaking fast round the scrum. The Scottish halves were the better pair, making some good breaks but while the centres tackled soundly they handled indifferently and the dangerous A.R. Smith had more or less to fend for himself. Stevenson, however, was throughout badly affected by a nasty knock he got after five minutes' play. The best score of the game was a try by Jaarsveldt who picked up a loose ball near mid field and outstripped everyone in a 50 yard dash.

FRANCE   Colombes   7 January 1961

SCOTLAND: Nil   0 Loss
FRANCE: 1 goal, 1 drop goal, 1 penalty goal   11

Scotland: K.J.F. Scotland (*London Scot.*); A.R. Smith (*Edin. Wrs.*), R.C. Cowan (*Selkirk*), G.D. Stevenson (*Hawick*), R.H. Thomson (*London Scot.*); G.H. Waddell* (*Camb. Univ.*), R.B. Shillinglaw (*KOSB*); H.F. McLeod (*Hawick*), N.S. Bruce (*London Scot.*), D.M.D. Rollo (*Howe of Fife*), F.H. ten Bos (*Oxford Univ.*), M.J. Campbell-Lamerton (*Blackheath*), G.K. Smith (*Kelso*), C.E.B. Stewart (*Kelso*), J. Douglas (*Stewart's FP*)

France: R. Martine (*Lourdes*); J. Dupuy (*Tarbes*), J. Bouquet (*Vienne*), G. Boniface (*Mont-de-Marsan*), J. Gachassin (*Lourdes*); P. Albaladejo (*Dax*); P. Lacroix (*Agen*); A. Domenech (*Brive*), J. de Gregoria (*Grenoble*), A. Roques (*Cahors*), L. Echave (*Agen*), M. Celaya (*Biarritz*), F. Moncla (*Pau*), R. Crancee (*Lourdes*), M. Crauste (*Lourdes*)

Referee: R.C. Williams (*Ireland*)   **Touch judges:** D.C.J. McMahon, B. Marie

No scoring at half time. P. Albaladejo dropped a goal and kicked a penalty (0–6); G. Boniface scored and P. Albaladejo converted (0–11).

C.E.B. Stewart suffered a leg injury in the first minute and although he returned he was merely a passenger for the rest of the afternoon. In spite of this the Scottish pack played so well that there was no scoring during the first half although the French forwards showed their customary flair for handling. It was well on in the second half before Boniface scored the only try and meantime Scotland came near to scoring; Waddell was held under the posts and Thomson got over only to be recalled for a previous infringement.

SOUTH AFRICA Murrayfield 21 January 1961

SCOTLAND: 1 goal 5 **Loss**

SOUTH AFRICA: 2 penalty goals, 2 tries 12

Scotland: K.J.F. Scotland (*London Scot.*); A.R. Smith* (*Edin. Wrs.*), E. McKeating (*Heriot's FP*), G.D. Stevenson (*Hawick*), R.H. Thomson (*London Scot.*); I.H.P. Laughland (*London Scot.*), R.B. Shillinglaw (*Gala*); H.F. McLeod (*Hawick*), N.S. Bruce (*London Scot.*), D.M.D. Rollo (*Howe of Fife*), F.H. ten Bos (*Oxford Univ.*), M.J. Campbell-Lamerton (*Blackheath*), G.K. Smith (*Kelso*), J. Douglas (*Stewart's FP*), K.I. Ross (*Boroughmuir FP*)

South Africa: D.A. Stewart (*WP*); J.P. Englebrecht (*WP*), J.L. Gainsford (*WP*), A.I. Kirkpatrick (*Orange FS*), H.J. Van Zyl (*T*); K. Oxlee (*Natal*), P. de W. Vys (*NT*); S.P. Kuhn (*T*), G.F. Malan (*WP*), P.S. du Toit (*Boland*), G.H. Van Zyl (*WP*), A.S. Malan* (*T*), J.T. Claassen (*WT*), F.C. Du Preez (*NT*), D.J. Hopwood (*WP*)

Referee: L.M. Boundy (*England*) **Touch judges:** G. Burrell, P.J. Van Zyl

D.J. Hopwood scored but F.C. Du Preez failed (0–3); J.T. Claassen scored but F.C. Du Preez failed (0–6).(H.T.). A.R. Smith scored and K.J.F. Scotland converted (5–6); F.C. Du Preez kicked 2 penalties (5–12).

Both sides played open rugby in a most exhilarating game. The heavier and faster South African forwards produced some great handling and backing up movements, but an improved Scottish pack, beaten in the scrums and line outs, were by no means outshone in the loose and the splendid tackling of the whole team did much to counter the great combined play of the visitors. K.J.F. Scotland was again at his best, his positioning and long accurate touch kicking being first rate. It was 25 minutes before Hopwood broke from a scrum to score and shortly afterwards he made an opening for another forward to score. Scotland's score came after a long run by Shillinglaw, Laughland, McKeating and Thomson. From a line out Laughland's drop at goal went wide but A.R. Smith raced in to touch down just short of the dead ball line and the conversion left Scotland one point behind. It is a measure of Scotland's resistance that South Africa could only manage two penalty kicks after that.

WALES   Murrayfield   11 February 1961

SCOTLAND: 1 try   3   **Win**

WALES: Nil   0

Scotland: K.J.F. Scotland (*London Scot.*); A.R. Smith* (*Edin. Wrs.*), E. McKeating (*Heriot's FP*), G.D. Stevenson (*Hawick*), R.H. Thomson (*London Scot.*); I.H.P. Laughland (*London Scot.*), A.J. Hastie (*Melrose*); H.F. McLeod (*Hawick*), N.S. Bruce (*London Scot.*), D.M.D. Rollo (*Howe of Fife*), F.H. ten Bos (*London Scot.*), M.J. Campbell-Lamerton (*Halifax*), K.I. Ross (*Boroughmuir FP*), J. Douglas (*Stewart's FP*), G.K. Smith (*Kelso*)

Wales: T.J. Davies* (*Llanelli*); P.M. Rees (*Newport*), G. Britton (*Newport*), H.M. Roberts (*Cardiff*), D.I. Bebb (*Swansea*); K. Richards (*Bridgend*), A. O'Connor (*Aberavon*); P.E.J. Morgan (*Aberavon*), B.V. Meredith (*Newport*), K.D. Jones (*Cardiff*), W.R. Evans (*Bridgend*), D.J.E. Harris (*Cardiff*), G.D. Davidge (*Newport*), D. Nash (*Ebbw Vale*), H.J. Morgan (*Abertillery*)

Referee: R.C. Williams (*Ireland*)   Touch judges: G.K. Rome, E.M. Lewis

A.R. Smith scored but K.J.F. Scotland failed (3–0).(H.T.).

This was mainly a hard forward battle played in wind and rain. The Scottish pack held their own in the scrums and were clearly on top in the open and with their backs tackling accurately, the Welsh threes had a profitless afternoon. After half an hour Hastie set his backs away and Scotland came into the line to make a break and send A.R. Smith in far out. Scotland failed with the long conversion and had an off day with his place kicking, missing some penalties also, but in the second half he saved a certain score when at the corner he felled Bebb after a great 50 yards run. Bebb at once threw the ball in and getting it back went over only to have the score refused by the referee who ruled that the throw-in was short.

IRELAND   Murrayfield   25 February 1961

SCOTLAND: 2 goals, 1 penalty goal, 1 try   16   **Win**

IRELAND: 1 goal, 1 try   8

Scotland: K.J.F. Scotland (*London Scot.*); A.R. Smith* (*Edin. Wrs.*), E. McKeating (*Heriot's FP*), G.D. Stevenson (*Hawick*), R.H. Thomson (*London Scot.*); I.H.P. Laughland (*London Scot.*), A.J. Hastie (*Melrose*); H.F. McLeod (*Hawick*), N.S. Bruce (*London Scot.*), D.M.D. Rollo (*Howe of Fife*), F.H. ten Bos (*London Scot.*), M.J. Campbell-Lamerton (*Halifax*), K.I. Ross (*Boroughmuir FP*), J. Douglas (*Stewart's FP*), G.K. Smith (*Kelso*)

Ireland: T.J. Kiernan (*UC Cork*); A.C. Pedlow (*CIYMS*), D. Hewitt (*QU Belfast*), J.C.

246

Walsh (*UC Cork*), N.H. Brophy (*Blackrock*); M.A.F. English (*Bohemians*), J.W. Moffett (*Ballymena*); B.G.M. Wood (*Lansdowne*), A.R. Dawson* (*Wanderers*), S. Millar (*Ballymena*), W.A. Mulcahy (*UC Dublin*), M.G. Culliton (*Wanderers*), J.R. Kavanagh (*Wanderers*), P.J.A. O'Sullivan (*Galwegians*), N.A.A. Murphy (*Garryowen*)

Referee: M.H.R. King (*England*) Touch judges: G.W.D. Hastie, J. Bell

J.R. Kavanagh scored and J.W. Moffett converted (0–5); K.J.F. Scotland kicked a penalty (3–5); J. Douglas scored and K.J.F. Scotland converted (8–5).(H.T.). K.I. Ross scored and K.J.F. Scotland converted (13–5); D. Hewitt scored but J.W. Moffett failed (13–8); K.I. Ross scored but K.J.F. Scotland failed (16–8).

This was a fast spectacular game with a great exhibition of forward play by two splendid packs, the Scottish back row in particular showing excellent form both in attack and defence. In spite of a greasy ball and slippery surface, Ireland played well to their wingers, who only failed against some firm tackling. They began, however, by keeping the ball amongst the fowards and it was Kavanagh who scored inside ten minutes. Good play by the pack regained the lead for Scotland and in the second half a sally into the line by K.J.F. Scotland saw him finish a touch line run by putting Ross over for a good try. Ireland retaliated with a tremendous passing movement which flowed to and fro across the field before Hewitt held on to a doubtful pass and scored what was really a lovely try. Ross, however, capped a fine afternoon's work with another score in the last ten minutes.

ENGLAND   Twickenham   18 March 1961

SCOTLAND: Nil   0   **Loss**

ENGLAND: 1 penalty goal, 1 try   6

Scotland: K.J.F. Scotland (*Heriot's FP*); A.R. Smith* (*Edin. Wrs.*), E. McKeating (*Heriot's FP*), G.D. Stevenson (*Hawick*), R.H. Thomson (*London Scot.*); I.H.P. Laughland (*London Scot.*), A.J. Hastie (*Melrose*); H.F. McLeod (*Hawick*), N.S. Bruce (*London Scot.*), D.M.D. Rollo (*Howe of Fife*), F.H. ten Bos (*London Scot.*), J. Douglas (*Stewart's FP*), K.I. Ross (*Boroughmuir FP*), G.K. Smith (*Kelso*), J.C. Brash (*Camb. Univ.*)

England: J.G. Willcox (*Oxford Univ.*); P.B. Jackson (*Coventry*), W.M. Patterson (*Sale*), M.P. Weston (*Richmond*), J. Roberts (*Sale*); J.P. Horrocks-Taylor (*Leicester*), R.E.G. Jeeps* (*Northampton*); C.R. Jacobs (*Northampton*), E. Robinson (*Coventry*), T.P. Wright (*Blackheath*), R.J. French (*St Helen's*), V.S.J. Harding (*Saracens*), D.P. Rogers (*Bedford*), W.G.D. Morgan (*Medicals*), L.I. Rimmer (*Bath*)

Referee: K.D. Kelleher (*Ireland*) Touch judges: J.R. Hunter, L.M. Boundy

J. Roberts scored but J.G. Willcox failed (0–3).(H.T.). J.P. Horrocks-Taylor kicked a penalty (0–6).

Once again at Twickenham Scotland failed to lift the Triple Crown for the whole team turned in a lack lustre performance. Undoubtedly the enforced rearrangement of their pack was not a success; the backs never got going and even K.J.F. Scotland could not raise his game and missed several penalties normally within his range. In contrast J.P. Horrocks-Taylor (coming in at half for Sharp) played brilliantly, exhibiting a vast range of attacking moves and he certainly made life utterly miserable for one Scottish back row man of whom a disgruntled critic later said that not only did he fail to tackle Horrocks and Taylor but never once even caught the bloody hyphen. There was one flurry of excitement near the close when Douglas close to the line tried to pick up the slippy ball, but knocked on when a tap over would surely have produced a touch down.

| **FRANCE** | **Murrayfield** | **13 January 1962** |

| **SCOTLAND:** | 1 penalty goal | 3 | **Loss** |
| **FRANCE:** | 1 goal, 2 penalty goals | 11 | |

Scotland: K.J.F. Scotland (*Leicester*); A.R. Smith* (*Edin. Wrs.*), J.J. McPartlin (*Oxford Univ.*), I.H.P. Laughland (*London Scot.*), R.C. Cowan (*Selkirk*); G.H. Waddell (*London Scot.*), J.A.T. Rodd (*London Scot.*); H.F. McLeod (*Hawick*), N.S. Bruce (*London Scot.*), D.M.D. Rollo (*Howe of Fife*), F.H. ten Bos (*London Scot.*), M.J. Campbell-Lamerton (*Halifax*), R.J.C. Glasgow (*Dunfermline*), J. Douglas (*Stewart's FP*), K.I. Ross (*Borough-muir FP*)

France: L. Casaux (*Tarbes*); J. Dupuy (*Tarbes*), J. Pique (*Pau*), J. Bouquet (*Vienne*), H. Rancoule (*Tarbes*); P. Albaladejo (*Dax*), P. Lacroix* (*Agen*); A. Domenech (*Brive*), J. de Gregorio (*Grenoble*), A. Roques (*Cahors*), B. Mommejat (*Albi*), J.P. Saux (*Pau*), M. Crauste (*Lourdes*), H. Romero (*Montauban*), R. Gensane (*Beziers*)

Referee: R.C. Williams (*Ireland*) **Touch judges:** H.W. Leach, M.J. Meynard

A.R. Smith kicked a penalty (3–0); P. Albaladejo kicked a penalty (3–3).(H.T.). P. Albaladejo kicked a penalty (3–6); H. Rancoule scored and P. Albaladejo converted (3–11).

The Scottish pack showed up well but their great efforts were wasted by a lack of initiative behind. Waddell, seemingly slower, was worried by the cover defence and concentrated on gaining territorial advantage by some powerful kicking. As a result the backs were never given a chance. Laughland managed to engineer one good break which failed when his winger knocked on a vital pass. Then Scotland only converted one of five reasonably easy penalty kicks. In the second half the match swung as the result of one incident. Defending grimly France kicked a penalty given against Campbell-Lamerton for his treatment of an opponent. If justice had been done France should have been penalised for the offence which stung the Scot into an open but understandable retaliation. France gained heart from their lead and Crauste and Gensane broke away from a line out in a dribbling run which put the ball over the line. Rancoule outpaced the defence to touch down just short of the dead ball line. Before the whistle Albaladejo narrowly missed with two drop kicks.

| **WALES** | **Cardiff** | **3 February 1962** |

| **SCOTLAND:** | 1 goal, 1 try | 8 | **Win** |
| **WALES:** | 1 drop goal | 3 | |

Scotland: K.J.F. Scotland (*Leicester*); A.R. Smith* (*Edin. Wrs.*), J.J. McPartlin (*Oxford Univ.*), I.H.P. Laughland (*London Scot.*), R.C. Cowan (*Selkirk*); G.H. Waddell (*London Scot.*), S. Coughtrie (*Edin. Acads.*); H.F. McLeod (*Hawick*), N.S. Bruce (*London Scot.*), D.M.D. Rollo (*Howe of Fife*), F.H. ten Bos (*London Scot.*), M.J. Campbell-Lamerton (*Halifax*), R.J.C. Glasgow (*Dunfermline*), J. Douglas (*Stewart's FP*), K.I. Ross (*Boroughmuir FP*)

Wales: K. Coslett (*Aberavon*); D.R.R. Morgan (*Llanelli*), D.K. Jones (*Llanelli*), H.M. Roberts (*Cardiff*), D.I. Bell (*Swansea*); A. Rees (*Maesteg*), L.H. Williams* (*Cardiff*); D. Greenslade (*Newport*), B.V. Meredith (*Newport*), L.J. Cunningham (*Aberavon*), W.R. Evans (*Bridgend*), B.E.V. Price (*Newport*), R.H. Davies (*London Welsh*), A. Pask (*Abertillery*), H.J. Morgan (*Abertillery*)

Referee: N.M. Parkes (*England*) **Touch judges:** R.P. Burrell, J.P. Evans

R.J.C. Glasgow and F. ten Bos scored and K.J.F. Scotland converted the second (8–0).(H.T.). A. Rees dropped a goal(8–3).

In wretched conditions a storming display by the pack brought Scotland its first win at Cardiff since 1927 and although they started with the wind and rain behind them there was no weakening of effort in the second half when some Welsh pressure could only manage a drop goal. The massive Scottish second row, totalling 34½ stones, was most effective but there was little back play for under the conditions Coughtrie concentrated mainly on some accurate and lengthy kicking to touch. After fifteen minutes the pack held the ball in the scrum and then Douglas with ten Bos broke away and sent Glasgow over for the first score. Five minutes later Waddell put up a high kick which was misfielded; ten Bos picked up the rebound and his momentum did the rest.

IRELAND Lansdowne Road 24 February 1962

SCOTLAND:	1 goal, 1 drop goal, 2 penalty goals, 2 tries	20	**Win**
IRELAND:	1 penalty goal, 1 try	6	

Scotland: K.J.F. Scotland (*Leicester*); A.R. Smith* (*Edin. Wrs.*), J.J. McPartlin (*Oxford Univ.*), I.H.P. Laughland (*London Scot.*), R.C. Cowan (*Selkirk*); G.H. Waddell (*London Scot.*), S. Coughtrie (*Edin. Acads.*); H.F. McLeod (*Hawick*), N.S. Bruce (*London Scot.*), R. Steven (*Edin. Wrs.*), F.H. ten Bos (*London Scot.*), M.J. Campbell-Lamerton (*Halifax*), R.J.C. Glasgow (*Dunfermline*), J. Douglas (*Stewart's FP*), K.I. Ross (*Boroughmuir FP*)

Ireland: F.G. Gilpin (*QU Belfast*); W.R.H. Hunter (*CIYMS*), M.K. Flynn (*Wanderers*), D. Hewitt (*Instonians*), N.H. Brophy (*Blackrock*); G.G. Hardy (*Bective Rangers*), J.T.M. Quirke (*Blackrock*); S. Millar (*Ballymena*), A.R. Dawson (*Wanderers*), R.J. McLoughlin (*UC Dublin*), W.A. Mulcahy* (*Bohemians*), D. Scott (*Malone*), M.L. Hipwell (*Terenure*), M.G. Culliton (*Wanderers*)

Referee: N.M. Parkes (*England*) **Touch judges:** G.K. Rome, J. Griffin

K.J.F. Scotland kicked a penalty (3–0); A.R. Smith and R.C. Cowan scored but K.J.F.

Scotland failed to convert (9–0).(H.T.). W.R. Hunter kicked a penalty (9–3); W.R. Hunter scored but failed (9–6); K.J.F. Scotland kicked a penalty (12–6); A.R. Smith scored and K.J.F. Scotland converted (17–6); S. Coughtrie dropped a goal (20–6).

Scotland, while deserving to win, were rather flattered by the margin. The pack were rather beaten in the scrums but did rally strongly in the latter stages when Ireland with the wind staged a revival. The Scottish backs were very sound. Again Waddell, greatly helped by the fine form shown by Coughtrie, made good use of the touch line but did set his threes moving more than usual. Ireland started well against the wind and Hunter just failed to beat Cowan to the touch following a missed drop kick by Hardy. Then after a Scotland penalty Waddell burst through and when his long pass went to ground McPartlin snapped up the bouncing ball and sent Smith in at the corner. Shortly before half-time Waddell began another movement which finished with Cowan scoring. Soon after the interval Hunter got a penalty and a try, and Ireland looked dangerous. Flynn also touched down but he was brought back for offside. At this stage the Scottish pack held the challenge off. Then Scotland kicked a penalty before Smith scored after a good run by Coughtrie, Waddell and McLeod, and near full time Coughtrie dropped a goal from a wide angle.

ENGLAND   **Murrayfield**   **17 March 1962**

SCOTLAND:	1 penalty goal	**3**	**Draw**
ENGLAND:	1 penalty goal	**3**	

Scotland: K.J.F. Scotland (*Leicester*); A.R. Smith* (*Edin. Wrs.*), J.J. McPartlin (*Oxford Univ.*), I.H.P. Laughland (*London Scot.*), R.C. Cowan (*Selkirk*); G.H. Waddell (*London Scot.*), S. Coughtrie (*Edin. Acads.*); H.F. McLeod (*Hawick*), N.S. Bruce (*London Scot.*), D.M.D. Rollo (*Howe of Fife*), F.H. ten Bos (*London Scot.*), M.J. Campbell-Lamerton (*Halifax*), R.J.C. Glasgow (*Dunfermline*), J. Douglas (*Stewart's FP*), K.I. Ross (*Boroughmuir FP*)

England: J.G. Willcox (*Oxford Univ.*); A.C.B. Hurst (*Wasps*), A.M. Underwood (*Northampton*), J.M. Dee (*Hartlepool Rovers*), J. Roberts (*Sale*); J.P. Horrocks-Taylor (*Leicester*), R.E.G. Jeeps* (*Northampton*); P.E. Judd (*Coventry*), S.A.M. Hodgson (*Durham City*), T.P. Wright (*Blackheath*), T.A. Pargetter (*Coventry*), V.S.J. Harding (*Sale*), P.G.D. Robbins (*Coventry*), P.J. Taylor (*Northampton*), S.J. Purdy (*Rugby*)

    Referee: K.D. Kelleher (*Ireland*)   **Touch judges:** D.C.J. McMahon, A.E.R. Cotterill

J.G. Willcox kicked a penalty (0–3); K.J.F. Scotland kicked a penalty (3–3).(H.T.).

Once again England prevented Scotland from lifting the Triple Crown with the third penalty draw in five seasons. Scotland had their chances but let them slip for they held a definite territorial advantage especially during the last twenty minutes. Neither of two heavy packs could claim dominance and both sides made great use of the kick ahead as a form of attack so that back play was restricted. England were never really in a position to dictate the run of play yet were always capable of holding any Scottish attack and always ready to set up a counterattack; indeed Hurst nearly scored in the dying moments. Near half time Willcox kicked a good 50 yard penalty cancelled out almost at once by K.J.F. Scotland who had failed with three previous attempts.

FRANCE   Colombes   12 January 1963

SCOTLAND: 1 goal, 1 drop goal, 1 penalty goal 11 **Win**

FRANCE: 1 drop goal, 1 penalty goal   6

Scotland: K.J.F. Scotland* (*Leicester*); R.H. Thomson (*London Scot.*), J.A.P. Shackleton (*London Scot.*), D.M. White (*Kelvinside Acads.*), G.D. Stevenson (*Hawick*); I.H.P. Laughland (*London Scot.*), S. Coughtrie (*Edin. Acads.*); A.C.W. Boyle (*London Scot.*), N.S. Bruce (*London Scot.*). D.M.D. Rollo (*Howe of Fife*), F.H. ten Bos (*London Scot.*), M.J. Campbell-Lamerton (*Halifax*), K.I. Ross (*Boroughmuir*), J. Douglas (Stewart's FP), W.R.A. Watherston (*London Scot.*)

France: J.P. Razat (*Agen*); P. Besson (*Brive*), A. Boniface (*Mont-de-Marsan*), G. Boniface (*Mont-de-Marsan*), C. Darrouy (*Mont-de-Marsan*); P. Albaledejo (*Dax*), P. Lacroix* (*Agen*); F. Mas (*Beziers*), J. de Gregorio (*Grenoble*), A. Roques (*Cahors*), B. Mommejat (*Albi*), J.P. Saux (*Pau*), R. Gensane (*Beziers*), J. Fabre (*Toulouse*), M. Crauste (*Lourdes*)

Referee: R.C. Williams (*Ireland*) **Touch judges:** J.R. Hunter, B. Marie

A Boniface dropped a goal (0–3); P. Albaladejo kicked a penalty (0–6).(H.T.). K.J.F. Scotland dropped a goal and kicked a penalty (6–6); R.H. Thomson scored and K.J.F. Scotland converted (11–6).

Because of the severe frost the pitch, in spite of the protective straw, had remained uncomfortably hard so the ground staff left an inch or so of the straw lying, set fire to it and then swept the ashes off so that the game was played on a brownish grassless pitch. France started with the wind but their pack was so outweighted and outplayed that all they could manage by half time was a drop goal from A. Boniface (who halted in the middle of a passing movement to make his successful pot at goal) and a penalty by Albaladejo. In the second half Scotland took a firm grip on the game but it was twenty mintues before K.J.F. Scotland caught a faulty kick to touch and dropped a superb goal from near the line and fifteen minutes later equalised with a penalty yielded by a desperate defender handling the ball on the ground. Then right on 'no side' from a line out Campbell-Lamerton got possession and the ball went via Rollo to Laughland who from 45 yards out dropped at goal. The ball dropped short of the left hand post only to bounce wickedly high over Besson's head and Thomson, the right winger, appeared, seemingly from nowhere, gathered the ball in full cry to score in the left corner one of the most sensational tries on record, for the whistle went after the conversion.

WALES   Murrayfield   2 February 1963

SCOTLAND: Nil   0 **Loss**

WALES: 1 drop goal, 1 penalty goal   6

Scotland: K.J.F. Scotland* (*Heriot's FP*); R.H. Thomson (*London Scot.*), J.A.P. Shackle-

251

ton (*London Scot.*), D.M. White (*Kelvinside Acads.*), G.D. Stevenson (*Hawick*); I.H.P. Laughland (*London Scot.*), S. Coughtrie (*Edin. Acads.*); A.C.W. Boyle (*London Scot.*), N.S. Bruce (*London Scot.*), D.M.D. Rollo (*Howe of Fife*), F.H. ten Bos (*London Scot.*), M.J. Campbell-Lamerton (*Halifax*), K.I. Ross (*Boroughmuir*), J. Douglas (*Stewart's FP*), W.R.A. Watherston (*London Scot.*)

Wales: G.T.R. Hodgson (*Neath*); D.R.R. Morgan (*Llanelli*), R. Evans (*Bridgend*), D.B. Davies (*Llanelli*), W.J. Morris (*Pontypool*); D. Watkins (*Newport*), D.C.T. Rowlands* (*Pontypool*); D. Williams (*Ebbw Vale*), N.R. Gale (*Llanelli*), K.D. Jones (*Cardiff*), B.E.V. Price (*Newport*), B.E. Thomas (*Camb. Univ.*), G. Jones (*Ebbw Vale*), A.E.I. Pask (*Abertillery*), H.J. Morgan (*Abertillery*)

Referee: R.C. Williams (*Ireland*)   **Touch judges:** J.G.R. Howie, T. Pritchard

G.T.R. Hodgson kicked a penalty (0–3).(H.T.). D.C.T. Rowlands dropped a goal (0–6).

This must rank as the dreariest match ever played. The Welsh pack gave Rowlands a major share of the ball but the Welsh captain embarked on a rigid policy of kicking to touch and it was recorded later that there were 111 line outs during the afternoon. At least he could claim that his tactics broke a run of four defeats at Murrayfield. Unfortunately the Scottish halves with less of the ball also tended to kick and it was not until far on in the second half that their backs were set moving. Then too late it was obvious that they had the ability to worry the opposition. In the first half Hodgson kicked a good penalty against the wind and after the interval Rowlands, from the line, dropped a very good angled goal.

IRELAND   Murrayfield   23 February 1963

SCOTLAND:	1 penalty goal	3	Win
IRELAND:	Nil	0	

Scotland: C.F. Blaikie (*Heriot's FP*); R.H. Thomson (*London Scot.*), I.H.P. Laughland (*London Scot.*), D.M. White (*Kelvinside Acads.*), G.D. Stevenson (*Hawick*); K.J.F. Scotland* (*Heriot's FP*), S. Coughtrie (*Edin. Acads.*); A.C.W. Boyle (*London Scot.*), N.S. Bruce (*London Scot.*), D.M.D. Rollo (*Howe of Fife*), F.H. ten Bos (*London Scot.*), M.J. Campbell-Lamerton (*Halifax*), R.J.C. Glasgow (*Dunfermline*), J. Douglas (*Stewart's FP*), W.R.A. Watherston (*London Scot.*)

Ireland: T.J. Kiernan (*UC Cork*); W.R. Hunter (*CIYMC*), J.C. Walsh (*UC Cork*), P.J. Casey (*UC Dublin*), A.J.F. O'Reilly (*Old Belvedere*); M.A.F. English (*Lansdowne*), J.C. Kelly (*UC Dublin*); S. Millar (*Ballymena*), A.R. Dawson (*Wanderers*), R.J. McLoughlin (*Gosforth*), W.A. Mulcahy* (*Bective Rangers*), W.J. McBride (*Ballymena*), E.P. McGuire (*UC Galway*), C.J. Dick (*Ballymena*), M.D. Kiely (*Lansdowne*)

Referee: G.J. Trehavre (*Wales*)   **Touch judges:** P.A. Macdonald, G.A. Jamieson

S. Coughtrie kicked a penalty (3–0).(H.T.).

Ireland could be regarded as unlucky for they ran the ball frequently and indeed came near to scoring more than once, but the intrusion of the penalty goal into the modern game was marked. Coughtrie missed three long range kicks before kicking a penalty after 36 minutes.

252

Scotland played a forward game but the pack, already suspect after the Welsh game, never got on top — they were, however, handicapped by an injury to Boyle. He changed places with ten Bos who was clearly not suited to the prop position. Glasgow, the oldest man on the field, again shone in the open, his fiercesome tackling being much in evidence. K.J.F. Scotland, handicapped by slow heeling, was much troubled by the Irish back row and had to kick more often than pass.

ENGLAND   Twickenham   16 March 1963

SCOTLAND:	1 goal, 1 drop goal	8	Loss
ENGLAND:	2 goals	10	

Scotland: C.F. Blaikie (*Heriot's FP*); C. Elliot (*Langholm*), B.C. Henderson (*Edin. Wrs.*), D.M. White (*Kelvinside Acads.*), R.H. Thomson (*London Scot.*); K.J.F. Scotland* (*Heriot's FP*), S. Coughtrie (*Edin. Acads.*); J.B. Neill (*Edin. Acads.*), N.S. Bruce (*London Scot.*), D.M.D. Rollo (*Howe of Fife*), F.H. ten Bos (*London Scot.*), M.J. Campbell-Lamerton (*Halifax*), R.J.C. Glasgow (*Dunfermline*), J.P. Fisher (*RHSFP*), K.I. Ross (*Boroughmuir*)

England: J.G. Willcox (*Harlequins*); P.B. Jackson (*Coventry*), M.S. Phillips (*Fylde*), M.P. Weston (*Durham City*), J. Roberts (*Sale*); R.A.W. Sharp* (*Wasps*), S.J.S. Clarke (*Camb. Univ.*); P.E. Judd (*Coventry*), H.O. Godwin (*Coventry*), N.J. Drake-Lee (*Camb. Univ.*), A.M. Davis (*Torquay A.*), J.E. Owen (*Coventry*), D.P. Rogers (*Bedford*), D.G. Perry (*Bedford*), D.C. Manley (*Exeter*)

Referee: G. Walters (*Wales*)   **Touch judges:** T.E. Grierson, W.J. Willeard

R.J.C. Glasgow scored and S. Coughtrie converted (5–0); K.J.F. Scotland dropped a goal (8–0); N.J. Drake-Lee scored and J.G. Willcox converted (8–5).(H.T.). R.A.W. Sharp scored and J.G. Wilcox converted (8–10).

Both teams showed changes, England having a new front row while Scotland made alterations to the threes and brought two new caps into the pack. Scotland with the wind made an impressive start and after some strong forward play Glasgow broke from a long line out to score. Later Willcox was caught with the ball and a quick heel let K.J.F. Scotland drop a goal. Before half time Sharp started a movement and passed to Jackson whose kick ahead was taken on by his forwards for Drake-Lee to go over. Early in the second half from a scrum close to the right touch line Clarke put out a good pass to Sharp who feinted to pass out to Weston but cutting back into the gap ran some 40 yards to score a classic try. Scotland fought back desperately but a stern defence kept them out.

FRANCE   Murrayfield   4 January 1964

SCOTLAND:	2 goals	10	Win
FRANCE:	Nil	0	

Scotland: S. Wilson (*Oxford Univ.*); C. Elliot (*Langholm*), B.C. Henderson (*Edin. Wrs.*), I.H.P. Laughland (*London Scot.*), R.H. Thomson (*London Scot.*); G. Sharp (*Stewart's FP*); J.A.T. Rodd (*London Scot.*); J.B. Neill* (*Edin. Acads.*), N.S. Bruce (*London Scot.*), D.M.D. Rollo (*Howe of Fife*), W.J. Hunter (*Hawick*), P.C. Brown (*West of Scot.*), J.W. Telfer (*Melrose*), T.O. Grant (*Hawick*), J.P. Fisher (*RHSFP*)

France: C. Lacaze (*Angouleme*); J. Gachassin (*Lourdes*), G. Boniface (*Mont-de-Marsan*), A. Boniface (*Mont-de-Marsan*), J. Dupuy (*Tarbes*); P. Albaladejo (*Dax*), J.C. Lasserre (*Dax*); J.C. Berejnoi (*Tulle*), J.M. Cabanier (*Montauban*), J. Bayardon (*Chalon*), D. Dauga (*Mont-de-Marsan*), J.le Droff (*Auch*), J.J. Rupert (*Tyrosse*), J. Fabre* (*Toulouse*), M. Crauste (*Lourdes*)

Referee: R.C. Williams (*Ireland*)   **Touch judges:** D. Hill, M. Laurent

I.H.P. Laughland scored and S. Wilson converted (5–0).(H.T.). R.H. Thomson scored and S. Wilson converted (10–0).

Conditions were unpleasant for a heavy rain left surface water on the pitch. Nevertheless France handled often and well especially in the second half when both backs and forwards indulged in some spectacular interpassing with sudden changes in direction and they only failed against a very strong defence. Wilson was sound at full back, Henderson's tackling was as murderous as ever and the back row of Telfer, Grant and Fisher were good in the line out and cover defence. Midway through the first half Fisher and Henderson moved onto a loose pass and started a rush which ended in Laughland scoring. The second try came just before full time. A. Boniface, caught in possession parted with the ball but Thomson intercepted and ran from the 25 to score.

NEW ZEALAND   Murrayfield   18 January 1964

SCOTLAND:	Nil	**0**	**Draw**
NEW ZEALAND:	Nil	**0**	

Scotland: S. Wilson (*Oxford Univ.*); C. Elliot (*Langholm*), J.A.P. Shackleton (*London Scot.*), I.H.P. Laughland (*London Scot.*), R.H. Thomson (*London Scot.*); G. Sharp (*Stewart's FP*), J.A.T. Rodd (*London Scot.*); J.B. Neill* (*Edin. Acads.*), N.S. Bruce (*London Scot.*), D.M.D. Rollo (*Howe of Fife*), W.J. Hunter (*Hawick*), P.C. Brown (*West of Scot.*), J.W. Telfer (*Melrose*), T.O. Grant (*Hawick*), J.P. Fisher (*RHSFP*)

New Zealand: D.B. Clarke (*Waikato*); R.W. Coulton (*Wellington*), P.F. Little (*Auckland*), M.J. Dick (*Auckland*); M.A. Herewini (*Auckland*); B.A. Watt (*Canterbury*), K.C. Briscoe (*Taranaki*); K.F. Gray (*Wellington*), D. Young (*Canterbury*), W.J. Whineray* (*Auckland*), B.J. Lochore (*Wairarapa*), A.J. Stewart (*Canterbury*), C.E. Meads (*King Country*), D.J. Graham (*Canterbury*), K.R. Tremain (*Hawkes Bay*)

Referee: R.C. Williams (*Ireland*)   **Touch judges:** A.S.R. Davidson, E.W. Kirton

This was a splendid performance by Scotland for the tourists finished by beating all the other Home Countries and France. Indeed with a bit of luck Scotland might have won, for at least three times they seriously threatened the New Zealand line whereas only once did the visitors look like scoring. For the first fifteen minutes the powerful New Zealand pack set about softening up the opposition only to meet with a completely successful resistance. The lighter Scottish pack beaten in the scrums, were quicker onto the ball in the loose and their backing up and cover defence were first rate. In view of the poor conditions Sharp preferred to kick and this reduced the chances for New Zealand who had shown themselves masters at attacking from their opponents' mistakes. All the wingers had a lean time. In a final bid to win New Zealand made much use of high speculative kicks only to find that Wilson was not only dead safe but also capable and willing to come forward with the ball in attack.

WALES   Cardiff   1 February 1964

SCOTLAND:	1 try	3	**Loss**
WALES:	1 goal, 1 penalty goal, 1 try	11	

Scotland: S. Wilson (*Oxford Univ.*); C. Elliot (*Langholm*), J.A.P. Shackleton (*London Scot.*), I.H.P. Laughland (*London Scot.*), R.H. Thomson (*London Scot.*); G. Sharp (*Stewart's FP*), J.A.T. Rodd (*London Scot.*); J.B. Neill* (*Edin. Acads.*), N.S. Bruce (*London Scot.*), D.M.D. Rollo (*Howe of Fife*), W.J. Hunter (*Hawick*), P.C. Brown (*West of Scot.*), J.W. Telfer (*Melrose*), T.O. Grant (*Hawick*), J.P. Fisher (*RHSFP*)

Wales: G.T.R. Hodgson (*Neath*); S.J. Watkins (*Newport*), D.K. Jones (*Llanelli*), K. Bradshaw (*Bridgend*), D.I. Bebb (*Swansea*); D. Watkins (*Newport*), D.C.T. Rowlands* (*Pontypool*); D. Williams (*Ebbw Vale*), N.R. Gale (*Llanelli*), L.J. Cunningham (*Aberavon*), B. Price (*Neath*), B.E. Thomas (*Neath*), G.J. Prothero (*Bridgend*), A.I.E. Pask (*Abertillery*), D.J. Hayward (*Cardiff*)

Referee: P.G. Brook (*England*)   **Touch judges:** J. Dun, A.I. Griffiths

I.H.P. Laughland scored but S. Wilson failed (3–0).(H.T.). K. Bradshaw scored and converted (3–5); K. Bradshaw kicked a penalty (3–8); B.E. Thomas scored but K. Bradshaw failed (3–11).

Scotland played far below their standard of the New Zealand game and the score did not exaggerate the Welsh supremacy but at least there was no cracking up under the continual pressure of the latter stages. Rowlands this year changed his tactics and used high attacking kicks rather than aiming at touch. Scotland, starting with the sun and wind at their backs made a good start. Sharp hoisted an up and under, and when the clearance was missed Laughland came up fast enough to dive on the ball and score. Early in the second half Rowlands broke away and sent Bradshaw in. The scorer converted the try and a penalty soon afterwards. Continual pressure saw Thomas plunge over but although Scotland fought on their pack could not beat a strong Welsh eight.

IRELAND   Lansdowne Road   22 February 1964

SCOTLAND:	2 penalty goals	6	**Win**
IRELAND:	1 penalty goal	3	

Scotland: S. Wilson (*Oxford Univ.*); C. Elliot (*Langholm*), B.C. Henderson (*Edin. Wrs.*), I.H.P. Laughland (*London Scot.*), W.D. Jackson (*Hawick*); D.H. Chisholm (*Melrose*), A.J. Hastie (*Melrose*); J.B. Neill* (*Edin. Acads.*), N.S. Bruce (*London Scot.*), D.M.D. Rollo (*Howe of Fife*), P.C. Brown (*West of Scot.*), M.J. Campbell-Lamerton (*London Scot.*), J.W. Telfer (*Melrose*), J.P. Fisher (*RHSFP*), R.J.C. Glasgow (*Dunfermline*)

Ireland: T.J. Kiernan (*Cork Const.*); P.J. Casey (*UC Dublin*), M.K. Flynn (*Wanderers*), J.C. Walsh (*UC Cork*), K.J. Houston (*QU Belfast*); C.M.H. Gibson (*Camb. Univ.*), J.C. Kelly (*UC Dublin*); P.J. Dwyer (*UC Dublin*), A.R. Dawson (*Wanderers*), R.J. McLoughlin (*Gosforth*), W.A. Mulcahy* (*Bective Rangers*), W.J. McBride (*Ballymena*), E.P. McGuire (*UC Galway*), M.G. Culliton (*Wanderers*), N.A.A. Murphy (*Cork Const.*)

Referee: A.C. Luff (*England*) **Touch judges:** C.R.G. Reid, M. Barry

S. Wilson kicked two penalties (6–0).(H.T.). T.J. Kiernan kicked a penalty (6–3).

Scotland started with the rain and wind in their favour but could only manage two 40 yard penalties by Wilson before the interval. Early in the second half Kiernan, who was timed to take a deliberate 105 seconds to place the ball, also kicked a penalty but against the elements Scotland, with their pack clearly in control, closed the game up — a style of play at which the Melrose halves excelled. The young and gifted Gibson got little chance against a vigorous defence by Glasgow but it must be noted that McLoughlin was sadly handicapped by a leg injury sustained during the first half.

ENGLAND Murrayfield 21 March 1964

SCOTLAND:	3 goals	15	**Win**
ENGLAND:	1 penalty goal, 1 try	6	

Scotland: S. Wilson (*Oxford Univ.*); C. Elliot (*Langholm*), B.C. Henderson (*Edin. Wrs.*), I.H.P. Laughland (*London Scot.*), G.D. Stevenson (*Hawick*); D.H. Chisholm (*Melrose*), A.J. Hastie (*Melrose*); J.B. Neill* (*Edin. Acads.*), N.S. Bruce (*London Scot.*), D.M.D. Rollo (*Howe of Fife*), P.C. Brown (*West of Scot.*), M.J. Campbell-Lamerton (*London Scot.*), J.P. Fisher (*RHSFP*), J.W. Telfer (*Melrose*), R.J.C. Glasgow (*Dunfermline*)

England: J.G. Willcox (*Harlequins*); R.W. Hosen (*Northampton*), M.S. Phillips (*Fylde*), M.P. Weston (*Durham City*), J.M. Ranson (*Rosslyn Park*); T.J. Brophy (*Liverpool*), S.R. Smith (*Blackheath*); C.R. Jacobs* (*Northampton*), H.O. Godwin (*Coventry*), D.F.B. Wrench (*Harlequins*), C.M. Payne (*Harlequins*), A.M. Davis (*Torquay A*), P.J. Ford (*Gloucester*), T.G.A.H. Peart (*Hartlepool Rovers*), D.P. Rogers (*Bedford*)

Referee: R.C. Williams (*Ireland*) **Touch judges:** D. McIntyre, J. Burgum

R.J.C. Glasgow and N.S. Bruce scored and S. Wilson converted both (10–0).(H.T.). R.W. Hosen kicked a penalty (10–3); J.W. Telfer scored and S. Wilson converted (15–3); D.P. Rogers scored but R.W. Hosen failed (10–6).

This was a very convincing win with much of the credit going to the Scottish forwards. They were solid in the scrums and well in top in the loose, being faster on to the ball and showing an ability to handle. Their aggressive back row was again in evidence; Fisher exhibiting his basket ball skills at the tail of the line out. The backs too played well Henderson being especially effective with his hearty tackling while Wilson again played an attacking game from full back. After half an hour Telfer picked up and passed to Glasgow who fairly crashed over for the opening score and near the interval further passing between Brown and Telfer put Bruce over. Early in the second half Hosen kicked a good 45 yard penalty but Scotland were not disturbed and Stevenson was nearly in at the corner before a break by Hastie was finished off by a spectacular try by Telfer. In spite of this the English pack fought back and near the close succeeded in scoring a pushover try credited to Rogers.

FRANCE Colombes 9 January 1965

SCOTLAND: 1 goal, 1 try   8   **Loss**

FRANCE: 2 goals, 2 tries   16

Scotland: K.J.F. Scotland (*Aberdeenshire*); C. Elliot (*Langholm*), B.C. Henderson (*Edin. Wrs.*), I.H.P. Laughland (*London Scot.*), G.D. Stevenson (*Hawick*); B.M. Simmers (*Glas. Acads.*), J.A.T. Rodd (*London Scot.*); J.B. Neill* (*Edin. Acads.*), F.A.L. Laidlaw (*Melrose*), D.M.D. Rollo (*Howe of Fife*), P.K. Stagg (*Sale*), M.J. Campbell-Lamerton (*London Scot.*), D. Grant (*Hawick*), J.W. Telfer (*Melrose*), J.P. Fisher (*London Scot.*)

France: P. Dedieu (*Beziers*); J. Gachassin (*Lourdes*), G. Boniface (*Mont-de-Marsan*), J. Pique (*Pau*), C. Darrouy (*Mont-de-Marsan*); J.P. Capdouze (*Pau*), L. Camberabero, (*La Voulte*); A. Gruarin (*Toulon*), J.M. Cabonier (*Montauban*), J.C. Berejnoi (*Tulle*), W. Spanghero (*Narbonne*), D. Dauga (*Mont-de-Marsan*), M. Lira (*La Voulte*), A. Herrero (*Toulon*), M. Crauste (*Lourdes*)

Referee: K.D. Kelleher (*Ireland*)   Touch judges: I. Young, B. Marie

J. Gachassin scored and P. Dedieu converted (0–5); B.C. Henderson scored and K.J.F. Scotland converted (5–5).(H.T.). C. Darrouy and J. Pique scored but P. Dedieu failed (5–11); B.C. Henderson scored but K.J.F. Scotland failed (8–11); C. Darrouy scored and P. Dedieu converted (8–16).

With the new hooker doing well Scotland tried to play an open game but France with a clear edge in pace and team work fully deserved their win. Almost at once a well placed kick ahead bounced kindly for Pique who gave Gachassin a clear run in. Following some broken play Laughland made a break and the ball went via Fisher to Henderson who ran in his most aggressive style for 40 yards past and through several opponents to bring the scores level at half time. Soon after restarting a clearance kick was blocked by Darroux who went on to score and then Pique with a neat switch of direction beat the defence. Simmers broke from well inside his own half; the ball went along the line to Elliot and back to Simmers who sent Henderson over. Finally a bad pass by Rodd to Laughland arrived with Crauste who unceremoniously upended the centre and the ball was quickly worked clear to Darrouy for his second score.

WALES Murrayfield 6 February 1965

SCOTLAND: 2 drop goals, 2 penalty goals   12   **Loss**

WALES: 1 goal, 2 penalty goals, 1 try   14

Scotland: S. Wilson (*London Scot.*); C. Elliot (*Langholm*), B.C. Henderson (*Edin. Wrs.*), I.H.P. Laughland (*London Scot.*), D.J. Whyte (*Edin. Wrs.*); B.M. Simmers (*Glas. Acads.*), J.A.T. Rodd (*London Scot.*); N. Suddon (*Hawick*), F.A.L. Laidlaw (*Melrose*), D.M.D. Rollo (*Howe of Fife*), P.K. Stagg (*Sale*), M.J. Campbell-Lamerton* (*London Scot.*), J.P. Fisher (*London Scot.*), J.W. Telfer (*Melrose*), R.J.C. Glasgow (*Dunfermline*)

Wales: T.G. Price (*Llanelli*); S.J. Watkins (*Newport*), J.R. Uzzell (*Newport*), S.J. Dawes (*London Welsh*), D.I. Bebb (*Swansea*); D. Watkins (*Newport*), D.C.T. Rowlands* (*Pontypool*); D. Williams (*Ebbw Vale*), N.R. Gale (*Llanelli*), R. Waldron (*Neath*), B. Price (*Newport*), W.J. Morris (*Newport*), G.J. Prothero (*Bridgend*), A.I.E. Pask (*Abertillery*), H.J. Morgan (*Abertillery*)

Referee: R.W. Gilliland (*Ireland*)   **Touch judges:** G.G. Murray, O.P. Bevan

B.M. Simmers dropped a goal (3–0); T.G. Price kicked a penalty (3–3); S. Wilson kicked a penalty (6–3); S.J. Watkins scored and T.G. Price converted (6–8).(H.T.). T.G. Price kicked a penalty (6–11); S. Wilson kicked a penalty (9–11); B.M. Simmers dropped a goal (12–11); N.R. Gale scored but T.G. Price failed (12–14).

This was a most exciting game won by Wales in the dying minutes. The forward exchanges were always vigorous but one gave as good as the other. Again Fisher's skill at the tail of the line was evident and Glasgow's tackling worried Watkins at half. Simmers started well and dropped a nice long goal after a pass from a set scrum but his knee gave way so that his play and that of the backs was unsettled. After an exchange of penalties Watkins went away on the blind side and stabbed the ball on. A lame Simmers failed to get the ball into touch and Watkins was able to collect and go on to score.

After half time and another exchange of penalties Scotland took the lead with another drop by Simmers after a set scrum in front of the posts. Then in the last minutes a Scottish throw in was badly deflected and Gale grabbed the ball and crashed over for the winning score.

IRELAND   Murrayfield   27 February 1965

SCOTLAND: 1 drop goal, 1 penalty goal   6   Loss

IRELAND: 2 goals, 1 drop goal, 1 try   16

Scotland: S. Wilson (*London Scot.*); C. Elliot (*Langholm*), B.C. Henderson (*Edin. Wrs.*), J.A.P. Shackleton (*London Scot.*), D.J. Whyte (*Edin. Wrs.*); I.H.P. Laughland (*London Scot.*), J.A.T. Rodd (*London Scot.*); N. Suddon (*Hawick*), F.A.L. Laidlaw (*Melrose*), D.M.D. Rollo (*Howe of Fyfe*), P.C. Brown (*West of Scot.*), M.J. Campbell-Lamerton* (*London Scot.*), J.P. Fisher (*London Scot.*), J.W. Telfer (*Melrose*), R.J.C. Glasgow (*Dunfermline*)

Ireland: T.J. Kiernan (*Cork Const.*); P.J. Casey (*Lansdowne*), J.C. Walsh (*UC Cork*), M.K. Flynn (*Wanderers*), P.J. McGrath (*UC Cork*); C.M.H. Gibson (*Camb. Univ.*), R.M. Young (*QU Belfast*); S. MacHale (*Lansdowne*), K.W. Kennedy (*QU Belfast*), R.J. McLoughlin* (*Gosforth*), W.J. McBride (*Ballymena*), W.A. Mulcahy (*Bective Rangers*), M.G. Doyle (*UC Dublin*), H. Wall (*Dolphin*), N.A.A. Murphy (*Cork Const.*)

I.H.P. Laughland dropped a goal (3–0); P.J. McGarth and R.M. Young scored and T.J. Kiernan converted the second (3–8).(H.T.). C.M.H. Gibson dropped a goal (3–11); N.A.A. Murphy scored and T.J. Kiernan converted (3–16); S. Wilson kicked a penalty (6–16).

Ireland, greatly helped by defensive weaknesses, were clear winners. Neither pack could claim domination in the line outs or scrums but the swift heeling from the set scrums gave Gibson a freedom which let him dictate the run of play. Scotland scored from the first scrum in front of the Irish posts but a swift passing run amongst the Irish threes put McGrath in and then a dummy scissors move by Flynn let Young clear away. In the second half Gibson dropped a goal before Murphy, peeling off on the blind side of a scrum, took Young's pass and found himself clear away for a score.

ENGLAND   Twickenham   20 March 1965

SCOTLAND:	1 drop goal	3	**Draw**
ENGLAND:	1 try	3	

Scotland: S. Wilson* (*London Scot.*); D.J. Whyte (*Edin. Wrs.*), B.C. Henderson (*Edin. Wrs.*), I.H.P. Laughland (*London Scot.*), W.D. Jackson (*Hawick*); D.H. Chisholm (*Melrose*), A.J. Hastie (*Melrose*); N. Suddon (*Hawick*), F.A.L. Laidlaw (*Melrose*), D.M.D. Rollo (*Howe of Fife*), P.K. Stagg (*Sale*), M.J. Campbell-Lamerton (*London Scot.*), J.P. Fisher (*London Scot.*), P.C. Brown (*West of Scot.*), D. Grant (*Hawick*)

England: D. Rutherford (*Gloucester*); E.L. Rudd (*Oxford Univ.*), D.W.A. Rosser (*Camb. Univ.*), G.P. Frankcorn (*Camb. Univ.*), A.W. Hancock (*Northampton*); M.P. Weston (*Durham City*), S.J.S. Clarke (*Blackheath*); A.L. Horton (*Blackheath*), S.B. Richards (*Richmond*), P.E. Judd (*Coventry*), J.E. Owen (*Coventry*), C.M. Payne (*Harlequins*), N. Silk (*Harlequins*), D.G. Perry* (*Bedford*), D.P. Rogers (*Bedford*)

Referee: D.G. Walters (*Wales*)   **Touch judges:** D. Haultain, D.L. Head

There was no scoring before half time. D.H. Chisholm dropped a goal (3–0); A.W. Hancock scored a try but D. Rutherford failed (3–3).

This was Hancock's match, for it was his extraordinary last minute try which denied Scotland a much desired win at Twickenham. After an early thrust by England, Scotland held the advantage during the first half and had such an obvious grip on the game later that the single score made shortly after half time seemed adequate especially as Chisholm and Hastie came near to scoring. Then in injury time Whyte got the ball inside the English 25. Had he kicked the ball dead the whistle may well have gone for no side but he, being relatively clear, ran for the line and was tackled. From the ensuing rush Weston got the ball, moved to the blind side and still inside the 25 passed to Hancock who set off along the left touch line. At least three defenders came across at him but a hand off and change of pace kept him free and with Laughland at his heels he crossed the line and was content to touch down at once. Rutherford failed with the kick from the touch line and the whistle went.

Murrayfield   **17 April 1965**

SCOTLAND: 1 goal, 1 drop goal   8   **Win**

SOUTH AFRICA: 1 goal   5

Scotland: S. Wilson* (*London Scot.*); D.J. Whyte (*Edin. Wrs.*), J.A.P. Shackleton (*London Scot.*), I.H.P. Laughland (*London Scot.*), W.D. Jackson (*Hawick*); D.H. Chisholm (*Melrose*), A.J. Hastie (*Melrose*); N. Suddon (*Hawick*), F.A.L. Laidlaw (*Melrose*), D.M.D. Rollo (*Howe of Fife*), P.K. Stagg (*Sale*), M.J. Campbell-Lamerton (*London Scot.*), J.P. Fisher (*London Scot.*), P.C. Brown (*West of Scot.*), D. Grant (*Hawick*)

South Africa: L.G. Wilson (*WP*); J.P. Englebrecht (*WP*), W.J. Mans (*WP*), J.L. Gainsford (*WP*), C.W. Dirksen (*EN Transvaal*); J.H. Barnard (*T*), D.J. De Vos (*WP*); S.P. Kuhn (*T*), D.C. Walton (*Natal*), J.F.K. Marais (*WP*), A.S. Malan* (*T*), G. Carelse (*EP*), J. Schoeman (*WP*), D.J. Hopwood (*WP*), M.R. Suter (*Natal*)

Referee: D.G. Walters (*Wales*)   **Touch judges:** J.A.H. Blake

J.A.P. Shackleton scored and S. Wilson converted (5–0).(H.T.). J.P. Englebrecht scored and W.J. Mans converted (5–5); D.H. Chisholm dropped a goal (8–5).

South Africa had undertaken a short tour of Ireland and Scotland at the beginning of their season and were obviously short of match practice. This was a narrow but sound win for Scotland for the visitors clearly tired before the finish and there was no doubt that the Scottish pack did well at the line out and in the loose. Again the Melrose halves had a good game, Chisholm making many fine breaks but was not so well supported as usual by the back row. After ten minutes Chisholm hoisted a high kick to the posts and when the full back failed to hold a swinging ball Shackleton was up to pick and score. Soon after the interval De Vos made a good break from a ruck and the ball went via Gainsford to Engelbrecht who beat the full back with alarming ease. Tremendous Scottish pressure followed but all that was achieved was a good drop goal from a wide angle by Chisholm after a quick heel. South Africa had one last attack: De Vos put Engelbrecht away but this time Wilson tackled him firmly and an inside pass was intercepted by Shackleton whose kick to touch finished the match.

FRANCE   **Murrayfield**   **15 January 1966**

SCOTLAND: 1 try   3   **Draw**

FRANCE: 1 penalty goal   3

Scotland: S. Wilson* (*London Scot.*); A.J.W. Hinshelwood (*London Scot.*), B.C. Henderson (*Edin. Wrs.*), I.H.P. Laughland (*London Scot.*), D.J. Whyte (*Edin. Wrs.*); D.H. Chisholm (*Melrose*), A.J. Hastie (*Melrose*); J.D. Macdonald (*London Scot.*), F.A.L. Laidlaw (*Melrose*), D.M.D. Rollo (*Howe of Fife*), P.K. Stagg (*Sale*), M.J. Campbell-Lamerton

(*London Scot.*), J.P. Fisher (*London Scot.*), J.W. Telfer (*Melrose*), D. Grant (*Hawick*)

France: C. Lacaze (*Angouleme*); J. Gachassin (*Lourdes*), G. Boniface (*Mont-de-Marsan*), A. Boniface (*Mont-de-Marsan*), C. Darrouy (*Mont-de-Marsan*); J.C. Roques (*Brive*), M. Puget (*Brive*); A. Gruarin (*Toulon*), J.M. Cabanier (*Montauban*), J.C. Berejnoi (*Tulle*), W. Spanghero (*Narbonne*), E. Cester (*TOEC*), J.J. Rupert (*Tyrosse*), D. Dauga (*Mont-de-Marsan*), M. Crauste* (*Lourdes*)

   Referee: D.M. Hughes (*Wales*)   **Touch judges:** G.V. Cooper, M. Laurent

C. Lacaze kicked a penalty (0–3); D.J. Whyte scored but S. Wilson failed (3–3).(H.T.).

Scotland played well but failed to turn their territorial and tactical advantages into points. Their pack was well on top. As Garcia puts it, '*c'est encore l'enfer pour les avants français*'. Laidlaw hooked very well, Stagg, Campbell-Lamerton and Fisher shone at the line out and the famous French peel at the tail never got going. As a result the French halves had an unhappy afternoon. In contrast the Scottish pair were very sound giving no loose chances for the French back row to snap up. Yet France scored first after fifteen minutes — admittedly by a penalty kick — before Chisholm sparked off a great handling movement. He moved inside G. Boniface and the ball went from Henderson and Laughland to Whyte who made a good run. When hemmed in by the cover defence the attack swung infield and a pass by Fisher reached Campbell-Lamerton before Hastie with a long pass set Whyte diving in at the corner. After half time Scotland missed three kickable penalties and Chisholm failed with two drops. On one occasion near the posts he kicked neatly on and was blatantly obstructed but the referee, understandably, was watching the ball and missed the incident.

WALES   Cardiff   5 February 1966

SCOTLAND: 1 penalty goal   3   **Loss**
WALES: 1 goal, 1 try   8

Scotland: S. Wilson* (*London Scot.*); A.J.W. Hinshelwood (*London Scot.*), B.C. Henderson (*Edin. Wrs.*), I.H.P. Laughland (*London Scot.*), D.J. Whyte (*Edin. Wrs.*); J.W.C. Turner (*Gala*), A.J. Hastie (*Melrose*); J.D. Macdonald (*London Scot.*), F.A.L. Laidlaw (*Melrose*), D.M.D. Rollo (*Howe of Fife*), P.K. Stagg (*Sale*), M.J. Campbell-Lamerton (*London Scot.*), J.P. Fisher (*London Scot.*), J.W. Telfer (*Melrose*), D. Grant (*Hawick*)

Wales: T.G.R. Hodgson (*Neath*); S.J. Watkins (*Newport*), D.K. Jones (*Cardiff*), K. Bradshaw (*Bridgend*), L. Davies (*Bridgend*); D. Watkins (*Newport*), A.R. Lewis (*Abertillery*); D. Williams (*Ebbw Vale*), N.R. Gale (*Llanelli*), D.J. Lloyd (*Bridgend*), B. Price (*Newport*), B.E. Thomas (*Neath*), G.J. Prothero (*Bridgend*), A.I.E. Pask* (*Abertillery*), H.J. Morgan (*Abertillery*)

   Referee: M.H. Titcomb (*England*)   **Touch judges:** T. Pearson, I. Davies

D.K. Jones scored but K. Bradshaw failed (0–3).(H.T.). D.K. Jones scored and K. Bradshaw converted (0–8); S. Wilson kicked a penalty (3–8).

This game was played on a sodden, sticky muddy field swept by driving rain and Scotland did well to hold the score down in the first half. After some 15 minutes Watkins, at a scrum,

261

ran left but Lewis fed Jones on the right. The ball went out to Watkins who passed back to Jones for his try. After the interval a typical bruising tackle by Henderson produced a loose ball which Hinshelwood picked up and hurled himself at the line. Instead of mauling the ball on over the line the pack heeled and nothing came of the move. Now against the wind Wales rallied and from a scrum Watkins, who had all through been most elusive, made a lovely break which finished with a try by Jones. Scotland were by no means overwhelmed but their pack lacked speed and cohesion and all that could be achieved was a penalty goal.

IRELAND   Lansdowne Road   26 February 1966

| **SCOTLAND:** | 1 goal, 2 tries | 11 | **Win** |
| **IRELAND:** | 1 penalty goal | 3 | |

Scotland: S. Wilson (*London Scot.*); A.J.W. Hinshelwood (*London Scot.*), B.C. Henderson (*Edin. Wrs.*), I.H.P. Laughland* (*London Scot.*), D.J. Whyte (*Edin. Wrs.*); D.H. Chisholm (*Melrose*), A.J. Hastie (*Melrose*); J.D. Macdonald (*London Scot.*), F.A.L. Laidlaw (*Melrose*), D.M.D. Rollo (*Howe of Fife*), P.K. Stagg (*Sale*), M.J. Campbell-Lamerton (*London Scot.*), J.P. Fisher (*London Scot.*), J.W. Telfer (*Melrose*), D. Grant (*Hawick*)

Ireland: T.J. Kiernan (*Cork Const.*); W.R. Hunter (*CIYMS*), M.K. Flynn (*Wanderers*), J.C. Walsh (*Sunday's Well*), P.J. McGrath (*UC Cork*); C.M.H. Gibson (*Camb. Univ.*), R.M. Young (*QU Belfast*); S. MacHale (*Lansdowne*), A.M. Brady (*Dublin Univ.*), R.J. McLaughlin* (*Gosforth*), W.J. McBride (*Ballymena*), O.C. Waldron (*Oxford Univ.*), N.A.A. Murphy (*Cork Const.*), R.A. Lamont (*Instonians*), M.G. Doyle (*Camb. Univ.*)

Referee: D.M. Hughes (*Wales*)   **Touch judges:** J.K. Hunter, T.B. Kearns

A.J.W. Hinshelwood scored and S. Wilson converted (5–0); T.J. Kiernan kicked a penalty (5–3).(H.T.). A.J.W. Hinshelwood and D. Grant scored but S. Wilson failed (11–3).

Chisholm's return to half brought an obvious improvement; even the pack seemed to benefit with the back row outstanding. Henderson as usual tackled ferociously. The Scottish pack dominated the scrums especially as the referee and the Irish hooker could not see eye to eye over Law Fifteen! Gibson, in spite of the scrum worries and a perturbed Young, was a constant threat. Scotland began with a blustery wind and saw Hunter go off injured early on. Hastie after a sustained shove and quick heel worked a dummy scissors with Henderson before putting Hinshelwood in at the corner. Before half time Kiernan kicked a penalty. In the second half Scotland often used a shortened line out with Fisher operating successfully at the tail. One throw he touched down to Campbell-Lamerton who was tackled but Telfer and Grant moved the ball on and it went from Stagg, Fisher and Hastie to Hinshelwood who scored at the corner. Towards the close another delayed but controlled heel let Hastie break sharply and send Grant over.

ENGLAND   Murrayfield   19 March 1966

SCOTLAND: 1 penalty goal, 1 try   6   **Win**

ENGLAND: 1 drop goal   3

Scotland: C.F. Blaikie (*Heriot's FP*); A.J.W. Hinshelwood (*London Scot.*), B.C. Henderson (*Edin. Wrs.*), I.H.P. Laughland* (*London Scot.*), D.J. Whyte (*Edin. Wrs.*); D.H. Chisholm (*Melrose*), A.J. Hastie (*Melrose*); J.D. Macdonald (*London Scot.*), F.A.L. Laidlaw (*Melrose*), D.M.D. Rollo (*Howe of Fife*), P.K. Stagg (*Sale*), M.J. Campbell-Lamerton (*London Scot.*), J.P. Fisher (*London Scot.*), J.W. Telfer (*Melrose*), D. Grant (*Hawick*)

England: D. Rutherford (*Gloucester*); E.L. Rudd (*Liverpool*), R.D. Hearn (*Bedford*), C.W. McFadyean (*Moseley*), K.F. Savage (*Northampton*); M.P. Weston (*Durham City*), T.C. Wintle (*Northampton*); A.L. Horton (*Blackheath*), W.T. Treadwell (*Wasps*), P.E. Judd (*Coventry*), J.E. Owen (*Coventry*), C.M. Payne (*Harlequins*), J.R.H. Greenwood (*Waterloo*), G.A. Sherriff (*Saracens*), D.P. Rogers* (*Bedford*)

Referee: K.D. Kelleher (*Ireland*)   **Touch judges:** I. Stirling, D.L. Head

C.F. Blaikie kicked a penalty (3–0).(H.T.). C.W. McFadyean dropped a goal (3–3); D.J. Whyte scored but C.F. Blaikie failed (6–3).

The English pack held a slight advantage in the scrums and indulged in a fair amount of obstructive play in the line out, none suffering more from this than Fisher at the tail. The Melrose pair exhibited their own brand of half back play, mixing sound defence with sudden attacking bursts. The Scottish defence also benefitted by some uncompromising tackles by both centres and by Grant from the back of the scrums. Early in the second half McFadyean equalised with a drop kick. Then from a line out Hastie flung a grand long pass to Chisholm who cut through. The ball travelled from Henderson to Laughland who was half checked but got a pass away to Grant who came up on the outside. A further pass sent Whyte off at full pace to score far out.

AUSTRALIA   Murrayfield   17 December 1966

SCOTLAND: 1 goal, 1 penalty goal, 1 try   11   **Win**

AUSTRALIA: 1 goal   5

Scotland: S. Wilson (*London Scot.*); A.J.W. Hinshelwood (*London Scot.*), J.W.C. Turner (*Gala*), B.M. Simmers (*Glas. Acads.*), D.J. Whyte (*Edin. Wrs.*); D.H. Chisholm (*Melrose*), A.J. Hastie (*Melrose*); N. Suddon (*Hawick*), F.A.L. Laidlaw (*Melrose*), D.M.D. Rollo (*Howe of Fife*), P.K. Stagg (*Sale*), P.C. Brown (*West of Scot.*), J.P. Fisher* (*London Scot.*), A.H.W. Boyle (*St Thomas's*), D. Grant (*Hawick*)

Australia: J.K. Lenehan (*NSW*); A.M. Cardy (*NSW*), J.E. Brass (*NSW*), R.J. Marks (*Queensland*), S. Boyce (*NSW*); P.R. Gibbs (*Victoria*), K.W. Catchpole* (*NSW*); J.M. Miller (*NSW*), P.G. Johnson (*NSW*), A.R. Miller (*NSW*), R.G. Teitzel (*Queensland*), P.C. Crittle (*NSW*), M.P. Purcell (*Queensland*), J.F. O'Gorman (*NSW*), G.V. Davis (*NSW*)

Referee: M. Joseph (*Wales*)   **Touch judges:** A.J.K. Monro, D.J.S. Spink

S. Wilson kicked a penalty (3–0); J.E. Brass scored and J.K. Leneham converted (3–5); D.H. Chisholm scored and S. Wilson converted (8–5).(H.T.). A.H.W. Boyle scored but S. Wilson failed (11–5).

Australia, having just beaten Wales for the first time, were fairly confident and, although forced to replace the injured Hawthorne at stand-off, might well have won this game had his replacement, Gibbs, not been injured in the last ten minutes. Scotland, playing with the wind, had a tremendous start for Wilson kicked a 35 yard penalty for an offence at the first scrum, but after twenty minutes Australia went into the lead when Brass charged down a clearance and scored. Ten minutes before half time and after some good work by Fisher and Brown, Chisholm wrong-footed the defence to score a fine solo try.

In the second half Australia with the wind did a lot of attacking but their backs, rather inclined to run across the field, could not break a good defence and it was their forwards who looked more dangerous. With ten minutes to go Gibbs suffered a leg injury but stayed on the field as an extra full back and O'Gorman came out of the pack. This undoubtedly helped Scotland for the forwards made some tremendous rushes and Boyle got over for the last score.

FRANCE   Colombes   14 January 1967

SCOTLAND:	2 penalties, 1 drop goal	9	**Win**
FRANCE:	1 goal, 1 try	8	

Scotland: S. Wilson (*London Scot.*); A.J.W. Hinshelwood (*London Scot.*), J.W.C. Turner (*Gala*), B.M. Simmers (*Glas. Acads.*), D.J. Whyte (*Edin. Wrs.*); D.H. Chisholm (*Melrose*), A.J. Hastie (*Melrose*); J.D. MacDonald (*London Scot.*), F.A.L. Laidlaw (*Melrose*), D.M.D. Rollo (*Howe of Fife*), P.K. Stagg (*Sale*), W.J. Hunter (*Hawick*), J.P. Fisher* (*London Scot.*), A.H.W. Boyle (*St Thomas's*), D. Grant (*Hawick*)

France: C. Lacaze (*Angouleme*); B. Duprat (*Bayonne*), C. Dourthe (*Dax*), J. Maso (*Perpignan*), C. Darrout* (*Mont-de-Marsan*); J. Gachassin (*Lourdes*), J.C. Lasserre (*Dax*); A. Gruarin (*Toulon*), J.M. Cabanier (*Montauban*), J.C. Berejnoi (*Tulle*), W. Spanghero (*Narbonne*), D. Dauga (*Mont-de-Marsan*), J.P. Salut (*Toulouse*), A. Herrero (*Toulon*), C. Carrere (*Toulon*)

Referee: K.D. Kelleher (*Ireland*)   **Touch judges:** J.W.A. Ireland, B. Marie

S. Wilson kicked a penalty (3–0): B. Duprat scored but J. Gachassin failed (3–3); S. Wilson kicked a penalty (6–3).(H.T.). B.M. Simmers dropped a goal (9–3); C. Carrere scored and J. Gachassin converted (9–8).

Within two minutes a 40 yard penalty kick by Wilson put Scotland into the lead but the French backs were moving the ball beautifully and a half break by Gachassin, carried on by Dourthe, put Duprat over for a fine try. The lead was short lived for after five minutes Wilson kicked another penalty. Both sets of backs, with their full backs coming into the line, were running well but grim defence prevented any further score. Just before the interval Maso hurt a leg and Salut came out to act as an extra threequarter. France resumed fiercely but fell further behind when Simmers dropped a goal after a line out at the 25. However, the seven French forwards came away with some fine rushes and Carrere got over for what proved to be the last score.

WALES   **Murrayfield**   **4 February 1967**

SCOTLAND: 1 goal, 1 drop goal, 1 try   11   **Win**
WALES: 1 goal   5

Scotland: S. Wilson (*London Scot.*); A.J.W. Hinshelwood (*London Scot.*), J.W.C. Turner (*Gala*), B.M. Simmers (*Glas. Acads.*), D.J. Whyte (*Edin. Wrs.*); D. H. Chisholm (*Melrose*), A.J. Hastie (*Melrose*); J.D. MacDonald (*London Scot.*), F.A.L. Laidlaw (*Melrose*), D.M.D. Rollo (*Howe of Fife*), P.K. Stagg (*Sale*), W.J. Hunter (*Hawick*), J.P. Fisher* (*London Scot.*), J.W. Telfer (*Melrose*), D. Grant (*Hawick*)

Wales: T.G. Price (*Leicester Univ.*); D.I. Bebb (*Swansea*), T.G.R. Davies (*Cardiff*), W.H. Raybould (*Camb. Univ.*), S.J. Watkins (*Newport*); B. John (*Llanelli*), W. Hullin (*Cardiff*); J. O'Shea (*Cardiff*), B. Rees (*London Welsh*), D.J. Lloyd (*Bridgend*), B. Price (*Newport*), W. Mainwaring (*Aberavon*), K. Braddock (*Newbridge*), A.E.I. Pask* (*Abertillery*), J. Taylor (*London Welsh*)

Referee: K.D. Kelleher (*Ireland*)   **Touch judges:** T.F.E. Grierson, A.H.D. North

S.J. Watkins scored and T.G. Price converted (0–5).(H.T.). A.J.W. Hinshelwood scored but S. Wilson failed (3–5); D.H. Chisholm dropped a goal (6–5); J.W. Telfer scored and S. Wilson converted (11–5).

Wales held some territorial advantage early on but there was little back play, only grim mauling between the two packs. Whyte had to go off with an injured hand and Grant was taken out of the pack. At a line out the ball shot back off a Scottish hand and Watkins caught it and ran fifteen yards unopposed to score at the corner. Whyte returned just after the interval to find Scotland defending but a good clearance put them into Welsh territory and from a scrum the ball was whipped along the line to Hinshelwood who had a fine sprint to throw himself in at the corner. Hereabout the Scottish pack began to improve and the ball coming to Chisholm he dropped a neat goal on the run. Near the close the Scottish forwards took the ball up field and from a scrum near the line Hastie sold a dummy and passed to Telfer who crashed his way over.

IRELAND   **Murrayfield**   **25 February 1967**

SCOTLAND: 1 penalty goal   3   **Loss**
IRELAND: 1 goal   5

Scotland: S. Wilson (*London Scot.*); A.J.W. Hinshelwood (*London Scot.*), J.W.C. Turner (*Gala*), R.B. Welsh (*Hawick*), D.J. Whyte (*Edin. Wrs.*); B.M. Simmers (*Glas. Acads.*), A.J. Hastie (*Melrose*); J.D. MacDonald (*London Scot.*), F.A.L. Laidlaw (*Melrose*), A.B. Carmichael (*West of Scot.*), P.K. Stagg (*Sale*), W.J. Hunter (*Hawick*), J.P. Fisher* (*London Scot.*), J.W. Telfer (*Melrose*), D. Grant (*Hawick*)

Ireland: T.J. Kiernan (*Cork Const.*); N.H. Brophy (*Blackrock*), J.C. Walsh (*Sunday's*

265

Well), F.P.K. Bresnihan (*UC Dublin*), A.T.A. Duggan (*Lansdowne*); C.M.H. Gibson (*NIFC*), B.F. Sherry (*Terenure Coll.*); S. MacHale (*Lansdowne*), K.W. Kennedy (*CIYMS*), S.A. Hutton (*Malone*), W.J. McBride (*Ballymena*), M.G. Malloy (*UC Galway*), N.A.A. Murphy* (*Cork Const.*), K.G. Goodhall (*Newcastle Univ.*), M.G. Doyle (*Edin. Wrs.*)

Referee: D.M. Hughes (*Wales*) **Touch judges:** J.A.S. Taylor, M. Barry

No scoring at half time. N.A.A. Murphy scored and T.J. Kiernan converted (0–5); S. Wilson kicked a penalty (3–5).

Ireland ran the ball from the beginning and it was soon obvious that Gibson was going to be a real danger for he continually stretched the defence with well placed kicks or attacking runs. The Irish score, half way through the second half, came from a fierce burst away from a lineout by Kiernan and all that Scotland could manage in reply was a 45 yard penalty by Wilson. Once again Fisher at the tail of the line out showed his skill at catching and distributing the ball.

ENGLAND   Twickenham   18 March 1967

SCOTLAND: 1 goal, 2 penalty goals, 1 try   14   **Loss**

ENGLAND   3 goals, 1 drop goal,   27
                2 penalty goals, 1 try

Scotland: S. Wilson (*London Scot.*); A.J.W. Hinshelwood (*London Scot.*), J.W.C. Turner (*Gala*), R.B. Welsh (*Hawick*), D.J. Whyte (*Edin. Wrs.*); I.H.P. Laughland (*London Scot.*), I.G. McCrae (*Gordonians*); J.D. MacDonald (*London Scot.*), F.A.L. Laidlaw (*Melrose*), D.M.D. Rollo (*Howe of Fife*), P.K. Stagg (*Sale*), W.J. Hunter (*Hawick*), J.P. Fisher* (*London Scot.*), J.W. Telfer (*Melrose*), D. Grant (*Hawick*)

England: R.W. Hosen (*Bristol*); K.F. Savage (*Northampton*), R.D. Hearn (*Bedford*), C.W. McFadyean (*Moseley*), R.C. Webb (*Coventry*); J.F. Finlan (*Moseley*), R.D.A. Pickering (*Bradford*); P.E. Judd* (*Coventry*), S.B. Richards (*Richmond*), M.J. Coulman (*Moseley*), J.N. Pallant (*Notts*), D.E.J. Watt (*Bristol*), D.P. Rogers (*Bedford*), D.M. Rollitt (*Bristol*), R.B. Taylor (*Northampton*)

Referee: D.P. D'Arcy (*Ireland*) **Touch judges:** R.S. Waddell, R.F. Johnson

R.W. Hosen kicked a penalty (0–3); J.W.C. Turner scored but S. Wilson failed (3–3); A.J.W. Hinshelwood scored and S. Wilson converted (8–3); C.W. McFadyean scored and R.W. Hosen converted (8–8); S. Wilson kicked a penalty (11–8).(H.T.). R.B. Taylor scored and R.W. Hosen converted (11–13); S. Wilson kicked a penalty (14–13); R.W. Hosen kicked a penalty (14–16); R.E. Webb scored but R.W. Hosen failed (14–19); C.W. McFadyean scored and R.W. Hosen converted (14–24); J.F. Finlan dropped a goal (14–27).

Scotland held their own in the first half but crumbled during the last half hour, when the English forwards took a firm grip in the scrums and loose mauls.

NEW ZEALAND   Murrayfield   2 December 1967

SCOTLAND: 1 drop goal   3   **Loss**

NEW ZEALAND: 1 goal, 2 penalties, 1 try   14

Scotland: S. Wilson (*London Scot.*); A.J.W. Hinshelwood (*London Scot.*), J.W.C. Turner (*Gala*), J.N.M. Frame (*Edin. Univ.*), R.R. Keddie (*Watsonians*); D.H. Chisholm (*Melrose*), A.J. Hastie (*Melrose*); A.B. Carmichael (*West of Scot.*), F.A.L. Laidlaw (*Melrose*), D.M.D. Rollo (*Howe of Fife*), P.K. Stagg (*Sale*), G.W.E. Mitchell (*Edin. Wrs.*), J.P. Fisher* (*London Scot.*), A.H.W. Boyle (*London Scot.*), D. Grant (*Hawick*)

New Zealand: W.F. McCormick (*Canterbury*); A.G. Steel (*Canterbury*), I.R. MacRae, (*Hawkes Bay*), W.L. Davis (*Hawkes Bay*), W.M. Birtwhistle (*Waikato*); E.W. Kirton (*Otago*), C.R. Laidlaw (*Otago*); K.F. Gray (*Wellington*), B.E. McLeod (*Counties*), A.E. Hopkinson (*Canterbury*), S.C. Strahan (*Manawata*), C.E. Meads (*King County*), K.R. Tremain (*Hawkes Bay*), B.J. Lochore* (*Wairarapa*), G.C. Williams (*Wellington*)

Referee: K.D. Kelleher (*Ireland*)   **Touch judges:** R.P. Burrell, J.G. Dow

D.H. Chisholm dropped a goal (3–0); W.F. McCormick kicked a penalty (3–3); I.R. MacRae scored but W.F. McCormick failed (3–6); W.F. McCormick kicked a penalty (3–9).(H.T.). W.L. Davis scored and W.F. McCormick converted (3–14).

Scotland did remarkably well against their very powerful opponents who were held in check by some determined tackling. The forwards, although beaten in the loose, had some success at the line outs where Fisher at the tail did a lot of fine catching and cover tackling. It was unpleasant to note that before Davis scored the only try in the second half, Fisher could not cover Kirton from the line out for he was quite clearly put out of the game by a nudge that laid him flat. It was a hard vigorous game yet not dirty in spite of the incident at the end of play. Chisholm stopped to pick up a rolling ball only to recoil to avoid a swinging kick aimed by Meads in the direction of the ball. The referee (and many others) regarded this as dangerous play and since he had already warned the player for dangerous foot work in the ruck, had no option but to send him off; a sad ending to an exciting game which the visitors deserved to win.

FRANCE   Murrayfield   13 January 1968

SCOTLAND: 1 penalty goal, 1 try   6   **Loss**

FRANCE: 1 goal, 1 try   8

Scotland: S. Wilson (*London Scot.*); A.J.W. Hinshelwood (*London Scot.*), J.W.C. Turner (*Gala*), J.N.M. Frame (*Edin. Univ.*), G.J. Keith (*Wasps*); D.H. Chisholm (*Melrose*), A.J. Hastie (*Melrose*); A.B. Carmichael (*West of Scot.*), F.A.L. Laidlaw (*Melrose*), D.M.D. Rollo (*Howe of Fife*), P.K. Stagg (*Sale*), G.W.E. Mitchell (*Edin. Wrs.*), J.P. Fisher* (*London Scot.*), A.H.W. Boyle (*London Scot.*), D. Grant (*Hawick*)

France: C. Lacaze (*Angouleme*); A. Campaes (*Lourdes*), J. Trillo (*Begles*), J. Maso (*Perpignan*), B. Duprat (*Bayonne*); G. Camberabero (*La Voulte*), L. Camberabero (*La Voulte*); A. Abadie (*Graulhet*), J.M. Cabanier (*Montauban*), A. Gruarin (*Toulon*), D. Dauga (*Montde-Marsan*), E. Cester (*TOEC*), J.J. Rupert (*Tyrosse*), W. Spanghero (*Narbonne*), C. Carrere* (*Toulon*)

Referee: K.D. Kelleher (*Ireland*) **Touch judges:** H.B. Laidlaw, R. Calmet

B. Duprat scored but G. Camberabero failed (0–3); G.J. Keith scored but S. Wilson failed (3–3).(H.T.). S. Wilson kicked a penalty (6–3); A. Compaes scored and G. Camberabero converted (6–8).

Inside five minutes France took the lead. From a line out G. Camberabero dropped a goal. The ball flew wide but Duprat had followed up so fast that he just beat Wilson to the touch down. Play thereafter tended to be in the French half although their backs handled well and even attacked from behind their own line. Right on the half hour the ball came from a line out to Chisholm who made a good burst, handed on to Turner who ripped through the defence and then the ball went via Frame to Keith who scored in the corner. Soon after the interval Wilson put Scotland into the lead with a penalty but after fifteen minutes France snatched a try when Dauga picked up a bad pass, crashed through the forwards and passed to Trillo who put Campaes in at the corner for Camberabero to convert. Scotland pressed but could not break down a fast covering defence.

WALES   Cardiff   3 February 1968

SCOTLAND:	Nil	0	**Loss**
WALES:	1 goal	5	

Scotland: S. Wilson (*London Scot.*); A.J.W. Hinshelwood (*London Scot.*), J.W.C. Turner (*Gala*), J.N.M. Frame (*Edin. Univ.*), G.J. Keith (*Wasps*); D.H. Chisholm (*Melrose*), A.J. Hastie (*Melrose*); A.B. Carmichael (*West of Scot.*), F.A.L. Laidlaw (*Melrose*), D.M.D. Rollo (*Howe of Fife*), P.K. Stagg (*Sale*), G.W.E. Mitchell (*Edin. Wrs.*), J.P. Fisher* (*London Scot.*), A.H.W. Boyle (*London Scot.*), T.G. Elliot (*Langholm*)

Wales: D. Rees (*Swansea*); S.J. Watkins (*Newport*), K.S. Jarrett (*Newport*), T.G.R. Davies (*Cardiff*), W.K. Jones (*Cardiff*); B. John (*Cardiff*), G.O. Edwards* (*Cardiff*); J. O'Shea (*Cardiff*), J. Young (*Harrogate*), D.J. Lloyd (*Bridgend*), M. Wiltshire (*Aberavon*), W.D. Thomas (*Llanelli*), W.D. Morris (*Neath*), R.E. Jones (*Coventry*), A.J. Gray (*London Welsh*)

Referee: G.C. Lamb (*England*) **Touch judges:** R.F. King, G.D. Francis

W.K. Jones scored and K.S. Jarrett converted (0–5).(H.T.).

The opening exchanges were mainly confined to the forwards with the halves kicking to touch and it was early seen that the new Welsh pack were faster on the ball and holding their own at the line outs. After twenty minutes following a scrum on the Scottish 25 Jarrett made a half break and gave a pass (which seemed well forward) to Davies who put Jones in at the corner for the only score of the match. There were many exciting runs from both sides which produced near misses. Edwards had one lovely break up the left touch line but his kick over Wilson's head beat him to the dead ball line. Fisher who had a good game at the line out and in the loose was held up more than once on the line. Jarrett, although kicking a good conversion, had an off day with penalty kicks.

IRELAND   Lansdowne Road   24 February 1968

SCOTLAND: 2 penalty goals   6   **Loss**

IRELAND: 1 goal, 1 penalty goal, 2 tries   14

Scotland: S. Wilson (*London Scot.*); A.J.W. Hinshelwood (*London Scot.*), J.W.C. Turner (*Gala*), J.N.M. Frame (*Edin. Univ.*), C.G. Hodgson (*London Scot.*); D.H. Chisholm (*Melrose*), I.G. McCrae (*Gordonians*); A.B. Carmichael (*West of Scot.*), F.A.L. Laidlaw (*Melrose*), D.M.D. Rollo (*Howe of Fife*), P.K. Stagg (*Sale*), A.F. McHarg (*West of Scot.*), J.P. Fisher* (*London Scot.*), A.H.W. Boyle (*London Scot.*), R.J. Arneil (*Edin. Acads.*)

Ireland: T.J. Kiernan (*Cork Const.*); A.T.A. Duggan (*Lansdowne*), B.A.P. O'Brien (*Shannon*), F.P.K. Bresnihan (*UC Dublin*), R.D. Scott (*QU Belfast*); C.M.H. Gibson (*NIFC*), J. Quirke (*Blackrock*); S. Millar (*Ballymena*), A.M. Brady (*Malone*), P. O'Callaghan (*Dolphin*), M.G. Malloy (*UC Galway*), W.J. McBride (*Ballymena*), M.G. Doyle (*Blackrock*), T.J. Doyle (*Wanderers*), K.G. Goodall (*Derry*)

Referee: M. Joseph (*Wales*)   **Touch judges:** K.A.G. Boxer, J.E. Leslie

T.J. Kiernan kicked a penalty (0–3); A.T.A. Duggan scored but T.J. Kiernan failed (0–6).(H.T.). S. Wilson kicked a penalty (3–6); F.P.K. Bresnihan scored but T.J. Kiernan failed (3–9); S. Wilson kicked a penalty (6–9); A.T.A. Duggan scored and T.J. Kiernan converted (6–14).

Again the Scottish pack did not come up to expectations; the new half back combination was not a success and although there was some bad luck there was too much mishandling by the backs. Ireland, on the other hand, took their chances when scoring their tries. The first came from an O'Brien run and crosskick which Duggan caught and although well tackled managed to fall over the line for the score. The second followed a charged down clearance kick which broke to Bresnihan for a gift try. Towards the close, three points behind, Scotland put in a fighting finish and Chisholm had a short run and pass inside to Boyle who charged into a ruck. Suddenly from this Quirke emerged with the ball and had a clear run up to Wilson. He collected his kick ahead and set up a passing run by O'Brien which gave Duggan his second score.

ENGLAND   Murrayfield   16 March 1968

SCOTLAND: 1 drop goal, 1 penalty goal   6   **Loss**

ENGLAND: 1 goal, 1 penalty goal   8

Scotland: S. Wilson (*London Scot.*); A.J.W. Hinshelwood (*London Scot.*), J.W.C. Turner (*Gala*), J.N.M. Frame (*Edin. Univ.*), C.G. Hodgson (*London Scot.*); I. Robertson (*London Scot.*), G.C. Connell (*Trinity Acads.*); N. Suddon (*Hawick*), D.T. Deans (*Hawick*), A.B. Carmichael (*West of Scot.*), P.K. Stagg (*Sale*), A.F. McHarg (*West of Scot.*), J.P. Fisher (*London Scot.*), J.W. Telfer* (*Melrose*), R.J. Arneil (*Edin. Acads.*)

England: R.B. Hiller (*Harlequins*); R.E. Webb (*Coventry*), R.H. Lloyd (*Harlequins*), T.J. Brooke (*Richmond*), K.F. Savage (*Northampton*); M.P. Weston* (*Durham City*), R.D.A. Pickering (*Bradford*); B.W. Keen (*Newcastle Univ.*), J.V. Pullin (*Bristol*), M.J. Coulman (*Moseley*), P.J. Larter (*Northampton*), M.J. Parsons (*Northampton*), P.J. Bell (*Blackheath*), D.J. Gay (*Bath*), B.R. West (*Loughborough*)

Referee: D.P. d'Arcy (*Ireland*) **Touch judges:** D.C.J. McMahon, Dr C.R. Narkham

S. Wilson kicked a penalty (0–3); G.C. Connell dropped a goal (6–0).(H.T.). M.J. Coulman scored and R.B. Miller converted (6–5); R.B. Hiller kicked a penalty (6–8).

Scotland began with a strong wind behind them and after fifteen minutes Wilson kicked a penalty. The new pair of half backs started well, Robertson placing some dangerous diagonal kicks and then after half an hour Connell, almost under the posts, stopped a rolling ball, whipped round and dropped a neat goal.

Against the wind England had barely been over the Scottish 25 line but immediately on restarting one kick from Weston found touch far upfield. Fortunately the Scottish back row was giving both Pickering and him a harassing time. Then from a four man line out Coulman ran onto the throw and had a 35 yard run through a flat defence for a splendid try. With ten minutes to go Hiller kicked a lovely penalty from the right touchline, a kick which emphasised Scotland's continual failures with penalties, not only in this game but throughout the whole season.

AUSTRALIA   Murrayfield   2 November 1968

SCOTLAND:	2 penalty goals, 1 try	9	**Win**
AUSTRALIA:	1 penalty goal	3	

Scotland: C.F. Blaikie (*Heriot's FP*); A.J.W. Hinshelwood (*London Scot.*), J.W.C. Turner (*Gala*), C.W.W. Rea (*West of Scot.*), W.D. Jackson (*Hawick*); C.M. Telfer (*Hawick*), G.C. Connell (*Trinity Acads.*); N. Suddon (*Hawick*), F.A.L. Laidlaw (*Melrose*), A.B. Carmichael (*West of Scot.*), P.K. Stagg (*Sale*), A.F. McHarg (*London Scot.*), T.G. Elliot (*Langholm*), J.W. Telfer* (*Melrose*), R.J. Arneil (*Edin. Acads.*)

Australia: B.D. Honan (*Queensland*); J.W. Cole (*NSW*), J.E. Brass (*NSW*), P.V. Smith (*NSW*), T.R. Forman (*NSW*); J.P. Ballesty (*NSW*), J.N.B. Hipwell (*NSW*); K.R. Bell (*Queensland*), P.G. Johnson* (*NSW*), R.B. Prosser (*NSW*), P.N.P. Reilly (*Queensland*), S.C. Gregory (*Queensland*), H.A. Rose (*NSW*), D.A. Taylor (*Queensland*), G.V. Davis (*NSW*)

Referee: M.H. Titcomb (*England*) **Touch judges:** R.B. Burrell, F. Parker

C.F. Blaikie kicked a penalty (3–0); A.J.W. Hinshelwood scored but C.F. Blaikie failed (6–0); J.E. Brass kicked a penalty (6–3); C.F. Blaikie kicked a penalty (9–3).(H.T.).

The Scottish pack held the whip hand throughout and Colin Telfer with a good share of the ball, played well in his first game. The solitary try came from a short penalty taken by Connell. The ball went from Colin Telfer to Rea who made a nice break and a further passing run by Jim Telfer and Arneil saw Hinshelwood score far out. The Australian attack was not much seen but in the second half the Scottish threes produced a lot of fine constructive play and were unlucky not to score although they did have the ball over the line twice but recalled for an infringement.

FRANCE	Colombes	11 January 1969

SCOTLAND:	1 penalty goal, 1 try	6	Win
FRANCE:	1 penalty goal	3	

Scotland: C.F. Blaikie (*Heriot's FP*); A.J.W. Hinshelwood (*London Scot.*), J.W.C. Turner (*Gala*), C.W.W. Rea (*West of Scot.*), W.D. Jackson (*Hawick*); C.M. Telfer (*Hawick*), G.C. Connell (*London Scot.*); N. Suddon (*Hawick*), F.A.L. Laidlaw (*Melrose*), A.B. Carmichael (*West of Scot.*), P.K. Stagg (*Sale*), A.F. McHarg (*London Scot.*), T.G. Elliot (*Langholm*), J.W. Telfer* (*Melrose*), R.J. Arneil (*Edin. Acads.*) Sub: I.G. McCrae (*Gordonians*)

France: P. Villepreux (*Toulouse*); J.M. Bonal (*Toulouse*), J.-P. Lux (*Tyrosse*), J. Maso (*Narbonne*), A. Campaes (*Lourdes*); J. Gachassin (*Lourdes*), J.L. Berot (*Toulouse*), M. Lasse, M. Yachvili (*Tulle*), J.M. Esponda (*Perpignan*), E. Cester (*TOEC*), B. Dauga (*Mont-de-Marsan*), J. Iracabal (*Bayonne*), W. Spanghero (*Narbonne*), C. Carrere* (*Toulon*)

Referee: G.C. Lamb (*England*)

C.F. Blaikie kicked a penalty (3–0).(H.T.). P. Villepreux kicked a penalty (3–3); J.W. Telfer scored but C.F. Blaikie failed (6–3).

Even before the game began Salut twisted his ankle running onto the pitch and was replaced by Iracabal so causing a shuffle in the pack. Then after Blaikie had kicked a penalty Connell had to retire hurt and McCrae came on as substitute as allowed under the new law. For the remainder of the half France were very active and dangerous for Dauga and Carrere were nearly over while Maso came near with a drop. Early in the second half Villepreux, who had not been kicking well, equalised with a tremendous penalty from mid field and there followed some fine French handling, one move sweeping the length of the field. Then towards the close Scotland grabbed a try when a French heel on their 25 let McCrae pounce on a loose ball and pass to Jim Telfer who fairly crashed over for the winning score.

WALES	Murrayfield	1 February 1969

SCOTLAND:	1 penalty goal	3	Loss
WALES:	1 goal, 2 penalty goals, 2 tries	17	

Scotland: C.F. Blaikie (*Heriot's FP*); A.J.W. Hinshelwood (*London Scot.*), J.N.M. Frame (*Gala*), C.W.W. Rea (*West of Scot.*), W.D. Jackson (*Hawick*); C.M. Telfer (*Hawick*), I.G. McCrae (*Gordonians*); N. Suddon (*Hawick*), F.A.L. Laidlaw (*Melrose*), A.B. Carmichael (*West of Scot.*), P.K. Stagg (*Sale*), A.F. McHarg (*London Scot.*), T.G. Elliot (*Langholm*), J.W. Telfer* (*Melrose*), R.J. Arneil (*Edin. Acads.*)

Wales: J.P.R. Williams (*London Welsh*); M.C.R. Richards (*Cardiff*), T.G.R. Davies (*Cardiff*), K.S. Jarrett (*Newport*), S.J. Watkins (*Newport*); B. John (*Cardiff*), G.O. Edwards (*Cardiff*); D. Williams (*Ebbw Vale*), J. Young (*Harrogate*), D.J. Lloyd (*Bridgend*), B. Price* (*Newport*), B.E. Thomas (*Neath*), W.D. Morris (*Neath*), T.M. Davies (*London Welsh*), J. Taylor (*London Welsh*)

Referee: K.D. Kellaher (*Ireland*) **Touch judges:** D.C.J. McMahon, E.R. Morgan

K.S. Jarrett kicked two penalty goals (0–6).(H.T.). G.O. Edwards scored but K.S. Jarrett failed (0–9); C.F. Blaikie kicked a penalty (3–9); M.C.R. Richards scored but K.S. Jarrett failed (3–12); B. John scored and K.S. Jarrett converted (3–17).

The Welsh team, with a trip to the Antipodes coming off, had taken to squad training under a national coach but they won this match not so much by team work as by capitalising on blunders by their opponents. In the first half Jarrett kicked two fine penalties awarded for simple offences. In the second half Edwards scored by pouncing on a bad Scottish heel on their line; Richards was given a clear run in along the line from a ball knocked back to him at a line out and then John having half charged down a kick, picked up and got over as he was tackled. Scotland, however, could not break through a good defence but Blaikie who eventually kicked a 45 yard penalty had hard lines in the first half when each of three long range kicks went narrowly past — kicks that could have given Scotland a 9–6 lead at half time.

IRELAND   Murrayfield   22 February 1969

| **SCOTLAND:** | Nil | 0 | **Loss** |
| **IRELAND:** | 2 goals, 2 tries | 16 | |

Scotland: C.F. Blaikie (*Heriot's FP*); A.J.W. Hinshelwood (*London Scot.*), J.N.M. Frame (*Gala*), C.W.W. Rea (*West of Scot.*), W.D. Jackson (*Hawick*); C.M. Telfer (*Hawick*), R.C. Allan (*Hutchesons' GSFP*); N. Suddon (*Hawick*), F.A.L. Laidlaw (*Melrose*), A.B. Carmichael (*West of Scot.*), P.C. Brown (*Gala*), A.F. McHarg (*London Scot.*), W. Lauder (*Neath*), J.W. Telfer* (*Melrose*), R.J. Arneil (*Edin. Acads.*) Subs: P.K. Stagg (*Sale*), W.G. Macdonald (*London Scot.*)

Ireland: T.J. Kiernan* (*Cork Const.*); A.T.A. Duggan (*Lansdowne*), F.P.K. Bresnihan (*UC Dublin*), C.M.H. Gibson (*NIFC*), J.C.M. Moroney (*London Irish*); B.J. McGann (*Lansdowne*), R.M. Young (*QU Belfast*); S. Millar (*Ballymena*), K.W. Kennedy (*London Irish*), P. O'Callaghan (*Dolphin*), W.J. McBride (*Ballymena*), M.G. Molloy (*London Irish*), J.C. Davidson (*Dungannon*), K.G. Goodall (*Derry*), N.A.A. Murphy (*Cork Const.*) Sub: M.L. Hipwell (*Terenure*)

Referee: M. Joseph (*Wales*) **Touch judges:** H.B. Laidlaw, F.I. Howard

A.T.A. Duggan scored but J.C.N. Moroney failed (0–3).(H.T.). B.J. McGann, C.M.H. Gibson and F.P.K. Bresnihan scored and J.C.M. Moroney converted the last two (0–16).

After some wintry weather, conditions were harsh and there were many stoppages for injury with three substitutes coming on during the match. W.G. Macdonald, incidentally, must hold some kind of record for he only played during the final two minutes of the game. Scotland lost their captain after fifteen minutes but frankly could not match a very experienced Irish team which mustered a fantastic total of 287 caps. McGann had a good game, placing the ball over the line to give Duggan a simple try and scoring a fine solo try himself. The other two scores came after strong running by the Irish backs.

ENGLAND   Twickenham   15 March 1969

SCOTLAND: 1 penalty goal   3   **Loss**
ENGLAND: 1 goal, 1 try   8

Scotland: C.F. Blaikie (*Heriot's FP*); W.C.C. Steele (*Langholm: RAF*), J.N.M. Frame (*Gala*), I. Robertson (*Watsonians*), W.D. Jackson (*Hawick*); C.M. Telfer (*Hawick*), G.C. Connell (*London Scot.*); J. McLauchlan (*Jordanhill Coll.*), F.A.L. Laidlaw (*Melrose*), A.B. Carmichael (*West of Scot.*), P.C. Brown (*Gala*), A.F. McHarg (*London Scot.*), W. Lauder (*Neath*), J.W. Telfer* (*Melrose*), R.J. Arneil (*Edin. Acads.*)

England: R.B. Hiller (*Harlequins*); K.J. Fielding (*Moseley*), J.S. Spencer (*Camb. Univ.*), D.J. Duckham (*Coventry*), R.E. Webb (*Coventry*); J.F. Finlan (*Moseley*), T.C. Wintle (*Northampton*); D.L. Powell (*Northampton*), J.V. Pullin (*Bristol*), K.E. Fairbrother (*Coventry*), N.E. Horton (*Moseley*), P.J. Larter (*Northampton*), R.B. Taylor (*Northampton*), D.M. Rollitt (*Bristol*), D.P. Rogers* (*Bedford*) Sub: T.J. Dalton (*Coventry*)

Referee: C. Durand (*France*)   **Touch judges:** D.H. Collier, Major C. Tyler

D.J. Duckham scored and R.B. Hiller converted (0–5).(H.T.). D.J. Duckham scored but R.B. Hiller failed (0–8); P.C. Brown kicked a penalty (3–8).

Although Scotland had the better of the first half they found themselves trailing at half time when Duckham snatched a score after Blaikie failed to hold a very high attacking kick. Duckham also finished off a fine handling run by the English backs in the second half. The Scottish pack although heavily outweighed showed considerable improvement and were well supported by their halves but no break through was achieved. Again many penalty kicks were not converted and Brown was the third to be tried when he scored at the end of the match.

ARGENTINA   Buenos Aires   13 September 1969

SCOTTISH XV: 1 try   3   **Loss**
ARGENTINA   1 goal, 2 drop goals,   20
                   1 penalty, 2 tries

Scotland: C.F. Blaikie (*Heriot's FP*); M.A. Smith (*London Scot.*), I.R. Murchie (*West of Scot.*), A.V. Orr (*London Scot.*), A.D. Gill (*Gala*); I. Robertson (*Watsonians*), D.S. Paterson (*Gala*); J. McLauchlan (*Jordanhill Coll.*), F.A.L. Laidlaw (*Melrose*), A.B. Carmichael (*West of Scot.*), P.K. Stagg (*Sale*), A.F. McHarg (*London Scot.*), R.J. Arneil (*Edin. Acads.*), J.W. Telfer* (*Melrose*), W. Lauder (*Neath*)

Argentina: D. Morgan (*Old Georgian*); M. Pascual (*Pucara*), A. Travaglini (*CASI*), A.R. Jurado (*San Isidro*), M. Walther (*San Isidro*); T. Harris-Smith (*Old Georgian*), A. Etchegaray (*CASI*); M. Farina (*CASI*), R. Handley (*Old Georgian*), L.G. Yanez (*San Fernando*), B. Otano (*Pucara*), A. Anthony (*San Isidro*), R. Loyola (*Belgrano*), H. Silva* (*Los Tilos*), H. Miguens (*CUBA*)

Referee: R. Colombo

A. Travaglini scored and T. Harris-Smith converted (0–5); M. Walther scored but T. Harris-Smith failed (0–8).(H.T.). T. Harris-Smith kicked a penalty and dropped a goal (0–14); M.A. Smith scored but C.F. Blaikie failed (3–14); A. Travaglini scored but T. Harris-Smith failed (3–17); T. Harris-Smith dropped a goal (3–20).

Scotland were early handicapped for I.R. Murchie took a bad blow on his shoulder in the opening minutes and after A. Travaglini had scored, had to leave the field with a broken collar bone. W. Lauder came out of the pack to play at centre. Thereafter in a scorching heat and on a hard pitch they gradually wilted and tired visibly later in the second half. Nevertheless, the Scottish pack took a major share of the ball in the line outs and scrums and it took firm tackling by a lively Puma team to keep control during the first half.

ARGENTINA	Buenos Aires	27 September 1969	
SCOTTISH XV:	1 penalty goal, 1 try	6	**Win**
ARGENTINA:	1 try	3	

Scotland: C.F. Blaikie (*Heriot's FP*); M.A. Smith (*London Scot.*), B. Laidlaw (*RHSFP*), C.W.W. Rea (*West of Scot.*), W.C.C. Steele (*Langholm*); I. Robertson (*Watsonians*), D.S. Paterson (*Gala*); J. McLauchlan (*Jordanhill Coll.*), F.A.L. Laidlaw (*Melrose*), A.B. Carmichael (*West of Scot.*), P.K. Stagg (*Sale*), A.F. McHarg (*London Scot.*), R.J. Arneil (*Edin. Acads.*), J.W. Telfer* (*Melrose*), W. Lauder (*Neath*)

Argentina: D. Morgan (*Old Georgian*); M. Pascual (*Pucara*), A. Travaglini (*CASI*), D. Benzi (*Duendez*), M. Walther (*San Isidro*); T. Harris-Smith (*Old Georgian*), A. Etchegaray (*CASI*); M. Farini (CASI), R. Handley (*Old Georgian*), L.G. Yanez (*San Fernando*), B. Stano (*Pucara*), A. Anthony (*San Isidro*), R. Loyola (*Belgrano*), H. Silva* (*Los Tilos*), H. Miguens (*CUBA*)

Referee: C.A. Pozzi

B. Otano scored but T. Harris-Smith failed (0–3); A.B. Carmichael scored but C.F. Blaikie failed (3–3); C.F. Blaikie kicked a penalty (6–3).(H.T.).

A more settled Scottish team, playing on a softer pitch, shrugged off an early score and gradually asserted their authority in all departments during the remainder of a fast but distinctly rugged match. Extremely close and hard marking by the Scots upset the fluency of the Puma's fast backs, especially as the forwards gave Harris-Smith a hard time.

Right away Blaikie grabbed a bouncing ball five yards out and when tackled passed back to Smith but the ball went wide and Stano got to it first. Ten minutes later Telfer broke from a loose maul at midfield and started a fine run in which at least half of the team handled before Carmichael went over at the corner. Just before half time Blaikie kicked a fine penalty from midfield for a lead which was safely held during the second half.

SOUTH AFRICA   Murrayfield   6 December 1969

SCOTLAND: 1 penalty goal, 1 try   6   **Win**

SOUTH AFRICA: 1 penalty goal   3

Scotland: I.S.G. Smith (*London Scot.*); A.G. Biggar (*London Scot.*), J.N.M. Frame (*Gala*), C.W.W. Rea (*West of Scot.*), A.J.W. Hinshelwood (*London Scot.*); I. Robertson (*Watsonians*), D.S. Paterson (*Gala*); J. McLauchlan (*Jordanhill Coll.*), F.A.L. Laidlaw (*Melrose*), A.B. Carmichael (*West of Scot.*), P.K. Stagg (*Sale*), G.L. Brown (*West of Scot.*), W. Lauder (*Neath*), J.W. Telfer* (*Melrose*), R.J. Arneil (*Leicester*)

South Africa: H.O. de Villiers (*WP*); S.H. Nomis (*T*), O.A. Roux (*NT*), E.Olivier (*WP*), G.H. Muller (*WP*); P.J. Visagie (*GW*), D.J.J. de Vos (*WT*); J.B. Neethling (*WP*), C.H. Cockrell (*WP*), J.F.K. Marais (*NE*), F.C.H. du Preez (*NT*), G. Carelse (*EP*), P.J.F. Greyling (*T*), T.P. Bedford* (*Natal*), J.H. Ellis (*SWA*). Sub: A.E. Van der Watt (*WP*)

Referee: M. Joseph (*Wales*)   **Touch judges:** R.P. Burrell, G.O. McInnes

P.J. Visagie kicked a penalty (0–3).(H.T.). I.S.G. Smith kicked a penalty, then scored a try which he failed to convert (6–3).

Straight away mention must be made of the almost intolerable strain placed on the tourists throughout the entire tour by the actions of those who professed to oppose the apartheid policy of the South African Government. For this match some 25,000 spectators were contained in the stand or in one section of the terracing directly opposite where a highly efficient group of policemen assisted by Stewards saw to it that the game was never interrupted by those militants who did come inside. The tourists were further handicapped by the late withdrawal of their captain, Dawie de Villiers but really Scotland deserved their narrow win. They dominated the line out where the South African throw in was completely disrupted by placing the 6 feet 10 inch Stagg at Number Two and they more than held their own in the light and loose scrums. But again they lacked a goal kicker for Smith could only convert one of the six penalties. However, he did make a well-timed entry into the line when five minutes from the end Frame, fed by Robertson, made a powerful break through and then left Smith with a clear run in for the winning try.

FRANCE: **Murrayfield**   **10 January 1970**

SCOTLAND: 2 penalty goals, 1 try   **9** **Loss**
FRANCE: 1 goal, 1 drop goal, 1 try   **11**

Scotland: I.S.G. Smith (*London Scot.*); A.G. Biggar (*London Scot.*), J.N.M. Frame (*Gala*), C.W.W. Rea (*West of Scot.*), A.J.W. Hinshelwood (*London Scot.*); I. Robertson (*Watsonians*), G.C. Connell (*London Scot*); J. McLauchlan (*Jordanhill Coll.*), F.A.L. Laidlaw (*Melrose*), A.B. Carmichael (*West of Scot.*), P.K. Stagg (*Sale*), G.L. Brown (*West of Scot.*), W. Lauder (*Neath*), J.W. Telfer* (*Melrose*), R.J. Arneil (*Leicester*)

France: P. Villepreux (*Toulouse*); J. Sillieres (*Tarbes*), J.-P. Lux (*Tyrosse*), A. Marot (*Brive*), R. Bougarel (*Toulouse*); L. Paries (*Biarritz*), G. Sutra (*Narbonne*); J. Iracabal (*Bayonne*), R. Benesis (*Narbonne*), J.-L. Azarete (*Dax*), J.-P. Bastiat (*Dax*), E. Cester (*TOEC*), C. Carrere* (*Toulon*), G. Viard (*Narbonne*), B. Dauga (*Mont-de-Marsan*)

Referee: G.C. Lamb (*England*) **Touch judges:** J. Young, C. Durand

B. Dauga scored and L. Paries converted (0–5); I.S.G. Smith scored but W. Lauder failed (3–5); L. Paries dropped a goal (3–8); W. Lauder kicked a penalty (6–8); J.P. Lux scored but P. Villepreux failed (6–11).(H.T.). W. Lauder kicked a penalty (9–11).

Scotland started well but after eighteen minutes Dauga picked the ball up from a scrum fifteen yards out and literally bulldozed his way in for a score. Scotland struck back with a try from Smith who made a well timed entry into a handling run. Then Paries failed to kick a penalty only to find a bad return kick come into his hands whereupon he dropped a good goal. Lauder then kicked a 35 yard penalty before Lux receiving from Sillieres crashed past three defenders for a spectacular try right on half time. Play was fairly even after restarting, but with twenty minutes to go Lauder kicked a penalty and then Scotland fairly put the pressure on a somewhat rattled French side, but several chances and one penalty were missed and the match lost.

WALES   **Cardiff**   **7 February 1970**

SCOTLAND: 1 drop goal, 1 penalty goal, 1 try **9** **Loss**
WALES: 3 goals, 1 try   **18**

Scotland: I.S.G. Smith (*London Scot.*); M.A. Smith (*London Scot.*), J.N.M. Frame (*Gala*), C.W.W. Rea (*West of Scot.*), A.J.W. Hinshelwood (*London Scot.*); I. Robertson (*Watsonians*), R.G. Young (*Watsonians*); J. McLaughlan (*Jordanhill Coll.*), F.A.L. Laidlaw (*Melrose*), A.B. Carmichael (*West of Scot.*), P.K. Stagg (*Sale*), P.C. Brown (*Gala*), W. Lauder (*Neath*), J.W. Telfer* (*Melrose*), R.J. Arneil (*Leicester*). Sub: G.L. Brown (*West of Scot.*)

Wales: J.P.R. Williams (*London Welsh*); L.C.T. Daniel (*Newport*), S.J. Davies (*London Welsh*), P. Bennett (*Llanelli*), I. Hall (*Aberavon*); B. John (*Cardiff*), G.O. Edwards*

276

(*Cardiff*); D.B. Llewelyn (*Newport*), V.C. Perrins (*Newport*), D. Williams (*Ebbw Vale*), W.D. Thomas (*Llanelli*), T.G. Evans (*London Welsh*), W.D. Morris (*Neath*), T.M. Davies (*London Welsh*), D. Hughes (*Newbridge*)

Referee: D.P. D'Arcy (*Ireland*) **Touch judges:** R.A. Macdonald, E.M. Lewis

I. Robertson dropped a goal (3–0); W. Lauder kicked a penalty (6–0); I. Robertson scored but I.S.G. Smith failed (9–0); L.C.T. Daniel scored and converted (9–5).(H.T.). D.B. Llewelyn, S.J. Davies and W.D. Morris scored and G.O. Edwards converted the last two (9–18).

For the first twenty minutes the Scottish pack provided some good ball and, with the wind, their backs responded well. Robertson dropped a neat goal and Lauder kicked a penalty before Robertson, fielding a weak kick, set P.C. Brown and Young away and he was up to get the final pass to beat two defenders and score a good try. But just before the interval a short penalty move put Daniel in at the corner for a try which he converted. Just after restarting P.C. Brown limped off to be replaced by his brother (one wit suggested that the family could collect a good few caps if they pursued this act further!) but with the wind the Welsh pack really began to dominate play. Another short penalty move using the forwards saw Llewelyn crash over, Davies collected a charged down kick and scored, and later Morris scored when the pack shoved the scrum over the Scottish line.

IRELAND   Lansdowne Road   28 February 1970

SCOTLAND:	1 goal, 1 drop goal, 1 try	11	**Loss**
IRELAND:	2 goals, 2 tries	16	

Scotland: I.S.G. Smith (*London Scot.*); M.A. Smith (*London Scot.*), J.N.M. Frame (*Gala*), C.W.W. Rea (*West of Scot.*), A.G. Biggar (*London Scot.*); I. Robertson (*Watsonians*), D.S. Paterson (*Gala*); N. Suddon (*Hawick*), F.A.L. Laidlaw (*Melrose*), A.B. Carmichael (*West of Scot.*), P.K. Stagg (*Sale*), G.L. Brown (*West of Scot.*), W. Lauder (*Neath*), J.W. Telfer* (*Melrose*), R.J. Arneil (*Leicester*)

Ireland: T.J. Kiernan* (*Cork Const.*); A.T.A. Duggan (*Lansdowne*), F.P.K. Bresnihan (*London Irish*), C.M.H. Gibson (*NIFC*), W.J. Brown (*Malone*); B.J. McGann (*Cork Const.*), R.M. Young (*Collegians*); S. Millar (*Ballymena*), K.W. Kennedy (*London Irish*), P. O'Callaghan (*Dolphin*), W.J. McBride (*Ballymena*), M.G. Malloy (*London Irish*), R.A. Lamont (*Instonians*), K.G. Goodall (*Derry*), J.F. Slattery (*UC Dublin*)

Referee: C. Durand (*France*) **Touch judges:** E.J. Mentiplay, G.A. Jamison

M.G. Malloy scored but C.M.H. Gibson failed (0–3); I. Robertson dropped a goal (3–3); K.G. Goodall and C.M.H. Gibson scored and T.J. Kiernan converted both (3–10).(H.T.). W.J. Brown scored but R.M. Young failed (3–16); W. Lauder and M.A. Smith scored and I.S.G. Smith converted the first only (11–16).

Ireland dominated this game until the last fifteen minutes when Scotland staged a tremendous rally to score twice and come close a few times, Biggar in particular running robustly. The first Irish score was a solo effort by Malloy who grabbed a loose ball at a line out ten yards out and crashed his way over for the try. The other three scores were the result of some fine running and passing by the Irish backs. The Irish team raised its total of caps to a new level of 315!

ENGLAND   Murrayfield   21 March 1970

SCOTLAND: 1 goal, 2 penalty goals, 1 try   14   **Win**
ENGLAND: 1 goal   5

Scotland: I.S.G. Smith (*London Scot.*); M.A. Smith (*London Scot.*), J.N.M. Frame (*Gala*), J.W.C. Turner (*Gala*), A.G. Biggar (*London Scot.*); I. Robertson (*Watsonians*), D.S. Paterson (*Gala*); N. Suddon (*Hawick*), F.A.L. Laidlaw* (*Melrose*), A.B. Carmichael (*West of Scot.*), P.K. Stagg (*Sale*), G.L. Brown (*West of Scot.*), T.G. Elliot (*Langholm*), P.C. Brown (*Gala*), R.J. Arneil (*Leicester*)

England: R.B. Hiller* (*Harlequins*); M.J. Novak (*Harlequins*), J.S. Spencer (*Camb. Univ.*), D.J. Duckham (*Coventry*), M.P. Bullpitt (*Blackheath*); I.R. Shackleton (*Camb. Univ.*), N.C. Starmer-Smith (*Harlequins*); C.B. Stevens (*Penzance-Newlyn*), J.V. Pullin (*Bristol*), K.E. Fairbrother (*Coventry*), A.M. Davis (*Harlequins*), P.J. Larter (*Northampton*), A.L. Bucknall (*Richmond*), R.B. Taylor (*Northampton*), B.R. West (*Northampton*) Sub: B.S. Jackson (*Broughton Park*)

Referee: M. Joseph (*Wales*)   **Touch judges:** T.F.E. Grierson, R.A.B. Crowe

P.C. Brown kicked a penalty (3–0); A.G. Biggar scored but P.C. Brown failed (6–0).(H.T.). P.C. Brown kicked a penalty (9–0); J.S. Spencer scored and R.B. Hiller converted (9–5); J.W.C. Turner scored and P.C. Brown converted (14–5).

Scotland, who had dropped two of their back row including their ex-captain, started briskly for within ten minutes Brown had kicked a long range penalty followed by a good run by Robertson and Frame which finished with Biggar racing in at the corner. There was no further scoring before half time although Hiller had hard luck with four mammoth kicks at goal. Another good penalty by Brown seemed to make things safe but with seven minutes left England took a swift short penalty which set Spencer off on a magnificent 75 yard run to score at the corner; Hiller's great conversion put England back in the game.

At this point West went off with a leg injury and was replaced by Jackson but Turner clinched the match in the last minutes by scoring after taking a well-timed reverse pass from Robertson.

AUSTRALIA   Sydney   6 June 1970

SCOTLAND: 1 penalty goal   3   **Loss**
AUSTRALIA: 1 goal, 1 penalty goal, 5 tries   23

Scotland: J.W.C. Turner (*Gala*); M.A. Smith (*London Scot.*), J.N.M. Frame (*Gala*), C.W.W. Rea (*West of Scot.*), A.G. Biggar (*London Scot.*); I. Robertson (*Watsonians*), D.S. Paterson (*Gala*); N. Suddon (*Hawick*), F.A.L. Laidlaw* (*Melrose*), A.B. Carmichael (*West of Scot.*), P.K. Stagg (*Sale*), G.L. Brown (*West of Scot.*), W. Lauder (*Neath*), G.K. Oliver (*Gala*), R.J. Arneil (*Leicester*)

Australia: A.N. McGill (*NSW*); J.W. Cole (*NSW*), S.O. Knight (*NSW*), G.A. Shaw (*NSW*), R.P. Batterham (*NSW*); R.G. Rosenblum (*NSW*), J.N.B. Hipwell (*NSW*); J.L. Howard (*NSW*), P.G. Johnson (*NSW*), J.R. Roxburgh (*NSW*), A.J. Skinner (*NSW*), O.F. Butler (*NSW*), G.V. Davis* (*NSW*), H.A. Rose (*NSW*), B.S. McDonald (*NSW*)

Referee: R. Vanderfield

J.N.B. Hipwell and R.P. Batterham scored and A.N. McGill converted the first (0–8); W. Lauder kicked a penalty (3–8).(H.T.). R.G. Rosenblum scored but A.N. McGill failed (3–11); A.N. McGill kicked a penalty (3–14); J.W. Cole, R.P. Batterham and J.W. Cole scored but A. McGill failed to convert (3–23).

Scotland finished off a short tour to Australia by being completely overrun in the one International played. They started well but mishandling let them down and Australia soon took command of the play. With the wind in the second half their backs made good use of a plentiful supply of the ball and ran in four unconverted tries to finish convincing winners.

FRANCE   Colombes   16 January 1971

SCOTLAND:	1 goal, 1 penalty goal	8	**Loss**
FRANCE:	2 goals, 1 penalty goal	13	

Scotland: I.S.G. Smith (*London Scot.*); A.G. Biggar (*London Scot.*), J.N.M. Frame (*Gala*), C.W.W. Rea (*Headingley*), W.C.C. Steele (*Bedford*); J.W.C. Turner (*Gala*), D.S. Paterson (*Gala*); J. McLauchlan (*Jordanhill Coll.*), F.A.L. Laidlaw (*Melrose*), A.B. Carmichael (*West of Scot.*), A.F. McHarg (*London Scot.*), G.L. Brown (*West of Scot.*), N.A. MacEwan (*Gala*), P.C. Brown* (*Gala*), R.J. Arneil (*Leicester*) Sub: B.M. Simmers (*Glas. Acads.*)

France: P. Villepreux (*Toulouse*); J. Sillieres (*Tarbes*), J. Trillo (*Begles*), J.-P. Lux (*Tyrosse*), J. Cantoni (*Beziers*); J.-L. Berot (*Toulouse*), M. Barrau (*Beaumont*); M. Etchevery (*Pau*), R. Benesis (*Narbonne*), J.-L. Azarete (*St Jean de Lux*), J.-P. Bastiat (*Dax*), Y. le Droff (*Auch*), G. Viard (*Narbonne*), B. Dauga* (*Mont-de-Marsan*), D. Dubois (*Begles*)

Referee: K.D. Kellehar (*Ireland*)   **Touch judges:** D.C.J. McMahon, R. Calmet

P. Villepreux kicked a penalty (0–3); I.S.G. Smith kicked a penalty (3–3).(H.T.). W.C.C. Steele scored and P.C. Brown converted (8–3); J. Sillieres scored and P. Villepreux converted (8–8); P. Villepreux scored and converted (8–13).

At the end of a fairly even first half Smith had to leave the field injured by a hard late tackle. He was replaced in the second half by Simmers who, however, was placed at stand off and Turner who had been playing well there, went to full back. This move was not really a success and came in for much criticism later. The Scottish try started when Rea, inside his own 25, pounced on a loose pass and the ball went via Frame to Steele who chipped ahead, gathered and scored in the corner. The French backs kept running the ball and inside the last ten minutes ran in two fine tries to win the match.

WALES	Murrayfield	6 February 1971

SCOTLAND: 4 penalties, 2 tries 18 **Loss**

WALES: 2 goals, 1 penalty goal, 2 tries 19

Scotland: I.S.G. Smith (*London Scot.*); W.C.C. Steele (*Bedford*), J.N.M. Frame (*Gala*), C.W.W. Rea (*Headingley*), A.G. Biggar (*London Scot.*); J.W.C. Turner (*Gala*), D.S. Paterson (*Gala*); J. McLauchlan (*Jordanhill Coll.*), F.A.L. Laidlaw (*Melrose*), A.B. Carmichael (*West of Scot.*), A.F. McHarg (*London Scot.*), G.L. Brown (*West of Scot.*), N.A. MacEwan (*Gala*), P.C. Brown* (*Gala*), R.J. Arneil (*Leicester*)

Wales: J.P.R. Williams (*London Welsh*); T.G.R. Davies (*Camb. Univ.*), S.J. Dawes* (*London Welsh*), A.J. Lewis (*Ebbw Vale*), J.C. Bevan (*Cardiff CE*); B. John (*Cardiff*), G.O. Edwards (*Cardiff*); D.B. Llewelyn (*Llanelli*), J. Young (*Harrogate*), D. Williams (*Ebbw Vale*), W.D. Thomas (*Llanelli*), M.G. Roberts (*London Welsh*), W.D. Norris (*Neath*), T.M. Davies (*London Welsh*), J. Taylor (*London Welsh*)

Referee: M.H. Titcomb (*England*) **Touch judges:** J. Young, D.L. Daniels

P.C. Brown kicked a penalty (3–0); B. John kicked a penalty (3–3); P.C. Brown kicked a penalty (6–3); J. Taylor scored and B. John converted (6–8).(H.T.). G.O. Edwards scored but J. Taylor failed (6–11); A.B. Carmichael scored but P.C. Brown failed (9–11); P.C. Brown kicked a penalty (12–11); B. John scored but failed (12–14); P.C. Brown kicked a penalty (15–14); C.W.W. Rea scored but P.C. Brown failed (18–14); T.G.R. Davies scored and J. Taylor converted (18–19).

This must rank as one of the most exciting matches ever played. Scotland, very much the underdogs, held the lead four times and only lost by what was virtually the last kick of the game. The Welsh team whose half backs were outstanding was undoubtedly good and with a try tally of 4–2 could not really be grudged their win, but credit must be given to a Scottish XV which never gave in. The Scottish tries came from powerful and determined solo efforts by Carmichael and Rea while the Welsh scores savoured more of team work superbly finished off by the gifted individuals concerned. In the last minutes Wales won a line out inside the 25 and the ball went across the line to the right. The inside centre was missed out and Williams came into the line to put Davies over at the corner. Taylor won the match with a left-footed kick which has been described elsewhere as 'the greatest conversion since St Paul's!

IRELAND	Murrayfield	27 February 1971

SCOTLAND: 1 goal 5 **Loss**

IRELAND: 1 goal, 2 penalty goals, 2 tries 17

280

Scotland: I.S.G. Smith (*London Scot.*); W.C.C. Steele (*Bedford*), J.N.M. Frame (*Gala*), A.G. Biggar (*London Scot.*), R.S.M. Hannah (*West of Scot.*); J.W.C. Turner (*Gala*), D.S. Paterson (*Gala*); J. McLauchlan (*Jordanhill Coll.*), F.A.L. Laidlaw (*Melrose*), A.B. Carmichael (*West of Scot.*), A.F. McHarg (*London Scot.*), G.L. Brown (*West of Scot.*), N.A. MacEwan (*Gala*), P.C. Brown* (*Gala*), R.J. Arneil (*Leicester*)

Ireland: B.J. O'Driscoll (*Manchester*); A.T.A. Duggan (*Lansdowne*), F.P.K. Bresnihan (*London Irish*), C.M.H. Gibson* (*NIFC*), E.L. Grant (*CIYMS*); B.J. McGann (*Cork Const.*), R.M. Young (*Collegians*); R.J. McLoughlin (*Blackrock*), K.W. Kennedy (*London Irish*), J.F. Lynch (*St Mary's*), W.J. McBride (*Ballymena*), M.G. Molloy (*London Irish*), M.L. Hipwell (*Terenure*), D.J. Hickie (*St Mary's*), J.F. Slattery (*UC Dublin*)

Referee: W.K.M. Jones (*Wales*)   Touch judges: T.F.E. Grierson, P. Beatty

C.H.M. Gibson kicked a penalty (0–3); A.T.A. Duggan scored but B.J. O'Driscoll failed (0–6); C.M.H. Gibson kicked a penalty (0–9).(H.T.); J.N.M. Frame scored and P.C. Brown converted (5–9); E.L. Grant scored but C.M.H. Gibson failed (5–12); A.T.A. Duggan scored and C.M.H. Gibson converted (5–17).

The first half belonged to Ireland who, with an advantage in the scrums, continually ran the ball and a blind side run by Young and McGann put Duggan in for a try. Gibson also kicked two fine long range penalties before the interval. Scotland improved a little in the second half and several individual bursts narrowly failed before Frame crashed over to score. Heartened by this Scotland fought hard only to hand Ireland two gift tries in injury time. The first came when Young picked up a wretched Scottish heel from a scrum and gave Grant a clear run in. A minute later an interception near half field gave Duggan another try to finish the match.

ENGLAND   Twickenham   20 March 1971

SCOTLAND:	2 goals, 1 drop goal, 1 try	16	**Win**
ENGLAND:	3 penalty goals, 2 tries	15	

Scotland: A.R. Brown (*Gala*); W.C.C. Steele (*Bedford*), J.N.M. Frame (*Gala*), C.W.W. Rea (*Headingley*), A.G. Biggar (*London Scot.*); J.W.C. Turner (*Gala*); D.S. Paterson (*Gala*); J. McLauchlan (*Jordanhill Coll.*), Q. Dunlop (*West of Scot.*), A.B. Carmichael (*West of Scot.*), A.F. McHarg (*London Scot.*), G.L. Brown (*West of Scot.*), N.A. MacEwan (*Gala*), P.C. Brown* (*Gala*), R.J. Arneil (*Leicester*) Sub: A.S. Turk (*Langholm*)

England: R. Hiller (*Harlequins*); J.P. Janion (*Bedford*), C.S. Wardlow (*Northampton*), J.S. Spencer* (*Headingley*), D.J. Duckham (*Coventry*); A.R. Cowman (*Loughborough*), J.J. Page (*Bedford*); D.L. Powell (*Northampton*), J.V. Pullin (*Bristol*), F.E. Cotton (*Loughborough*), P.J. Larter (*Northampton*), N.E. Horton (*Moseley*), A.L. Bucknall (*Richmond*), R.B. Taylor (*Northampton*), A. Neary (*Broughton Park*) Sub: I.D. Wright (*Northampton*)

Referee: C. Durand (*France*)   Touch judges: H.B. Laidlaw, G.C. Lamb

R. Hiller scored but failed (0–3); P.C. Brown scored and converted (5–3); R. Hiller kicked two penalties (5–9).(H.T.). D.S. Paterson dropped a goal (8–9); A. Neary scored but R.

Hiller failed (8–12); R. Hiller kicked a penalty (8–15); D.S. Paterson scored but P.C. Brown failed (11–15); C.W.W. Rea scored and P.C. Brown converted (16–15).

For the second time in the season Scotland were involved in a match won by the last kick of the game but this time Brown's conversion gave them their first win at Twickenham since 1938. England opened the scoring when Janion fielded a kick ahead and beat several men before the ball passed from Cowman, Taylor and Spencer to Hiller who scored at the corner. Frame had previously gone off with an injured thigh and Turk now came on as substitute. Soon P.C. Brown followed a break by Rea and finished a handling run by Biggar and MacEwan to score a try which he converted to give Scotland the lead. However two penalties by Hiller put England in front at the interval. At this stage Wardlow was replaced by Wright who went on to the wing with Duckham at centre. Paterson soon had a smart drop goal but once again poor Scottish heeling gave Page a chance to pick up and send Neary in for a try and England looked very safe when Hiller kicked his third penalty with eight minutes to go. Then Paterson took advantage of a defensive fumble to score and in the last minute Rea, who had been the sharpest centre all afternoon, whipped through a gap to score a try which Brown converted to win the match.

ENGLAND   Murrayfield   27 March 1971

SCOTLAND: 4 goals, 1 penalty goal, 1 try   26   **Win**

ENGLAND: 1 drop goal, 1 penalty goal   6

Scotland: A.R. Brown (*Gala*); W.C.C. Steele (*Bedford*), J.N.M. Frame (*Gala*), C.W.W. Rea (*Headingley*), A.G. Biggar (*London Scot.*); J.W.C. Turner (*Gala*), D.S. Paterson (*Gala*); J. McLauchlan (*Jordanhill Coll.*), Q. Dunlop (*West of Scot.*), A.B. Carmichael (*West of Scot.*), A.F. McHarg (*London Scot.*), G.L. Brown (*West of Scot.*), N.A. MacEwan (*Gala*), P.C. Brown* (*Gala*), R.J. Arneil (*Leicester*) Sub: G.M. Strachan (*Jordanhill Coll.*)

England: R. Hiller (*Harlequins*); J.P. Janion (*Bedford*), C.S. Wardlow (*Northampton*), J.S. Spencer* (*Headingley*), D.J. Duckham (*Coventry*); A.R. Cowman (*Loughborough*), N.C. Starmer-Smith (*Harlequins*); D.L. Powell (*Northampton*), J.V. Pullin (*Bristol*), F.E. Cotton (*Loughborough*), P.J. Larter (*Northampton*), C.W. Ralston (*Richmond*), A.L. Bucknall (*Richmond*), R.B. Taylor (*Northampton*), A. Neary (*Broughton Park*)

Referee: M. Joseph (*Wales*) **Touch judges:** R.P. Burrell, T.F.E. Grierson

J.N.M. Frame scored and A.R. Brown converted (5–0); P.C. Brown kicked a penalty (8–0); A.R. Cowman dropped a goal (8–3); P.C. Brown scored but did not convert (11–3).(H.T.). J.N.M. Frame scored and A.R. Brown converted (16–3); R. Hiller kicked a penalty (16–6); W.C.C. Steele and C.W.W. Rea scored and A.R. Brown converted both (26–6).

This was an extra game played in Edinburgh to mark the Centenary of the first International at Raeburn Place on the same date in 1871. It was attended by the Prince of Wales and the Prime Minister. There was an extraordinary start to the match. Turner kicked off and Hiller fielded the ball near his right hand corner flag. He passed inside and left to Janion who at once handed on to Cowman. His pass to Spencer was dropped and Frame, moving up for the tackle, took the ball over the line to score in what was estimated to be 10–12 seconds after the kick-off — surely the quickest try ever scored in an International match! By half time a penalty and a try by P.C. Brown against a drop goal by Cowman made the score 11–3. In the second half some fine combined play by the Scots produced three good tries and England could only reply with a penalty by Hiller to make the score 26–6. Just after Steele's try an injured G.L. Brown was replaced by Strachan.

FRANCE   **Murrayfield**   **15 January 1972**

SCOTLAND: 1 goal, 1 drop goal,   20   **Win**
                 1 penalty goal, 2 tries

FRANCE: 1 goal, 1 penalty goal   9

Scotland: A.R. Brown (*Gala*); W.C.C. Steele (*Bedford*), J.N.M. Frame (*Gala*), J.M. Renwick (*Hawick*), A.G. Biggar (*London Scot.*); C.M. Telfer (*Hawick*), I.G. MacCrae (*Gordonians*); J. McLauchlan (*Jordanhill Coll.*), R.L. Clark (*Edin. Wrs.*), A.B. Carmichael (*West of Scot.*), A.F. McHarg (*London Scot.*), G.L. Brown (*West of Scot.*), N.A. MacEwan (*Gala*), P.C. Brown* (*Gala*), R.J.Arneil (*Northampton*) Sub: A.J.M. Lawson (*Edin. Wrs.*)

France: P. Villepreux (*Toulouse*); R. Bertranne (*Bagneres*), J. Trillo (*Begles*), J.-P. Lux (*Dax*), J. Cantoni (*Beziers*); J.-L. Berot (*Toulouse*), J.-M. Aguirre (*Bagneres*); A. Vacquerin (*Beziers*), R. Benesis (*Agen*), J.-L. Martin (*Beziers*), J.-P. Bestiat (*Dax*), B. Dauga* (*Mont-de-Marsan*), O. Saisset (*Beziers*), C. Spanghero (*Narbonne*), V. Boffelli (*Aurillac*)

Referee: M. Joseph (*Wales*) **Touch judges:** T.F.E. Grierson, J. Saint-Guilhem

C.M. Telfer scored but P.C. Brown failed (4–0); C.M. Telfer dropped a goal (7–0); P.C. Brown kicked a penalty (10–0).(H.T.). P. Villepreux kicked a penalty (10–3); J.M. Renwick scored but P.C. Brown failed (14–3); B. Dauga scored and P. Villepreux converted (14–9); J.N.M. Frame scored and A.R. Brown converted (20–9).

The French backs were full of running but the defence was solid and over all the Scottish pack were splendid in the loose and line out. Their first try came from a rush that was halted; MacEwan pounced on a bad heel and got the ball out to Biggar who sent Telfer in. Then a Telfer drop goal came from fine possession at a line out on the 25 yard line. MacCrae had to go off with rib trouble after ten minutes of the second half. Villepreux kicked a penalty just before Lawson came on as substitute. Then Arthur Brown picked up a French kick through, ran the ball out to link with Biggar who put Renwick over near the left corner. The French replied with a fierce rush by their forwards finished off by the powerful Dauga crashing over. Right on time Telfer got good possession from a line out and slipped a reverse pass to Frame who smashed his way through four or five tackles to score at the posts. After the whistle for the conversion the delighted crowd erupted onto the field and had to be sent back for another minute of injury time.

WALES   **Cardiff**   **5 February 1972**

SCOTLAND: 1 goal, 2 penalty goals   12   **Loss**

WALES: 3 goals, 3 penalty goals, 2 tries 35

Scotland: A.R. Brown (*Gala*); W.C.C. Steele (*Bedford*), J.N.M. Frame (*Gala*), J.M. Renwick (*Hawick*), A.G. Biggar (*London Scot.*); C.M. Telfer (*Hawick*), D.S. Paterson (*Gala*); J. McLauchlan (*Jordanhill Coll.*), R.L. Clark (*Edin. Wrs.*), A.B. Carmichael (*West of Scot.*), I.R. Barnes (*Hawick*), G.L. Brown (*West of Scot.*), N.A. MacEwan (*Gala*), P.C. Brown* (*Gala*), R.J. Arneil (*Northampton*) Sub: L.G. Dick (*Loughborough*)

Wales: J.P.R. Williams (*London Welsh*); T.G.R. Davies (*London Welsh*), R.T.E. Bergiers (*Cardiff*), A.J. Lewis (*Ebbw Vale*), J.C. Bevan (*Cardiff*); B. John (*Cardiff*), G.O. Edwards (*Cardiff*); D.J. Lloyd* (*Bridgend*), J. Young (*RAF*), D.B. Llewelyn (*Llanelli*), W.D. Thomas (*Llanelli*), T.G. Evans (*London Welsh*), W.D. Morris (*Neath*), T.M. Davies (*London Welsh*), J. Taylor (*London Welsh*) Sub: P. Bennett (*Llanelli*)

Referee: G.A. Jamieson (*Ireland*) **Touch judges:** F. Parker, E.M.Lewis

J.M. Renwick kicked a penalty (3–0); B. John kicked a penalty (3–3); T.G.R. Davies scored but B. John failed (3–7); P.C. Brown kicked a penalty (6–7); B. John kicked a penalty (6–10).(H.T.). R.L. Clark scored and P.C. Brown converted (12–10); G.O. Edwards scored twice and B. John converted the first only (12–20); B. John kicked a penalty (12–23); R.T.E. Bergiers and J. Taylor scored and B. John converted both (12–35).

In spite of some hard running by the Welsh backs who were given good possession by their pack, Scotland held grimly onto a narrow lead until fifteen minutes after the restart when Edwards scored a somewhat suspect try following a peel from a line out on the Scottish line. Then the Welsh pack, with Davies prominent in the line out, dominated the game with the result that their threes smashed through the Scottish defence for three fierce tries, Edwards and T.G.R. Davies being particularly dangerous. J.P.R. Williams was replaced by P. Bennett after twenty minutes of the first half whilst Dick came on for Biggar after six minutes of the second half.

ENGLAND   Murrayfield   18 March 1972

SCOTLAND: 1 drop goal, 4 penalty goals, 2 tries   23   **Win**

ENGLAND: 3 penalty goals   9

Scotland: A.R. Brown (*Gala*); W.C.C. Steele (*Bedford*), J.N.M. Frame (*Gala*), J.M. Renwick (*Hawick*), L.G. Dick (*Loughborough*); C.M. Telfer (*Hawick*), A.J.M. Lawson (*Edin. Wrs.*); J. McLaughlan (*Jordanhill Coll.*), R.L. Clark (*Edin. Wrs.*), A.B. Carmichael (*West of Scot.*), A.F. McHarg (*London Scot.*), G.L. Brown (*West of Scot.*), N.A. MacEwan (*Gala*), P.C. Brown* (*Gala*), R.J. Arneil (*Northampton*)

England: P.M. Knight (*Bristol*); K.J. Fielding (*Moseley*), J.P.A.G. Janion (*Bedford*), G.W. Evans (*Coventry*), D.J. Duckham (*Coventry*); A.G.B. Old (*Middlesbrough*), L.E. Weston (*West of Scot.*); C.B. Stevens (*Harlequins*), J.V. Pullin (*Bristol*), M.A. Burton (*Gloucester*), A. Brinn (*Gloucester*), C.W. Ralston (*Richmond*), P.J. Dixon* (*Harlequins*), A.G. Ripley (*Rosslyn Park*), A. Neary (*Broughton Park*)

N.A. MacEwan scored but A.R. Brown failed (4–0); A.G.B. Old kicked a penalty (4–3); P.C. Brown kicked a penalty (7–3); P.C. Brown scored but A.R. Brown failed (11–3); C.M. Telfer dropped a goal (14–3).(H.T.). A.G.B. Old kicked two penalties (14–9); A.R. Brown kicked a penalty (17–9); P.C. Brown kicked two penalties (23–0).

This was not a great exhibition of open rugby yet Scotland could be moderately satisfied with a try tally of 2–0. The first came from a bad pass to Old which Telfer tapped on to catch Knight with the ball and MacEwan was there to snap up the ball and score. Well through the first half P.C. Brown took a clean catch at the tail of the line out and charged over from three yards out. Right on the interval another clean catch by Brown let Telfer drop a nice goal. The second half was marked by five penalty goals although Steele and Janion each had exciting solo runs.

NEW ZEALAND Murrayfield 16 December 1972

SCOTLAND: 1 drop goal, 2 penalty goals 9 Loss
NEW ZEALAND: 1 goal, 2 tries 14

Scotland: A.R. Irvine (*Heriot's FP*); W.C.C. Steele (*Bedford*), I.W. Forsyth (*Stewart's FP*), J.M. Renwick (*Hawick*), D. Shedden (*West of Scot.*); I.R. McGeechan (*Headingley*), I.G. McCrae (*Gordonians*); J. McLauchlan (*Jordanhill Coll.*), R.L. Clark (*Edin. Wrs.*), A.B. Carmichael (*West of Scot.*), A.F. McHarg (*London Scot.*), G.L. Brown (*West of Scot.*), N.A. MacEwan (*Gala*), P.C. Brown* (*Gala*), R.J. Arneil (*Northampton*)

New Zealand: J.F. Karam (*Wellington*); B.G. Williams (*Auckland*), B. Robertson (*Counties*), R.M. Parkinson (*Poverty Bay*), G.B. Batty (*Wellington*); I.N. Stevens (*Wellington*), S.M. Going (*North Auckland*); J.D. Matheson (*Otago*), R.W. Norton (*Canterbury*), G.J. Whiting (*King Country*), P.J. Whiting (*Auckland*), H.H. McDonald (*Canterbury*), I.A. Kirkpatrick* (*Poverty Bay*), A.I. Scown (*Taranaki*), A.J. Wyllie (*Canterbury*) Sub: K.K. Lambert (*Manawata*)

Referee: G. Domercq (*France*) **Touch judges:** A.M. Hosie, J.G. Dow

A. Scown scored and J.F. Karam converted (0–6).(H.T.). A.R. Irvine kicked a penalty (3–6); G.B. Batty scored but J.F. Karam failed (3–10); I.R. McGeechan dropped a goal (6–10); A.R. Irvine kicked a penalty (9–10); S.M. Going scored but J.F. Karam failed (9–14).

Play was mainly confined to the Scottish half for the powerful and active New Zealand forwards dominated play in the loose although Scotland did quite well in the set scrums and line out. Behind his fine pack Going was a constant menace, setting up the first try for Wyllie and scoring the vital try in the last minute by intercepting a dangerous pass at midfield and running on to score. The second New Zealand try came when Robertson, after a wandering run in the Scottish 25 area, placed a lovely kick to the corner which allowed Batty to run on to the ball and score. For Scotland, the new caps defended well, Irvine making a particularly impressive debut, but really the whole team raised their game and were making a tremendous fight to score in injury time when Going clinched the match with his runaway score.

FRANCE Parc des Princes **13 January 1973**

SCOTLAND: 1 drop goal, 2 penalties, 1 try 13 **Loss**

FRANCE: 1 drop goal, 3 penalties, 1 try 16

Scotland: A.R. Irvine (*Heriot's FP*); W.C.C. Steele (*Bedford*), I.W. Forsyth (*Stewart's FP*), J.M. Renwick (*Hawick*), D. Shedden (*West of Scot.*); I.R. McGeechan (*Headingley*), A.J.M. Lawson (*Edin. Wrs.*); J. McLauchlan (*Jordanhill Coll.*), R.L. Clark (*Edin. Wrs.*), A.B. Carmichael (*West of Scot.*), A.F. McHarg (*London Scot.*), R.W.J. Wright (*Edin. Wrs.*), N.A. MacEwan (*Gala*), P.C. Brown* (*Gala*), W. Lauder (*Neath*)

France: J. Cantoni (*Beziers*); J.-P. Lux (*Dax*), C. Dourthe (*Dax*), J. Trillo (*Begles*), R. Bougarel (*Toulouse*); J.-P. Romeu (*Montferrand*), M. Barrau (*Toulouse*); A. Vaquerin (*Beziers*), A. Lubrano (*Beziers*), J.J. Iracabal (*Bayonne*), E. Cester (*Valence*), A. Esteve (*Beziers*), O. Saisset (*Beziers*), W. Spanghero* (*Narbonne*), P. Biemouret (*Agen*)

Referee: K. Pattinson (*England*), M.F. Palmade (*France*) **Touch judges:** J. Dun, M.F. Palmade

J.-P. Romeu kicked two penalties (0–6); P.C. Brown kicked a penalty (3–6); C. Dourthe scored but J.-P. Romeu failed (3–10); I.R. McGeechan dropped a goal (6–10).(H.T.). A.J.M. Lawson scored but P.C. Brown failed (10–10); J.-P. Romeu kicked two penalties (10–16); P.C. Brown kicked a penalty (13–16).

This was the first match in the new stadium at Parc des Princes. Although there was only a penalty difference between the scores France deserved to win because of their extra sharpness in the broken play. Back play was dominated by too much kicking. The French try came from a loose ball picked up by Cester and passed through several hands to Dourthe who went through a Scotland defence. The Scottish try started from a high kick by McGeechan; Renwick flattened the catcher and Clark got the loose ball away to Lawson who scored. After thirteen minutes Mr Pattinson had to retire with a leg injury and was replaced by the French touchjudge who proved to be a most impartial and strict referee.

WALES Murrayfield **3 February 1973**

SCOTLAND: 1 goal, 1 try 10 **Win**

WALES: 3 penalties 9

Scotland: A.R. Irvine (*Heriot's FP*); W.C.C. Steele (*Bedford*), I.R. McGeechan (*Headingley*), I.W. Forsyth (*Stewart's FP*), D. Shedden (*West of Scot.*); C.M. Telfer (*Hawick*), D.W. Morgan (*Melville Coll. FP*); J. McLauchlan* (*Jordanhill*), R.L. Clark (*Edin. Wrs.*), A.B. Carmichael (*West of Scot.*), A.F. McHarg (*London Scot.*), P.C. Brown (*Gala*), N.A. MacEwan (*Gala*), G.M. Strachan (*Jordanhill*), J.G. Millican (*Edin. Univ.*)

Wales: J.P.R. Williams (*London Welsh*); T.G.R. Davies (*London Welsh*), R.T.E. Bergiers (*Llanelli*), A.J.L. Lewis* (*Ebbw Vale*), J.C. Bevan (*Cardiff*); P. Bennet (*Llanelli*), G.O.

Edwards (*Cardiff*); G. Shaw (*Neath*), J. Young (*London Welsh*), D.J. Lloyd (*Bridgend*), W.D. Thomas (*Llanelli*), D.L. Quinnell (*Llanelli*). W.D. Morris (*Neath*), T.M. Davies (*Swansea*), J. Taylor (*London Welsh*)

Referee: M.F. Palmade (*France*)   **Touch judges:** J. Young, J. Mescall

C.M. Telfer and W.C.C. Steele scored and D.W. Morgan converted the first only (10–0); P. Bennett and J. Taylor kicked penalties (10–6).(H.T.). P. Bennett kicked a penalty (10–9).

Wales with nine Lions in their team and five successive wins against Scotland arrived as favourites but found themselves up against a pack which held them, especially at the line outs, nor could their backs break through a defence which covered their every move and tackled ruthlessly.

Wales attacked from the start but a fine follow up tackle by McGeechan on Williams resulted in a scrum won by Scotland and Telfer, with Forsyth running outside him, dummied, and broke inside for a fine try. Some more strong Welsh running broke against a solid defence and then a fast run from defence by Irvine ended by Wales having to carry over and touch down. Scotland won the strike; Telfer went off on a decoy run and the ball was passed instead to Steele who shot through a scattered defence to score. For the rest of the match Scotland fairly held their own, putting in strong attacks while halting every Welsh move. All that Wales could manage was three good penalties which closed the scoring but Irvine came close with a drop at goal while a late penalty attempt by Morgan went so close that the touch judges hesitated before deciding against it.

IRELAND	Murrayfield	24 February 1973

SCOTLAND:	3 drop goals, 2 penalty goals, 1 try	19	**Win**
IRELAND:	2 penalty goals, 2 tries	15	

Scotland: A.R. Irvine (*Heriot's FP*); W.C.C. Steele (*Bedford*), I.R. McGeechan (*Headingley*), I.W. Forsyth (*Stewart's FP*), D. Shedden (*West of Scot.*); C.M. Telfer (*Hawick*), D.W. Morgan (*Melville Coll. FP*); J. McLauchlan* (*Jordanhill Coll.*), R.L. Clark (*Edin. Wrs.*), A.B. Carmichael (*West of Scot.*), A.F. McHarg (*London Scot.*), P.C. Brown (*Gala*), N.A. MacEwan (*Gala*), G.M. Strachan (*Jordanhill Coll.*), J.G. Millican (*Edin. Univ.*) Sub: R.D.H. Bryce (*West of Scot.*)

Ireland: T.J. Kiernan* (*Cork Const.*); T.O. Grace (*St Mary's*), R.A. Milliken (*Bangor*), C.M.H. Gibson (*NIFC*), A.W. McMaster (*Ballymena*); B.J. McGann (*Cork Const.*), J.J. Maloney (*St Mary's*); R.J. McLoughlin (*Blackrock*), K.W. Kennedy (*London Irish*), J.F. Lynch (*St Mary's*), K.M.A. Mays (*UC Dublin*), W.J. McBride (*Ballymena*), J.F. Slattery (*Blackrock*), T.A.P. Moore (*Highfield*), J.H. Buckley (*Sunday's Well*)

Referee: R. Lewis (*Wales*)   **Touch judges:** T.F.E. Grierson, J.R. West

D.W. Morgan kicked a penalty (3–0); B.J. McGann kicked two penalties (3–6); D.W. Morgan dropped a goal and kicked a penalty (9–6); A.W. McMaster scored but B.J. McGann failed (9–10).(H.T.). I.R. McGeechan dropped a goal (12–10); T.J. Kiernan scored but B.J. McGann failed (12–14); I.W. Forsyth scored but D.W. Morgan failed (16–14); D.W. Morgan dropped a goal (19–14).

287

Ireland, who had not lost at Murrayfield since 1963, came with a very experienced tea~
captained by Kiernan whose 54th and last cap this was to be. However, the Scottish pac
gave as good as they got in a hard uncompromising forward battle while their backs we~
probably more dangerous than their opponents especially as McGann tended to overkick ~
half. The play opened with a series of penalties and a drop goal for Morgan who managed ~
hold on to a desperate clearance by Kiernan and get in his kick. Just before half tim~
McLauchlan had to go off with a cracked fibula and from a scrum McGann went blind an~
put McMaster in at the corner to regain the lead. Bryce came on for the second half and ~
nice drop by McGeechan put Scotland back in the lead. Then Gibson made a nice break an~
the ball went from McMaster to Kiernan who crossed at the corner only to be crashed in~
touch in goal. To the dismay of all Scots he was adjudged to have scored and so Ireland too~
the lead for the third time. With some ten minutes to go Scotland fairly raised their gam~
Steele was halted by a firm tackle and then just lost the touch down to Grace, but in the la~
minutes Irvine came up with the ball, was supported by a galloping McHarg who passed ~
Forsyth and the burly centre crashed over in the left corner. Morgan missed the lon~
conversion but right on time dropped a fine goal from near the left touch line to finish th~
game.

ENGLAND   Twickenham   17 March 197~

| **SCOTLAND:** | 1 goal, 1 penalty goal, 1 try | 13 | Los |
| **ENGLAND:** | 2 goals, 2 tries | 20 | |

Scotland: A.R. Irvine (*Heriot's FP*); W.C.C. Steele (*Bedford*), I.R. McGeechan (*Heading*
ley), I.W. Forsyth (*Stewart's FP*), D. Shedden (*West of Scot.*); C.M. Telfer (*Hawick*
D.W. Morgan (*Melville Coll. FP*); J. McLauchlan* (*Jordanhill Coll.*), R.L. Clark (*Edin*
Wrs.), A.B. Carmichael (*West of Scot.*), A.F. McHarg (*London Scot.*), P.C. Brown (*Gala*
N.A. MacEwan (*Gala*), G.M. Strachan (*Jordanhill Coll.*), J.G. Millican (*Edin. Univ.*) Sub
G.L. Brown (*West of Scot.*)

England: A.M. Jorden (*Blackheath*); P.J. Squires (*Harrogate*), G.W. Evans (*Coventry*
P.S. Preece (*Coventry*), D.J. Duckham (*Coventry*); M.J. Cooper (*Moseley*), S.J. Smit
(*Sale*); C.B. Stevens (*Penzance–Newlyn*), J.V. Pullin* (*Bristol*), F.E. Cotton (*Lough*
borough), R.M. Uttley (*Gosforth*), C.W. Ralston (*Richmond*), P.J. Dixon (*Gosforth*), ~
Neary (*Broughton Park*), A.G. Ripley (*Rosslyn Park*)

  Referee: J.C. Kelleher (*Wales*)   **Touch judges:** Dr K.B. Slawson, M.H. Titcomb

P.J. Squires and P.J. Dixon scored but A.M. Jorden failed to convert (0–8).(H.T.). P.J
Dixon scored and A.M. Jorden converted (0–14); D.W. Morgan kicked a penalty (3–14)
W.C.C. Steele scored twice but D.W. Morgan failed with the first and A.R. Irvin
converted the second (13–14); G.W. Evans scored and A.M. Jorden converted (13–20).

Scotland went to Twickenham with high hopes of lifting the Triple Crown but foundere~
against an English pack which was on top in all phases of forward play. J. McLauchlan
who had had no match play since his injury against Ireland, was quite determined to play,
decision that many both before and after the game considered to be most unwise. Howeve~
Cooper, with an ample supply of the ball, tended to kick rather than release an obvious~
active set of backs and it was some twenty minutes before a run saw Squires score. Almos
from the kick off Evans set Duckham off on a run halted by McHarg on the line, but Dixo~

was up to score. Soon after the interval a peel from a line finished with Dixon scoring again. With ten minutes to go Scotland came right back into the game. Morgan kicked a 50 yard penalty and then Steele, hemmed in on the touch line, kicked ahead, charged down Smith's attempted clearance and was first to the ball for a score. Here a concussed Millican was replaced by G.L. Brown. Duckham was again halted on the line and then from a sluggish English heel Morgan hacked the ball on and it reached McGeechan who fed P.C. Brown. The latter threw a long pass to Steele who got in with three men hanging onto him. Irvine's conversion from the touch line brought the score to 13–14 but almost at once a punt over the line by Preece bounced awkwardly and Evans was able to beat the defence for the last score.

SRU PRESIDENT'S XV Murrayfield   31 March 1973

SCOTLAND:	2 goals, 1 penalty goal, 3 tries	37	**Win**
PRESIDENT'S XV:	2 goals, 1 try	16	

Scotland: A.R. Irvine (*Heriot's FP*); A.D. Gill (*Gala*), I.R. McGeechan (*Headingley*), I.W. Forsyth (*Stewart's FP*), D. Shedden (*West of Scot.*); C.M. Telfer (*Hawick*), D.M. Morgan (*Melville Coll. FP*); J. McLauchlan* (*Jordanhill Coll.*), R.L. Clark (*Edin. Wrs.*), A.B. Carmichael (*West of Scot.*), A.F. McHarg (*London Scot.*), G.L. Brown (*West of Scot.*), N.A. MacEwan (*Gala*), P.C. Brown (*Gala*), G.M. Strachan (*Jordanhill Coll.*) Sub: J.N.M. Frame (*Gala*)

President's XV: R.A. Carlson (*South Africa*); J.J. McLean (*Australia*), D.R. Burnet (*Australia*), D.A. Hales (*New Zealand*), G.B. Batty (*New Zealand*); I.N. Stevens (*New Zealand*), G.L. Colling (*New Zealand*); J. Iracabal (*France*), R. Benesis (*France*), D.A. Dunworth (*Australia*), B. Dauga (*France*), A.R. Sutherland (*New Zealand*), J.H. Ellis (*South Africa*), A.J. Wyllie* (*New Zealand*), P.J.F. Greyling (*South Africa*)

Referee: M. Joseph (*Wales*) **Touch judges:** T.F.E. Grierson (*Hawick*), A.M. Hosie (*Hillhead HSFP*)

D. Shedden scored but P.C. Brown failed (4–0); J.J. McLean scored and converted (4–6); A.D. Gill scored and A.R. Irvine converted (10–6).(H.T.). A.D. Gill scored but A.R. Irvine failed (14–6); A.F. McHarg scored but D.W. Morgan failed (18–6); D.A. Hales and D.R. Burnet scored and J.J. McLean converted the second only (18–16); A.R. Irvine kicked a penalty (21–16); C.M. Telfer scored and A.R. Irvine converted (27–16).

Caps were awarded for this fixture arranged as part of the Centenary celebrations and the XVs were presented to Sir Alec Douglas Home before the kick off. This overseas XV did remarkably well for a group which had only a few day's preparation and it was not surprising that Scotland finished the stronger, especially on a blustery, rain-swept day. Gill, a last minute substitute for an injured Steele, had a fine debut. McHarg, as he had done all season, showed up well in the loose but Irvine was particularly prominent, making many searing runs from full back, two of which produced the first two tries. McGeechan hurt his neck after thirteen minutes play and was replaced by Frame.

ARGENTINA Murrayfield **24 November 1973**

SCOTTISH XV: 1 drop goal, 3 penalty goals 12 **Win**
ARGENTINA: 2 tries, 1 drop goal 11

Scottish XV: A.R. Irvine (*Heriot's FP*); W.C.C. Steele (*Bedford*), J.M. Renwick (*Hawick*), M.D. Hunter (*Glas. HSFP*), A.D. Gill (*Gala*); C.M. Telfer (*Hawick*), D.W. Morgan (*Stewart's FP*); J. McLauchlan* (*Jordanhill Coll.*), D.F. Madsen (*Gosforth*), A.B. Carmichael (*West of Scot.*), A.F. McHarg (*London Scot.*), G.L. Brown (*West of Scot.*), N.A. MacEwan (*Highland*), W.S. Watson (*Boroughmuir*), G.M. Strachan (*Jordanhill Coll.*)

Argentina: M.F. Alonzo (*San Isidro*), R. Matarazzo (*San Isidro*), A. Travaglini (*San Isidro*), A.R. Jurado (*San Isidro*), E..R Morgan (*Old Georgians*); H. Porta (*Banco Nacion*), L. Gradin (*Belgrano*); F.G. Insua (*San Isidro*), J.E. Dumas (*Universitario*), R. Fariello (*Mendoza*), J.A. Virasoro (*San Martin*), J.J. Fernandez (*Deportiva Francesa*), N. Carbone (*Puchara*), H.R. Miguens* (*Universitario*), J. Carracedo (*San Isidro*)

  Referee: J.S.P. Evans (*Wales*) **Touch judges:** T.F.E. Grierson, J.M. Buchan

H. Porta scored but E.R. Morgan failed (0–4); A. Travaglini scored but E.R. Morgan failed (0–8); D.W. Morgan kicked two penalties (6–8); H. Porta dropped a goal (6–11).(H.T.). D.W. Morgan kicked a penalty (9–11); C.M. Telfer dropped a goal (12–11).

This Scottish XV, practically a fully capped team, were most fortunate to finish as winners. They had to yield two good tries and could not penetrate an excellent defence to score themselves. Porta was an excellent half while Travaglini proved a powerful centre both in attack and defence. The Argentine forwards, however, although splendid in the loose, were overshadowed in the scrums and line outs. The game finished sourly. The referee had continually to penalise the visitors for an assortment of offences which included a stiff arm tackle on Irvine, and Morgan eventually placed three good goals to keep Scotland in contention. Inside the last seven minutes Telfer dropped a goal to put Scotland in the lead and almost at once an ugly brawl developed which left Madsen with a head wound that required stitching. The visitors then put in a great finish, running the ball continually from all positions but narrowly failed to save the game. Then as they left the field one of their forwards felled Gordon Brown standing in the tunnel and later their manager complained that the Welsh referee was not neutral — in fact, could not be neutral since he came from the British Isles — a comment where the logic was as false as the initial statement.

WALES Cardiff **19 January 1974**

SCOTLAND: Nil 0 **Loss**
WALES: 1 goal 6

Scotland: A.R. Irvine (*Heriot's FP*); A.D. Gill (*Gala*), J.M. Renwick (*Hawick*), I.R. McGeechan (*Headingley*), L.G. Dick (*Jordanhill Coll.*); C.M. Telfer (*Hawick*), A.J.M.

Lawson (*Edin. Wrs.*); J. McLauchlan* (*Jordanhill Coll.*), D.F. Madsen (*Gosforth*), A.B. Carmichael (*West of Scot.*), A.F. McHarg (*London Scot.*), G.L. Brown (*West of Scot.*), N.A. MacEwan (*Highland*), W.S. Watson (*Boroughmuir*), W. Lauder (*Neath*)

Wales: J.P.R. Williams (*London Welsh*); T.G.R. Davies (*London Welsh*), K. Hughes (*London Welsh*), I. Hall (*Aberavon*), J.J. Williams (*Llanelli*); P. Bennett (*Llanelli*), G.O. Edwards* (*Cardiff*); G. Shaw (*Neath*), R. Windsor (*Pontypool*), P.D. Llewellyn (*Swansea*), A.J. Martin (*Aberavon*), D.L. Quinnell (*Llanelli*), W.D. Morris (*Neath*), T.M. Davies (*Swansea*), T. Cobner (*Pontypool*)

Referee: R.F. Johnson (*England*) **Touch judges:** W.B. Watt, J.C. Kelleher

T. Cobner scored and P. Bennett converted (0–6).(H.T.).

After some early pressure by Scotland, during which Irvine came close with a penalty, Wales, with the wind, came into the game. After 22 minutes they heeled against the head and a lovely side stepping run by T.G.R. Davies put Cobner in for the only score of the match.

Both sides attacked throughout the second half but the defences were sound. The Scottish pack played much better especially in the loose where the back five of the pack were often in evidence. J.P.R. Williams, however, was in fine form and like Irvine frequently joined his threes in attack.

ENGLAND Murrayfield 2 February 1974

SCOTLAND: 1 goal, 2 penalty goals, 1 try 16 **Win**

ENGLAND: 1 drop goal, 1 penalty goal, 2 tries 14

Scotland: A.R. Irvine (*Heriot's FP*); A.D. Gill (*Gala*), J.M. Renwick (*Hawick*), I.R. McGeechan (*Headingley*), L.G. Dick (*Jordanhill Coll.*); C.M. Telfer (*Hawick*), A.J.M. Lawson (*Edin. Wrs.*); J. McLauchlan* (*Jordanhill Coll.*), D.F. Madsen (*Gosforth*), A.B. Carmichael (*West of Scot.*), A.F. McHarg (*London Scot.*), G.L. Brown (*West of Scot.*), N.A. MacEwan (*Highland*), W.S. Watson (*Boroughmuir*), W. Lauder (*Neath*)

England: P.A. Rossborough (*Coventry*); P.J. Squires (*Harrogate*), D. Roughley (*Liverpool*), G.W. Evans (*Coventry*), D.J. Duckham (*Coventry*); A.G.B. Old (*Leicester*), J.G. Webster (*Moseley*); C.B. Stevens (*Penzance-Newlyn*), J.V. Pullin* (*Bristol*), F.E. Cotton (*Coventry*), C.W. Ralston (*Richmond*), N.E. Horton (*Moseley*), P.J. Dixon (*Gosforth*), A.G. Ripley (*Rosslyn Park*), A. Neary (*Broughton Park*)

Referee: M.J. Saint Guilhem (*France*) **Touch judges:** N.R. Sanson, J. Straughan

A.R. Irvine kicked a penalty (3–0); W. Lauder scored and A.R. Irvine converted (9–0); F.E. Cotton scored but P.A. Rossborough failed (9–4); A.G.B. Old kicked a penalty (9–7).(H.T.). A. Neary scored but P.A. Rossborough failed (9–11); A.R. Irvine scored but failed to convert (13–11); P.A. Rossborough dropped a goal (13–14); A.R. Irvine kicked a penalty (16–14).

For the first time since 1880 the Calcutta Cup match, because of a new system of cycling

International games, lost its traditional placing as the last game of the season in March. This proved to be a fast hard game with a story book finish. Scotland began well scoring nine points within twelve minutes. Irvine took three long range penalties and converted one from about 45 yards out. Then Madsen pounced on a loose ball from a line out and a pass to Lauder left him with an easy score far out but beautifully converted by Irvine. England rallied strongly and a run by Squires was carried on by Ripley, Neary and Cotton who crashed over for a try. Just short of half time Old kicked a penalty. After restarting England attacked continuously but were halted by some great tackling, especially by McGeechan. In the last 20 minutes the lead changed four times. Firstly a short penalty manoeuvre by Webster and Ripley put Neary over. There followed a fine dodging run by Irvine who scored a try he could not convert. With some three minutes left Rossborough caught a bad clearance and dropped a good 35 yard goal to put England ahead 11–14. Then in the third minute of injury time Irvine kicked a magnificent penalty from 40 yards out on the touch line — and the final whistle went.

IRELAND Lansdowne Road 2 March 1974

SCOTLAND:	2 penalty goals	6	**Loss**
IRELAND:	1 goal, 1 penalty goal	9	

Scotland: A.R. Irvine (*Heriot's FP*); A.D. Gill (*Gala*), J.M. Renwick (*Hawick*), I.R. McGeechan (*Headingley*), L.G. Dick (*Jordanhill Coll.*); C.M. Telfer (*Hawick*), D.W. Morgan (*Stewart's FP*); J. McLauchlan* (*Jordanhill Coll.*), D.F. Madsen (*Gosforth*), A.B. Carmichael (*West of Scot.*), A.F. McHarg (*London Scot.*), G.L. Brown (*West of Scot.*), N.A. MacEwan (*Highland*), W.S. Watson (*Boroughmuir*), W. Lauder (*Neath*)

Ireland: A.H. Ensor (*Lansdowne*); T.O. Grace (*UC Dublin*), R.A. Milliken (*Bangor*), C.M.H. Gibson (*NIFC*), A.W. McMaster (*Ballymena*); M.A. Quinn (*Lansdowne*), J.J. Moloney (*St Mary's*); R.J. McLoughlin (*Blackrock*), K.W. Kennedy (*London Irish*), J.F. Lynch (*St Mary's*), M.I. Keane (*Lansdowne*), W.J. McBride* (*Ballymena*), S.A. McKinney (*Dungannon*), T.A.P. Moore (*Highfield*), J.F. Slattery (*Blackrock*)

Referee: F. Palmade (*France*) **Touch judges:** J.W. McLeod, D.P. D'Arcy

S.A. McKinney kicked a penalty (0–3); R.A. Milliken scored and C.M.H. Gibson converted (0–0).(H.T.). A.R. Irvine kicked two penalties (6–9).

Scotland had a poor first half but eventually their pack began to take control and play was mainly inside the Irish half for the last twenty minutes. The only try came from a long throw in taken by Slattery who after a nice run gave the ball to Milliken. The centre went for the line and when tackled was bundled over the line by his own forwards. After the restart Ireland began strongly and twice they came near to scoring but then came the final rally by Scotland who failed, however, to get the ball over the line and Irvine's two penalties were not enough to win the match.

FRANCE Murrayfield 16 March 1974

SCOTLAND:	1 goal, 3 penalty goals, 1 try	19	**Win**

FRANCE: 1 drop goal, 1 penalty goal   6

Scotland: A.R. Irvine (*Heriot's FP*); A.D. Gill (*Gala*), J.M. Renwick (*Hawick*), M.D. Hunter (*Glas. HSFP*), L.G. Dick (*Jordanhill Coll.*); I.R. McGeechan (*Headingley*), D.W. Morgan (*Stewart's FP*); J. McLauchlan* (*Jordanhill Coll.*), D.F. Madsen (*Gosforth*), A.B. Carmichael (*West of Scot.*), A.F. McHarg (*London Scot.*), G.L. Brown (*West of Scot.*), N.A. MacEwan (*Highland*), W.S. Watson (*Boroughmuir*), W. Lauder (*Neath*) Sub: I.A. Barnes (*Hawick*)

France: M. Droitecourt (*Montferrand*); J.-F. Gourdon (*RCF*), J.-P. Lux (*Dax*), J. Pecune (*Tarbes*), R. Bertranne (*Bagneres*); J.-P. Romeu (*Montferrand*), M. Barrau (*Agen*); J. Iracabal (*Bayonne*), C. Benesis (*Agen*), A. Vaquerin (*Beziers*), E. Cester* (*Valence*), A. Esteve (*Beziers*), J.-C. Skrela (*Toulouse*), C. Spanghero (*Narbonne*), V. Boffelli (*Aurillac*)

Referee: K.H. Clark (*Ireland*)   Touch judges: A.M. Hosie, F. Flingou

J.-P. Romeu kicked a penalty (0–3); D.W. Morgan kicked a penalty (3–3); A.F. McHarg scored and A.R. Irvine converted (9–3).(H.T.). J.-P. Romeu dropped a goal (9–6); A.R. Irvine kicked two penalties (15–6); L.G. Dick scored but A.R. Irvine failed (19–6).

France came needing a win to head the International table but met a Scottish team which played well to win comfortably. The visitors began with some brisk handling amongst their forwards before Romeu put them in the lead with a penalty but it was not long before Morgan levelled the scores. A succession of penalties were missed by Irvine and Morgan but right on half time a magnificent handling run involving ten pairs of hands criss-crossed the field three times before Irvine came into the line and his pass saw McHarg crash over for a wonderful try. Scotland restarted briskly only to see Romeu seize a chance to drop a neat goal. Irvine restored the lead with a penalty and saw an injured MacEwan replaced by Barnes before he repeated the feat. For the last fifteen minutes a confident Scotland attacked and inside the final ten minutes Irvine ran from inside his own half and yet another fine passing run which involved McHarg, Carmichael, Lauder, McGeechan and Renwick put Dick in for a great try. The Scottish pack were very good: the front three were solid, Brown and McHarg were good in the line outs and the back row sound in defence and attack. Yet McHarg deserved extra notice for his ability to get out and about in the open.

TONGA   **Murrayfield**   **28 September 1974**

SCOTTISH XV: 5 goals, 2 penalty goals, 2 tries   44 **Win**

TONGA: 2 tries   8

Scottish XV: A.R. Irvine (*Heriot's FP*); W.C.C. Steele (*London Scot.*), J.M. Renwick (*Hawick*), I.R. McGeechan (*Headingley*), L.G. Dick (*Jordanhill Coll.*); C.M. Telfer (*Hawick*), D.W. Morgan (*Stewart's FP*); J. McLauchlan* (*Jordanhill Coll.*), D.F. Madsen (*Gosforth*), A.B. Carmichael (*West of Scot.*), A.F. McHarg (*London Scot.*), G.L. Brown (*West of Scot.*), N.A. MacEwan (*Highland*), W.S. Watson (*Boroughmuir*), W. Lauder (*Neath*)

Tonga: Valita Ma'ake; Isikeli Vave, Samiuela Lata, Sitafoti 'Aho, Talilotu Ngaluafe; Malakai 'Alatini, Ha'unga Fonua; Siosaia Fifita, Tevita Pulumufila, Lialeni Pahulu, Fa'aleo Tupi, Polutele Tu'ihalamaka, Saimone Vaea, Sione Mafi*, Fakahau Valu

Referee: G. Domercq (*France*) **Touch judges:** A.M. Hosie, E.N. Sheret

A.R. Irvine kicked two penalties (6–0).(H.T.). W.C.C. Steele (2) and L.G. Dick scored and A.R. Irvine converted two (22–0); S. Fifita scored but V. Ma'ake failed (22–4); W.C.C. Steele (2), D.W. Morgan and J. McLauchlan scored and A.R. Irvine converted three (44–4); I. Vave scored but V. Ma'ake failed (44–8).

No caps were awarded for this match although a full Scottish XV was put out. Throughout the game Scotland maintained control of the scrums and line outs but in the first half all their attacks failed against a stout defence and they could only manage two penalties. In the second half the Tongan defence tired and some fine passing runs saw Scotland's wingers run in five of the seven tries scored. Yet the visitors never ceased to play their own style of adventurous running rugby and one such move brought them their first score. In the last minutes Vave intercepted a pass near his own line and the winger ran some 90 yards, throwing off tackles by Irvine and Gill, to score a great solo try.

IRELAND: Murrayfield   1 February 1975

SCOTLAND: 2 drop goals, 2 penalty goals, 2 tries   20   **Win**

IRELAND: 1 goal, 1 penalty goal, 1 try   15

Scotland: A.R. Irvine (*Heriot's FP*); W.C.C. Steele (*London Scot.*), J.M. Renwick (*Hawick*), D.L. Bell (*Watsonians*), L.G. Dick (*Jordanhill Coll.*); I.R. McGeechan (*Headingley*), D.W. Morgan (*Stewart's FP*); J. McLauchlan* (*Jordanhill Coll.*), D.F. Madsen (*Gosforth*), A.B. Carmichael (*West of Scot.*), A.F. McHarg (*London Scot.*), G.L. Brown (*West of Scot.*), M.A. Biggar (*London Scot.*), D.G. Leslie (*Dundee HSFP*), W. Lauder (*Neath*)

Ireland: A.H. Ensor (*Wanderers*); T.O. Grace (*St Mary's*), R.A. Milliken (*Bangor*), C.M.H. Gibson (*NIFC*), J.P. Dennison (*Garryowen*); W.M. McCombe (*Bangor*), J.J. Maloney (*St Mary's*); R.J. McLoughlin (*Blackrock*), P.C. Whelan (*Garryowen*), R.J. Clegg (*Bangor*), W.J. McBride* (*Ballymena*), M.I. Keane (*Lansdowne*), J.F. Slattery (*Blackrock*), W.P. Duggan (*Blackrock*), S.A. McKinney (*Dungannon*)

Referee: R.F. Johnson (*England*) **Touch judges:** A.M. Hosei, S.A. Causland

D.W. Morgan dropped a goal (3–0); J. Dennison scored and W.M. McCombe converted (3–6); I.R. McGeechan dropped a goal (6–6); J.M. Renwick and W.C.C. Steele scored but A.R. Irvine failed to convert (14–6).(H.T.). W.M. McCombe kicked a penalty (14–9); A.R. Irvine kicked a penalty (17–9); T.O. Grace scored but W.M. McCombe failed (17–13); A.R. Irvine kicked a penalty (20–13).

Last season's champions, Ireland, came to their happy hunting ground at Murrayfield in their Centenary season with a win over England behind them but met a Scottish team whose pack more than held its own and whose backs ran and defended well. Scotland had a great start for within a minute Dick went down the left wing, was halted but from the ruck Biggar got the ball out to Morgan who dropped a goal. Another fine run saw Steele nearly in but then Ireland began to run the ball and a fine handling movement by their forwards got the ball out to Gibson who gave Dennison a clear run in. Scotland, however, struck back before half time. McGeechan dropped a goal from a Scottish heel; Bell with a dummy scissors move put Renwick through and right on half time a splendid dash by Steele brought a second score. After restarting Ireland came back into the game with a McCombe penalty which, however, was cancelled out by another from Irvine. Both sides kept on attacking without success until inside the last ten minutes poor line out play let the Irish backs whip the ball along the line fast enough to allow Grace to get round the defence and score far out but just short of time Irvine made the win safe by kicking another penalty.

FRANCE   Parc des Princes   15 February 1975

SCOTLAND: 3 penalty goals   9   **Loss**

FRANCE: 1 drop goal, 1 penalty, 1 try   10

Scotland: A.R. Irvine (*Heriot's FP*); W.C.C. Steele (*London Scot.*), J.M. Renwick (*Hawick*), D.L. Bell (*Watsonians*), L.G. Dick (*Jordanhill Coll.*); I.R. McGeechan (*Headingley*), D.W. Morgan (*Stewart's FP*); J. McLauchlan* (*Jordanhill Coll.*), D.F. Madsen (*Gosforth*), A.B. Carmichael (*West of Scot.*), A.F. McHarg (*London Scot.*), G.L. Brown (*West of Scot.*), M.A. Biggar (*London Scot.*), D.G. Leslie (*Dundee HSFP*), W. Lauder (*Neath*)

France: M.M. Taffary (*RCF*); J.-F. Gourdon (*RCF*), C. Dourthe* (*Dax*), R. Bertranne (*Bagneres*), J.L. Averous (*La Voulte*); L. Paries (*Narbonne*), R. Astre (*Beziers*); A. Vaquerin (*Beziers*), J.P. Ugartemendia (*St. Jean de Luz*), G. Cholly (*Castres*), A. Guilbert (*Toulon*), C. Spanghero (*Narbonne*), J.-P. Rives (*Toulouse*), V. Boffelli (*Aurillac*), J.C. Skrela (*Toulouse*)

     Referee: S.M. Lewis (*Wales*)   **Touch judges:** R.E.W. Thomas, N.J. Saint Guilhem

A.R. Irvine kicked a penalty (3–0); R. Astre dropped a goal (3–3).(H.T.). C. Dourthe scored but L. Paries failed (3–7); A.R. Irvine kicked a penalty (6–7); L. Paries kicked a penalty (6–10); A.R. Irvine kicked a penalty (9–10).

This was a scrappy, bad tempered match which Scotland could well have won if one or two of them had kept cool throughout. Straight away there was scrapping amongst the forwards and the mood persisted, but another factor was the tactics of the halves who were prone to kick rather than get their backs going. This of course left Irvine out as an attacking force. In addition the full back had an off day with his kicking, converting three out of nine penalties, one of the last at short range. The single try came from a line out from which Skrela and Rives, two fast and skilful flankers, broke away to let Dourthe cut through. Scotland did have bad luck on two occasions when a final pass did not go to hand. Following one of the near misses the Scottish pack went for a push over score only to find Rives diving in amongst Scottish feet. The scrum collapsed and France got a penalty!

WALES   Murrayfield   1 March 1975

SCOTLAND: 1 drop goal, 3 penalty goals   12   **Win**

WALES: 2 penalty goals, 1 try **10**

Scotland: A.R. Irvine (*Heriot's FP*); W.C.C. Steele (*London Scot.*), J.M. Renwick (*Hawick*), D.L. Bell (*Watsonians*), L.G. Dick (*Jordanhill Coll.*); I.R. McGeechan (*Headingley*), D.W. Morgan (*Stewart's FP*); J. McLauchlan* (*Jordanhill Coll.*), D.F. Madsen (*Gosforth*), A.B. Carmichael (*West of Scot.*), A.F. McHarg (*London Scot.*), G.L. Brown (*West of Scot.*), M.A. Biggar (*London Scot.*), D.G. Leslie (*Dundee HSFP*), N.A. MacEwan (*Highland*)

Wales: J.P.R. Williams (*London Welsh*); T.G.R. Davis (*Cardiff*), S.P. Fenwick (*Bridgend*), R.W.R. Gravell (*Llanelli*), J.J. Williams (*Llanelli*); J.D. Bevan (*Aberavon*), G.O. Edwards (*Cardiff*); A.G. Faulkner (*Pontypool*), R.W. Windsor (*Pontypool*), G. Price (*Pontypool*), A.J. Martin (*Aberavon*), M.G. Roberts (*London Welsh*), T.J. Cobner (*Pontypool*), T.M. Davies* (*Swansea*), T.P. Evans (*Swansea*) Sub: P. Bennett (*Llanelli*), W.R. Blyth (*Swansea*)

Referee: J.R. West (*Ireland*) Touch judges: N.R. Sanson, A.B. Daniel

D.W. Morgan kicked a penalty (3–0); S.P. Fenwick kicked a penalty (3–3); D.W. Morgan kicked a penalty (6–3); S.P. Fenwick kicked a penalty (6–6); D.W. Morgan kicked a penalty (9–6).(H.T.). I.R. McGeechan dropped a goal (12–6); T.P. Evans scored but A.J. Martin failed (12–10).

Wales who had already had comfortable wins against France and England brought an enormous following to Edinburgh. Two hours before the kick off Murrayfield and its approaches were jammed solid and it was later revealed that the game was watched by a world record crowd of 104,000 plus with several thousands eventually locked out.

The match proved to be a hard, bruising and exciting one but the standard of rugby was really not very high. The first half was mainly a tale of brief runs and kicks at goal — five successful penalties, three misses by Wales and a near drop by McGeechan, but Wales had to replace both Bevan and Fenwick by Bennett and Blyth, the latter normally a full back. The second half produced two more missed penalties but also a neat successful and valuable drop by McGeechan but again there was little running till in the fourth minute of injury time J.P.R. Williams burst into the line and Gerald Davies put Evans over far out for a good try. To Scotland's relief Martin's long range kick just failed and the whistle went.

ENGLAND Twickenham 15 March 1975

SCOTLAND: 2 penalty goals **6** **Loss**

ENGLAND: 1 penalty goal, 1 try **7**

Scotland: A.R. Irvine (*Heriot's FP*); W.C.C. Steele (*London Scot.*), J.M. Renwick (*Hawick*), D.L. Bell (*Watsonians*), L.G. Dick (*Jordanhill Coll.*); I.R. McGeechan (*Headingley*), D.W. Morgan (*Stewart's FP*); J. McLauchlan* (*Jordanhill Coll.*), D.F. Madsen (*Gosforth*), A.B. Carmichael (*West of Scot.*), A.F. McHarg (*London Scot.*), G.L. Brown (*West of Scot.*), M.A. Biggar (*London Scot.*), D.G. Leslie (*Dundee HSFP*), N.A. MacEwan (*Highland*) Sub: I.A. Barnes (*Hawick*)

England: A.M. Jorden (*Bedford*); P.J. Squires (*Harrogate*), P.J. Warfield (*Camb. Univ.*), K. Smith (*Roundhay*), A.J. Morley (*Bristol*); W.N. Bennett (*Bedford*), J.J. Page (*Northampton*); C.B. Stevens (*Penzance–Newlyn*), J.V. Pullin (*Bristol*), F.E. Cotton* (*Coventry*), R.M. Uttley (*Gosforth*), C.W. Ralston (*Richmond*), D.M. Rollitt (*Bristol*), A. Neary (*Broughton Park*), A.G. Ripley (*Rosslyn Park*)

Referee: D.P. D'Arcy (*Ireland*)   Touch judges: W.K. Burrell, R.F. Johnson

D.W. Morgan kicked a penalty (3–0); W.N. Bennett kicked a penalty (3–3).(H.T.). D.W. Morgan kicked a penalty (6–3); A.J. Morley scored but W.W. Bennett failed (6–7).

For the fourth time since the War, Scotland's attempt to win the Triple Crown failed at Twickenham. This was a game that they could have won but once again this season they could not score except by penalties. They had much the better of play in the first half but finished poorly. They played equally well during the second half and were shocked when Morley chased an awkward kick ahead and beat Irvine to the rolling ball for a try. They continued to press for the last fifteen minutes but a heartened English pack gave nothing away and when two late penalties by Morgan and a snap at goal by McGeechan failed the match was lost. MacEwan came off after two minutes of play and was replaced by Barnes.

NEW ZEALAND   Auckland   14 June 1975

SCOTLAND:	Nil	0	**Loss**
NEW ZEALAND:	4 goals	24	

Scotland: B.H. Hay (*Boroughmuir*); A.R. Irvine (*Heriot's FP*), G.A. Birkett (*Harlequins*), J.M. Renwick (*Hawick*), L.G. Dick (*Jordanhill Coll.*); I.R. McGeechan (*Headingley*), D.W. Morgan (*Stewart's FP*); J. McLauchlan* (*Jordanhill Coll.*), C.D. Fisher (*Waterloo*), A.B. Carmichael (*West of Scot.*), I.R. Barnes (*Hawick*), A.F. McHarg (*London Scot.*), D.G. Leslie (*Dundee HSFP*), W.S. Watson (*Boroughmuir*), W. Lauder (*Neath*) Sub: W.C.C. Steele (*London Scot.*)

New Zealand: J.F. Karam (*Horowhenua*); B.G. Williams (*Auckland*), W.N. Osborne (*Wanganui*), L.L. Jaffray (*Otago*), G.B. Batty (*Wellington*); D.J. Robertson (*Otago*), S.M. Going (*N Auckland*); K.E.R. Tanner (*Canterbury*), T.E. Norton (*Canterbury*), W.K. Bush (*Canterbury*), J.A. Callesen (*Manawata*), H.H. Macdonald (*N. Auckland*), K.W. Stewart (*Southland*), A.N. Leslie* (*Wellington*), I.A. Kirkpatrick (*Poverty Bay*)

Referee: P. McDavitt (*Wellington*)   Touch judges: R.F. McMullen, M.G. Farnworth

H. McDonald scored and J.F. Karam converted (0–6).(H.T.). B.G. Williams (2) and D.J. Robertson scored and J.F. Karam converted all three (0–24).

This was a match which should never have been played, for something like four inches of rain had fallen in less then twelve hours and large areas of the field lay under pools of water. But the Scots were flying home the next day; no alternative date was possible; 45,000 spectators had braved the conditions and so the decision to play was taken. Scotland started facing into a gale of torrential rain only to find after half time that the wind had veered right round and once again they had to face into icy lashing rain. Having found that excuse, one must admit that the New Zealand pack was in the conditions much superior. Then there were some vital fielding errors by the Scottish backs which yielded scores but it is difficult to be too critical considering the circumstances.

Within fifteen minutes Scotland lost Hay who had an arm broken when he stood his ground claiming a fair catch which was not granted and the forward rush that followed let Macdonald in for the first score. Irvine then went to full back and Steele came out to play on the wing. In the second half Steele having taken a difficult high kick slipped and the ball which rolled back over the line was touched down by Williams. Then in their own in-goal Irvine and Dick collided going for a high kick and Robertson was left to touch down. Finally Dick flykicked the ball for touch only to see it land and stop dead in a pool of water. Williams was at hand to pick it out and charge past a surprised defence for a try.

Three after-match comments may be quoted. Leslie, the New Zealand captain, remarked that 'this was one of the greatest moment in New Zealand swimming'. McLauchlan congratulated Leslie on the win but said that 'it is just sheer luck that nobody was drowned!' while Carmichael actually said that he had played in worse conditions, 'I once played in four inches of snow and that was worse, but I was worried because I can't swim very well'.

AUSTRALIA	Murrayfield	6 December 1975	
SCOTLAND:	1 goal, 1 try	10	**Win**
AUSTRALIA:	1 penalty goal	3	

Scotland: B.H. Hay (*Boroughmuir*); A.R. Irvine (*Heriot's FP*), J.M. Renwick (*Hawick*), I.R. McGeechan (*Headingley*), L.G. Dick (*Jordanhill Coll.*); C.M. Telfer (*Hawick*), D.W. Morgan (*Stewart's FP*); J. McLauchlan* (*Jordanhill Coll.*), C.D. Fisher (*Waterloo*), A.B. Carmichael (*West of Scot.*), A.F. McHarg (*West of Scot.*), G.L. Brown (*West of Scot.*), W. Lauder (*Neath*), G.Y. Mackie (*Highland*), D.G. Leslie (*West of Scot.*)

Australia: P.E. McLean (*Queensland*); P.G. Batch (*Queensland*), R.D. L'Estrange (*Queensland*), J. Berne (*NSW*), L.E. Monaghan (*NSW*); J.C. Hindmarsh (*NSW*), J.N.B. Hipwell* (*NSW*); J.E.C. Meadows (*Victoria*), P.A. Horton (*NSW*), R. Graham (*NSW*), G. Fay (*NSW*), R.A. Smith (*NSW*), G. Cornelsen (*NSW*), D.W. Hillhouse (*Queensland*), A.A. Shaw (*Queensland*) Sub: L.T. Weatherstone (*Capital Territory*)

Referee: R.F. Johnson (*England*)   **Touch judges:** A.M. Hosie, A. Bryce

L.G. Dick scored but D.W. Morgan failed (4–0); J.M. Renwick scored and D.W. Morgan converted (10–0).(H.T.). P.E. McLean kicked a penalty (10–3).

Sandy Carmichael was given the honour of leading the team onto the field, this being his record 41st full cap. Scotland started well but soon found that the tourists were very fast in their counter attacking and Hay in particular had to tackle well to prevent possible scores. However, a break away by Morgan and Mackie set up a ruck from which Morgan put McGeechan and Hay away to finish with Dick scoring. Right on half time McGeechan intercepted a pass and set Renwick away on a 35 yard scoring run.

In the second half the Scottish pack was well in command and halted many Australian moves by winning loose mauls, but their backs although having some good runs, could not score. Midway through the half McLean kicked a fine angled penalty, all of 50 yards.

One writer, noting Irvine's appearance as a winger, commented that it was many years ago since Scotland fielded three full backs, this being a humourous reference to McHarg's habit of appearing, both in defence and attack, anywhere amongst the backs — but it must be remembered that the same character was always a more than useful performer at the line outs.

FRANCE   Murrayfield   10 January 1976

SCOTLAND: 1 drop goal, 1 penalty goal   6   **Loss**

FRANCE: 1 try, 3 penalty goals   13

Scotland: B.H. Hay (*Boroughmuir*); A.R. Irvine (*Heriot's FP*), J.M. Renwick (*Hawick*), I.R. McGeechan (*Headingley*), L.G. Dick (*Jordanhill Coll.*); C.M. Telfer (*Hawick*), D.W. Morgan (*Stewart's FP*); J. McLauchlan* (*Jordanhill Coll.*), D.F. Madsen (*Gosforth*), A.B. Carmichael (*West of Scot.*), A.F. McHarg (*London Scot.*), G.L. Brown (*West of Scot.*), W. Lauder (*Neath*), G.Y. Mackie (*Highland*), D.G. Leslie (*West of Scot.*)

France: M. Droitecourt (*Montferrand*); J.-F. Gourdon (*RCF*), R. Bertranne (*Bagneres*), F. Sangali (*Narbonne*), A. Dubertrand (*Montferrand*); J.P. Romeu (*Montferrand*), J. Fouroux* (*La Voulte*); G. Cholley (*Castres*), A. Paco (*Beziers*), R. Paparemborde (*Pau*), F. Haget (*Agen*), M. Palmie (*Beziers*), J.P. Rives (*Toulouse*), J.P. Bastiat (*Dax*), J.C. Skrela (*Toulouse*)

Referee: K.A. Pattinson (*England*)   **Touch judges:** N.R. Sanson, Dr A. Cuny

D.W. Morgan dropped a goal (3–0); J.P. Romeu kicked a penalty (3–3); A. Dubertrand scored but J.P. Romeu failed (3–7).(H.T.). J. Romeu kicked a penalty (3–10); J.M. Renwick kicked a penalty (6–10); J.P. Romeu kicked a penalty (6–13).

Scotland's run of ten home wins was halted by a side which was competent enough but gradually took heart as they saw their opponents fail with their goal kicking and handling. The game, however, seldom got moving, play being continually halted by unsuccessful shots at goal. Morgan missed four and Irvine five before Renwick, who was as competent a club kicker as the other two, put one over. In fairness it must be said some of the misses were long range efforts taken under very windy conditions and Irvine's second attempt went over only to be cancelled by the referee who decided that it was a fault for McLauchlan to lie in front of the ball while holding it in place — an erroneous and sad decision — for another Scottish score at that stage might have lifted their game. As it happened a neat drop by Morgan was cancelled out by a touch line penalty by Romeu before Gourdon snatched up a loose pass and crosskicked to set off a handling run that put Dubertrand over at the other wing. It could be noted that Romeu who tied the win up with three penalties, missed the conversion and two other penalties.

WALES   Cardiff   7 February 1976

SCOTLAND: 1 goal   6   **Loss**

WALES: 2 goals, 1 drop goal, 2 penalty goals, 1 try   28

Scotland: A.R. Irvine (*Heriot's FP*); W.C.C. Steele (*London Scot.*), J.M. Renwick (*Hawick*), A.G. Cranston (*Hawick*), D. Shedden (*West of Scot.*); I.R. McGeechan (*Headingley*), D.W. Morgan (*Stewart's FP*); J. McLauchlan* (*Jordanhill Coll.*), C.D. Fisher (*Waterloo*), A.B. Carmichael (*West of Scot.*), A.F. McHarg (*London Scot.*), G.L. Brown (*West of Scot.*), M.A. Biggar (*London Scot.*), G.Y. Mackie (*Highland*), D.G. Leslie (*West of Scot.*)

Wales: J.P.R. Williams (*London Welsh*); T.G.R. Davies (*Cardiff*), R.W.R. Gravell (*Llanelli*), S.P. Fenwick (*Bridgend*), J.J. Williams (*Llanelli*); P. Bennett (*Llanelli*), G.O. Edwards (*Cardiff*); A.G. Faulkner (*Pontypool*), R.W. Windsor (*Pontypool*), G. Price (*Pontypool*), A.J. Martin (*Aberavon*), G.A.D. Wheel (*Swansea*), T.J. Cobner (*Pontypool*), T.M. Davies* (*Swansea*), T.P. Evans (*Swansea*)

Referee: Dr A. Cuny (*France*)   **Touch judges:** A. Bryce, M. Joseph

J.J. Williams scored and P. Bennett converted (0–6); A.R. Irvine scored and D.W. Morgan converted (6–6); P. Bennett kicked 2 penalties (6–12).(H.T.). P. Bennett kicked a penalty (6–15); S.P. Fenwick dropped a goal (6–19); T.P. Evans and G.O. Edwards scored and P. Bennett converted the second only (6–28).

Wales made a great start; a lovely diagonal kick beat the defence and J.J. Williams dived in to score inside two minutes. However, good possession from a maul saw McHarg make a run and put Irvine in at the corner but before half time the accurate Bennett had added two penalties. In the second half Wales were clearly on top but met with some stern defending and it was well on before some fine handling gave them two good tries. This latter stage was clearly affected by the refusal of the referee to leave the field after he had injured a leg muscle and during the last half hour he limped along well behind play, often missing offences with a resultant exasperation among the players.

ENGLAND   Murrayfield   21 February 1976

SCOTLAND: 2 goals, 2 penalty goals, 1 try   22   **Win**

ENGLAND: 1 goal, 2 penalty goals   12

Scotland: A.R. Irvine (*Heriot's FP*); W.C.C. Steele (*London Scot.*), A.G. Cranston (*Hawick*), I.R. McGeechan (*Headingley*), D. Shedden (*West of Scot.*); R. Wilson (*London Scot.*), A.J.M. Lawson (*London Scot.*); J. McLauchlan* (*Jordanhill Coll.*), C.D. Fisher (*Waterloo*), A.B. Carmichael (*West of Scot.*), A.J. Tomes (*Hawick*), G.L. Brown (*West of Scot.*), M.A. Biggar (*London Scot.*), A.F. McHarg (*London Scot.*), D.G. Leslie (*West of Scot.*) Sub: J.M. Renwick (*Hawick*)

England: A.J. Hignell (*Camb. Univ.*); K.C. Plummer (*Bristol*), A.W. Maxwell (*Headingley*), D.A. Cooke (*Harlequins*), D.J. Duckham (*Coventry*); A.G.B. Old (*Middlesbrough*), M.S. Lampkowski (*Headingley*); F.E. Cotton (*Sale*), P.J. Wheeler (*Leicester*), M.A. Burton (*Gloucester*), W.B. Beaumont (*Fylde*), R.M. Wilkinson (*Bedford*), M. Keyworth (*Swansea*), A.G. Ripley (*Rosslyn Park*), A. Neary* (*Broughton Park*) Sub: D.M. Wyatt (*Bedford*), W.N. Bennet (*Bedford*)

Referee: D.M. Lloyd (*Wales*)   **Touch judges:** T.F.E. Grierson, Reverend R.N. Newell

A.W. Maxwell scored and A.G.B. Old converted (0–6); A.R. Irvine kicked a penalty (3–6); A.G.B. Old kicked a penalty (3–9); A.J.M. Lawson scored and A.R. Irvine converted (9–9); A.G.B. Old kicked a penalty (9–12).(H.T.). A.R. Irvine kicked a penalty (12–12); D.G. Leslie and A.J.M. Lawson scored and A.R. Irvine converted the second only (22–12).

Her Majesty the Queen attended and the XV's were presented to her before the start. With Prince Philip, she and a capacity all-ticket crowd of 70,000 watched a match full of incident. The English pack dominated for long periods especially in the set scrums but the Scottish forwards rallied well in the line outs and the loose mauls and gave their backs some good possession. England had a fine start for within six minutes some broken play finished with Old putting Maxwell over for a converted try. Half way through Shedden caught an attacking kick ahead and sparked off a splendid handling run by Biggar, Carmichael and Tomes which put Lawson over but Old, by kicking two penalties to Irvine's one, put England in the lead at the interval. During this half Duckham and Shedden, both injured in tackles, were replaced by Wyatt and Renwick. England restarted strongly winning a string of rucks to set their backs running well only to be firmly held, Cranston in particular putting in some bruising tackles. Irvine had levelled the scores with a penalty when Leslie charged down a hurried defensive kick by Old, picked up the bounce and ran 25 yards to score. More Scottish pressure gave Lawson a chance to whip through a gap for his second try. England counter attacked for the last ten minutes but uncompromising tackling held them out. During this second half Bennet replaced Maxwell.

IRELAND   Lansdowne Road   20 March 1976

SCOTLAND: 1 drop goal, 4 penalty goals   15   **Win**

IRELAND: 2 penalty goals   6

Scotland: A.R. Irvine (*Heriot's FP*); W.C.C. Steele (*London Scot.*), A.G. Cranston (*Hawick*), I.R. McGeechan (*Headingley*), D. Shedden (*West of Scot.*); R. Wilson (*London Scot.*), A.J.M. Lawson (*London Scot.*); J. McLauchlan* (*Jordanhill Coll.*), C.D. Fisher (*Waterloo*), A.B. Carmichael (*West of Scot.*), A.J. Tomes (*Hawick*), G.L. Brown (*West of Scot.*), M.A. Biggar (*London Scot.*), A.F. McHarg (*London Scot.*), D.G. Leslie (*West of Scot.*)

Ireland: L.A. Moloney (*Garryowen*); T.O. Grace* (*St Mary's*), J.A. Brady (*Wanderers*), C.M.H. Gibson (*NIFC*), S.E.F. Blake-Knox (*NIFC*); B.J. McGann (*Cork Const.*), J.J. Moloney (*St Mary's*); P.A. Orr (*Old Wesley*), J. Cantrell (*UC Dublin*), P. O'Callaghan (*Dolphin*), M.I. Keane (*Lansdowne*), R.F. Hakin (*CIYMS*), S.M. Deering (*Garryowen*), W.P. Duggan (*Blackrock*), S.A. McKinney (*Dungannon*) Sub: C.H. McKibbin (*Instonians*)

Referee: M.S. Lewis (*Wales*) **Touch judges:** J.A. Short, J.R. West

B.J. McGann kicked a penalty (0–3); A.R. Irvine kicked two penalties (6–3); B.J. McGann kicked a penalty (6–6).(H.T.). A.R. Irvine kicked two penalties (12–6); R. Wilson dropped a goal (15–6).

This was Scotland's first away win since Twickenham in 1971 and their first at Lansdowne Road since 1966, but it was achieved without a try being scored. True, continuous rain and a heavy pitch was against handling but the game was continually halted by a succession of penalty kicks and here Irvine converted four out of eight attempts while McGann succeeded with two out of six. The Scottish pack more than held their own while their backs,

301

seldom seen in attack, were solid in defence. Near the close Gibson went off with a pulled muscle and was replaced by McKibbin.

JAPAN   Murrayfield   25 September 1976

SCOTTISH XV: 3 goals, 4 tries   34   **Win**

JAPAN: 1 goal, 1 penalty goal   9

Scottish XV: A.R. Irvine (*Heriot's FP*); W.B.B. Gammell (*Edin. Wrs.*), K.W. Robertson (*Melrose*), I.R. McGeechan* (*Headingley*), D.M. Ashton (*Ayr*); R. Wilson (*London Scot.*), A.J.M. Lawson (*London Scot.*); J. Aitken (*Gala*), C.D. Fisher (*Waterloo*), N.E.K. Pender (*Hawick*), A.J. Tomes (*Hawick*), J.G. Carswell (*Jordanhill Coll.*), M.A. Biggar (*London Scot.*), W.S. Watson (*Boroughmuir*), D.G. Leslie (*West of Scot.*) Sub: G.Y. Mackie (*Highland*)

Japan: N. Tanaka; M. Fujiwara, S. Mori, M. Yoshida, K. Aruga; S. Hoshino, R. Imazato; T. Takata, T. Wada, T. Yasui, K. Shibata, T. Terai, Y. Izawa, I. Kobayashi, H. Akama Sub: K. Muraguchi

Referee: K.H. Clark (*Ireland*) **Touch judges:** A.M. Hosie, F. Parker

N. Tanaka kicked a penalty (0–3); W.B.B. Gammell, I.R. McGeechan and A.R. Irvine scored but A.R. Irvine converted the first only (14–3).(H.T.). C.D. Fisher and W.B.B. Gammell scored and A.R. Irvine converted the second (24–3); M. Fujiwara scored and N. Tanaka converted (24–9); A.J.M. Lawson and D.M. Ashton scored and A.R. Irvine converted the first (34–9).

The visitors whose forwards were giving away an average of two stones and three inches per man, were obviously handicapped in the set scrums and line outs. They were, however, very fast in the loose, ran the ball whenever possible and tackled firmly until they tired a bit towards the end. Their try was the reward for a succession of good handling moves which set up a scrum from which their halves gave Fujiwara a chance to run hard and force his way over. Tanaka, a small ten stone full back, not only defended well but was always ready and able to run out of defence. Mackie replaced Leslie in the second half and Aruga also came off near the end.

ENGLAND   Twickenham   15 January 1977

SCOTLAND: 2 penalty goals   6   **Loss**

ENGLAND: 2 goals, 2 penalty goals, 2 tries   26

Scotland: A.R. Irvine (*Heriot's FP*); W.C.C. Steele (*London Scot.*), I.R. McGeechan* (*Headingley*), A.G. Cranston (*Hawick*), L.G. Dick (*Swansea*); R. Wilson (*London Scot.*), A.J.M. Lawson (*London Scot.*); J. Aitken (*Gala*), D.F. Madsen (*Gosforth*), A.B. Carmichael (*West of Scot.*), A.J. Tomes (*Hawick*), A.F. McHarg (*London Scot.*), W. Lauder (*Neath*), D.S.M. Macdonald (*Oxford Univ.*), A.K. Brewster (*Stewart's FP*)

England: A.J. Hignell (*Camb. Univ.*); P.J. Squires (*Harrogate*), B.J. Corless (*Moseley*), C.P. Kent (*Rosslyn Park*), M.A.C. Slemen (*Liverpool*); M.J. Cooper (*Moseley*), M. Young (*Gosforth*); R.J. Cowling (*Leicester*), P.J. Wheeler (*Leicester*), F.E. Cotton (*Sale*), W. B. Beaumont (*Fylde*), N.E. Horton (*Moseley*), P.J. Dixon (*Gosforth*), R.M. Uttley* (*Gosforth*), M. Rafter (*Bristol*)

Referee: M. Joseph (*Wales*)   **Touch judges:** R.C. Quittenton (*London*), K. Kelleher (*Wales*)

A.R. Irvine kicked a penalty (3–0); M.A.C. Slemen scored but A.G. Hignell failed (3–4); A.G. Hignell kicked a penalty (3–7); A.R. Irvine kicked a penalty (6–7); M. Young scored and A.G. Hignell converted (6–13).(H.T.). A.G. Hignell kicked a penalty (6–16); C.P. Kent scored but A.G. Hignell failed (6–20); R.M. Uttley scored and A.G. Hignell converted (6–26).

Scotland's recast team was badly shown up; the English forwards dictated play all afternoon and took full advantage of a very shaky back row defence. As a result the Scottish backs were barely seen as an attacking force and again our only scores came from penalties by Irvine, his second being a colossal effort from inside his own half. Fortunately his opposite number only converted two out of seven penalty attempts.

IRELAND   Murrayfield   19 February 1977

SCOTLAND: 1 drop goal, 2 penalty goals,
                 3 tries   21   **Win**

IRELAND: 1 goal, 1 drop goal,
                 3 penalty goals   18

Scotland: A.R. Irvine (*Heriot's FP*); W.B.B. Gammell (*Edin. Wrs.*), I.R. McGeechan* (*Headingley*), J.M. Renwick (*Hawick*), D. Shedden (*West of Scot.*); R. Wilson (*London Scot.*), D.W. Morgan (*Stewart's FP*); J. Aitken (*Gala*), D.F. Madsen (*Gosforth*), N.E.K. Pender (*Hawick*), I.A. Barnes (*Hawick*), A.F. McHarg (*London Scot.*), M.A. Biggar (*London Scot.*), D.S.M. McDonald (*London Scot.*), W.S. Watson (*Boroughmuir*) Sub: A.B. Carmichael (*West of Scot.*)

Ireland: F. Wilson (*CIYMS*); T.O. Grace* (*St Mary's*), A.R. McKibbin (*Instonians*), C.M.H. Gibson (*NIFC*), D. St.J. Brown (*Cork Const.*); M.A. Quinn (*Lansdowne*), J.C. Robbie (*Dublin Univ.*); P.A. Orr (*Old Wesley*), P.C. Whelan (*Garryowen*), E.M.J. Byrne (*Blackrock*), M.I. Keane (*Lansdowne*), C.W. Murtagh (*Portadown*), S.A. McKinney (*Dungannon*), W.P. Duggan (*Blackrock*), J.F. Slattery (*Blackrock*)

Referee: M. Joseph (*Wales*)   **Touch judges:** P.J. Wilmshurst, C.A.P. Thomas (*Wales*)

A.R. Irvine kicked a penalty (3–0); C.M.H. Gibson kicked a penalty (3–3); W.B.B.

Gammell scored but A.R. Irvine failed (7–3); M.A. Quinn dropped a goal (7–6); C.M.H. Gibson kicked a penalty (7–9).(H.T.). W.B.B. Gammell scored but A.R. Irvine failed (11–9); A.R. Irvine kicked a penalty (14–9); D.F. Madsen scored but A.R. Irvine failed (18–9); M.A. Quinn kicked a penalty (18–12); D.W. Morgan dropped a goal (21–12); C.M.H. Gibson scored and converted (21–18).

Scotland made eight changes to Ireland's five, each including two new caps. The pitch was soft after heavy rain and was soon cutting up, and both sides opened their scoring with penalties, Irvine's being a 45 yard effort. After fifteen minutes Pender went off with a rib injury and was replaced by a warmly welcomed Carmichael. Soon after McGeechan had a fine run and his blocked pass went to Gammell who crashed over for a good try. Almost at once Quinn caught a poor drop out and dropped a neat goal and with a Gibson penalty Ireland led at the interval. Ireland attacked on the restart but in one run Wilson missed a pass which Gammell seized and ran 30 yards to score. The Irish pack reacted vigorously but the defence held and in fact the Scottish backs were often quick to counter attack. However, it was Madsen who scored next from an Irish error at a line out and then Barnes gave Morgan the chance to drop a neat goal. In the last minute the score was made to look respectable for Ireland when an attacking kick by Grace bounced wickedly for the defence and Gibson scored a try which he converted.

FRANCE   Parc des Princes   5 March 1977

SCOTLAND: 1 penalty goal   3   **Loss**

FRANCE: 2 goals, 1 penalty goal, 2 tries   23

Scotland: A.R. Irvine (*Heriot's FP*); W.B.B. Gammell (*Edin. Wrs.*), I.R. McGeechan* (*Headingley*), J.M. Renwick (*Hawick*), D. Shedden (*West of Scot.*); R. Wilson (*London Scot.*), D.W. Morgan (*Stewart's FP*); J. Aitken (*Gala*), D.F. Madsen (*Gosforth*), A.B. Carmichael (*West of Scot.*), I.A. Barnes (*Hawick*), A.F. McHarg (*London Scot.*), M.A. Biggar (*London Scot.*), D.S.M. Macdonald (*London Scot.*), W.S. Watson (*Boroughmuir*)

France: J.M. Aguirre (*Bagneres*); D. Harize (*Toulouse*), R. Bertranne (*Bagneres*), F. Sangalli (*Narbonne*), J.L. Averous (*La Voulte*); J.P. Romeu (*Montferrand*), J. Fouroux* (*Auch*); G. Cholley (*Castres*), A. Paco (*Beziers*), R. Paperemborde (*Pau*), M. Palmie (*Beziers*), J.F. Imbernon (*Perpignan*), J.P. Rives (*Toulouse*), J.P. Bastiat (*Dax*), J.C. Skrela (*Toulouse*)

   Referee: M. Joseph (*Wales*) **Touch judges:** M. Thomas (*Wales*), J.-P. Bonnet (*France*)

A.R. Irvine kicked a penalty (3–0); A. Paco scored and J.P. Romeu converted (3–6); J.P. Romeu kicked a penalty (3–9).(H.T.). D. Harize, R. Bertranne and R. Paperemborde scored and J.P. Romeu converted the last (3–23).

The game opened with a magnificent punch by Cholley which felled Macdonald and since he was penalised later for his equally rough treatment of Renwick and Wilson he was lucky to be left on the field. Not that he was alone in this for a good few of the Scots had to halt for recovery, which was a pity for this French team was very much on top and perfectly capable of scoring by fine handling. Scotland never came into the game. They held their own at the line out but the ball seldom got out to the threes and the French pack was well on top in the loose play.

WALES **Murrayfield** **19 March 1977**

SCOTLAND: 1 goal, 1 drop goal 9 **Loss**

WALES: 2 goals, 2 penalty goals 18

Scotland: A.R. Irvine (*Heriot's FP*); W.B.B. Gammell (*Edin. Wrs.*), J.M. Renwick (*Hawick*), A.G. Cranston (*Hawick*), D. Shedden (*West of Scot.*); I.R. McGeechan* (*Headingley*), D.W. Morgan (*Stewart's FP*); J. McLauchlan (*Jordanhill Coll.*), D.F. Madsen (*Gosforth*), A.B. Carmichael (*West of Scot.*), I.A. Barnes (*Hawick*), A.F. McHarg (*London Scot.*), M.A. Biggar (*London Scot.*), D.S.M. Macdonald (*London Scot.*), W.S. Watson (*Boroughmuir*)

Wales: J.P.R. Williams (*Bridgend*); T.G.R. Davies (*Cardiff*), S.P. Fenwick (*Bridgend*), D.H. Burcher (*Newport*), J.J. Williams (*Llanelli*); P. Bennett* (*Llanelli*), G.O. Edwards (*Cardiff*); C. Williams (*Aberavon*), R.W. Windsor (*Pontypool*), G. Price (*Pontypool*), A.J. Martin (*Aberavon*), G.A.D. Wheel (*Swansea*), T.J. Cobner (*Pontypool*), D.L. Quinnell (*Llanelli*), R.C. Burgess (*Ebbw Vale*)

Referee: G. Domercq (*France*) **Touch judges:** P.C. Robertson, F. Palmade (*France*)

I.R. McGeechan dropped a goal (3–0); P. Bennett kicked a penalty (3–3).(H.T.). A.R. Irvine scored and converted (9–3); T.G.R. Davies scored and P. Bennett converted (9–9); P. Bennett kicked a penalty (9–12); P. Bennett scored and converted (9–18).

Scotland made a sensational start for inside the first minute Biggar got the ball away from a ruck to Morgan whose pass let McGeechan drop a goal. There followed two near penalty misses, Bennett hitting the post from near the touch line and Irvine narrowly missing from five yards inside his own half. Then Bennett, after a foul on Quinnell, levelled the scores with a fine 40 yard penalty. There was no further scoring before half time although both sides produced some good handling runs. Scotland restarted well for early on Morgan breaking from a scrum set Renwick off on a fine run which ended with Irvine joining in to score a try which he converted. Within five minutes Wales drew level when Edwards and J.P.R. Williams combined to put J.J. Williams over and Bennett converted from the touch line. Another Bennett penalty put them into the lead before Fenwick, taking the ball in his own 25, started an attack which set Davies off on a great run up the touch line continued by Burcher with Edwards and Bennett in support. A final pass to Bennett saw him make a clear run to score between the posts and convert. The fact that many Scots were certain that the final pass was forward could not detract from the qualify of such a fine attacking run from defence.

JAPAN **Tokyo** **18 September 1977**

SCOTTISH XV: 9 goals, 4 penalty goals, 2 tries 74 **Win**

JAPAN: 1 goal, 1 penalty goal   9

Scotland: C.D.R. Mair (*West of Scot.*); W.B.B. Gammell (*Edin. Wrs.*), J.M. Renwick (*Hawick*), A.G. Cranston (*Hawick*), L.G. Dick (*Swansea*); R. Wilson (*London Scot.*), R.J. Laidlaw (*Jedforest*); J. McLauchlan (*Jordanhill Coll.*), C.T. Deans (*Hawick*), R.F. Cunningham (*Gala*), A.J. Tomes (*Hawick*), I.A. Barnes (*Hawick*), M.A. Biggar* (*London Scot.*), D.S.M. Macdonald (*London Scot.*), G. Dickson (*Gala*). Subs: R.A. Moffat (*Melrose*), G.M. McGuinness (*West of Scot.*)

Japan: S. Tanaka; H. Ujino, M. Yoshida, S. Mori, M. Fujiwara; Y. Matsuo, J. Matsumoto; T. Yasui, T. Takada*, T. Hatakeyama, N. Kumagai, K. Segawa, H. Akama, H. Ogasawara, I. Kobayashi

Referee: P.E. Hughes (*England*)

W.B.B. Gammell (4), R.J. Laidlaw (2), A.G. Cranston, G. Dickson, R.A. Moffat, G.M. McGuinness and R. Wilson scored. C.D.R. Mair kicked nine goals and four penalties. For Japan, H. Ujino scored and S. Tanaka converted. Y. Matsuo kicked a penalty.

Japan resisted well up to half-time when the score was only 15–3 but thereafter the taller and heavier Scottish forwards wore down their opponents and some penetrative running by the Scottish backs, Laidlaw, Renwick and Gammell in particular, put Scotland in complete command.

This was the final match in a short tour to Thailand, Hong Kong and Japan.

IRELAND   Lansdowne Road   21 January 1978

SCOTLAND: 3 penalty goals   9   Loss

IRELAND: 1 goal, 2 penalty goals   12

Scotland: B.H. Hay (*Boroughmuir*); A.R. Irvine (*Heriot's FP*), J.M. Renwick (*Hawick*), I.R. McGeechan (*Headingley*), D. Shedden (*West of Scot.*); R. Wilson (*London Scot.*), D.W. Morgan* (*Stewart's FP*); J. McLauchlan (*Jordanhill Coll.*), D.F. Madsen (*Gosforth*), A.B. Carmichael (*West of Scot.*), A.J. Tomes (*Hawick*), A.F. McHarg (*London Scot.*), M.A. Biggar (*London Scot.*), D.S.M. Macdonald (*West of Scot.*), C.B. Hegarty (*Hawick*)

Ireland: A.H. Ensor (*Wanderers*); T.O. Grace (*St Mary's*), A.R. McKibben (*London Irish*), P.P. McNaughton (*Greystones*), A.C. McLennan (*Wanderers*); A.J.P. Ward (*Garryowen*), J.J. Moloney* (*St Mary's*); P.A. Orr (*Old Wesley*), P.C. Whelan (*Garryowen*), M.P. Fitzpatrick (*Wanderers*), M.I. Keane (*Lansdowne*), D. Spring (*Dublin Univ.*), J.B. O'Driscoll (*London Irish*), W.P. Duggan (*Blackrock*), J.F. Slattery (*Blackrock*) Sub: S.A. McKinney (*Dungannon*), L.A. Moloney (*Garryowen*)

Referee: P.E. Hughes (*England*)   **Touch judges:** A. Welsby (*England*), O.E. Doyle (*Ireland*)

D.W. Morgan kicked a penalty (3–0); A.J.P. Ward kicked a penalty (3–3); D.W. Morgan kicked a penalty (6–3); A.J.P. Ward kicked a penalty (6–6); S.A. McKinney scored and A.J.P. Ward converted (6–12). (H.T.). D.W. Morgan kicked a penalty (9–12).

Ireland started strongly and it was ten minutes before Scotland got to the Irish 25 whereupon the new Scottish captain promptly kicked a penalty. Scrappy play followed with Ireland having the better of the loose play and at the end of 40 minutes the scores were level at two penalties each. Here Driscoll retired hurt and was replaced by McKinney who at once took part in a fierce forward rush and then from the resulting scrum took a pass from Slattery and scored. The second half was slightly more open with the Irish backs being more in evidence mainly because their forwards were clearly better in the line out and loose play. Irvine, clearly isolated on the wing, was allowed to take one shot at goal and narrowly missed with a tremendously long kick. Later Morgan kicked another penalty but missed another in the 44th minute. Hegarty then nearly got in at the corner. From the line out Scotland got a penalty, obviously kickable, but Morgan elected to run the ball for a winning try. The Irish defence killed the move and the whistle went. This was a long match for the first half lasted 47 minutes and the second one 48 minutes. Ensor, badly concussed in a collision, was replaced by L.A. Moloney half way through the second half.

FRANCE: Murrayfield 4 February 1978

SCOTLAND: 1 goal, 1 drop goal,
1 penalty goal, 1 try 16 **Loss**

FRANCE: 1 goal, 3 penalty goals, 1 try 19

Scotland: A.R. Irvine (*Heriot's FP*); B.H. Hay (*Boroughmuir*), J.M. Renwick (*Hawick*), I.R. McGeechan (*Headingley*), D. Shedden (*West of Scot.*); R. Wilson (*London Scot.*), D.W. Morgan* (*Stewart's FP*); J. McLauchlan (*Jordanhill Coll.*), C.T. Deans (*Hawick*), N.E.K. Pender (*Hawick*), A.J. Tomes (*Hawick*), A.F. McHarg (*London Scot.*), M.A. Biggar (*London Scot.*), G.Y. Mackie (*Highland*), C.B. Hegarty (*Hawick*) Sub: A.G. Cranston (*Hawick*), C.G. Hogg (*Boroughmuir*)

France: J.M. Aguirre (*Bagneres*); J.F. Gourdon (*Bagneres*), R. Bertranne (*Bagneres*), C. Belascain (*Bayonne*), J.-L. Averous (*La Voulte*); B. Vives (*Agen*), J. Gallion (*Toulon*); G. Cholley (*Castres*), A. Paco (*Beziers*), R. Paparemborde (*Pau*), M. Palmie (*Beziers*), F. Haget (*Agen*), J.P. Rives (*Toulouse*), J.-P. Bestiat* (*Dax*), J.-C. Skrela (*Toulouse*)

Referee: C.P.G. Thomas (*Wales*) **Touch judges:** A. Bryce, C. Norling (*Wales*)

D.W. Morgan kicked a penalty (3–0); D. Shedden scored but D.W. Morgan failed (7–0); A.R. Irvine scored and D.W. Morgan converted (13–0); J. Gallion scored but J.M. Aguirre failed (13–4).(H.T.). J.M. Aguirre kicked a penalty (13–7); F. Haget scored and J.M. Aguirre converted (13–13); J.M. Aguirre kicked a penalty (13–16); D.W. Morgan dropped a goal (16–16); J.M. Aguirre kicked a penalty (16–19).

During the first half in wet conditions Scotland harried the French by being fast onto the loose ball. Shedden came through after a diagonal kick by Morgan, charged down Gourdon's kick and scored. Then Irvine followed up a long kick ahead by Morgan, kicked the ball over the line and although blatantly impeded, got to the ball first. Unfortunately he landed awkwardly and hurt his shoulder. While he was off, Gallion made a break and kicked a high ball into the ingoal area where Hegarty (playing on the wing with Hay at full back) could not hold the wet ball and a kindly bounce gave Gallion a try. Irvine returned but early in the second half both he and Shedden had to retire to be replaced by Cranston and Hogg. France, even in the rain, kept up the attack and a good handling run by Belascain, Skrela and Averous put Haget in at the corner but Aguirre made a fine conversion and then kicked a penalty to put France ahead. Morgan levelled the scores with a drop goal taken after a non-scoring penalty award and certainly some of the French team protested that he had omitted the tap kick before making the drop! Minutes later Aguirre kicked another penalty and although Scotland put in a great attacking finish they could not get the vital score.

WALES   Cardiff   18 February 1978

SCOTLAND: 2 penalty goals, 2 tries   14 **Loss**

WALES: 1 drop goal, 1 penalty goal, 4 tries   22

Scotland: B.H. Hay (*Boroughmuir*); W.B.B. Gammell (*Edin. Wrs.*), J.M. Renwick (*Hawick*), A.G. Cranston (*Hawick*), D. Shedden (*West of Scot.*); I.R. McGeechan (*Headingley*), D.W. Morgan* (*Stewart's FP*); J. McLauchlan (*Jordanhill Coll.*), C.T. Deans (*Hawick*), N.E.K. Pender (*Hawick*), A.J. Tomes (*Hawick*), A.F. McHarg (*London Scot.*), M.A. Biggar (*London Scot.*), D.S.M. Macdonald (*West of Scot.*), C.B. Hegarty (*Hawick*) Sub: C.G. Hogg (*Boroughmuir*)

Wales: J.P.R. Williams (*Bridgend*); T.G.R. Davies (*Cardiff*), R.W.R. Gravell (*Llanelli*), S.P. Fenwick (*Bridgend*), J.J. Williams (*Llanelli*); P. Bennett* (*Llanelli*), G.O. Edwards (*Cardiff*); A.G. Faulkner (*Pontypool*), R.W. Windsor (*Pontypool*), G. Price (*Pontypool*), A.J. Martin (*Aberavon*), G.A.D. Wheel (*Swansea*), T.J. Cobner (*Pontypool*), D.L. Quinnell (*Llanelli*), J. Squire (*Newport*)

Referee: J.R. West (*Ireland*) **Touch judges:** D.M.D. Rea (*Ireland*), A.W. Bevan (*Wales*)

D.W. Morgan kicked a penalty (3–0); G.O. Edwards scored but P. Bennett failed (3–4); J.M. Renwick scored but D.W. Morgan failed (7–4); R.W.R. Gravell scored but P. Bennett failed (7–8).(H.T.). P. Bennett dropped a goal (7–11); S.P. Fenwick scored but P. Bennett failed (7–15); P. Bennett kicked a penalty (7–18); D.L. Quinnell scored but P. Bennett failed (7–22); D.W. Morgan kicked a penalty (10–22); A.J. Tomes scored but D.W. Morgan failed (14–22).

Wales chose to play against the wind in the first half and were content with their narrow half-time lead for although the Scottish pack were on top in the line out Wales were controlling the scrums and loose play. Inside three minutes Scotland lost Shedden and once again he was replaced by Hogg. After a 40 yard penalty by Morgan, Edwards from a ten yards scrum dummied and crashed his way through for a score. After Morgan had missed two penalties, he sent McGeechan away and with Hay coming into the line Renwick was given a scoring pass. Almost at once Edwards took a short penalty which led to Gravell barging through the defence for a determined try. Restarting with the wind Wales scored fourteen points in as many minutes and appeared to have the match won, yet for the last twenty minutes Scotland fought back most determinedly but could not make up the deficit.

308

ENGLAND   Murrayfield   4 March 1978

SCOTLAND: Nil   0   **Loss**

ENGLAND: 2 goals, 1 penalty goal   15

Scotland: A.R. Irvine (*Heriot's FP*); W.B.B. Gammell (*Edin. Wrs.*), J.M. Renwick (*Hawick*), A.G. Cranston (*Hawick*), B.H. Hay (*Boroughmuir*); R.W. Breakey (*Gosforth*), D.W. Morgan* (*Stewart's FP*); J. McLauchlan (*Jordanhill Coll.*), C.T. Deans (*Hawick*), N.E.K. Pender (*Hawick*), A.J. Tomes (*Hawick*), D. Gray (*West of Scot.*), M.A. Biggar (*London Scot.*), D.S.M. Macdonald (*West of Scot.*), C.B. Hegarty (*Hawick*)

England: D. Caplan (*Headingley*); P.J. Squires (*Harrogate*), B.J. Corless (*Moseley*), P.A. Dodge (*Leicester*), M.A.C. Slemen (*Liverpool*); J.P. Horton (*Bath*), M. Young (*Gosforth*); B.G. Nelmes (*Cardiff*), P.J. Wheeler (*Leicester*), F.E. Cotton (*Sale*), W.B. Beaumont* (*Fylde*), M. Colclough (*Angouleme*), P.J. Dixon (*Gosforth*), J.P. Scott (*Rosslyn Park*), M.J. Rafter (*Bristol*)

Referee: J.R. West (*Ireland*)   **Touch judges:** J.A. Short, D.I.H. Burnett (*Ireland*)

P.J. Squires scored and M. Young converted (0–6); P.A. Dodge kicked a penalty (0–9). (H.T.). B.G. Nelmes scored and M. Young converted (0–15).

Both countries came to Murrayfield without a win but it was England who returned with the Calcutta Cup leaving Scotland with the wooden spoon. Again the Scottish pack did well at the line out only to be outplayed in the scrums and loose mauls. England started with the wind and their new full back nearly scored in the first minutes. It was a full twenty minutes before Scotland got into their opponents' half but poor finishing ruined their attacks. After 30 minutes Slemen broke away to initiate a splendid handling run by his forwards which ended by Squires on the opposite wing scoring a fine try. Just on half time Dodge kicked a massive 55 yard penalty. With the wind Scotland did some attacking, Gammell and Renwick both being caught at the corner but again poor finishing let them down and with 10 minutes to go England clinched the win when a scissors movement by their centres was completed by Nelmes who fairly smashed his way over.

NEW ZEALAND   Murrayfield   9 December 1978

SCOTLAND: 1 goal, 1 drop goal   9   **Loss**

NEW ZEALAND: 2 goals, 2 penalty goals   18

Scotland: A.R. Irvine (*Heriot's FP*); K.W. Robertson (*Melrose*), J.M. Renwick (*Hawick*), A.G. Cranston (*Hawick*), B.H. Hay (*Boroughmuir*); I.R. McGeechan* (*Headingley*), A.J.M. Lawson (*London Scot.*); J. McLauchlan (*Jordanhill Coll.*), C.T. Deans (*Hawick*), R.F. Cunningham (*Gala*), A.J. Tomes (*Hawick*), A.F. McHarg (*London Scot.*), M.A. Biggar (*London Scot.*), D.G. Leslie (*Gala*), G. Dickson (*Gala*) Sub: I.K. Lambie (*Watsonians*)

New Zealand: B.J. McKechnie (*Southland*); S.S. Wilson (*Wellington*), B.J. Robertson (*Counties*), W.M. Osborne (*Wanganui*), B.G. Williams (*Auckland*); D.D. Bruce (*Canterbury*), M.W. Donaldson (*Manawata*); B.R. Johnstone (*Auckland*), A.G. Dalton (*Counties*), G.A. Knight (*Manawata*), A.M. Haden (*Auckland*), F.J. Oliver (*Otaga*), L.M. Rutledge (*Southland*), G.A. Seear (*Otago*), G.N.K. Mourie* (*Taranaki*)

Referee: J.R. West (*Ireland*) **Touch judges:** P.C. Robertson, D.I.H. Burnett (*Ireland*)

B.H. Hay scored and A.R. Irvine converted (6–0); B.J. McKechnie kicked a penalty (6–3); G.A. Seear scored and B.J. McKechnie converted (6–9).(H.T.). B.J. McKechnie kicked a penalty (6–12); I.R. McGeechan dropped a goal (9–12); B.J. Robertson scored and B.J. McKechnie converted (9–18).

In a day of rain visibility became so poor that the kick off was actually advanced by five minutes but the game finished in a very dim light. The wet conditions caused many handling errors and the opening score came when Bruce slithered past a loose ball which Hay kicked on and gathered to dive over for a try converted from the touch line by Irvine. Strong New Zealand forward play followed and after McKechnie had kicked a penalty Seear drove over for a try. Early in the second half Leslie limped off to be replaced by Lambie. Scotland came away strongly and a McKechnie penalty was cancelled out by a drop goal by McGeechan. The Scots continued to attack only to give away a most unlucky score. McGeechan, with his threes up in attack, dropped at goal only to find the ball bouncing off Bruce. Robertson shot on to the rebound and with two long hacks ahead was able to put the ball the length of the field and keep ahead of a shocked defence to score under the posts.

WALES: Murrayfield   20 January 1979

| **SCOTLAND:** | 3 penalty goals, 1 try | 13 | **Loss** |
| **WALES:** | 1 goal, 3 penalty goals, 1 try | 19 | |

Scotland: A.R. Irvine (*Heriot's FP*); K.W. Robertson (*Melrose*), J.M. Renwick (*Hawick*), I.R. McGeechan* (*Headingley*), B.H. Hay (*Boroughmuir*); J.Y. Rutherford (*Selkirk*), A.J.M. Lawson (*London Scot.*); J. McLauchlan (*Jordanhill Coll.*), C.T. Deans (*Hawick*), R.F. Cunningham (*Gala*), A.J. Tomes (*Hawick*), A.F. McHarg (*London Scot.*), M.A. Biggar (*London Scot.*), I.K. Lambie (*Watsonians*), G. Dickson (*Gala*)

Wales: J.P.R. Williams* (*Bridgend*); H.E. Rees (*Neath*), R.W.R. Gravell (*Llanelli*), S.P. Fenwick (*Bridgend*), J.J. Williams (*Llanelli*); W.G. Davies (*Cardiff*), T.D. Holmes (*Cardiff*); A.G. Faulkner (*Pontypool*), R.W. Windsor (*Pontypool*), G. Price (*Pontypool*), A.J. Martin (*Aberavon*), G.A.D. Wheel (*Swansea*), P. Ringer (*Llanelli*), D.L. Quinnell (*Llanelli*), J. Squire (*Pontypool*)

Referee: F. Palmade (*France*) **Touch judges:** J.W. Dinsmore, G. Chevrier (France)

S.P. Fenwick kicked a penalty (0–3); A.R. Irvine kicked two penalties (6–3); A.R. Irvine scored but failed to convert (10–3); S.P. Fenwick kicked a penalty (10–6); A.R. Irvine kicked a penalty (13–6).(H.T.). S.P. Fenwick kicked a penalty (13–9); H.E. Rees and T.D. Holmes scored and S.P. Fenwick converted the second (13–19).

In spite of the very wintry conditions the electric blanket had kept the pitch in beautiful condition. For the first half Scotland had the benefit of a bitterly cold wind blowing down the pitch from the clock end, but a heavy and active Welsh pack dominated the line out and scrums. The Scottish backs had always to work with a limited supply of good ball, yet their try was as fine a combined effort as one could wish to see. Irvine, having fielded a kick ahead, side stepped and ran on to link with Hay. The ball went loose but Lawson pounced on it and set Rutherford racing through a gap to link up with McGeechan and Tomes. The big lock then flung out an overhead pass which Irvine took and side stepped over for a great score.

With the wind in the second half Wales attacked continually. Fenwick, who had kicked a third penalty, combined with Gravell to set J.P.R. Williams away. A nice chip ahead let Rees go in for the equalising score. Scotland held on grimly but in the dying minutes a powerful surge by the Welsh pack put Holmes over for the winning score.

ENGLAND   Twickenham   3 February 1979

SCOTLAND: 1 penalty goal, 1 try   7   **Draw**

ENGLAND: 1 penalty goal, 1 try   7

Scotland: A.R. Irvine (*Heriot's FP*); K.W. Robertson (*Melrose*), J.M. Renwick (*Hawick*), I.R. McGeechan* (*Headingley*), B.H. Hay (*Boroughmuir*); J.Y. Rutherford (*Selkirk*), A.J.M. Lawson (*London Scot.*); J. McLauchlan (*Jordanhill Coll.*), C.T. Deans (*Hawick*), R.F. Cunningham (*Gala*), A.J. Tomes (*Hawick*), A.F. McHarg (*London Scot.*), M.A. Biggar (*London Scot.*), I.K. Lambie (*Watsonians*), G. Dickson (*Gala*)

England: A.J. Hignell (*Bristol*); P.J. Squires (*Harrogate*), A.M. Bond (*Sale*), P.W. Dodge (*Leicester*), M.A.C. Slemen (*Liverpool*); W.N. Bennett (*London Welsh*), M. Young (*Gosforth*); R.J. Cowling (*Leicester*), P.J. Wheeler (*Leicester*), G.S. Pearce (*Northampton*), W.B. Beaumont (*Fylde*), N.E. Horton (*Toulouse*), A. Neary (*Broughton Park*), R.M. Uttley* (*Gosforth*), M. Rafter (*Bristol*) Sub: J.P. Scott (*Cardiff*)

Referee: C. Norling (*Wales*) **Touch judges:** C. Thomas (*Wales*), A. Welsby

M.A.C. Slemen scored but W.N. Bennett failed (0–4); W.N. Bennett kicked a penalty (0–7); J.Y. Rutherford scored but A.R. Irvine failed (4–7).(H.T.). A.R. Irvine kicked a penalty (7–7).

A capacity crowd which included Prince Philip saw England make a great start, for after a straightforward threequarter run, Slemen went over at the corner inside five minutes play. The home pack was dominating both the line out and second phase play but their backs did not make effective use of the possession. The Scottish backs looked good but were given few real chances to attack. Bennett had kicked a long range penalty before Renwick seized a loose ball and Irvine in the line kicked ahead only to be rather obviously tripped. Rutherford, however, followed up for the score which was not converted. The second half followed much the same pattern with the English backs failing to make use of a plentiful supply of the ball and eventually an Irvine penalty levelled the scores. Near the close Uttley was hurt and replaced by Scott.

IRELAND Murrayfield 3 March 1979

SCOTLAND: 1 penalty goal, 2 tries   11   **Draw**

IRELAND: 1 penalty goal, 2 tries   11

Scotland: A.R. Irvine (*Heriot's FP*); K.W. Robertson (*Melrose*), J.M. Renwick (*Hawick*), I.R. McGeechan* (*Headingley*), B.H. Hay (*Boroughmuir*); J.Y. Rutherford (*Selkirk*), A.J.M. Lawson (*London Scot.*); J. McLauchlan (*Jordanhill Coll.*), C.T. Deans (*Hawick*), I.G. Milne (*Heriot's FP*), A.J. Tomes (*Hawick*), D. Gray (*West of Scot.*), M.A. Biggar (*London Scot.*), W.S. Watson (*Boroughmuir*), G. Dickson (*Gala*)

Ireland: W.R.J. Elliott (*Bangor*); C.M.H. Gibson (*NIFC*), A.R. McKibbin (*London Irish*), P.P. McNaughton (*Greystones*), A.C. McLennan (*Wanderers*); A.J.P. Ward (*Garryowen*), C.S. Patterson (*Instonians*); P.A. Orr (*Old Wesley*), P.C. Whelan (*Garryowen*), G.A.J. McLoughlin (*Shannon*), M.I. Keane (*Lansdowne*), D.E. Spring (*Dublin Univ.*), W.P. Duggan (*Blackrock*), M.E. Gibson (*Lansdowne*), J.F. Slattery* (*Blackrock*)

Referee: C. Thomas (*Wales*)   **Touch judges:** J.R. Colquhoun, K. Rowlands (*Wales*)

J.Y. Rutherford scored but A.R. Irvine failed (4–0); C.S. Patterson scored but A.J.P. Ward failed (4–4); A.R. Irvine kicked a penalty (7–4).(H.T.). A.R. Irvine scored but failed to convert (11–4); A.J.P. Ward kicked a penalty (11–7); C.S. Patterson scored but A.J.P. Ward failed (11–11).

There was a strong swirling wind which baffled the kicks at goal but made attacking kicks doubly dangerous, Ward in particular hoisting some wicked ones. Yet there were some fine runs especially by the Scottish threes. Both Irish tries followed good work by their fowards and Patterson scored with typical scrum half's fast breaks near the line. Ireland were unlucky that Ward's last conversion effort swung to strike a post. The first Scottish score followed an interception by Lawson who covered at least 50 yards before failing to reach Renwick with a pass. From a line out thereafter nice running by Milne, Deans and Lawson put Rutherford in at the corner. Their second score came from a neat kick ahead by Renwick which Robertson took on the run and then put Irvine in.

FRANCE Parc des Princes 17 March 1979

SCOTLAND: 1 goal, 1 penalty goal, 2 tries   17   **Loss**

FRANCE: 1 drop goal, 2 penalty goals, 3 tries   21

Scotland: A.R. Irvine (*Heriot's FP*); K.W. Robertson (*Melrose*), J.M. Renwick (*Hawick*), I.R. McGeechan* (*Headingley*), B.H. Hay (*Boroughmuir*); J.Y. Rutherford (*Selkirk*), A.J.M. Lawson (*London Scot.*); J. McLauchlan (*Jordanhill Coll.*), C.T. Deans (*Hawick*), I.G. Milne (*Heriot's FP*), A.J. Tomes (*Hawick*), D. Gray (*West of Scot.*), M.A. Biggar (*London Scot.*), G. Dickson (*Gala*), W.S. Watson (*Boroughmuir*)

312

France: J.M. Aguirre (*Bagneres*); J.F. Gourdon (*Bagneres*), R. Bertranne (*Bagneres*), C. Belascain (*Bayonne*), F. Costes (*Montferrand*); R.R. Aguerre (*Biarritz*), J. Gallion (*Toulon*); G. Cholley (*Castres*), A. Paco (*Beziers*), R. Paparemborde (*Pau*), F. Haget (*Biarritz*), J.F. Marchal (*Lourdes*), J.P. Rives* (*Toulouse*), J.L. Joinel (*Brive*), Y. Malquier (*Narbonne*)

Referee: R.C. Quittenton (*England*)   **Touch judges:** Welsby (*England*), St Guilhern (*France*)

C. Belascain scored but Aguerre failed (0–4); K.W. Robertson scored but Irvine failed (4–4); R. Aguerre kicked a penalty and dropped a goal (4–10); G. Dickson scored and Irvine converted (10–10).(H.T.). A.R. Irvine kicked a penalty (13–10); Y. Malquier scored but Aguerre failed (13–14); A.R. Irvine scored but failed (17–14); Y. Malquier scored but Aguerre failed (17–18); R. Aguerre kicked a penalty (17–21).

This was a game which could have gone either way yet France with a strong pack always looked the more dangerous. R. Aguerre, although scoring nine points, had an off day with his place kicking but clinched the match in the last four minutes by kicking a penalty from beyond the centre line.

NEW ZEALAND   Murrayfield   10 November 1979

SCOTLAND: 2 penalty goals   6   Loss
NEW ZEALAND: 2 goals, 2 tries   20

Scotland: A.R. Irvine (*Heriot's FP*); K.W. Robertson (*Melrose*), J.M. Renwick (*Hawick*), D.I. Johnston (*Watsonians*), B.H. Hay (*Boroughmuir*); J.Y. Rutherford (*Selkirk*), A.J.M. Lawson (*Heriot's FP*); J. McLauchlan* (*Jordanhill Coll.*), C.T. Deans (*Hawick*), I.G. Milne (*Heriot's FP*), A.J. Tomes (*Hawick*), D. Gray (*West of Scot.*), M.A. Biggar (*London Scot.*), I.K. Lambie (*Watsonians*), G. Dickson (*Gala*)

New Zealand: R.G. Wilson (*Canterbury*); S.S. Wilson (*Wellington*), G. Cunningham (*Auckland*), M. Taylor (*Waikato*), B.F. Fraser (*Wellington*); E. Dun (*North Auckland*), D.S. Loveridge (*Taranaki*); B.R. Johnstone (*Auckland*), A.G. Dalton (*Counties*), J.E. Spiers (*Counties*), A.M. Haden (*Auckland*), J.K. Fleming (*Wellington*), K.W. Stewart (*Southland*), M.G. Mexted (*Wellington*), G.N.K. Mourie* (*Taranaki*) Sub: M. Donaldson (*Manawatu*)

Referee: R.C. Quittenton (*England*)   **Touch judges:** J.M. Prideaux, C.J. High (*England*)

D.S. Loveridge scored; R.G. Wilson failed (0–4).(H.T.). M.G. Mexted scored; R.G. Wilson converted (0–10);A.R. Irvine kicked two penalties (6–10); S.S. Wilson and E. Dunn scored; R.G. Wilson converted the second (6–20).

The Scottish pack held its own in the line out and scrums but was no match for the New Zealand pack in loose play. The Scottish backs did little handling and against a solid defence never really looked like scoring. In contrast some of the Scottish tackling was poor; Mexted scored his try by a solo breakaway from a two man line out on the Scottish 22 metre line.

IRELAND Lansdowne Road **2 February 1980**

SCOTLAND: 2 goals, 1 penalty goal 15 **Loss**

IRELAND: 1 goal, 1 drop goal,
3 penalty goals, 1 try 22

Scotland: A.R. Irvine (*Heriot's FP*); S. Munro (*Ayr*), J.M. Renwick (*Hawick*), D.I. Johnston (*Watsonians*), B.H. Hay (*Boroughmuir*); J.Y. Rutherford (*Selkirk*), R.J. Laidlaw (*Jedforest*); J.N. Burnett (*Heriot's FP*), C.T. Deans (*Hawick*), I.G. Milne (*Heriot's FP*), W. Cuthbertson (*Kilmarnock*), D. Gray (*West of Scot.*), M.A. Biggar* (*London Scot.*), J.R. Beattie (*Glas. Acads.*), A.K. Brewster (*Stewart's FP*)

Ireland: R.C. O'Donnell (*St Mary's*); T.J. Kennedy (*St Mary's*), A.R. McKibbin (*London Irish*), P.P. McNaughton (*Greystones*), A.C. McLennan (*Wanderers*); S.O. Campbell (*Old Belvedere*), C.S. Patterson (*Instonians*); P.A. Orr (*Old Wesley*), C.F. Fitzgerald (*St Mary's*), M.P. Fitzpatrick (*Wanderers*), J.J. Glennon (*Skerries*), M.I. Keane (*Lansdowne*), J.B. O'Driscoll (*London Irish*), D.E. Spring (*Dublin Univ.*), J.R. Slattery* (*Blackrock*)

Referee: G. Chevrier (*France*) **Touch judges:** F. Palmade, J.P. Bonnet (*France*)

A.R. Irvine kicked a penalty (3–0); D.I. Johnston scored and A.R. Irvine converted (9–0); S.O. Campbell kicked 2 penalties (9–6); M.I. Keane scored but S.O. Campbell failed (9–10).(H.T.). T.J. Kennedy scored and S.O. Campbell converted (9–16); S.O. Campbell kicked a penalty and dropped a goal (9–22); D.I. Johnston scored and A.R. Irvine converted (15–22).

Yet again the Scottish pack held their own in the line out and scrums only to be beaten in the loose and show weaknesses in their cover defence. Their backs looked sharp enough, but never really got good possession and it was disheartening to find their early lead being frittered away. Campbell had missed three penalties before kicking his first but here Irvine was most unlucky to be penalised in front of the posts. Having called for a mark he stood his ground only to be penalised for not releasing the ball on being tackled.

FRANCE Murrayfield **16 February 1980**

SCOTLAND: 2 goals, 2 penalty goals, 1 try 22 **Win**

FRANCE: 1 drop goal, 1 penalty goal, 3 tries 14

Scotland: A.R. Irvine (*Heriot's FP*); S. Munro (*Ayr*), J.M. Renwick (*Hawick*), D.I. Johnston (*Watsonians*), B.H. Hay (*Boroughmuir*); J.Y. Rutherford (*Selkirk*), R.J. Laidlaw (*Jedforest*); J.N. Burnett (*Heriot's FP*), C.T. Deans (*Hawick*), I.G. Milne (*Heriot's FP*), A.J. Tomes (*Hawick*) D. Gray (*West of Scot.*), M.A. Biggar* (*London Scot.*), J.R. Beattie (*Glas. Acads.*), A.K. Brewster (*Stewart's FP*)

France: S. Gabernet *(Toulouse)*; D. Bustaffa *(Carcassonne)*, R. Bertranne *(Bagneres)*, D. Cordorniou *(Narbonne)*, J.L. Averous *(La Voulte)*; A. Caussade *(Lourdes)*, J. Gallion *(Toulon)*; A. Vaquerin *(Beziers)*, P. Dintrans *(Tarbes)*, R. Paparemborde *(Pau)*, F. Haget *(Biarritz)*, J.F. Marchal *(Lourdes)*, J.P. Rives* *(Toulouse)*, M. Clement *(Oloron)*, J.L. Joinel *(Brive)*

Referee: J.R. West *(Ireland)* **Touch judges:** A. O'Sullivan, M. Reddan *(Ireland)*

J. Gallion scored but A. Caussade failed (0–4); J.Y. Rutherford scored but A.R. Irvine failed (4–4); S. Gabernet kicked a penalty (4–7).(H.T.). S. Gabernet scored but A. Caussade failed (4–11); A. Caussade dropped a goal (4–14); A.R. Irvine scored and converted (10–14); A.R. Irvine scored and J.M. Renwick converted (16–14); A.R. Irvine kicked 2 penalties (22–14).

After thirteen games without a win it was an extraordinary and very late revival by Scotland that broke the sequence. Initially France got much reasonable possession from the loose play but did not make good use of it. Their first try was a typical scrum half's move following a fine rush by the pack while the second followed a long defensive kick which Gabernet fielded and then made a very fast break up the touch line. Interpassing with Averous gave the full back a fine score. A.R. Irvine took a series of penalty kicks which were so off target that the crowd began to shout for a change of kicker. Then with some fifteen minutes to go the Scottish backs began to handle and run and after some eight people had taken part in a movement, Irvine was right up to get in at the corner — and this time he kicked a goal. Inside five minutes backs and forwards combined beautifully at pace and again Irvine was right up to take a scoring pass. Renwick converted this and in the closing minutes Irvine completely re-established himself as the hero of the crowd by kicking two penalty goals. So Scotland pulled off an amazing win by scoring 18 points inside 12 minutes to change the score from 4–14 to 22–14!

WALES   Cardiff   1 March 1980

SCOTLAND:	1 goal	6	**Loss**
WALES:	1 goal, 1 penalty goal, 2 tries	17	

Scotland: A.R. Irvine *(Heriot's FP)*, K.W. Robertson *(Melrose)*, J.M. Renwick *(Hawick)*, D.I. Johnston *(Watsonians)*, B.H. Hay *(Boroughmuir)*; B.M. Gossman *(West of Scot.)*, R.J. Laidlaw *(Jedforest)*; J.N. Burnett *(Heriot's FP)*, K.G. Lawrie *(Gala)*, N.A. Rowan *(Boroughmuir)*, A.J. Tomes *(Hawick)*, D. Gray *(West of Scot.)*, M.A. Biggar* *(London Scot.)*, J.R. Beattie *(Glas. Acads.)*, G. Dickson *(Gala)* Sub: A.J.M. Lawson *(Heriot's FP)*

Wales: W.R. Blyth *(Swansea)*; H.E. Rees *(Neath)*, D.S. Richards *(Swansea)*, S.P. Fenwick *(Bridgend)*, D. Keen *(Aberavon)*; W.G. Davies *(Cardiff)*, T.D. Holmes *(Cardiff)*; C. Williams *(Swansea)*, A.J. Phillips *(Cardiff)*, G. Price *(Pontypool)*, A.J. Martin *(Aberavon)*, G.A.D. Wheel *(Swansea)*, J.M. Lane *(Cardiff)*, E.T. Butler *(Pontypool)*, J. Squire* *(Pontypool)* Sub: P. Morgan *(Llanelli)*

Referee: L.M. Prideaux *(England)* **Touch judges:** R.C. Quittenton, C.J. High *(England)*

S.P. Fenwick kicked a penalty (0–3); T.D. Holmes scored but S.P. Fenwick failed (0–7).(H.T.). D. Keen scored but S.P. Fenwick failed (0–11); D.S. Richards scored and W.R. Blyth converted (0–17); J.M. Renwick scored and A.R. Irvine converted (6–17).

The teams were presented to the Prince of Wales. The Scots were forced to make three changes and in fact Gossman was a third choice at half. The forwards did well enough in the scrums and line out but Laidlaw (who retired hurt after twenty minutes) had always to put up with some very untidy ball. The Welsh pack, however, were clearly superior in the loose, giving their backs much clear possession and aided by some rather weak tackling they ran in three tries. Yet the Scottish defence held out twice when the Welsh pack were literally encamped on their line. Just before half time one five minute siege finished when the Scottish backs ran the ball from behind the line to gain touch near midfield. Just before the end these backs again showed their potential when a dropped pass by Fenwick went via Gossman, Beattie and Irvine to Robertson who after a mazy run gave Renwick a pass to complete a fine handling movement. Shortly before half time P. Morgan replaced an injured G. Davies.

ENGLAND   Murrayfield   15 March 1980

SCOTLAND: 2 goals, 2 penalty goals   18 **Loss**

ENGLAND: 2 goals, 2 penalty goals, 3 tries   30

Scotland: A.R. Irvine* (*Heriot's FP*), K.W. Robertson (*Melrose*), J.M. Renwick (*Hawick*), D.I. Johnston (*Watsonians*), B.H. Hay (*Boroughmuir*); J.Y. Rutherford (*Selkirk*), R.J. Laidlaw (*Jedforest*); J.N. Burnett (*Heriot's FP*), K.G. Lawrie (*Gala*), N.A. Rowan (*Boroughmuir*), A.J. Tomes (*Hawick*), D. Gray (*West of Scot.*), D.G. Leslie (*Gala*), J.R. Beattie (*Glas. Acads.*), M.A. Biggar (*London Scot.*) Sub: J.S. Gossman (*West of Scot.*)

England: W.H. Hare (*Leicester*); J. Carleton (*Orrell*), C.R. Woodward (*Leicester*), P.W. Dodge (*Leicester*), M.A.C. Slemen (*Liverpool*); J.P. Horton (*Bath*), S.J. Smith (*Sale*); F.E. Cotton (*Sale*), P.J. Wheeler (*Leicester*), P.J. Blakeway (*Gloucester*), W.B. Beaumont* (*Fylde*), M.J. Colclough (*Angouleme*), R.M. Uttley (*Wasps*), J.P. Scott (*Cardiff*), A. Neary (*Broughton Park*)

Referee: J.P. Bonnet (*France*)   **Touch judges:** F. Palmade and G. Chevrier (*France*)

J. Carleton (2) and M.A.C. Slemen scored; W.H. Hare converted the first two (0–16); A.R. Irvine kicked a penalty (3–16); W.H. Hare kicked a penalty (3–19).(H.T.). A.R. Irvine kicked a penalty (6–19); S.J. Smith scored but W.H. Hare failed (6–23); A.J. Tomes scored and A.R. Irvine converted (12–23); W.H. Hare kicked a penalty (12–26); J. Carleton scored but W.H. Hare failed (12–30); J.Y. Rutherford scored and A.R. Irvine converted (18–30).

The foundation of a good English win was laid during the first half during which period their pack was clearly on top in all phases of play. The English backs enjoyed plenty clear possession and aided by some poor cover defence ran in three tries before half time and another soon after the restart. Yet the Scots never ceased to attack whenever they got the ball in their hands and indeed looked most dangerous running in two excellent tries and narrowly failing at least twice. As a result the second half was a most exhilarating exhibition of attacking rugby.

316

Some Post-war Notes

World War 2 which in effect stretched across seven seasons, inevitably cut into many rugby careers. Thus, of the fifteen pre-war caps who died on active service, nine may well have gained further recognition. Of the 53 who played in the Services Internationals (1942–45), eleven were pre-war caps but only fifteen of the others continued to be capped later. Of the eleven pre-war caps, I.C. Henderson, J.R.S. Innes, W.C.W. Murdoch, R.W.F. Sampson and W.B. Young bridged the years to win post-war caps and Murdoch's span of thirteen years (1935–48) stands as a record. No caps were awarded for the six Victory Internationals in 1946 and of the 21 who played, four — J. Anderson (London Scottish), J. Kirk (Edin. Acads.-Wrs.), J.R. McClure (Ayr) and K.H.S. Wilson (London Scottish) — were unfortunate in not being reselected when the official International matches began again in the year 1946–47.

Since that restart it is interesting to note how the front row of the scrum has been dominated by a relatively few long-serving players. Two in I.C. Henderson (1939–48) and R.W.F. Sampson (1939–47) have already been mentioned while T.P.L. McGlashan, who played in two Services Internationals in 1945, was later capped in the widely separated seasons of 1947 and 1954. The trend was really started by J.C. Dawson (1947–53) and continued by T. Elliot (1955–58) but their fine services are completely overshadowed by those of four of Scotland's most capped players.

Firstly there was the almost unobtrusive but extremely competent H.F. McLeod (1954–62) whose unbroken run of 40 caps is a record. After fourteen games with T. Elliot he was partnered for a further fourteen with D.M.D. Rollo (1959–68), a vigorous, unyielding but mobile farmer who only missed two games through injury in his own total of 40 caps. This sequence was almost at once continued by a most formidable pair in A.B. Carmichael (1967–77) and J. McLaughlan (1969–79). Carmichael (6 feet 2 inches in height and weighing 16 stone) ranks as one of the game's finest props and deservedly earned his Scottish record of 50 caps. His partner in 34 games, McLaughlan, was a mere 5 feet 9 inches but weighed fifteen and a half stone. Any apparent deficiency in build was covered by an unwavering and aggressive conviction that no other prop could trouble him — and he spent 80 minutes of every match proving it.

During this same period Scotland was equally well served by their hookers. After running through some ten specialists up to 1953, stability was established with R.K.G. MacEwen (1954–58) before the position was taken over by two outstanding hookers in N.S. Bruce (1958–64) and F.A.L. Laidlaw (1965–71), who, supported by the props already mentioned, provided Scotland with as good front rows as they ever had.

The second row has also had its share of outstanding players. J.W.Y. Kemp was continually praised for his skill in the line out and in the loose. It is doubtful if Scotland have ever had a more massive yet active pair than M.J. Campbell-Lamerton and F. ten Bos. P.C. Brown added to an all-round vigour an ability to kick goals in a highly individualistic manner. Having made a heel mark and casually placed the ball upright therein he would abruptly turn away with a gesture that established that his nose was still in position. Then equally abruptly he turned back for the kick. Usually the result was as good as could be desired but on occasions the ball followed a wavering trajectory which left the result in doubt until the last minute. G.L. Brown, his younger brother, was another good line out performer who shone in open play as South Africa found out when he scored a record eight tries on the 1977 Lions Tour. Away back in the 1920s a Hawick man of prewar vintage, asked for his opinion of a certain player who was very successfully demonstrating the relatively new arts of a wing forward, rather sourly commented 'Hei scores fer ower mony tries'. A.F. McHarg has had to put up with something of the same criticism. Certainly he has shown a remarkable ability to pop up all over the field both in defence and in attack but no one can really deny the general effectiveness of his intrusions and more over he was always a highly competent jumper in the line out.

Immediately after the War W.I.D. Elliot at once established himself as one of the best all-round forwards Scotland has produced. Strong in the line out, excellent with hands or feet in the open and a ruthless tackler he was really a splendid throwback to the pre-1914 type of forward. Other back row players may be briefly remembered: P.W. Kininmonth for his extraordinary drop goal against Wales; A. Robson for sound defence and fine handling; R.J.C. Glasgow for his really destructive tackling; J.P. Fisher whose Olympic basketball skills were evident in his catching of the ball at the tail of the line out and his handling in the open and lastly J.W. Telfer, a hard, vigorous Border forward who was always up with the play. P.K. Stagg who finished at 6 feet 10 inches (and was known to the French as M. Tour Eiffel) is the tallest player to be capped. He barely needed to jump in the line out and on occasions greatly disturbed the opponent's throw in by placing himself at the front of the line out.

A check on the half backs selected in the 33 seasons from 1947–1980 reveals that 22 scrum halves have partnered 25 stand offs, 14 of whom were also capped at centre or full back and it is only too easy to argue that there has been a lack of steady partnerships. For example — A.F. Dorward between 1950 and 1957 played with eight different partners in his fifteen matches while later C.M. Telfer had six partners during his run of seventeen caps. By contrast D.H. Chisholm, with fourteen caps, played thirteen times with his club partner, A.J. Hastie, during one of Scotland's more successful periods. This argument, however, must not be taken as a condemnation of the individual halves of the time, the longer serving of whom in addition to the two already mentioned were J.A.T. Rodd, S. Coughtrie (surely at 6 feet 1 inch the tallest ever) and D.S. Paterson. Since 1972 the choice has wavered between the contrasting styles of A.J.M. Lawson and D.W. Morgan.

The problem seems to have been at stand off. There A. Cameron and G.H. Waddell, both tall and burly, while capable of breaking through will probably be remembered for the excellence of their tactical and defensive kicking. D.H. Chisholm, benefitting from his club understanding, could create openings and drop goals. C.M. Telfer, also a good attacker, was often noted for his fine supporting play. I.R. McGeechan, as often placed at centre as at half, was a strong runner who, however, was a most successful drop kicker.

When one comes to consider the threequarters a choice has to be made from some 80 players and it is easier, and probably wiser, to name only the most capped men. So at centre there were three Borderers in J.M. Renwick (34), G.D. Stevenson (24) and J.W.C. Turner (20) (all born in Hawick!), two Anglo-Scots in I.H.P. Laughland (31) and I.R. McGeechan (32) and the Edinburgh born J.N.M. Frame (23). J.M. Renwick, now the most capped Scottish back should surely have been on the 1977 Lions tour and many Scots reckon that his omission was due to an excessive Welsh influence exerted by S.J. Dawes. Laughland, McGeechan and Turner often found themselves at stand off. It may be noted that Laughland was one of the stars in the brilliant and successful London Scottish Sevens of the 1960s. Stevenson, as whimsical and forthright a character on the field as off, was fast enough to play six times on the wing. I believe that it was N.G.R. Mair who commented that the opposition's delight in Stevenson's odd blunder was tempered by an uneasy suspicion as to what was coming next. Frame, whose clubs ranged from Highland to Gala must surely hold the record for the quickest score when he touched down within thirteen seconds of the kick off against England at Murrayfield in 1971.

From the wingers we have A.R. Smith (33), A.J.W. Hinshelwood (21) and W.C.C. Steele (23), all three were on the 6 foot mark, all knew where the corner flag was and had the pace and determination to get there. A.R. Smith, a man of many clubs, was a most powerful and controlled runner and it was his magnificient solo try up the Stand touchline against Wales in 1955 that sparked off the win which ended the dreadful run of losses.

For years the full back was nothing other than the last line of defence. He was expected to produce the crunching try saving tackle, to cover and field cleanly the attacking kicks ahead and reply with a long and sure kick to touch. W.E. Maclagan, the second to play as a solo full back, was a magnificent example of this type. The attacking feats of H.J. Stevenson, normally a brilliant centre half, were much admired during the early 1890s but not imitated by others of lesser genius. Between the Wars D. Drysdale (the first of a remarkable succession of eight Heriot's players to fill the position) was another classical full back but just after World War 2 K.I. Geddes frequently employed the attacking run from the rear position. This was continued by K.J.F. Scotland who was not only a sound full back but also a fine handler of the ball and he made many decisive intrusions into the line of the backs to set up a scoring overlap. A.R. Irvine has taken this move a stage further for he takes every chance to come forward and with his extra pace has not only set up scores for others but has himself scored a record number of tries as a full back.

Lastly we may note that S. Wilson, like Scotland, was a sound and successful goal kicker although now both have been surpassed by Irvine whose ability to convert long range penalties has helped him to a record total of points in International games.

Key to Abbreviations

GENERAL
A Albion
Acads. Academicals
Coll. College
FP Former Pupils
GS Grammar School
HS High School
Inst. Institution
OB Old Boys
UC University College
Univ. University

SCOTLAND
Fet.-Lor. Fettesian-Lorettonians
KOSB King's Own Scottish Borderers
London Scot. London Scottish
RE Royal Engineers
RHS Royal High School
SFU Scottish Football Union
SRU Scottish Rugby Union
Stewart's FP Stewart's College Former Pupils

ARGENTINA
CASI Club Atletico, San Isidro
CUBA Club Universitario, Buenos Aires

ENGLAND
Bradford N Bradford Northern
Guy's Guy's Hospital
Hull KR Hull Kingston Rovers
Marl. Nomads Marlborough Nomads
N Durham North Durham
Newcastle N Newcastle Northern
OMT Old Merchant Taylors
RIEC Royal Indian Engineering College
RMA Royal Military Academy (Woolwich)
RMC Royal Military College (Sandhurst)
RN Royal Navy
RNAS Royal Naval Air Service
RNEC Royal Naval Engineering College
Bart's St Bartholomew's Hospital
St Thomas's St Thomas's Hospital
Un. Services United Services

FRANCE
A Bayonnais Aviron Bayonnais
BEC Bordeaux Etudiants Club
CASG Club Athlétique des Sports Généraux
Castres O Castres Olympique
Lyon OU Lyon Olympique Universitaire
PUC Paris Université Club
RCF Racing Club de France
SBUC Stade Bordelais Université Club
SCUF Sporting Club Universitaire de France
SF Stade Français
TOEC Toulouse Olympique Employés Club

IRELAND
CIYMS Church of Ireland Young Men's Society
Cork Const. Cork Constitutional
NIFC North of Ireland Football Club
QC Cork Queen's College Cork

NEW ZEALAND
RNZAF Royal New Zealand Air Force

SOUTH AFRICA
B Border
EN Transvaal Eastern and Northern Transvaal
EP Eastern Province
GW Griqualand West
NE Cape North Eastern Cape
NT Northern Transvaal
Orange FS Orange Free State
SA Services South African Services
SWA South West Africa
T Transvaal
WP Western Province
WT Western Transvaal

WALES
Camarthen TC Camarthen Technical College
Pontypridd CS Pontypridd County School

Appendix 1

Overall Results 1
England

	P	W	D	L	O
1871–1914	41	17	9	15	3
1920–1939	20	8	1	11	0
1947–1980	35	10	5	20	0
	96	35	15	46	3

Ireland

	P	W	D	L	O
1871–1914	38	25	4*	9	1
1920–1939	20	9	0	11	0
1947–1980	33	11	1	21	1
	91	45	5*	41	2

* Includes the abandoned match of 1885

Wales

	P	W	D	L	O
1871–1914	30	13	1	16	2
1920–1939	20	11	1	8	0
1947–1980	34	10	0	24	0
	84	34	2	48	2

France

	P	W	D	L	O
1871–1914	4	3	0	1	1
1920–1939	12	8	1	3	8
1947–1980	34	13	1	20	0
	50	24	2	24	9

Appendix 1
Overall Results 2
New Zealand

	P	W	D	L
1871–1914	1	0	0	1
1920–1939	1	0	0	1
1947–1980	7	0	1	6
	9	0	1	8

South Africa

	P	W	D	L
1871–1914	2	1	0	1
1920–1939	1	0	0	1
1947–1980	5	2	0	3
	8	3	0	5

New South Wales & Australia

	P	W	D	L
1920–1939	1	1	0	0
1947–1980	6	4	0	2
	7	5	0	2

Scottish XV Matches

		P	W	D	L
Argentine	1969–1973	3	2	0	1
Barbarians	1970	1	0	0	1
Tonga	1974	1	1	0	0
Japan	1976–1977	2	2	0	0

Appendix 2: Chronology of Scottish References

1424 Act of Parliament: James I.

1458 Act of Parliament: James II.

1471 Act of Parliament: James III.

1491 Act of Parliament: James IV.

1487 Treasury Accounts: James IV.

1497 St Andrews: Ban on the playing of football.

1500 Gavin Douglas: Game mentioned in his poem 'King Hart'.

1511 Perth: Complaint to the Privy Council about players at Kirkmichael.

1537 at Andrews: Shrove Tuesday games permitted.

1540 Sir David Lyndsay: References in two of his works.

1546 Perth: Company of Hammermen: Game played by apprentices.

1552 St Andrews: Archbishop allowed to breed rabbits on the Links but the citizens retain their right to use the area for golf, futball and shuteing.

1570 Peebles: Town Council bans play in the Hie Gait.

1575 Glasgow: Burgh Council permits Shrove Tuesday football and donates two pence for a ball.

1585 Lothians: Synod rebukes John Law, the minister of Kirkliston, for playing on the Lord's Day.

1591 Perth: Kirk Session rebukes the heir of Luncarty and others for playing at Muirton on the Sunday of the Fast in the time of preaching.

1595 Kelso: Sir Robert Carey records 'a

great match made at footeball at Shel-say'.

1599 Bewcastle: Record of a six-a-side football match between Scottish and English borderers which degenerated into a brawl. There was a Roman fort at Bewcastle connected by a road to Hadrian's Wall.

1600 Archibald Douglas, Earl of Argyll, played at the football.

1600 Blairgowrie: Football opposed by the local minister.

1600 Borders: Sir John Carmichael murdered on his way home on a Sunday from a football meeting.

1600 Fife: The men of Kincaple warned for playing football on Trinity Sunday.

1607 Aberdeen: Youths accused of 'drinking, playing football, dancing and roving from parish to parish' on the Sabbath.

1609 Glasgow: Burgh Accounts: 'gifen upon the xxviii day of February to John Neill, cordoner, younger, for fute balls to the toune at fasterins evin conforme to the old use . . . xxvi.s. viii.d'.

1618 Elgin: Kirk Session bans football during 'the season called Yewle'.

1618 Lanark: Football played in the churchyard of Dalserf on the first Sunday in May.

1620 Perth: Two men of Exmagirdle admit to playing football on the Sabbath.

1628 Carstairs: The minister rebukes his parishioners for indulging in 'footballing, dancing and barley-breaks'.

1630 David Wedderburn: Produced a Latin grammar with references to football.

1648 Aberdeen: Various parishioners of Rayne and Culsalmond guilty of 'scandalous behaviour in convening themselves upon the Lord's Day to a public footballing'.

1650 Orkney: Football known in Kirkwall.

1656 Parliament: On the Borders Sunday football matches were common and led at times to raids. Act passed prohibiting all boisterous games on the Lord's Day.

1659 Edinburgh University: Second year students forbidden to play on the Burghmuir.

1670 Kirkwall: 'It is reported that severall idle boyes playes at football in tym of and after sermon'.

1682 Banff: Players fined 40s. for playing in the streets.

1684 Leith: Football played on the Links.

1700 Stirling: The minister of Kippen deliberately ruined a game by indulging in an overlong preliminary prayer.

1700 Jedburgh: Fleshers Corporation fine several brethren as 'guiltie at the rastling at the football'.

1704 Jedburgh: Burgh Council attempt to ban the annual Fastern's Eve Ball game.

1724 Duns: Bailies complain of tumults on Fastern's Even when football is played.

1738 Rev. J. Skinner: Reference in poem: 'The Moneymusk Christmas Ba'ing'.

1769 Hawick: Football played on Fastern's Eve.

1774 Ayr: Ball game played at the school.

1784 Kilmarnock: Ball game played at the school. The same reference also mentions Thurso Institute and Geo. Heriot's Hospital but gives no date.

1787 Kirkwall: Football is the principal diversion of the common people.

1796 Scone: The annual Shrove Tuesday game described in the 'Statistical Account of Scotland'.

 * Kielder: Thirty-a-side game played over several days between Scottish and English teams. Kielder lay on one of the paths over the Cheviots into Scotland used by the later Roman patrols.

1800 Glasgow: Football played in the Old College grounds in the High Street.

1801 Joseph Strutt: Comments that the game has fallen into disrepute and is but little practised.

c.1810 Edinburgh: Football played in the High School Yards at the foot of Infirmary Street.

1815 Selkirk: Sir Walter Scott organises a great football match at Carterhaugh.

c.1815 Rev. T. Somerville notes that many games are less generally practised than when he was younger.

1819 Dollar Academy opened.

1820 Musselburgh: Dr Langhorne starts a private school.

1823 Rugby: Date of the W. Webb Ellis legend.

1824 Edinburgh: The new Academy opened. Football played in the Academy Yards.

1827 Musselburgh: Dr Langhorne moves his school to Loretto House.

Dollar: Headmaster prohibits football

324

and other games liable to destroy property

1828 Yarrow: Annual match recorded between the men of Ettrick and Yarrow at Mount Benger.

1829 Edinburgh: The new High School opens on Calton Hill.

1833 Edinburgh: Merchiston Castle now used as a school with its playing field across Colinton Road where Abbotsford Park now stands. Cricket, football and shinty played.

1835 Yarrow: Another ball game noted.

1836 Edinburgh: Two twenties of the 71st Light Infantry play at Grange Loan. The Colonel attended and 'settled all appeals made to him in the most condescending manner'. This would probably be played on the original Grange C.C. field.

1837 Edinburgh: The tenants of St Ann's Yards, Holyrood Palace, appeal against the playing of cricket, quoits, foot or hand ball.

1840 East Lothian: At Tantallon Castle, Old Handsel Monday in January was celebrated by sports which included a football match between married and single men.

Edinburgh: Irish residents celebrated St Patrick's Day with a game of football on King's Park behind the palace. This had taken place for several years but this game ended in a general fight.

Dumfries: Football recorded in that area.

1842 Hawick: The annual Ba' game reintroduced.

1843 The Edinburgh–Glasgow (Haymarket-Queen Street), railway line opened.

1844 Dollar: Football still played but no particular rules used.

1846 Glasgow Academy is opened. Rugby School prints its Laws of Football. The Edinburgh–Berwick and Edinburgh–Carstairs–Carlisle railway lines opened.

1847 Glenalmond: Trinity College opened. The Winchester football rules are used.

Thos. Harvey comes to Edinburgh Academy.

1849 William Purdie and others charged by Jedburgh Council for playing handball in the town.

The Edinburgh-Hawick railway line opened.

1850 Edinburgh: The 93rd Highlanders play a match (31 v. 37) on Grange's second cricket ground at Grove Street.

The Royal Border railway bridge opened at Berwick-on-Tweed. Durham Grammar School using the Rugby School Laws.

1852 The two Crombie brothers come to Durham GS from Thornton Castle, Kincardine.

1853 Alex. (Joe) Crombie returns to Edinburgh to study Law.

1854 The Edinburgh Academy acquires Raeburn Place as a cricket ground. Francis Crombie also comes to Edinburgh and enters the Academy.

1856 Thos. Harvey becomes Headmaster of Merchiston. Francis Crombie becomes the first Captain of football at the Academy.

1857 H.H. Almond arrives at Loretto. Dr D. Murray recorded that football was played at Glasgow University and every season hereafter.

1857–58 Edinburgh Academicals and Edinburgh University play a match spread over four Saturday afternoons.

1858 Edinburgh Academicals play a military team. After their first AGM they have their rules printed. Merchiston play High School in the first interschool game. The Merchiston captain was A. Van Der Byl from Cape Town. Later Merchiston played the Academy — a fixture which has continued to this day. H.H. Almond and J.J. Rogerson come to Merchiston.

1859 The Glasgow University Review records that Football 'was a rough and tumble sort of game in which the contending sides swept across the low green from Blackfriars Street to the New Vennel and back like the hordes of Attila'.

1860 The High School acquire a cricket ground beside the Palace at Holyrood. The Merchistonians appear as an adult club.

1861 A High School FP and PP team play an Edinburgh University team at Holyrood.

1862 H.H. Almond moves to Loretto as Headmaster. In London, Blackheath print their rules. A. Van Der Byl plays

325

in the first recorded match in Cape Town.

1863 Thos. Harvey becomes Rector of The Edinburgh Academy and J.J. Rogerson is now Headmaster at Merchiston. At Kirkwall, their annual Ba' game is regarded as long established.
In London the Football Association is formed.

1865 West of Scotland FC formed and plays on the Cricket Club's field at Hamilton Crescent.
Dreghorn College, Edinburgh, plays football. Their school magazine *The Echo* describes play. The rules of local football in the Blairgowrie area are published. In Glasgow Queen's Park becomes the first Association Club in Scotland.

1866 Glasgow Academical FC formed, playing at Burnbank.

1867 Edinburgh Academicals play West of Scotland and St Salvator's (St Andrew).

1868 Edinburgh Academicals print the Green Book of Rules for use by the Scottish clubs. The Royal High School FP Club formed. Kilmarnock Club exists. Edinburgh Wanderers Club exists. Glasgow University plays on the old College Green. Many schools now playing rugby football.

1869 Games between Alloa and Dollar noted. The Edinburgh–Glasgow Caledonian railway line opened.

1870 Fettes College opened. Aberdeen University Club exists. Glasgow University play Edinburgh University at Gilmorehill. England v. Scotland play an association match at the Oval. Scottish clubs issue a challenge to the English rugby clubs.

1871 The English rugby clubs form their union. Several Scottish clubs join. The first Rugby International played at Raeburn Place on a Monday. The Langholm Club exists.

1872 Edinburgh Institution FP Club formed. Aberdeen University play Dalhousie FC on Queen's Links. The second Rugby International played on Kennington Oval. British residents form a club at Le Havre, France.

1873 Scottish Football Union formed. St Andrews University Club formed. Hamilton Crescent used for the third International. Glasgow Academicals move to Kelvinside. The Hawick and Greenock Wanderers Clubs and the first Kirkcaldy club formed.

1874 Scottish team noted for heeling the ball out of the maul and passing amongst the back players. Rugby Unions formed in Dublin and New South Wales.

1875 Watsonian FC formed. Donaldson's Hospital plays Heriot's Hospital. Games noted at Inverness, Fort George and Cupar.

1875–76 Tries now recognised in the scoring. Gala Club formed. Another Union formed in Belfast. England plays Ireland in London.

1876 Glenalmond changes to Rugby Rules. Kelso Club exists. Kelso High School plays rugby. Wick Club plays Thurso and Kirkwall.

1877 England, Ireland and Scotland all change to fifteens. H.H. Johnston becomes the first to play as a single full back. Melrose Club formed.

1878 Black's *Scottish Football Calendar* produced. Kelvinside Academicals Club formed. London Scottish Club formed. Merchiston move field to Colinton Road. Football played under electric light at Hampden Park and rugby at Coltbridge, near Murrayfield.

1879 Hawick v. Melrose at Hawick, Kelso v. Earlston at Kelso, played under electric light. First Calcutta Cup match at Raeburn Place. Rugby recorded at Lerwick and Kirkwall. Fettes play three backs and encourage interpassing. A single Irish Rugby Union established.

1880 Internationals now played on Saturdays. W.H. Masters and W. Sorley Brown form an interpassing pair of quarter backs for their club and Scotland. Loretto playing a definite interpassing game among their backs. The Merchiston forwards noted for their play as an interpassing and dribbling pack. Dundee HSFP and Panmure Clubs formed.

1881 Scotland play three backs against Ireland and England. Edinburgh Academy have a schoolboy playing in both the Scottish and English teams. England plays Wales. Fettesian-Lorettonian Club formed.

1882 Neutral referee used for English match. Ireland plays Wales.

1883 Scotland plays Wales. Glasgow Academicals move to Old Anniesland. First Melrose Sevens.

1884 Game of the Dispute v. England at Blackheath. First Gala Sevens.

1885 Irish Rugby Union initiates the idea of an International Board. Jedforest Club formed. Referee given a whistle but can only act if an umpire raises his stick. Irish game in Belfast abandoned because of appalling conditions. No game with England so a second Irish game played in Edinburgh. First Hawick Sports.

1886 The International Board formed. The RU introduces a points scoring system, not accepted by the other unions. Stewart's College FP Club formed. Wales try four back system.

1887 G.C. Lindsay scores five tries v. Wales.

1888 No match with England. Three Hawick players in British tour to New Zealand. R. Bruce Lockhart, Headmaster, starts rugby at Spier's School, Beith. North of Scotland RFU. Calendar issued.

1889 No match with England. South and North now represented on SFU committee. Maori tourists play Hawick on their new field at Mansfield Park. South African Football Board formed.

1890 Fettes College Governors refuse lease to SFU for field at Comely Bank. Heriot FP Club formed. IB firmly established by arbitration. Forth Bridge opened. Barbarian FC formed.

1891 New scoring values: Try 2: Penalty goal 3: Goal after try 5: Other goals 4. British tour (W.E. Maclagan, Captain) to South Africa. Umpires replaced by touch judges.

1893 England faced with 'broken time' controversy. Wales establish the four back system.

1893–94 Glasgow HSFP and Aberdeen GSFP Clubs formed. Kirkcaldy Club reformed. Scotland play four back system. First Jedforest Sevens.

1894–95 Try now worth 3 points.

1895 Last International at Raeburn Place. Referees now in sole control without appeal. Northern Union formed in Leeds.

1896 Old Hampden Park used for English match. London representative on SFU committee. An Edinburgh XV plays in Paris. The Gould Testimonial controversy begins. Second British tour in South Africa.

1897 Powderhall, Edinburgh, used for Irish match. No Welsh match played. Ayr Club formed.

1898 Powderhall used for English match. No Welsh match played. French team plays in Edinburgh and Glasgow.

1899 The first Union ground at Inverleith opened. Welsh fixture resumed.

1903 Gordonians Club formed. British tour (M.C. Morrison capt.) to South Africa.

1904 Dunfermline and Hillhead HSFP Clubs formed. British tour (D.R. Bedell-Sivright) to Australia and New Zealand.

1905 SFU take over control of Sevens. First New Zealand tour in Great Britain.

1906 Mark goal value now three. First South African tour in Great Britain.

1907 Selkirk Club formed. RU purchase Twickenham: French Sports Association seeks recognition.

1908 First Langholm Sevens: Irish Union acquire Lansdowne Road ground.

1909 First Australian tour in Great Britain.

1910 Scotland v. France at Inverleith. A.D. Flett becomes first paid official of SFU.

1911 Haddington Club formed.

1913 South Africa tour in Great Britain.

1914 SFU reconstituted. A.D. Flett now Secretary and Treasurer. Relations broken with France.

1919 Boroughmuir FP Club formed. First Selkirk Sevens.

1920 First Kelso Sevens. Fédération Française de Rugby formed. Edinburgh Northern RFC formed.

1921–22 Leith Academicals and Trinity Academicals Clubs formed.

1922–23 Highland club formed. Hutchesons' GSFP Club formed.

1923 Edinburgh Infirmary Sevens at Inverleith. Neil Macpherson case opened.

1924 Title changed to Scottish Rugby Union. British tour in S.A.

1925 Murrayfield opened with record crowd at English match. New Zealand tour in Great Britain except Scotland. Broughton FP Club formed.

1926 IB admit Dominion representation. First Middlesex Sevens at Twickenham. Harris Academy FP Club formed.

1927–28 Preston Lodge FP Club formed. NSW tour in Great Britain.

1930 British tour to Australia and New Zealand.

1932 Sheriff Watt presents Flagstaff and Flag to SRU. Relations broken with France. South African tour in Great Britain. Players in trials numbered. S.R.U. Committee nominate 5 members as team selectors.

1933 Scottish players now numbered. Italian Rugby Federation formed.

1935–36 Extensions added to stand at Murrayfield. New Zealand tour in Great Britain.

1936–37 Penalty try introduced.

1937 Calcutta Cup match broadcast. Clarkston Club formed.

1938 British tour to South Africa.

1939 War halts tour by Australian team.

1940 Field and offices at Murrayfield commandeered by army.

1946 Victory Internationals played; no caps awarded. New Zealand Army team tour in Great Britain.

1947 Internationals, including France, resumed. A.E. Sellars completes 50 years service as groundsman to SRU.

1948 Drop goal reduced to three points. NSW tour in Great Britain.

1950 British tour in Australia and New Zealand.

1951 South African tour in Great Britain.

1954 New Zealand tour in Great Britain.

1955 British tour to South Africa. Touch judges now chosen from active referees.

1957 Australian tour in Great Britain.

1959 Under soil heating installed at Murrayfield. British tour to Australia and New Zealand.

1960–61 South African tour in Great Britain.

1960 Scottish make first short tour to South Africa. Madras College FP Club formed.

1961 Poynder Park, Kelso, equipped with floodlighting.

1962 British tour (A.R. Smith, captain) in South Africa.

1963 New Zealand tour in Great Britain.

1964 Scotland make short tour in Canada.

1966 British tour (M.J. Campbell-Lamerton) to Australia and New Zealand. Australia tour in Great Britain.

1967 New Zealand tour in Great Britain. Scottish Border Club visits South Africa.

1968 Replacements in International matches permitted. British tour to South Africa.

1969 Scotland make short tour to Argentina. South African tour in Great Britain. I.G. McCrae becomes first substitute in an International game.

1970 Fiji tour in Great Britain. Scotland make a short tour in Australia.

1971 British tour in Australia and New Zealand.

1971–72 RU Centenary celebrations. Wales and Scotland do not play in Ireland because of political situation. Try is increased from three to four points.

1972 Jordanhill Club formed. New Zealand tour in Great Britain.

1972–73 SRU Centenary year celebrations, including first International Sevens tournament at Murrayfield. Stewarts–Melville College FP amalgamate.

1973–74 League football started in Scotland. British tour in South Africa. Argentina tour in Ireland and Scotland.

1974 Tonga tour in Great Britain.

1975 Scottish short tour in New Zealand. Australia tour in Great Britain.

1976 Japan tour in Great Britain. One touch judge now a neutral active referee.

1977 Scottish short tour in Far East. British tour to New Zealand and Fiji. N.A. MacEwan appointed by SRU as 'adviser to the captain'.

1978–79 New Zealand tour to Great Britain.

1979–80 New Zealand tour to Great Britain. Referee and both touch judges all from same neutral country.

Appendix 3: Acts of the Parliament of Scotland

James I: Perth: May 1424
It is statute and the King forbiddis, that na man play at the fute ball under the pane of xI.s. to be rasit to the Lord of the land, als oft as he be taintit, or to the Schiref of the land or his ministers gif the Lordis will not punis sic trespassouris.

James II: Edinburgh: March 1457
It is decretyt and ordanyt, that the wapinschawings be haldin be the Lordis and Barronis spirituall and temporall foure tymis in the zeir. And that the futball and golf be utterly cryit downe, and not to be usit.

James III: Edinburgh: May 1471
And that ilk sherif, stewart, bailze and uther officiares mak wapinschawying within the bondes of thar office eftir the tenor of the Act of Parliament. Swa that in defawt of the said wapinschawying our Souvran Lordes leiges be nocht destitut of harnes quhe that neid and at the futball and gold be abusit in tym cumyng . . .

James IV: Edinburgh: May 1491
It is statute and ordanit, that ilk Schiref, stewart or Baillie of the Realme gar wappinschawings be maid foure tymes in the zeir in all placis convenient within his Baillierie . . . And attour that in na place of the Realme there be usit futball, golf, or other sic unproffitabill sportis . . .

Appendix 4: Laws of Football at Rugby School 1846

1. Kick off from Middle must be a place kick.
2. Kick out must not be from more than 25 yards out of goal, nor from more than 10 yards if a place kick.
3. Fair catch is a catch direct from the foot.
4. Charging is fair, in the case of a place kick, as soon as the ball has left the ground; in the case of a kick from a catch, as soon as the player offers to kick, but he may always draw back, unless he has actually touched the ball with his foot.
5. Offside — A player is off his side if the ball has touched one of his own side behind him until the other party kick it.
6. A player being off his side is to consider himself as out of the game, and is not to touch the ball in any case whatever (either in or out of touch); or in any way to interrupt the play, and is, of course, incapable of holding the ball.
7. Knocking on, as distinguished from throwing on, is altogether disallowed under any circumstances whatsoever. In case of this rule being broken, a catch from such a knock on shall be equivalent to a fair catch.
8. It is not lawful to take the ball off the ground, except in touch, either for a kick or throw on.
9. First of His Side is the player nearest the ball on his side.
10. Running In is allowed to any player on his side, provided he does not take the ball off the ground, or through touch.
11. If, in the case of a run in, the ball is held in a scrummage, it shall not be lawful for the holder to transmit it to another of his own side.
12. No player may be held, unless he is himself holding the ball.
13. It is not fair to hack and hold at the same time.
14. No hacking with the heel, or unless below the knee is fair.

15. No one wearing projecting nails or iron plates on the soles or heels of his shoes or boots shall be allowed to play.
16. Try at Goal — A ball touched down between the goal posts may be brought up to either of them but not between.
17. The ball when punted must be within, and when caught without the line of goal.
18. The ball must be placed kicked and not dropped and if it touches two hands the try will be lost.
19. It shall be a goal if the ball goes over the bar (whether it touches or not) without having touched the dress or person of any player; but no player may stand on the goal bar to interrupt it going over.
20. No goal may be kicked from touch.
21. Touch — A player may not in any case run with the ball in touch.
22. A player standing up to another may hold one arm only, but may hack him or knock the ball out of his hand if he attempts to kick it, or go beyond the line of touch.
23. No agreement between two players to send the ball straight out shall be allowed.
24. A player having touched the ball straight for a tree and touched the tree with it, may drop from either side if he can, but one of the opposite side may oblige him to go to his own side of the tree.
25. In case of a player getting a fair catch immediately in front of his own goal, he may not retire behind the line to kick it.
26. No player may take the ball out of the Close.
27. No player may stop the ball with anything but his own person.
28. If a player takes a punt or drop when he is not entitled to it, the opposite side may take a punt or drop, without running (after touching the ball on the ground) if the ball has not touched two hands, but such a drop may not be a goal.
29. That part of the Island which is in front of the line of goal is in touch, that behind is in goal.
30. The discretion of sending into goal rests with heads of sides and houses or their deputies.
31. Heads of sides, or two deputies appointed by them, are the sole arbiters of all disputes.
32. All matches are drawn after 5 days or after 3 days if no goal has been kicked.

Laws 33— 37 are of local interest only.

Some amendments of 1847
4. Charging is fair, in the case of a place kick, as soon as the ball has touched the ground.
5. Off side — A player is off his side, if the ball had been kicked or thrown on by one of his own side behind him, until the other party kick it, thrown it on or run with it.
26. No player may take the ball out of the Close, i.e. behind the line of trees beyond the goal.

Appendix 5: Edinburgh Academicals FC Rules 1858

A foreword states 'The following Rules are taken from the Book of Rules used at Rugby'.

1. KICK OFF must be from MIDDLE and a place kick.
2. When the ball is touched down behind goal, if touched by the side behind whose goal it is, they have a KICK OUT; but if by the opposite side, they may have a TRY AT GOAL.
3. KICK OUT must not be from more than 25 yards out of goal.
4. FAIR CATCH is a catch direct from the foot, or a knock on from the HAND of the opposite side only.

5. A CATCH from a throw on is not a fair catch.
6. CHARGING is fair, in the case of a place kick, as soon as the ball has touched the ground; in case of a kick from a catch, as soon as the player offers to kick, but he may always draw back unless he has actually touched the ball with his foot.
7. OFF SIDE. A player is off his side when he is behind all the players on the opposite side, or in front of the kicker of his own side.
8. A player being off his side is to consider himself as out of the game and is not to touch the ball in any case whatever (either in or out of touch) or in any way to interrupt the play, and is of course incapable of holding the ball.
9. It is not lawful to take the ball off the ground, except in touch, for any purpose whatsoever.
10. It is not lawful to take the ball when rolling as distinguished from bounding.
11. RUNNING IN is allowed to any player on his side, provided he does not take the ball off the ground, or through touch.
12. RUNNING IN: If, in the case of a run in, the ball be held in a maul, it shall be lawful for a player on either side to take it from the runner in.
13. No player out of a maul may be held, or pulled over, unless he is himself holding the ball.
14. Though it is lawful to hold any player in a maul, this holding does not include attempts to throttle or strangle, which are totally opposed to all the principles of the game.
15. No one wearing projecting nails or iron plates on the soles or heels of his boots or shoes shall be allowed to play.
16. TRY AT GOAL: A ball touched between the goal posts may be brought up to either of them, but not between; but if not touched between the posts must be brought up in a straight line from where it is touched.
17. The ball, when punted, must be within, and when caught, without the line of goal.
18. The ball must be place kicked or dropped, but if it touches two players' hands the try will be lost.
19. It shall be a goal if the ball goes over the bar (whether it touch or no) without having touched the dress or person of any player; but no player may stand on the goal bar to interrupt it going over.
20. No goal may be kicked from touch or by a punt at any time.
21. TOUCH: A ball in touch is dead; consequently the first player on his side must in any case touch it down, bring it to the edge of touch and throw it straight out, but may take it himself if he can.
22. No player may stop the ball with anything but his own person.
23. Heads of sides, or two deputies appointed by them, are the sole arbiters of all disputes.

Appendix 6: Blackheath Club Rules 1862

1. That the ball be started from the centre of the ground by a place kick.
2. A fair catch is a catch direct from the foot or a knock on from the hand of one of the opposite side, when the catcher may either run with the ball or make his mark by inserting his heel in the ground on the spot where he catches it; in which case he is entitled to a free kick.
3. It is not lawful to take the ball off the ground, except in touch, for any purpose whatever.
4. A ball in touch is dead, and the first player who touches it down must kick it out straight from the place where it entered touch.
5. A catch out of touch is not a fair catch, but may be run off.
6. Running is allowed to any player on his side if the ball be caught or taken off the first bound.
7. Any player holding the ball unless he has made his mark after a fair catch, may be hacked; and running is not allowed after the mark is made.

8. No player may be hacked and held at the same time — and hacking above or on the knees or from behind is unfair.
9. No player can be held or hacked unless he has the ball in his hands.
10. Though it is lawful to hold a player in a scrummage, this does not include attempts to throttle or strangle, which are totally opposed to the principles of the game.
11. A player whilst running or being held may hand the ball to one of his own side who may continue to run with it, but after the ball is grounded it must be hacked through, not thrown or lifted.
12. When a player running with the ball grounds it, it cannot be touched by anyone until he lifts his hand from it.
13. If the ball goes behind the goal it must be kicked out by the party to whom the goal belongs from in a line with the goals; but a catch off a kick behind goal is not a fair catch, but may be run off.
14. No player is to get before the ball on the side furthest from his own goal; but if he does he must not touch the ball as it passes him until touched by one of the opposite side, he being off-side.
15. A goal must be a kick through or over and between the poles, and if touched by the hands of one of the opposite side before or whilst going through, is no goal.
16. No one wearing projecting nails, iron plates or gutta-percha on the soles or heels of his boots be allowed to play.

Appendix 7: Laws of Blairgowrie, Rattray and Neighbourhood 1865

1. The maximum length of the ground shall be 200 yards, the maximum breadth shall be 100 yards; the length and breadth shall be marked off with flags; and the goal shall be defined by two upright posts, 8 yards apart, without any tape or bar across.
2. The game shall be commenced by a place kick from the centre of the ground by the side winning the toss; the other side shall not approach within 10 yards of the ball until it is kicked off. After a goal is won the losing side shall be entitled to kick off.
3. The two sides shall change goals after each goal is won.
4. A goal shall be won when the ball passes over the space between the goal posts (at whatever height), not having been thrown, knocked on or carried.
5. When the ball is in touch, the first player who touches it shall kick or throw it from the point on the boundary line where it left the ground, in a direction at right angles with the boundary line.
6. A player shall be out of play immediately he is in front of the ball, and must return behind the ball as soon as possible. If the ball is kicked past a player by his own side, he shall not touch or kick it, or advance until one of the other side has first kicked it or one of his own side on a level with or in front of him has been able to kick it.
7. In case the ball goes behind the goal line, if a player on the side to whom the goal belongs first touches the ball, one of his side shall be entitled to a free kick from the goal line at the point opposite the place where the ball shall be touched. If a player of the opposite side first touches the ball, one of his side shall be entitled to a free kick from a point 15 yards outside the goal line opposite the place where the ball is touched.
8. If a player makes a fair catch he shall be entitled to a free kick, provided he claims it by making a mark with his heel at once; and in order to take such a kick he may go as far back as he pleases, and no player on the opposite side shall advance beyond his mark until he has kicked.
9. A player shall be entitled to run with the ball towards his adversaries' goal if he makes a fair catch or catches the ball on the first bound; but in the case of a fair catch, if he makes his mark, he shall not then run.

10. If a player shall run with the ball towards his adversaries' goal, any player on the opposite side shall be at liberty to charge, hold, trip or hack him, or to wrest the ball from him; but no player shall be held and hacked at the same time.

11. Neither tripping nor hacking shall be allowed and no player shall use his hands or elbows to hold or push his adversary, except in the case provided for by Law 10.

12. Any player shall be allowed to charge another, provided they are both in active play. A player shall be allowed to charge even if he is out of play.

13. A player shall be allowed to throw the ball or pass it to another if he makes a fair catch, or catches the ball on the first bound.

14. No player shall be allowed to wear projecting nails, iron plates, or gutta-percha on the soles or heels of his boots.

Some definitions of terms follow, of which the most interesting are:

HACKING: Is kicking an adversary on the front of the leg below the knee.

CHARGING: Is attacking an adversary with the shoulder, chest or body, without using the hands or legs.

TRIPPING: Is throwing an adversary by the use of the legs without the hands, and without hacking or charging.

KNOCKING ON: Is when a player strikes or propels the ball with his hands, arms or body without kicking or throwing it.

These extracts are from W.P. Ireland & Isaac Donald: *Handbook to Blairgowrie, Rattray and Neighbourhood*, 1865

Appendix 8: Kilmarnock FC Rules of Play 1869

1. The length of the ground shall be 200 yards, the breadth 100 yards, and the distance between the goal posts 15 feet.

2. Before the commencement of the Game, the Captain of each side, or their representatives, shall toss for choice of goals and the kick off. They shall also fix the time for leaving off playing.

3. In a Match, when half the time agreed upon has elapsed, the sides shall change goals the next time the ball is out of play. In ordinary games the change shall be made after every goal.

4. The ball shall be put in play as follows:

a. At the commencement of the game, and after every goal, by a place kick, from a point 25 yards in advance of the goal, by either side alternately.

b. If the ball has been played behind the goal line, the side owning the goal shall have a free kick from behind the goal line, at their discretion. But it is not permissable for one of a side wilfully to play the ball behind his own goal.

c. If the ball has been played across the side line, the player first touching it with his *hand* shall have a free kick from the point at which the ball crossed the line; the ball must be kicked into the ground at right angles to the side line.

5. In all the above cases the side starting the ball shall be *out of play* until one of the opposite side has played it; and in the last two, the ball shall not be considered *in play* until it has touched the ground.

6. When any player catches the ball by a fair and full catch, he is entitled to a free kick; and if caught when bouncing above the knee, he may, if he choses, take a run with it.

7. Any player may hold, push with his hands, or trip any player of the opposite side, when within 4 yards of the ball.

8. Though it is lawful to hold any player with the ball, this holding does not include attempts to throttle or strangle, which are, of course, opposed to all the principles of the game.

9. It is not lawful to pick up the ball for *any* purpose whatever (except in touch, or after it has been touched down in goal, to take it out).

10. No player may wear iron plates or projecting nails on his boots or shoe.

11. No hacking allowed.

12. A goal is gained when the ball is kicked in between the two flags which mark out the goals.

13. In case of any distinct and wilful violation of these rules of play, by one of either side, the opposite side may claim a fresh kick off.

Definition of terms
A 'place kick' is a kick at the ball while it is at rest on the ground.
'Touch' is that part of the field on either side of the ground, which is beyond the line of flags.
'Hacking' is kicking an adversary intentionally.

These extracts are from J.F.T. Thomson: *More Than a Game: Kilmarnoch R.F.C. Centenary History 1868—1973*

Appendix 9: The Scotsman November 1937

Extract from a letter to the Editor.

Many years ago, when I had occasion to hunt for the origin of Rugby, I discovered that the High School played a carrying game round about 1810. This fact I mentioned to some of my old English football friends and others when we gathered at Rugby in 1923 as representatives of the carrying game to help to celebrate the centenary — so-called. When told that they had given the name 'Rugby' to the game, but that they certainly did not invent it as it had been played in Scotland for unknown years before 1823 and by the High School about 1810, some of them were very annoyed.

I am not an old High School boy and in fact was one of her 'enemies' in the football world and only wish I could claim that my old school was as close to the origin of rugby as was the High School.

H.J. Stevenson

Harry Stevenson W.S. (Edin. Acads.) was one of the most outstanding backs of his time, playing fifteen times for Scotland between 1888 and 1893.

Appendix 10: The Merchistonian January 1859

Comments on the first Edinburgh Academy-Merchiston match

Football at Merchiston this year is very different and superior to the game as played last year (i.e. 1857–58). For this improvement we have to thank the Rugby rules and those who introduced them. Last year there was no order in the game whatever; it was each for himself, each kicking recklessly ahead, very little running with the ball and 'off side' scarcely heard of. Now it is far different, each one has that place assigned to him for which he is most suited, whether goalkeeper, muddler, dodger or as a member of that useful body, the light brigade.

Last year we were disappointed in playing the Academy but now it was fixed as the first match of the season. Accordingly, at about 11 a.m. of Saturday, 11th December last an omnibus drew up at the gate of the Academy field and discharged the 20 Merchistonians eager for the fight and a few who had come as spectators.

. . . we could not help observing that the Academy goals were a good deal easier to kick over than ours, being both lower and broader . . .

Lyall . . . runs into touch right behind our goal. Here an expostulation was made on the plea that the rules prohibited running into touch but finding that it only related to side touch, we were obliged to yield and allow the try at goal.

We had always been accustomed to play over the area of the whole field, our only boundaries being the goals and the school wall on one side and the paling at the bottom of the field on the other.

. . . we thought we had a goal, for McFie kicked the ball easily over, but it stood for nothing as it was handed to him 'off his side'.

. . . Willie Tennent comes in for his share of kudos . . . the agility he displayed in leaping through the wires round the cricket ground after the ball (in touch!)

Our captain must not be forgotten, his way of ridding himself of those who press upon him too closely in a maul by stamping on their toes is admirable.

Appendix 11: The Merchiston Chronicle February 1859

Comments on the second Edinburgh Academy-Merchiston match

'The Academy had two former Academicals on their side, Merchiston confining itself strictly to the residents at the school. This was, perhaps, the best way of settling an amicable controversy we have had for some time with the Academy, relative to the right of playing masters.'

The Merchiston XX is known and included Mr Almond.

Appendix 12: Comparison of Players 1876–1976

The first team selection recorded in the SFU minutes was that for the English game in 1876. The individual weights taken in uniform on the day of the match were also noted and it is interesting to compare these 'giants of the past' with the players in the corresponding match 100 years later. (Weights are given in stones and pounds.)

1876: T. Chalmers 11.1, J.S. Carrick 11.7, M. Cross 10.1, N.J. Finlay 12.4, G.Q. Paterson 8.12, A.K. Stewart 10.7; A. Arthur 12.2, W.H. Bolton 12.1, N.T. Brewis 11.1, C.W. Cathcart 12.4, D. Drew 11.8, G.R. Fleming 11.0, J.H.S. Graham 11.8, R.W. Irvine 12.4, J.E. Junor 11.2, D. Lang 11.3, A.G. Petrie 12.12, J. Reid 14.4, C. Villar 12.12, D.H. Watson 11.4

1976: A.R. Irvine 12.4, W.C.C. Steele 12.2, A.G. Cranston 13.9, I.R. McGeechan 11.5, D. Shedden 11.0, R. Wilson 12.10, A.J.M. Lawson 12.2; J.McLauchlan 14.7, C.D. Fisher 12.12, A.B. Carmichael 16.0, A.J. Tomes 15.10, G.L. Brown 16.12, M.A. Biggar 14.4, A.F. McHarg 15.3, D.G. Leslie 14.5

Average weights

Year	Backs	Forwards
1876	10.10	11.13
1976	12.2	14.3

Even in 1896 a writer in *Rugby Football* was stating that the ideal weight for a forward was 13.0 with a height of 5'10". It is known that in the 1876 team Read and Petrie, both about 6'3", were head and shoulders above the others, whereas in 1976 the pack *averaged* 6'2".

Appendix 13: International Grounds

SCOTLAND
(Numbers in brackets indicate frequency)
Edinburgh: Raeburn Place
England (10) 1871. 75. 77. 79. 81. 83. 86. 90. 92. 94
Ireland (7) 1884. 85. 86. 88. 90. 92. 95
Wales (6) 1883. 87. 89. 91. 93. 95
Glasgow: Hamilton Crescent
England (1) 1873
Ireland (2) 1880. 82
Wales (1) 1885
Glasgow: Old Hampden Park
England (1) 1896
Glasgow: New Hampden Park
South Africa (1) 1906
Edinburgh: Powderhall
Ireland (1) 1897
England (1) 1898
Edinburgh: Inverleith
Ireland (11) 1899. 1901. 03. 05. 07. 09. 11. 13. 20. 22. 24
Wales (11) 1899. 1901. 03. 05. 07. 09. 11. 13. 20. 22. 24
England (10) 1900. 02. 04. 06. 08. 10. 12. 14. 21. 23
New Zealand (1) 1905
France (5) 1910. 12. 21. 23. 25
South Africa (1) 1912
*Services Games (2) E. 1942. 43
Edinburgh: Murrayfield
England (26) 1925. 27. 29. 31. 33. 35. 37. 39. 48. 50. 52. 54. 56. 58. 60. 62. 64. 66. 68. 70. 71. 72. 74. 76. 78. 80
Wales (24) 1926. 28. 30. 32. 34. 36. 38. 47. 49. 51. 53. 55. 57. 59. 61. 63. 65. 67. 69. 71. 73. 75. 77. 79
Ireland (24) 1926. 28. 30. 32. 34. 36. 38. 47. 49. 51. 53. 55. 57. 59. 61. 63. 65. 67. 69. 71. 73. 75. 77. 79
France (20) 1927. 29. 31. 48. 50. 52. 54. 56. 58. 60. 62. 64. 66. 68. 70. 72. 74. 76. 78. 80

New South Wales (1) 1927
South Africa (5) 1932. 51. 61. 65. 69
New Zealand (7) 1935. 54. 64. 67. 72. 78. 79
*Services Games (2) E. 1944. 45
*New Zealand Army (1) 1946
*Victory Games (3) 1946: I.W.E.
Australia (5) 1947. 58. 66. 68. 75
*Barbarians (1) 1970
President's XV (1) 1973
*Argentine (1) 1973
*Tonga (1) 1974
*Japan (1) 1976

ENGLAND
London: *Kennington Oval*
(4) 1872. 74. 76. 78
Manchester: Whalley Range
(3) 1880. 82. 87
London: Blackheath
(4) 1884. 99. 1901. 07
Manchester: Fallowfield
(1) 1897
London: Richmond
(5) 1891. 95. 1903. 05. 09
Leeds: Headingley
(1) 1893
London: Twickenham
(29) 1911. 13. 20. 22. 24. 26. 28. 30. 32. 34. 36. 38. 47. 49. 51. 53. 55. 57. 59. 61. 63. 65. 67. 69. 71. 73. 75. 77. 79
London: Wembley
(1) *Services Game: E. 1942
Leicester
(3) *Services Games: E. 1943. 44. 45

IRELAND
Belfast: Ormeau
(5) 1877. 79. 81. 85. 87
Ulster Ground
(3) 1889. 91. 93

Balmoral
(2) 1898. 1902
Royal Ulster Agric. Soc.
(1) 1910
Ravenhill
(1) 1954
Dublin: Lansdowne Road
(33) 1894. 96. 1900. 04. 06. 08. 12. 14. 21.
23. 25. 27. 29. 31. 33. 35. 37. 39. 48. 50.
52. 56. 58. 60. 62. 64. 66. 68. 70. 74. 76.
78. 80

WALES
Newport
(3) 1884. 88. 94
Swansea
(12) 1892. 1900. 04. 08. 12. 21. 25. 29. 33.
37. 50. 54
Cardiff
(27) 1886. 90. 96. 1902. 06. 10. 14. 23. 27.
31. 35. 39. 48. 52. 56. 58. 60. 62. 64. 66.
68. 70. 72. 74. 76. 78. 80

FRANCE
Colombes
(17) 1911. 22. 26. 28. 30. 47. 49. 51. 53. 57.
59. 61. 63. 65. 67. 69. 71
Parc des Princes
(6) 1913. 20. 73. 75. 77. 79
Stade Pershing
(1) 1924

SOUTH AFRICA
Port Elizabeth
(1) 1960

ARGENTINA
*Buenos Aires
(2) 1969. 69

AUSTRALIA
Sydney
(1) 1970

NEW ZEALAND
Auckland
(1) 1975

Appendix 14: Scottish Captains

A = Australia; Ar = Argentina; Barb = Barbarians; E = England; F = France; I =
Ireland; J = Japan; NZ = New Zealand; NSW = New South Wales; P = President's XV;
SA = South Africa; W = Wales

F.J. Moncreiff	Edin. Acads	(3)	1871: E 1872: E 1873: E
W.D. Brown	Glas. Acads.	(2)	1874: E 1875: E
R.W. Irvine	Edin. Acads.	(8)	1876: E 1877: I.E. 1878: E
			1879: I.E. 1880 I.E.
J.H.S. Graham	Edin. Acads	(2)	1881: I.E.
R. Ainslie	Edin.Inst. F.P.	(1)	1882: I
D.Y. Cassels	West of Scot.	(4)	1882: E 1883: W.I.E.
W.E. Maclagan	London Scottish	(8)	1884: W.I.E. 1885: W.I.I.
			1890: W.E.
J.B. Brown	Glas. Acads.	(3)	1886: W.I.E.
C. Reid	Edin. Acads.	(4)	1887: W.I.E. 1888: W.
A.R. Don Wauchope	Fettesians-Lorettonians	(1)	1888: I.
D.S. Morton	West of Scot.	(2)	1889: W.I.
M.C. McEwan	Edin. Acads.	(4)	1890: I 1891: W.I.E.
C.E. Orr	West of Scot.	(3)	1892: W.I.E.
R.G. Macmillan	London Scottish	(6)	1893: W 1894: W 1895: I.E.
			1897: I.E.
J.D. Boswell	West of Scot.	(4)	1893: I.E. 1894: I.E.
W.R. Gibson	RHSFP	(1)	1895: W
G.T. Neilson	West of Scot.	(3)	1896: W.I.E.
A.R. Smith	Oxford Univ.	(2)	1898: I.E.
W.P. Donaldson	West of Scot.	(1)	1899: I.

M.C. Morrison	RHSFP	(15)	1899: W.E. 1900: W.E.
			1901: W.I.E. 1902: W.I.E.
			1903: W.I. 1904: W.I.E.
T. Scott	Hawick	(1)	1900: I.
J.R.C. Greenlees	Cambridge Univ.	(1)	1903: E
W.P. Scott	West of Scot.	(2)	1905: W.I.
A.B. Timms	Edin. Univ.	(1)	1905: E
D.R. Bedell-	Edin. Univ.	(1)	1905: NZ
Sivright			
L. West	Hartlepool;		
	L. Scot.	(3)	1906: W.I.E.
L.L. Greig	Glas. Acads.;		
	Un. Services	(4)	1906: SA 1907: W 1908: W.I.
P. Munro	London Scot.	(5)	1907: I.E. 1911: F.W.I.
I.C. Geddes	London Scot.	(1)	1908: E
J.M.B. Scott	Edn. Acads.	(2)	1909: W.I.
G. Cunningham	Oxford Univ.	(4)	1909: E 1910: F.I.E.
G.M. Frew	Glas. HSFP	(1)	1910: W
J.C. MacCallum	Watsonians	(5)	1911: E 1912:F.W.I.E.
F.H. Turner	Liverpool;		
	Oxford Univ.	(5)	1912: SA 1913: F.W.I.E
D.M. Bain	Oxford Univ.	(1)	1914: W
E. Milroy	Watsonians	(2)	1914: I.E.
A.W. Angus	Watsonians	(1)	1920: F
C.M. Usher	London Scot.;		
	Edn. Wrs.	(7)	1920: W.I.E 1922: F.W.I.E
A.T. Sloan	Edn. Acads.	(1)	1921: F
J. Hume	RHSFP	(3)	1921: W.I.E.
A.L. Gracie	Harlequins	(4)	1923: F.W.I.E.
J.C.R. Buchanan	Stewart's Coll.; FP	(4)	1924: F.W.I.E
G.P.S.	Oxford Univ.	(12)	1925: F.W.E 1927: F.W.I
Macpherson	Edin. Acads.		1930: F.W.I.E 1931: E
			1932: E
D. Drysdale	Heriot's F.P.;	(11)	1925: I 1926: F.W.I.E.
	Oxford Univ.		1927: E.NSW 1928: F.I.E.
	London Scot.		1929: F
J.M. Bannerman	Glasgow HSFP	(4)	1928: W 1929: W.I.E.
W.N. Roughead	London Scottish	(3)	1931: F.W.I.
W.M. Simmers	Glas. Acads.	(3)	1932: SA.W.I
I.S. Smith	London Scottish	(3)	1933: W.E.I
H. Lind	Dunfermline	(1)	1934: W
M.S. Stewart	Stewart's Coll. FP	(2)	1934: I.E
K.C. Fyfe	Camb. Univ.	(1)	1935: W
R.W. Shaw	Glasgow HSFP	(9)	1935: I.E.NZ 1938: W.I.E.
			1939: W.I.E.
R.C.S. Dick	Guy's	(2)	1936: W.I
J.A. Beattie	Hawick	(1)	1936: E
W.R. Logan	Edn. Wndrs.	(3)	1937: W.I.E
C.L. Melville*	Army	(*4)	*1942: E.E *1943: E.E
J.A. Waters	Selkirk	(*2)	*1944: E.E
K.I. Geddes	RAF; Wasps;	(*6+2)	*1945: E.E *1946: NZ.W.I.E
	London Scots.		1947: F.W
D.W. Deas*	Heriot's FP	(*2)	*1946: W.E
W.H. Munro	Glas. HSFP	(1)	1947: I
C.R. Bruce	Glas. Acads.	(1)	1947: E
J.R.S. Innes	Aberdeen GSFP	(5)	1948: A.F.W.I.E

338

D.H. Keller	London Scot.	(4)	1949: F.W.I.E
W.I.D. Elliot	Edn. Acads.	(7)	1950: F.W.I
			1954: NZ.I.E.W
P.W. Kinimonth	Richmond	(8)	1950: E 1951: F.W.I.E
			1952: F.W.I
A. Cameron	Glasgow HSFP	(9)	1951: SA 1953: I.E
			1955: W.I.E. 1956: F.W.I.
A.F. Dorward	Gala.	(3)	1952: E 1953: F.W
J.N.G. Davidson	Edn. Univ.	(1)	1954: F
J.T. Greenwood	Dunfermline:		
	Perth Acads.	(9)	1955: F 1956: E 1957: F.W.E
			1958: E 1959: F.W.I
A.R. Smith	Camb. Univ:		
	Gosforth	(15)	1957: I 1958: F.W.A.I
			1960: F.W.
	Ebbw Vale:		
	Edn. Wrs.		1961: SA.W.I.E
			1962: F.W.I.E
G.H. Waddell	Cam. Univ.	(4)	1959: E 1960: I.E.SA
K.J.F. Scotland	Heriot's FP	(4)	1963: F.W.I.E
J.B. Neill	Edn. Acads.	(6)	1964: F.NZ.W.I.E 1965: F
M.J. Campbell-Lamerton	London Scottish	(2)	1965: W.I
S. Wilson	London Scot.	(4)	1965: E.SA 1966: F.W
I.H.P. Laughland	London Scot.	(2)	1966: I.E
J.P. Fisher	London Scot.	(9)	1966: A 1967: F.W.I.E.NZ
			1968: F.W.I
J.W. Telfer	Melrose	(*2+10)	1968: E.A 1969: F.W.I.E.SA
			*1969: Ar.Ar. 1970: F.W.I
F.A.L. Laidlaw	Melrose	(2)	1970: E.A *1970: Barb
P.C. Brown	Gala.	(9)	1971: F.W.I.E
			1972: F.W.E.NZ 1973: F
J. McLauchlan	Jordanhill	(*2+19)	1973: W.I.E.P *1973: Ar.
			1974: W.E.I.F. *1974: T
			1975: I.F.W.E.NZ.A.
			1976: F.W.E.I. 1979: NZ
I.R. McGeechan	Headingley	(9)	*1976: J 1977: E.I.F.W.
			1978: NZ. 1979: W.E.I.F
D.W. Morgan	Stew.-Mel. FP	(4)	1978: I.F.W.E
M.A. Biggar	London Scottish	(3)	1980: I.F.W.
A.R. Irvine	Heriot's FP	(1)	1980: E

Captain with first cap

F.J. Moncreiff 1871: E **D.H. Keller** 1949: F

Since no caps were awarded for NZ.1905, F.1912, F.1920, F.1921 and in 1946 the following three players could be placed in this group:
L.L. Greig 1905: NZ 1906: SA*
J. Hume 1912: F 1920: F 1921: F 1921: W*
K.I. Geddes 1946: NZ.I.E(2): 1947: F*

Appendix 15: Scoring details

Points 1

OVERALL

Scottish matches were not decided by points until the 1889–90 season and several values have been altered since then, the two latest being the down grading in 1948–49 of the drop goal from four to three and the upgrading in 1971–72 of the try from three to four. So in this table a player has been placed according to the present day value of his scores (B) while also showing its original value (A).

G = Goal; DG = Drop Goal; MG = Mark Goal; PG = Penalty Goal; T = Try

	G	DG	MG	PG	T	(A)	(B)
A.R. Irvine	16			38	9	182	182
I.S. Smith					24	72	96
K.J.F. Scotland	7	4		15		71	71
D.W. Morgan	4	6		15		71	71
S. Wilson	10			16		68	68
P.C. Brown	4			15	3	64	65
A.R. Smith	2			6	12	58	64
H. Waddell	2	5			7	45	47
D. Drysdale	19	1		1		45	44
A.C. Wallace					11	33	44
R.W. Shaw	2				8	28	36
W.A. Stewart					8	24	32
J.C. MacCallum	10				2	26	28
K.C. Fyfe	5			2	3	25	28
J.M. Renwick	1			2	5	28	28
K.G. MacLeod	1		1	2	4	23	27
A.B.H.L. Purves		1			6	22	27
A.C. Gillies	7			3	1	26	27
A. Browning	2			1	5	22	27
J.W. Allan	9			3		27	27
I.H.M Thomson	6			5		27	27

		G	DG	PG	T	(A)	(B)
A.R. Don Wauchope					6	*	24
W.C.C. Steele					6	24	24
D.J. McFarlan		3			4	*	22

Points 2

MATCH

		G	DG	PG	T	(A)	(B)
G.C. Lindsay	1887: Wales				5	*	20
R.C. MacKenzie	1872: Ireland		2		3	*	18
W.A. Stewart	1913: Ireland				4	12	16
I.S. Smith	1925: France				4	12	16
	1925: Wales				4	12	16
A.R.Irvine	1980: France	1		2	2	16	16
F.H. Turner	1912: France	5			1	13	14
P.C. Brown	1972: England			3	1	13	13
A.R. Irvine	1979: Wales			3	1	13	13
J.M. Tennent	1910: France				3	9	12
W.A. Stewart	1913: France				3	9	12
A.C. Wallace	1920: France				3	9	12
I.S. Smith	1924: Wales				3	9	12
W. Wotherspoon	1891: Ireland				3	6	12
A.R. Irvine	1974: England	1		2	1	12	12
	1976: Ireland			4		12	12
D. Drysdale	1924: Wales	4		1		11	11
J.W. Allan	1931: England	5				10	10
A.R. Irvine	1976: England	2		2		10	10
	1980: England	2		2		10	10

Tries

Conversions

Drop Goals

Penalty Goals

OVERALL

38 **A.R. Irvine**
16 **S. Wilson**
15 **K.J.F. Scotland: P.C. Brown: D.W. Morgan**
6 **A.R. Smith**
5 **I.H.M. Thomson: C.F. Blaikie**
4 **W.H. Crawford: W. Lauder**
3 **F. Kennedy: A.C. Gillies: J.W. Allan: A. Cameron: M.K. Elgie**

MATCH

A.R. Irvine 1976: Ireland 4; 1975: France 3; 1979: Wales 3
K.J.F. Scotland 1960: England 3
P.C. Brown 1972: England 3
D.W. Morgan 1975: Wales 3; 1978: Ireland 3

First Scorers

	For Scotland	*Against Scotland*
Try	**A. Buchanan** (*E*)1871	**R.H. Birkett** (*E*)1871
Conversion	**M. Cross** (*E*)1871	**F.W. Isherwood** (*E*)1872
Drop Goal	**C.W. Cathcart** (*E*)1872	**H. Freeman** (*E*)1872
Penalty Goal	**G.T. Neilson** (*E*)1895	**W.J. Bancroft** (*W*)1893
Mark Goal	**C.W. Berry** (*I*)1887	**A. Beguet** (*F*)1923

Appendix 16: Relatives Capped

Father & Son

J.B. Waters (1904); F.H. Waters (1930)
H.T.S. Gedge (1894); P.M.S. Gedge (1933)
J.H. Bruce Lockhart (1913); R.B. Bruce Lockhart (1937); L. Bruce Lockhart (1948)
R.A. Gallie (1920); G.H. Gallie (1939)
I.C. Geddes (1906); K.I. Geddes (1947)
A.T. Sloan (1914); D.A. Sloan (1950)
H. Waddell (1924); G.H. Waddell (1957)
W.M. Simmers (1927); B.M. Simmers (1965)
A.T. Fisher (1947); C.D. Fisher (1975)
J.J. Hegarty (1951); C.B. Hegarty (1978)

Brothers

G.T. Neilson (1891); W. Neilson (1891); W.G. Neilson (1894); R.T. Neilson (1898)
J.F. Finlay (1871); A.B. Finlay (1875); N.J. Finlay (1875)
J.W. Arthur (1871); A. Arthur (1875)
W. Cross (1871); M. Cross (1875)
R.W. Irvine (1871); D.R. Irvine (1878)
T.R. Marshall (1871); W. Marshall (1872)
T.R. Marshall (1871); W. Marshall (1872)
J.H. McClure (1872); G.B. McClure (1873)
J. Reid (1874); C. Reid (1881)
R. Ainslie (1879); T. Ainslie (1881)
R. Maitland (1881); G. Maitland (1885)
A. Walker (1881); J.G. Walker (1882)

A.R. Don Wauchope (1881); P.H. Don Wauchope (1885)
M.C. McEwan (1886); W.M.C. McEwan (1894)
C.E. Orr (1887); J.E. Orr (1889)
J.H. Dods (1895); F.P. Dods (1901)
D.R. Bedell-Sivright (1900); J.V. Bedell-Sivright (1902)
J.E. Crabbie (1900); G.E. Crabbie (1904)
J. Ross (1901); E.J. Ross (1904)
L.M. MacLeod (1904); K.G. MacLeod (1905)
A.B.H.L. Purves (1906); W.D.C.L. Purves (1912)
D.G. McGregor (1907); J.R. McGregor (1909)
C.D. Stuart (1909); L.M. Stuart (1923)
D.D. Howie (1912); R.A. Howie (1924)
G.M. Murray (1921); R.O. Murray (1935)
J.C. Dykes (1922); A.S. Dykes (1932)
J.M. Henderson (1933); I.C. Henderson (1939)
R.W. Shaw (1934); I. Shaw (1937)
R.B. Bruce Lockhart (1937); L. Bruce Lockhart (1948)
T.F. Dorward (1938); A.F. Dorward (1950)
D.D. Valentine (1947); A.R. Valentine (1953)
A. Cameron (1948); D. Cameron (1953)
R.W.T. Chisholm (1955); D.H. Chisholm (1964)
C. Elliot (1958); T.G. Elliot (1968)
T.O. Grant (1960); D. Grant (1965)
A.C.W. Boyle (1963); A.H.W. Boyle (1966)
P.C. Brown (1964); G.L. Brown (1969)
B.M. Gossman (1980); J.S. Gossman (1980)
D.S.M. Macdonald (1977); D.A. Macdonald (1974) for South Africa

Half Brothers

P. Turnbull (1901); G.B. Crole (1920)

Cousins

R.W. Irvine (1871); D.R. Irvine (1878); T.W. Irvine (1885)
R. Welsh (1895); W.H. Welsh (1900)
E.D. Simson (1902); J.T. Simson (1905)
A.G. Biggar (1969); M.A. Biggar (1975)

Uncles & Nephews

A. Buchanan (1871); F.G. Buchanan (1910)
D. Patterson (1896); W. Burnet (1912)
J.M. Dykes (1898); J.C. Dykes (1922); A.S. Dykes (1932)
G. Thom (1920); J.R. Thom (1933)
J.W. Allan (1927); J.L. Allan (1952)
J.G. Watherston (1934); W.R.A. Watherston (1962)
H.F.McLeod (1954); C.M. Telfer (1968)
C. McDonald (1947); D.M. Rose (1951)

Appendix 17: Roll of Honour

The Boer War 1899–1902
1900: D.B. Monypenny

The 1914–1918 War
1914: R.F. Simson: J.L. Huggan: J. Ross:
L. Robertson
1915 F.H. Turner: J. Pearson: D.M. Bain:
W.C. Church: E.T. Young: P.C.B.
Blair: W.M. Wallace: D.R. Bedell-
Sivright: W.M. Dickson
1916: D.D. Howie: A. Ross: C.H.
Abercrombie: J.S. Wilson: R. Fraser: E.
Milroy
1917: J.G.Will: T.A. Nelson: W.T.
Forrest: A.L. Wade: J.Y.M.
Henderson: J.A. Campbell: S.S.L.
Steyn
1918: G.A.W. Lamond: W.R. Hutchison:
R.E. Gordon: W.R. Sutherland

The 1939–45 War
1940: D.K.A. Mackenzie
1941: T.F. Dorward: A.W. Symington
1942: P. Munro: J.M. Ritchie: R.M.
Kinnear: W.A. Ross: J.G.S. Forrest: D.
St.C. Ford
1943: G. Roberts: W.M. Penman
1944: A.S.B. McNeil: W.N. Renwick:
G.H. Gallie
1945: E.H. Liddell

Players Who Bridged the Wars

1914–1919
A.W. Angus *(1910–1920)*: A.S. Hamilton
(1914–1920): J. Hume *(1912–1922)*:
A.D. Laing *(1914–1921)*: J.H. Bruce
Lockhart *(1913–1920)*: J.B. Macdougall
(1913–1921): G.H.H.P. Maxwell
(1913–1922): A.T. Sloan *(1914–1921)*:
C.M. Usher *(1912–1923)*: A. Wemyss
(1914–1922)

1939–1945
I.C. Henderson *(1939–1948)*: J.R.S. Innes
(1939–1948): W.C.W. Murdoch
(1935–1948): R.W.F. Sampson
(1939–1947): W.B. Young *(1937–1948)*

Surviving Caps pre-1914
W.M. Milne *(27.7.1883)*: C.D. Stuart
(18.5.1887): G.A. Ledingham
(8.3.1890): C.M. Usher *(26.9.1891)*:
A.R. Ross *(13.1.1892)*
I shall be delighted to learn of any other
pre-war survivors.

Appendix 18: Ages of Caps

Youngest First Cap

	School	Date of Birth	Date of Match	Age
N.J. Finlay*	Edin. Academy	31.1.1858	8.3.1875	17y 36 days
C. Reid*	Edin. Academy	14.1.1864	19.2.1881	17y 36 days
W.G. Neilson*	Merchiston	1.10.1876	17.3.1894	17y 5m
W. Neilson*	Merchiston	18.8.1873	7.2.1891	17y 5m
K.G. MacLeod	Fettes	2.2.1888	18.11.1905	17y 9m
L.M. Balfour	Edin. Academy	9.3.1854	5.2.1872	17y 10m
A. Arthur	Glas. Academy	3.4.1857	8.3.1875	17y 11m
R.W. Irvine	Edin. Academy	19.4.1853	27.3.1871	17y 11m

The reader is invited to check why N.J. Finlay is placed ahead of C. Reid. The first four
marked by an asterisk, were capped while still at school, as were the following five players:

W. StC. Grant	Craigmount	*c.*1853	3.3.1873	*c.*20y
J.A. Campbell	Merchiston	*c.*1858	4.3.1878	*c.*20y
T. Anderson	Merchiston	17.5.1863	18.2.1882	18y 9m
M.F. Reid	Loretto	3.8.1864	17.2.1883	18y 5m
D.M. Grant	Elstow	*c.*1893	4.2.1911	*c.*18y

Oldest First Cap
T. Gray *(33y.2m)*: C.J.G. Mackenzie *(32y.1m)*: F.O. Turnbull *(31y.7m)*: R.H.D. Bryce *(31y.3m)*: R.J.C. Glasgow *(31y.2m)*

Oldest Cap
J. McLauchlan *(37y.6m)*: A.F. McHarg *(34y.7m)*: R.J.C. Glasgow *(34y.3m)*: T. Gray *(34y.2m)*

Appendix 19: Leading Caps

(Number of caps given in brackets)

A.B. Carmichael *(50)*: A.F. McHarg *(44)*: J. McLauchlan *(43)*: H.F. McLeod *(40)*: D.M.D. Rollo *(40)*: A.R. Irvine *(37)*: J.M. Bannerman *(37)*: J.M. Renwick *(35)*: A.R. Smith *(33)*: I.S. Smith *(32)*: F.A.L. Laidlaw *(32)*: I.R. McGeechan *(32)*: N.S. Bruce *(31)*: I.H.P. Laughland *(31)*: G.L. Brown *(30)*

Appendix 20: Double Caps

Cricket: Pre-1909
T. Anderson: A.G.G. Asher: L.M. Balfour-Melville: E.M. Bannerman: A. Buchanan: J.S. Carrick: T. Chalmers: W. St.C. Grant: F. Hunter: W.E. Maclagan: T.R. Marshall: G. MacGregor: D. Somerville: H.J. Stevenson: J.G. Walker: A.R. Don Wauchope

Cricket Post-1909
A.W. Angus: D.L. Bell: G.B. Crole: J.N.G. Davidson: M.R. Dickson: A.W. Duncan: T.M. Hart: J.R. Kerr: J.H. Bruce Lockhart: R.B. Bruce Lockhart: W.R. Logan: I.J.M. Lumsden: A.S.B. McNeil: N.G.R. Mair: K.W. Marshall: K.J.F. Scotland: J.M. Tennent

Other Sports
Athletics
R.H. Lindsay-Watson *(Hammer Throw)* (Olympic Team): F.G. Buchanan *(Long Jump)*: E.H. Liddell *(Track Events)* (Olympic Team): G.P.S. Macpherson *(Long Jump)*: P.M.S. Gedge *(Fencing)*: D.D. Mackenzie *(Relay Team)*
Hockey: W.E. Bryce
Golf: G. Roberts
Water Polo: J.M. Ritchie
Basketball: J.P. Fisher (Olympic Team)

This list is nowhere near complete and I should welcome additional entries.